CliffsNotes®

*AP European History with CD-ROM

2ND EDITION

by
Michael J. Romano, Ph.D.

WILEY

Wiley Publishing, Inc.

About the Author

Michael J. Romano has a Ph.D. in history and is an adjunct professor at various local N.Y. colleges. He has been an educator and supervisor of social studies in the New York state system. Dr. Romano is also a presenter at local, regional, and national social studies councils.

Dedication

To my parents, Giuseppe and Concetta, whose immigrant experiences influenced my love of history and education. To my family, especially Linda, who was a great help, and my wife, Lucy, who has been my constant source of encouragement and support.

Editorial

Acquisitions Editor: Greg Tubach

Project Editor: Suzanne Snyder, Ph.D.

Copy Editor: Marylouise Wiack

Technical Editor: Marcus Stadelmann, Ph.D.

Composition

Proofreader: Cynthia Fields

Wiley Publishing, Inc. Composition Services

CliffsNotes® AP European History with CD-ROM, 2nd Edition

Published by:
Wiley Publishing, Inc.
111 River Street
Hoboken, NJ 07030-5774
www.wiley.com

Copyright © 2010 Wiley Publishing, Inc.

Published by Wiley, Hoboken, NJ
Published simultaneously in Canada

Library of Congress Cataloging-in-Publication Data is available from the publisher upon request.

ISBN: 978-0-470-55100-4

Printed in the United States of America
10 9 8 7 6 5 4 3 2 1

For general information on our other products and services or to obtain technical support, please contact our Customer Care Department within the U.S. at (877) 762-2974, outside the U.S. at (317) 572-3993, or fax (317) 572-4002.

Wiley also publishes its books in a variety of electronic formats. Some content that appears in print may not be available in electronic books. For more information about Wiley products, please visit our web site at www.wiley.com.

Table of Contents

PART II: AP EUROPEAN HISTORY PRACTICE EXAMS

Introducing the AP European History Examination

What Is the Advanced Placement Program?

The Advanced Placement (AP) Program has been established by the College Board, a nonprofit organization that oversees college admission examinations. The AP Program allows highly motivated secondary-school students to take college-level courses in more than 30 subjects in which AP examinations are available. Students who take these high school AP courses, such as European History, and receive a satisfactory grade on the AP examination (usually a 3 or higher) receive college credit. AP credit is accepted by more than 3,600 colleges and universities worldwide for college credit. Some institutions even grant sophomore status to students who have taken a number of these AP examinations and receive a grade of 3 or better.

Approximately 60 percent of the high schools participate in the AP program. The number of AP exams that students took increased by 45 percent, from 1.1 million for the school year ending 2004 to 1.6 million for the school year ending 2008. Three high school and three college history teachers design the AP European History course and other AP courses. The committee outlines the content of the courses as well as what should be on the examinations. They also meet to update the curriculum, to reflect the latest changes and events in the world, as well as to make changes in the format of the exam. In 1998, the committee altered the number of Document-Based Questions (DBQs) from 14 to approximately 10 or 12 questions.

AP examinations are offered every May at participating schools. Below is a suggested timeline for registration for the AP examinations:

- **JANUARY:** Consult your AP teachers, guidance counselor, and AP coordinator for specific dates and fees for the examinations. If any special exam modifications are needed, you should notify the AP coordinator at this time.
- **MARCH/APRIL:** Check with your counselor/AP coordinator to determine if the special modifications have been established or if you need to take the exam at another school.
- **MAY:** The AP European History examination and other AP examinations are administered.
- **JUNE:** Examinations are graded.
- **JULY 1:** Students can receive their exam grades via telephone. The College Board mails the exam results to the individual schools.

Students can get additional information about the AP European History examination and programs on-line at www.collegeboard.org. Students can ask their teachers for a copy of the Advanced Placement Course Description: European History, which is also available at the College Board Web site.

Themes of the AP European History Course

The College Board designed AP programs in European History for students to develop an understanding of the important themes in European history from 1450 to the present and how these themes helped shape the world in which we live. The themes revolve around the following:

- Intellectual and cultural history
- Political and diplomatic history
- Social and economic history

Intellectual and Cultural History

The intellectual history theme focuses on the changes in attitudes towards religious institutions that began in Europe in the fifteenth century. Such changes led to a secularization of learning as well as changes in attitude toward education, literature, arts, politics, and social values. These intellectual developments are responsible for the scientific and technological advances within European society.

The cultural history theme provides an analysis of how these new intellectual concepts influenced different social groups and impacted areas of popular culture such as attitudes, family, religion, and work. Cultural history also examines the influence of global expansion on European culture.

Political and Diplomatic History

The political history theme explores the rise of the nation state and nationalism, as well as the rise of political elites in different countries and their ideologies. Political history also examines the forms of political protests, reform, and revolution, and the extension and limitations of political and civil liberties in Europe.

The diplomatic history theme includes not only a study of foreign policy but also how domestic and political events influence relations with other countries. The theme examines ways roles of international law, balance of power, and collective security determine how the failure of diplomacy can lead to conflict, and evaluates the importance and consequences of technology in relation to these conflicts. The theme also analyzes the rise of colonialism (and subsequent decolonization), imperialism, and global interdependence as part of diplomacy.

Social and Economic History

The social history theme includes an analysis of the shift in social classes from a hierarchical order to one of social mobility. Changes in gender roles, attitudes towards race, ethnicity, and influence of sanitation, urbanization, diet, and changes in food are examined within the scope of social history.

The economic history theme entails an examination of changes in agricultural production and organization and the development of commercial practices such as mass production and consumption. Economic history also includes the study of the consequences of industrialization, competition, the role of the state in economic activity, and the importance of global interdependence in our world.

The examination questions are broken down as follows:

Themes of the AP European History Examination		
Intellectual and cultural themes	30–35%	24–28 questions
Political and diplomatic themes	30–35%	24–28 questions
Social and economic themes	30–35%	24–28 questions

Fifty percent of the multiple-choice questions cover the period from 1450 to 1815; see Chapter 1, "The Renaissance (c. 1350–c. 1550)" through to Chapter 5, "The Age of Revolution: The French Revolution and Napoleonic Era," and 50 percent cover the period from 1815 to 2000; see Chapter 6, "Mercantilism and the Agricultural and Industrial Revolutions," through Chapter 14, "Contemporary Europe."

Although the AP European History examination tests specific themes, there will always be questions that are cross-topical and require you to draw on a bank of knowledge that may relate to events before 1450 but impact post-1450 events. For example, the Black Death occurred during the Medieval period but impacted society during the fifteenth century. However, there are no questions in any of the sections that specifically ask about events that took place before 1450 or the post-2001 period (p. 4 of the *College Board Bulletin*).

The AP European History Exam Format

The AP examination is 3 hours and 5 minutes in length. The examination is divided as follows:

- **Section I:** 80 Multiple-Choice Questions—55 minutes. These questions test your knowledge of the three major themes. It is anticipated that the students will not be familiar with all the material covered.
- **Section II:** Free-Response portion of the exam—130 minutes.
  - **Part A:** A mandatory 15-minute reading of the Document-Based Question (DBQ). Students then have 45 minutes to answer the DBQ.
  - **Part B:** Students have 70 minutes to answer two thematic essay questions. It is recommended, but not mandatory, that students spend 5 minutes planning for each essay and 30 minutes writing each essay.

The thematic essays cover a variety of historical periods and change every year to ensure that different time periods are addressed. The groupings are not necessarily chronological.

The AP European History Exam's Scoring Procedure

The critique for grading the AP European History exam is as follows:

Section I

Multiple Choice: This section is worth 50 percent of the total grade. The raw score of the multiple-choice section is obtained by adding up the number of correct questions minus the number you answered incorrectly and multiplying by 0.25. Thus, you can answer 51 questions correctly out of 60 questions, leave 20 blank and still be on track to get a score of 3. Usually, if you get a raw score of 48 out of 80 for multiple-choice and do well on the essays, you can earn a score of 3.

Section II (Free-Response Section)

- **Part A:** DBQ—worth 45 percent of the grade.
- **Part B:** Thematic Essays—worth 55 percent of the grade.

AP Grades

The total raw scores are converted to a 5-point scale.

Scoring	
5	Extremely Well Qualified
4	Well Qualified
3	Qualified
2	Possibly Qualified
1	No Recommendation

Students who achieve a score of 3 or better usually receive college course credits for their AP scores. However, some colleges require that students achieve a score of 4 or 5 to receive credit. Students should contact their college directly for their AP policies and should also go on-line for a college search (www.collegeboard.com) to try to get information about a particular school's AP policies.

How to Use this Book

This book has various features that will enable you to score well on the AP exam. To get the most out of your review:

- **Review the format of the AP examination as outlined in the Introduction.**
- **Read the section on "Preparing for the Examination."**
- **Study the review chapters.** Focus on those sections that you think are your weak areas. Complete the sample questions at the end of each chapter.
- **Take the three Sample Practice Tests.** Once again, check your answers with the correct responses in the book.
- **Check all your answers for the Multiple-Choice Questions.** Carefully read all explanations for the correct and incorrect answers as well as for the ones you were unable to answer.
- **Read your essay answers for the DBQ and Thematic Essays.** Compare your responses with the models outlined in the book.

Preparing for the Examination

Helpful Hints for Studying for the AP European History Examination

There is no set way to study for the AP European History exam. However, the following procedures can help you:

Keep the big picture in mind: The writers of this examination design questions to determine if you have mastered the main ideas or generalizations about a particular period or event in history. What are the main events associated with this question? Who are the key personalities? What are the important results? An example of this type of question is as follows:

1. Which was one of the factors that contributed to Adolf Hitler's rise to power?

    A. The Communist Party supported the Weimar Republic.
    B. The Nationalist Socialist Party (NSDAP) won an absolute majority of votes in the Reichstag.
    C. Hitler used military power to seize direct control of the government.
    D. An alliance with the Nationalists gave Hitler a parliamentary majority.
    E. France and England supported the Nazi Party.

The correct answer is **D.** The Nationalist Party supported Hitler's Nazi Party because they were anti-communists and Hitler had promised to restore the greatness of Germany.

This question requires students to understand the economic, political, and social conditions within Germany during the 1920s, and the anger of the German people towards the Versailles Treaty, as well as Germany's relations with its former enemies from World War I (France and England). This illustrates the "big picture of events" — the broad context within which student must frame his or her response.

Avoid studying trivial information: This exam assesses how well you know information in the context of the broad political, social, and economic trends of the historical era. There are no rote-memory questions on the exam that require little historical analysis. There will never be a question such as the following:

1. Who was the Russian Czar in 1917?

   A. Nicholas I
   B. Nicholas II
   C. Alexander I
   D. Alexander II
   E. Alexander III

The correct answer is **B.**

Avoid studying straight military history: Military battles are only important as they relate to political, economic, and social events or as an introduction of technology.

Look for chronology and order of difficulty: Exam questions are organized in chronological order in the multiple-choice questions. Each group of questions will be more difficult than the preceding group of questions. The first group of questions is usually on the Renaissance and the Reformation, the Enlightenment, the French Revolution, and so on. You will notice a break when you go from one group to another. The first 20 to 25 questions are usually the easiest, and the most difficult are given at the end of the exam. Usually the questions from 30 to 60 are in the middle range of difficulty.

Focus on the connections in history: History should not be studied as a collection of incidents in isolation but as a series of strands that are connected by cause and effect and interconnecting events. For example, students should try to understand how the importance of individuals as well as reasons in society contributed to the Renaissance and also to the Scientific Revolution and the Enlightenment. The belief in reason led to the idea that not only kings, but individuals could rule government, which led to the growth of democracy. In analyzing the causes of World War I, students should assess this event in the context of the growth of nationalism, imperialism, and industrialization in the world of the nineteenth century. This approach to history helps students understand how the events are connected in history and to comprehend the big picture in history.

Types of Multiple-Choice Questions

There are several types of European History multiple-choice questions on the examination. They include the following:

- Identification questions
- Analysis questions
- Reading/quotation questions
- Skill-based questions, including maps, graphs, and charts
- Illustration-type questions, including political cartoons, posters, photographs, works of art, and sculpture
- "Except"-type questions

Identification Questions

The majority of the questions are of this direct and straightforward variety: Identify a person and connect that person to an historical event or idea, a group of people, an invention, or a development. You need to have a basic knowledge of the topic — there is little historical analysis required to answer this type of question. Approximately 40 to 45 percent of the questions are of this type.

1. Which was an immediate result of the Protestant Reformation?

   A. Breaking of the religious unity of Europe
   B. Strengthening the political power of the pope
   C. Increasing the influence of the Roman Catholic Church
   D. Restoration of political unity to Western Europe
   E. The growth of mercantilism

The correct answer is **A**. You need to know what the Protestant Reformation was and how it influenced Europe. If you had known that the Protestants were against strong papal authority and religious wars were fought during the sixteenth century, it would help you eliminate choices B, C, D, and E.

---

2. The main purpose of the Congress of Vienna was to

    A.   establish strategies to rebuild the Russian economy.

    B.   turn back the clock in Europe to conditions that existed prior to the French Revolution.

    C.   create a European Court of Justice.

    D.   promote the ideals of the French Revolution.

    E.   establish collective security systems to ensure peace.

The correct answer is **B**. You must know that the Congress of Vienna was convened to help end the chaos in Europe after the upheavals of the French Revolution and Napoleon's domination of Europe. You can also answer this question correctly by knowing that the Congress of Vienna was a conservative reaction to the democratic ideals of the French and Napoleonic revolutions.

These questions are very direct and you must have specific information about these events.

Analysis Questions

This type of question requires less specific information but tests your ability to draw conclusions by considering cause and effect. In this type of question, you need less specific information but must have a broader understanding of the historic period, trend, or relationship. Knowing the time frame of the events and the chronology of the period will help you determine how one event influenced another and can help you select the correct answer. Approximately 20 to 25 percent are analysis-type questions.

---

3. Which of the following resulted from the revocation of the Edict of Nantes?

    A.   France succeeded in breaking up the Triple Alliance.

    B.   Huguenots were granted the right to freedom of worship in France.

    C.   The French aristocracy vigorously opposed the revocation.

    D.   The Catholic Church in France was freed from the domination of Louis XIV.

    E.   Many French Protestants emigrated to England and Holland.

The correct answer is **E**. The French Protestants or Huguenots escaped France and settled in England and Holland. Many of them were craftsmen and business people and their loss hurt the French economy. This is an analysis question of the cause-and-effect variety. This question requires you to evaluate and assess each choice to determine its validity. If you recall that the Edict of Nantes granted religious freedom to the Protestants and that Louis XIV's revocation in 1685 was part of his effort to assume absolute control, you would know that Choice D is incorrect because Louis XIV wanted absolute power to extend over all aspects of society. Choice C is incorrect because the French aristocrats had long petitioned the king to crack down on the Protestants.

---

4. The Thermidorian Reaction refers to

    A.   the Metternich System.

    B.   the restoration of Charles II of England.

    C.   the fall of Robespierre.

    D.   Napoleon's Hundred Days.

    E.   the *Declaration of the Rights of Man and of the Citizen*.

The correct answer is **C**. You can answer this question if you are able to connect the Thermidorian Reaction to the time period of the French Revolution of 1789 and how it affected the country. By putting the events in order, you can eliminate other choices. The Metternich System refers to efforts by Prince Metternich of Austria after the Congress of Vienna (1814–1815) to stop the spread of the revolutionary ideas of the French. You can also eliminate choices B, D, and E because the time frame for the restoration of Charles II took place in the seventeenth century, Napoleon's Hundred Days in 1815, and the *Declaration of the Rights of Man and of the Citizen* in 1789. This elimination process leaves Choice C. The Thermidorian Reaction of 1794 was the successful effort of the French moderates and conservatives to depose Robespierre because of the excesses of the Reign of Terror.

Reading/Quotation Questions

This type of question requires you to read a quote or a passage from pieces of literature and identify the author or the philosophy of that school of thought. It does not require specific information and is not too difficult to answer. You should look for key words or ideas to help you understand the passage. About 10 percent of the questions are of this type.

---

5. **Statement:** A prince being thus obliged to know well how to act as a beast must imitate the fox and the lion . . . one must therefore be a fox to recognize traps, and a lion to frighten wolves.

   This quotation is from the writings of

   A. Machiavelli.
   B. Rousseau.
   C. Locke.
   D. Darwin.
   E. Adam Smith.

The correct answer is **A.** The theme of the passage is how a ruler should rule. You should be able to associate this idea with Machiavelli to help you select Choice A. If you do not recognize the passage, you can use the process of elimination. Rousseau and Locke are associated with the social contract and natural rights. Darwin's theme is survival of the fittest, and Smith supported capitalism. By eliminating all of the other choices, you are left with A.

Skill-Based Questions (Maps, Graphs, and Charts)

This type of question requires map skills and limited information to answer the question. When answering this type of question, be sure to note the title, legend, or key before answering. Maps usually present information about social, economic, and political issues. Approximately 10 percent are this type of question.

Graph and chart questions are usually easy to answer because they contain all the data necessary to arrive at the correct answer. Graphs and charts are useful in determining patterns of change over a period of time. Approximately 10 percent are this kind of question.

A chart/graph question is below:

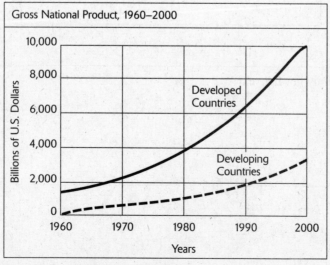

Courtesy of Wizard Test Maker, Eduware, Inc.

6. Which of the following conclusions can be drawn from the graph about economic growth in developing and developed countries?

    A. By 2000, the economic growth rate in developing countries will be greater than that of developed countries.

    B. Between 1990 and 2000, the economic growth rate will decrease in developed countries.

    C. Between 1980 and 1990, the economic growth rate was faster in developing countries than in developed countries.

    D. Between 1960 and 2000, the difference in the economic growth rate between developed and developing countries has increased.

    E. Between 1980 and 2000, the GNP remained steady in developed countries.

The correct answer is **D**. The graph shows that the GNP in developed countries has grown progressively larger than in developing countries between 1960 and 2000. By looking at the chart, you can see that there has been a continuous growth in both developed and developing countries but the difference between the two types of countries has increased in favor of developed countries. There is no evidence that any of the other choices can be supported by the chart/graph.

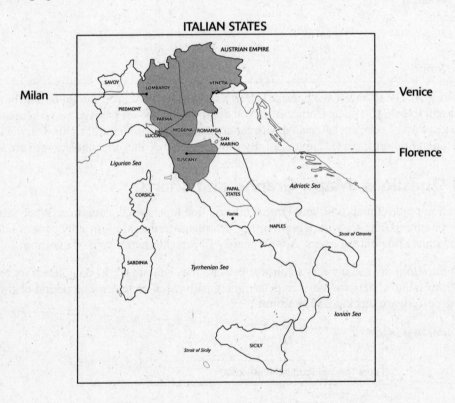

7. This map represents Italy in what year?

    A. 1861

    B. 1815

    C. 1950

    D. 1970

    E. 1890

The correct answer is **B.** You have to remember that Italy was divided into many different states and did not become a united country until 1861; thus A, C, D, and E are incorrect. That leaves Choice B. In 1815, northern Italy was part of the Austrian Empire and cities such as Venice, Milan, and Florence were controlled by Austria.

Illustration-Type Questions (Political Cartoons, Posters, Photographs, Works of Art, and Sculpture)

Political cartoons are distorted to emphasize a point of view. This type of question is relatively easy if you avoid reading too much into the question. Read the captions and titles carefully. Like political cartoons, poster questions are very straightforward and easy to answer. Once again you must read the document carefully and try to place it in the context of the time period. Questions related to photographs, works of art, and sculpture ask you to identify what is taking place or to put the work of art in historical perspective.

Courtesy of Wizard Test Maker, Eduware, Inc.

8. Which political system is best represented in this cartoon?

   A. Absolutism
   B. Democracy
   C. Communism
   D. Feudalism
   E. Theocracy

The correct answer is **C.** There is no reference in this cartoon to absolutism, democracy, feudalism, or theocracy. The key object in the cartoon is the hammer and sickle representing communism. The quote reflects the inability of communism to meet the demands of its people, which led to its fall in 1989.

"Except"-Type Questions

This type of question can be confusing because you are being asked which of the five choices does not belong. When you see the question, immediately circle the word EXCEPT. Cross out the choices that would be correct if you leave out EXCEPT. Then you are left with the correct choice. Approximately 10 percent of the questions on the exam are of this type.

9. All of the following were totalitarian states in the 1930s EXCEPT

    A. Germany.
    B. Italy.
    C. Spain.
    D. France.
    E. Russia.

The correct answer is **D.** Germany under Hitler, Italy under Mussolini, Spain under Franco, and Russia under Stalin represented forms of totalitarianism. France was unlike the totalitarian regimes of Germany, Italy, Spain, and Russia. France's traditional policy of political pluralism and democracy avoided totalitarianism. The key to this question is to circle EXCEPT and then cross out all the examples of totalitarian government. This will leave you with Choice D.

Hints and Strategies for Mastering the Multiple-Choice Questions

- **Read the questions carefully and underline the key words in each question.** This helps you to avoid careless mistakes. Focus on the main idea of the question and what is being asked.

- **Answer the easy questions first.** This strategy will instill confidence and enable you to budget your time more efficiently.

- **Read all choices carefully before making a selection.** Sometimes the initial choice may seem correct, but only by being patient can you choose the best answer.

- **Go with your first instincts.** Most of the time your first choice is the best. Don't change any answers unless you are absolutely certain.

- **Use the process of elimination.** Cross out the incorrect answers so that you can narrow down the possible correct choices. This technique will increase the possibility of getting the right answer.

- **Make educated guesses.** If you can eliminate two or three choices, your odds of getting the correct answer improve. Multiple-choice scores are based on the number of questions answered correctly. Points are not deducted for incorrect answers, and no points are awarded for unanswered questions. Because points are not deducted for incorrect answers, students are encouraged to answer all multiple-choice questions.

- **Budget your time.** Don't get stuck on one question. Circle the questions you can't answer and return to them after you finish the 80 questions. Sometimes, you might find clues or hints in other questions. Remember, you are not penalized for unanswered questions.

The Free-Response Section

Students have two hours and ten minutes to write three essays in this section of the exam.

- **Part A:** Document-Based Question (DBQ)—Comprises 45 percent of the free-response section. There is a 15-minute mandatory reading of the documents provided in the exam, and 45 minutes is allowed for writing the essay.

- **Part B:** Thematic Essay—Comprises 55 percent of the Free-Response Section. You will have 70 minutes to write two thematic essays.

In order to write the DBQ or the thematic essays, it is important that you understand the meaning of the key words and what is being asked. Below is a list of frequently used terms on the AP essay questions:

- **Analyze:** To explain or the give reasons for the cause of an event; to show relationships between events. *Example:* Analyze the way in which society was changed as a result of the ideas contained in the *Communist Manifesto*.

- **Assess/Evaluate:** To judge the validity of a statement; to determine the advantages and disadvantages of a generalization. *Example:* Democracy developed in England through evolution, while in France democracy developed through revolution. Include facts in your evaluation to support your argument.

- **Compare/Contrast:** To identify similarities and differences between two or more things. *Example:* Compare and contrast the totalitarian regime of Adolf Hitler in Germany with that of Joseph Stalin in Russia.
- **Describe:** To tell about or to draw a picture about a particular event. *Example:* Describe the political, economic, and social consequences of the Protestant Reformation.
- **Discuss:** To examine various points of view or present different sides of the subject; to write about a topic. *Example:* Discuss the extent to which the Versailles Treaty influenced the spread of nationalism and totalitarianism in Italy and Germany.
- **Explain:** To make clear or plain; to give greater detail or to tell the meaning of something. *Example:* Explain how political, economic, and social factors contributed to the French Revolution of 1789.
- **Identify:** To refer to specific events or developments; to make connections to historical events. *Example:* Identify the political and social conditions before 1914 that contributed to the fall of the Romanov Dynasty.

Strategies for Writing the Essays

Part A: Document-Based Question (DBQ)

The Document-Based Question is an exercise that tests your ability to analyze and synthesize different historical viewpoints. The primary purpose of the DBQ is to evaluate how students can answer a question from the documentary evidence. It is not a test of a student's prior knowledge. In writing the DBQ, a student acts like an historian who must arrive at a conclusion from the available writings. There is no single correct answer. By using a variety of documents, you can defend or refute a particular viewpoint. There are approximately 10 to 12 documents on the examination.

The following is a helpful set of steps for writing the DBQ:

1. Read the questions/historical background carefully. Determine your task. Underline the keywords in the question (Analyze, Discuss). Write down any information that you can connect to the question or to the historical background.
2. Read all the documents. Circle key phrases or words in the documents that are related to the main theme.
3. Take note of the source of the document, and the author's point of view or bias. Make a chart of the key ideas of each document. Separate them to reflect both sides of the question.
4. Decide on your thesis statement. Outline the essay. Include an introductory statement that leads up to your thesis.
5. DO NOT summarize or give a laundry list of documents. Remember to include relevant outside historical facts as long as they are accurate.
6. Weave or incorporate the documents together.
7. Write a conclusion to show that you have proven the thesis.

Scoring the DBQ

The DBQ is graded on a 0-to-9 scale. Since 2000, the College Board has introduced a core-scoring method to grade the DBQ. Core-scoring means that you may earn a total of six Basic Core points if you demonstrate basic competence, such as having an acceptable thesis statement or using a majority of documents. You may earn an additional three points in Expanded Core points only if you successfully earn all six Basic Core points. The following chart specifically identifies the two cores of points. You should use this scoring guide or rubric when you are writing your practice DBQ essay contained in this book. Compare your essay to the rubric to make sure you have provided all the required information.

Generic Core-Scoring Guide for AP European History Document-Based Questions (Score Scale 0–9)			
Basic Core	**Points**	**Expanded Core**	**Points**
1. Has an acceptable thesis that addresses all aspects of the question. The thesis should not restate the question.	1	Expands beyond the basic core of 1–6 points. A student must earn points in the basic core area before earning points in the expanded core area.	0–3
2. Uses a majority of documents.	1	Gives examples	
3. Supports the thesis with appropriate evidence from documents.	1	Addresses all parts of the question thoroughly.	
4. Understands the basic meaning of the documents cited in the essay.	1	Provides a clear, analytical, and comprehensive thesis.	
		Uses all or almost all documents.	
5. Provides an analysis of bias or point of view in at least two or three documents.	1	Provides an insightful analysis of the documents.	
6. Demonstrates an analysis of the documents by grouping them according to a particular viewpoint.	1	Evaluates bias or point of view in at least four documents cited in the essay.	
		Analyzes the documents by creating additional groupings or other forms of analysis.	
		Incorporates relevant "outside" historical content.	
Subtotal	6	Subtotal	3
		Total	9

A Practice DBQ

Directions: The following question is based on the accompanying Documents 1 to 10.

---

1. Analyze the responsibility of the European powers towards the outbreak of World War I.

   Historical Background: From 1815 to 1914, Europe enjoyed a period of peace and prosperity. However, the arms race, the alliance system, and the issue of nationalism in the Balkans created tension. The assassination of Archduke Ferdinand of Austria-Hungary in June 1914 in Sarajevo by a Bosnian youth was the spark that led to World War I.

Document 1

Per Capita Expenditures of the Great Powers on Armaments						
	1870	**1880**	**1890**	**1900**	**1910**	**1914**
Great Britain	$3.54	$3.46	$3.84	$12.60*	$7.29	$8.23
France	2.92	4.02	4.66	5.21	6.47	7.07
Russia	1.28	1.50	1.26	1.44	2.32	3.44
Germany	1.28	2.16	2.80	4.06	4.06	8.19
Austria-Hungary	1.08	1.70	1.50	1.46	1.68	3.10
Italy	1.38	1.74	2.52	2.34	3.36	3.16

*Boer War costs

Source: From *Europe, 1815–1914*, by Gordon A. Craig, 1966.

Document 2

Heir to Austria's Throne Is Slain with His Wife by a Bosnian Youth to Avenge Seizure of His Country

Sarajevo, Bosnia, June 28 . . . Archduke Francis Ferdinand, heir to the throne of Austria-Hungary, and his wife, the Duchess of Hohenberg, were shot and killed by a Bosnian student here today. The fatal shooting was the second attempt upon the lives of the couple during the day, and is believed to have been the result of a political conspiracy.

Later details show that the assassin darted forth from his hiding place behind a house and actually got on the motor car in which the Archduke and his wife were sitting. He took close aim first at the Archduke, and then at the Duchess. The fact that no one stopped him, and that he was allowed to perpetrate the dastardly act indicate that the conspiracy was carefully planned and that the Archduke fell a victim to a political plot. The aspiration of the Serbian population in Bosnia to join with Serbia and form a great Serbian kingdom is well known. No doubt today's assassination was regarded as a means of forwarding the plan. . . .

Source: *New York Times*, June 29, 1914. 1. c. 1914 by The New York Times Company.

Document 3

Gavrilo Princip, arrested and tried, gives his reasons for the assassination:

No, I am not sorry. I have cleared an evil out of the way. He (Francis Ferdinand) is a German and an enemy of the South Slavs. He treated them badly . . . Every day a high treason trial. Every day it went worse with our people. They are impoverished . . . I killed him and I am not sorry. . . . I regarded him as an energetic man who as ruler would have carried through definite ideas and reforms which stood in our way . . . For union (of the South Slavs) one must sacrifice many lives, and it was for this reason that Franz Ferdinand fell. Nevertheless, the main motive, which guided me in my deed was: the avenging of the Serbian people . . .

Source: *Current History,* August 1927, pp. 703–706.

Document 4

German Chancellor Bethmann-Hollweg notifies the German Ambassador of the Kaiser's position:

Finally, concerning Serbia, His Majesty naturally can not take any stand in the questions between Austria and Serbia, for they are beyond his competence, but (Austrian Emperor) Francis Joseph may be sure that His Majesty, in accordance with his treaty obligations and old friendship, will stand true by Austria's side.

Source: *Kautsky Documents,* published in December, 1919, by Weimar Republic.

Document 5

. . . the Royal Serbian Government has done nothing to repress these movements. It has permitted the criminal machinations of various societies and associations directed against the Monarchy, and has tolerated unrestrained language on the part of the press, the glorification of the perpetrators of outrages and the participation of officers and functionaries in subversive agitation. . . .

. . . (The) Royal Governments see themselves compelled to demand from the Royal Serbian Government a formal assurance that they condemn this dangerous propaganda against the Monarchy. . . .

. . . To accept the collaboration in Serbia of representatives of the Austro-Hungarian Government for the suppression of the subversive movement . . . the Austrian Hungarian Government expects the reply of the Royal Government no later than 6 o'clock on Saturday morning.

Source: This is an excerpt from the *Austro-Hungarian Red Book No. 7,* sent to Serbia on July 23, 1914.

Document 6

Sir George Buchanan, British Ambassador to Russia, notes:

I had a telephone message this morning from [Russian Foreign Minister] Sazonof . . . [who] said that Austria's conduct was both provocative and immoral; she would never have taken such action unless Germany had first been consulted; some of her demands were quite impossible of acceptance. He hoped that His Majesty's Government would not fail to proclaim their solidarity with Russia and France.

The French Ambassador gave me to understand that France would fulfill all the obligations entailed by her alliance with Russia, if necessity arose, besides supporting Russia strongly in any diplomatic negotiations.

Source: *British Blue Book, No. 6,* Official Diplomatic Documents, 87.

Document 7

Emperor William II's telegram to Czar Nicholas II on July 29, at 1 a.m., a day after Austria-Hungary declared war on Serbia (July 28):

It is with the gravest concern that I hear of the impression, which the action of Austria against Serbia is creating in your country. The unscrupulous agitation that has been going on in Serbia for years has resulted in the outrageous crime, to which Archduke Franz Ferdinand fell a victim. The spirit that led Serbians to murder their own king and his wife [in 1903] still dominates the country. You will doubtless agree with me that we both . . . have a common interest as well as all Sovereigns to insist that all the persons morally responsible . . . should receive their deserved punishment. In this case politics play no part at all. . . .

I am exerting my utmost influence to induce the Austrians to deal straightly to arrive at a satisfactory understanding with you. I confidently hope you will help me in my efforts to smooth over difficulties that may still arise.

Source: *Schilling Diary,* "How the War Began in 1914: Diary of a Russian," Foreign Document Office, p. 45.

Document 8

Nicholas II replies to William II's telegram:

. . . In this most serious moment, I appeal to you to help me. An ignoble war has been declared to a weak country. The indignation in Russia shared fully by me is enormous. I foresee that very soon I shall be overwhelmed by the pressure brought upon me and be forced to take extreme measures which will lead to war. To try and avoid such a calamity as a European war I beg you in the name of our old friendship to do what you can to stop your allies from going too far.

Source: *Schilling Diary,* p. 46.

Document 9

The Allied and Associated Governments affirm and Germany accepts the responsibility of Germany and her allies for causing all the loss and damage to which the Allied and Associated Governments and their nationals have been subjected as a consequence of the war imposed upon them by the aggression of Germany and her allies.

Source: Article 231 of the Treaty of Versailles.

Document 10

In this excerpt from May 7, 1919, Count Brockdorff-Rantzau, leader of the German delegation to the Versailles Peace Conference, protested:

It is demanded of us that we shall confess ourselves to be alone guilty of the war. Such a confession from my lips would be a lie. We are far from declining all responsibility for the fact that this great World War took place or that it was fought in the way that it was. . . . But we energetically deny that Germany and its people, who were convinced that they fought a war of defense, were alone guilty. No one would want to assert that the disaster began only at that disastrous moment when the successor of Austria-Hungary fell a victim to murderous hands. In the last fifty years, the imperialism of all European states has chronically poisoned international relations. Policies of retaliation, polices of expansion, and disregard for the right of peoples to determine their own destiny, have contributed to the European malady, which came to a crisis in the World War. The mobilization of Russia deprived statesmen of the opportunity of curing the disease, and places the issue in the hands of the military powers. . . .

Source: *German White Book,* pp. 3–4.

Analysis of the DBQ Question and Documents

Analysis of the Question

This question presents you with the task of determining who was responsible for World War I. You must decide if the Versailles Treaty, Article 231, placing the blame solely on Germany, is accurate. To determine the validity of Article 231, you have to assess whether England, France, Austria-Hungary, and Russia bear responsibility and how conditions prior to World War I contributed to its outbreak. You should include relevant outside information to help support and reinforce your thesis statement.

Analysis of the Documents

- **Document 1:** This chart shows that Germany and Great Britain spent the most per person on armaments. The chart could be used to show that the countries were preparing for war and that this arms race led to fear among neighboring countries.
- **Document 2:** The headline clearly shows that the Archduke Ferdinand was killed because of political conspiracy. It is important to note that this is an American viewpoint; the U.S. declared its neutrality in 1914.
- **Document 3:** Princip's statement that he killed Archduke Ferdinand for national reasons might be relevant in assessing responsibility.
- **Document 4:** Bethmann-Hollweg's statement affirms his decision to support Austria. This document could be used to show Germany's responsibility towards the war.
- **Document 5:** This Austrian-Hungarian excerpt contains specific demands on Serbia. This document may be used to show how Austria's ultimatum was either reasonable or unreasonable.
- **Document 6:** This document states how Great Britain had decided to stand firm with Russia and France.
- **Document 7:** Emperor William II's telegram demonstrates his efforts to prevent Russian action against Austria. This document can be used to contrast Germany's attitude with her position in Document 4.
- **Document 8:** Nicholas II's reply shows how he was appealing to William II to help him stop Austria. This document can be useful to show how Russia was trying to contain the force of the war.
- **Document 9:** According to the Versailles Treaty, Germany accepted the sole responsibility for the war. This statement should be evaluated in light of other documents.
- **Document 10:** This excerpt shows that Germany rejected that it alone was responsible for the war. The Count's claim that the imperialism of all European nations caused the war can be used to show how all the nations were responsible.

First Student DBQ Essay

The origin of the outbreak of World War I has been a source of controversy. The question of who was responsible was raised during the war and answered specifically in the Versailles Treaty. In Article 231 of the Versailles Treaty, Germany and her allies accepted the responsibility for causing all the losses and damages associated with World War I (Doc. 9). Rather than Germany being blamed as the sole cause of the war, the responsibility for World War I was the result of conditions in Europe at the beginning of the twentieth century as well as the failure of European diplomacy to effectively deal with the crisis that developed after the assassination of Archduke Ferdinand in 1914 (Doc. 10).

In the period between 1871 and 1914, a number of developments took place that created tension between the major powers. In 1871, the Unification of Germany upset the balance of power, and the decision of Emperor William II in 1890 to build up a navy comparable to that of Great Britain created an arms race that haunted Europe (Doc. 1). From 1890 to 1914, England, France, and Germany substantially increased their per capita expenditures on armaments (Doc. 1). Germany's decision to add an expensive fleet of gun battleships to its expanding navy heightened tensions with England. German nationalists, like Admiral Alfred von Tirpitz, saw a large navy as a source of pride and patriotic unity. However, the British saw it as a military challenge.

By 1914, Europe had developed an alliance system of England, France, and Russia (Triple Entente) and the Triple Alliance (Austria-Hungary, Germany, and Italy). These alliances divided Europe into rival camps. Thus, the alliances and armaments pursued for defense proved to be a means of creating tension. The alliance systems also guaranteed that the crisis would be Europe-wide. The immediate crisis that threatened the peace of Europe occurred on June 28, 1914, when Gavrilo Princip, a Serbian nationalist, assassinated the heir to the Austrian-Hungarian throne, Archduke Ferdinand, and his wife, while they were visiting Sarajevo, the capital of the Austrian province of Bosnia (Doc. 2). Princip, who later was proven to be a member of the Black Hand, a radical Serbian nationalist group, assassinated the Archduke because he wanted an independent state free of Austrian-Hungarian control. Austria-Hungary resisted this movement in order to preserve their empire. Since Princip was loosely connected with the Serbian government, Austria-Hungary wanted to punish Serbia. Austria sought Germany's help and Chancellor Bethmann-Hollweg offered Austria a blank check of support (Doc. 4).

Subsequently, Austria issued an ultimatum requiring Serbia to cease all subversion in Austria and all anti-Austrian propaganda in Serbia. They also wanted a joint commission to investigate all aspects of the assassination at Sarajevo (Doc. 5). These demands amounted to Austrian control of the Serbian state. Serbia turned to its big Slavic brother, Russia, for assistance. The British Ambassador to Russia began to inform the government in England that the Russians wanted their support and that France was going to support Russia.

It was apparent that the diplomatic situation was out of control. Military plans and timetables began to dictate policy. When Austria-Hungary declared war on Serbia on July 28, William II tried to prevent Russian mobilization against Austria (Doc. 7). However, Nicholas II, Czar of Russia, realized that once Austria had mobilized its troops, Russia would be forced to take action that would lead to war (Doc. 8). Count Brockdorff-Rantzau, leader of the German delegation at the Versailles Treaty, believed that the mobilization of Russian troops had made political efforts secondary to military considerations (Doc. 10).

The march toward war could not be stopped. On August 1, Germany declared war on Russia; on August 3, France declared war on Germany; on August 4, England declared war on Germany after she violated Belgium neutrality in her attempt to invade France. Sidney Bradshaw Fay in his book The Origins of the World War claims that none of the great powers wanted war and all of them must bear responsibility for the conflict. Serbia wanted Austro-Hungarian territories and subject nationalities in the Austria-Hungary empire wanted their independence. Russia and Germany were rivals in the Balkans and each wanted to dominate the area. Britain and Germany were competing for world dominance and saw each other as threats to their security. Finally, in August of 1914, each country believed that they had been wronged and they rallied to defend it. The majority of the population enthusiastically embraced the outbreak of war.

Reader's Comments on the First Student DBQ Essay

- The student makes effective use of the documents and adds relevant outside information, such as mention of the Alliance System.
- The various points of view of each of the documents are clearly addressed.
- The student identifies the documents with the proper number assigned to them.
- Sentence structure flows smoothly.
- The thesis is clearly stated within the first paragraph and put into historical context.
- The student makes a strong argument to show that the responsibility for World War I was shared by all the European powers.

Possible student score: 8–9

Second Student DBQ Essay

I agree that Germany was solely responsible for World War I. Document 9 Article 231 of the Versailles Treaty states that Germany accepts the responsibility for causing all the "loss and damage to which the Allied government . . . and their nationals have been subjected."

In Document 1, the increased spending on armaments by Germany would indicate that she was preparing for war. In 1910, Germany was spending $8.19 per capital expenditures which was only four cents less than Great Britain's amount of $8.23.

When Archduke Ferdinand was assassinated, Germany promised, as stated in Document 4, "that His Majesty, in accordance with his treaty obligations and old friendship, will stand true by Austria's side." With this blank check from Germany, Austria-Hungary issued an ultimatum that demanded that the Serbian Government "condemn this dangerous propaganda against the Monarchy . . ." (Doc. 5). The ultimatum also demanded that Serbia accept the "collaboration in Serbia of representatives of the Austro-Hungarian Government for the suppression of the subversive movement . . ."

In Document 6, the British Ambassador to Russia notifies his government in London that Austria's stand was provocative and that she would never have taken this stand unless Germany had been consulted.

Based on the documents presented, I believe that Germany was solely responsible for World War I. The large arms buildup, the alliance system, and the blank check to Austria encouraged Austria to take a hard line. If Germany had not been so forceful, World War I would not have happened.

Reader's Comments on the Second Student DBQ Essay

- The student discusses the documents superficially and merely lists the documents.
- The student strings the documents together to create an essay but there is no analysis of the documents.
- The student's thesis fails to analyze the responsibility of other European countries and merely focuses on Germany.
- There is no outside information.

Possible student score: 1–3

Part B: The Thematic Essay

The Thematic Essay part of the Free-Response Section requires students to answer two essays from a set of three questions from Group I and three questions from Group II. You must select one question from each group. The first group of questions covers the period from the Renaissance to the Napoleonic era, and the second group covers the period from the Napoleonic era to the present. Students have 70 minutes to answer both questions. It is usually suggested that they use 5 minutes as planning time for each question and 30 minutes for writing time. Most thematic essays are descriptive because you are asked to analyze, assess/evaluate, and compare/contrast the causes and effects of an historical subject. The Thematic Essay, unlike the DBQ, requires you to incorporate all relevant outside information and to represent it in an organized and coherent fashion.

Topics of Thematic Essays

The three themes — intellectual/cultural, political/diplomatic, and social/economic — have all been equally represented in this section of the examination in recent years. The common topics have been the Renaissance, Reformation, Enlightenment, French Revolution, Napoleon, art interpretation, economic/political issues of the nineteenth century, Marxism, imperialism, nationalism, communism, Cold War, and post-World War II economic changes in Europe.

The following is a list of strategies for writing the thematic essays:

1. Read the questions in each group. Jot down key facts that you know about each question. Select the question for which you have the most information. Focus on those questions which you may have previewed or which you may have discussed in class.
2. Underline the key directive words such as assess, evaluate, explain, compare, and contrast.
3. Make your choice and begin to organize your information.
4. Develop your thesis statement (your position) and outline the facts you want to include in your essays.
5. Check the facts in your outline to be sure you are correct. DO NOT include any incorrect or unsure information.
6. Begin to write. Include an introductory paragraph, a supporting paragraph, and a summary/conclusion of your position. Be sure to use concrete historical examples to support your ideas.
7. Proofread your essays. Check to see if they are organized; look for factual inconsistencies, poor sentence structure, or anything that may weaken the support of your thesis statement.

A Practice Thematic Essay

> Assess the validity of the following statement: The Bolshevik Revolution of 1917 directly influenced the Russian people and other nations.

Before writing this essay, check the preceding strategies for writing the thematic essay and follow these three steps:

1. Jot down what you know about the topic: causes, personalities, and effects of the Russian Revolution on people and countries of the world.
2. Underline the key word, assess, which means to determine if the statement is accurate.
3. Frame certain questions in your mind, such as: Did the Russian Revolution really change the lives of the people and the government? Did the Russian Revolution influence other nations?

First Student Thematic Essay

The Russian or Bolshevik Revolution of 1917 had a major impact on the people of Russia and other nations. An underlying cause of the Russian Revolution was that compared to Western Europe, the country was an undeveloped nation. The Romanov czars who had ruled Russia for close to 300 years were absolute rulers. Through the secret police, the czars vigorously suppressed demands for reform and punished reformers by imprisonment, execution, or exile to Siberia. Economically, Russia had not been industrialized. Serfs or farmers made up more than 75 percent of the population. They were still bound to the lands like the serfs of the Middle Ages.

In the late nineteenth century, Alexander II and his son Nicholas II began the process of industrializing Russia. The landless peasants provided the cheap labor and French investors provided the resources. The Russians constructed iron and steel mills, textile factories, and railroads. Russia's Industrial Revolution created two new economic classes: workers and capitalists. The workers and the middle class business owners began to demand more rights. Both groups desired a voice in the government and opposed Czarist absolutism.

The immediate cause of the Russian Revolution was Russia's involvement in World War I. The country was unprepared for war. Russian industries were not developed enough to meet the demands for war supplies. The transportation system could not supply the armies at the front. At one time, only one out of three soldiers had a rifle. Poorly equipped troops suffered enormous losses. Especially in the cities, people faced shortages of food and other goods because of the war. Czar Nicholas II ignored demands to withdraw from the war and did nothing to improve these conditions. In March, 1917, riots and strikes erupted in St. Petersburg; crowds protested the war and shortage of food. When Czar Nicholas II's troops refused to fire on the striking city workers and some joined the protest, the Russian Revolution had officially begun. Nicholas II abdicated and a new provisional government of Alexander

Kerensky was established. This new government guaranteed civil liberties but refused to withdraw from the war. When the Kerensky government was unable to solve the food crisis and refused to support the land seizures by the peasants, the Bolsheviks under the leadership of Lenin began to gain supporters using the slogan of Peace, Land, and Bread. The Bolsheviks gained followers because they promised to end the war, provide food for the people, and obtain land for the peasants. On November 6/7, 1917, armed Bolsheviks seized power and set up a communist government.

Immediately upon seizing power, the Bolsheviks (who later became known as the Communists) sought to transfer Russia's economic system from capitalism to communism. Under a program called War Communism, the government nationalized mines, factories, railroads, and land and prohibited most private ownership. War Communism proved a failure. Factory workers failed to maintain production schedules and farmers curtailed their production because the state seized their surplus crops without payment. In 1921, Lenin was forced to crush riots by peasants and workers and an open rebellion by previously pro-Bolshevik soldiers at Kronstadt. Lenin put to death 15,000 soldiers. In March, 1921, Lenin introduced the New Economic Policy which re-established limited economic freedom in an attempt to rebuild agriculture and industry. Peasants and small retail traders were allowed to sell their products in free markets for profit. However, heavy industry, railroads, and banks were wholly nationalized. By 1928, the NEP had revived Russia's economy, and agriculture and industrial output had reached pre-World War I levels.

The transformation of Soviet society had a profound impact on the lives of women. The Russian Revolution immediately proclaimed complete equality for women. In the 1920s, divorce was made easily available and women were urged to work outside the home and liberate themselves sexually.

The Revolution turned Russia into a communist country which affected Europe as well as the rest of the world. In 1922, the communists reorganized Russia into four republics and renamed the country the Union of Soviet Socialist Republics (USSR) or the Soviet Union.

The Russian Revolution also created fear that communism would spread to other countries. According to Karl Marx, the Father of Communism, communism could only be successful if there was a worldwide revolution to spread their ideas. In Italy, the Fascist dictator Benito Mussolini and in Germany, the Nazi dictator Adolf Hitler claimed that only their form of totalitarianism could save their nations from the evils of communism. By battling the communist movement, the Nazis, like the Fascists in Italy, gained the support of property holders, bankers, and industrialists.

The Communist Revolution also affected Russia's relationship with the United States. The United States did not recognize the USSR until 1933. Although the United States and Russia were allies in World War II against Germany, they reverted back to their pre-war hostilities at the end of the war in 1945. The United States and Russia entered a Cold War which lasted from 1947 to 1989. The Cold War, which has often been described as a war of words between the forces of democracy and communism, led to tension in Europe, Asia, Latin America, and Africa. The ideas of communism also led to the rise of Mao-Tse-Tung in China and Fidel Castro in Cuba. Both of these leaders were successful in establishing communist governments in their countries. The fear of communism also led to the development of nuclear arsenals that threatened the safety of the world.

Although the Soviet Union collapsed in 1991, communism still exists in Cuba and China. The fall of communism in Russia has left the country with unresolved economic, social, and political issues. Poverty is still a problem in Russia and the quality of life continues to decline.

Evaluating the Sample Thematic Essay

- Did the essay show a thorough understanding of the theme of the question?
- Did the essay include relevant facts, examples, and details to support the theme?
- Were the facts, references, and examples accurate?
- Was the essay well developed and did it demonstrate a logical and clear plan of organization?
- Did the essay contain an introductory and concluding statement that support the theme or refute the question?
- Did the essay show an ability to analyze and evaluate events?

Reader's Comments on the First Student Thematic Essay

- The thesis statement is clear.
- The essay provides specific background on the causes of the Russian Revolution and how War Communism and the NEP changed the economic life in Russia.
- The reference to the Kronstadt Rebellion demonstrated the ruthlessness of communism.
- The changing role of women in the Soviet Union also provided concrete facts about how communism influenced Russia.
- The essay uses historical facts such as a reference to how communism influenced events in the United States, Italy, Germany, China, and Cuba.
- The essay structure is logical and well developed.
- A weakness of the essay was the failure to include how Stalin affected Soviet life through the Five Year Plans and collectivization policies.

Possible score: 8–9

Second Student Thematic Essay

The Russian or Bolshevik Revolution took place on November 6/7, 1917. Lenin, the leader of the Bolshevik (Communist Party), gained the support of the people by promising land, peace, and bread.

When he was in office, Lenin began to change the economy. He introduced the New Economic Policy, which allowed Russians some economic freedom but heavy industry was still nationalized. The Russian Revolution also created fear in other countries. Benito Mussolini in Italy and Adolf Hitler in Germany rose to power because they claimed that they would save the country from communism.

The Communist Revolution also led to a Cold War with the United States and led to the rise of communism in China and Cuba. The fear of communism also contributed to the nuclear arms race, resulting in the fear of nuclear warfare.

Reader's Comments on the Second Student Thematic Essay

- The thesis is absent or never really stated.
- The student neglects to discuss or evaluate any specific information.
- The student really does not have the factual information to write and develop the answer.
- There is no logical development of ideas.

Possible score: 2–3

Some Frequently Asked Questions about the AP European History Exam

Q. What should I do on the day of the exam?

A. Relax. Have a good breakfast but not a huge one. You need energy for the exam, but avoid eating too much because it could make you sleepy. Don't drink too much coffee, tea, or soda, which might lead to frequent use of the rest room during the examination. Bring a healthy snack for the break. The additional food will give you extra energy. Remember to turn off your cell phone.

Bring two sharpened No. 2 pencils for the multiple-choice section of the examination. Bring an eraser or be sure that your pencils have good erasers. If you change a response on the multiple-choice questions, you must erase the answers thoroughly in order to ensure that there are no stray marks. For safety's sake, bring additional pencils. Be sure to have two pens with dark blue or black ink. All the essays must be written in pen.

Bring a watch so that you can monitor your own time. Normally, the proctor will keep you informed of the time.

Bring your high school code with you. Your guidance counselor will have this information.

Relax and be positive. Don't cram information a few minutes before the examination.

Q. How long is the exam?

A. The exam is three hours and five minutes.

Section I: 80 multiple-choice questions—55 minutes

Section II: Free-response questions—130 minutes

> Part A: Mandatory reading of the Document Based Question (DBQ)—15 minutes; Suggested writing time—45 minutes
>
> Part B: Students will have to answer two thematic essays—70 minutes

The total examination takes about 3½ hours, which includes the reading of the instructions, collecting the papers, and the 5–10 minute break.

Q. Will guessing hurt my score?

A. No. Make an educated guess. If you are able, narrow down the choices to two or three, then go for it. The odds of getting the correct answer will improve. Remember, points are not deducted for incorrect answers, so students are encouraged to answer all the multiple-choice questions. Do not leave any questions unanswered. No points are given for unanswered questions.

Q. Is there a specific length for the free-response questions?

A. The readers grade your responses on content, not length. It is important that your essay be organized and hit the essential points of the questions. The reader is looking for specific information and it is important that you avoid information that is not relevant to the topic. Budget your time so that you can devote sufficient time to answer the questions. Remember that there are six free-response questions for Part B. The proctor will suggest that you move on to the next section, but you will not be mandated to go on to the next part. Remember that the readers are looking for how well you organize and synthesize your information. Do not just present a collection of facts.

Q. Is it necessary to use all the documents for the DBQ question?

A. You should use as many documents as necessary to answer the question. Obviously, you should use more than half of the documents in order to fully support your thesis or the focus of the essay. It is also important that you analyze and evaluate the documents rather than merely list them. The reader is looking to see how well you use the documents to analyze the information to support your historical thesis.

Q. Do penmanship, spelling, and neatness count?

A. The readers will not penalize you for poor handwriting, lack of neatness, and misspelled words. The readers are looking at your essay holistically and understand that you are pressed for time and have to write quickly. However, if your penmanship is poor and your essay is illegible, it becomes harder to get the best score when the readers are not exactly sure of what you are stating. If you have poor handwriting, spend a few extra minutes in writing the essay. The graders are marking thousands of essays and cannot devote too much time to trying to decipher each paper. You should also avoid last-minute revisions inserted in different places because it can confuse the readers and gives the impression that you are not organized. Usually, your first draft contains the essential information. Do not doubt yourself.

Q. Where can I outline my ideas for the essay questions?

A. Most students use the green booklet that contains the DBQ and the Thematic Essays. All your writing is done in the pink booklet. You should underline key phrases or terms for each of the questions, such as discuss, analyze, and compare, and any key facts that you associate with the questions. This simple technique will help you to focus on the main idea of the question. Use the green booklet only to outline the key ideas. If the proctor provides you with additional scrap paper, do not write an entire question and then rewrite it in the pink booklet. Remember, you are only graded for the information in the pink booklet.

Q. How much should I prepare for the examination?

A. Preparing for the examination is something that you will be doing with your class and teacher during the entire year. Take good notes on all your readings and make sure that your assignments are done thoroughly and completely. Make a list of authors or historians and their viewpoints on the different topics which you have discussed during the year. This summary can be used to briefly review the highlights about each time period.

Q. How much should I review?

A. Start studying for the exam at least a month in advance. Start slowly, perhaps ½ hour once or twice a week. Become familiar with the format of the exam. Organize a study group with your class to discuss practice essays and how to rate them. Use the guide in this book as your model.

Don't cram. Get a good night's sleep and relax on the day of the exam.

Q. **When are the scores reported and who receives them?**

A. The examination is graded in June and the scores are sent to the high school and colleges that students have designated by the middle of July. If you want to get your scores earlier (July 1) by phone, you can call toll free (888) 308-0013. There is a fee for this service which is payable by credit card. You will also need your AP number as well as your Social Security number.

Q. **Can I withhold or cancel my scores?**

A. Yes. If you want to withhold or cancel a score, you must contact the College Board by June 15 of the year that you take the examination. There is a $5 fee for withholding the score but not for cancelling the score. Be sure that you have your AP number, and the name of your high school, city, and state. Before you consider either withholding or cancelling a score, consider that college officers are looking for students who are willing to challenge themselves rather than just at the results.

How to Make Effective Use of this Book

1. The purpose of this book is to give you an overview of the AP European History Examination. The book will provide you with the structure and format of the examination.

2. This book is not a textbook but a tool to help you prepare for the examination by providing you with the essential information that you need to prepare for the exam.

3. Throughout the year you should use the review chapters in this book to help you study for unit exams and quizzes. You should also analyze the questions at the end of each chapter to help reinforce the material that you are studying. Always read the reasons for the correct as well as the incorrect choices to help you better understand why a particular response is right.

4. Refer throughout the year to the strategies for answering the Multiple Choice, DBQ, and Thematic Essay.

5. Do the practice examinations in the back of this book so that you become familiar with the format of the exam.

6. Follow the specific directions (time allotments and so on) for each practice examination in this book. This will give you a good barometer on how to budget your time for the examination.

PART I

SUBJECT AREA REVIEWS WITH SAMPLE QUESTIONS AND ANSWERS

The Renaissance (c. 1350–c. 1550)

The word **Renaissance** means *rebirth* in French. The Renaissance was a period of artistic and cultural achievement in Europe from the fourteenth to the sixteenth century. It was characterized by a number of distinctive ideas about life, specifically secularism, individualism, Humanism, and materialism. The spirit of the Renaissance influenced European society for generations, making the Renaissance truly a golden age in European history.

If the Renaissance was a rebirth of culture, you might think that the period before the Renaissance was one of gloom and darkness. Actually, historians have shown that the Medieval Era, or Middle Ages, did produce art, architecture, literature, and other ideas in law, languages, and economics that influenced Europe in the fourteenth century and provided the foundation for the Renaissance. However, during the Middle Ages, writers and philosophers viewed society as a preparation for the afterlife. Renaissance writers were interested in the present or secular world.

The table below explains some of the important differences between the Middle Ages and the Renaissance:

Differences between the Middle Ages and the Renaissance		
	Middle Ages	**Renaissance**
Purpose of art	Glorify God	Glorify the individual
Politics	Local/feudal lords ruled	Kings in England, France, and Spain centralized power
Society	Church as center of activity	Secular/material world became a vital part of life
Religion	Focus of one's life	Important but not most dominant
Education	Church promoted education to prepare students for religious life	Stressed teaching of history, arts, ethics, and public speaking

Italian Renaissance

The Renaissance began in Florence, Italy, and subsequently spread to the rest of Italy and then to Northern Europe. Unlike other areas of Europe, Italian cities had survived the economic crises of the late Middle Ages. Italian towns had remained important centers of Mediterranean trade and boosted their production of textiles and luxury goods. Furthermore, Italy was the center of ancient Roman history. Architectural remains, statues, and amphitheatres were visible reminders to Italians of the "Glory of Rome."

The Italian City-States

At the time of the Renaissance, Italy was made up of numerous **city-states** that were geographically situated to benefit from the revival of trade that had developed as a result of the Crusades. The northern city-states of Florence, Venice, and Genoa acted as middlemen in the lucrative trade with the East. These northern, independent city-states marketed goods such as wool, silk, and other products to countries in Europe and Asia. They became prosperous centers of banking, trade, and manufacturing.

The cities of northern Italy also benefited from being able to absorb stimulating new ideas from their advanced Byzantine and Muslim neighbors on the Mediterranean Sea. By 1350, the city-states of Florence, Venice, and Genoa were urban regions with populations of about 100,000, a large figure by medieval standards. The conditions were right for these cities to undergo a cultural explosion.

At the height of the Renaissance, several city-states, including the Republic of Genoa, the Republic of Florence, the Duchy of Milan, the Venetian Republic, the Papal States, and the Kingdom of Naples, were important. Within these city-states, merchants used their wealth as steppingstones to economic and political leadership. Bankers made loans to kings and supported other commercial ventures that contributed to economic growth across Europe. Men like Francesco Sforza in Milan and Cosimo de' Medici in Florence, who gained power because of their own merit and not based on birth, became sponsors of the arts. They began to realize that their wealth enabled them to enjoy the material pleasures of life as well as fine fashion, arts, and architecture.

Florence: The Symbol of the Renaissance

Florence, the most dominant of the Italian cities, became known as the symbol of the Renaissance. Like ancient Athens, Florence attracted people of talent from other Italian city-states. The **Quattrocento,** a common historical term for the Golden Age of the Renaissance, began in the 1400s when the Medici family of Florence exerted power over that city. The Medicis were a merchant family who amassed a fortune in the wool trade and expanded into banking. They provided Florence with political and artistic leadership.

Through marriages, the Medici family became affiliated with the major houses of Europe. Besides acquiring the "Grand Dukes of Tuscany" title, the Medici family produced three popes (Leo X, Clement VII, and Leo XI), two queens of France (Catherine de' Medici and Marie de' Medici), and several cardinals of the Roman Catholic Church. The rise of the Medicis in Florence coincided with the triumph of the capitalist class over the guild merchants and artisans. The Medicis also exerted control over the government without holding any permanent official position, ruling Florence as part of the Grand Duchy of Tuscany until the 1700s. However, the Medicis were driven from power and expelled from Florence three times: from 1433 to 1434, from 1494 to 1512, and from 1527 to 1530. The attempts (such as the Pazzi conspiracy of 1478) of the Florentine republicans to restore their former liberties ultimately failed because of the Medicis' wealth and connections.

In 1434, **Cosimo de' Medici** (1389–1464) took control of the government of Florence. He was a shrewd political leader who was also the wealthiest man of his time but chose to rule Florence by staying behind the scenes. He controlled local politics by ensuring that all eight members of the city council were loyal to him. He ruled for thirty years as a dictator and won the support of the people by championing popular causes.

Cosimo's grandson, **Lorenzo de' Medici** (1449–1492), also known as Lorenzo the Magnificent, was a clever politician who never held any public office but ruled with absolute control behind the scenes. Lorenzo represented the Renaissance ideal. He was a generous patron of the arts who saw the beauty of present life as complete fulfillment. Poets and philosophers visited the Medici palace. Lorenzo, who wrote poetry, supported artists such as Michelangelo (1475–1564) and Botticelli (1445–1510) and encouraged them to visit Florence.

Lorenzo's son, **Giovanni de' Medici** (1475–1521), who became Pope Leo X from 1513 to 1521, was also an important patron of the arts. He is remembered more for his interest in art than as a pope. He was a patron of Raphael (1483–1520), who was one of the Renaissance's greatest Italian painters. Raphael painted a number of Madonnas, mostly during his time in Florence. Giovanni also promoted the rebuilding of St. Peter's Church in Rome.

Humanism and Society

The defining concept of the Renaissance was **Humanism,** a literary movement that began in Italy during the fourteenth century. Humanism was a distinct movement because it broke from the medieval tradition of having pious religious motivation for creating art or works of literature. Humanist writers were concerned with worldly or secular subjects rather than strictly religious themes. Such emphasis on secularism was the result of a more materialistic view of the world. Unlike the Medieval Era, Renaissance people were concerned with money and the enjoyment of life and all its worldly pleasures. Humanist writers glorified the individual and believed that man was the measure of all things and had unlimited potential.

Humanism had far-reaching effects throughout Italy and Europe. The advent of Humanism ended Church dominance of written history. Humanist writers secularized the view of history by writing from a nonreligious viewpoint.

The Humanists also had a great effect on education. They believed that education stimulated the creative powers of the individual. They supported studying grammar, poetry, and history, as well as mathematics, astronomy, and music. Humanists promoted the concept of the well-rounded, or Renaissance, man who was proficient in both intellectual and physical endeavors.

Humanist writers sought to understand human nature through the study of classical writers such as Plato and Aristotle. They believed that the classical writers of ancient Greece and Rome could teach important ideas about life, love, and beauty. The revival of interest in the classical models of Greece and Rome was concentrated primarily among the educated people of the Italian city-states and focused on literature and writing.

During the Middle Ages in Western Europe, Latin was the language of the Church and educated people. The Humanist writers began to use the *vernacular,* the national languages of a country, in addition to Latin.

Some important Italian Humanists of the Renaissance included the following:

- **Giovanni Pico della Mirandola** (1463–1494) was an Italian who lived in Florence and expressed in his writings the belief that there were no limits to what man could accomplish.

- **Francesco Petrarca,** known as **Petrarch** (1304–1374), was the Father of Humanism, a Florentine who spent his youth in Tuscany and lived in Milan and Venice. He was a collector of old manuscripts, and through his efforts the speeches of Cicero and the poems of Homer and Virgil became known to Western Europe. Petrarch's works also led to the rise of the **Civic Humanists,** those individuals who were civic-minded and looked to the governments of the ancient worlds for inspiration. Petrarch also wrote sonnets in Italian. Many of these sonnets expressed his love for a beautiful woman named Laura. His sonnets greatly influenced other writers of the time.

- **Leonardo Bruni** (1369–1444), who wrote a biography of Cicero, encouraged people to become active in the political as well as the cultural life of their cities. He was a historian who today is most famous for the *History of the Florentine People,* a 12-volume work. He was also the Chancellor of Florence from 1427 until 1444.

- **Giovanni Boccaccio** (1313–1375) wrote *The Decameron.* These hundred short stories were presented within the framework of a group of young men and women who fled to a villa outside Florence to escape the Black Death. Boccaccio's work is considered to be the best prose of the Renaissance.

- **Baldassare Castiglione** (1478–1529) wrote one of the most widely read books, *The Courtier,* which set forth the criteria on how to be the ideal Renaissance man. Castiglione's ideal courtier was a well-educated, mannered aristocrat who was a master in many fields, from poetry to music to sports.

Humanism and Women

Humanism represented some advances for women. During the Middle Ages, few women could read or write outside of the convents. In the cities of the Italian Renaissance, upper-class girls received an education somewhat similar to boys. Young ladies studied the writings of ancient Greece and Rome. Some women could also speak one or two modern languages such as French or Spanish, and a small minority achieved some fame. In the latter sixteenth century, at least 25 women published books in Italy. Leonardo Bruni created an educational program for women. However, it did not include a provision for public speaking, which was essential for men but not considered vital for a woman's education. **Christine de Pisan** (1364–1430), born in Venice and the daughter of the physician to French King Charles V, was schooled by her father in Latin, philosophy, and various branches of science. In 1405, she wrote *The Book of the City of Ladies,* which was an attempt at a dialogue with male philosophers and writers who claimed that women had no capacity for education and were inferior to men in mind, body, and soul. Pisan used historical examples to show how women had been unjustly oppressed and how historic women had contributed to society. **Laura Cereta** (1469–1499) reflected the success and failure of Humanist women. Educated in a convent, she learned languages, philosophy, theology, and mathematics. However, by 15, like other educated women, she had to choose between marriage and full participation in social life, and study and withdrawal from the world. Although Cereta chose marriage, she was widowed after only eighteen months and spent the remaining twelve years studying and withdrawing from society.

Although some Renaissance women were better educated than their medieval counterparts, their education prepared them for the social functions of domestic or home life. They were expected to use their education to run a household. Educated men, however, were supposed to know how to rule and to participate in public affairs. The Renaissance ideal was different for men and women. The ideal woman offered balance to man. She was vibrant and not too reserved. She also had to be beautiful because that was a sign of goodness.

Spreading Humanism

Two inventions helped spread the ideas produced by the Humanists across Italy and the rest of Europe. About 1450, **Johannes Gutenberg** (c. 1398–1468) a German printer, invented printing through the development of a movable metal-type press. The first European book printed by machine was the **Gutenberg Bible** (1455). With the Gutenberg Bible, the European age of printing had begun. As compared to the medieval practices of hand copying or block printing books at a tediously slow pace, the movable-type press tremendously increased output and decreased costs. As books became more readily available, more people learned to read and write. The increased circulation of books by Italian writers helped to spread more of the ideas of the Renaissance to other parts of Europe.

Northern Renaissance

In the last quarter of the fifteenth century, the ideas of the Italian Renaissance spread to Northern Europe. Northern writers interpreted Italian ideas and attitudes toward classical antiquity in terms of their own traditions. These writers in Holland, England, Germany, and France were more Christian, or at least more pious, than those of Italy. The secular and pagan themes of Greece and Rome received more attention from the Italians. In Northern Europe, the Renaissance had a distinct religious character and stressed biblical and early Christian themes along with the original works of the classical world. These writers tried to create a more perfect world by combining the best elements of the ancient world with Christian culture. Unlike the Italian Humanists, who stressed secularism and individualism, the Northern Humanists focused on broad programs of social reform based on Christian ideals.

Some of the most important writers of the Northern Renaissance include the following:

- **Sir Thomas More** (1478–1535) of England, wrote his *Utopia* (which means "nowhere") in 1516 to describe a fictional, ideal society somewhere off the main land of the New World. In More's *Utopia,* all children received an education in the Greco-Roman classics. There was also social equality since all profits from business and property were held in common. *Utopia* asserts that man, through his own efforts, can construct a perfect world. More's ideas were original in that he contradicted the long-standing view that evil existed in society because man was basically corrupt. Instead, More maintained that the acquisition of private property promoted vice and corruption. If a society could reform or change the institution that molded an individual, society could improve. More played a major role in introducing Humanism into England. He was decapitated in 1535 by Henry VIII for not supporting Henry's break with the Catholic Church. In 1935 the Catholic Church made him a saint.

- **Desiderius Erasmus** (c. 1466–1536) of Holland, known as "The Prince of Humanists," dominated the intellectual thought of the northern Renaissance. His *The Praise of Folly* satirized ignorance, superstition, and many Church practices. He criticized the religious abuses of the Church and called for men to lead lives exemplifying simple Christian piety. In the book *Handbook of a Christian Knight,* he stressed the importance of Christians to act in accordance with the Christian faith rather than merely performing the necessary rites of the sacraments. Erasmus also wrote Greek and Latin editions of the Bible. Both he and Sir Thomas More are often referred to as **Christian Humanists** who criticized the Church but preached reason and reform rather than radical changes like Martin Luther.

- **William Shakespeare** (1564–1616) of England is often considered the greatest poet and playwright of all time. Shakespeare's best-known plays include the histories, *Henry IV* and *Henry V,* and the tragedies, *Romeo and Juliet, Hamlet, Julius Caesar,* and *Macbeth.* Shakespeare helped set the standards for the English language.

- **François Rabelais** (1494–1553) of France, a friar and classicist, wrote the romances *Gargantua* and *Pantagruel.* With tongue-in-cheek humor, he portrayed a comic world of giants whose adventures satirized education, politics, and philosophy.

- **Michel Eyquem de Montaigne** (1533–1592) of France introduced the essay as a literary form to Europe. He expressed skepticism towards accepted beliefs and urged people to reject superstition and intolerance.

- **Geoffrey Chaucer** (c. 1342–1400) of England wrote *The Canterbury Tales,* a collection of witty short stories. This is one of the early classics of English literature.

Politics of the Renaissance

Italy

During the Middle Ages, the test of a good government was whether it provided justice, law, and order. Politically, the Renaissance produced a different approach to power. During the Renaissance, the test of a good government was whether it was effective as well as able to increase the power of the ruler. The Florentine **Niccolo Machiavelli** (1469–1527) put this new approach into practice. Machiavelli served the Florentine Republic as secretary and diplomat but was dismissed from office when the Medici family came back to power in 1512. In an attempt to regain the favor of the government, Machiavelli wrote *The Prince* (1513), a virtual instruction manual for a prince or ruler on the manner in which he should rule. This major work, which focuses on ethics and government, describes how rulers maintain power by methods that ignore right or wrong. Rulers need to accept the philosophy that "the end justifies the means." Machiavelli believed that politicians should manipulate people and use any means to gain power. He did not advocate amoral behavior, but thought that a politician's actions should not be governed by moral consideration. A prince had to combine the cunning of a fox and the power of a lion to achieve his goals. Machiavelli dedicated the book to Lorenzo de Medici in the hopes that that he would restore Italy to its former greatness. Throughout the sixteenth century, Italy was a battleground in which France and Spain fought for dominance. Machiavelli believed that Lorenzo was in the best situation to unite Italy because of his family's great influence in Florence and over the Church, since Lorenzo's uncle was Pope Leo X.

The most able practitioners of Machiavelli's approach to politics were the fifteenth- and sixteenth-century monarchs: Louis XI of France, Henry VII and Henry VIII of England, and Ferdinand and Isabella of Spain. These leaders acted according to the principles discussed in *The Prince*. They invested in their government a strong sense of authority and leadership. In the sixteenth century, **Jean Bodin's** (1530–1596) work, *The Six Books of the Commonwealth,* outlined the first systematic and clear conception that absolute sovereignty resided in the nation, regardless of the forms of government. The "state" was an absolute sovereign that tolerated no rival legal authority above it except God. Bodin's ideas would contribute to the rise of absolutism in Europe.

France

Although France won the **Hundred Years' War** (1337–1453), a series of wars fought between France and England, the French country was left devastated. Farmland was destroyed and many French nobles lost their lives. Yet, the French monarchy became stronger since the war had weakened the power of the nobles. A revival of commerce, leading to the rise of the *bourgeoisie* (middle class), further strengthened the power of the king. Throughout the late fifteenth and early sixteenth centuries, the French kings consolidated their power. Louis XI, who ruled from 1461 to 1483, was the most successful of these monarchs. He curbed feudal anarchy, set up an efficient government, and is considered to be the architect of French absolutism.

England

After the Hundred Years' War, England struggled to rebuild its economy. Unfortunately, the end of this war led to a civil war, known as the **War of the Roses** (1455–1485), between the House of York (symbolized by a white rose) and the House of Lancaster (symbolized by a red rose). After a 30-year struggle, a Lancasterian, Henry Tudor (1457–1509), gained control of England and his line ruled England until the seventeenth century. Called **Henry VII,** he reestablished the monarch's authority over the nobles and promoted trade and prosperity. His most famous accomplishment was the establishment of the **Star Chamber,** a court to check aristocratic power. There was no jury, and torture was a common remedy for all problems.

Spain

Spain, unlike France and England, was divided into many separate kingdoms. The various groups who lived on the peninsula lacked a common tradition. Muslims (Moors) and Jews had significantly influenced Spanish society. Until the 1100s, the Moors had controlled most of the country and many Jews had achieved high positions in finance, government, and medicine. The **Reconquista** was nearly an 800-year struggle to drive the Muslims out of Spain. By the late 1400s, the Muslims held only the kingdom of Granada. **Ferdinand V of Aragon** (1452–1516) married **Isabella of Castile** (1451–1504), in 1469, thus uniting the Christian kingdom of Spain and laying the foundation for the final stage of the Reconquista. In 1492 (the same year that Columbus landed in America) the combined armies of these kingdoms drove the Moors from Granada and from Europe, bringing the entire Iberian peninsula under Christian leadership. Ferdinand and Isabella worked together to consolidate royal authority and to strengthen the Spanish kingdom, although during their reign, Spain remained a loose confederation of separate states. Ferdinand and Isabella used the *hermandades,* a collection of local police forces, to strengthen royal justice. They also used the Church as a vehicle of state authority, reviving in 1478 the **Inquisition,** a religious court controlled by the monarchy. The Inquisition, which ultimately led to the expulsion of all Jews, monitored and persecuted those who were suspected of heresy, especially converted Jews, known as the *marranos* or *conversos.* By the end of their reign, Ferdinand and Isabella had established a strong central government, which enabled Spain to become a leader in the exploration of Asia and the discovery of the New World in the Americas.

Artistic Achievements of the Renaissance

Renaissance art has the following characteristics:

- It imitates the classical work of ancient Greece and Rome and rejects the medieval forms of art.
- It is very realistic. Artists studied human anatomy in detail and worked from live models. They also created the technique of three-dimensional perspective.
- It portrays secular themes and glorifies the achievements of the individual.

Some Renaissance artists include the following:

- **Giotto** (1267–1337) was born in Florence and helped to make it the first great center of the Renaissance. He is famous for his frescoes (paintings on walls), such as *St. Francis Preaching to the Birds.* His realistic paintings replaced the artificial two-dimensional art represented in the Middle Ages. He also designed a bell tower, usually called Giotto's Tower, for the Cathedral of Florence.
- **Lorenzo Ghiberti** (1378–1455) was a Florentine sculptor. He is famous for the bronze doors of the Baptistery, a great cathedral in Florence. The ten panels on the door depict realistic scenes from the Bible and took 21 years to complete.
- **Donatello** (1386–1466) was the most influential Florentine artist before Michelangelo. He revived the classical figure of the nude body with its balance and self-awareness. His *David* was the first nude statue of the Renaissance.
- **Filippo Brunelleschi** (1377–1446) was born in Florence and was one of the pioneers of early Renaissance architecture in Italy. His most prestigious work was the Cathedral of Florence in 1434 because of its dome or cupola, which was supported without scaffolding, columns, arches, or pilasters. The dome was the biggest innovation in Renaissance architecture and the first to be completed in Western Europe since the fall of the Roman Empire.
- **Leonardo da Vinci** (1452–1519) is today known as an example of a "Renaissance man," an expert in many fields who has a wide range of interests. He was a painter, sculptor, inventor, architect, musician, engineer, and scientist. He dissected human corpses to see how muscles and bones worked. His sketchbooks include plans for a flying machine and underwater boats. His paintings also include *The Last Supper,* which was painted with oil on a plaster wall. His most famous painting is the *Mona Lisa.*
- **Michelangelo** (1475–1564), like da Vinci, was skilled in many areas. He was a sculptor, engineer, poet, painter, and architect. His murals of biblical figures and scenes on the ceiling of the Sistine Chapel are his most famous works. His sculptured masterpiece of the fourteen-foot statue of *David* in the city of Florence is considered to have been a propaganda tool to inspire the citizens in their struggle against Milan. Michelangelo also carved the *Pieta,* showing Mary grieving over the dead Jesus, and designed the dome of St. Peter's Church in Rome.
- **Raphael** (1438–1520) worked in Florence and Rome. He is considered to be the greatest painter of the Renaissance. Although he is famous for his beautiful Madonnas, especially *Sister Madonna,* his fresco, *The School of Athens,* is considered to be the greatest masterpiece of Renaissance art. Raphael's realistic portrayal of Aristotle and Plato, combined with God, the Father, holding the globe and St. Augustine dictating *The City of God,* exemplify the realistic religious themes of the Renaissance. His use of proportion and perspective adds to the quality of the fresco.

Raphael's fresco, *The School of Athens.*

- **Frans Hals** (c. 1580–1666) painted portraits of everyday life that captured the spirit of the Dutch people. His well-known work, *The Laughing Cavalier,* is probably one of the most reproduced paintings in art.
- **Rembrandt** (1606–1669) is considered the greatest Dutch painter. He is famous for his realism and dramatic use of light and shade. His paintings include religious subjects and scenes from everyday life. His most famous works include *The Night Watch* and *Aristotle Contemplating a Bust of Homer.*
- **El Greco** (The Greek) (1541–1614) was a Spanish artist. He painted religious scenes, such as *The Assumption of the Virgin,* and landscapes, such as *View of Toledo.*
- **Albrecht Dürer** (1471–1528) was a German artist who is famous for his metal and wood engravings. His most noteworthy work is *Praying Hands.*

Chronology of the Renaissance

1337–1453	Hundred Years' War between England and France. The war leaves both nations crippled.
c. 1353	Boccaccio's *Decameron* becomes the first great prose work of the Renaissance.
c. 1390	Geoffrey Chaucer's *The Canterbury Tales* becomes one of the first works written in the vernacular (language of the people) of England, his homeland. Chaucer had become familiar with the works of Dante and Boccaccio while traveling in Italy.
1434	Cosimo de' Medici establishes his family's dominance in Florence.
1436	Filippo Brunelleschi finishes the Cathedral of Florence.
c. 1450	German Johannes Gutenberg revolutionizes the world of the written word with the introduction of the movable-type printing press.
1453	Ottoman Turks capture Constantinople; end of the Byzantine Empire.
1455–1485	The English House of York and House of Lancaster fight each other for political control in the War of the Roses.
1469	The marriage of Isabella of Castile and Ferdinand of Aragon.
1478	The Inquisition is introduced into Spain to control the activity of the *marranos* (Jews who had converted to Christianity).
1485	The Tudor dynasty is established in England with the end of the War of the Roses.
1492	Completion of the Reconquista; expulsion of the Jews from Spain.
1501–1504	Michelangelo creates the sculpture *David*.
1503–1506	Leonardo da Vinci labors on his signature piece, the *Mona Lisa*.
1508–1512	Michelangelo paints the Sistine Chapel ceiling.
1509	Erasmus publishes *In Praise of Folly*.
1513	Niccolo Machiavelli writes *The Prince*.
1516–1519	Desiderius Erasmus produces his Greek and Latin translations of the New Testament.
1527	The sack of Rome by Holy Roman Emperor, Charles V.

Sample Multiple-Choice Questions

1. Which situation contributed most to the beginning of the Renaissance?

    A.   Strong rulers censored new ideas.
    B.   Europe became increasingly isolated from other regions.
    C.   The emphasis on religious uniformity increased.
    D.   A wealthy class that supported the arts emerged.
    E.   Europe began to discover the writings of St. Thomas Aquinas.

2. An important characteristic of Renaissance Humanists was their emphasis on

    A.   accepting ideas based on Confucian thought.
    B.   the teachings of the Roman Catholic Church.
    C.   magic and alchemy.
    D.   the idea that the glorification of the individual was sinful.
    E.   classical Roman and Greek writings.

3. The above painting of the painter known as Masaccio demonstrates what characteristics of Renaissance art?

    A.   Elaborate ornamentation
    B.   Realistic portrayal of individuals
    C.   One-dimensional perspective of individuals
    D.   Lack of inner perspective
    E.   Gothic style of color and detail

4. Which of the following families used its powerful influence in banking to promote the creative artists in Florence during the Renaissance?

    A.   Medici
    B.   Sforza
    C.   Donatello
    D.   Bellini
    E.   Condottieri

5. The Northern Humanists were different from the Southern Humanists because they emphasized

   A. economic gain and materialism.
   B. social reform based on Christian ideals.
   C. pagan virtues.
   D. scholastic dogma over reason.
   E. emphasis on democracy as a political system.

6. The best description of Machiavelli's *The Prince* is

   A. a satire on sixteenth-century politics.
   B. a call for Italian nationalism.
   C. an outline of constitutional principles for establishing a government.
   D. a handbook on politics as practiced in Renaissance Italy.
   E. a brief history of city-states of Florence.

7. "Tedious were it to recount, how citizen avoided citizen, how among neighbors was scarce found any that shewed fellow-feeling for another, how kinsfolk held aloof, and never met, or but rarely; enough that this sore affliction entered so deep into the minds of men and women, that in the horror thereof brother was forsaken by brother, nephew by uncle, brother by sister, and oftentimes husband by wife; nay, what is more, and scarcely to be believed, fathers and mothers were found to abandon their own children, untended, unvisited, to their fate, as if they had been strangers. . . . "

   The author of this passage was

   A. Baldassare Castiglione
   B. François Rabelais
   C. Leonardo Bruni
   D. Giovanni Boccaccio
   E. Giovanni Pico della Mirandola

8. Which of the following themes was dominant in the work of Erasmus?

   A. A complete break with the Catholic Church
   B. Support of classical literature
   C. A belief in the monastic life of contemplation and divorce from the material world
   D. A belief in scholasticism
   E. The importance of Christian education for moral and intellectual development

9. Renaissance men's view of educated women was that they should

   A. be encouraged and given an equal place in society.
   B. have a voice in the affairs of the city.
   C. not be encouraged in any manner.
   D. be allowed to add a social touch to the household, but otherwise remain subservient to men.
   E. be treated as equals in all activities.

10. A basic idea contained in Sir Thomas More's *Utopia* was that

    A. evil exists because men and women are basically corrupt.
    B. political leaders must learn how to manipulate their subjects.
    C. social order is only an unattainable ideal.
    D. corruption and war are due to acquisitiveness and private property.
    E. government derives power from a social contract with the people.

Multiple-Choice Questions: Answers and Explanations

1. **D.** In the fifteenth century, a wealthy class of merchants and bankers, such as the Medici family who had amassed large fortunes in Florence, became the major sponsors of Renaissance artists. Art was used as a way to glorify the success of the sponsors and their families. Strong Renaissance rulers were more concerned with developing countries into nations than with censoring new ideas. The Catholic Church, however, was more concerned with censorship, such as with Galileo and Copernicus. Religious uniformity declined in the Renaissance. Writers such as Erasmus criticized some of the abuses of the Church. These criticisms gave rise to the Protestant Reformation, which destroyed the religious unity of Europe. Humanism rejected the Scholastic philosophy of St. Thomas Aquinas and focused on the writings of the Greeks and Romans. Europe became less isolated as it increased trade with Asia and explored new lands in the Americas.

2. **E.** Renaissance Humanists and writers emphasized classical Roman and Greek writings, examining the worldly subjects that the Romans and Greeks had studied. These Humanist writers hoped to use these ancient writings to increase their knowledge about their own times. Petrarch, a Humanist writer, saw the fourteenth century as a time of rebirth for ancient Roman culture. Humanism was not concerned with the ideas of Confucius nor with magic and alchemy. A basic tenet of Humanism was the importance of the individual as a unique personality capable of fulfilling all of his potential.

3. **B.** *Masaccio*, means "fat, clumsy or messy." Masaccio was the first great painter of the Quattrocento period of the Italian Renaissance art. He rejected the elaborate ornamentation and the Gothic style of bold colors. Masaccio used linear perspective and a more natural mode that provided a more realistic image of the individual. His self portrait shows a subject who is proportionally presented with a distinct individual identity, unlike the cardboard figures of the Middle Ages. His realistic art inspired great artists of the Renaissance such as Leonardo da Vinci, Michelangelo, and Raphael.

4. **A.** The Medici family dominated Florence. They were a merchant family that amassed a fortune in trade and expanded into banking. Through their wealth, the Medici family provided Florence with political and artistic leadership. The Medicis supported artists such as Michelangelo, Botticelli, and Raphael. Through the efforts of the Medici family, Florence became the center of the Renaissance. The Medicis dominated politics in Florence throughout the fifteenth and sixteenth centuries. The Sforza family controlled Milan. Donatello and Bellini were artists from Florence and Venice, respectively. *Condottieri* was the term used for Italian mercenary leaders or warlords that were contracted by the Italian city-states and the papacy.

5. **B.** The Northern Humanists promoted social reform based on Christian ideals as a way to develop an ethical way of life combining the best elements of classical and Christian cultures. The Dutch writer Erasmus ridiculed upper-class privileges in the hope of getting people to think about reforms in society. He stressed reason over scholastic dogma. Sir Thomas More of England wrote about an ideal country (*Utopia*) that was free from war, injustices, and poverty. His works did not consider democracy a viable form of government. The Northern Humanists based their program on Christian ideals, not economic gain and materialism. They stressed biblical and Christian themes and not the pagan themes characterized by the Italian Renaissance.

6. **B.** Machiavelli wrote *The Prince* to describe the competitive politics of the Italian city-states in the sixteenth century. Machiavelli was writing his book at the time when Italy was being invaded by the Spanish and French. He was calling for a strong leader to unite Italy and defeat the foreign invaders who were destroying the country. *The Prince* is neither a satire nor a plan for constitutional government. The book does not describe the politics of the Renaissance and does not provide a detailed history of Florence. Machiavelli calls for a strong leader who will use whatever means necessary to achieve success and help Italy restore its greatness.

7. **D.** Giovanni Boccaccio wrote *The Decameron*. These short stories describe the breakdown of social order during the Black Death. Groups of men and women fled from Florence to escape the bubonic plague. In his short stories, Boccaccio describes how individuals abandoned all forms of civilization in order to survive. Baldassare Castiglione wrote a handbook on how courtiers should behave. François Rabelais wrote *Gargantua* and *Pantagruel,* which satirized political life in France in the sixteenth century. Leonardo Bruni wrote a 12-volume work on the history of Florence. Giovanni Pico della Mirandola's writings focused on the ability of an individual to achieve success.

8. **E.** One of the fundamental themes in all of Erasmus' scholarly works was the importance of Christian education for moral and intellectual development. As a Dutch Humanist, Erasmus rejected the paganism of classical literature and advocated the "philosophy of Christ." He had been forced to enter a monastery as a young orphan and disliked the monastic life. He also disliked the formalism of scholastic philosophy and the laws of the Church. Although Erasmus was critical of the Church, he remained loyal to it.

9. **D.** During the Renaissance, women did receive a better education, but this education was intended to adorn the home of the husband, not to challenge men intellectually. Renaissance men believed that educated women violated nature and thus ceased to be women. They felt they were a threat to male dominance and did not want them to have an equal place in society or a voice in the affairs of the city, or to be encouraged in any manner.

10. **D.** Sir Thomas More promoted the concept that corruption and war were due to society's flawed institutions, such as ownership of private property. His approach was extremely radical in that he contended that society, not the inherently corrupt nature of humanity, was responsible for corruption. Machiavelli, not More, stated that political leaders should learn how to manipulate their subjects. Exemplified by his *Utopia,* More believed that society could be perfected through the reform of the social institutions that mold the individual. John Locke and Jean Jacques Rousseau, not More, promoted the belief that government was a contract between government and the people.

The Reformation (1517–1640)

The Protestant Reformation, led by such figures as Martin Luther, Ulrich Zwingli, and John Calvin, was a turning point in the history of Western Europe. Followers of the Protestant Reformation were known as **Protestants** because they protested abuses within the Roman Catholic Church. The protest of these abuses led to a revolution that destroyed the religious unity of Europe and established various Protestant denominations or sects, a large concentration of which were located in Northern Europe. The Renaissance of Southern and Northern Europe contributed to the environment that promoted a religious revolt. The spirit of individuality fostered by the Renaissance led to criticism of certain Church practices and usages.

Protestantism also led to a series of religious wars in Western Europe and to the dominance of religious leaders by political rulers. The underlying tone of the Reformation was one of national pride. Kings questioned whether they had to follow the leadership of a distant pope who lived in Italy. In Germany, local rulers supported Martin Luther's attacks on the Church because they saw it as an opportunity to increase their power. Outside of Germany, the Protestant reformer, John Calvin, who was influenced by Ulrich Zwingli, had a great impact on the rest of Europe. Calvin's ideas spread from Geneva, Switzerland, to Northern Europe, England, and Scotland. The invention of the printing press after 1450 led to the further spread of the Protestant Reformation. Since books could now be reproduced inexpensively and in large quantities, they could be easily obtained throughout Europe shortly after Protestant authors such as Luther completed them.

The Catholic Reformation, or Counter Reformation—officially launched by the Council of Trent—was an attempt to stop the spread of Protestantism and to end the abuses within the Church. The Church reestablished its authority and renewed the Inquisition, a secret order of Church officials, to rid the Church of heretics, Jews, and Moslems. The efforts of the Jesuits under the leadership of Ignatius Loyola led to warfare between Catholics and Protestants throughout the first half of the seventeenth century and created a religious split between the Protestant countries of Northern Europe and the Catholic countries of Southern Europe. Protestantism allowed for greater religious freedom for some individuals but ultimately led to spiritual disunity and political disorganization for Europe.

Background of the Protestant Reformation

The causes of the Protestant Reformation were religious, political, economic, and intellectual.

- **Religious:** Many people were critical of certain Church abuses or practices, such as the following:
- **Simony:** Catholic Church officials sold positions to the highest bidders, who used these positions for their own personal gain. Many Church leaders also held multiple positions that made it difficult for them to take care of their parishioners.
- **Immorality:** Many Church leaders violated the law of celibacy and neglected their religious duties for more worldly activities. Outspoken critics like the Italian Dominican priest **Girolamo Savonarola** (1452–1498) preached against the moral corruption of the clergy. He was burned at the stake. His main opponent was Pope Alexander VI, who was a member of the infamous Borgia family of Florence.
- **Nepotism:** Catholic Church officials appointed relatives to high offices, regardless of their abilities.
- **Sales of indulgences:** The selling of indulgences was a practice that originated in the time of the Crusades. Church leaders sold indulgences as pardons, supposedly to reduce the punishment in the hereafter for certain sins. The sale of indulgences was often used as a way to raise money to fund certain Church activities.
- **Clerical ignorance:** The Black Death in Europe in the fourteenth century had destroyed one-third of the population of Europe, including many members of the clergy. The Catholic Church was forced to recruit many priests who could barely read or write and knew little or no Latin. Many of these peasant priests were unable to intelligently deal with Luther's challenge.

- **Decline of Church prestige:** During the early 1300s, the papacy came under the influence of the French monarch. In 1305, Philip IV of France persuaded the College of Cardinals to choose a French bishop as the new pope. Clement V, who wanted to escape the civil wars that were disrupting Italy and was critically ill with cancer, was convinced to settle in Avignon, a small city in southern France. For the next sixty years, the popes lived in Avignon under the control of the French king and never entered the city of Rome. This long period of exile is known as the **Babylonian Captivity** (1309–1378), after the period of exile of the Jews in Babylon in the 500s B.C.E. The seven popes at Avignon concentrated on monetary and bureaucratic matters to the exclusion of spiritual concerns, causing people to lose respect for the Church. Furthermore, the general atmosphere at Avignon of luxury and extravagance hurt the prestige of the pope.

- **The Great Schism** (1378–1417): Popes were elected by two different factions of the Italian and French Cardinals within the Catholic Church, and the embarrassment of two popes excommunicating each other did little to help the Church. In 1377, Pope Gregory XI ended the Babylonian Captivity when he returned to Rome. However, he died shortly after he returned. After his death, the Roman mobs forced the College of Cardinals to elect an Italian as Pope (Urban VI, who ruled from 1378 to 1389). Some Cardinals, however, declared that the election was invalid because they had voted under duress. In addition, Urban VI had alienated some members of the Church hierarchy with his proposals to reform the Church. The Cardinals then selected a new pope (**Clement VII,** who ruled from 1378 to 1394), who settled in Avignon. The powers of Europe aligned themselves with either Urban or Clement, along political lines. England and the Holy Roman Empire (Germany) recognized Pope Urban VI; Scotland, France, Aragon, Castile, and Portugal recognized Pope Clement VII; the Italian city-states at first recognized Urban and then after being alienated by his reform policies, opted for Clement. In the 1400s, Western European leaders were committed to the idea that the Church was ruled not by the pope but by a General Council representing bishops, cardinals, theologians, and lay people. In 1409, the Council of Pisa met to unite the Church behind one pope. It resulted in the election of a third pope, since neither the pope in Rome nor in Avignon wanted to resign. In 1414, the **Council of Constance**—convened at the request of Emperor Sigismund of the Holy Roman Empire—forced all three popes to resign. The Council chose Martin V, ending the Great Schism. This period of disunity weakened the political influence of the Church as many Europeans began to feel a greater sense of loyalty to their monarchs than to the pope.

- **Failure of Reform Leaders: John Wycliffe** (1328–1384) in England and **Jan Hus** (1369–1418) in Bohemia (today the Czech Republic) were forerunners to Luther. Wycliffe denied the pope's supreme religious authority, translated the Bible into English, and encouraged people to read the Bible themselves. Wycliffe was condemned as a heretic (one who denies the basic teachings of the Church) in 1380 and again in 1384. He was persuaded to moderate his views and received only a mild punishment. He died peacefully in 1384 in retirement. Hus, who advocated ideas similar to Wycliffe, was burned at the stake for his beliefs. Hus's execution led to a rebellion against the Church that took years to resolve.

- **Political:** By the sixteenth century, many secular leaders resented the interference of clergy in state affairs and wanted to reduce the Church's influence. These leaders were also jealous of the wealth and power of the Church. National-minded rulers considered the pope to be a foreign ruler.

- **Economic:** Members of the rising middle class, peasants, and rulers disliked Church taxes such as Peter's Pence (a yearly tax on all Christians) and the fact that a good portion was being sent to Rome. Many of the kings also wanted to take control of the vast landholdings of the Church throughout Europe.

- **Intellectual:** The Renaissance, which had weakened a respect for authority, encouraged some people to question the Church's teachings in science, history, and religious dogma. Humanists, especially in Northern Europe, attacked the abuses of the Church. Dutch humanist **Desiderius Erasmus** (1466–1536), who wanted an orderly change, argued for the revival of simple piety based on a renewed study of the Bible. These movements convinced many people that it was time for change.

Protestant Leaders

Martin Luther

Martin Luther (1483–1546) was a German Augustinian friar and a theologian at the University of Wittenberg. Luther, who had studied for a law degree, underwent a religious conversion in 1505. Caught in a terrible thunderstorm, he promised St. Ann that he would enter the seminary if he survived. He kept his promise and by 1512, received a doctorate in theology. Although a popular teacher at the university, Luther was still troubled by the question of his own salvation and felt that he was not worthy of it. He also believed that salvation was earned by faith, not by good works such as prayers, sacraments, or fasting. Furthermore, Luther had traveled to Rome in 1510 and was shocked by the immoral behavior of the Catholic clergy.

The issue that initiated the Protestant Reformation concerned the sale of indulgences, mentioned earlier in this chapter. Indulgences had often been used as a means of raising money for Church activities. In 1517, **Pope Leo X,** who was eager to construct St. Peter's Basilica in Rome, was hard-pressed for funds. Furthermore, Albrecht, Archbishop of Mainz, had borrowed money from the Fuggers, a wealthy banking family in Augsburg, to pay for a papal dispensation that allowed him to hold several Church positions. Pope Leo X authorized **Johann Tetzel** (1465–1519), a Dominican friar, the right to preach and sell indulgences, the proceeds of which were to go to build the new cathedral at St. Peter's Church and to repay the loan to the Fuggers. One of the popular beliefs of the time, which became Tetzel's slogan, was "As soon as gold in the basin rings, the souls in purgatory spring." This slogan created much business and horrified people such as Luther, who condemned the sale of indulgences and were critical of the pope getting wealthy from the money collected in Germany. On October 31, 1517, Luther nailed his **Ninety-Five Theses** (statements), written in Latin, to the door of the castle church at Wittenberg, a medieval way of indicating that an issue should be debated. Pope Leo X initially ignored Luther's pleas for reform and refused to get involved, considering Luther's action a local issue.

From 1517 to 1520, Luther wrote a series of works, such as *On Christian Liberty* (1520), *The Babylonian Captivity of the Church* (1520), and *The Freedom of Christian Man* (1520), which outlined his basic beliefs. These beliefs were as follows:

- **Salvation is through faith alone.** Influenced by the words of St. Paul in Romans 1:17, Luther rejected the Church's position that a combination of good works and faith was necessary for salvation.

- **Religious authority rests with the Bible, not the pope.** Luther considered the Bible the final authority because each individual could read it and thus determine Church doctrine and practices. There was no need for a pope or any higher authority.

- **The Church consists of the entire community of Christian believers.** The Catholic Church identified the Church only with the clergy.

- **All work is sacred and each person should serve God in his or her own individual calling.** The monastic or religious life is not better than the secular life.

- **Marriage of clergy should be permitted.** Luther married a former nun and had seven children.

- **Baptism, Communion, and Extreme Unction are the only sacraments instead of the seven Roman Catholic Church sacraments (Baptism, Communion, Confirmation, Penance, Matrimony, Holy Orders, and Extreme Unction).** Luther also disagreed with the Church's doctrine of **transubstantiation** (the idea that the bread and wine of the Eucharist are transformed into the actual body and blood of Christ). Luther supported **consubstantiation,** the belief that the bread and wine undergo a spiritual change whereby Christ is really present but the elements themselves are not transformed.

- **Secular rulers are the supreme authority in all matters except theological ones.** Political leaders supported Luther's belief because it gave them an opportunity to gain control of the vast Church lands and wealth, and limited the power of the pope.

45

In 1520, Pope Leo X issued a **Papal Bull** (or official statement by the pope) demanding that Luther recant his ideas or be burned at the stake as a heretic. In an act of defiance, Luther publicly burned the Bull and claimed that he no longer recognized papal authority. The pope excommunicated him in 1521 and ordered him to appear before the **Diet of Worms,** a meeting of German nobility and Holy Roman Emperor **Charles V** in Worms, a city along the Rhine. Luther had not been arrested because he was under the protection of **Frederick the Wise of Saxony** who was sympathetic to many of Luther's ideas. At the Diet, Emperor Charles V ordered Luther to recant his beliefs. In dramatic fashion, Luther proclaimed that he would not recant, stating, "To go against conscience is neither right nor safe." Declared a heretic and banned from the Empire, Luther was hidden by his protector Frederick of Saxony and did not leave Germany. In Saxony, he organized a new branch of Christianity, known as **Lutheranism,** based on his ideas. He also translated the Bible into German, which influenced the spread of Lutheranism. Charles V did not attend the Second Diet (**Diet of Speyer**) in 1529, but sent instructions to his brother Ferdinand to pursue a more conciliatory line. His advice did not reach his brother in time and Ferdinand rejected any compromise and demanded that the empire return to the Catholic religion. The Lutheran princes issued a defiant protest about the final document; hence, the origins of the term "Protestant."

During the 1520s, Lutheranism spread throughout northern Germany, Denmark, Norway, and Sweden, where rulers seized Church property and closed down monasteries. The German princes of the North protected Luther from the pope and the Holy Roman Emperor while gaining political power by assuming many of the privileges once reserved for the Church. In southern Germany, Catholicism prevailed in the Rhine Valley in the direct possession of the Hapsburg dynasty, which reached as far north as the Netherlands.

Many peasants in Germany followed Lutheranism because they were suffering economic hardship. The peasants looked to Luther for support, mistakenly believing that Luther's idea of the priesthood of all believers was a call for social justice. Christian liberty for them meant the end of harsh manorial burdens. In 1524, German peasants, excited by the prospects of freedom, demanded an end to serfdom. Bands of angry peasants went about the countryside pillaging and burning and ransacking monasteries. However, Luther was terrified by the **Peasant Revolts** (beginning in 1524) against the feudal system and attacked the extremists in his tract entitled, "Against the Murdering and Thieving Hordes of Peasants." He exhorted the nobility to put down the rebellion, which resulted in the deaths of 70,000 to 100,000 peasants. Feeling betrayed by Luther, many peasants rejected his religious leadership.

Luther rejected the ideas of a number of other religious sects (which together comprise what is called the **Radical Reformation**) that developed out of his challenge to religious authority. One such sect was the **Anabaptist,** which denied the validity of child baptism and believed that children had to be rebaptized when they became adults. Anabaptists also proposed the radical idea of separation of Church and state. Another sect, known as the **Anti-Trinitarians,** denied the validity of the Holy Trinity. They rejected the idea that the Holy Spirit could be considered one of three persons in God, saying it had no scriptural validity. Luther was a conservative and supported efforts by the Catholics and Lutherans to persecute those who held these beliefs.

Ulrich Zwingli

A combination of Luther's incredible skill with languages and the development of the printing press made his ideas well known outside of Germany. **Ulrich Zwingli** (1484–1531) introduced religious reform ideas in Switzerland, campaigning against Church abuses and preaching against all practices that were not found specifically in the Scriptures. Like Luther, Zwingli rejected celibacy of priests, the worship of saints, fasting, and confession, and regarded the Bible—not the pope—as the final authority. However, he disagreed with Luther by denying all the sacraments and insisting that the Eucharist, which he called the Last Supper or Communion, was only a symbol and that Christ was not actually present.

Zwingli set up a **theocracy** (a government that is led by religious leaders or ruled by someone who is said to have divine authority) from 1523 until 1525. He required church attendance by all citizens and regulated many aspects of their personal lives. Zwingli's brand of Protestantism spread from Zurich to all but five of Switzerland's thirteen cantons. Civil war broke out between Protestants and Catholics. In 1531, Zwingli died in battle fighting a religious war against the Swiss Catholic cantons. In 1531, the **Peace of Cappel** was signed, which allowed each canton to determine its own religion. This agreement served as a model for the other European countries fighting religious wars.

John Calvin

John Calvin (1509–1564) was another influential reformer in Switzerland. Trained as a lawyer, he fled from Catholic France to safety in Geneva because he feared persecution for being a Protestant. In 1536, he published *Institutes of the Christian Religion.* He was a generation younger than Luther, and was influenced by Luther's writings, which first appeared in France in 1518. Like Luther, he believed that the Bible was the final authority and salvation was possible by faith alone. However, Calvin had his own views on the power of God and the nature of human beings as well as the role of the state:

- **Predestination:** Calvin viewed man as sinful and corrupt and believed that God had already determined from the beginning who was going to be saved (the Elect) and who was going to be damned. Since God was all-powerful and predetermined our fate, there was no room for free will. Those predestined for salvation could be identified by the virtue of their moral life. In time, the Elect would also be identified by their material and economic success. The belief that poverty was a sign of damnation contributed to the idea known as the *Protestant work ethic* and served as a justification for capitalism. The Calvinist doctrine permitting the charging of interest on loans also helped to support the ideals of capitalism.

- **Unity of Church and state:** Unlike Luther, Calvin did not believe that the Church should be ruled by the state. He insisted that it should be a moral force in the secular government. Under his theocratic state, Calvinism became the official religion of Geneva. He imposed laws that controlled the religious and secular life of the people. He closed down all the taverns, outlawed card playing or any other forms of amusement, and was intolerant of anyone who did not follow these rules.

During the 1540s and 1550s, Calvinism spread throughout Europe under different names. In Scotland, where John Knox helped to make it a state religion, it was called **Presbyterianism.** In England, the Calvinists were called **Puritans;** they later brought Calvinism to America. In France, Calvin's followers were known as the **Huguenots.** Many were attracted to Calvinism by its simplicity and strict moral life.

Women in Protestantism

The abolition of monasticism for Protestants led to the glorification of the home, which Luther and other reformers stressed as the special domain of the wife where gentler virtues were upheld. The Protestants also established schools where girls as well as boys became literate in the Bible and religious teachings. Luther argued that all vocations had equal merit in the sight of God, giving dignity to those who performed ordinary, routine, domestic tasks. However, Luther believed that marriage was a woman's career. He married an ex-nun, **Katharina von Bora** (1499–1552). He believed that women should concern themselves exclusively with the children, kitchen, and the Church. Luther believed that the husband should rule the household while the wife controlled its economy. The wives of other reformers, though they exercised no leadership in the reforms, shared their husbands' work and concerns. Some women of nobility, however, did play a role in the Reformation. In France, **Marguerite of Navarre** (1492–1549), the sister of King Francis I, protected several Protestant preachers. Educated women wrote treatises on religious issues that were widely read. **Margaret More** (1505–1544), daughter of Sir Thomas More, was a recognized scholar. **Catherine Parr** (1512–1548), the last wife of Henry VIII, wrote a book that evaluated the idea of justification by faith. On the whole, there were limited opportunities for women to act as leaders.

The English Reformation (1517–1640)

In England, political and emotional considerations, rather than religious reasons, were the causes for the reform movement. **King Henry VIII** (who reigned from 1509 to 1547) led the English Reformation. In 1509, Henry married **Catherine of Aragon**—the aunt of the powerful Emperor Charles V, King of Spain and the Holy Roman Empire. After twenty years of marriage, Catherine failed to produce a male heir to the throne; all of her sons died in infancy (one daughter, Mary, survived). Henry, meanwhile, had fallen in love with **Anne Boleyn,** a young woman at the Court, who he wanted to marry. As a Catholic, however, he was unable to obtain a divorce. In 1527, Henry appealed to the pope for an annulment, thinking that the pope would grant it because of Henry's past service and the fact that he had written a pamphlet in 1521, entitled *Defence of the Seven Sacraments,* against Luther and had even received the title, "Defender of the Faith."

When **Pope Clement VII** (who reigned from 1523 to 1534), under the control of the Holy Roman Emperor Charles V (Catherine's nephew), refused to grant the annulment, Henry took matters into his own hands. Between 1529 and 1533, Henry used Parliament to dissolve ties with the Church in Rome. Parliament cut off all revenue to Rome and no longer recognized the pope's supreme authority in religious matters in England. In April 1533, Henry appointed Thomas Cranmer as Archbishop of Canterbury, who declared Henry's marriage to Catherine null and void. Henry had already secretly married Anne who was three months pregnant. In September, Anne gave birth to a baby girl (Elizabeth) who later ruled England from 1558 to 1603 as **Elizabeth I.** Still seeking a male heir, Henry married a total of six more times. His third wife, **Jane Seymour,** finally produced his male heir, Edward, who ruled from 1547 to 1553 as **Edward VI.**

In 1534, Parliament passed the **Act of Supremacy,** which made the king of England, not the pope, the head of the Church of England. As the leader of the Church of England (known as the Anglican Church), Henry did not change any of the doctrines or rituals except the one regarding the authority of the pope. However, he seized the monasteries, which were Catholic and represented 25 percent of the country's wealth. He also distributed the Catholic Church's land to the nobles who supported him, while persecuting Protestants as heretics. In 1539, Parliament passed **The Act of the Six Articles** that made Catholic beliefs obligatory in England. After Henry's death in 1547, there were some doctrinal changes. His son, Edward VI (who reigned from 1547 and died from tuberculosis in 1553), introduced Calvinism. During this time (in 1549), Archbishop Thomas Cranmer prepared the *Book of Common Prayer.* This book, a version of which is still used today, includes the order for all services of the Church of England.

Mary (who reigned from 1553 to 1558), Edward's half sister and daughter of Catherine of Aragon, tried to restore the links with the papacy but was unsuccessful. Mary had many Protestants killed. She earned the nickname "Bloody Mary" from her opponents. Finally, under Elizabeth, a religious settlement (the **Elizabethan Settlement**) was worked out, in which the Church of England followed a moderate course that provided for a Church of England (or Anglican Church) that was Protestant with Catholic features and made concessions to both Protestants and Catholics:

- **Protestant concession:** Priests in the Church of England were allowed to marry.
- **Catholic concession:** The Church of England kept some of the symbols of Catholicism, such as the golden crucifix and rich robes.

The *Book of Common Prayer* also was revised to be somewhat more acceptable to Catholics. While Elizabeth restored religious peace, she was threatened by Catholic Spain. In 1588, Philip II assembled the **Spanish Armada,** a fleet of 130 ships and 19,000 sailors, who were ready to invade England. When they reached the southwest coast of England in July, the bad weather and the strength of the English fleet defeated the Armada.

The Catholic Reformation

The Catholic Reformation or **Counter Reformation** is the term used to describe the efforts taken by the Roman Catholic Church to combat Protestantism during the sixteenth and seventeenth centuries. The reform of the Church began under the leadership of **Pope Paul III** (who reigned from 1534 to 1549). He supported the creation of the **Index of Prohibited Books** in Catholic countries, which listed heretical works that Catholics were forbidden to read, including the writings of Erasmus and Galileo. The Church, under Pope Paul III, also revived the medieval **Inquisition** (Church courts), which put heretics on trial for their religious beliefs and killed many of them.

The centerpiece of the Counter Reformation was the **Council of Trent,** which met sporadically from 1545 to 1563. The Council, convened by Pope Paul III, reaffirmed the dogma of the Church. Its main resolutions were the following:

- The rejection of the Protestant belief that salvation was obtained solely by faith. Salvation, instead, was obtained by a combination of good works and faith.
- The Bible, Church tradition, and Church law were sources of religious authority and faith. To that end, the individual needs the guidance of the Church in understanding the Bible. The only valid interpretation of the Bible was the **Vulgate**, the Latin translation by St. Jerome.

- The reaffirmation of the seven sacraments, celibacy, the monastic life, and transubstantiation.
- The condemnation of abuses, such as nepotism and simony, within the Church, although the principle of indulgences was upheld.
- The mandatory seminary education of the clergy in each diocese.
- The call for more religious art. (Some believe that these efforts played a role in the development of the Baroque style of art.) The Catholic Church had decided that art should communicate religious themes by direct and emotional involvement. Palaces and churches became ornately decorated with gold cherubs, murals, and ceilings. The Church demanded that paintings and sculptures in church should appeal to the illiterate as well as the educated.

The **Jesuits (Society of Jesus)** became the spiritual soldiers of the Counter Reformation to combat Protestantism. **Saint Ignatius Loyola** (1491–1556), a former Spanish soldier and nobleman, founded the Jesuits in 1534. They were committed to pious living and Loyola demanded absolute obedience and absolute faith. They were a tight-knit organization and received rigorous training in education and philosophy. The Jesuits played a significant role in upholding the Church's dogma for the following reasons:

- They won political influence as advisors to kings.
- They educated the youth in schools and universities.
- They carried the Christian message to Latin America, Asia, and Africa and preserved Catholicism in southern Germany and much of Eastern Europe.
- They used the Inquisition, especially in Italy and Spain, to suppress heresy, to control Protestantism, and to reassure the dominance of Catholicism.

Although the Council of Trent had reestablished the power and influence of the papacy, the Protestant Reformation had dealt the Church a serious blow in the following ways:

- The religious unity of Europe was destroyed.
- Northern Europe (England, Scotland, Wales, Holland, northern Germany, Switzerland, Denmark, Norway, and Sweden) was Protestant and Southern Europe (southern Germany, Italy, Spain, Portugal, Austria, Hungary, and southern Poland) was predominantly Catholic.
- Civil authority gained control over Church authority. The idea that the state was superior to the Church in all matters except spiritual led to the rise of nationalism.
- The importance of the individual reading the Bible encouraged the growth of education and the rise of capitalism. Max Weber, a nineteenth-century German sociologist, claimed that the Calvinistic stress on hard work and material success as a symbol of salvation contributed to the growth of capitalism in many Protestant countries.
- In the sixteenth and seventeenth centuries, wars of religion erupted in Europe between Protestants and Catholics.

Religious Wars and Revolts

The Reformation resulted in a series of wars between Protestants and Catholics in Germany, the Netherlands, France, and Central Europe.

War in Germany

In 1531, Protestant rulers formed the **League of Schmalkalden** to defend themselves against the efforts of Charles V, the Holy Roman Emperor, to establish Catholicism in Germany. Charles V was the most powerful of the Hapsburg rulers and controlled land in Spain, the Netherlands, Austria, and Central Europe. He appealed to Pope Clement VII for help in trying to regain control of these German provinces, but the pope refused because he resented the Hapsburgs' power and still blamed Charles V for the sack of Rome in 1527. After two decades of warfare, Charles was forced to accept the **Peace of Augsburg** (1555), establishing the permanent division of Germany into Lutheran and Catholic areas. As a compromise, the ruler accepted the statement, "*Cius regio, eius religio*" ("whose region his religion"), which meant the political ruler would determine the religion of the area.

Dutch Revolt against Spain

In 1556, Charles V retired to a monastery and divided his empire between his brother Ferdinand (who became the new Holy Roman Emperor and received Austria, Hungary, and Bohemia) and his son Philip (who received Spain, Milan, Naples, the colonies in the Americas, and the Netherlands). **Philip II** (who reigned from 1556 to 1598) was a deeply religious ruler who worked very hard and whose goal was to make Europe Catholic. Philip wanted to impose a more centralized government on the Netherlands as well as strengthen Catholicism in response to the growing strength of Calvinism. He sent the **Duke of Alva** (1508–1583) with 20,000 soldiers to deal with the threat. Alva established the **Council of Troubles** (called the Council of Blood by its opponents) and executed 18,000 people as heretics. He also revived the Inquisition.

At first, the Calvinist and Catholic provinces of the Netherlands united in 1576. They ultimately separated into two sections: the Calvinist Union of Utrecht (modern-day Netherlands) and the Catholic Union of Arras (modern-day Belgium). Led by **William of Orange** (1533–1584), the Dutch declared their political and religious independence in 1581. After 1584, the English began to support the Dutch rebels with money because they resented Philip's effort to restore Catholicism in England. Spain was driven out of the northern Netherlands in the 1590s and the war ended in 1609. In 1648, Spain officially recognized the independence of the northern provinces (the Netherlands) but still retained control of the southern provinces (Belgium).

Civil War in France

Francis I, who ruled France from 1515 to 1547, inherited a strong monarchy and extended his control over the country by establishing a *taille* (a direct tax on all land and property). He also gained control of the French Church when he signed the **Concordat of Bologna,** in which he recognized the supremacy of the Papacy in return for the right to appoint French bishops. This understanding gave the monarchy a rich supplement of money and power over the Church that lasted until the Revolution of 1789. The Concordat also established Catholicism as France's state religion. Since French rulers possessed control over appointments and had a financial interest in Catholicism, they had no need to revolt against the Church. Despite this state of affairs, John Calvin's ideas—written in French, not Latin—gained wide circulation in France, especially among the nobles who used Calvinism to support their opposition to the monarchy as a way to gain power. Some also were attracted to the piety of the Calvinist religion in contrast to the corruption and wealth of the Catholic Church. These French Calvinists, known as the **Huguenots,** sought to regain power over a series of weak monarchs.

When the French King Henry II (who was a member of the Valois dynasty that ruled France since 1328) died in 1559 from wounds in a jousting tournament, he left three young, incompetent sons to rule. Sickly Francis II, who ruled from 1559 to 1560, died after seventeen months. Charles IX succeeded at the age of ten and died in 1574 from tuberculosis. His younger brother, Henry III, reigned from 1574 to 1589 and was destined to be the last Valois king of France; he divided his time between religious piety and debaucheries. These three boys were dominated by their strong-willed mother, **Catherine de' Medici,** who really ruled France in their names. Between 1562 and 1589 there were nine civil wars that both divided and shattered France.

Two ambitious French families further inflamed the tensions between Catholics and Huguenots. On one side was the House of Bourbon, a family of French nobles who had become Protestants, and on the other side was the House of Guise, who were militant Catholics. In an attempt to reconcile Catholics and Huguenots, King Charles IX's sister was married to Protestant Henry of Navarre. However, Catherine de' Medici, who was not a religious zealot but was fearful that she was losing her influence over her weak son, King Charles IX, was determined to protect her son's interests. When the Huguenot gentry gathered in Paris on August 24, 1572, Catherine encouraged her son to give the orders that led to the **St. Bartholomew's Day Massacre.** It is estimated that over 20,000 Huguenots were killed in organized attacks throughout France.

The St. Bartholomew's Day Massacre led to the fight that launched the **War of the Three Henrys,** a civil conflict among factions led by the Catholic Henry of Guise, the Protestant King Henry of Navarre, and King Henry III, who succeeded Charles IX in 1574. Although Henry III was Catholic, he was more concerned that the Guises wanted a "Holy League" of Catholic nobles that would not only destroy Calvinism but also wanted to replace him with a member of the Guise family. Henry turned to Huguenot Henry of Navarre to assassinate Henry of Guise. In revenge, a Dominican friar stabbed King Henry III to death. In 1589 Prince Henry of Navarre became King Henry IV and established the Bourbon dynasty that ruled France until the French Revolution. Henry IV tried to unite France but was unable to convince Paris (a stronghold of Catholicism) to support him. Henry was more interested in political unity than religious unity and converted to Catholicism in 1593. He was allowed to enter Paris and is claimed to have said, "Paris is worth a Mass." In 1598, he issued the **Edict of Nantes,** which granted religious and civil freedom to the Protestant minority. This was the first significant recognition by a major country that there could be more than one legalized religion in a state. The Edict led to a truce in the religious wars in France.

Thirty Years' War (1618–1648)

The most important and bloodiest of the religious wars was the **Thirty Years' War.** An uneasy truce had existed in Germany since the Peace of Augsburg in 1555. This agreement allowed Lutheran and Catholic rulers to determine the religion of their subjects, but it did not make any provisions for the inroads of Calvinism. Catholics were alarmed that the Lutherans were gaining conversions and territory in violation of the settlement. Lutherans feared that the Peace of Augsburg would be undermined by Calvinist and Catholic gains. In the early seventeenth century, Catholics and Protestants formed armed alliances to preserve their rights: the Catholic League under Maximilian I of Bavaria and the Protestant Union under Frederick V of the Palatinate. The Thirty Years' War was the first continental war in which all the major European nations were involved. It was a struggle between emperors and the states of Germany; the French and the Hapsburgs; the Spanish and the Dutch; as well as efforts by Denmark and Sweden to extend control over the Baltics. Historians have divided the Thirty Years' War into four phases.

Phases of the Thirty Years' War			
Phase	**Causes**	**Highlights**	**Results**
Bohemian (1618–1625)—Takes place in the modern-day Czech Republic and the Slovak Republic	Calvinists demand more freedom from the Catholic Hapsburg ruler.	Defenestration of Prague: Two of the Emperor's officials are thrown out of a window in Prague during negotiations; the rebels are defeated at the Battle of White Mountain (1620).	Bohemia becomes Catholic by 1635.
Danish (1625–1629)	King Christian IV, Protestant leader of Denmark, intervenes to defend fellow Protestants in northern Germany.	Albert of Wallenstein, leader of the Holy Emperor's (Ferdinand's) forces, scores major victories and defeats the Danes.	Edict of Restitution (1629): Calvinism is outlawed and Lutherans are required to return all Catholic property seized since 1552.
Swedish (1629–1635)	Gustavus Adolphus, King of Sweden and a Protestant leader, intervenes to support fellow Protestants.	Adolphus, a military genius, dies in the Battle of Luetzen (1632); this ends Sweden's effectiveness; the Swedes are supported by the French.	The Edict of Restitution is revoked; southern Germany remains Catholic; the war continues; Cardinal Richelieu of France provides aid to Sweden as a way to destroy Hapsburg power.
Swedish/French (1635–1648)	The French want to destroy Hapsburg power; religious issues become secondary to political; Cardinal Richelieu wants to keep the Hapsburgs from becoming too powerful.	A coalition of Catholic France and Protestant countries (Holland and Switzerland) fight Catholic Hapsburg; this is the most destructive phase.	The Peace of Westphalia ends the Thirty Years' War.

The **Peace of Westphalia** (1648) marked an end to the Thirty Years' War with the following results:

- The Peace of Augsburg was renewed and Calvinism was recognized.
- The Edict of Restitution was revoked.
- German princes were granted sovereignty and the right to raise armies and conclude alliances with foreign powers. With the power in the hands of 300 princes and no central government, the power of the Holy Roman Empire was ineffective and unification of Germany was delayed until the nineteenth century.
- France and Sweden obtained some territory from the Holy Roman Empire.
- Switzerland and Holland were guaranteed independence, free from Hapsburg domination.
- The Papacy was denied the right to participate in German religious affairs, a restriction symbolizing the reduced role of the Church in European politics.

As a result of the Thirty Years' War, over 8 million of Europe's inhabitants were killed. All of Germany was destroyed and much of its culture was lost. Agricultural areas suffered catastrophically. The Hapsburg and Holy Roman Empires were greatly weakened. The age of religious wars ended permanently and Protestantism was established in Europe. Finally, the concept of the balance of power emerged as a force in international diplomacy, whereby nations went to war with one another, not for religion but to ensure that one power did not dominate the continent.

Chronology of the Reformation

1517	Luther's Ninety-Five Theses are posted on the door of Wittenberg Castle.
1519	Luther debates John Eck, a theologian, on the authority of the pope. Ulrich Zwingli begins his teaching of Protestantism in Switzerland.
1521	Pope Leo I excommunicates Luther. Luther is declared an outlaw by Emperor Charles V at the Diet of Worms.
1524	Peasants' rebellion in Germany is partly stirred by Luther's writing. Luther condemns their actions.
1527	Henry VIII of England petitions Pope Clement II for a divorce from Catherine of Aragon.
1529	German Lutheran princes meet at the Diet of Speyer to protest imperial decrees against their faith (contributing to the origins of the term "Protestant").
1531	Ulrich Zwingli is killed.
1533	Archbishop of Canterbury Thomas Cranmer annuls the marriage of Henry VIII and Catherine of Aragon.
1534	The Act of Supremacy recognizes Henry VIII as the head of the Church of England. The English Reformation is complete.
1536	John Calvin publishes Institutes of the Christian Religion in Geneva.
1539	Six Articles are passed by the British Parliament reaffirming many sacraments of the Catholic Church.
1540	The Jesuits, founded by Ignatius Loyola (1534), are recognized and encouraged by Rome to fight the spread of Protestantism.
1543	John Knox begins the Calvinist Movement in Scotland.
1545	Pope Paul III calls the Council of Trent, which reaffirms traditional Catholic doctrines on the seven sacraments and the authority of the pope.
1547	The British Parliament repeals the Six Articles.
1549	The British Parliament adopts the Anglican Mass and Book of Common Prayer as the models for the new state religion.
1555	The Peace of Augsburg allows German princes the right to choose the religion of their subjects. There is no mention of Calvinism.
1558	Elizabeth I of England ascends to the throne and reigns for 45 years.
1568	William of Orange leads a rebellion against Spanish powers.
1584	William of Orange is assassinated.
1588	The Spanish Armada is defeated by the English.
1589	The reign of Henry of Navarre (Henry IV of France) begins; he converts to Catholicism in 1593.
1598	The Edict of Nantes is passed, granting religious toleration to the French Protestants (the Huguenots).
1618	The Thirty Years' War begins.
1620	Holy Roman Emperor Ferdinand II defeats the Bohemians at the Battle of White Mountain.
1632	Gustavus Adolphus, the Swedish Protestant King, wins a military victory at Luetzen, though he is fatally wounded.
1633	France enters the Thirty Years' War.
1648	The Peace of Westphalia is signed; the Thirty Years' War ends.

Sample Multiple-Choice Questions

1. Salvation by faith alone, the supreme authority of the Bible, and ministry of all believers is a basic tenet of

    A. Lutheranism.
    B. Calvinism.
    C. Anglicanism.
    D. Catholicism.
    E. Presbyterianism.

2. All of the following are central ideas of Calvinism EXCEPT that

    A. human nature is evil.
    B. salvation is predestined.
    C. the Church should be subordinate to the state.
    D. the chosen Elect could be identified by material success.
    E. the state should rule according to God's Plan.

3. Which of the following was one of Martin Luther's beliefs about the role of Christian women in society? That they should

    A. lead a life devoted to prayer and meditation.
    B. teach reading and writing in religious schools.
    C. become a wife and mother.
    D. preach the word of God in church on Sunday.
    E. minister to the sick and poor.

4. The goal of the Peace of Augsburg (1555) was to

    A. resolve the issue of Calvinism.
    B. end the Thirty Years' War.
    C. restore Catholicism in Germany.
    D. end the civil war between Lutherans and Catholics in the German states.
    E. unite the German states.

5. Which of the following was not a result of the Council of Trent (1545–1563)?

    A. Abolition of indulgences
    B. Insistence on replacement of the vernacular with Latin as the language of worship
    C. Reaffirmation of the seven sacraments
    D. Preservation of the Papacy as the supreme authority in the Church
    E. Promotion of the Latin Vulgate as the only translation of the Bible

6. Luther disagreed with the Church's doctrine of transubstantiation, which states that

    A. the bread and wine undergo a spiritual change whereby Christ is present but the elements themselves are not changed.
    B. salvation is earned by passing through a good-works phase, coupled with ongoing faith.
    C. man has certain basic rights that exist independently of all man-made laws.
    D. the bread and wine of the Eucharist are transformed into the actual body and blood of Christ.
    E. clergy members can and should be encouraged to marry and produce offspring.

7. The Edict of Nantes allowed for

    A. recognizing the importance of the military in state affairs.
    B. granting religious toleration to the French Huguenots.
    C. providing for religious services for Jews.
    D. limiting the power of the king in religious matters.
    E. establishing control of the Estates General over the king.

8. The phrase, "Paris is well worth a Mass," attributed to Henry IV of France, reflects

   A. his decision to convert to Protestantism.
   B. his reaction to the pope's visit to France.
   C. his putting aside religious principles and converting to Catholicism for political principles.
   D. his belief that religion should dominate politics.
   E. his desire to meet with the Catholic and Protestant nobility.

9. The Peace of Westphalia, which ended the Thirty Years' War, led to which of the following developments?

   A. The Holy Roman Empire was further strengthened.
   B. The Holy Roman Empire was completely undermined as a viable state.
   C. Local German economies became stronger.
   D. German Catholicism flourished in northern Germany.
   E. Europe refused to recognize the independence of the united provinces of the Netherlands.

10. "He who desires to fight for God under the banner of the Cross in our society . . . shall realize that every part is fighting for God under the faithful obedience to one's most holy lord, the pope, and to other roman pontiffs who succeed him."

    This quotation best reflects the philosophy of

    A. Ignatius Loyola.
    B. Martin Luther.
    C. John Calvin.
    D. Henry VIII.
    E. Ulrich Zwingli.

Multiple-Choice Questions: Answers and Explanations

1. **A.** In his Ninety-Five Theses, Luther denied the pope's supremacy and claimed that the Bible was the final authority. He also believed that the Church consisted of the entire Christian community, not just the clergy, and that every individual could read and interpret the Bible. He also stated that Christianity is the priesthood of all believers. Predestination is the basic tenet of Calvinism. Anglicanism, which was founded by Henry VIII, broke with the Church over the question of papal authority. However, Anglicanism did not promote the ministry of all believers. John Knox, the founder of Presbyterianism, was a student of John Calvin who firmly believed in predestination. Catholicism rejected the basic ideas of Lutheranism.

2. **C.** Calvin emphasized the doctrine of predestination and that human nature was evil. He believed that an all-powerful God had predetermined who was to be saved and who was to be damned. Calvin believed that the Elect could be identified by their economic success and that the state should rule and be a moral force in the secular government. He also stated that the Church should not be ruled by the state. Calvin preached a state in which religion dominated the government and controlled the lives of the people.

3. **C.** Luther believed that marriage was the focal point of a woman's life and that they should focus primarily on the rearing of children and ensure domestic tranquility. Luther thought that next to God's Word (the Bible), matrimony was the most important treasure on earth. Luther envisioned traditional roles for women in marriage. Luther rejected the idea of monasticism, and Protestantism did not encourage women to preach the word of God or render help to the sick and poor. Although Protestantism promoted education for women, it did not consider education the most important role for women.

4. **D.** The Peace of Augsburg was signed in 1555 after two decades of civil war between Lutherans and Catholics in Germany. This agreement provided a compromise permitting German rulers to choose the religion of their subjects, either Catholicism or Lutheranism. It did not mention Calvinism, did not unite Germany, and did not restore Catholicism. The Peace of Westphalia (1648) ended the Thirty Years' War.

5. **A.** The Council of Trent (1545–1563) did not abolish the sale of indulgences but reaffirmed the basic Catholic doctrine of papal authority and the exclusive right of the Church to interpret the Bible. The Council reaffirmed the seven sacraments as well as celibacy. The Council rejected the use of the vernacular and insisted that only the Latin Vulgate could be used as a source to interpret the Bible. The Council sought to reform abuses such as simony but continued to promote indulgences as a way to help people achieve salvation.

6. **D.** Transubstantiation refers to the idea that the bread and wine of the Eucharist are transformed into the actual body and blood of Christ. Luther instead believed in consubstantiation, which is the belief that the bread and wine undergo a spiritual change whereby Christ is present but the elements themselves are not changed.

7. **B.** In 1598, Henry IV issued the Edict of Nantes, which granted religious toleration to the minority French Protestants, the Huguenots. The Edict of Nantes helped to end the civil war between Catholics and Protestants that had engulfed France for 27 years. The Edict did not address issues such as the importance of the military, or religious toleration for Jews, nor did it provide any control to the Estates General over the king. The Edict of Nantes helped Henry IV lay the foundation for French absolutism.

8. **C.** Henry IV of Navarre was a Calvinist and member of the Bourbon family. In 1593, he converted to Catholicism in order to end the civil war between Catholics and Protestants. Henry was willing to sacrifice his religious principles for political necessity. He was a politique, more interested in political unity than religious unity. Henry IV was not expecting the pope to visit France, nor was he meeting with the Catholic and Protestant nobility to seek their support. He also firmly believed that politics, not religion, should be the dominant force in government.

9. **B.** The Thirty Years' War weakened the power of the Holy Roman Empire. Individual German states, numbering over 300, obtained complete independence from the Holy Roman Empire. The treaty also ensured that the emperor would remain an ineffectual force within German politics and that Germany would remain divided for the next 200 years. In Spain, the Hapsburgs became a second-rate power. The Thirty Years' War also destroyed the economy of Germany and ensured that Protestantism would flourish in northern Germany and Catholicism would flourish in southern Germany. The Peace of Westphalia also ensured that the United Netherlands (Holland) was an independent state.

10. **A.** Ignatius Loyola was the founder of the Society of Jesus in 1534. Known as the Jesuits, they became the spiritual soldiers fighting Protestantism. Ignatius Loyola was a former Spanish soldier who developed Jesuits into a highly centralized organization devoted to the pope and committed to go anywhere for the help of souls and the prevention of the spread of Protestantism. Luther, Calvin, Henry VIII, and Zwingli were Protestant leaders who rejected allegiance to the pope.

The Age of Discovery and the Rise of Absolutism and Constitutionalism (1400–1700)

The Renaissance spirit of inquiry not only led to changes in religion, but also led Europeans to explore the outside world. Beginning in the fifteenth century, European nations undertook expeditions to find a direct water route to India, believing that control of the trade route with East Asia would bring vast wealth. Asian traders and Italian merchants from the city-states of Venice and Genoa held a monopoly on the existing trade routes and prices were very high. Many Europeans wanted to bypass the Mediterranean and trade directly with the East as a way to increase profits. Others sought fame and fortune and the titles that went with the exploration of new lands. Finally, some saw these expeditions as an opportunity to spread the glory of God.

Technological development during the fourteenth and fifteenth centuries also contributed to this age of increased exploration. Notable improvements in map making and shipbuilding, which gave rise to the *caravel,* a ship with both square and triangular sails that enabled it to sail more effectively against the wind than the square-rigged ships, enabled Europeans to sail farther than ever before. The caravel also had an improved rudder that enabled it to achieve easier turns than earlier ships, plus a larger cargo area, which enabled the caravel to carry the amount of supplies needed for longer voyages. Navigational improvements, moreover, such as the mariner's compass, the sextant, and the astrolabe, made ocean voyages less dangerous.

The financial capital that was needed to promote these explorations supported the need for strong leadership with the ability to centralize and consolidate power. This consolidation of power contributed to the rise of the absolute rulers who controlled every aspect of their respective governments. In France, the reign of Louis XIV (1643–1715) symbolized absolutism at its height. There would be absolute rulers in Eastern Europe, like Peter the Great of Russia, but none would surpass the power of the French monarchs. While France represented the classic model of absolutism, England provided the example of a constitutional parliamentary government, which defined the limits of the king. Spain, similar to France, developed a strong absolutist government, but had a short period of greatness, which ended at the close of the sixteenth century.

The Age of Discovery

Historians have called the period from 1415 to 1650 the **Age of Discovery.** This term refers to the era's phenomenal advances in geographical knowledge and technology. Portugal, situated on the extreme southwestern edge of the European continent, had a head start in overseas exploration before the rest of Europe. **Prince Henry** (1394–1460), the son of the Portuguese king, was called **"the Navigator"** because of the annual expeditions that he sent down the western coast of Africa. He established a school of navigation along the southwestern coast of Portugal. Prince Henry gathered mapmakers, shipbuilders, and trained captains at the school to help them perfect their trade. In 1415, he encouraged Portugal to search for a direct water route to India around the south coast of Africa. Some important **Portuguese explorers** included the following:

- **Bartholomew Diaz** (1450–1500). In 1488, Diaz was the first man to sail around the Cape of Good Hope in Africa.
- **Vasco da Gama** (1469–1524). In 1498, da Gama discovered an all-water route to India by sailing around the southern tip of Africa, and was the first European to reach India by water. By doing so, he showed that it was possible for Europeans to obtain Asian goods without having to use an overland route. In 1502, on a second voyage, da Gama returned home with Asian spices that were worth more than $1 million in gold and 60 times the cost of the actual voyage. This voyage generated a great deal of excitement in Western Europe.

Portugal gained control of the rich spice trade of the Indian Ocean by overpowering Muslim forts and deploying squadrons of naval ships to defeat the Arab fleets that patrolled the Indian Ocean. A scholar once commented that Christianity came to India on cannonballs. The Portuguese successfully mounted cannons on ships, using them in 1509 to blast open Goa, a port city on India's west coast, and in 1511, Malacca, near modern Singapore. These battles ended Arab domination of the South Asian trade and established a Portuguese foundation for a trading empire for most of the 1500s. In capturing the port city of Malacca, the Portuguese seized the waterway that gave them control of the Spice Islands, just west of New Guinea. Portugal's control of these areas broke the old trade route from the East. In 1504, spices could be bought in Lisbon for only one-fifth of what it cost when they had been purchased from the Arabs and Italians.

The success of Portugal inspired Spain to gain a share of the rich trade with the East. However, the Spanish decided to try the westward route, or the Atlantic route, rather than down around the Cape of Good Hope to reach the treasures of the East. The Spanish were hoping to beat the Portuguese to the East, which da Gama had not yet reached, and they also wanted to break the Muslim-Italian monopoly of the spice trade. Some important Spanish explorers included the following:

- **Christopher Columbus** (1451–1506). Convinced that he could reach Asia by sailing west, Columbus managed to persuade Ferdinand and Isabella of Spain to provide three ships for a journey. In October 1492, after a 36-day voyage from the Canary Islands, Columbus landed in the Bahamas instead of the East Indies. Undeterred, he named the territory the "Indies." In three subsequent voyages, Columbus explored all of the Caribbean islands.

- **Ferdinand Magellan** (1480–1521). In 1519, Magellan led several ships from Spain, rounded the southern tip of South America, and crossed the Pacific. However, Magellan became involved in a local war between two rival tribes and was killed in the Philippine Islands. By 1522, one of Magellan's ships managed to return to Spain, thereby completing the first circumnavigation of the globe. Magellan's voyage proved that the territory where Columbus landed was not part of the Far East but an entirely new continent. This new island group gave Spain a base from which to trade with China and spread Catholicism in Asia.

The Spanish also sent out *conquistadors* (or conquerors) who sought fame, wealth, and power in the unexplored lands in the New World. These included the following:

- **Hernando Cortés** (1485–1547). Cortés landed in Mexico in 1519. By 1521, he had formed an alliance with the enemies of the Aztec and defeated the mighty Aztec Empire. The Aztecs controlled their vast empire of 38 provinces of central Mexico through terror. Their state religion, the Cult of Huitzilopochtli, which required human sacrifice, led to constant warfare against their neighbors in order to obtain sacrifices for these religious practices. When Cortés arrived in 1519, the provinces were in revolt against the Aztecs, who were demanding higher tribute. Thus, many of these subjugated people joined the Spanish against the Aztecs.

- **Francisco Pizarro** (1476–1541). Between 1531 and 1533, Pizarro conquered the Inca Empire of Peru and established Spanish control in western Latin America.

Spain's conquests were successful for the following reasons:

- **Superior technology.** The Spanish used armor, horses, and muskets—all of which the Indians had never seen.
- **Introduction of disease.** The Spanish carried diseases, such as measles, mumps, and smallpox, to which the natives had never been exposed and had no natural immunity, thus killing millions.
- **Support.** Spain found allies among the natives, such as the Tlaxcaltec in Mexico, who disliked the Aztecs.

The results of Spain's conquests in the Americas were the following:

- There was an influx of gold and silver from the New World, which contributed to Spain's growth as a major power in the sixteenth century.
- New foods, such as potatoes and tomatoes, were introduced to Europe.
- Europeans began transporting slaves from Africa to the Americas to serve in the mines and farms in the New World. Over ten million slaves were involved in the trans-Atlantic slave trade from 1451 to 1870.
- Diseases destroyed about 25 million, or 80 percent, of the Native Americans. Syphilis appeared in Europe for the first time in 1493 because sailors and settlers returned to their homelands infected with this disease. The global transfer of plants, people, animals, and diseases that occurred during the European colonization of the Americas became known as the **Columbian Exchange.**

The Rise of Absolutism in France

The foundation of French absolutism was established in the seventeenth and eighteenth centuries. The following people helped achieve the foundation of French absolutism:

- **Henry IV** (b. 1553, ruled 1589–1610). The **Duke of Sully** (Maximilien de Bethune, 1560–1641), Henry IV's chief minister, established economic growth and financial stability for France, reducing the crushing debt that had accumulated during the religious wars between the Catholics and the Calvinists (Huguenots) by reforming the tax system and tax collection. The Duke also instituted a program of economic improvement by constructing new roads and bridges that improved transportation and promoted economic prosperity. Henry IV strengthened the power of the monarch by limiting the power of the nobles over the regional parliaments. In 1610, Henry IV was assassinated by a fanatic who thought that Henry was a menace to the Catholic Church.

- **Louis XIII** (b. 1601, ruled 1610–1643). Louis was only nine years old when he became king. His mother, Marie de' Medici, replaced the Duke of Sully and ran the government inefficiently until her son was 23, spending money lavishly on court expenditures as well as pensions to discontented nobles. In 1617, Louis XIII forced his mother into retirement because she had excluded him from running the government even though he had been declared of age in 1614. They were reconciled in 1624 and she was able to secure the appointment of her protégé, Cardinal Richelieu. (At this time, religious leaders held official positions in the government in many Catholic countries.) By 1630, she became jealous of Richelieu's influence and urged Louis to dismiss him. Instead, the king sent his mother into exile and she never returned to France. Afterwards, the king gave full support to Richelieu, who was appointed prime minister.

- **Cardinal Richelieu** (1585–1642). Richelieu's goal was to establish the supremacy of the king and French domination of the European continent. He achieved these objectives by destroying the fortified castles of the French nobles, which had long been a symbol of their independence. He also crushed the political power of the Huguenots. When the Huguenots revolted in 1625, Richelieu personally supervised the siege of their walled city, La Rochelle, and forced it to surrender. By the Peace of Alais in 1629, the Huguenots were allowed to keep their religion but they lost their fortified cities, military, and territorial rights. Richelieu did not want the Huguenots to ever again be able to defy the king and then withdraw behind a strong defense. Through his spy system, he efficiently destroyed any conspiracy that threatened royal power. By the use of the **intendant system,** he transferred local government functions from the nobles to royal officials, further weakening the power of the nobles. The intendants were royal officials who collected taxes, recruited soldiers, and carried out government policies in the provinces. All of these officials regularly communicated to Richelieu. He also levied taxes without the consent of the Estates General, the French parliament. All these steps served to strengthen the power of the king. In foreign affairs, Richelieu involved France in the Thirty Years' War, supporting the Protestants in order to weaken the domination of the Hapsburgs and establish French control on the continent.

- **Louis XIV** (b. 1638, ruled 1643–1715). Louis was only four when his father died and his mother Queen Anne selected **Cardinal Mazarin** as Prime Minister. Mazarin, resented by the people because he was Italian, continued Richelieu's strategies for centralizing power; however, he lacked Richelieu's shrewdness. Mazarin's attempts to increase the royal revenue led to civil wars, called the **Fronde,** which lasted intermittently from 1648 to 1653. The term *fronde* means a slingshot, and *frondeurs* were originally mischievous street children who threw mud or shot rocks at passing carriages of the rich. The term came to symbolize anyone who opposed the policies of the government. In 1648, a bitter civil war ensued between the monarchy and the **Frondeurs** (the nobility and the middle class). Riots wrecked Paris and violence continued intermittently for a number of years, resulting in Louis XIV and Cardinal Mazarin fleeing the city. However, internal differences between the nobles and the middle class and the overall chaos in the country contributed to Louis XIV's eventual return. The Frondeurs had no systematic program other than the overthrow of Mazarin.

The rebellions had a traumatic effect on Louis XIV, who became convinced that the sole alternative to anarchy and the power of the nobles was to establish an absolute monarchy. After the death of Mazarin in 1661, Louis became his own prime minister and adopted the ideal of the **Divine Right of Kings.** This concept had been developing in France since the sixteenth century. According to **Bishop Jacques Bossuet** (1627–1704), one of Louis' advisers, the king was chosen by God to rule, and only God had authority over the king, not a parliamentary body or any group of nobles. This Divine Right Theory of rule provided the justification for the absolute sovereignty of Louis and his monarchy. Louis' statement, "L'état, c'est moi" ("I am the state"), represents his belief that there was no higher authority that could ever control him.

During Louis XIV's 72-year reign, France became a dominant power in Europe. European countries envied France's success in industry and agriculture. **Jean-Baptiste Colbert** (1619–1683), the son of a wealthy merchant, was Louis' able finance minister who helped revive trade and the economy. While he did not invent the system of mercantilism, discussed in Chapter 6, "Mercantilism and the Agricultural and Industrial Revolutions," he rigorously applied it to France. Colbert's central principle was that the wealth and the economy of France should serve the state. To advance prosperity, Colbert promoted good farming methods, internal improvements (roads and canals), and support of both old and new industries. Colbert sponsored the established cloth industries and gave special privileges to the newly developing ones like silk, rugs, and tapestries. Colbert also set up large areas of free trade zones known as the Five Great Farms, but enacted high tariffs to prevent foreign products from competing with French ones. Colbert's goal was to make France militarily stronger and to create a strong merchant marine that could help France compete with the overseas empires of the English and Dutch in North America as well as Asia. Another goal was to make France self-sufficient by centralizing the economy through government control of trade and industry. Unfortunately, France did not have the resources to support a powerful army and navy. Thus, Louis XIV established a strong army and ceded naval dominance to the British.

Louis XIV also sought to control religion, believing that more than one religion could not exist and that religious unity was essential for absolute control. In 1685, he revoked the **Edict of Nantes.** He destroyed Huguenot schools and churches and took away their civil rights. The Huguenots escaped France and settled in Holland, England, and America. Many of those who fled were craftsmen and businesspeople, and their departure hurt the French economy.

Louis kept France at war for much of the time that he ruled. He pursued an aggressive foreign policy, wanting France to achieve its natural boundaries along the Rhine River. To this end, Louis created a personal army that was employed by the state instead of the nobles. The French armies were able to gain some territory in Germany and its surrounding areas. France was engaged in the following wars: the War of Devolution or the First Dutch War (1667–1668); the Second Dutch War (1672–1678); and the War of the League of Augsburg (1688–1697). By the end of the fourth war, the **War of the Spanish Succession** (1701–1714), fought because of Louis' efforts to lay claim to the Spanish throne for his grandson, the European countries of Holland, Great Britain, and Austria were able to contain Louis' territorial ambitions. In 1713, France signed the **Peace of Utrecht,** which forbade the union of France and Spain, stating that the two countries could not be ruled by the same monarch. The treaty also made Louis XIV's grandson, Philip V, the new king of Spain. The treaty ended French expansionism and left France on the brink of bankruptcy.

The reign of Louis XIV is considered the Golden Age of France. French became the language of polite society and replaced Latin as the language of diplomacy and scholarship. Louis—who was referred to as the Grand Monarch or the Sun King, because, like the sun, he was the center of all power—was a strong patron of the arts. He loved the stage and encouraged writers like Molière, Racine, and Louis de Rouvroy, duc de Saint-Simon, to pursue their crafts. The French style of classicism and fashion were the models for all of Europe.

Louis XIV's palace at Versailles influenced the architectural style of Europe. It was built 12 miles outside of Paris, at a cost of over $100 million, and was filled with 1,400 fountains—this palace served as a fundamental tool of state policy under Louis. He was able to control the nobles who were forced to live at Versailles and also used the elaborate architecture to impress his subjects and foreign visitors. Versailles became a reflection of French genius. Peter the Great of Russia and Frederick the Great of Prussia would try to model their palaces on the one in Versailles. By the time of Louis' death in 1715, France was the leading nation on the European continent. However, his extravagant lifestyle at Versailles burdened the peasants with taxes, and the long war emptied the treasury, drained the manpower of the country, and held back economic development of the country.

Source: Versailles Palace, Versailles, France—Eric Pouhier; February 2007

The Rise of Constitutionalism in England

While France witnessed the rise of Absolutism in the 1600s, England would develop a parliamentary system of government limiting the power of the king. The foundation for the development of constitutionalism in England was established in the Middle Ages. The **Magna Carta** (1215) limited royal power by stating that the king could not tax without the consent of the Grand Council (consisting of the nobility and the high clergy). The Grand Council later evolved into the Parliament, which alone levied taxes. By the 1300s, the Parliament (or the Grand Council) included middle-class representation. Because the enlarged council served as a model for England's future legislature, it is often called the **Model Parliament.** By the fourteenth century, Parliament had compelled English monarchs to accept guidelines on the question of taxes as well as other issues. In the fifteenth century, after the War of the Roses (1455–1485), **Henry Tudor** established the Tudor Dynasty following the defeat of Richard III of the House of York in 1485, becoming **Henry VII** (b. 1457, ruled 1485–1509) after he married Elizabeth of York, and was crowned King.

The Tudors

After the death of Henry VII, **Henry VIII** (b. 1491, ruled 1509–1547) and **Elizabeth I** (b. 1533, ruled 1558–1603) strengthened the power of the Tudor monarchy by governing intelligently and following a popular foreign policy. The Tudors were successful because they skillfully mastered Parliament by outwardly consulting it, but actually dominating the legislature. They also aided the middle class by providing law and order and encouraging trade. Elizabeth, who was the daughter of Henry VIII and his second wife Ann Boleyn, was the last and greatest of the Tudor monarchs. Elizabeth was the first woman to successfully occupy the British throne. Sometimes called the **"Virgin Queen,"** referring to her choice not to marry, she used the prospects of marriage as a political tool. Elizabeth's potential eligibility as a wife may have also kept foreign powers from attacking England due to the fact that foreign leaders may have wanted to keep their options open. Elizabeth firmly established Protestantism in England. **The Act of Uniformity of 1559** and the **Thirty-Nine Articles** of 1563 defined the **English Reformation.** The Act of Uniformity established a common prayer book and set the basic ceremonies of the Church. The Thirty-Nine Articles established the religious doctrine that governed the Church until the English Revolution of the 1640s. Both acts were compromises favoring the view of the more conservative Protestant groups. Throughout most of her reign, powerful Catholic nobles in northern England rose in rebellion but were savagely repressed.

In 1571, an international conspiracy was uncovered to assassinate her in favor of her cousin, Mary, Queen of Scots. Although Mary was beheaded in1587, the plot against Elizabeth did not end until England defeated the Spanish Armada in 1588. Elizabeth's reign was a period of cultural flowering. The Elizabethan Age was the era of William Shakespeare, Edmund Spenser, Christopher Marlow, and John Donne. Although Elizabeth may not have directly promoted the arts, she created a stable environment allowing the arts to flourish. When Elizabeth died in 1603, childless, her cousin King James Stuart of Scotland (James VI) ascended to the throne.

The Stuart Monarchs

James I (b. 1566, ruled 1603–1625) created resentment and hostility by telling Parliament at their first session that his power could not be challenged. Although the king had the power to summon and dismiss the Parliament, he needed its support to raise money for additional revenue that was beyond his ordinary expenses. Parliament refused to grant him additional revenue. James I squandered his revenue on an extravagant lifestyle at the court and was unable to live within the fixed and customary level of the crown. From 1610 to 1611, James I and Parliament were involved in continuous debates on how to finance the government.

In religious matters, the **Puritans** (a Calvinist sect) viewed James I as the enemy. They wanted to purify the Anglican Church of all traces of Catholicism. In 1604, when they petitioned James I to reform the Church of England, he refused to make any changes. James I presided at the **Hampton Court Conference** (1604). The goal of the conference was to examine the different versions of the English Bible, which had been translated from the original Hebrew and Greek. From this conference originated the movement from which came the authorized **King James Version** of the Bible, the first edition of which appeared in 1611. James also followed an unpopular foreign policy of friendship with Catholic Spain.

Like his father James I, **Charles I** (b. 1600, ruled 1625–1649) wanted to rule by Divine Right. Yet Charles was more politically inept than his father, running into friction with Parliament when they refused to grant him a lifetime of custom duties, instead granting him a one-year period. Charles used his wife's dowry to fight a war against Spain, which was a failure. However, when he needed additional money for his military expedition against Spain, he requested a forced loan from his wealthier subjects. Several members of the gentry refused to vote for the loans and Charles threw them into jail. In 1628, Parliament again declined to give Charles additional resources unless he signed the **Petition of Right,** which forbade the king to do the following:

- Levy taxes without the Parliament's consent
- Proclaim martial law in peacetime
- Imprison anyone without a specific charge
- Quarter troops in the home of private citizens without their permission

Charles ended up signing the petition in order to get his funds. Charles ruled without the Parliament for eleven years (1629–1640).

In 1637, Charles tried to impose Anglican practices on Calvinist Scotland. The people revolted and Charles was forced to call upon Parliament, referred to as the **Short Parliament** because it lasted only three weeks, to raise money for the war against the Scots. They turned down his request unless Charles addressed their grievances. The Scots defeated Charles' army and invaded northern England. They then demanded money in order to leave northern England. Thus, in 1640, Charles again appealed to the Parliament for money. This Parliament, known as the **Long Parliament** because it lasted 20 years, managed to pass laws limiting the power of the king. The king was compelled to summon Parliament every three years and could not dissolve Parliament without its consent. Parliament also impeached Charles' chief advisors, supporting what was known as the **Grand Remonstrance,** a list of 204 Parliamentary grievances from the past decades. In 1642, Charles I charged five Parliament members with high treason and tried to arrest them. When Parliament refused to hand the members over, the king decided to personally arrest them. The five members fled, having received information in advance. Parliament then demanded sole command of the military forces. Charles refused and in August he fled London to Nottingham to recruit and gather his army, declaring war against Parliament. The English Civil War had begun.

Highlights of the English Civil War (1642–1649)

The English Civil War concerned religious differences and also centered on whether authority or sovereignty rested in England with the monarchy or the Parliament. It had two phases: Phase I (1642–1646) and Phase II (1646–1649).

The participants in the English Civil War were:

- **Cavaliers or Royalists.** These were supporters of the king. This group consisted of the wealthy landowners, the Anglican clergy, and the Catholics.
- **Roundheads.** These were supporters of the Parliament. This faction was generally made up of the middle class, merchants, small nobility, Puritans, and the Presbyterian Scots who had opposed Charles' efforts to impose his religion on them.

Phase I (1642–1646)

At first, the Cavaliers gained victory until Scotland intervened on the side of Parliament and **Oliver Cromwell** (1599–1658), a Puritan leader in Parliament, emerged as a leader. Cromwell organized the **New Model Army,** which was composed of well-paid and disciplined soldiers. In 1644, Cromwell's Model Army defeated Charles and the Royalists at Marston Moor. In 1646, Charles gave himself up to the Scots, who turned him over to Parliament, which was led by Cromwell.

Phase II (1646–1649)

The victors then quarreled among themselves. The Presbyterian wing of the Puritan movement, supported by the Scots, decided to set up a constitutional monarchy, with Charles at the head and Presbyterianism as the established church. They were opposed by the army—which was more radical than Parliament and wanted a republic—some of whose members, like Cromwell, were Independents who favored some religious toleration for all groups except Catholics and were opposed to Presbyterianism as the established church. To add to the confusion, Parliament refused to pay the troops. Charles took advantage of this situation between Parliament and the army and fled London. In 1647, the Scots allied with Charles, who promised that he would support Presbyterianism in England. In August, 1648, the Scots invaded England but the army, led by Cromwell, defeated them at the Battle of Preston. Charles was captured. The second civil war had made Cromwell the undisputed leader. In 1648, the **Rump Parliament** was established which removed all Presbyterian members and was under the control of Cromwell. After a formal trial, Charles I was accused of treason and condemned to death. Charles I was beheaded on January 30, 1649. The Civil War was over.

From 1649 to 1653, the Rump Parliament claimed to have supreme power. The monarchy was abolished and a **Commonwealth,** a Republican form of government, was established. In 1653, Cromwell expelled the Rump Parliament because the Parliament was lax in paying the troops, had been accused of accepting bribes, and filled vacancies in Parliament by nominations and not by elections. In 1653, Cromwell took the title of Lord Protectorate and established a military dictatorship. He suppressed rebellions in Ireland and Scotland, advanced English trade, and greatly increased English power. However, Cromwell's rule did not gain popular support because people resented the severe moral code of the Puritans. The Anglicans, who were more numerous than the Puritans, also opposed Cromwell's policy of intolerance. When Cromwell died in 1658, people were tired of his stern military rule and deposed his son Richard in 1660. Charles II, son of Charles I, was invited to return from exile and accept the throne.

The Stuart Restoration (1660–1688)

Mindful of his father's fate, **Charles II** (b. 1630, ruled 1660–1685) pledged to work with Parliament. He accepted the Parliament's right to levy taxes and agreed to call Parliament into regular sessions. During his reign, the Cavalier Parliament restored the Church of England as the official church. In 1670, Charles signed a secret treaty with Catholic France in which he received a subsidy in return for some vague promise that England may become

Catholic. In 1673, Parliament passed the Test Act, which excluded all Catholics from public office. It also tried to pass a law excluding James, Charles' Catholic brother, from inheriting the throne; it failed. At this time, Parliament was divided into two groups: the **Whigs,** who wanted a constitutional monarchy under a Protestant king; and the **Tories,** who supported the king, but feared the restoration of Catholicism. The Whigs, fearful of Charles II's pro-Catholic tendencies, did what they could to limit his power. In 1679, under the control of the Whigs, the Parliament passed the **Habeas Corpus Act.** This act prohibited imprisonment without due cause and guaranteed a fair trial.

Upon the death of Charles II in 1685, **James II** (who reigned from 1685 to 1688) assumed the throne. As a converted Catholic, James antagonized the Parliament by appointing pro-Catholic ministers to important posts, which angered the Whigs who supported the Church of England. James' efforts to set up a standing army created fears among the Tories. When James' wife gave birth to a son, Parliament was fearful that Catholicism would be reestablished in England.

The Glorious Revolution

In 1688, Parliament secretly offered the English crown to **William,** the Protestant ruler of Holland, and his wife **Mary,** the Protestant daughter of James II. They accepted. When William arrived in England, James II fled to France. In 1689, Parliament proclaimed William and Mary the new king and queen of England, under the conditions that they accept the **Declaration of Rights,** which later was enacted into law as the **Bill of Rights.** This bloodless overthrow of the previous monarch in 1688 is called the **Glorious Revolution** because there was so little violence.

The Glorious Revolution had the following effects upon English government:

- It ended the Divine Right Theory in England.
- It re-established the principle of supremacy of the Parliament over the monarch.
- Parliament passed the **Bill of Rights** (1689), a series of laws stating that the king could not levy taxes, make laws, or maintain an army without the consent of the Parliament. People were guaranteed basic civil liberties such as freedom of speech, right to petition, and protection against excessive bail or unusual punishment.
- Parliament passed the **Toleration Act** (1689) granting freedom of worship to Protestants who were dissenters from the Church of England, such as Baptists and Congregationalists, but not to Catholics or Quakers.
- English rulers had to be Anglican.
- It laid the foundation for the constitutional monarchy. Over the centuries, the British monarchy would be permitted to reign, but not to rule completely.

The Golden Age of Spain and Its Decline

In the sixteenth century, Spain became a rich and powerful country as a result of its vast empire in the New World. **Charles V** (b. 1500, ruled 1519–1556), Charles of Hapsburg, was the grandson of King Ferdinand and Queen Isabella. As king of a united Spain and the Holy Roman Empire, he was the most powerful ruler of Europe during the first half of the sixteenth century. He controlled lands in Spain and its colonial empire as well as the Netherlands, southern Italy, Austria, and other lands in Central Europe.

Charles V abdicated the Spanish throne to his son, **Philip II** (b. 1527, ruled 1556–1598). Throughout his reign, Philip, who considered himself the champion of Catholicism, was involved in religious wars resulting from the Protestant Reformation. The country's wealth was drained as Philip tried to halt the Reformation. He was unable to put down the Dutch religious revolt. In 1588, the defeat of the seemingly invincible **Spanish Armada** prevented an invasion of England and ended all efforts to restore Catholicism, as well as Spain's dominance of the sea. Spain lost large portions of her empire to England and Holland. Royal expenditures increased but income from the Americas suffered. Spanish kings seemed to lack the will to reform. **Philip III** (b. 1578, ruled 1598–1621), a deeply pious man whose only virtue seemed to be the total absence of vice, drew criticism from his reliance on the advice of his corrupt chief minister, the lazy Duke of Lerma, who was more concerned with promoting the wealth of his family over the interest of the country. **Philip IV** (b.1605, ruled 1621–1665) was a patron of the arts and not interested in politics. Spain's participation in the Thirty Years' War during his reign also contributed to its decline. Spain no longer had the wealth or the military power to become involved in any war on the European continent. By 1640, Portugal regained its independence after a revolt and, in 1648, Holland was lost by the **Treaty of Westphalia.** By the Treaty of the Pyrenees in 1659, which ended the French-Spanish war, Spain was compelled to surrender extensive territory to France. The treaty marked the end of Spain as a great power.

During the sixteenth century, Spain produced one of the world's greatest literary masterpieces. **Miguel de Cervantes** (1547–1616) wrote *Don Quixote,* a book that describes the fabric of Spanish society in the sixteenth century. The main character, Don Quixote, a knight, lives in a world of dreams traveling around the countryside seeking military glory. Cervantes is considered the greatest of all Spanish authors. In English, the term *quixotic* means idealistic, but impractical. This term describes Spain in the seventeenth century.

Chronology of the Age of Discovery and the Rise of Absolutism and Constitutionalism

1415	Prince Henry the Navigator establishes his school of navigation.
1445	The Portuguese conquer Cape Verdi, Africa.
1488	Bartholomew Diaz reaches the Cape of Good Hope.
1492	Christopher Columbus sails for India.
1493	Pope Alexander VI establishes the Line of Demarcation. Spain receives everything west of the line between the Azores and Cape Verdi. Portugal receives everything east of the line between the Azores and Cape Verdi.
1494	The Treaty of Tordesillas moves the Papal Demarcation Line of 1493 west to give Brazil to Portugal.
1497	Giovanni Cabazo (John Cabot) explores Nova Scotia, Newfoundland, and New England.
1500	Pedro Cabral reaches Brazil.
1513	Vasco Nunez de Balboa reaches the Pacific.
1519	Ferdinand Magellan sets out to circumnavigate the globe.
1519	Hernando Cortés conquers the Aztecs of Mexico.
1531–1533	Francisco Pizarro conquers the Incas of Peru.
1534–1541	Jacques Cartier explores the St. Lawrence River in Canada.
1542–1543	The Portuguese land in Japan.
1558	Elizabeth I of England ascends to the throne as the last Tudor monarch.
1588	The Spanish Armada, under Philip II, is defeated by the English Navy.
1589	Henry of Navarre becomes King Henry IV and begins the Bourbon Dynasty.
1603	James VI of Scotland, cousin of Elizabeth I, becomes James I of England, the first Stuart king.
1610	Louis XIII and Cardinal Richelieu reign.
1618	The Thirty Years' War begins.
1625	Charles I becomes king.
1629	Charles I accepts the Petition of Right prohibiting taxation without parliamentary approval.
1637	Charles I forces a new prayer book upon Scotland's Presbyterians.
1643	Louis XIV becomes king of France.
1648	Peace of Westphalia ends the Thirty Years' War.
1649	Charles I is beheaded on the charge of treason.
1653	Oliver Cromwell establishes the Commonwealth of England.
1658	Oliver Cromwell dies.
1660	Restoration: Charles II becomes king.
1685	Louis XIV revokes the Edict of Nantes.
1688–1689	Parliament deposes James II and replaces him with Protestant leader William of Orange and his wife, Mary; this bloodless overthrow is known as the Glorious Revolution.
1689	Peter the Great becomes Czar of Russia.
1715	Louis XIV dies.

Sample Multiple-Choice Questions

1. Which of these events during the Age of Exploration was a cause of the others?

   A. Europeans brought food, animals, and ideas from one continent to another.

   B. European diseases had an adverse effect on the native populations of new territories.

   C. Warfare increased as European nations competed for land and power.

   D. Advances in learning and technology made long ocean voyages possible.

   E. Christianity was brought to the Native Americans.

2. Which of these European nations was the first to send ships into the Indian Ocean and establish colonies?

   A. Britain
   B. Portugal
   C. Holland
   D. France
   E. Spain

3. "The person of the king is sacred, and to attack him in any way is an attack on religion itself. Kings represent the Divine Majesty and have been appointed by Him to carry out His purposes. Serving God and respecting kings are bound together."

   Which of these men would support this statement?

   A. Thomas Hobbes
   B. Bishop Jacques Bossuet
   C. John Locke
   D. Jean Jacques Rousseau
   E. Baron de Montesquieu

4. Colbert supported all of the following to promote the French economy EXCEPT

   A. improvement of internal transportation in France.

   B. encouragement of the growth of new industries.

   C. establishment of a strong maritime fleet to transport goods.

   D. creation of a central bank.

   E. setting up of tariffs to protect French industries.

5. Louis XIV was able to control the nobility by

   A. working closely through the Estates General.

   B. appointing them to higher positions within the government.

   C. gaining their support for his foreign policy.

   D. requiring them to live at Versailles for at least part of the year.

   E. gaining the support of the Huguenots.

6. Cardinal Richelieu was able to establish absolute control for Louis XIII of France by all of the following EXCEPT

   A. destroying the castles of the nobles.

   B. levying taxes without the consent of the Estates General.

   C. disbanding the intendant system.

   D. eliminating the nobility from any government position.

   E. crushing any group of nobles who threatened royal power.

7. The decline of Spain in the seventeenth century can be attributed to

   A. an overexpansion of industry and trade.

   B. the rise of an urban middle class.

   C. weak and ineffective monarchs.

   D. the growth of slave labor in America.

   E. the growth of an intellectual movement that questioned the authority of the king.

8. Which is the best way to describe Oliver Cromwell's Protectorate?

   A. Constitutional monarchy
   B. Democracy
   C. Puritan military dictatorship
   D. Absolute monarchy
   E. Parliamentary democracy

9. Which was a result of the Glorious Revolution of 1689?

    A. It restored the Puritans to office.
    B. It established democracy.
    C. It restored the supremacy of Parliament over the king.
    D. The king gained power at the expense of the nobility.
    E. The Stuarts were allowed to remain in power.

10. Therefore, the Parliament declares:

    "That the (king's) pretended power of suspending laws . . . without consent of Parliament is illegal. That levying money (taxes) for or to the use of the crown (king) . . . without grant (consent) of Parliament . . . is illegal."

    This seventeenth-century excerpt can be found in which of the following?

    A. English Bill of Rights (1689)
    B. *Declaration of the Rights of Man and of the Citizen*
    C. Napoleonic Code
    D. Magna Carta
    E. Locke's *Two Treatises of Government*

Multiple-Choice Questions: Answers and Explanations

1. **D.** The Renaissance spirit of inquiry and the development of navigational devices such as the compass and astrolabe made better navigation possible for Europeans. Advances in geographic knowledge due to the improvement in the field of cartography also encouraged explorers to venture farther away from home. Finally, new and improved ships such as the caravel provided the vessels that Europeans needed to launch their voyages. The Age of Exploration led to the Columbian Exchange in which Europe brought horses, cattle, and sheep to the Americas and returned with corn, potatoes, peanuts, and tobacco. Europeans also brought diseases such as smallpox to the Americas. These advances also contributed to the Europeans engaging in a series of wars from the sixteenth to the eighteenth centuries. They were caused partly by colonial rivalry. The English defeated the Spanish Armada in 1588 and England and France fought in four major wars. Missionaries also saw exploration as a struggle to convert Native Americans to Christianity.

2. **B.** Prince Henry the Navigator of Portugal set up a school for sailing that inspired Portugal to search for a direct all-water route around Africa to the East. In 1498, Vasco da Gama rounded the Cape of Good Hope and sailed on to India. He established trading posts at Goa and Calicut. Spain would explore efforts to reach a direct water route in 1492 when Columbus sailed westward and landed in the Bahamas. Britain, Holland, and France would begin their exploration of the New World in the sixteenth century.

3. **B.** Bishop Jacques Bossuet believed in the Divine Right Theory. This theory was used to justify unlimited royal power. Bossuet summed up the theory in his book, *Discourse on Universal History* (1681). Bossuet claimed that the king was an agent of God and his authority to rule came directly from God. The king was entitled to unquestioning obedience. The Divine Right Theory supported the idea that we are given basic rights from God. Thomas Hobbes supported an absolute monarchy but not the divine right of government. John Locke and Jean Jacques Rousseau rejected absolutism and supported the idea that government was a social contract between the people and the government. Baron de Montesquieu believed in limiting royal absolutism.

4. **D.** Colbert supported the principle of mercantilism that depended upon making France self-sufficient. To achieve this goal, Colbert wanted France to develop its internal transportation system and promote the growth of new industries. To protect these industries, he supported a protective tariff. He also believed that France could become self-sufficient only if it developed a strong merchant marine fleet that could transport the goods necessary for the economy. The establishment of a national bank was not one of Colbert's economic goals.

5. **D.** Louis XIV required all the great nobility of France to live at the Versailles Palace, at great cost to the Royal Court. The nobles were free from paying any taxes. Left at their own estates, the nobles could be a threat to the power of the monarch. By luring the nobles to Versailles, he turned them into courtiers, battling for privilege rather than power. Louis never called a meeting of the Estates General, and he appointed members of the upper middle class, not the nobles, to high positions of power within the government. Louis also never needed the support of the nobles for the war. In 1685, he revoked the Edict of Nantes, which had granted the French Huguenots religious toleration. Louis exiled many of the Huguenots, and others fled to Holland and the Americas. He wanted their support only if they converted.

6. **C.** Cardinal Richelieu did not eliminate the intendant system. He introduced the institution of the intendants, who were state-appointed officials. These officials held a wide range of powers over the local area that they administered. The intendants were used to enforce royal orders in the provinces and to weaken the power and influence of regional nobility. Richelieu destroyed the fortified castles, which had long been a symbol of noble independence. Although a few nobles held important offices, a majority of state officials were members of the middle class. Richelieu crushed aristocratic conspiracies ruthlessly.

7. **C.** After Philip II's rule ended in 1598, his successor Philip III allowed the Duke of Lerma to run the country on his behalf. He used this power to advance his personal and familial wealth. Philip IV left the management of his several kingdoms to his favorite nobles. Many of them clung to the belief that the solution to restoring Spain's greatness was to revive its involvement in the religious wars of Europe. Spain became involved in the Thirty Years' War, which emptied its treasury and brought disaster. The decadence of the Spanish rulers and the lack of effective royal councilors contributed to Spain's failure. The incredible

wealth of South America destroyed any efforts to expand Spain's industry and trade and destroyed what remained of the Spanish middle class. The gold and silver of the colonies created contempt for business and manual labor. The growth of slave labor helped to create Spanish absolutism because its power was built upon the slaves who produced the gold and silver in the colonies. There was limited intellectual growth in Spain, as the Spanish ignored new scientific or mercantile ideas because they came from the heretical nations of Holland and England.

8. **C.** Oliver Cromwell was designated as a Lord Protectorate in 1652 to restore law and order. He ruled as a military dictator through his army. Cromwell levied heavy taxes, divided England into 12 military districts, and proclaimed quasi-martial law. He ruled until his death in 1658. Cromwell's government was not a parliamentary democracy since all power in his government resided in him.

9. **C.** The Glorious Revolution was a bloodless and successful revolution. In 1688, Parliament secretly offered the English crown to William, the Protestant ruler of Holland and his wife Mary (also Protestant), daughter of James II. Parliament was fearful that James II would reestablish Catholic rule in England. When William and Mary accepted and arrived in England, James II fled the country. Parliament proclaimed William and Mary the new king and queen. This relatively bloodless revolution ended divine-right rule in England and established the supremacy of Parliament. The Glorious Revolution ended the Stuarts' power, but did not restore the Puritans to office, or establish democracy. The Glorious Revolution provided for a constitutional monarchy in which the king's power was limited and not increased at the expense of the nobility. The wealthy landowners through Parliament were the dominant force in the government.

10. **A.** This seventeenth-century excerpt is found in the English Bill of Rights. This excerpt rejected the idea that the king is an absolute ruler. In 1689, James II of England was forced to abdicate his throne because of his Catholicism and his wish to become an absolute ruler. The British Parliament invited William and Mary to rule provided that they agreed to sign a series of acts that became known as the Bill of Rights. This bill limited the power of the king to repeal any law, levy taxes, or maintain an army without the consent of Parliament. The monarch also agreed not to interfere with parliamentary elections and debates. The people were also guaranteed basic civil rights. The Bill of Rights guaranteed the superiority of Parliament over the king. The National Assembly of France in 1789 issued the *Declaration of the Rights of Man and of the Citizen.* It proclaimed that the government rested on the consent of the people, not on the divine right of the king. This declaration ended the absolutism of Louis XVI and turned France into a constitutional monarchy. The Napoleonic Code consisted of laws that consolidated the achievements of the French Revolution, such as social equality, religious toleration, and trial by jury. The Magna Carta (1215) was signed by King John and was passed to protect the feudal nobles against the tyranny of the king. John Locke's *Two Treatises on Government* was written to justify the Glorious Revolution and that government was organized to protect the life and liberty of all.

The Scientific Revolution of the sixteenth and seventeenth centuries changed the way educated people looked at the world. It evolved from the Renaissance's stress on the importance of individuals to understand the world around them, and was the key factor that moved Europe from a worldview that was primarily religious to one that was primarily secular. Although a more secular society was likely not their goal, Luther's and Calvin's attacks against the authority of the pope provided a powerful example of how to challenge traditional authority. Their questioning attitudes produced an environment that encouraged the inquiry necessary for science to flourish.

Science in the Middle Ages was designed to help a person reach a better understanding of God and not the world. A medieval scientist would have found it inconceivable to examine the universe outside the realm of religion. During the Renaissance from the 1300s until the early 1500s, science was still considered a branch of religion, and scientific thought held that the earth was a stationary object at the center of the universe. Beginning with Copernicus, however, who taught that the earth revolved around the sun, Europeans began to reject Aristotelian-medieval scientific thought. Copernicus, Galileo, and Newton developed a new concept of a universe based on natural laws, not a mysterious God.

The new scientific approach promoted critical thinking. Nothing was to be accepted on faith. Belief in miracles and superstition was replaced by reliance on reason and the idea that rational thinking would uncover a plan governing the universe. This critical analysis of everything in society from religion to politics and the optimism that the human mind could find the solution to everything was known as the **Enlightenment.** Sixteenth- and seventeenth-century intellectuals, writers, and philosophers were optimistic that they could change society for the better. Writers, such as David Hume and Immanuel Kant, were primarily interested in teaching people how to think critically about everything, while philosophers, such as Voltaire, Montesquieu, Rousseau, Smith, and Diderot, were not revolutionaries but reformers who criticized the existing social, political, and economic structures in order to improve them. They found their hope in **Enlightened Despots,** or monarchs, the most important of whom were Frederick the Great of Prussia, Joseph II of Austria, and Catherine the Great of Russia, who would improve the lives of their subjects and encourage the pursuit of knowledge. However, societal reform was not accomplished by these despots, but came instead through the revolutionary forces that were instrumental to the French Revolution at the end of the eighteenth century.

The Scientific Revolution

To understand how the Scientific Revolution dramatically altered the way society viewed the world and the role of man in society, you must realize that the medieval worldview was ruled by the ideas of the third-century B.C.E Greek philosopher, Aristotle, the second-century B.C.E. Egyptian philosopher, Ptolemy, and theologians. Their ideas had been recovered during the Middle Ages as Western Europe began to trade with the East. Medieval theologians, such as St. Thomas Aquinas, brought these writings into harmony with Christian doctrines. The philosophy of Aquinas was known as **scholasticism**. The Aristotelian view of the world supported the Ptolemaic view of a motionless earth at the center of the universe, and this world was made up of four elements: earth, air, fire, and water. This view offered a common-sense approach for Christians, who put human beings at the center of the universe. Although widely accepted during the Renaissance, the traditional view of science began to be questioned by various rulers, such as Florence's Medici family, who supported the investigations of Galileo.

The views of Aristotle and Ptolemy were shattered by **Nicholas Copernicus** (1473–1543). In his book *On the Revolutions of the Heavenly Spheres* (not published until after his death in 1543 because he feared the ridicule of fellow astronomers), Copernicus suggested that the sun was the center of the universe and that the earth and planets revolved in circular orbits. This **Heliocentric Theory** that the sun—and not the earth—was the center of the universe contradicted contemporary scientific thought and challenged the traditional teachings of hundreds of years. Copernicus' book had enormous scientific and religious consequences. By characterizing the earth as just another planet, he destroyed the impression that the earthly world was different from the heavenly world.

Religious leaders understood the significance of Copernicus' findings all too well; of him, Luther is reported to have said, "The fool wants to turn the world of astronomy upside down." Calvin, like Luther, also condemned Copernicus. The Catholic Church, however, reacted slowly and did not declare Copernicus' theory false until 1616, continuing to hold to the view that the earth was the center of the universe. The slow reaction of the Church reflected the slow acceptance of Copernicus' theory. Other events created doubts about traditional astronomic ideas as well, such as the discovery of a new star in 1572 and the appearance of a comet in 1577. These events began to dramatically alter the acceptance of the earth as a motionless object.

Copernicus' ideas influenced others in the field of science. A Danish astronomer, **Tycho Brahe** (1546–1601), set the stage for the study of modern astronomy by building an observatory and collecting data for over twenty years on the location of the stars and planets. His greatest contribution was this collection of data, yet his limited knowledge of mathematics prevented Brahe from making much sense out of the data.

Johannes Kepler (1571–1630), a German astronomer and assistant to Brahe, used his data to support Brahe's data and Copernicus' idea that the planets move around the sun in elliptical, not circular, orbits. Kepler's three laws of planetary motion were based on mathematical relationships and accurately predicted the movements of planets in a sun-centered universe. His work demolished the old systems of Aristotle and Ptolemy.

While Kepler was examining planetary motion, **Galileo Galilei,** a Florentinian (1564–1642), continued the attack on traditional views of science. Using observation rather than speculation to help him formulate ideas—such as his laws on the motion of falling bodies—Galileo established **experimentation,** the cornerstone of modern science. He applied experimental methods to astronomy by using the newly invented telescope. Using this instrument, he discovered the four moons of Jupiter, and that the moon had a mountainous surface, much like the earth. His discovery destroyed an earlier notion that planets were crystal spheres (the earth was the center of the universe and around it moved separate, transparent crystal spheres: the moon, the sun, five planets, and fixed stars), and challenged the traditional belief in the unique relationship between the earth and the moon. Galileo's evidence reinforced and confirmed the theory of Copernicus. Following the publication of his book, *Dialogue Concerning the Two Chief World Systems* (1632), which openly criticized the works of Aristotle and Ptolemy, Galileo was arrested, imprisoned, tried for heresy by the Papal Inquisition, and forced to publicly recant his views. In modern times, Galileo's trial has come to symbolize the conflict between religious beliefs and scientific knowledge.

The greatest figure of the Scientific Revolution was **Sir Isaac Newton** (1642–1727), an Englishman. In his book *Principia Mathematica* (1687), he integrated the ideas of Copernicus, Kepler, and Galileo into one system of mathematical laws to explain the orderly manner in which the planets revolved around the sun. The key feature of his thesis was the **law of universal gravitation.** According to this law, every body in the universe attracts every other body in precise mathematical relationships. Newton's law mathematically proved that the sun, moon, earth, planets, and all other bodies moved in accordance with the same basic force of gravitation. Such proof showed that the universe operated by rules that could be explained through mathematics and that a religious interpretation was not the sole means of comprehending the forces of nature.

The Scientific Revolution also led to a better way of obtaining knowledge. Two important philosophers were **Francis Bacon** (1561–1626) and **René Descartes** (1596–1650). Both were responsible for key aspects in the improvement of scientific methodology. Francis Bacon was an English politician and writer, who advocated that new knowledge had to be acquired through an **inductive,** or experimental, reasoning process (using specific examples to prove or draw a conclusion from a general point) called **empiricism.** Bacon rejected the medieval view of knowledge based on tradition, and believed instead that it was necessary to collect data, observe, and draw conclusions. This approach is the foundation of the scientific method.

René Descartes was a French mathematician and philosopher. Like Bacon, he scorned the traditional science and broke with the past by writing the *Discourse on the Method* (1637) in French rather than Latin, which had been the intellectual language of the Middle Ages. Unlike Bacon, Descartes stressed deductive reasoning. He believed that it was necessary to doubt everything that could be doubted. His famous quote—"*Cogito ergo sum*" ("I think therefore I am")—proved his belief in his own existence and nothing else. He believed that, as in geometry, it is necessary to use deductive reasoning and logic to determine scientific laws governing things. Descartes' view of the world (now called **Cartesian Dualism**) reduced natural law to matter and the mind, or the physical and the spiritual. Bacon's inductive experimentalism and Descartes' deductive, mathematical, and logical thinking combined into the scientific method, which began taking hold of society in the late seventeenth century.

Some consequences of the Scientific Revolution include the following:

- A scientific community emerged whose primary goal was the expansion of knowledge. Learned societies like the French Academy of Sciences and the Royal Society of London were founded to promote the growth of scientific ideas among different countries.

- A modern scientific method arose that was both theoretical and experimental, and its practitioners refused to base their conclusions on traditional and established sources or ancient texts. The belief that human reason was the vehicle that would unlock the secrets of the universe ended the dominance of religion on society. The Age of Reason in the eighteenth century, with its faith in the rational and skeptical mind, would provide the background for the Enlightenment.

There was little connection, however, between science and technology. The Scientific Revolution had little effect on daily life before the nineteenth century. The revolution in science in the sixteenth and seventeenth centuries was primarily an intellectual one.

The Enlightenment

The Scientific Revolution was the single most important event that fostered the creation of a new intellectual movement in the late seventeenth and early eighteenth centuries called the **Enlightenment,** or, sometimes, the **Age of Reason**—a time period defining the generation that came of age between the publication of Newton's ideas in 1687 and the death of Louis XIV in 1715. The Enlightenment's core tenet was that natural law could be used to examine and understand all aspects of society.

The Enlightenment's leaders believed that by using scientific methods, they could explain the laws of society and human nature. It was an optimistic creed—armed with the proper methods of discovering the laws of human nature, enlightened thinkers were convinced they could solve all problems. They believed it was possible to create a better society and people and that progress was inevitable. They were free from the restraints of religion and focused instead on improving economic and social conditions. Consequently, the movement was profoundly secular.

Some important enlightened thinkers include the following:

- **Thomas Hobbes** (1588–1679). An English writer, Hobbes was influenced by the experimental attitude toward nature and decided to apply it to politics. Writing at the time of the English Civil War, Hobbes was forced to flee London to Paris in 1648 because he feared for his life. In 1651 he wrote *Leviathan,* a title he chose after the sea monster from the Book of Job. Hobbes believed that humans in their original state of nature were unhappy. In the state of nature, Hobbes asserted that man was quarrelsome, turbulent, and forever locked in a war against all. He supported an absolute monarch (although he did not support the Divine Right Theory of government) because he thought that man needed protection from destroying himself and an all-powerful ruler was the best source of such protection. Thus, man enters a social contract to surrender his freedom to an absolute ruler, in order to maintain law and order. The subject could never rebel and the monarchs had the right to put down any rebellion by any means possible.

  Hobbes's ideas never won great popularity. In England, **Royal Absolutism,** a cause he supported, never gained acceptance. He was overshadowed by his contemporary John Locke.

- **John Locke** (1632–1704). Like Hobbes, Locke was interested in the world of science. His book, *Two Treatises of Government* (1690), was written as a philosophical justification for the Glorious Revolution, which refers to the bloodless overthrow of James II in 1689 and the end of absolutism in England. This work translated his belief in natural law into a theory of government that became known as **The Social Contract.** Locke argued that man is born basically good and has certain natural rights of life, liberty, and property. To protect these natural rights, people enter into a social contract to create a government with limited powers. Locke believed that if a government did not protect these rights or exceeded its authority, the people have a right to revolt, if necessary. Locke's ideas of **consent of the governed,** a social contract, and the right of revolution influenced the writing of the United States' Declaration of Independence and the Constitution of the United States. Locke's ideas also laid the foundation for the criticisms of absolute government in France.

It was in France that the Enlightenment reached its highest development. Some of the reasons for this were the following:

- French was the international language of the educated class.
- In addition to being the wealthiest and most populous country, France was the cultural center of Europe.
- Although critical books were often banned by the French censors and their authors jailed or exiled, the writers were not tortured or executed for their statements. Thus, the French intellectuals battled powerful forces but did not face the overwhelming difficulties of writers in Eastern or Central Europe.

The French used the term **philosophe** (*philosopher*) to describe the thinkers of the age. The philosophes were committed to bringing new thought to all of Europe. They wanted to educate the economic and social elite but not necessarily the masses. Philosophes, who were not allowed to criticize either the Church or state openly, circulated their work in the form of books, plays, novels, dictionaries, and encyclopedias, using satire and double meaning to spread their messages and thus preventing their writings from being burned or banned. **Salons,** gatherings organized by wealthy women held in large drawing rooms in their homes, were also used to help philosophes avoid trouble with authorities. At these meetings, philosophes would gather to discuss politics, philosophy, and current issues. These discussions allowed the writers greater freedom to spread their words. Enlightened thinkers considered themselves part of an intellectual community. They shared their ideas through books, personal letters, and visits back and forth amongst themselves.

Some of the important French philosophes included the following:

- **Baron de Montesquieu** (1689–1755) was a French aristocrat who wanted to limit royal absolutism. In his book, *The Spirit of Laws* (1748), he urged that power be separated among three branches of government: executive, legislative, and judicial. Each branch would check the other branches, thus preventing despotism and preserving freedom. Montesquieu admired the British system of government and was critical of the absolutism of the French monarchy because all power was concentrated in one person. His theory of the separation of powers greatly influenced the framers of the United States Constitution.
- **Voltaire** (1694–1778): Born François-Marie Arouet, Voltaire is considered to be the greatest of all the Enlightened philosophes. Educated by Jesuits, he challenged the authority of the Catholic Church. Although he believed in God, his God was a distant deistic God—a clockmaker who built an orderly universe and then let it operate under the laws of science. Voltaire hated religious intolerance, urged religious freedom, and thought that religion crushed the human spirit. In his book, *Candide,* he wrote against the evils of organized religion, and in his *Treatise on Toleration,* he argued for religious tolerance. Voltaire denounced organized religion because it exploited people's ignorance and superstitions. Deism was intended to construct a more natural religion based on reason and natural law. His most famous anti-religious statement was "*écrasez l'infâme*" ("crush the horrible thing").

    In 1717, he was imprisoned in the Bastille for eleven months, after which he was forced to live in exile for three years in Great Britain, a period of time that greatly influenced the rest of his life. Like Montesquieu, Voltaire came to admire Britain's system of government. He praised their limited monarchy, respect for civil liberties, and freedom of thought. He promoted freedom of thought and respect for all. Typical of his outlook is the statement attributed to him: "I disapprove of what you say, but I will defend to the death your right to say it." Voltaire became a European celebrity who in 1743 lived in the court of Frederick the Great of Prussia, and became a supporter of Enlightened Despotism.
- **Jean-Jacques Rousseau** (1712–1778). Like other Enlightened writers, Rousseau was committed to individual freedom. However, he attacked rationalism and civilization, considering them to be destroying rather than liberating man. Instead, spontaneous feeling was to replace and complement the coldness of intellectualism. According to Rousseau, man was basically born good and needed protecting from the corrupting influences

of civilization. These ideas would later greatly influence the Romantic Movement of the nineteenth century, which rebelled against the culture of the Enlightenment.

Rousseau's book, *The Social Contract,* published in 1762, begins with the famous line, "All men are born free but everywhere they are in chains." He believed that as social inequalities develop, people enter into a social contract agreeing to surrender their individual rights to the community and the general will, or the will of the majority, in order to be free—thus creating a government as a necessary evil to carry out the general will. If the government fails, people have the right to replace it. Although Rousseau's concept of the general will appealed to democrats and nationalists after the French Revolution of 1789, it has also been used by dictators like Adolf Hitler to justify totalitarian rule by claiming that a dictator or one-party ruler speaks for the general will to which all citizens owe obedience.

In 1762, Rousseau also published *Émile,* a book that stirred controversy because of its attacks on civilization and its new theory of education. He criticized education that focused on the development of reason and logical thinking and advocated greater love, tenderness, and understanding towards children. Rousseau argued for more humane treatment of children and for children to develop naturally and spontaneously. Children had to explore nature as a way to raise their emotional awareness. *Émile* helped to change the educational and child-rearing practices in eighteenth-century Europe.

- **Denis Diderot** (1713–1784) published his writings and the ideas of many Enlightened philosophers in his *Encyclopedia* (1751). This 25-volume collection of political and social critiques, which included writers such as Voltaire and Montesquieu, attacked abuses of the French government, including religious intolerance and unjust taxation. The *Encyclopedia* was an example of the eighteenth-century belief that all knowledge could be organized in a systematic and scientific fashion. Diderot hoped that this information would help people to think and act rationally and critically.

The **physiocrats** were economic thinkers in eighteenth-century France who developed the first complete system of economics. Like the philosophes, the physiocrats looked for natural laws to define a rational economic system. However, the physiocrats, unlike the philosophes, were close to the government as advisors. Some famous physiocrats include the following:

- **François Quesnay** (1694–1774) was the French leader of the physiocrats and a physician to Louis XV. He supported a hands-off, or *laissez-faire,* approach to the government's involvement in the economy.
- **Adam Smith** (1727–1790) was a Scottish economist. While not an actual physiocrat member, Smith had met with the physiocrats on the continent and adopted and refined many of their ideas. In his *Wealth of Nations,* published in 1776, the same year as the United States' Declaration of Independence, Smith argued against strict government control of mercantilism. He outlined the nucleus of the economic system that came to be known as **capitalism.** Smith believed in a *laissez-faire* approach to business. He argued that individuals should be left to pursue their own economic gain. The role of the state is to act as a policeman who intervenes only when necessary. Smith thought that the invisible hand of supply, demand, and competition would ensure that people would act in the best interest of everyone.

Women and the Enlightenment

French women helped spread the Enlightenment through their salons where the philosophes mixed with the most brilliant thinkers of Europe. Women helped to promote the careers of the philosophes. As Louis XIV grew closer to death, the Court of Versailles had begun to lose its luster. Thus, many wealthy aristocratic ladies began to host small gatherings in their Paris townhouses. Women like **Marie-Thérèse Geoffrin** (1699–1777) and **Claudine Tencin** (1682–1749) gave the philosophes access to useful social and political contacts. Madame Geoffrin, who hosted two dinners each week, became so well known that she regularly corresponded with the king of Sweden and Catherine the Great of Russia.

The women of the Enlightenment were also able to help the philosophes avoid trouble with authorities and even secured pensions for some of them. The **Marquise de Pompadour** (1721–1764), the mistress of Louis XV, played a role in preventing the censoring of the *Encyclopedia Britannica* and blocked the circulation of work attacking the philosophes. However, the philosophes were not on the whole strong supporters of women's rights. Although many criticized the overly religious education of women, they did not advocate any radical changes in the social conditions of women. Although Montesquieu believed that women were not inferior to men and should have a wider role in society, he supported a traditional view of family and marriage and expected men to dominate these institutions. The writings of the authors in the *Encyclopedia* were also unfavorable to women. The editors almost exclusively recruited men and saw no need to include articles about women. The writers may have disagreed about the social equality of women, but in general, women were discussed primarily in traditional roles (daughters, wives, and mothers) and motherhood was their most important occupation. Rousseau, who was a political radical, urged a traditional role for women. In his novel, *Émile,* he claimed there should be separate spheres for men and women. Women were assigned the domestic sphere because of their physiological limitations. Rousseau excluded women from political life and felt they should not be granted equal education with men. Inspired partially by the French Revolution, **Mary Wollstonecraft** (1759–1797), who wrote *A Vindication of the Rights of Woman* in 1792, criticized Rousseau for seeking to limit the hopes of women. Wollstonecraft was demanding the basic rights and liberties that the Enlightened male writers had been advocating throughout the century.

Enlightened Despotism

Many philosophes believed that Enlightened reform would come by way of Enlightened monarchs. **Enlightened Despots** were rulers who tried to justify their absolute rule by claiming to rule in the people's interest by making good laws, promoting human happiness, and improving society. Encouraged and instructed by philosophes like Voltaire who did not trust the masses and believed that change had to come from above and not from the people, the monarchs of Prussia, Russia, and Austria were able to mesh their need for a more effective state with the need for economic, educational, and social reform. The most notable Enlightened Despots of these countries include the following:

- **Frederick the Great** (b. 1712, ruled 1740–1786) of Prussia. As King of Prussia, Frederick invited Voltaire to his court and sought his advice on how to be an Enlightened ruler. He did away with the torture of accused criminals, improved the educational system, allowed his subjects to believe as they wished in religion, and promoted industry, agriculture, and commerce. He was an efficient statesman and made Prussia into the best-ruled nation in Europe. **Immanuel Kant** (1724–1804) of Germany, the greatest German philosopher of his age, suggested that Frederick was an Enlightened ruler because he allowed freedom of the press and gave Catholics and Jews permission to settle in Prussia.

- **Peter the Great** (b. 1672, ruled 1682–1725) of Russia was a contemporary of Louis XIV of France. Technically, he might not be considered an Enlightened Despot because he never tried to justify his absolutism by claiming to rule in the people's interest. Nevertheless, he was responsible for trying to make Russia a part of Europe after centuries of domination by the Mongols. Peter's efforts to westernize Russia included introducing his country to Western ideas in science, education, military training, and industry. He ordered his male subjects to shave their traditional long beards and discard their oriental garments. He also extended control over the Russian Byzantine Church. Western artisans were invited to the country and, with their workers, helped to build a new seaport on the Gulf of Finland called St. Petersburg, his "window to the West." This seaport provided a trade route with Western Europe.

- **Catherine the Great** (b. 1729, ruled 1762–1796) of Russia. The German wife of the Russian czar, Peter III, Catherine deposed her husband and ruled as an autocrat. She read the works of Montesquieu and Voltaire and imported Western culture to Russia. She also revised and codified Russian law, patronized the arts, created hospitals, and undertook other public welfare projects. The Pugachev serf uprising of 1773 led her to reverse her trend towards reform of serfdom and return to nobles the absolute control of their serfs.

- **Maria Theresa** (b. 1717, ruled 1740–1780) of Austria realized upon inheriting the throne that Austria was weak, and so she began a series of reforms. She established a national army, limited the power of the Catholic Church, revised the tax system and the bureaucracy, and reduced the power of the lord over the serfs. She also improved the educational system.

- **Joseph II** (b. 1741, ruled 1780–1790) of Austria furthered the reforms of his mother, Maria Theresa. He abolished serfdom and introduced a single tax for everyone, a physiocratic idea. He granted religious tolerance to Calvinists and Lutherans, and eliminated many of the restrictions on Jews. Joseph abolished capital punishment, reformed the educational and judicial system, and established hospitals. After his death, his brother **Leopold II** (b. 1747, ruled 1790–1792) was forced to back away from these reforms as a way to quell a series of peasant and aristocratic revolts.

Chronology of the Scientific Revolution and the Enlightenment

1543	Posthumous publication of *On the Revolution of the Heavenly Spheres* by Copernicus.
1590	The first microscope is made by Zacharias.
1605	Publication of *The Advancement of Learning* by Sir Francis Bacon.
1608	The telescope is invented.
1609	Publication of *On the Motion of Mars* by Johannes Kepler.
1616	The Catholic Church bans Copernicus' ideas.
1628	Publication of William Harvey's theory of blood circulation.
1632	Publication of *Dialogue Concerning the Two Chief World Systems* by Galileo.
1633	Galileo is imprisoned for heresy.
1637	Publication of René Descartes' *Discourse on Method*.
1642–1646	The Civil War in England.
1642	The birth of Isaac Newton.
1651	Thomas Hobbes' *Leviathan* is published.
1655	Evangelista Torricelli constructs the first mercury barometer.
1682	Edmond Halley observes a "new" comet.
1687	Publication of Isaac Newton's *Principia*.
1690	John Locke publishes *Two Treatises on Government*.
1694	François Arouet (Voltaire) is born.
1712	Jean-Jacques Rousseau is born.
1734	Voltaire publishes *Letters on the English*.
1739–40	David Hume publishes *A Treatise of Human Nature*.
1743	Antoine Lavoisier, "father of modern chemistry," is born.
1748	Baron de Montesquieu publishes *The Spirit of Laws*.
1751	Denis Diderot publishes the first volume of the *Encyclopedia*.
1756	Wolfgang Amadeus Mozart, composer, is born in Austria.
1759	Voltaire publishes *Candide*.
1762	Catherine the Great begins her rule in Russia.
1768–1771	*The Encyclopedia Britannica* is published.
1776	America's Declaration of Independence is created; Adam Smith publishes *The Wealth of Nations*.

Sample Multiple-Choice Questions

1. During the Scientific Revolution and the Enlightenment, the works of many scientists and philosophers were similar in that they

   A. relied heavily on the idea of medieval thinkers.
   B. favored an absolute monarchy as a way of improving economic conditions.
   C. received support from the Catholic Church.
   D. supported the Divine Right Theory of government.
   E. examined natural laws governing the universe.

2. Which statement was a belief of many writers of the Enlightenment?

   A. The wealthy class should govern society.
   B. Democracy is the best form of government.
   C. Kings are responsible only to God.
   D. Ideas can be proven by reason.
   E. Traditional values are important.

3. Which of the following European rulers cannot be considered an Enlightened monarch or despot?

   A. Catherine the Great
   B. Maria Theresa of Austria
   C. Joseph II
   D. Frederick the Great
   E. Elizabeth I

4. John Locke and Jean-Jacques Rousseau would be most likely to support

   A. a return to feudalism in Europe.
   B. a government ruled by a Divine Right monarchy.
   C. a society ruled by the Church.
   D. the right of citizens to decide the best form of government.
   E. a government ruled by Enlightened Despots.

5. Which of these men proposed the Heliocentric Theory of the universe?

   A. Aristotle
   B. Descartes
   C. Copernicus
   D. Kepler
   E. Ptolemy

6. "In every government, there are three sorts of power . . . when the legislative and executive are united in the same person or in the same body of magistrates, there can be no liberty because . . . the same monarch or senate . . . (may) enact tyrannical laws."

   The author of this passage was

   A. Montesquieu
   B. Bossuet
   C. Voltaire
   D. Hobbes
   E. Louis XIV

7. Voltaire's statement, "*écrasez l'infâme*" ("crush the horrible thing"), refers to

   A. the government of Louis XIV.
   B. the Catholic Church.
   C. the military.
   D. the middle class.
   E. the poor.

8. In what way did women in the Enlightenment play an important role?

   A. They wrote books supporting the ideals of the Enlightenment.
   B. They acted as representatives of the royal families in Europe.
   C. They spread the ideals of the Enlightenment in their salons.
   D. They were supported by men in their goal for equal rights.
   E. They were encouraged by the rising middle class to play a greater role in society.

9. "Every individual generally neither intends to promote the public interest, nor knows how much he is promoting it. . . . . He is . . . led by an invisible hand to promote an end, which was no part of his intention."

   This passage reflects the ideas of

   A. Adam Smith.
   B. Thomas Hobbes.
   C. Baron Montesquieu.
   D. John Locke.
   E. Jean-Jacques Rousseau.

10. The phrase, "*Cogito ergo sum*" ("I think, therefore I am"), has been attributed to

    A. Galileo Galilei.
    B. William Harvey.
    C. René Descartes.
    D. Johannes Kepler.
    E. Sir Francis Bacon.

Multiple-Choice Questions: Answers and Explanations

1. **E.** Scientists of the sixteenth and seventeenth centuries believed that by using reason and observation, one could determine the natural laws that governed the universe. The English scientist Sir Isaac Newton, for instance, calculated the natural law of gravity to help explain the operation of the forces of nature. The philosophers of the eighteenth-century Enlightenment believed that science and reason could explain the laws of society, and in their writings tied together the ideas of the Scientific Revolution. Both scientists and philosophers of this period rejected the ideas of the Middle Ages, which they believed were based on superstition and not reason. They also challenged the authority of the Catholic Church, which had rejected the ideas of Copernicus and Galileo, and were critical of the Divine Right Theory. These scientists and philosophers instead supported absolute monarchs who promoted economic and social progress for the people.

2. **D.** A belief of the Enlightenment was that ideas can be proven by reason. In the eighteenth century, French philosophes believed that one could use reason to understand the universe and rejected traditional ideas based on authority. They also believed that government existed not for the wealthy but was a social contract between the people and the government. Most of the philosophes opposed democracy. According to Voltaire, the best form of government was monarchism or Enlightened Despotism. They also rejected the notion that the king was responsible only to God. These writers criticized traditional values that were based on superstition and blind obedience to the past.

3. **E.** Elizabeth I (1558–1603), Queen of England, was born before the era of Enlightened Despotism. She preserved Protestantism in England and achieved world power for England. Catherine the Great of Russia, Maria Theresa of Austria, Joseph II of Austria, and Frederick the Great of Prussia were Enlightened Despots. They justified their absolutism by claiming to govern in the people's interest, and sought to advance society by promoting social justice. Catherine the Great encouraged legal reforms; Maria Theresa created a system of compulsory education in every community; Joseph II wanted to make all persons equal before the law; and Frederick the Great promoted religious freedom.

4. **D.** John Locke and Jean-Jacques Rousseau would be most likely to support the citizens' right to decide the best form of government. Locke and Rousseau believed that people entered into social contracts to protect their basic rights and create a government; hence Enlightened Despotism was anathema to their way of thinking. According to Locke, if the government fails to live up to its obligations, people have a right to change it. Rousseau asserted that people make the laws and the rule of the majority is supreme. Both philosophers were widely influential: Locke's ideas influenced the framers of the Constitution of the United States, while Rousseau has been hailed as a champion of democracy for advocating that political authority lies with the people. Neither of these writers supported a society governed by the Catholic Church; instead, they rejected feudalism and challenged the Church's authority.

5. **C.** Copernicus proposed the Heliocentric Theory of the universe, which stated that the earth revolved around the sun and that the sun was the center of the universe. Aristotle was a Greek philosopher who believed that a motionless earth was fixed at the center of the universe. Descartes was a French scientist and mathematician who today is considered the founder of analytic geometry. Kepler, a German astronomer and mathematician, determined that planets follow an elliptical, not a circular, path about the sun. Ptolemy was an Egyptian astronomer who placed the earth as a stationery object with the sun revolving around it.

6. **A.** The author of this passage is Montesquieu, who argued in his work *The Spirit of Laws* that governmental power had to be separated among three branches—executive, legislative, and judicial, each checking the other—instead of permitting power to be concentrated in one person, the king. This type of government would prevent despotism. Bossuet and Louis XIV believed in a Divine Right Theory in which all power was bestowed on the king by God. Voltaire believed in Enlightened Despotism and was a member of the Court of Frederick the Great. Hobbes claimed that only an absolute ruler with unlimited power could restore order to society.

7. **B.** Voltaire's statement refers to the Catholic Church. Although educated by Jesuits, Voltaire was critical of the perceived bigotry and narrow-mindedness that he felt was at the core of all religious tradition. He was a Deist who believed that God created the universe and then allowed it to act according to scientific law. Concerning choices A, C, D, and E, Voltaire wrote *The Age of Louis XV* in 1745 and portrayed him as a dignified ruler. Voltaire did not write about the military but did praise the poor for their simple piety.

8. **C.** The salons or townhouses of wealthy women provided the meeting places for the philosophes to discuss their ideas and how these ideas could become a vehicle for correcting the abuses of society. These salons provided the philosophes with the opportunity to meet important political people. Through the efforts of these wealthy women, the ideals of the Enlightenment became known and they also protected many writers from censorship. The women of the Enlightenment did not write books about the Enlightenment nor did they act as representatives of the royal families. In France, Madame Pompadour protected Enlightenment writers from persecution by the royal family. Neither the male writers, like Rousseau, nor the rising middle class encouraged women to play a greater role in society.

9. **A.** This passage reflects the ideas of Adam Smith in *The Wealth of Nations* (1776). Smith's ideas embodied a policy called *laissez-faire,* which enabled the bourgeoisie to further their own economic interests, but also increased the national wealth. Smith argued that the "invisible hand" of free competition for one and for all disciplined the greed of selfish individuals and provided the most effective means of increasing the wealth of both rich and poor. Hobbes believed in absolute government. Montesquieu proposed that separation of powers provided the best form of government. Locke and Rousseau promoted the Social Contract theory of government in which the government was formed to protect the rights of the people.

10. **C.** René Descartes was the French scientist and mathematician who wrote *Discourse on Method,* in which he claimed that all experience is validated by observation of natural phenomena. Descartes stripped away his belief in everything except his own existence. The other choices are incorrect for the following reasons: Galileo Galilei's observation of the heavens confirmed Copernicus' theory; William Harvey was an English physician who demonstrated that blood circulated through the body; Johannes Kepler was a German astronomer whose observations showed that the planets followed an elliptical orbit around the sun; and Sir Francis Bacon popularized the scientific method of observation.

The Age of Revolution: The French Revolution and Napoleonic Era

In 1789, France was widely considered a nation to be envied. It was the center of the intellectual movement of the Enlightenment. French scientists—such as **François Lavoisier** (1743–1794), the "Father of Modern Chemistry," and **Jean-Baptiste Lamarck** (1744–1829), who were the first to study how forms of life adjust to the environment—led the world, French books were read everywhere, and French was the international language spoken among the educated and aristocratic circles of many countries. With a population of about 25.5 million, France was the most populous nation in Europe, and Paris, although smaller than London, was the cultural center of Europe. French exports to Europe were greater than those of Great Britain. Nearly half of the gold pieces circulating in Europe at the time were French.

Despite its power and appearance of wealth, France had deep-rooted problems. The French government had become corrupt and ineffective, clinging to an outdated social structure that carried over from the Middle Ages. Under this old order, or *Ancien Régime* (Old Regime), there were three *estates*, or orders, in society. The structure of this old order no longer corresponded to the real distribution of power or influence among the French. The government was also heavily in debt and unable to balance its budget or deal with the crisis of doing so.

Efforts to reform the country led to a series of events that ultimately ended in the bloody French Revolution that destroyed the Old Regime. As the French Revolution progressed from its moderate stage to its more radical phase, known as the "Reign of Terror," other European nations became concerned because the Revolution's slogan of "Liberty, Equality, and Fraternity" threatened the established social order of the nineteenth century. The monarchs of England, Austria, Russia, and Prussia thus formed the Grand Alliance to stop the spread of the Revolution. The forming of this Alliance led to war with France.

The French Revolution also led to the rise of the legendary leader, Napoleon. In 1799, Napoleon, who called himself a "son of the Revolution," seized control of France. From 1800 to 1815, Napoleon dominated the European continent. He was a military genius who established a French empire that controlled every European country except England. He was an efficient administrator who instituted a number of Enlightened reforms that captured the support of the people. He spread the idea of the French Revolution throughout Europe, but his ambition and repression of liberty contributed to his downfall. After losing many troops in the disastrous Russian campaign of 1812, Napoleon was defeated at the Battle of Nations in 1813 by a coalition of European forces.

In 1814, the European nations met at the Congress of Vienna in an effort to undo the effects of the French Revolution and to turn back the clock to the way the world was prior to 1789. The representatives also sought to establish a policy of a balance of power to ensure that one person or country such as Napoleon or France would never dominate the European continent. This balance of power led to a hundred years of peace and prosperity in Europe. During this time, Europe became a powerful force in the world and extended its control over the areas of Asia and Africa.

The French Revolution

In 1789, the structure of French society, which fostered great inequalities among the people, led to a revolt against Louis XVI. The French Revolution led to a period of reform, chaos, and conservative reaction. Historians, such as Crane Brinton, acknowledge that democratic revolutions, such as the English Puritan Revolution of 1689, the American Revolution of 1776, and the French Revolution, may have a set of individual characteristics that are different from each other, but they follow a sequel of events that are similar to all democratic revolutions.

France under the Old Regime

The political, economic, and social conditions of eighteenth-century France was called the **Old Regime.** The class structure of France was divided along the following lines:

- **The First Estate.** The clergy of the Catholic Church represented about 1 percent of the population but owned about 10 to 15 percent of the land. They paid no direct taxes to the government except for a voluntary tax every five years. The Roman Catholic clergy of the First Estates included bishops and abbots but not the parish priests, who were often as poor as their parishioners.

- **The Second Estate.** Nobles and landowners in France consisted of less than 2 percent of the population and owned about 20 percent of the land. They also were exempt from taxes. Like the First Estate, the Second Estate was a privileged class. It collected feudal dues from the peasants, and its members held the best government jobs and army positions.

- **The Third Estate.** The middle class (*bourgeoisie*), urban lower classes, and peasant farmers comprised 98 percent of France's total population and owned about 40 percent of the land. Although the middle class had grown in France, the majority of the Third Estate consisted of the peasants who lived on the land. The bulk of the taxes fell on the Third Estate. The most burdensome taxes were the *taille* (a tax on agricultural goods such as produce), capitation (poll tax), a tithe (a Church tax of about 10 percent), a *gabelle* (a salt tax), a *vingtième* (an income tax), and dues to the local lord for the use of his mill (wine press and so on). The bourgeoisie, the rising commercial and professional classes, paid fewer taxes than the peasants but felt unjustly treated. They were denied good jobs and wanted to reform a system that was outdated and did not give them political and social rights that were on par with their economic conditions.

The absolutism of the king denied the people both a voice in the government and a way for them to make their grievances known. By using *lettres de cachet* (letters bearing the royal seal), the king was able to put his opponents into jail indefinitely without charges, bail, or trial.

The immediate cause of the French Revolution was financial. In 1789, France was sinking under a mound of debts. The French debt stood at four billion livres and it could not be carried because revenue fell short of expenditures. France was not poor, but tax exemptions and tax evasions by the wealthy, as described in the Estates list earlier, had led the country to a serious financial crisis. The extravagant cost of maintaining the Versailles Court and the debts incurred from the wars of Louis XIV as well as the money raised to support the American War of Independence against France's rival, Britain, added to the problem. By 1789, half of the income tax went just to pay off the interest on this enormous debt. The French debt was being held by aristocrats, merchants, manufacturers, and financiers.

However, the financial crisis was not due to national poverty; France was not bankrupt. **Louis XVI** (b. 1754, ruled 1774–1793) was a weak and indecisive ruler whose unpopular wife, **Marie Antoinette** (1755–1793), was considered a foreigner (she was a Hapsburg from Austria) and a vain, frivolous person who refused to cut expenses. Louis appointed a number of advisers, such as Swiss financier Jacques Necker who proposed to abolish tax privileges, but they were forced to resign after they proposed taxing the First and Second Estates. The king was fearful that taxing the First and Second Estates would weaken his royal power because these Estates wanted to exert greater political influence in the government. By 1786, the depressed economy and the lack of public confidence made it increasingly difficult for the government to obtain new loans. Louis XVI had no other option but to raise taxes. His adviser, Calonne, convened an "Assembly of Notables" (composed of high-ranking nobles and clergy) in 1787, hoping to gain endorsement for a general tax on all landowners. The nobles insisted that they wanted to share in the control of the government. A deadlock ensued and Louis dismissed his adviser. He tried to push the same program through the Paris Parlement (composed of 13 regional royal courts, and not to be confused with the English "Parliament"). When the Paris Parlement refused to grant Louis XVI the power to raise taxes unless a meeting of the Estates General was called, the king had run out of options. He was forced to reconvene the Estates General (described in the next section), a legislative body that included the representatives from all three Estates.

The Meeting of the Estates General and Creation of the National Assembly

On May 5, 1789, the **Estates General** met at Versailles. The Estates General was first summoned in 1302 to Paris by Philip IV in order to obtain national approval for his anti-clerical program. The power of the Estates General was never clearly defined, nor did that body ever obtain the financial control which made the English Parliament a powerful institution. The Estates General did not meet as a single body but convened separately as regional units, and its power varied inversely with the power of the king. Thus, as royal absolutism gained greater control in France, the Estates General became less significant. The Estates General had not met since 1614 and people looked to the meeting with enthusiasm because conditions in the country were bad. Peasants were starving and there were riots in Paris. People looked to the Estates General to save the country.

The Estates General was made up of the First (clergy), Second (nobles), and Third (middle class, workers, and peasants) Estates. Each Estate had drawn up a list of grievances called *cahiers de doléances.* As part of the electoral process of 1789, the *cahiers* were intended to inform and instruct the deputies of local views and authorize reform. There was general consensus among the three Estates that the royal power had to be limited, that the Estates General had to meet regularly, and that the individual liberties had to be guaranteed by law. However, the middle class, especially the lawyers who primarily made up the Third Estate, placed a greater emphasis on protecting the citizens' rights than the needs of the peasants. An immediate issue arose over the voting procedure.

The Estates General voted by unit and not by individual members. Each Estate had one vote. Therefore, the privileged classes—the First and Second Estates combined—could outvote the Third Estate. On June 17, 1789, after six weeks of deadlock over voting procedures, the Third Estate declared itself the National Assembly and was joined by much of the low-ranking clergy and some of the nobles. The renaming was effectively a claim that this new body was now sovereign.

Louis XVI locked the National Assembly's members out of the meeting hall. In retaliation, they met at an indoor tennis court at Versailles and took the **Tennis Court Oath** (June 20, 1789) not to disband until they had written a constitution for France.

The Tennis Court Oath officially began the French Revolution because power was coming from the National Assembly and not the king. On June 27, 1789, the king rejected violence and ordered the delegates to meet with the National Assembly. The National Assembly had become the legal form of government without resorting to violence. This body was to function as the legislative branch of government until the end of September 1791 and charged itself with writing a constitution. To reflect this mission, it called itself the **National Constituent Assembly** where the voting would be per capita and not by unit.

The Moderate Stage (1789–1792)

In the summer of 1789, food shortages, rising bread prices, and rumors that the king had sent troops to Versailles to dissolve the National Assembly incited people to action. On July 14, Paris mobs, looking for weapons, stormed the **Bastille,** a fortress symbolic of the Old Regime. The crowd cut off the head of the commander and marched around Paris with his decapitated head. This was a foreshadowing of the future. Disorder spread throughout France and set off what became known as **The Great Fear.** Peasants rose up against the nobles, burned castles, and destroyed records of feudal dues.

On August 4, 1789, at a stormy all-night session, the National Assembly's legislators took two preliminary legal steps to end the abuses of the Old Regime:

- **They abolished feudalism** in terms of feudal dues and tithes owed by the peasants; nobles were forced to give up special status and their exemption from taxes; all male citizens could hold government, army, or Church office.

- **They created the *Declaration of the Rights of Man and of the Citizen.*** Issued by the Assembly on August 26, 1789, this document shows the influence of Enlightenment thinkers such as Locke. It was modeled in part on the American Declaration of Independence, and contains the following decrees:
  - Men are born free and equal before the law.
  - Men are guaranteed freedom of speech, religion, and due process before the law.
  - Taxes have to be paid according to the ability to pay.
  - The right to rule rests not only on the king but also on the general will of the people.

The principles of the Declaration were captured in the slogan, "Liberty, Equality, and Fraternity." It became the symbol of the French Revolution.

In October, about 7,000 women marched to Versailles demanding bread. After protesting in front of an audience and the king, they eventually forced the royal family to return to the **Tuileries,** their palace in Paris. The royals were virtually prisoners there until their execution in 1793.

The National Assembly, fearful of the mob, returned to Paris. The Assembly now had a two-fold function: Solve the financial crisis and draw up a new constitution for France. The members, who were largely made up of the bourgeoisie class, addressed the following issues:

- **Financial measures.** To pay off the huge debt, they seized Church property and sold the land to aid the government.
- **Religious matters.** The National Assembly abolished Church titles. They seized the land of the Church, and religious freedom was granted to all groups. In 1790, the **Civil Constitution of the Clergy** was approved, which subjected the Catholic Church to state control. The Civil Constitution declared that the Church was independent from the pope and that the Catholic clergy was to be paid by the government and elected by the people. The Civil Constitution ended papal authority over the Church in France and dissolved monasteries and convents.

  Pope Pius VI and a majority of the French clergy denounced the Civil Constitution, as well as the Declaration of Rights. This attack on the Catholic Church turned many people against the Revolution and made the Church the Revolution's bitter enemy.

- **Legislative matters.** In 1791, the National Assembly (also called the Constituent for its work on the new constitution) completed its task by producing a constitution. The Constitution of 1791 provided for a constitutional monarchy, limited the powers of the monarch, and created a legislative assembly. The elected legislative assembly passed the nation's laws, collected taxes, and decided on issues of war and peace. Members of the assembly had to be property owners and were elected by taxpaying citizens. The National Assembly also divided France into 83 departments ruled by local assemblies, thus eliminating the provincial system. The assembly also extended rights to Protestants and Jews, and abolished slavery in France, but not in the colonies. This sparked an uprising by **Toussaint L'Ouverture** (1744–1803), a self-educated former slave, against the plantation owners in Hispaniola (Haiti). By 1794, slavery ended in all the French colonies and Haiti became the first independent state in the Caribbean.

Meanwhile, Louis XVI's brother, who was a leader of the émigré nobles and had fled the country in order to actively restore the Old Regime, convinced the king to flee France. On June 20, 1791, the royal family was captured near the French border town of Varennes and was escorted back to Paris by a taunting mob.

News of the Revolution created excitement and fear in Europe. European liberals and radicals hoped that the Revolution would lead to a reordering of society everywhere. However, conservatives, such as **Edmund Burke** (1729–1797) of Great Britain, in *Reflections on the Revolution in France* (1790), predicted that it would lead to chaos and tyranny. Marie Gouze known to history as **Olympe de Gouges** (1745–1793), a butcher's daughter, became a major radical in Paris and was disappointed with *The Declaration of the Rights of Man and of the Citizen,* which did not grant equal rights for women. In her *Declaration of the Rights of Woman* (1791), which de Gouges addressed to Queen Marie Antoinette, she argued that women should be regarded as citizens and that they should have the right to own property and have equality of sexes in marriage. She also wanted improved education and the right to initiate divorces for women, and asserted that women are born free and have the same rights as men. De Gouges' book directly influenced the publication of the Englishwoman **Mary Wollstonecraft's** (1759–1797) *A Vindication of the Rights of Woman* (1792). Wollstonecraft argued that women should have the same political rights to vote and hold office as men. De Gouges was guillotined in 1793 in part because of her royalist policies and her criticism of Robespierre, the leader of the Reign of Terror. The works of Wollstonecraft and de Gouges marked the birth of the modern women's movement for equal rights. In 1797, Wollstonecraft died of puerperal fever shortly after childbirth.

Some European monarchs were fearful that these revolutionary ideas would spread and endanger their countries. In August 1791, Frederick William II, the king of Prussia, and Emperor Leopold II of Austria (the brother of Marie Antoinette) issued the **Declaration of Pillnitz.** They threatened to intervene if necessary to protect the French monarchy. In retaliation, France declared war on Austria in 1792. The Revolution entered a new stage.

The Radical Stage (1792–1795)

The war went badly for the poorly equipped French soldiers. Prussia joined immediately with Austria, and by the summer of 1792, the two powers were on the verge of invading Paris. On July 25, Austria and Prussia issued the **Brunswick Manifesto** promising to destroy Paris if any harm came to the French king. The legislative assembly declared the country in danger. In Paris, the *sans-culottes* (which literally means "without breeches," indicating their support of the trousers worn by the lower class) were committed to the working-class people and determined to push the Revolution in a more radical direction. Many believed that the king was conspiring with the invading army and was responsible for the battle disasters of the French army. On August 10, 1792, the Paris mob stormed the Tuileries and slaughtered the king's guard. In September, the *sans-culottes*, under the leadership of **Georges Danton,** who was the Minister of Justice and had organized the defense of Paris against the Prussians, carried out the September massacres. The mob attacked the prisons and killed over 1,000 people, including nobles and clergy who they believed were traitors to the cause of the Revolution. Danton subsequently was killed during the Reign of Terror.

The Radicals took control of the National Assembly and called for the election of a new legislative assembly— the **National Convention**—based on universal suffrage. Meeting for the first time in September 1792, the National Convention abolished the monarchy and proclaimed France a republic. All members of the National Convention were Jacobins. However, there was a split between two factions within the Jacobins at the convention: the **Girondists,** named after a department in southwestern France, and the **Montagnards ("mountains"),** so named because their members usually sat high in the hall. The Girondists favored a decentralization of power and were fearful of the powers of the *sans-culottes*. They supported voting rights based on property ownership.

The Montagnards were led by **Maximilien Robespierre** (1758–1794), a middle-class lawyer who represented the *sans-culottes*, the working class of Paris. Robespierre favored a strong central government with the power to help the poor and control the economy. Known as "Mr. Incorruptible," he wanted to create a "Republic of Virtue" and accused the Girondists of sympathy toward the king.

In 1793, the National Convention put Louis XVI on trial. The trial split the convention. The Girondists wanted to imprison the royal family and exile him after the European powers had been defeated. The Montagnards wanted to execute him. On January 21, 1793, Louis XVI was beheaded by the fast-falling blade of a brand-new *guillotine* (Dr. Joseph Guillotin, a member of the legislature, had introduced the device as a more humane method of beheading rather than the uncertainty of the axe), and later that same year Marie Antoinette was beheaded. The execution of Louis XVI sent shock waves throughout Europe. England, Spain, the Netherlands, Austria, and Prussia united in the first coalition to stop the spread of these revolutionary ideas. This became known as the **First Coalition.**

The Reign of Terror (1793–1794)

By 1793, France faced even greater problems. Not only was the country at war with countries in opposition to the Revolution, but rising prices, unemployment, and a rebellion in Vendee (the western part of France) led by royalists and priests, also threatened the government. In the face of these problems, the *sans-culottes* joined with the Montagnards to oust the Girondists from the National Convention in May 1793.

These Radical Jacobins centralized all control in a 12-man **Committee of Public Safety,** which had dictatorial powers. The goal of the Committee was to save the Revolution from foreign and domestic enemies. The Committee subjected the entire nation to compulsory military service, and the war against the Coalition became a national mission. Between August 1793 and September 1794, France raised an army of over 1.1 million men, the largest Europe had ever seen. Troops from the port city of Marseilles set the theme with the call for people to rally around the fatherland. The song sung by these troops would become **"La Marseillaise,"** the national anthem of the French nation.

The French were victorious over the European Coalition because they had the ability to draw on the power of patriotic dedication to the nationalist state and a national mission. This was the foundation of modern nationalism, as citizens, reinforced by the ideas of democracy, were stirred by the danger of a common enemy. The Committee had turned the concept of a gentlemanly eighteenth-century game of war into a struggle between good and evil.

To protect the Revolution against domestic enemies, the Committee of Public Safety instituted a **Reign of Terror,** which lasted from late summer of 1793 to August 1794. The Committee arrested all persons suspected of treason and sentenced them to death. It is estimated that about 40,000 people lost their lives to the guillotine or to gunfire, or were drowned on barges set out to sea. The Reign of Terror had no respect for class origin. About 8 percent were nobles, 14 percent were bourgeoisie, mainly of the rebellious southern cities, 6 percent were clergy, and no less than 70 percent were of the peasant and working classes.

The Committee of Public Safety also instituted price and wage controls, food rationing, monetary controls to stop inflation, the metric system, and censorship of all written material. In late 1793, Robespierre, who had become the chief architect of the Reign of Terror, proclaimed a **Republic of Virtue.** This was his bold scheme to de-Christianize France and to promote revolutionary values. He removed Christian symbols from public buildings, turned the Cathedral of Notre Dame into a Temple of Reason, and created a new non-Christian calendar. His actions alienated many people, especially the Catholic majority.

Revolutionary women made their efforts to fight domestic enemies of the revolution. In 1793, the Society of Revolutionary Republican Women sought stricter controls on the prices of food and worked to find women who horded food. The women of the Society also wanted to train for military service and wanted to wear the revolutionary cap or cockade, usually worn only by men. In 1793, they were officially excluded from the army and Jacobins, who had begun to fear the turmoil the Society was causing, banned all women's clubs and societies.

The Reactionary Stage (1795–1799)

By 1794, the Reign of Terror had spiraled out of control and its horrors turned the French people against the actions of the Jacobins. In March 1794, Robespierre executed Danton, one of the Jacobin Committee leaders, for arguing that it was time to end the Reign of Terror. Fearful that they might be next, the Convention decided to arrest Robespierre and he was guillotined on 8 Thermidor (July 28, 1794), one of the months of the new non-Christian calendar. The death of Robespierre began the **Thermidorian Reaction.** Tired of violence and virtue, the moderates regained control of the National Convention. A new constitution was written in 1795, which set up a republican form of government. The middle class was in control since only men of property could vote and hold office (women were not allowed to vote). The **New National Convention** set up two branches of the legislature: the **Council of 500** (the lower house) and the **Council of Elders** (an upper house of 250 members over the age of 40). The Convention removed all economic controls, closed the Jacobin clubs, allowed Catholic services to be held again, and granted amnesty to those who were considered enemies during the Reign of Terror.

In 1795, the National Convention chose a five-member executive group that became known as the **Directory.** Attacked by the aristocracy and the *sans-culottes*, who were critical of the government's economic policies, the Directory began to lose power. Unable to deal with the worsening inflation problem and fearful of a royalist uprising, it turned to the military for support. On October 5, 1795, a rebellion broke out in Paris and the Directory ordered a young general, Napoleon Bonaparte, to crush it. He saved the Republic, but the savior would ultimately be the destroyer of the government. Napoleon was rewarded for his loyalty with the command of the French army fighting the Austrians in Italy.

The Napoleonic Era (1799–1815)

Napoleon Bonaparte (1769–1821) was born on the Mediterranean island of Corsica (which had been owned by the Italians until annexed by the French), and was the son of a poor village lawyer. When the French Revolution began, he was a low-level military officer, but he quickly rose in rank and won important victories against the British and Austrians. He was a popular military general who appealed to the people who looked to a strong military leader to end the disorder and corruption that existed under the Directory.

In November 1799, he overthrew the Directory by a *coup d'état* (a swift overthrow of government by force) and formed a new government, the **Consulate.** The Consulate was made up of three Consuls, but all the power was vested in Napoleon as the First Consul. In 1802, the constitution made him Consul for life and in 1804, he was crowned Emperor. For each of these constitutional changes, Napoleon held a national **plebiscite** (a yes or no vote). The French people, hoping for stability, supported him at each step in his rise. Napoleon's popularity was due to his effective domestic policies, as described in the following list. His reforms provided efficient government and furthered the revolutionary principle of equality.

- **The Concordat of 1801** made peace with the Catholic Church. Pope Pius VII renounced claims to Church property confiscated during the Revolution. The government could nominate bishops but the pope confirmed them and could remove them. Napoleon acknowledged that Catholicism was the religion of the majority of the French people but reaffirmed religious toleration for all. By this agreement, Napoleon protected the peasant owners of former Church land and pleased the overwhelmingly Catholic French population.

- **The Napoleonic Code** (1804) established a uniform legal system to replace an outdated and inequitable medieval system. Emphasizing the revolutionary principles of equality, the Code created equal treatment before the law, providing religious toleration for Protestants and Jews, and abolishing serfdom and feudalism. However, the Code undid some reforms of the French Revolution. Women lost most of their rights under the Code. Male heads of households regained complete authority over their wives and children.

- **Free public education** was expanded by Napoleon. He established a government-supervised public school system of uniform educational standards. The University of France, a government agency and not an educational institute of higher learning, controlled all levels of education.

- **The "Legion of Honor"** was a society created by Napoleon for public recognition of those who had rendered distinguished military and civilian service to France. Membership was based on merit, not social status, which was in accord with the principle of equality. Nevertheless, he practiced nepotism, placing his relatives on the thrones of countries that he conquered. Napoleon centralized government and directly placed local governments under national authority.

- **The Bank of France** was founded in 1800, and introduced a sound currency and balanced budget. Everyone was expected to pay taxes and there were no tax exemptions because of birthright. By collecting taxes fairly and paying off the debt, Napoleon restored the government to financial health. These measures pleased the bourgeoisie. Napoleon also encouraged business enterprises.

Napoleon Dominates Europe

When Napoleon assumed power in 1799, Russia, Austria, Prussia, and Great Britain formed the **Second Coalition.** Napoleon took command of the French forces, which were at war with the Second Coalition. He was able to win significant victories and by 1802 ended the war favorably for France. Napoleon was a military genius who was able to take advantage of the changes brought about by the French Revolution. He effectively used the *levée en masse* (the call to use all able-bodied men to rally around the country) to help spread the ideals of Liberty, Equality, and Fraternity, with the emphasis on fighting for the fatherland. The troops called him the "little Corporal" because he defeated four armies larger than his own. They trusted him because he allowed them independence on the battlefield and combined the forces of light artillery, infantry, and cavalry to develop an effective fighting tool.

In 1805, France resumed war with the **Third Coalition** (Austria, Sweden, Russia, and Great Britain), and between 1805 and 1807 France had defeated all these countries except England. In 1805, Napoleon defeated the Austrian and Russian armies at Austerlitz. He then abolished the **Holy Roman Empire** and created the **Confederation of the Rhine,** reducing the number of German states from 300 to fewer than 100, an act for which he has sometimes been called the "Grandfather of German Unity." In October 1806, Napoleon defeated the Prussian forces at the **Battle of Jena** and the Russians at **Friedland** in June 1807. Shortly after, Tsar Alexander I and Napoleon met privately on a raft in the middle of the Niemen River, not far from Tilsit, a border area between Prussia and Russia. The result of this meeting was the signing of the **Treaty of Tilsit** in July 1807, by which the French and Russian empires became allies against Great Britain. Alexander accepted Napoleon as the Emperor of the West and Napoleon continued to occupy Berlin with his troops, taking away about one-half of Prussian territory. In return, Russia received a free hand in its design on Switzerland, then a Swedish possession. King Frederick William II of Prussia, who was originally restricted to pacing nervously along the banks of the Niemen River, was eventually drawn into the negotiations as a mere formality. He had been defeated at Jena and had little military resources to resist any agreement.

By 1807, Napoleon's Grand Empire dominated continental Europe from the Atlantic coast to the Russian plains. His empire included Spain, northern Italy, Naples, and parts of Germany and the newly independent Confederation of the Rhine. As Napoleon took control of each area, he instituted reforms. He stripped away the power of the nobles and their privileges in order to destroy the last vestiges of the Old Regime. In 1805, the British forces led by **Horatio Nelson** (1758–1801) destroyed the French navy at the **Battle of Trafalgar** during which he was killed. This battle gave England command of the seas and put an end to Napoleon's plan to invade the British Isles. Unable to defeat the British navy, Napoleon decided to wage economic warfare through the **Continental System** instead. He forbade the European nations to import British goods. Napoleon considered England "a nation of shopkeepers" and believed that the Continental System would ruin the British economy. In the end, the Continental System was a failure. European nations needed British goods, and the French navy was not strong enough to prevent widespread smuggling. French commerce lost much of its business, and unemployment spread while the British found new markets in North America.

Resentment against the Continental System was one of the causes of nationalistic revival, which eventually ended Napoleon's dream of complete European domination. Some other reasons for Napoleon's decline include:

- **The Peninsular War** (1808–1814). Napoleon's decision to put his brother Joseph on the throne of Spain's Bourbon King Charles V angered the Spanish people and they revolted, waging a guerrilla war that tied down the French soldiers for a number of years. Eventually British and Spanish forces under the **Duke of Wellington** drove the French out of Spain.

- **The Invasion of Russia.** When Alexander I of Russia withdrew from the Continental System in 1812, Napoleon invaded, leading an army of about 600,000 men into Russia. The Russian army retreated and adopted a scorched-earth policy of burning crops and villages as they went along. Napoleon captured Moscow in September but found the city in ashes. Napoleon ordered the Grand Army to retreat because there was not enough food to supply his army during the winter. The 1,000-mile retreat from Moscow was a disaster in which Napoleon lost three-quarters of his army. In 1813, the combined forces of Russia, Prussia, and Austria defeated Napoleon at the **Battle of the Nations.**

On April 11, 1814, Napoleon abdicated his throne and after an attempted suicide was exiled to **Elba,** a small island off the Italian coast. The Bourbons were restored to power and **Louis XVIII** (1755–1824), brother of Louis XVI, was crowned the new king of France. The king accepted the Napoleonic Code and honored the land settlements made during the Revolution. However, in 1815, Napoleon escaped from Elba and marched to France. The king fled and Napoleon was welcomed back as a hero. His return lasted only 100 days, however. On June 18, the Allied army of Russia, Austria, Prussia, and Great Britain defeated Napoleon at the **Battle of Waterloo.** Louis XVIII returned and Napoleon was exiled to the remote island of **St. Helena** where he died in 1821.

The Congress of Vienna (1814–1815)

After Napoleon's defeat, the four great powers (England, Russia, Prussia, and Austria) and France met in Vienna in November 1814 (the **Congress of Vienna**) to draw up a peace settlement. Their goal was to redraw the map of Europe as it existed pre-1789 in order to ensure order and stability.

Congress of Vienna		
Diplomat	**Country**	**Objectives**
Prince Klemens von Metternich	Austria	To restore Europe to the way it was before the French Revolution. Metternich dominates the Congress and rejects the ideas of the French Revolution. He is a conservative who despises democracy and nationalism; his ideas influence Europe between 1815 and 1848 and his anti-democratic policies are followed by leaders in Western Europe.
Lord Castlereagh	England	To ensure that France does not become a powerful nation again.
Czar Alexander I	Russia	To organize an alliance system (Holy Alliance) of Christian monarchs to fight revolutions throughout the world; also to become king of Poland.
Périgord Talleyrand	France	To ensure that France retains the rank of a major power. Talleyrand proves to be the great mediator among the other major powers attending the Congress.
Karl von Hardenberg	Prussia	To recover Prussian territory lost to Napoleon in 1807 and gain additional territory in northern Germany (Saxony).

Despite their different goals, the leaders of the Congress of Vienna agreed to establish a balance of power in Europe to ensure that one nation, like France, would never become politically and militarily strong enough to dominate the continent. The diplomats encircled France through the following:

- Adding Belgium and Holland to create the kingdom of the Netherlands, a much larger state north of France
- Giving Prussia lands along the Rhine River
- Enhancing Austrian influence over the Germans by creating the **German Confederation** of 39 states, with Austria designated as its official head.
- Allowing Austria to again take control of lands in Italy

The leaders also wanted to restore the power to monarchs based on the **principle of legitimacy.** This meant returning to power the ruling families deposed by more than two decades of revolutionary movement. Bourbon rulers were restored in France, Spain, and Naples. Dynasties were restored in Holland, and the Papal States were returned to the pope. The Congress recognized the British possession of overseas territories of Malta and Ceylon that were conquered during the Napoleonic wars. The Congress also acknowledged the status of Switzerland as an independent and neutral nation.

The Congress also provided for compensation, rewarding those states that had made considerable sacrifice to defeat Napoleon: Austria was given Lombardy and Venetia; Russia was given most of Poland and Finland; and Prussia was awarded the Rhineland and part of Poland. To enforce this settlement, Metternich organized the **Quadruple Alliance** of Austria, Prussia, Russia, and Britain. The purpose of the Alliance was to maintain the balance of power and to stop and suppress any revolutionary ideas of nationalism and democracy, which threatened to upset the Vienna settlement. The cooperation among the major nations of Europe is often referred to as the Concert of Europe. Alexander I organized the **Holy Alliance**, consisting of most European monarchs who pledged to rule by Christian principles. The Holy Alliance was ineffective, idealistic, and existed only on paper.

Even though the Congress of Vienna denied the principles of nationalism and democracy, the settlement lasted for 100 years. Europe would not see another war on the Napoleonic scale until World War I in 1914. During this hundred years' period, Europe was able to direct its resources toward an Industrial Revolution that would directly affect the political, economic, and social fabric of the continent. The statesmen of Vienna, however, underestimated how this new Industrial Revolution would lead to the creation of a new alignment of social classes and the development of new needs and issues.

Chronology of the French Revolution

May 5, 1789	The Estates General meets for the first time in 175 years.
June 17, 1789	The Estates General becomes the National Assembly.
June 20, 1789	The Tennis Court Oath. Members of the Third Estate meet on tennis courts at Versailles and promise not to disband before they write a new constitution.
June 27, 1789	Louis XVI recognizes the National Assembly.
July 14, 1789	Storming of the Bastille (celebrated as French Independence Day today).
July–August, 1789	The Great Fear sweeps the countryside.
August 4, 1789	The National Assembly ends feudalism in France.
August 27, 1789	*Declaration of the Rights of Man and of the Citizen* is published.
October 5 and 6, 1789	Women march on Versailles; the royal family is forced to return to Paris.
November, 1789	The National Assembly confiscates Church property.
July 12, 1790	The Civil Constitution of the Clergy is adapted.
June 20 to 25, 1791	The royal family is caught and arrested at the French border in a failed effort to escape.
August 27, 1791	Declaration of Pillnitz. Austria, Prussia, and other European monarchies express willingness to intervene in France.
1791–1792	Legislative Assembly convenes. It abolishes slavery and grants religious tolerance to Protestants and Jews.
April 20, 1792	France declares war on Austria.
August 10, 1792	*Sans-culottes* storm the Tuileries.
September 2–7, 1792	The September Massacre.
September 21, 1792	The National Convention meets. It abolishes the monarchy and creates a new government and constitution.
January 21, 1793	Execution of Louis XVI of France.
October 16, 1793	Execution of Marie Antoinette.
1793–1794	Reign of Terror.
July 28, 1794	Maximilien Robespierre is arrested and executed.
1795–1799	The Directory rules France ineffectively and inefficiently.
November 9, 1799	Napoleon overthrows the Directory and seizes control of the government.
July 15, 1801	Napoleon signs the Concordat with Pope Pius VII, giving the French government control over the Church in France.
March 27, 1802	The Treaty of Amiens with Great Britain.
May 18, 1804	Napoleon crowns himself Emperor.
October 21, 1805	Nelson defeats Napoleon at the Battle of Trafalgar.
1806	Battle of Jena—Prussia is defeated.
1807	Battle of Friedland—Russia is defeated; the Treaty of Tilsit is signed between France and Russia.
March 1810	Napoleon marries Marie Louise.
June 24, 1812	France invades Russia.
October 1813	The Grand Alliance defeats France at the Battle of Nations.
April 11, 1814	Napoleon is exiled to Elba; Louis XVIII is crowned king of France.
November 1814	The Congress of Vienna meets.
1815	Napoleon escapes Elba and begins his rule of 100 days.
June 1815	Wellington defeats Napoleon at the Battle of Waterloo.

Sample Multiple-Choice Questions

1. Which of the following was the basic cause of the French Revolution?

   A. A majority of the French people wanted to replace the monarchy with the republic.
   B. France was a weak country and in economic decline in 1789.
   C. The past abuses of the Old Regime.
   D. The support of nobles for the absolute government of Louis XVI.
   E. The invasion of France by foreign countries.

2. The French bourgeoisie supported the French Revolution mainly because

   A. they believed in the Theory of Divine Right of Kings.
   B. they were not allowed to own property under the Old Regime.
   C. they resented their lack of political power under the Old Regime.
   D. they wanted a democratic form of government.
   E. the government set up a voting system based on universal male suffrage.

3. The *Declaration of the Rights of Man and of the Citizen* adapted by the National Assembly in the French Revolution was

   A. a declaration of war against Austria and Prussia.
   B. a statement of the main principles of the French Revolution.
   C. a constitution establishing a republican form of government.
   D. a set of laws that confiscated Church property.
   E. an announcement of the French military victory over the enemies of the Revolution.

4. Which of these positions does Mary Wollstonecraft support in her book, *A Vindication of the Rights of Woman*?

   A. Edmund Burke's belief that the revolution was creating chaos on the European continent
   B. That women should focus on economic progress over political progress
   C. That the ideas of Olympe de Gouges were too radical
   D. That inherited privileges were important in society
   E. That the ideals of the French Revolution of liberty and equality should be applied equally to men and women

5. Which social group had the greatest number of victims during the Reign of Terror (1793–1794)?

   A. Bourgeoisie
   B. Clergy
   C. Nobility
   D. Foreigners
   E. Peasants

6. Which was an important result of the Civil Constitution of the Clergy (1790)?

   A. The Pope continued to appoint Church officials.
   B. The Church was made a department of the French states.
   C. The clergy were given power to open more monasteries and convents.
   D. Church officials received privileged positions in the Estates General.
   E. The Pope was required to pay the salary of the clergy.

7. All of the following are true about the Napoleonic Code EXCEPT that

    A. it provided equal treatment before the law.

    B. it guaranteed religious toleration and trial by jury.

    C. it abolished what remained of serfdom and feudalism.

    D. it is the basis of law in Latin America and is still used in France.

    E. it improved the rights of women.

8. In Goya's painting, *The Third of May 1808,* the painter depicts the shooting of Spanish civilians by

    A. Napoleon's troops.

    B. those involved in the Decembrist Revolution.

    C. Bismarck's troops trying to eliminate Austria's influence over Germany.

    D. Garibaldi's Red Shirts trying to unify Sicily.

    E. the Estates General.

9. What was a major goal of the Congress of Vienna?

    A. To establish democratic governments in all European nations

    B. To maintain a balance of power in Europe

    C. To preserve the reforms of the French Revolution

    D. To encourage nationalism

    E. To reestablish the Holy Roman Empire

10. The most influential figure at the Congress of Vienna was

    A. Talleyrand.

    B. Metternich.

    C. Napoleon Bonaparte.

    D. Nicholas II.

    E. Otto von Bismarck.

Multiple-Choice Questions: Answers and Explanations

1. **C.** The Old Regime, which described the political, economic, and social conditions in Europe before 1789, was marked by absolutism in government, inequality among classes, and unequal and burdensome taxation. In 1789, France was divided into Three Estates. The First Estate was made up of the clergy and the Second Estate was composed of the nobles. They made up about 2 percent of the population, but owned about 40 percent of the land and paid no taxes. The Third Estate was made up of the middle class (bourgeoisie), city workers, and the peasants who comprised 98 percent of the population, controlled 60 percent of the land, and paid a variety of different taxes, such as the tithe to the clergy and feudal dues to the nobles. A majority of the French people supported the monarchy until 1791. In 1789, France was one of the wealthiest countries in Europe and not in economic decline. The nobles supported Louis XVI but wanted more influence in the decision-making process. The foreign powers invaded France in 1792, two years after the French Revolution had begun.

2. **C.** The French bourgeoisie supported the French Revolution mainly because they resented their lack of political power under the Old Regime. The bourgeoisie (middle class) included prosperous bankers, merchants, and manufacturers who propped up the French economy. They also included the officials who staffed the royal bureaucracy. The estates system allowed the clergy and the nobles to monopolize all the benefits while the majority received very little. The French bourgeoisie did not support the belief in the Divine Right Theory. They still were loyal to the monarchy but one with less absolute power. They did not support democracy. The middle class owned about 40 percent of the land but had little or no political influence.

3. **B.** The *Declaration of the Rights of Man and of the Citizen* was a statement of the main principles of the French Revolution. The declaration guaranteed basic civil rights and that all political sovereignty rested in the hands of the people, not the king. It also proclaimed that all male citizens were equal before the law. Its principles captured the slogan of the French Revolution, "Liberty, Equality, and Fraternity." The declaration established a constitutional monarchy, not a republican form of government. The Civil Constitution of the clergy led to the confiscation of Church land. The declaration was a statement of political principles and not an announcement of any military victories.

4. **E.** Mary Wollstonecraft was directly influenced by the ideas of Olympe de Gouges. She accepted her belief that women should have the same rights as men. Wollstonecraft also stressed, like de Gouges, that women should be given improved educational opportunities in conjunction with political rights. Her goals were to achieve economic and political freedom and to not sacrifice economic freedom for political gains. As a firm believer in liberty and equality, Wollstonecraft rejected Edmund Burke's ideas about the fear of freedom and the ideas of privileges based on birth.

5. **E.** Of the 40,000 who died during the Reign of Terror, about 70 percent were from the peasant class. About 15 percent were bourgeoisie and the remaining 15 percent were clergy and nobility. There were no major executions of foreigners.

6. **B.** The Civil Constitution of the Clergy, which was passed by the National Assembly, denied the power of the pope's control of the Catholic Church in France. The clergy became salaried officials of the state. The clergy were elected by the people and were independent from the pope. The clergy were denied special privileges and the government dissolved monasteries and convents.

7. **E.** The Napoleonic Code did not improve the rights of women. The Code had several weaknesses in regard to women: Women could not vote; a wife owed obedience to her husband, who had total control over property; and an unmarried woman could not be a legal guardian. The Code recognized civil marriages and divorces; however, it was easier for a man to sue for divorce than a woman. Male heads of households regained complete authority over their wives and children. The Napoleonic Code embodied the Enlightenment principle of equality of all citizens before the law, religious toleration, and trial by jury. The Code also abolished the remnants of serfdom and feudalism. It is still the basis of law in Latin America and France.

8. **A.** The painting, *The Third of May 1808,* shows the execution of Spaniards by Napoleon's troops. In 1808, Napoleon replaced the king of Spain with Napoleon's brother, Joseph, who introduced liberal reforms that sought to undermine the Spanish Catholic Church. The Spanish remained loyal and conducted a campaign of hit-and-run raids. These attacks kept Napoleon bogged down when troops were needed elsewhere. The painting does not depict events associated with the Decembrist Revolution, Bismarck, programs of Nicholas I, or the Estates General.

9. **B.** A major goal of the Congress of Vienna was to maintain a balance of power in Europe. Following Napoleon's defeat, diplomats of the victorious nations and France met in Vienna from 1814 until 1815. This was a peace conference to reconstruct war-torn Europe. Although the leaders of the Congress had different objectives, they were determined to turn back the clock of Europe to the time before the French Revolution. They wanted to establish a balance of power, or a distribution of military and economic power, to prevent any one nation from becoming too strong. To ensure this balance of power, Prince Metternich of Austria created the Concert of Europe. The Concert included all the major European states and pledged to maintain the balance of power and to suppress any uprising inspired by the ideas of the French Revolution. The representatives of the Congress of Vienna did not support establishing democratic governments in all European nations. They opposed the French revolutionary ideas of equality and democratic governments. Napoleon brought about the end of the Holy Roman Empire. The leaders of the Congress of Vienna were interested in stopping the spread of democracy and nationalism and not interested in reestablishing the Holy Roman Empire, which Napoleon had destroyed.

10. **B.** Prince Metternich of Austria was the most influential figure at the Congress of Vienna. This is because Metternich set a pattern of anti-democratic policies that was followed by most of the rulers of Europe. For 50 years, he was the most influential diplomat in Europe. Talleyrand of France was not the most influential figure at the Congress because he played a secondary role to Metternich. Napoleon Bonaparte was exiled at St. Helena and did not attend the meeting in Vienna. Nicholas II of Russia and Otto von Bismarck of Germany were leaders of their respective countries in the middle of the late nineteenth or early twentieth centuries.

Mercantilism and the Agricultural and Industrial Revolutions

The Age of Exploration—besides leading to the discovery and conquest of new lands such as the Americas, and overseas expansion and new trade routes such as with Asia—brought about national economic changes. The fierce competition for trade and empire among European monarchs led to the widespread adoption of **mercantilism,** an economic policy under which nations sought to increase their wealth and power by obtaining large amounts of gold and silver and by exporting more goods than they imported. The increased gold and silver flowing into Europe from the Spanish colonies contributed to a price revolution known as **inflation,** which encouraged trade and businesses of all types. As prices of goods went up, businessmen were willing to take risks to invest money in the hope of making more money. This new attitude spurred the growth of early European capitalism. As trade routes shifted in the sixteenth century from the Mediterranean and the Baltic to the Atlantic, Venice and Genoa soon declined and Portugal and Spain became the dominant powers. In the seventeenth century, cities like London, Paris, and Amsterdam became the centers of commercial activity. These changes were part of the Commercial Revolution that influenced Europe.

The Agricultural and Industrial revolutions, like the Commercial Revolution, also impacted European society. The discovery of new machinery and advancements in farming had far-reaching effects. The use of new crops and techniques, and the introduction of better methods of soil rotation enabled Europe to grow more food. This helped to raise the standard of living. The Agricultural Revolution provided the food for the expanding city populations and directly led to a population explosion in Europe. The Industrial Revolution, which started in Great Britain, had a greater effect on society than the French Revolution. The transformation from an agrarian to an industrial society influenced the European political, economic, and social structure. The landed aristocracy, which had begun to lose influence because of the rise of the middle class, would be completely overshadowed by the birth of a new capitalist class of businessmen. The shift from a rural society to an urban society created new problems, such as how to deal with the conditions created by the factory system. New philosophies and economic ideas such as Romanticism, Socialism, Nationalism, and Communism arose to meet the problems created by industrialization. The Agricultural and Industrial revolutions not only transformed Europe in the nineteenth century but also had a major impact on the world in the twentieth century.

Mercantilism and Capitalism

From the sixteenth through the seventeenth centuries, European monarchs adopted a policy of mercantilism aimed at strengthening their national economies. Mercantilists supported several basic ideas:

- **A nation's wealth is measured by the gold and silver (bullion) it possesses.**
- **A nation must export more goods than it imports.** In other words, there must be a favorable balance of trade in order for a nation to build up its supply of gold and silver.
- **Colonies exist for the benefit of the mother country.** Colonies supply raw materials not available in Europe for manufacture and trade, and also serve as a market for the mother country's manufactured goods.
- **Strict laws must regulate trade with the colonies.** The regulation of trade strengthened the nation's economy because, in addition to providing gold and silver, the colonies could not set up industries to manufacture goods nor buy goods from foreign countries. This strict regulation ensured that all revenue went to the government.
- **The government must promote and protect local industries by taxing imported goods.**
- **Governments can increase revenue by imposing a single national currency and selling monopolies to large producers in certain industries as well as big overseas trading companies.**
- **Self-sufficiency must be promoted.** A country had to use everything it needed within its own borders and not depend on other countries for goods.

The establishment of European colonies in the Americas, the direct trade with Asia and Africa, and the continued expansion of the Commercial Revolution led to some major changes in Europe:

- Large quantities of gold and silver from the New World during the 1500s affected the economy of Western Europe. Since consumers had more money to spend, it drove up prices and this led to **inflation,** which led to a decline in the value of money as the prices of goods and services increased. The purchasing power of the people declined.

- The traditional divisions of societal classes were affected. Because the growing demand for goods led to increased production, Western Europe's guild system was impacted. The guild system originated in medieval times; it was an association of people who all worked at the same occupation, and the guild controlled membership, wages, and prices. The institution of the guild had to change to meet the growing production needs of a nation-centered economic system. A middle class of merchants, bankers, and capitalists thus emerged who were devoted to the goal of making profits. This new social class grew in number and began to resent the fact that it lacked political influence in the government. This discontent led to conditions that gave rise to the French Revolution, as was discussed in the preceding chapter.

Although farmers benefited from the changing market because they were able to sell surplus crops, they lacked political power. The nobility whose income still depended on a fixed asset suffered a decline in economic power; as a class, however, the nobility still ranked high on the social scale.

The economic changes of the sixteenth and seventeenth centuries led to the rise of **capitalism,** or using money to make a profit, or more money. The Dutch, who controlled the major trade routes in the seventeenth century, were the first people to practice capitalism. The merchants of Amsterdam bought surplus grain and sold it at the highest prices when they heard about poor harvests in other parts of Europe. Since they controlled the trading routes, they were able to enforce a monopoly and control all the shipments to other parts of Europe. In the mid-1630s, the Dutch replaced the Italians as the bankers of Europe.

Expanded trade and the push for building overseas empires promoted capitalism's growth. Entrepreneurs organized, managed, and assumed the risk of doing business by hiring craftsmen, supplying them with raw materials, and selling the finished goods. It was the beginning of the **domestic system,** in which weavers and crafters produced goods at home. When entrepreneurs were unable to raise money for a project or thought it was too risky, capitalists developed new ways to create wealth by forming **joint stock** (also known as **trading) companies** that allowed people to pool large amounts of capital needed for overseas ventures. The Dutch, British, and French founded trading companies, such as the Dutch East India Company and the British East India Company, in the 1600s. Capitalists also reduced the risk of liability from dangerous investments during the seventeenth century by creating insurance companies such as Lloyd's of London.

In the ways mentioned above, the European expansion of money and goods revolutionized Europe's economy and transformed its society. These changes in trade, manufacturing, and investments laid the foundation for the Agricultural and Industrial revolutions.

The Agricultural Revolution

Up until the middle of the eighteenth century, farming remained very much as it had been under the manorial system of the Middle Ages. Although farmers labored hard and long, they produced scanty crops. Before the Agricultural Revolution, farmers did the following:

- Worked to raise food for themselves and their landlords instead of making a profit by selling produce on the markets
- Relied upon a few ancient tools such as the wooden plow, the hoe, the rake, and the shovel
- Continued the three-field system, which kept one-third of the land idle at any one time
- Knew very little about fertilizers, crop rotation, and animal breeding

The Dutch led the way in the Agricultural Revolution. In the 1600s, they built dikes or dams to reclaim land by draining it and thus making it useable. They also used fertilizers from livestock to renew the soil and combined fields into larger ones to make better use of the land.

During the eighteenth and nineteenth centuries, the British and Americans improved on the Dutch experiment by inventing new tools and processes that led to the mechanization of agriculture. The following is a table that lists some of the improvements in agriculture.

Inventor	Invention
Jethro Tull (English) 1674–1741	Seed drill (1701). This device planted seeds in rows, replacing planting the seed by hand. This method also permitted cultivation between rows, increasing the amount of food produced per acre.
Charles "Turnip" Townshend (English) 1675–1738	Crop rotation (1750). This helped to conserve soil fertility and made more land available for production. It alternated grain with soil-enriching plants such as turnips and clover.
Robert Bakewell (English) 1725–1795	Scientific breeding of animals.
Charles Newbold (American) 1764–1835	Cast-iron plow (1797). This turned soil deeper and more easily than the wooden plow.
John Deere (American) 1804–1886	Self-cleaning steel plow (1837). This improved upon the cast-iron plow.

The **enclosure movement** contributed to large-scale farming. Between 1760 and 1830, the English Parliament—the majority of whom were large landowners—passed a series of laws called the Enclosure Acts, in which they took over and fenced off land formerly shared by peasant farmers. In the 1500s, enclosed lands gained pasture for sheep and increased work output. By the 1700s, the land-owning aristocracy began to fence in the common lands of villages and replace the strip farms of medieval times with larger fields that could be cultivated more efficiently. The large landowners employed new farming techniques that led to increased production, but at a price. Machines displaced many farm laborers. Small farmers were forced off the land because they could not compete with the larger, more efficient farmers. They migrated to the towns and cities in large numbers to seek factory jobs.

The Agricultural Revolution contributed to a rapid growth of population in Europe. In Great Britain alone, the population soared from 8.6 million in 1700 to almost 15 million in 1800. Similarly, the population in Europe rose from 120 million to about 190 million by the beginning of the 1800s. Reasons for this population explosion included the following:

- The risk of famine was reduced because of the vast quantities of food being produced by the new agricultural methods.
- People ate a more balanced diet, contributing to overall better health.
- A better diet for women made them able to have stronger babies.
- Vaccines were developed against diseases such as smallpox. Improved medical care further reduced deaths from diseases.

The Industrial Revolution

The Agricultural Revolution helped to trigger the **Industrial Revolution.** The Industrial Revolution can be viewed in two ways:

1. A slow, gradual process that began during the Stone Age and continues to evolve to the present with changes in technology.
2. A shift that took place between 1750 and 1830 in the production of goods from handmade items to items made by more expensive and complicated machines. These changes also resulted in the transfer of work from home (the domestic system) to the factory system.

Although both views are valid, this book adopts the second view. The Industrial Revolution began in England in the second half of the eighteenth century for the following reasons:

- England was rich in raw materials secured from the colonies and worldwide trade. It was also rich in natural resources such as coal, which was used to power steam engines and iron ore, which was used to build the machines.

- Wealthy men had the capital to invest in machinery and factories.

- The Agricultural Revolution provided a large pool of displaced workers needed to run the mines, build factories, and run machines.

- A stable government encouraged science, inventions, and the application of new methods of industry. The **Royal Society of London** (1660), the world's oldest scientific society, spurred scientific research.

- As an island, England was cut off from the wars of continental Europe. The country was unharmed and free to develop its new industries.

The Industrial Revolution in England began with a series of technological developments in the textile industry, improvements in the sources of power (steam), and revolutions in transportation. The following table lists important inventions that improved production, provided sources of power, and instituted changes in transportation.

Textile Industry	Inventions	Impact
John Kay (English) 1704–1764	Flying shuttle (1733)	Sped up weaving and increased production power.
James Hargreaves (English) 1720–1778	Spinning jenny (1764)	Made it possible to spin several threads at once. This mechanized the spinning wheel.
Sir Richard Arkwright (English) 1732–1792	Water frame (1771)	This water-powered spinning machine increased the rapidity of spinning.
Samuel Crompton (English) 1753–1827	Spinning mule (1779)	This combination of spinning jenny and water frame produced strong, fine thread. It spurred the invention of better weaving machines.
Edmund Cartwright (English) 1743–1823	Power loom (1785)	This water-powered loom provided rapid and automatic weaving.
Eli Whitney (American) 1765–1825	Cotton gin (1793)	This quick method of separating the seed from the cotton fiber increased the supply of cotton for factories.

The improvement of production in the textile industry opened up new markets, and the adoption of Watt's steam engine meant that factories could now be built in any convenient location, not just near bodies of water. The development of the steam locomotive paved the way in England for the growth of the railroads (1830–1850), which meant lower transportation costs, larger markets, and cheaper goods. The railroads did not have to follow the course of a river. This meant that goods could go places rivers did not, allowing factory owners and merchants to ship goods over land. Building railroads also took workers from their rural life and made them more inclined to become urban dwellers.

Steam Power	Inventions	Impact
Thomas Newcomen (English) 1663–1729	Steam engine (1712)	Served chiefly to operate a pump to drain water from coal mines.
James Watt (English) 1736–1819	Improved Newcomen's work (1769)	This opened up the age of steam. Watt's engine was adapted for textile-mill use and for transportation.
Robert Fulton (American) 1765–1815	Steamship (1807)	Sped up shipping and lowered costs.
George Stephenson (English) 1781–1848	First steam engine locomotive (1814)	Paved the way for the railroad era.

Industrialization swept across Europe from west to east, from England in the eighteenth century to Holland, Belgium, France, and the United States by 1830. By the 1850s, Germany, Italy, and Austria became industrialized and by the end of the nineteenth century, industrialization had spread to Eastern Europe and Russia. In the twentieth century, it spread to Asia, Africa, and Latin America.

Results of the Industrial Revolution

The Industrial Revolution brought about many economic and social changes, of which the most dramatic were increased production and availability of goods. Mass-produced goods were cheaper than those in pre-industrial Europe, and therefore more people were able to purchase them. The increased purchase of goods brought great riches to the entrepreneurs and also led to the growth of more jobs. Families migrated to the cities as the demand for workers increased, and entrepreneurs built factories around small market towns. In 1750 the population of Manchester, England, was 17,000 people, and by 1800 there were over 70,000 inhabitants. By the middle of the nineteenth century, England had more people living in cities or urban areas than in the countryside.

Unfortunately, the rapid and unplanned growth of the cities contributed to deplorable living conditions. The working class, or poor, lived in crowded and unhealthy conditions with no running water, no sewage or sanitation system, and garbage rotting in the streets. Cholera and other diseases spread rapidly. Although life in rural areas had always been difficult for the poor, the new concentration of so many people in one spot made it even worse. The lack of transportation within the cities and the slowness of the government to address the need for new sanitary codes contributed to the problems.

Industrialization also affected the family structure. Before, entire families had worked together as a unit under the domestic system. Under the factory system, family members held different jobs and did not work together; moreover, women and children frequently worked under horrible conditions—often 12 to 14 hours per day. In 1821, Michael Sadler, a British legislator, began Parliamentary investigations into the textile industry. The **Sadler Committee** discovered that children were regularly beaten and abused by factory owners. These investigations led to the passage of legislation regulating the employment of children in factories as well as in mines. In 1833, the first **Factory Act** restricted the number of hours that children under nine could work. Perhaps the most influential reform was the **Ten Hours Act** of 1847, which limited women and children to ten-hour shifts. Unfortunately, many parents did not support these laws because they needed the earnings of their children since their own wages were so low.

The Industrial Revolution was a mixed blessing for women. It opened up new economic opportunities for them while creating other problems. Women earned less than one-half of what men earned. Poorer than men, women were also forced, after twelve-hour shifts in the factory, to return to their homes to deal with the daily tasks of feeding and clothing their families and coping with sickness and other problems.

Family life was hard in rural England, but became even more difficult during this era of industrialization. The pre-industrial pattern of women working with their husbands disappeared except for poor women. In earlier times, middle class women often helped with the family business out of the home. By the mid-1800s, women became full-time mothers and not wage earners. Middle-class husbands went to work in an office or shop, and the successful husband was one whose wife did not need to work outside the home.

A woman's new main responsibility was to rear the children, make all major domestic decisions, and do some religious or charity service. This ideal that women were supposed to sacrifice everything for the welfare of the husband and family led to the rise of what became known as the "cult of domesticity" during the Victorian period, which spanned from 1837 to 1901—the years in which Queen Victoria ruled England. The glorification of the domestic life became popularized in books, songs, and sayings such as "A Man's Home Is His Castle." Unfortunately, as was previously mentioned, the ideal of domesticity rarely applied to poor working-class women.

Many individuals saw industrialization as a threat to their way of life. Hand-loom weavers, for instance, lost their jobs and were replaced by machines. A group of anti-industrialists known as the **Luddites** opposed the new technology. They smashed machines to preserve their jobs and burned factories. Luddites were named after a mythical figure, Ned Lud, who destroyed machines in the 1780s. Luddites were treated harshly and were hanged or sent to penal colonies in Australia.

Another group that opposed industrialization was known as the **Romantics.** The Romantics were composed of artists, writers, and composers who rebelled against the Enlightenment's emphasis on reason and stressed emotion. Some important Romantic writers were **Samuel Coleridge** (1772–1834), **Sir Walter Scott** (1771–1832), and **Victor Hugo** (1802–1885). Hugo expressed the French revolutionary spirit and fascination with history in his novel *The Three Musketeers,* and the struggle of the individual against a historical backdrop in works such as *Les Misérables* and *The Hunchback of Notre Dame.* The French novelist, **Amandine Aurore Dupin** (1804–1876), who wrote under the pen name **George Sand,** was the most successful woman writer of the nineteenth century. She earned much notoriety for her Bohemian lifestyle and smoked cigars, dressed like a man, and had affairs with married men and famous artists like Frédéric Chopin. Her first independent novel, *Indiana,* describes the story of an unhappy wife whose struggle to free herself from the imprisonment of marriage, which Sand called a form of slavery, made her an overnight celebrity.

Some Romantic composers included **Frédéric Chopin** (1810–1849), **Franz Liszt** (1811–1886), and **Hector Berlioz** (1803–1869). One of the most famous was **Ludwig van Beethoven** (1770–1827). This German composer combined classical forms with a stirring range of sound. At first, Beethoven wrote in the style of the music popular during the Enlightenment, then progressed to his *Ninth Symphony,* which celebrates freedom, dignity, and triumph. In all, Beethoven produced nine symphonies, five piano concertos, a violin concerto, an opera, and two masses. His expanded use of the orchestra was a revolutionary movement from the controlled and formal compositions of the Enlightenment.

Romantic artists included **J. M. Turner** (1775–1851) and **Eugène Delacroix** (1798–1863). Delacroix, in *Liberty Leading the People,* dramatically depicts the revolutionary tricolore flag as French citizens rally to the cause of freedom after the overthrow of Charles X in 1830. Poets such as **William Blake** (1757–1827) and **William Wordsworth** (1770–1850) wrote about the horrors of the Industrial Revolution. They viewed modern industry as ugly and as a brutal attack on nature and humanity. By emphasizing feelings, the Romantics helped create humanitarian movements to fight poverty and industrial evils.

The hardships and changes brought about by the Industrial Revolution gave rise to various solutions that led to new theories of economics. One of them was the **Classical School of Economics**, which rejected the government restriction of mercantilism in favor of free trade. Classical economics appealed to the new middle class since they looked upon tariffs and other government restrictions as obstacles to progress. Some important leaders in this movement are listed in the following table.

Leader	Writings	Main Ideas
Adam Smith (Scottish) 1723–1790	*The Wealth of Nations* (1776)	*Laissez-faire:* The government should not get involved with the national economy. It should act as an agency to ensure that everyone is following the laws of society. The "invisible hand" of supply and demand will promote the best interest of society. Smith's ideas became the basis of the economic system of capitalism during the Industrial Revolution.
Thomas Malthus (English) 1776–1834	*An Essay on the Principle of Population* (1798)	Poverty and misery were unavoidable because population growth was increasing faster than food supply. War, disease, and famine were checks on population growth. Smaller families could stop the population growth.
David Ricardo (English) 1772–1823	*On the Principles of Political Economy and Taxation* (1817)	Iron Law of Wages: Human wages must be sufficient to buy food. When wages are high, families have more children, but that increases the supply of labor, which leads to lower wages and higher unemployment. Like Malthus, Ricardo believed in limiting the size of the family and opposed governmental help for the poor for fear it would lead to greater suffering.

Leader	Writings	Main Ideas
Jeremy Bentham (English) 1748–1832	*Principles of Morals and Legislation* (1781)	Utilitarianism: The goal of society should be the greatest happiness for the greatest number. What is good for the individual is what gives him the most pleasure. However, if the individual harms the common good, government can intervene. This was a retreat from *laissez-faire*.
John Stuart Mill (English) 1806–1873	*On Liberty* (1859)	A follower of Bentham who supported freedom for the individual but feared pursuit of one's own interest might harm others. Mill wanted government to pass laws to remove the evils of society. He advocated the rights of workers to organize, equal rights for women, and universal suffrage.

Many nineteenth-century thinkers condemned the evils of industrialization and capitalism and offered socialism as a means to end the poverty and injustices in society. Socialism can be defined as state (rather than private) ownership of the means of production (farms, factories, and railroads) and other large businesses that produce and distribute goods. The goal of the socialists was a society that operated for the welfare of all the people, and they felt that state ownership was a means to that end.

Socialism began in France and England in the early 1800s. The early socialists were called **Utopian socialists** because they offered no practical plan for achieving their ideal society. They thought that industrialists would support socialism as soon as they realized how effective it could be. The most outstanding Utopian socialists were the following:

- **Henri Comte de Saint-Simon** (1760–1825) was a French socialist who advocated the end of private property. He believed that a cadre of skilled businessmen and scientists should run the state for the betterment of the lower classes.

- **Robert Owen** (1771–1858) was a successful English industrialist who created a model industrial community in Scotland at New Lanark, the site of cotton mills. Contrary to the prevailing practices, he paid high wages, reduced working hours, ended child labor, built decent homes, provided education for the workers, and permitted the workers to share in management and profits. His New Lanark community prospered, but he was disappointed that others did not follow his example.

- **Louis Blanc** (1811–1882) believed that every person had a right to a job and that the state should provide work for the unemployed in government-sponsored or national workshops. His ideas were successful for a short time in France during the Revolution of 1848.

- **Karl Marx** (1818–1883) was a German writer and economist who, in the 1840s, advocated a more militant form of socialism called Communism. He used this term to distinguish his views from those of the Utopian socialists, whom he condemned as unrealistic dreamers. His basic ideas are contained in *The Communist Manifesto,* a pamphlet he wrote in collaboration with **Friedrich Engels** (1820–1895) in which he called for a worldwide revolution to end the abuses of capitalism. *Das Kapital* is a three-volume work, with the first volume published in 1867, the second in 1885, and the third in 1895.

The basic theories of Marxism are as follows:

- **Economic View of History.** Marx argued that economics determines the course of history. Economic conditions shape the institutions of society such as religion and government.

- **Class Struggle.** History is a continuous class struggle between the "haves" and the "have nots." Marx's theory of historical evolution was built on ideas of the German philosopher **Georg Hegel** (1770–1831). Hegel believed that history was ideas in constant motion between the thesis and the antithesis. Marx accepted Hegel's view of history as the dialectic of the process of change but substituted economics as the driving force in history. Thus, in ancient times the struggle between the patricians and the plebeians; in the Middle Ages between the lords and the serfs; in industrial society between the capitalists and the workers (**proletariat**). Capitalists exploit the workers by paying them just enough wages to keep them alive. Marx predicted that the future would bring a violent revolution by the workers to overthrow the capitalists.

- **Inevitability of Revolution.** Marx predicted that the hostility between the classes would be aggravated as the rich get richer and the poor get poorer. As conditions worsen, especially during depression or war, the working class will inevitably revolt and establish a "dictatorship of the proletariat." This dictatorship will create a collective, classless society. Marx also believed that the revolution would first come to industrial nations such as the United States and England, not an agricultural country such as Russia.

- **Surplus Value.** Capitalists take advantage of workers by not paying them the true value of their labor. The workers receive only a small portion of their just price or just enough to keep them alive. The difference between the worker's wage and the price of the goods produced is the surplus value. This surplus value is the profits for the capitalist and contributes to the class struggle that inevitably leads to revolution.

- **Communist Society.** Once the proletariats establish a classless society, the "state will wither away" as it will no longer be needed as a result of the elimination of all other classes besides the proletariat. Private property will be abolished and the production of goods and availability of services would make the Marxist principle, "from each according to his ability to each according to his needs," a reality.

Marx brought a revolutionary zeal to the class struggle because he wanted to unite the workers of the world by organizing socialist parties. In 1864, a socialist organization was founded in London, which became known as the First International. However, internal struggles led to its dissolution in 1876. In 1889, socialist parties of many countries organized the Second International, and these parties became powerful across Europe.

Chronology of the Agricultural and Industrial Revolutions

1705	Thomas Newcomen builds the steam engine to pump water out of coal mines.
1733	John Kay invents the flying shuttle.
1764	James Hargreaves invents the spinning jenny.
1768	Richard Arkwright invents the water frame.
1769	James Watt patents the steam engine, allowing, for the first time in history, a steady and unlimited source of power.
1771	Robert Owen, one of the early Utopian socialists, is born.
1776	Adam Smith publishes *The Wealth of Nations*, which develops the theory of laissez-faire capitalism.
1779	Samuel Crompton combines the concept of the spinning jenny and water frame in the mills.
1785	Edmund Cartwright invents the power loom for machines.
1793	Eli Whitney invents the cotton gin.
1798	Thomas Malthus writes *An Essay on the Principle of Population*.
1803	The first steam wagon appears on the streets of London.
1807	Robert Fulton drives the steamboat *Clermont* up the Hudson from New York to Albany.
1832	The Great Reform bill is passed by British Parliament; rotten boroughs were eliminated and there was an increase of voters in industrial areas because property qualifications for voting were reduced.
1833	The Factory Act passes in England, limiting the number of hours that children can work.
1837	The telegraph is developed; the Chartist Movement is born.
1847	The Ten Hours Act is passed in England, permitting children and women to work only ten-hour shifts.
1848	*The Communist Manifesto* by Karl Marx and Friedrich Engels is published.
1849	The last of the Navigation Acts are repealed.
1851	England is connected to the European continent by telegraph wire.
1867	The Reform Bill of 1867 is passed in England and the franchise is increased by 124 percent.
1872	The secret ballot becomes a law in England.
1891	Pope Leo XII issues *Rerum Novarum*, which addresses the struggle between capitalists and workers.

Sample Multiple-Choice Questions

1. Which was one of the basic principles of mercantilism?

   A. Countries must export more than they import.

   B. Tariff barriers should be avoided.

   C. Colonies are not essential for the mother country.

   D. Government should limit its involvement in the economy.

   E. A country has to maintain a favorable balance of trade to build up its supply of gold and silver.

2. The Industrial Revolution began in England for all of the following reasons, EXCEPT that

   A. England had an adequate supply of raw materials.

   B. considerable money was available for investments.

   C. there was a large supply of available workers.

   D. the government was stable.

   E. prices were high due to an inadequate food supply.

3. A direct result of the eighteenth-century Enclosure Acts in Great Britain was

   A. an increase in agricultural efficiency.

   B. an increase in rural population.

   C. exports of food and fiber to the continent.

   D. an increase in small farms.

   E. a de-emphasis on scientific farming.

4. Most of the technological advances of the early Industrial Revolution occurred in the following area:

   A. Textiles

   B. Chemicals

   C. Railways

   D. Ships

   E. Heavy machinery

5. The Luddites of the nineteenth century were

   A. political liberals.

   B. apprentices.

   C. workers who smashed the machinery that eliminated their jobs.

   D. communists.

   E. union laborers.

6. "In the natural advance of society, the wages of labour will have a tendency to fall, as far as they are regulated by supply and demand; for the supply of labourers will continue to increase at the same rate, while the demand for them will increase at a slower rate . . . I say that, under these circumstances, wages would fall if they were regulated only by the supply and demand of labourers; but we must not forget that wages are also regulated by the prices of the commodities on which they are expended."

   This passage is best associated with the ideas of

   A. Robert Owen.

   B. Louis Blanc.

   C. David Ricardo.

   D. Karl Marx.

   E. Jeremy Bentham.

7. One of the goals of the Royal Society of London, founded in 1660, was to

   A. promote political democracy.

   B. foster social reforms.

   C. encourage scientific research.

   D. support the expansion of public education.

   E. develop programs for geographic exploration.

8. Which of the following is not associated with his contribution to the Agricultural Revolution?

   A. Jethro Tull—reaper

   B. Charles "Turnip" Townshend—crop rotation

   C. Robert Bakewell—scientific breeding of animals

   D. Charles Newbold—cast-iron plow

   E. John Deere—self-cleaning plow

9. Adam Smith would most likely have supported the belief that

   A. the government should regulate all businesses.
   B. the free market would benefit all members of society.
   C. monopolies would be good for a state.
   D. population would grow faster than production.
   E. the free market would benefit only the wealthy.

10. Which of the following is not associated with the ideas of Karl Marx?

   A. Inevitability of revolution
   B. Natural selection
   C. Class struggle
   D. Surplus value
   E. Economic view of history

Multiple-Choice Questions: Answers and Explanations

1. **E.** European monarchs adopted this economic policy from the sixteenth to the eighteenth centuries in their quest for colonies and trade. Under mercantilism, colonies existed for the benefit of the mother country. Colonies provided raw materials for the mother country, and in return the colonists were expected to serve as a market for manufactured goods. Mercantilism also required that a country achieve a favorable balance of trade by exporting more than it imported. European countries passed strict navigation laws to ensure that the colonies traded with the mother country and foreign goods were kept out of the country. Government was expected to closely regulate the economy so as to maximize exports.

2. **E.** High prices due to inadequate food supply was not one of the contributing factors that gave rise to the Industrial Revolution in England. The Agricultural Revolution in the first half of the eighteenth century had provided England with a surplus labor supply and the means to feed it, as well as surplus capital. These agricultural changes prepared England for what Professor W.W. Rostow in his study, *The Stages of Economic Growth* (1960), has termed "the industrial takeoff."

3. **A.** Enclosure, or fencing in of land, was a widespread practice in Great Britain after 1760. The Enclosure Acts allowed powerful landlords to use open fields, strips, and village commons, and evicted tenant farmers from leased lands. As millions of acres were enclosed, farm output increased. Profits also rose because large fields needed few people to work them. The improvement of agricultural efficiency had a human cost, however. Villages shrank as small farmers, who were forced off their land because they could not compete with large landholders, left in search of work. England did not export food to the continent, but instead used its improved food production to supply its growing population. The Enclosure Act contributed to the growth of scientific farming as the British continued to improve farm production. Charles Townshend's use of crop rotation and Robert Bakewell's experiments in scientific breeding highlighted the importance of science in agriculture.

4. **A.** The Industrial Revolution first took off in the textile industry. In the 1700s, as the demand for cotton goods grew, inventors came up with a string of devices that revolutionized the British textile industry. In 1733, John Kay's flying shuttle sped up weaving by the loom and created a demand for more thread. One invention led to another, such as the spinning jenny, the water frame, the power loom, and the cotton gin. The innovations in the textile industry improved productivity. Improvements in chemicals, railways, ships, and heavy machinery would occur in the nineteenth century as the need for markets led to the development of different sectors of the economy.

5. **C.** The Luddites were skilled artisans who resisted the new labor-saving machines that were costing them their jobs. They were conservatives and not political liberals. These men were reacting to industrialization by using violent methods and did not turn to communism or unions as a way to meet their demands.

6. **C.** These words are derived from David Ricardo's writings from *Principles of Political Economy and Taxation.* These ideas became known as the so-called Iron Law of Wages, which states that increased supply of labor leads to lower wages and higher unemployment. Robert Owen was an English Utopian socialist. Louis Blanc was a French socialist who believed that the state should provide national workshops for the unemployed. Karl Marx was the founder of communism. Jeremy Bentham was the founder of a utilitarian school of social philosophy.

7. **C.** The Royal Society of London had its beginnings in the English Civil War which engulfed much of Great Britain in the mid-1600s. In 1660, they obtained a charter from King Charles II and their goal was to discuss scientific topics. Their purpose was to promote mathematical and experimental learning. Early members included Sir Isaac Newton and Edmund Halley. The society has provided an impetus for scientific thoughts and research. Its publication, *Philosophical Transactions,* is the oldest scientific periodical in continuous publication. The Society has not been involved in promoting political democracy, social reform, education, or programs for geographical exploration.

8. **A.** Jethro Tull (1674–1741) invented the seed drill (1701). Tull's seed drill planted seeds in straight lines rather than by hand. The drill distributed seeds in an even manner and at the proper depth. This method also permitted cultivation between rows, increasing the amount of food produced per acre. Cyrus McCormick invented the reaper in 1834.

9. **B.** Adam Smith believed that the free market would benefit all members of society. In 1776, Smith wrote *The Wealth of Nations*. Smith argued that the free market, through the natural laws of supply and demand, should be allowed to operate and regulate all businesses. He tried to show how manufacturing, trade, wages, profits, and economic growth were all linked to the forces of supply and demand. The free market would produce more goods at lower prices, making them affordable to everyone. A growing economy would also encourage capitalists to reinvest and spur continued economic growth. Smith believed in *laissez-faire* (leave business alone) and that the marketplace was better off without any government regulation. Smith rejected monopolies and encouraged competition. Thomas Malthus discussed the relationship between population growth and production. Smith believed that a growing economy would benefit more members of society than the wealthy.

10. **B.** Charles Darwin's *Origins of the Species* is associated with natural selection and the theory of evolution. In 1848, Karl Marx outlined his ideas of history in *The Communist Manifesto*. He proposed a scientific theory of history in which economic conditions determine history. He wrote that history is a struggle between the *haves* and *have-nots*. In ancient times, the struggle was between plebeians and patricians. During the Middle Ages, the struggle was between lords and serfs. In industrial societies, the final struggle is between the factory owners, who are the *haves,* and the workers, who are the *have-nots.* Marx predicted that there will be a worldwide revolution in which the workers will rise up against the owners and form a classless society. He felt that the conflict was inevitable because workers worldwide are being oppressed by capitalist owners. The difference between the workers' wages and the prices of the goods produced is the surplus value (profits). The surplus value contributes to the class struggle and inevitably leads to revolution.

The years from the end of the Congress of Vienna (1815) to the revolutions of 1848 are often referred to as the **Age of Reaction,** or the **Age of Metternich.** Prince Klemens von Metternich of Austria set in motion a 30-year pattern of anti-democratic policies that was followed by the conservatives—monarchs, nobles, landowners, and Church elders—who dominated the continent of Europe. Metternich firmly believed that the American and French revolutions had been responsible for a generation of war, causing bloodshed and suffering in Europe. As a conservative, he had a passionate hatred of liberalism because it had generally become associated with national aspirations. The idea that each national group had a right to establish its own independent government threatened the very existence of the nobility as well as the Austrian Empire. Conservatives such as Metternich wanted to return the kings of Europe to power and restore the historic social class structure in society. Many peasants supported the conservatives because they wanted to preserve their traditional ways that were being threatened by industrialization.

In spite of the careful plans of the Congress of Vienna, there were a series of revolts inspired by nationalism or liberalism in countries such as Italy, Spain, Greece, and Portugal. These revolts spread to Austria, the German states, and France. Borrowing their ideas from the Enlightenment, the liberal thinkers of the 1820s and 1830s, many of whom represented the middle class, wanted a government based on a written constitution that guaranteed the natural rights of the people. The struggle between liberalism and conservatism erupted in full-scale revolts in 1848. The tidal wave of revolution ended the Age of Metternich, and for many opponents of the old order it was the springtime of the people. The revolutions of 1848, beginning in Paris, affected all the countries on the European continent except Great Britain and Russia.

In the German states, following the 1848 uprisings, Prussia's failure to accommodate democratic changes contributed to the growth of militarism within the country. Austria, meanwhile, struggled against the forces of democracy and nationalism threatened the foundation of its multilingual, multinational empire. In France, the revolutions of 1848 continued the nation's uneven march toward democracy as the country grappled with the forces of liberalism and conservatism.

In Russia, which was unaffected by the 1848 revolutions, efforts to modernize and reform the economy came into conflict with the goals of the Russian czar to retain absolute control. In Britain, however, different democratic reforms had evolved throughout the nineteenth century that helped to broaden the franchise and voter participation. By the end of the nineteenth century, both Britain and France had created the foundation for a liberal democratic government.

The Age of Metternich (1815–1848)

Prince Klemens von Metternich (1773–1859) of the Austrian Empire took stern measures to combat the spread of democracy and nationalism. He began his diplomatic career in 1801 as Ambassador to Saxony, and later to Prussia in 1803. In 1806, the Austrian Emperor appointed him Ambassador to Napoleon's court and by 1809, he was Foreign Minister, an office he held until 1848. In 1810, Metternich was successful in arranging the marriage of Marie Louise, the 18-year-old daughter of the emperor, to Napoleon, who had divorced his wife, Josephine. He also secured a temporary alliance with France. Metternich joined the War of the Sixth Coalition against Napoleon, after the French invaded Russia in 1812. Metternich reached the height of his power at the Congress of Vienna (see Chapter 5, "The Age of Revolution: The French Revolution and Napoleonic Era"), and after 1815, Metternich devoted his energies to upholding the settlements of the Congress of Vienna and maintaining the power of the Hapsburg Dynasty in Europe.

The **Metternich System** employed censorship of speech and the press, espionage, and the suppression of revolutionary and national movements. It also used secret police and spies to establish control. The **German Confederation,** as states under Metternich's control were called, was forced to adopt the **Carlsbad Decrees** (1819), which banned freedom of speech and the press. Other countries in Europe adopted similarly restrictive policies. In Britain, the **Six Acts** (1819) were designed to control radical leaders, and in France the **Four** (or **July**) **Ordinances** (1830) forbade freedom of the press and reduced the number of eligible voters. Britain, Austria, Russia, and Prussia also formed a **Quadruple Alliance** and were later joined by France in 1818 (**Quintuple Alliance**) to keep peace and maintain order of the existing status quo. This cooperation among the major powers became known as the "Concert of Europe."

Despite repression, reformers continued to demand democracy and independent governments. Frequent uprisings throughout the 1820s and 1830s weakened the Metternich System.

The Revolutions of the 1820s

From 1820 to 1823, revolutions broke out in Spain, Sardinia, Portugal, and Greece. The revolts in Spain and Sardinia were easily crushed by the members of the Quintuple Alliance. A constitutional monarchy was established in Portugal in 1822. In their rebellion against the Ottoman Empire, the Greek revolutionaries won worldwide support. The Greek revolt became tied to the so-called "**Eastern Question**" in European history: a term used to designate the political and diplomatic problems created by the decaying Ottoman Empire during the nineteenth and twentieth centuries. European countries, especially England, France, and Russia, feared the instability of the European territories controlled by the Ottoman Empire. Many Europeans wanted to support their cause because Christian Europe saw it as a struggle against the Muslims as well as a way to gain territory and weaken the Ottoman Empire. In 1824, the work of the Romantic painter **Eugène Delacroix** (1798–1863) entitled *The Massacre of Chios* glorified the struggle of Greek freedom fighters against the Ottomans and won the support of nationalists. In 1829, Greece won its independence.

The Revolutions of the 1830s

A series of revolutions broke out in the 1830s, first taking place in France and then spreading to Belgium, Poland, Italy, and Germany. After the fall of Napoleon, **Louis XVIII,** brother of Louis XVI, was returned to the throne. Although undemocratic, Louis protected the people against the return of absolutism and aristocratic privilege. When Louis died in 1824, his brother **Charles X** (who reigned from 1824 to 1830) inherited the throne and decided to reestablish the old order, believing in absolute rule. In 1830, he suspended the legislature, limited the right to vote, and restricted the press. This sparked the **July Revolution** (July 26–29, 1830). Angry students, workers, and intellectuals rioted in Paris for three days. Charles abdicated and fled to Britain. The workers and intellectuals wanted a republic, but the upper middle class, who retained control, wanted a constitutional monarchy. Through the efforts of Talleyrand and the Marquis de Lafayette, the lower house of the Chamber of Deputies agreed upon **Louis-Philippe** as king—Louis-Philippe was a cousin of Charles X, and in his youth had supported the revolution of 1789.

The French called Louis-Philippe the **"citizen king"**; he was plain spoken, dressed in a frock coat and top hat, carried an umbrella, and owed his throne to the people. He adopted the dress of the common man. He also replaced the Bourbon flag with the tricolore flag of the Revolution and increased the electorate to include the upper middle class. The vast majority of the people, however, could still not vote and Louis' policy favored the middle class at the expense of the workers.

The news of the successful July Revolution in France served as a spark to revolutions throughout Europe, leading Metternich to say, "When France sneezes, Europe catches a cold." In 1830, Belgium revolted against Dutch rule, protesting against being governed by people who had a different language and religion. The Belgians received support from Louis-Philippe in France and from England, and in 1831 they became an independent state. In 1839, all the great powers recognized Belgium as a neutral state. Nationalist uprisings also took place in Italy, Germany, and Poland; these revolts were easily crushed by Austria and Russia, however. The successful revolutions in France and Belgium showed that even in Western Europe, the Metternich System could not contain the forces of democracy and nationalism.

The Revolutions of 1848 and Their Aftermath

The specter of revolutions, which according to Karl Marx haunted Europe in 1848, was similar to the one that had previously haunted Europe in 1789 and 1830. In 1848, however—a time of social and economic change—the revolutionary demands were widespread and irrepressible. Agricultural disasters, such as the Irish potato famine, widespread unemployment, and tension between the urban workers and the new class of capitalists created by the Industrial Revolution added to the discontent. Moreover, the power of nationalism in the German and Italian states added fuel to an already smoldering fire.

France

As usual, France started the revolutionary tide by revolting early in February of 1848. King Louis-Philippe aroused the opposition of both the liberal and the radical **Republicans.** The liberal Republicans consisted of moderates and members of the middle class who supported the expansion of the suffrage for all male voters. The radical Republicans wanted to promote social and economic changes to help the lives of the workers. They opposed both a monarchy and the liberal Republicans, who had formerly supported Louis-Philippe, and they denounced the rampant corruption of his government and voting restrictions. Unemployed workers, who had no vote, were also unhappy with Louis-Philippe's government. In February, when the government prohibited a scheduled political meeting held by Republicans to honor George Washington, angry crowds took to the streets of Paris.

During the **February Days** (February 22–23), workers, students, and radicals rioted, and demonstrators clashed with troops. On February 24, as the turmoil spread and the workers took control of Paris, Louis-Philippe abdicated and fled to England. A provisional government was created, composed of Political Republicans (middle class liberals) and Social Republicans (the working-class group), who set national elections for April. Differences divided the government, however: The middle-class liberals in control of the government were led by **Alphonse de Lamartine** (1790–1869); they favored moderate reforms and had little sympathy for the working poor, although they gave some concessions to the workers. **Louis Blanc** (1811–1882), a Social Republican, was allowed to establish national workshops to provide jobs for the unemployed. In June of 1848, the upper and middle classes, who had won a majority of the votes in the April election (based on universal male suffrage), shut down the workshops, claiming that they were a waste of money. Angry crowds stormed the streets again. This time, however, the bourgeoisie and peasants, fearing that the Socialists might take their land, turned against the workers. The **June Riots** (June 23–26) were unlike previous uprisings in France in that they constituted full-scale class warfare involving half of Paris. After three terrible days and the death or injury of 10,000 people, the government, with the support of the army and the peasants, crushed the rebellion.

Seeking to restore order, the National Assembly issued a constitution for a **French Second Republic** (the first had lasted from 1792 to 1804 when Napoleon became emperor). The new constitution of this government created a strong president with a one-house legislature, elected by universal male suffrage. In November, **Louis Napoleon,** nephew of Napoleon Bonaparte, was elected. He was installed as president of the French Second Republic on December 20, 1848.

After his election, Louis Napoleon created a conservative government. He cooperated with the National Assembly, but when it refused to change the constitution so he could run for another term, he initiated a *coup d'état* in 1851 and assumed dictatorial powers. Napoleon was fearful that the radicals would win the 1852 election. He replaced the Second Republic with the **Second Empire** (the first was that of Napoleon I) and crowned himself **Emperor Napoleon III** in 1852. Like his uncle, his actions were approved by a **plebiscite** (an expression of the popular will) of the voters. Until 1860, Napoleon III's government retained the outward appearance of a democracy but it was a dictatorship. He exercised control through his secret police and enforced censorship of the press and state-controlled elections.

When the coup d'etat by Napoleon III took place in 1851, **Victor Hugo** (1802–1885), the great Romantic writer fled to Brussels because he believed his life in danger. His exile lasted for twenty years. During this time, he published

Les Misérables (1862), which became one of his most famous novels. The French word *misérables* means both "poor wretches" and/or "scoundrels or villains." The book paints a vivid picture of the social injustices that existed in France under Napoleon III. Hugo returned to France in 1871 when the Third Republic was proclaimed. When he died in Paris in 1882, he was given a national funeral that was attended by over two million people and was buried in the Pantheon.

After 1860, Napoleon III believed that economic progress would reduce political and social tensions, and by rebuilding much of Paris he would enhance the glory of the empire. He carried out a vast public-works policy, which included rebuilding roads, canals, and railroads. Working with **Georges Haussmann** (1809–1891), Napoleon III transformed Paris into a modern city, clearing slums and creating wide boulevards. Sanitary conditions improved and a sewage system was developed to remove waste. Napoleon III also gained the support of city workers by legalizing unions and granting them the right to strike.

Failures in foreign affairs, however, became a problem for Napoleon III. In 1862 he tried to place Maximilian, an Austrian Hapsburg prince, on the throne of Mexico. Although he committed a large number of troops and money, the venture failed. Opposition of the Mexican patriots and protests from the United States forced him to withdraw his French troops in 1866. Maximilian was overthrown and shot by Mexican leaders. The Second Empire fell when Napoleon III became involved in the ill-fated **Franco-Prussian War** (1870–1871) in which he was captured and exiled to Britain for his last years. The **National Assembly** (1871–1875) was established and met to decide on a new government. In March 1871, a radical government (the **Paris Commune**) took control of Paris. The **Communards,** as the rebels were called, included workers, socialists, and bourgeoisie Republicans. As patriots, they rejected the peace with Germany that the National Assembly had negotiated and refused to recognize the authority of the National Assembly. In May, the loyal troops of the National Assembly crushed the revolt, in which it is estimated that over 20,000 people were killed, and the city of Paris was burned.

By 1875, the National Assembly had agreed to establish a new government called the **Third Republic,** which consisted of a two-house legislature, a **Chamber of Deputies** elected by universal male suffrage, and a **Senate** chosen by an indirect election. Since many parties were represented in the Chamber of Deputies, no one party could dominate the government. This led to instability as governments rose and fell depending upon their ability to gain the support of the different political parties. The Third Republic was also threatened by domestic difficulties such as the Boulanger and Dreyfus affairs, described presently.

The Third Republic was also successful in the separation of Church and state and provided free education. Despite a bumpy road, France established a stable government providing many social benefits by the end of the nineteenth century. The Third Republic lasted for 65 years.

The Boulanger Affair (1887–1889)

In 1887, **General Georges Boulanger** (1837–1891), the Minister of War who had won the support of the army by improving its military life and who was a believer in a monarchial form of government, was encouraged by his supporters to overthrow the government. He waited too long and Republicans had enough time to expel him from the country. Boulanger fled to Belgium, where he later committed suicide. The successful handling of this affair improved the prestige of the government.

The Dreyfus Affair (1894–1906)

Alfred Dreyfus (1859–1935), a Jewish Republican Army captain, was court-martialed by royalist officers and declared guilty of selling secret military documents to the Germans. Many suspected an anti-Semitic conspiracy. The country was divided between his supporters and those who believed the charges were legitimate. In 1898, the French novelist **Émile Zola** (1840–1902) published an open letter entitled *J'accuse* ("*I accuse*"), denouncing the army for covering up the scandal. Zola was convicted of libel and sentenced to a year in jail. However, he fled into exile. Dreyfus was acquitted in 1906 and awarded the Legion of Honor. The Dreyfus affair strengthened the Third Republic because it showed the monarchists as being the faction guilty of anti-government activities.

The Dreyfus case and the pogroms, or violent attacks of the Jews in Russia, reflected the strength of anti-Semitism in Europe. These events convinced many Jews that they needed a separate homeland. In 1890, **Theodor Herzl**

(1860–1904), an Austrian journalist, launched modern **Zionism,** a movement devoted to rebuilding a Jewish state in Palestine. In his book, *The Jewish State* (1896), he argued for the establishment of a Jewish homeland. In 1897, Herzl organized the **First Zionist Congress** in Basel, Switzerland.

The Austrian Empire

The Austrian Empire consisted of many different national groups: Germans, Hungarians, Czechs, Romanians, Poles, Slavs, and Italians. Although the revolutions in the 1820s and 1830s had little effect on it as a whole, the Empire, headed by Emperor **Ferdinand I** (1793–1875; reigned 1835–1848), was vulnerable to revolutionary changes. With its collection of different nationalities, the specter of nationalism haunted the Austrian Empire. Its government was reactionary and the social system provided little hope for the people. As news of the February Days in France spread across Europe, people within the Austrian Empire began to revolt. Many demanded more democracy and students, supported by the workers, demonstrated in the streets of Vienna, manning the barricades and invading the Imperial Palace. In March, the revolution spread to Budapest. The Hungarian nationalist leader **Lajos Kossuth** (1802–1894) demanded independence. He also called for an end to serfdom and a written constitution to protect basic rights in Hungary. The Czechs made similar demands.

Fearing for his life, Metternich resigned and fled to England in disguise. Ferdinand I agreed to the reforms and abdicated. Conflicts among the different nationalities (Hungarians against Croats; Serbs against Romanians; Czechs against Germans) weakened the revolution, however. The alliance of the working class and the middle class soon collapsed and the Austrian army regained control of Vienna. In October of 1848, the Hungarians invaded Austria and by April 1849 a Hungarian Republic with Kossuth in charge was created. In June of 1849, with the aid of the Russians, Austria defeated the Hungarians. Kossuth fled into exile while thirteen of his guards were executed. In northern Italy, the two provinces of Milan and Venice revolted in favor of a united Italy. These revolutions were also crushed. The revolutions in the Austrian Empire had failed. However, the Austrian Empire still had to confront the problems associated with the rise of national aspirations within the different ethnic groups in its empire. By the end of the nineteenth century, these problems would have serious ramifications for the later-formed Austro-Hungarian Empire.

Prussia

After Austria, Prussia was the largest and most influential German kingdom. Prussia included the Rhineland, the central region around Berlin, West Prussia, and East Prussia. In the 1830s, Prussia had provided leadership in creating an economic union called the **Zollverein.** Prior to 1848, middle-class Prussian liberals desired to transform absolutist Prussia into a liberal constitutional government, with the goal of Prussia taking the lead in uniting all of Germany into a liberal unified government.

The events in France in 1848 had repercussions in Prussia, where Emperor **Friedrich Wilhelm IV** (b. 1795, ruled 1840–1861) had promised reforms but always hesitated. When riots broke out in Berlin on March 10, the king promised to grant Prussia a liberal constitution written by an elected assembly and merge it with a new national German state that was being created. Although the demands of the workers, which included a ten-hour workday and minimum wages, differed from those of the Prussian aristocracy who wanted to assert their power over the king, the king allowed the election of a constituent assembly to draw up a constitution. In December of 1848, the king drew up his own constitution that was very similar to what the assembly had planned, allowing for freedom of the press and a two-house legislature with universal male suffrage for the lower house. However, power still remained in the hands of the upper class because weighted votes were given to those who paid more taxes.

Meanwhile, delegates from many German states met in Frankfurt from May of 1848 until May of 1849 as part of the **Frankfurt Assembly** to discuss their vision of how a united Germany would be established. This meeting, which was not sanctioned by Friedrich Wilhelm IV, was hampered by conflicting aims and divisions. Although all agreed on a united Germany, delegates disagreed over whether it should be a republic or a monarchy. Moreover, a major dispute arose over what areas would be included in the new Germany. Those who supported the **Grossdeutsche** ("large Germany") view wanted to include the German-speaking province of Austria under German rule. The **Kleindeutsche** ("small Germany") wanted to exclude Austria and include only Prussia with the small German states. When the Austrians opposed any division of their territory, the delegates decided on a united Germany excluding Austria. They completed drawing up a liberal constitution and offered the Imperial Crown of a united Germany to Wilhelm IV. He contemptuously refused to accept the "crown from the gutter" and reestablished his authority by dissolving the assembly under threat from the Prussian military. The failure of the Frankfurt Assembly destroyed the hope of a united Germany under a liberal parliamentary government and laid the foundation for the rise of Prussian militarism that created a united Germany in 1871.

Russia

The European revolutions of the 1820s and 1830s had very little effect on Russia. The Russian czars had ruled for centuries with absolute power and the ideals of the Enlightenment and French Revolution had never taken hold in that country. **Alexander I** (b. 1777, ruled 1801–1825) initially was receptive to liberal ideas such as promoting education, ending censorship, and granting greater freedom for Jews, but he became very conservative after Napoleon's invasion in 1812. At the Congress of Vienna, he sided with the conservatives and opposed all efforts at liberal reform. He imposed strict censorship and insisted that all his subjects follow the Russian Orthodox Church.

When Alexander I died in December of 1825, his young brother **Nicholas I** (b. 1796, ruled 1825–1855), ascended to the throne. At the time of the succession, a group of young officers, henceforth known as the **Decembrists,** led a revolt. They supported **Constantine,** Nicholas' brother, who they believed would promote a more liberal government, a constitution, and the modernization of Russia. Nicholas I crushed the revolt, executed some of the Decembrists, and cracked down on all dissenters. Nicholas created the **Third Section,** the dreaded secret police, who hunted down all those critical of the government and strictly enforced the czar's decree that banned books from Western Europe. To bolster his regime, Nicholas I enthusiastically supported the ideals of Russian absolutism:

- **Orthodoxy,** the strong connection between the Russian Orthodox Church, of which the czar was the official head, and the government.
- **Autocracy,** the absolute power of the czar.
- **Nationalism,** respect for Russian tradition and suppression of non-Russians within the empire.

The autocratic regime of Nicholas I was not threatened by the revolutionary movements that dominated Europe in 1848. From 1848 to 1849, Russian troops put down a revolt by Polish nationalists and suppressed all democratic institutions. Nicholas also followed a policy of Russification, which forced Poles and other racial groups to use the Russian language and follow the approved Russian Orthodox religion. Many unsuccessful peasant revolts occurred during Nicholas' reign.

Alexander II (b. 1818, ruled 1855–1881) came to the throne during the **Crimean War** (1853–1856), which had developed at the end of the reign of Nicholas I, when Russia tried to seize Ottoman lands along the Danube River. Because neither France nor England wanted to see Russia expand into the Mediterranean, France joined England in supporting the **Ottoman Empire,** known as "the sick man of Europe," by sending fleets into the Black Sea. The term "the sick man of Europe" was used because after the loss of Hungary in 1699, the Ottoman Empire had entered a long period of territorial disintegration. In 1856, Russia's defeat in the Crimean War revealed how far Russia lagged behind the Western countries economically, technologically, and culturally. Alexander realized that he had to introduce reform and modernization.

In 1861, Alexander issued the **Emancipation Edict,** abolishing serfdom—an institution that had long disappeared from Western Europe. Although the serfs became free citizens and were no longer the personal possessions of the lords, freedom brought problems. Peasants now had to buy the land that they had worked on for so long, but were too poor to purchase it. Furthermore, the land allotted to the peasants was either too small to be efficient or not able to support a family. Peasant communities, not individual peasants, received approximately one-half of the land and each peasant community had 49 years to pay the government for the land it had received. The government had hoped that collective responsibility would prevent the development of a class of landless peasants. In reality, the serfs, while legally free, were still bound to the land since they could not leave until the village paid off the debt. Thus, discontent still festered within the peasant class. In 1917, the Bolshevik leader, Lenin, would build on this resentment to help him gain power; see Chapter XI, "Europe in Crisis (1917–1939)."

Alexander II also realized that in order to compete with Western Europe, he had to make some efforts to modernize and industrialize the economy. In 1860, the country had approximately 1,250 miles of railroads, but by 1880 it had 15,550 miles. Industrial suburbs developed around Moscow and St. Petersburg. Despite these changes, Russian intellectuals began to question the future of Russia. Some, known as **Westerners,** thought that Russia should model itself after Western Europe. Others, such as the **Slavophiles,** thought that Russia should retain its own spirit and tradition and avoid westernization. As the number of dissenters grew, terrorism became common. In 1881, Alexander II was assassinated and the era of reform came to an abrupt end.

Alexander III (b. 1845, ruled 1881–1894) was a reactionary, determined to avenge his father's death to ensure his autocratic rule by reinforcing the pillars of Russian absolutism through the secret police and censorship. Although Russian efforts at political reforms were frozen, Russia continued to industrialize because the czar realized that the country needed to develop its economy to remain a great power. The gigantic **Trans-Siberian Railway** connecting Moscow with Vladivostok on the Pacific Ocean, 5,000 miles away, was a source of pride for Russia. The success of the railroad encouraged foreign capitalists to build and develop steel and coal industries in Russia. By 1900, only Germany and the United States were producing more steel than Russia, and Russia was producing and refining half the world's steel output. While Russia was establishing itself as an industrial country, however, Alexander III failed to realize the problems created by industrialization, such as the need for political, constitutional, and economic reforms. These issues led to major changes in Russia at the beginning of the twentieth century.

Britain: Democracy through Evolution

Although England had established the framework for democracy during the seventeenth century, it still maintained many undemocratic features. For example, there was a Constitutional Monarch and a Parliament with two political parties, but the government was not representative of the people. Less than five percent of the population could vote and the British Parliament represented the interests of the wealthy. Parliament was made up of the **House of Lords,** which consisted of hereditary nobles and high-ranking clergy of the Anglican Church. The House of Lords had the power to veto any law passed by the **House of Commons.**

During the nineteenth century, however, England embarked on a series of evolutionary changes that gradually made the country more democratic. One such series of changes came at the conclusion of the Napoleonic War in 1815. England had regulated the price of grain since the seventeenth century to protect the wealthy landowners who ran Parliament. In 1815, Parliament passed **Corn Laws** to limit the import of foreign grain until domestic grain cost above 80 shillings per quarter ton. These restrictions sparked food riots in many cities. In 1819, the government met force with force, which led to the **Peterloo Massacre** in Manchester. Eventually in 1846, the **Anti-Corn Law League** headed a nationwide campaign for the repeal of the Corn Laws, which ended in success in 1846 when the Prime Minister, **Sir Robert Peel** (1788–1850), repealed the legislation. Throughout the 1820s and 1830s, reformers began to make other changes. Religious toleration was granted to Catholics, membership was allowed in unions, and the justice system was restructured, allowing for a revised penal code.

In the 1830s, a greater series of political reforms were enacted that had a lasting influence on the country. The **Whigs** (representing the middle class and concerned about business interests) and the **Tories** (representatives of the nobles and landowners) fought over a reform bill about representation, as the House of Commons had not been reapportioned since the seventeenth century. The Industrial Revolution had led to the growth of cities at the expense of the rural areas. Although the population of urban areas had increased dramatically, the rural areas were still sending the same number of representatives to the House of Commons even though fewer voters or sometimes no voters lived there. These areas became known as the so-called **"rotten boroughs"** because they were underpopulated and did not represent the people. **The Great Reform Bill of 1832** abolished the rotten boroughs. Adequate representation was given to the industrial areas and, by reducing property qualifications, there was an increase in the number of voters from 500,000 to 800,000. The Reform Bill of 1832 was the first step toward democracy. These changes began to put power in the hands of the industrial towns.

Because the Reform Bill did not enfranchise city workers, they organized the **Chartist Movement,** a reform movement representing the working class and some lower middle-class workers. In the **People's Charter of 1837,** from which the movement derived its name, the Chartists petitioned the government for the following:

- Universal male suffrage
- Secret ballots
- Equal election districts
- Elimination of property qualifications for members of Parliament
- Annual elections
- Salaries for members of Parliament

In 1848, as revolution swept across Europe, Chartists marched on Parliament and presented their petition. Parliament, as it had done in 1837, rejected the petition. The Chartists failed in the short run, but by the beginning of the twentieth century, all of their demands, with the exception of annual parliamentary elections, came to pass.

The efforts to expand the franchise continued throughout the latter half of the nineteenth century. In 1867, Prime Minister **Benjamin Disraeli** (1804–1881), who dominated the **Conservative Party** (formerly the Tories), was able to convince Parliament to approve a Reform Bill that doubled the number of voters by reducing property qualifications. The Reform Bill extended votes to men who either owned a house or paid rent. Disraeli had hoped that the newly enfranchised city voters would join together with the wealthy landowners and outvote the merchants and factory owners—the **Liberals** (formerly Whigs). However, Disraeli failed to change the voting behaviors of the city workers, and they continued to support the Liberals to achieve more democratic reforms. In 1884, the Liberals, under Prime Minister **William Gladstone** (1809–1898), enacted the **Reform Bill of 1884,** which extended the right to vote to agricultural workers. From the mid-1850s to the first two decades of the 1900s, either the Liberals or the Tories were in control of the government. Disraeli, in the 1880s, sponsored laws to improve public health and housing for workers in the cities. Gladstone supported free public education for all children; government jobs based on merit, and not on birth or wealth; and the legalization of unions, as well as the adaption of the secret ballot.

In the 1900s, unions and socialist members formed their own **Labour Party** that began to push for social legislation that protected the rights of workers. The Labour Party grew in strength and by 1924 gained a parliamentary majority with the support of the Liberal party. The efforts of the Labour party laid the foundation for such social legislation as unemployment insurance, old-age pensions, and disability insurance, which was eventually enacted after World War II.

Chronology of the Struggle for Democracy in Nineteenth-Century Europe (1815–1914)

1819	Metternich imposes the Carlsbad Decree upon the German Confederation.
1820–24	Revolutions take place in Spain, Sardinia, Portugal, and (in 1821–1824) Greece.
1824	Charles X becomes king of France; Eugène Delacroix's painting *The Massacre at Chios* celebrates the Greek struggle for freedom and independence.
1825	The Decembrist Revolt occurs in Russia.
1830	The Greeks gain independence; the Revolution begins in France; Charles X flees to England; Louis-Philippe becomes the "citizen king."
1832	The Reform Bill nearly doubles the electorate in England and abolishes "rotten boroughs."
1832	The Factory Act in Britain restricting child labor is established.
1837	The Chartist Petition passes.
1845–47	The potato famine occurs in Ireland.
1848	The *Communist Manifesto* is first published; Revolutions break out in Italy, France, Hungary, Austria, and Prussia—and all fail; Metternich resigns and flees to England.
1849	The Frankfurt Assembly selects Friedrich Wilhelm IV as emperor of the new German Empire, but he refuses the crown.
1852	Louis Napoleon becomes Emperor Napoleon III.
1861	Czar Alexander II of Russia issues the Emancipation Edict that abolishes serfdom.
1867	The Reform Bill in Britain reduces property qualifications for voters.
1870–1871	The Franco-Prussian War takes place; France is defeated and Napoleon III is exiled; the Second French Empire ends.
1884	A Reform Bill extends the right to vote to agricultural workers in Britain.
1894	The Dreyfus Affair divides France.

Sample Multiple-Choice Questions

1. The first great national rebellion of the 1820s broke out in

   A. Italy.
   B. Germany.
   C. Ireland.
   D. Poland.
   E. Greece.

2. The July Revolution of 1830 resulted in

   A. the rise of Louis Napoleon to power.
   B. the selection of Charles X as the new king.
   C. the appointment of Louis-Philippe as king by the Chamber of Deputies.
   D. conflict with England.
   E. the granting of universal suffrage to all men who owned property.

3. Which of the following statements is least accurate about the June Days in Paris in 1848?

   A. The peasants supported the workers.
   B. Class warfare broke out between the workers and bourgeoisie.
   C. The government, with the support of the army, crushed the rebellion.
   D. The government did not fully support the national workshops.
   E. The June Days led to the creation of the Second Republic.

4. Louis Napoleon (Napoleon III) gained popularity for all of the following EXCEPT

   A. granting workers the right to strike.
   B. sponsoring a public works program.
   C. modernizing Paris.
   D. having successful foreign policy victories.
   E. encouraging massive railroad building.

5. Which of the following was not a demand of the Chartists?

   A. Universal suffrage for men and women
   B. Secret ballots
   C. Elimination of property qualifications
   D. Annual election of Parliament
   E. Equal election districts

6. The Reform Act of 1832 in Britain

   A. granted universal suffrage for men.
   B. introduced the secret ballot.
   C. ended the rotten boroughs.
   D. limited the power of the House of Lords.
   E. increased the power of the monarchy.

7. The Frankfurt Assembly was

   A. a middle class body that wanted to write a constitution for a liberal, united Germany.
   B. united behind a republican form of government.
   C. supported by Austria.
   D. called by Bismarck to enhance Prussia's prestige.
   E. concerned primarily with economic issues.

8. The main purpose of the Corn Laws was to

   A. prohibit the exporting of British grain.
   B. improve the quality of British grain.
   C. weaken the power of the landed aristocracy.
   D. strengthen the influence of the rising middle class in England.
   E. protect the interests of the landed aristocracy (who grew the grain) from foreign imports.

9. The Decembrist Revolt of 1825 was

   A. an initial attempt by the middle class to gain greater influence.

   B. a revolt by young liberal officers and the upper class, who wanted to modernize Russia and promote a more liberal constitution.

   C. an early example of the Pan-Slavic movement in the Balkans.

   D. successful because Nicholas I supported the reform ideas.

   E. encouraged by the secret police's Third Section.

10. Which conclusion can be drawn from the table below? Base your answer to this question on data from the table and your knowledge of British history.

Year	Suffrage granted to
1815	less than 5 percent of the male Anglican population
1820s	wealthy male Roman Catholics and wealthy non-Anglican Protestants
1832	men with a certain amount of property
1860s	a large category of working-class men
1880s	farm workers and most other men

   A. Anglicans gained the right to vote after the Catholics.

   B. Revolutions gained the right for all men to vote.

   C. The right to vote was gradually extended over a period of time.

   D. By 1860, all men had the right to vote.

   E. All Roman Catholics could vote by 1830.

Multiple-Choice Questions: Answers and Explanations

1. **E.** The Greeks, with the assistance of the European powers (England, France, and Russia), successfully revolted against the Ottoman Empire, setting the stage for nationalists throughout Europe. The Europeans supported the Greeks' struggle for independence because Christian Europe saw it as a struggle against the Muslims as well as a way to weaken the Ottoman Empire. Ottoman atrocities towards the rebels also fanned the fires of Europe's outrage. In 1830, England, France, and Russia declared Greek independence. Italy and Germany became independent, united nations during the late 1860s and early 1870s. Ireland and Poland did not become independent nations until the twentieth century.

2. **C.** The July Revolution of 1830 resulted in the Chamber of Deputies appointing Louis-Philippe as king. Charles X, the successor to Louis XVIII, tried to reestablish the old order and repudiate the constitutional charter, which protected against a return to royal absolutism, in 1830. Angry students, city workers, and intellectuals rioted for three days in Paris. When Charles X fled to England, the Chamber of Deputies enthroned Louis-Philippe as a united monarch. Louis-Philippe, known as the "citizen king," replaced the Bourbon flag with the tricolore flag of the French Revolution. He enacted a liberal constitution and reduced the property qualifications to vote in order to enfranchise more members of the middle class. Louis Napoleon rose to power as a result of the revolution of 1848. Charles X was forced to abdicate and flee to England in 1830. After the Congress of Vienna, France and England were at peace with each other for the rest of the century. In 1848, not 1830, universal male suffrage was enacted in France. The provisional republic established in 1848 granted universal male suffrage.

3. **A.** The peasants did not support the workers. The peasants, like the middle and upper class, were frightened by the socialist outlook of the workers. Peasants who owned lands hated the radicals of Paris. Fearing the socialists might take their land, they attacked the workers and opposed the national workshops. In June 1848, the upper and middle class won control of the government and shut down the national workshops because they considered them to be a waste of money. When the city workers took to the streets, the bourgeoisie turned against the protesters. After three terrible days, the government put down the revolts. Over 10,000 people were either killed or injured. The government of moderate Republicans at first supported national workshops as a compromise solution for the socialists. However, as the workshops grew and became more radical, the government dissolved them on June 21. In 1848, the revolutionaries proclaimed the Second French Republic, and guaranteed universal male suffrage. The French people elected Louis Napoleon, the nephew of Napoleon Bonaparte, as president. The republic lasted until 1851.

4. **D.** Louis Napoleon (Napoleon III) was never successful in his foreign policy ventures. Nationalists were disappointed with Napoleon III's humiliating failure in Mexico (1862–1866). To revive his popularity, Napoleon III tried to check Prussian power, and opposed German unification. In the Franco-Prussian War (1870–1871), the French army was defeated and Napoleon III was taken prisoner and exiled. The defeat of Napoleon III led to the end of the Second French Empire and the Second Republic. After 1860, Napoleon III gained popularity by granting workers the right to form unions and the right to strike, both of which had been denied by the earlier government. Napoleon III tried to avoid social and economic tensions by promoting the welfare of all his subjects through government reforms. He believed that by modernizing Paris through a public works program, he could improve living conditions. Rebuilding Paris provided a model for urban planning. Napoleon III also promoted mass railroad building as a way to help promote economic growth.

5. **A.** The Chartists did not support universal suffrage for men and women. The Chartist movement was formed in 1838 to secure the vote for the working and lower middle class as part of their larger demand for universal suffrage for men. Although the Chartists did not call for women's rights, women in the Chartist movement organized the first British association to work for women's suffrage. The Chartist movement lasted about ten years. In subsequent years, the Chartist demands, such as secret ballots, elimination of property qualifications, and payment of regular salaries for members of Parliament, were eventually enacted. The annual election of Parliament was the only demand that never became a law.

6. **C.** The Reform Act of 1832 ended the rotten boroughs. The Reform Bill redistributed the seats in the House of Commons, giving representation to large towns and eliminating rotten boroughs—rural towns that had lost so many people that there were few or no voters. These rotten boroughs were still sending members to Parliament. Universal male suffrage and secret ballots were part of the demands of the Chartists in 1848. The Parliament Act of 1911 limited the power of the House of Lords. There was never any discussion to increase the power of the monarchy. The Glorious Revolution of 1689 had established a limited monarchy, which has continued to serve as a symbol of unity for the people of England up to the present.

7. **A.** The Frankfurt Assembly was supported by the middle class, who wanted a constitution for a liberal, united Germany. After the revolution broke out in France, the National Assembly, which met in Frankfurt and became known as the Frankfurt Assembly, met to write a constitution for a united Germany. Friedrich Wilhelm IV refused to accept the crown from the Assembly, and efforts to unite Germany failed. The Frankfurt Assembly did not support a republican form of government but wanted a liberal monarchial form of government modeled on England. Austria did not support the work of the Frankfurt Assembly and opposed any unification efforts that eliminated her influence in the German states. Bismarck was not in power during the time of the Frankfurt Assembly. The primary interest of the delegates was political, not economic, unification.

8. **E.** The Corn Laws of 1815 were designed to protect English landowners by prohibiting the importation of foreign grain unless the domestic price rose above a certain level. These laws were passed because the aristocracy feared that at the end of the Napoleonic War, there would be large imports of wheat from the continent and lower prices, which would directly affect them. The Corn Laws were passed at a time of widespread unemployment and hurt the middle and working classes. The Corn Laws did not have any scientific goal nor did they prohibit the export of British grain. These laws were selfishly designed to promote the economic advantage of the aristocracy.

9. **B.** In December 1825, following the death of Alexander I, a group of liberal members of the upper class and about 3,000 military officers staged an unsuccessful rebellion to prevent the accession of Nicholas I. These Decembrists supported Nicholas' brother Constantine. The poorly organized revolt was easily suppressed, since most of the troops remained loyal to Nicholas I and the rebels had no cannons and were outnumbered about four to one. The revolutionaries were banished to Siberia and some members of the Decembrists were executed. The middle class was not involved in the revolt since Russia was still primarily an agricultural economy and had not developed an urban middle class. Nicholas I, with the support of the secret police's Third Section, crushed the revolt.

10. **C.** The table supports the conclusion that the right to vote was gradually extended over a period of time. In the 1800s, political power remained with the landed aristocracy (male Anglican population), while the middle and working classes had no voting rights. The Reform Act of 1832 lowered the voting qualifications and gave more middle class people the right to vote. The proportion of voters increased from 1 in 100 to 1 in 32 men. City workers, however, were still deprived of their right to vote. In 1848, the Chartists, a reform group of the working class, petitioned the government for universal suffrage for men, as well as removal of property qualifications for members of Parliament. The Chartist Movement failed, but their reforms were eventually implemented. In 1867, property qualifications were reduced so that more city workers could vote. In 1884, Prime Minister William Gladstone supported a reform bill that extended the right to vote to all farm workers and other men. This bill increased the number of voters by one million men. By 1830, only wealthy male Catholics could vote.

The Age of Nationalism in Europe

Between 1850 and 1914, strong nation states developed in Germany and Italy. The nation states were built upon the principle of **nationalism:** the bonding of a people by a common language, history, traditions, beliefs, and goals. Nationalism originated with the French Revolution and with Napoleon, who helped to spread it throughout Europe. As it took hold in the emerging urban societies of the late nineteenth century, people began to transfer their allegiance from a monarch to a country and to put national interests above all considerations. Nationalism provided people with a sense of belonging and power, as well as a connection to the state, which had been disrupted by the Industrial Revolution. The Industrial Revolution had altered the relationship between the worker and the employer, and the allegiance that had once been directed to the employer was now refocused toward a unified state. The national states became a way of coping with the challenges of rapid economic and political changes. Strong leaders were able to direct this energy toward industrialization and modernization.

The revolutions of 1848 had not satisfied the demands of the nationalists in Italy and Germany. Camillo Benso, Count of Cavour, the moderate nationalist prime minister of Piedmont-Sardinia, realized that the independent Kingdom of Italy could be united into a single political state only by combining force with diplomacy. In Germany, Otto von Bismarck, chief minister of Prussia, skillfully fought three wars to unify Germany into one single nation under Prussian leadership. These men were the driving forces behind unification and were masters of the art of power politics, or **realpolitik.**

The spread of nationalism had negative as well as positive consequences, however. The emergence of a unified Germany threatened to upset the balance of power that had existed since the Congress of Vienna in 1815, and endangered the dominant role of Great Britain on the continent. In the multinational Austrian and Ottoman empires, nationalism had a divisive rather than a unifying effect. Competing nationalist factions in these empires promoted fragmentation, which sparked conflicts and bloodshed that dramatically affected Europe in the twentieth century.

Unification of Italy

Italy was not a united nation before 1861. Napoleon sparked dreams of national unity, but at the **Congress of Vienna** (see Chapter 5, "The Age of Revolution: The French Revolution and Napoleonic Era"), Prince Klemens von Metternich insisted that Italy be a geographic expression instead of a united nation. The Congress divided the country into the following separate states:

- The rich, northern industrialized provinces of Lombardy and Venetia were ruled by Austria.
- The duchies of Parma, Tuscany, and Modena were under local rulers but controlled by Austria.
- The Papal States in the middle were under Church control.
- The Kingdom of the Two Sicilies, also called Naples, in the southern half of the boot and the poorest section of the country, was under local rulers dominated by Austria.
- The Kingdom of Piedmont-Sardinia, consisting of the northwestern provinces of Nice, Savoy, and Piedmont, was the only independent state in Italy. (It bordered France and Switzerland and is referred to as Sardinia throughout this chapter.)

Between 1815 and 1848, the goal of a united Italy began to appeal to Italians. The **Carbonari** (chimney sweepers) was a secret society organized during the time of Napoleon I and was committed to establishing a united Italian republic. The Carbonari fermented uprisings in 1820, 1821, and 1831, but these revolts were crushed by Austria. After the failure of these revolutions, Italians began to lose faith in the Carbonari. By 1831, most of the Carbonari members had joined the **Young Italy society,** which was instrumental in provoking the uprisings of 1848 throughout Italy.

Map courtesy of *Frommer's Travel Guides.*

Stages of Italian unification.

The revolution of 1848 in Italy also led to hostility with the pope. Prior to the revolution of 1848, **Pope Pius IX** (b. 1792, ruled 1846–1878) was considered a liberal pope who had expressed support for Italian unification. However, his initial support gave way to fear and hostility when someone assassinated his minister. The pope was forced to temporarily flee from Rome when a Republic was proclaimed. Pope Pius IX was restored to power when French military forces were sent to protect him; these troops remained there for the next twenty years. The pope would not only become an opponent of national unity, but also of modernization. In 1864, Pope Pius IX issued *The Syllabus of Errors,* in which he denounced rationalism, liberalism, and modern civilization. He insisted that Catholics should not be aligned with current ideas or progress.

Only in Sardinia did the revolutionists gain any ground when King **Victor Emmanuel II (1820–1878)** granted a liberal constitution to the people in March 1848, complete with elections and parliamentary control of taxes. Thus, to many Italians, Sardinia appeared to be the logical state to achieve the goal of Italian unity.

Italian Nationalists

Desiring to free Italy from Austrian control, the following men were instrumental in promoting **Il Risorgimento,** or Italian unification:

- **Giuseppe Mazzini** (1805–1872) was a writer, an orator, a former member of the Carbonari, and the founder of the Young Italy society in 1831, a non-secret society dedicated to the liberation of Italy. Mazzini is considered the soul of Italian unification. His speeches and pamphlets stirred up the passions of the people for a united Italy with a democratic republic in Italy. In his most widely read book, *The Duties of Man,* he placed a pure duty to the nation between duty to family and duty to God. The failure of the 1848 revolutions forced him to flee from Italy. He continued his fight for freedom from abroad.

- **Giuseppe Garibaldi** (1807–1882) was a friend of Mazzini and also supported a democratic republic. Garibaldi was a military leader who personified the romantic, revolutionary nationalism of Mazzini and had fought in the jungles of Uruguay in that country's struggle for independence. Initially, he organized a guerrilla band of 1,000 **Red Shirts** that conquered Sicily in May 1860. The name "Red Shirts" came about because red was the symbol of revolution. Like Mazzini, Garibaldi supported a democratic republic for a united Italy. He is considered the military leader of Italian unification.

- **Camillo Cavour** (1810–1861) became prime minister of Piedmont-Sardinia in 1852. He strengthened the country by encouraging industrial development, building railroads, fostering education, and freeing the peasants. He sought to make Sardinia the model of a liberal, progressive constitutional government as a way to gain support. He understood that his goal of a united Italy could only be achieved by using force to get Austria out of northern Italy. However, Cavour realized that Sardinia under Victor Emmanuel II could never do it by itself. Cavour sought the support of the international community, especially Napoleon III of France, who believed in the principle of nationality as well as the expansion of France. From 1852 until his death in 1861, Cavour used power politics of war and diplomacy to achieve his goal of unifying Italy.

Steps to Italian Unity

In 1855, Sardinia, led by Cavour, allied with France and Great Britain in the Crimean War against Russia. Although Sardinia gained no territory from the war, Cavour established a rapport with France.

In 1858, Cavour negotiated a secret diplomatic alliance with Napoleon III to aid Sardinia in case Austria attacked it. In July 1859, Cavour goaded Austria into declaring war against Sardinia. With the assistance of Napoleon III, who had been promised Nice and Savoy, Austria was defeated. Napoleon III, however, did an about-face and pulled out of the war because of criticisms at home from French Catholics for supporting a war against Catholic Austria, as well as threats from the Prussians, who had mobilized and expressed sympathy for Austria. Furthermore, a detachment of French troops was still in Rome defending the pope, while the army fought Austria in the North. In July 1859, Napoleon III, without consulting Cavour, signed the Franco-Austria agreement that gave Lombardy to Piedmont but excluded Venetia. Cavour resigned but revolutions continued to spread across Italy. Tuscany, Modena, Parma, and Romagna drove out Austria. Cavour returned in early 1860 and after a plebiscite, he arranged for the annexation of these areas with Sardinia. The northern states, except Venezia, met at Turin, the Piedmontese capital, in 1860. Napoleon III recognized the expanded Kingdom of Sardinia-Piedmont in return for Sardinia's transferring Nice and Savoy to France, where a plebiscite by the people supported annexation to France.

In May 1860, Garibaldi, with his band of 1,000 Red Shirts, landed on the shores of Sicily. Garibaldi's guerrilla band captured the imagination of the Sicilian peasantry and with popular support was able to outwit the 20,000-man royal army. Within months, he had liberated the Kingdom of the Two Sicilies and Naples. He was prepared to attack Rome and the pope.

While Garibaldi conquered the Kingdom of the Two Sicilies, Cavour shrewdly sent Sardinian troops into the Papal States (but not Rome). Rome was protected by French troops and Cavour did not want to antagonize Napoleon III. Fearing Garibaldi's popular appeal, Cavour organized a plebiscite in the conquered territories; however, Garibaldi put aside his republican sentiments and did not oppose Cavour. The people of the Kingdom of the Two Sicilies voted to join Sardinia. In March 1861, Victor Emmanuel II was proclaimed the king of Italy—Cavour had succeeded.

The new Kingdom of Italy did not include Venetia or Rome. Venetia was ceded to Italy in 1866 and Rome was annexed in 1870 and designated as the capital of Italy in 1871. From 1870 to 1929, the pope adopted a policy of self-imprisonment on the Vatican grounds. In the **Lateran Treaty of 1929,** Italy recognized the existence of **Vatican City,** about a square mile in area, as an independent state and the pope as its sovereign leader. The treaty also made Catholicism the state religion in Italy and established a annual sum of money paid to the Vatican to compensate it for territorial losses. Italy was a parliamentary democracy but only a small minority of Italian males had the right to vote. Relations between the new government and the Church were strained. The pope had forbidden Catholics to participate in the new government, a ban that was not lifted until 1912.

Regional divisions still existed in Italy, despite unification. The industrial North had little in common with the agrarian South whose population was booming, and whose illiterate peasants were still dominated by large landowners. Living standards were low in the South and the government encouraged Italians to migrate to Canada, South America, and the United States. Italians entered the twentieth century with the hope of trying to play the role of a great world power, but the country's dire economic position would not allow it to realize its dreams. This frustration would dominate Italian society for many years.

Unification of Germany

Nationalism in the German states developed gradually in the 1800s. Napoleon had unintentionally aided its growth by abolishing the Holy Roman Empire and reducing the more than 300 German states to about 100. The Congress of Vienna in 1815 reduced the number of German states even further to 39 and organized them into the German **Confederation,** a weak body dominated by Austria. The failure of the Confederation to provide effective leadership stirred German nationalists to seek unity by other means. German unification was also helped by the following:

- The formation of the **Zollverein** in 1834, a German customs union under the leadership of Prussia. All of the German states except Austria were joined into a single economic union, similar to the European Common Market, which promoted free trade among the member states and maintained high tariffs against non-member states.
- The **Prussian aristocracy,** or **Junkers** (meaning "young master" of a noble family), began to support the efforts of the **Hohenzollerns,** the ruling dynasty of Prussia, in their efforts to lead the struggle for German unification.

There were obstacles to German unification, however:

- **Prussia,** with its booming industrial economy and militaristic Junker class, aroused the opposition of Austria and other German states in the South. These southern German states were agricultural and Catholic, unlike the northern states, which were predominately Protestant and led by Prussia.
- **France** viewed a unified Germany as a potential threat to its leadership in Europe. France also believed that a divided Germany would make France more militarily secure.

German Nationalists

The unsuccessful revolts of 1848 and the rise of industrialism in Germany contributed to the vigorous growth of a nationalist movement that had the support of the growing middle class and city workers. The failure of the Frankfurt Assembly in 1848 also paved the way for unification under autocratic and antidemocratic leadership. The leaders of German unification were:

- **Otto von Bismarck** (1815–1898), who became chief minister of Prussia in 1862. He was a Junker and a member of the conservative landowning class. Bismarck despised democracy and claimed that Germany could only be united "by blood and iron," not by speeches. Determined to avoid the blunders of 1848, Bismarck emphasized the importance of the military and was a master of power politics. He believed that the end justified the means, yet he was flexible and very pragmatic.
- **Wilhelm I** (ruled 1861–1888), who was the king of Prussia, and who became emperor in 1871. He fully supported Bismarck's policies that led to the formation of a unified German Empire.
- **Helmuth von Moltke** (1800–1891), who was a Prussian general and chief of staff. He built up a strong army and navy that enabled Bismarck to achieve success.

Steps to German Unification

The Rise of Prussian Military Power

In 1861, the Prussian parliament refused to grant the military budget that Bismarck and Wilhelm I requested. Many in Parliament were liberals who wanted Parliament to have control over government policies. These men did not like professional armies and they considered the Prussian Junkers, from whom the official corps were recruited, as their main rivals to the state government. Wilhelm I wanted to increase the efficiency of the army and make it the strongest in the world. Bismarck, also known as the **Iron Chancellor,** secured funds by ignoring the constitution and the legislature. He collected taxes and ruled illegally until 1866 when the Prussian Parliament sanctioned his actions.

The Danish War (1864)

Denmark's attempt to annex Schleswig-Holstein, which was largely inhabited by Germans, led to an alliance with Austria. Denmark was quickly defeated by Prussia, Holstein was given to Austria, and Schleswig was given to Prussia. Prussia and Austria disagreed over the administration of these provinces. This set the stage for the next step in Bismarck's plan.

Austro-Prussian War (1866)

Austria and Prussia's quarrels over the administration of Schleswig and Holstein included issues such as who should keep internal order and who should have the right of passage. Bismarck was able to provoke Austria into declaring war on Prussia. The Austro-Prussian War was also known as the **Seven Weeks' War** because the efficient Prussian army, under General Helmuth von Moltke, quickly crushed the Austrian forces. Realizing that Prussia might need Austria for an inevitable conflict with France, Bismarck granted lenient peace terms. Austria had to pay a small indemnity and recognize Prussia's dominance of the German states.

In 1867, Bismarck dissolved the German Confederation. Prussia and 21 other German states formed the **North German Confederation,** ruled by the Prussian king and a bicameral legislature. The bicameral legislature was composed of the lower house (the **Reichstag**), which represented all the people elected by universal male suffrage, and the upper house (the **Bundesrat**), which represented the German states. Bismarck, being practical and wanting to avoid any desire for revenge on the part of Austria, allowed Austria and the four southern states to remain independent. However, these four states were tied to Prussia by the Zollverein and by a defensive military alliance.

Franco-Prussian War (1870–1871)

Realizing that only a war could get the southern states to join the Northern Confederation, Bismarck provoked a war with France. The immediate cause was a dispute over the Spanish throne. When Prince Leopold, a relative of the Prussian king, became a candidate for the throne, Napoleon III protested. The French minister went to Ems to talk to Wilhelm I, who refused to settle the dispute. Wilhelm sent a telegram to Bismarck informing him of his decision, and Bismarck edited the telegraph so as to make it insulting to the French. Napoleon III declared war on Prussia in July 1870, and by September, the Emperor was captured and the French forces had been defeated. Unlike his treatment of Austria in the Austro-Prussian War, Bismarck treated France harshly, bringing Paris to submission by starving the city for over five months. By the **Treaty of Frankfurt** in May 1871, France ceded Alsace and Lorraine to Germany and agreed to pay a huge indemnity to Germany. The harshness of the treaty laid the foundation of hate and anger that would poison Franco-German relations for the next generation, and planted the seeds for World War I.

German Empire

As Bismarck expected, the four southern Catholic states, delighted by the victory over France, joined the Prussian-dominated North German Confederation. The **German Empire** was officially announced at Versailles in January 1871 with Bismarck as **Chancellor** and Wilhelm I as Emperor or **Kaiser.**

The German Empire was a federation of monarchies, a union of 25 German states, in which Prussia dominated. Although the Reichstag was popularly elected, real power remained in the hands of the Kaiser and the Chancellor. The Kaiser was not a figurehead, but instead commanded the armed forces, conducted foreign affairs, and appointed his choices to major government positions. The Chancellor (prime minister) and other cabinet members were responsible to the Kaiser, not the legislature.

In the German Empire, autocracy, not democracy, was the real form of government. As Chancellor, Bismarck pursued a policy that was conservative and nationalistic. In 1872, Bismarck launched his **Kulturkampf,** "the battle for civilization." His goal was to make Catholics put loyalty to the state above the Church. Bismarck's move against the Catholic Church backfired, however. Catholics rallied behind the Church, and the **Catholic Center Party** gained strength. Being a realist, Bismarck made peace with the Church. Bismarck also saw a threat to the new Germany in the growing power of the Socialists. In 1878, Bismarck tried to suppress the Socialists by securing laws that forbade Socialist meetings and subjected their leaders to arrest. His efforts failed and made the Socialists even more popular. Again, Bismarck changed his course, and between 1883 and 1889 secured the passage of social insurance programs, such as workmen's compensation, old age insurance, and sickness benefits that set an example for other industrial countries.

In 1888, **Wilhelm II** (b. 1859, ruled 1888–1918) became Kaiser. He was a strong defender of Divine Right and of autocracy in government. When he and Bismarck disagreed over policies in 1890, Bismarck was dismissed. Wilhelm II's rule was autocratic and his nationalist program helped lead to World War I.

Crisis in the Multinational Empires

The Austrian-Hungarian Empire

The rising spirit of nationalism in Europe directly affected the Austrian Empire, which was a multinational empire consisting of over 20 million people. Although less than one-third were German speaking (the Austrians), they were the dominant nationality and held leading positions in the government. The Hapsburgs, the empire's ruling family, were also Austrian. The other subjected nationalities in the empire included Hungarians (or Magyars), Czechs, Slovaks, Poles, Serbs, Croats, and Slovenes. Emperor **Francis Joseph I** (b. 1830, ruled 1848–1916) realized that the government had to make some reforms; throughout the 1850s, he tried hard to centralize the state and Germanize the language and culture of the different nationalities. Austria's efforts to repress its nationalities depleted its military strength, however. Her humiliating defeat against France and Sardinia in 1859 forced her to give up territory in Italy, and her disastrous defeat in 1866 in the war with Prussia brought renewed pressure for reforms.

To buttress the empire, Austria was forced to grant equal partnership with the Hungarians. The **Ausgleich,** or **Compromise of 1867,** established the **Dual Monarchy** under which Austria and Hungary were separate states, each having its own parliament and legislature. The two states were joined together under the leadership of Francis Joseph I, who became the Emperor of Austria and King of Hungary. Each half of the empire agreed to deal with its own nationalities as it saw fit. The chief problem for the empire was the question of governing the many nationalities and the many different minorities. Croats and Romanians in the Hungarian domains were oppressed even more than before the Ausgleich. By 1900, nationalist discontent had left the government paralyzed, especially in the Balkan regions.

The Ottoman Empire

The Ottoman Empire also was multinational in scope, extending from Eastern Europe and the Balkans to North Africa and the Middle East. The empire included Arabs in the Middle East, southern Slavs, Albanians, Romanians, Bulgarians, and Greeks in the Balkans. In the Balkans, Serbs had won their autonomy in 1829 and the Greeks their independence in 1830.

Many Serbs and Greeks still lived in the Balkans under Ottoman control, however. Other nationalist groups, such as the Bulgarians and the Romanians, wanted their independence. These nationalist stirrings became tied up with the ambitions of European powers. European countries, such as Great Britain, France, and Russia, sought to benefit from the "sick man of Europe," a term used because since the loss of Hungary in 1699, the Ottoman Empire had entered on a long process of territorial disintegration. Russia wanted the Dardanelles, which would provide access to the Mediterranean. Britain opposed these ambitions, while France, after gaining Algiers, sought additional territory.

The crumbling Ottoman Empire forced many moderate Ottoman statesmen to reform the empire on the European model. During the 1830s, reform, known as the **Tanzimat** or Reorganization, was introduced, calling for equality before the law for Jews, Muslims, and Christians, as well as modernizing the economy and the military. The Tanzimat reforms did not bring about revolutionary changes, however, nor did they halt the growth of nationalism. The adoption of western ideas, moreover, disturbed many conservative Muslims who saw them as a departure from Islamic tradition and holy laws. These Islamic conservatives became the supporters of **Sultan Abdülhamid** (b. 1842, ruled 1876–1909), who abandoned the European model and tried to rebuild the autocratic power of the earlier rulers. His repressive policies of intolerance towards minorities in the empire also led to the brutal genocide of the **Armenians,** a Christian people in the mountainous regions of the empire.

In 1878, when the Ottoman Empire was forced to grant independence to Serbia, Montenegro, Bulgaria, and Rumania, a group of reformers (mostly composed of army officers) known as the **Young Turks** insisted that the only way to save the empire was to change the government by establishing a constitutional monarchy and modernizing the military. In 1908, the Young Turks overthrew the Sultan and forced him to implement these reforms. Their efforts, however, were unable to stop the rising tide of nationalism in the Balkans that plunged Europe into war in 1914 and ultimately destroyed the remnants of the Ottoman Empire.

Chronology of the Age of Nationalism in Europe

1831	Young Italy society, a nationalist youth organization, is founded by Mazzini.
1834	The Zollverein, a German customs union, is formed.
1848	The Frankfurt Assembly meets in order to create a unified constitutional German state; revolutions break out across Italy.
1848	Pope Pius IX flees Rome after one of his ministers is assassinated.
1852	Camillo Benso, Count of Cavour, becomes prime minister of the Kingdom of Sardinia.
1859	Cavour tricks Austria into declaring war upon Sardinia.
1860	Giuseppe Garibaldi and his Red Shirts invade Sicily.
1861	Italy becomes unified under Victor Emmanuel II, excluding Rome and Venetia.
1862	Otto von Bismarck becomes chief minister of Prussia.
1864	During the Danish War, Prussia allies with Austria to prevent Denmark from annexing Schleswig-Holstein.
1864	Pope Pius IX issues *The Syllabus of Errors,* warning all Catholics against the dangers of liberalism.
1866	Bismarck provokes Austria into fighting the Austro-Prussian War; Prussian troops easily win the Seven Weeks' War; Venetia is added to the Kingdom of Italy.
1867	The Ausgleich, a compromise establishing a dual monarchy in Austro-Hungary, is created.
1870–1871	The Franco-Prussian War begins and ends.
	The German Empire is established after the conclusion of a peace treaty with France.
1872	Bismarck launches the Kulturkampf, an attack against Catholics.
1878	The Congress of Berlin sets ground rules for imperialism and grants independence to Serbia, Montenegro, and Romania, weakening the Ottoman Empire.
1890	Bismarck is dismissed as chancellor.
1890	The Young Turks organize to modernize the Ottoman Empire.
1908	The Young Turk Revolution takes place in the Ottoman Empire.

Sample Multiple-Choice Questions

1. Which of the Italian states was independent in 1850?

   A. The Kingdom of the Two Sicilies
   B. Piedmont-Sardinia
   C. Venetia
   D. Parma
   E. Papal States

2. Who is considered the architect and the diplomatic force behind Italian unification?

   A. Cavour
   B. Mazzini
   C. Garibaldi
   D. Victor Emmanuel II
   E. Gioberti

3. On which of the following did Mazzini and Garibaldi agree?

   A. United Italy should be a constitutional monarchy.
   B. United Italy should be a democratic republic.
   C. United Italy should be ruled by a dictatorship.
   D. The pope should be the leader of a united Italy.
   E. Foreign assistance was necessary to drive Austria from Italy.

4. The Zollverein (1834) was designed to do which of the following?

   A. Promote the interests of the Junkers.
   B. Create a uniform currency.
   C. Establish a large standing army.
   D. Set up a customs union to promote free trade.
   E. Set up an "all German Parliament."

5. Which of the following presented the greatest obstacle to unification of Italy and Germany?

   A. The middle class
   B. The papacy
   C. The landed aristocracy of each country
   D. Great Britain
   E. Austria

6. Bismarck's Kulturkampf in Germany was directed against

   A. liberals.
   B. the middle class.
   C. the Catholic Church.
   D. Socialists.
   E. Prussian landowners.

7. The Ausgleich was established by the Austrian government in 1867 to grant equal partnership to which of the following groups?

   A. Serbs
   B. Croats
   C. Magyars (Hungarians)
   D. Germans
   E. Italians

8. The "sick man of Europe," which European powers wanted to preserve, referred to

   A. the Russian Empire.
   B. the Austrian Empire.
   C. the Second French Empire.
   D. the German Empire.
   E. the Ottoman Empire.

9. Which of the following statements is most accurate about German unification in 1871?

   A. Austria was the chief architect.
   B. France supported unification.
   C. Russia was instrumental in providing military assistance.
   D. German unification was accomplished by democratic and liberal methods.
   E. Prussia used military methods and autocratic rule to unite Germany.

10. After the revolutions of 1848, who became an obstacle to the unification of Italy?

   A. Bismarck of Prussia
   B. Napoleon III
   C. Pope Pius IX
   D. Giuseppe Garibaldi
   E. Victor Emmanuel II

Multiple-Choice Questions: Answers and Explanations

1. **B.** Piedmont-Sardinia was the only independent Italian state in 1850. Piedmont-Sardinia took the lead in the process of unification. At the Congress of Vienna, Metternich was determined to keep Italy united merely as "a geographic expression." The kingdoms of Parma and the Two Sicilies were under local rulers controlled by Austria. Austria annexed Venetia, and the Papal States were under Church control.

2. **A.** Cavour is considered the diplomatic force behind Italian unification. Cavour became prime minister of Piedmont-Sardinia in 1852. He realized that he could not unify northern Italy without the help of France. Through a series of diplomatic maneuvers, he secured the help of Napoleon III for the war against Austria and seized on the nationalist fever in central Italy to get Parma, Modena, and Tuscany to vote for annexation to Piedmont-Sardinia. Cavour was also shrewd in getting Garibaldi to offer his conquests to Victor Emmanuel II, securing the unification of northern and southern Italy. Mazzini is considered the soul of Italian unification. Mazzini was forced into exile after the failure of the revolutions in Italy after 1848. Garibaldi was a military leader. Victor Emmanuel II was the first king of a united Italy. Gioberti was a Catholic priest who wanted a federation of Italian states under the presidency of the pope.

3. **B.** Mazzini and Garibaldi believed that Italy should be united as a democratic republic. In 1831, Giuseppe Mazzini founded Young Italy. The goal of this society was to make Italy one free, independent, democratic republican nation.

   From 1848 to 1849, Mazzini helped set up a republic in Rome but French forces crushed it. Garibaldi, a disciple of Mazzini, also wanted to create a republic. Garibaldi defended Mazzini's Roman Republic against the French in 1849. Neither Mazzini nor Garibaldi believed in a constitutional monarchy or a dictatorship. They were anticlerical and wanted to seize control of the Papal States. Neither of them thought foreign assistance was necessary to help drive Austria from Italy.

4. **D.** The Zollverein was a customs union designed to promote free trade among member nations. Under Prussian leadership, it was found to stimulate trade and increase revenues of member states. The Zollverein excluded Austria. The Junkers were the landowning aristocracy of Prussia. The Zollverein dealt only with free trade, not the establishment of a uniform currency, a large standing army, or an all-German Parliament.

5. **E.** Austria ruled the industrial provinces of Lombardy and Venetia. Italian nationalist leaders like Cavour and Garibaldi realized that a united Italy could only be achieved by forcing Austria out of northern Italy. In Germany, Austria resented the rise of Prussia as well as the efforts by Otto von Bismarck of Prussia to unify Germany. The Austro-Prussian War, or the Seven Weeks' War, established dominance of Prussia among the German states. The middle class in Germany and Italy did not oppose unification. The papacy opposed unification in Italy but was not an important influence in Germany. The landed aristocracy of each country did not oppose unification because there was not any effort to change the social order in either country. Great Britain supported Italian unification and feared a strong Germany, but unlike France, did not make any effort to prevent unification. France believed that a united Germany would be a direct threat to its national interest.

6. **C.** Kulturkampf was directed against the Catholic Church. Bismarck had laws passed that gave the state the right to supervise Catholics and approve the appointment of priests. Bismarck did not attack the liberals whom he had already won over by his unification of Germany. Nor did he attack the middle class or the Prussian landowners who had supported him since he became chancellor. Bismarck did attack the Socialists but that was not known as Kulturkampf. Bismarck's social welfare measures were an attempt to win the support of the working class from the Socialist Party.

7. **C.** The Ausgleich in 1867 granted equal partnership to the Magyars (Hungarians). Austria and Hungary were joined together under the leadership of Francis Joseph I. The Serbs, Croats, and Italians were different nationalities living in areas that were considered part of the Austrian-Hungarian Empire.

8. **E.** The term "sick man of Europe" was used to describe the feeble Ottoman Empire over the 100-year period from 1815 to 1914. In the 1800s, Europeans were eager to divide up the Ottoman lands. Russia wanted the Dardanelles, and Austria-Hungary took the provinces of Bosnia and Herzegovina, angering Serbia, which wanted the area. However, England and France sought to preserve the empire because they feared a general European war if the empire collapsed. The Ottoman Empire became a pawn among the powerful European nations. The Russian and Austrian empires had internal problems but each of them played an active role on the diplomatic scene in Europe during the nineteenth century. The Second French Empire of Napoleon III had a short life from 1852 to 1871. The German Empire began in 1871 and played an important role on the European continent from 1871 until 1918 when Germany was defeated in World War I.

9. **E.** In 1848, Otto von Bismarck, who was Prussia's chief minister and later Chancellor from 1862 to 1871, believed that Germany could only be united by "Blood and Iron," meaning military power. Bismarck did not believe in democracy. In a series of wars, he eliminated Austria as a factor in German unification and united north and south Germany by the Franco-Prussian War. Austria and France opposed unification of Germany. Austria feared a loss of influence and France wanted Germany as a weak, disunited neighbor. Russia played no major role in the unification of Germany. Bismarck skillfully used diplomacy to keep Russia friendly toward Germany. Bismarck rejected democracy and liberal methods to unite Germany.

10. **C.** After 1848, Pope Pius IX was an obstacle to the unification of Italy. Initially known as "the liberal pope," he rejected unification after he was temporarily driven from Rome during the upheavals of 1848. For many generations, the papacy would oppose national unification as well as modern trends. In 1864, Pope Pius IX, in *The Syllabus of Errors,* denounced liberalism and modern civilization. Bismarck and Cavour were allied in the Seven Weeks' War against Austria. By the peace treaty, Austria ceded Venetia to Italy. Napoleon III joined forces with Cavour to help Piedmont defeat Austria. Garibaldi secured the Kingdom of the Two Sicilies that helped unite northern and southern Italy. Victor Emmanuel II was the first king of united Italy.

The Age of Imperialism (1870–1914)

Although the Industrial Revolution and nationalism shaped European society in the nineteenth century, imperialism—the domination by one country or people over another group of people—dramatically changed the world during the latter half of that century.

Imperialism did not begin in the nineteenth century. From the sixteenth to the early nineteenth century, an era dominated by what is now termed **Old Imperialism,** European nations sought trade routes with the Far East, explored the New World, and established settlements in North and South America as well as in Southeast Asia. They set up trading posts and gained footholds on the coasts of Africa and China, and worked closely with the local rulers to ensure the protection of European economic interests. Their influence, however, was limited. In the **Age of New Imperialism** that began in the 1870s, European states established vast empires mainly in Africa, but also in Asia and the Middle East.

Unlike the sixteenth- and seventeenth-century method of establishing settlements, the new imperialists set up the administration of the native areas for the benefit of the colonial power. European nations pursued an aggressive expansion policy that was motivated by economic needs that were created by the Industrial Revolution. Between 1870 and 1914, Europe went through a "Second Industrial Revolution," which quickened the pace of change as science, technology, and industry spurred economic growth. Improvements in steel production revolutionized shipbuilding and transportation. The development of the railroad, the internal combustion engine, and electrical power generation contributed to the growing industrial economies of Europe and their need to seek new avenues of expansion.

The expansion policy was also motivated by political needs that associated empire building with national greatness, and social and religious reasons that promoted the superiority of Western society over "backward" societies. Through the use of direct military force, economic spheres of influence, and annexation, European countries dominated the continents of Africa and Asia. By 1914, Great Britain controlled the largest number of colonies, and the phrase, "the sun never sets on the British Empire," described the vastness of its holdings. Imperialism had consequences that affected the colonial nations, Europe, and the world. It also led to increased competition among nations and to conflicts that would disrupt world peace in 1914.

Old Imperialism

European imperialism did not begin in the 1800s. In their efforts to find a direct trade route to Asia during the age of Old Imperialism, European nations established colonies in the Americas, India, South Africa, and the East Indies, and gained territory along the coasts of Africa and China. Meanwhile, Europe's Commercial Revolution created new needs and desires for wealth and raw materials. Mercantilists maintained that colonies could serve as a source of wealth, while personal motives by rulers, statesmen, explorers, and missionaries supported the imperial belief in "Glory, God, and Gold." By 1800, Great Britain was the leading colonial power with colonies in India, South Africa, and Australia. Spain colonized Central and South America. France held Louisiana and French Guinea, and Holland built an empire in the East Indies.

In the first half of the nineteenth century, colonialism became less popular. The Napoleonic Wars, the struggle for nationalism and democracy, and the cost of industrialization exhausted the energies of European nations. Many leaders also thought that the costs to their respective empires outweighed the benefits, especially the cost of supervising the colonies. However, in the mid-nineteenth century, Europe—especially Great Britain and France— began an economic revival. During the Victorian Era, which lasted from 1837 to 1901, Great Britain became an industrial giant, providing more than 25 percent of the world's output of industrial goods. In France, Napoleon's investment in industry and large-scale ventures, such as railroad building, helped to promote prosperity. Thus the Industrial Revolution stirred ambitions in many European countries and renewed their confidence to embark on a path of aggressive expansion overseas.

New Imperialism

From the late 1800s through the early 1900s, Western Europe pursued a policy of imperialism that became known as New Imperialism. This New Imperialist Age gained its impetus from economic, military, political, humanitarian, and religious reasons, as well as from the development and acceptance of a new theory—Social Darwinism—and advances in technology.

Economic Reasons

By 1870, it became necessary for European industrialized nations to expand their markets globally in order to sell products that they could not sell domestically on the continent. Businessmen and bankers had excess capital to invest, and foreign investments offered the incentive of greater profits, despite the risks. The need for cheap labor and a steady supply of raw materials, such as oil, rubber, and manganese for steel, required that the industrial nations maintain firm control over these unexplored areas. Only by directly controlling these regions, which meant setting up colonies under their direct control, could the industrial economy work effectively—or so the imperialists thought. The economic gains of the new imperialism were limited, however, because the new colonies were too poor to spend money on European goods.

Military and Political Reasons

Leading European nations also felt that colonies were crucial to military power, national security, and nationalism. Military leaders claimed that a strong navy was necessary in order to become a great power. Thus, naval vessels needed military bases around the world to take on coal and supplies. Islands or harbors were seized to satisfy these needs. Colonies guaranteed the growing European navies safe harbors and coaling stations, which they needed in time of war. National security was an important reason for Great Britain's decision to occupy Egypt. Protecting the Suez Canal was vital for the British Empire. The **Suez Canal,** which formally opened in 1869, shortened the sea route from Europe to South Africa and East Asia. To Britain, the canal was a lifeline to India, the jewel of its empire. Many people were also convinced that the possession of colonies was an indication of a nation's greatness; colonies were status symbols. According to nineteenth-century German historian, Heinrich von Treitschke, all great nations should want to conquer barbarian nations.

Humanitarian and Religious Goals

Many Westerners believed that Europe should civilize their little brothers beyond the seas. According to this view, non-whites would received the blessings of Western civilization, including medicine, law, and Christianity. **Rudyard Kipling** (1865–1936) in his famous poem, "The White Man's Burden" expressed this mission in the 1890s when he prodded Europeans to take up "their moral obligation" to civilize the uncivilized. He encouraged them to "Send forth the best ye breed to serve your captives' need." Missionaries supported colonization, believing that European control would help them spread Christianity, the true religion, in Asia and Africa.

Social Darwinism

In 1859, **Charles Darwin** (1809–1882) published *On the Origin of Species*. Darwin claimed that all life had evolved into the present state over millions of years. To explain the long slow process of evolution, Darwin put forth the theory of *natural selection*. Natural forces selected those with physical traits best adapted to their environment. Darwin never promoted any social ideas. The process of natural selection came to be known as *survival of the fittest*. The Englishman Herbert Spencer (1820–1903) was the first to apply "survival of the fittest" to human societies and nations. **Social Darwinism** fostered imperialistic expansion by proposing that some people were more fit (advanced) than others. The Europeans believed that they, as the white race, were dominant and that it was only natural for them to conquer the "inferior" people as nature's way of improving mankind. Thus, the conquest of inferior people was just, and the destruction of the weaker races was nature's natural law.

Western Technology

Superior technology and improved medical knowledge helped to foster imperialism. Quinine enabled Europeans to survive tropical diseases and venture into the mosquito-infested interiors of Africa and Asia. The combination of the steamboat and the telegraph enabled the Western powers to increase their mobility and to quickly respond to any situations that threatened their dominance. The rapid-fire machine gun also gave them a military advantage and was helpful in convincing Africans and Asians to accept Western control. The following table summarizes the causes of the new imperialism:

Causes of New Imperialism			
Economic	**Military/Political**	**Humanitarian/Religious**	**Technological**
Need for markets	Need for military bases	White man's burden	New medicine
Raw materials	National security	Spread of Christianity	New weapons
Source of investments	Source of pride—nationalism	Social Darwinism (superiority of Western society)	Transportation

Imperialism in Africa

Africa was known as the **Dark Continent** and remained unknown to the outside world until the late nineteenth century because its interior—desert, mountains, plateaus, and jungles—discouraged exploration. Britain's occupation of Egypt and Belgium's penetration of the Congo started the race for colonial possessions in Africa.

Suez Canal

In 1875, Britain purchased a controlling interest in the **Suez Canal** from the bankrupt ruler of Egypt who was unable to repay loans that he had contracted for the canal and modernization. of the country. The French, who organized the building of the Suez Canal under Ferdinand de Lesseps in 1859, owned the other shares. The Suez Canal was important because it shortened the route from Europe to South and East Asia. The canal also provided a lifeline to India, which Britain had made part of the British Empire in 1858. In 1882, Britain established a protectorate over Egypt, which meant that the government leaders were officials of the Ottoman Empire, but were really controlled by Great Britain. The British occupation of Egypt, the richest and most developed land in Africa, set off "African fever" in Europe. To ensure its domination and stability in the area, Great Britain extended its control over the Sudan as well.

Exploration of the Congo

In 1878, **Leopold II of Belgium** (b. 1835, ruled 1865–1909) sent Anglo-American newspaperman **Henry Stanley** (1841–1904), to explore the Congo and establish trade agreements with leaders in the Congo River basin. Stanley, in 1871, had "found" the great Scottish explorer and missionary **David Livingstone** (1813–1873), who had traveled throughout Africa for over thirty years. When several years passed without a word from him, it was feared that he was dead. Stanley was hired in 1869 by the *New York Herald,* an American newspaper to find Livingstone. His famous greeting, "Dr. Livingstone, I presume" became legendary, even though there is some question about its authenticity. Stanley's account of their meeting made headlines around the world and helped make him famous. Stanley eventually sold his services to Leopold II, who had formed a financial syndicate entitled **The International African Association.** A strong-willed monarch, Leopold II's intrusion into the Congo area raised questions about the political fate of Africa south of the Sahara. Other European nations were fearful that Belgium wanted to extend control over the entire area.

The Scramble for Africa

Otto von Bismarck (1815–1898), Chancellor of Germany, and **Jules Ferry** (1832–1893), Premier of France and considered the builder of the modern French Empire, organized an international conference in Berlin to lay down the basic rules for colonizing Africa. The **Berlin Conference** (1884–1885) established the principle that European occupation of African territory had to be based on effective occupation that was recognized by other states, and that no single European power could claim Africa. The Berlin Conference led to the "Scramble for Africa." Between 1878 and 1914, European powers divided up the entire African continent except for the independent countries of Ethiopia and Liberia. Liberia was settled by free slaves from the United States and became an independent republic in 1847. Ethiopia, which was already independent, routed an Italian invasion in 1896. Defeating the Italians assured that the country would stay independent. European countries divided Africa as follows:

France

The French had the largest colonial empire in Africa, over 3 ½ million square miles, half of which contained the Sahara Desert. In 1830, France had conquered Algeria in North Africa. Between 1881 and 1912, France acquired Tunisia, Morocco, West Africa, and Equatorial Africa. At its height, the French Empire in Africa was as large as the continental United States.

Great Britain

Britain's holdings in Africa were not as large as France's but it controlled the more populated regions, particularly of southern Africa, which contained valuable mineral resources such as diamonds and gold. In 1806, the British displaced Holland in South Africa and ruled the Cape Colony. However, the British soon came into conflict with the **Boers** (farmers), the original Dutch settlers who resented British rule. In the 1830s, the Boers left British territory, migrated north, and founded two republics—the Orange Free State and Transvaal. The Boers soon came into conflict with the powerful **Zulus,** a native-African ethnic group, for control of the land. When the Zulus and the Boers were unable to win a decisive victory, the British became involved in The Zulu Wars and eventually destroyed the Zulu empire. In 1890, **Cecil Rhodes** (1853–1902)**,** who was born in Great Britain and had become a diamond mine millionaire, became prime minister of the Cape Colony. He wanted to extend the British African Empire from Cape Town to Cairo and decided to annex the Boer Republic. In the **Boer War** (1899–1902), the British, with great difficulty, defeated the Boers and annexed the two republics. In 1910, Britain combined its South African colonies into the Union of South Africa. Whites ran the government, and the Boers, who outnumbered the British, assumed control. This system laid the foundation for racial segregation that would last until the 1990s.

Germany

Late unification delayed Germany's imperialistic ventures, but it also wanted its place in the sun. Germany took land in eastern and southwestern Africa.

Italy

Italy was another late entry into the imperialistic venture. Italy took control of Libya, Italian Somaliland, and Eritrea, which is the north-most province of Ethiopia, near the Red Sea. Italy's efforts to gain control of Ethiopia ended in bitter defeat.

Portugal

Portugal carved out large colonies in Angola and Mozambique.

Imperialism in Asia

India

The British took control of India in 1763, after defeating the French in the **Seven Years' War** (1756–1763). The British controlled India through the **British East India Company,** which ruled with an iron hand. In 1857, an Indian revolt, led by native soldiers called *sepoys,* led to an uprising known as the **Sepoy Mutiny.** After suppressing the rebellion, the British government made India part of the empire in 1858, as mentioned previously. The British introduced social reforms, advocated education, and promoted technology. Britain profited greatly from India, which was called the "Crown Jewel of the British Empire." The Indian masses, however, continued to live close to starvation and the British had little respect for the native Indian culture.

The Dutch held the Dutch East Indies and extended their control over Indonesia, while the French took over Indochina (Cambodia, Laos, and Vietnam). The Russians also got involved and extended their control over the area of Persia (Iran).

China

Since the seventeenth century, China had isolated itself from the rest of the world and refused to adopt Western ways. The Chinese permitted trade but only at the Port of Canton, where the rights of European merchants were at the whim of the emperor. Imperialism in China began with the **First Opium War** (1839–1842), when the Chinese government tried to halt the British from importing opium. This resulted in a war in which Britain's superior military and industrial might easily destroyed the Chinese military forces. The **Treaty of Nanking** (1842) opened up five ports to the British, gave Britain the island of Hong Kong, and forced China to pay a large indemnity. In 1858, China was forced to open up eleven more treaty ports that granted special privileges, such as the right to trade with the interior of China and the right to supervise the Chinese custom offices. Foreigners also received the right of extraterritoriality, which meant that Western nations maintained their own courts in China and Westerners were tried in their own courts.

Between 1870 and 1914, the Western nations carved China into spheres of influence, areas in which outside powers claimed exclusive trading rights. France acquired territory in southwestern China, Germany gained the Shandong Peninsula in northern China, Russia obtained control of Manchuria and a leasehold over Port Arthur, and the British took control of the Yangzi valley. The United States, which had not taken part in carving up China because it feared that spheres of influence might hurt U.S. commerce, promoted the **Open Door Policy** in 1899. **John Hay,** the American Secretary of State, proposed that equal trading rights to China be allowed for all nations and that the territorial integrity of China be respected. The imperial nations accepted this policy in principle but not always in practice. For the United States, however, the Open Door Policy became the cornerstone of its Chinese policy at the beginning of the twentieth century.

By the 1900s, China was in turmoil. There was rising sentiment against foreigners because China had been forced to give up so many political and economic rights. This anti-foreign sentiment exploded into the **Boxer Rebellion** or **Uprising** (1899–1901). The **Boxers** were a secret Chinese nationalist society supported by the Manchu government, and their goal was to drive out all foreigners and restore China to isolation. In June 1900, the Boxers launched a series of attacks against foreigners and Chinese Christians. They also attacked the foreign embassies in Beijing. The imperialistic powers sent an international force of 25,000 troops to crush the rebellion, which ended within two weeks.

The Boxer Rebellion failed, but it convinced the Chinese that reforms were necessary. In 1911, revolutions broke out across the country and the Manchu emperor was overthrown. **Dr. Sun Yat-Sen** (1866–1925), the father of modern China, proclaimed a republic and was named the new president. He advocated a three-point program of nationalism (freeing China from imperial control); democracy (elected government officials); and livelihood (adapting Western industrial and agricultural methods). The Chinese republic faced many problems and for the next thirty-seven years, China would continue to be at war with itself and with foreign invaders.

Japan

Japan was the only Asian country that did not become a victim of imperialism. In the seventeenth and eighteenth centuries, the Japanese expelled Europeans from Japan and closed Japanese ports to trade with the outside world, allowing only the Dutch to trade at Nagasaki. In 1853, **Commodore Matthew Perry** (1866–1925), an American naval officer, led an expedition to Japan. He convinced the *shogun,* a medieval-type ruler, to open ports for trade with the United States. Fearful of domination by foreign countries, Japan, unlike China, reversed its policy of isolation and began to modernize by borrowing from the West. The **Meiji Restoration,** which began in 1867, sought to replace the feudal rulers, or the shogun, and increase the power of the emperor. The goal was to make Japan strong enough to compete with the West. The new leaders strengthened the military and transformed Japan into an industrial society. The Japanese adopted a constitution based on the Prussian model with the emperor as the head. The government was not intended to promote democracy but to unite Japan and make it equal to the West. The leaders built up a modern army based on a draft and constructed a fleet of iron steamships.

The Japanese were so successful that they became an imperial power. In the Sino-Japanese War of 1894–95, Japan defeated China and forced her to give up her claims in Korea. Japan also gained control of its first colonies—Taiwan and the Pescadores Islands—and shocked the world by defeating Russia in the **Russo-Japanese War** of 1904–1905. Japan's victory was the first time that an Asian country had defeated a European power in over 200 years.

Imperialism in the Middle East

The importance of the Middle East to the new imperialists was its strategic location (the crossroads of three continents: Europe, Asia, and Africa), vital waterways (canals and the Dardanelles), and valuable oil resources. The Europeans divided up the Middle East in the following manner:

- **Great Britain:** Britain's control of the Suez Canal forced her to take an active role in Egypt as well as to acquire the militarily valuable island of Cyprus to secure oil resources for industrial and military needs. The British also secured concessions in Iran, Iraq, Kuwait, Qatar, and Bahrain. Pipelines were built to the Mediterranean Sea and the Persian Gulf.
- **Russia:** Traditionally, Russia sought to gain control of the Dardanelles as an outlet to the Mediterranean Sea and an area of expansion. Russia helped to dismember the Ottoman Empire and gain independence for several Balkan states.
- **Germany:** In 1899, German bankers obtained the Ottoman Empire's consent to complete the Berlin-Baghdad Railroad.

Consequences of Imperialism

The new imperialism changed both Western society and its colonies. Through it, Western countries established the beginning of a global economy in which the transfer of goods, money, and technology needed to be regulated in an orderly way to ensure a continuous flow of natural resources and cheap labor for the industrialized world.

Imperialism adversely affected the colonies. Under foreign rule, native culture and industry were destroyed. Imported goods wiped out local craft industries. By using colonies as sources of raw materials and markets for manufactured goods, colonial powers held back the colonies from developing industries. One reason why the standard of living was so poor in many of these countries was that the natural wealth of these regions had been funneled to the mother countries.

Imperialism also brought confrontation between the cultures. By 1900, Western nations had control over most of the globe. Europeans were convinced that they had superior cultures and forced the people to accept modern or Western ways. The pressures to westernize forced the colonial people to reevaluate their traditions and to work at discouraging such customs as foot binding in China and *sati* in India. *Sati* was the custom in which a virtuous woman (*sati*) threw herself onto her husband's funeral fire in the hope that the sacrificial act would wipe away the sins of both her husband and herself. Although imperialism exploited and abused colonial people, Western countries introduced modern medicine that stressed the use of vaccines and more sanitary hygiene that helped to save lives and increase life expectancy.

Imperialism created many political problems. European nations disrupted many traditional political units and united rival peoples under single governments that tried to impose stability and order where local conflicts had existed for years, such as in Nigeria and Rwanda. Ethnic conflicts that developed in the latter half of the twentieth century in many of these areas, can be traced to these imperial policies. Imperialism also contributed to tension among the Western powers. Rivalries between France and Great Britain over the Sudan, between France and Germany over Morocco, and over the Ottoman Empire contributed to the hostile conditions that led to World War I in 1914.

European Society at the Turn of the Century

The latter half of the 1800s and the early 1900s saw great changes in all aspects of European society. In the earlier period, the arts had been restricted primarily to the wealthy, who had money and leisure time to enjoy culture. In most industrial countries, the working day had become limited to ten hours a day and a five-and-a-half-day work week. This created more leisure time which earlier generations never had the time to enjoy. A popular leisure activity was a trip to local music halls. These music halls offered a variety of different acts that included singers, dancers, comedians, and jugglers. By 1900, arts, music, and other forms of entertainment reached a wider audience. The invention of the phonograph and records brought music directly to people's homes. During the 1880s, new technology contributed to the rise of motion pictures. By the early 1900s movies quickly became a big business, and by 1910, close to five million Americans attended some 10,000 theatres each day to watch silent movies. The European movie industry experienced a similar growth.

Middle- and working-class people began to enjoy sports and outdoor activities. European professional soccer clubs were formed. In1913 at the Football Association Cup finals at the Crystal Palace Stadium in England, Burnet defeated Liverpool 1–0 before a crowd of 120,000 people. The growing interest in sports led to the revival of the ancient Olympic games among countries. In 1896, the first modern Olympics were held in Athens.

Travel, which formerly had been reserved for the wealthy, now became popular with the middle class as doctors, lawyers, teachers, and engineers became part of the industrial society. **Thomas Cook** (1808–1892), an Englishman who had organized his first excursion in 1841 for 500 people to attend a temperance rally for 1 shilling, popularized tours for the middle class. In 1851, he promoted day trips for over 150,000 to the Great Exhibition in London, which had been conceived to symbolize the industrial and economic superiority of Great Britain. Cook's excursions became so popular that he offered trips all over the British Isles, Europe, and North America. By the late 1870s, Cook had organized the first worldwide tour. The success of the Cook Travel Agency symbolized how travel had also become more popular with many segments of society, rather than just the upper class.

Changes in the Arts/Literature

In the early nineteenth century, Romantic artists and writers rejected the rationalism of the Enlightenment and stressed the importance of human emotions and feelings. In the latter half of the nineteenth and early twentieth centuries, realism, impressionism, and postimpressionism (expressionism) would dominate the artistic and literary worlds.

Realism

The writers and artists of the Realist movement focused on contemporary everyday life, especially of the urban working classes, neglected in imaginative literature before this time. These writers also stressed that human behavior was influenced by such factors as environment and heredity.

From Romanticism to Realism	
Goals	• To paint the world as it is • To focus on the harsh side of life and on the lives of working-class men and women • To improve the lives of the unfortunate • To reject the Romantic emphasis on imagination
Artists/Works	**Gustave Courbet** (French, 1819–1877) *The Stone Breakers* (1849). Colbert's truthful portrayal of two rough laborers on a country road—leaving out the glamour that most French painters at that time added to their works—helped him become the leader of the Realist movement in painting. **Jean François Millet** (French, 1814–1875) *The Sower* (1850). Millet's paintings focused on the world of the peasant.
Writers/Writings	**Charles Dickens** (English, 1812–1870) *Oliver Twist* (serial: 1837–1839), *Hard Times* (1854). Dickens' writing often portrayed the lives of slum dwellers and factory workers, including children. **Émile Zola** (French, 1840–1902) *Germinal* (1885). Exposed class warfare in French mining industry. **George Eliot** (Mary Ann Evans) (English, 1819–1880), *Middlemarch* (1871–1872). Depicted life in English countryside in the 1830s; underlying themes were the status of women, the nature of marriage, the hypocrisy of religion, and the slow pace of political reform to help improve the lives of ordinary people. **Gustave Flaubert** (French, 1821–1880) *Madame Bovary* (1856–1857). Described the disappointment of romantic view of marriage as opposed to real life. **Leo Tolstoy** (Russian, 1828–1910) *War and Peace*. Depicted how the Napoleonic War affected the ordinary lives of people in Russia.

Impressionism

Impressionism	
Goals	• Advent of photography • To avoid realism when a camera could do the same thing better • To capture the first fleeting or personal impression made at a certain instant
Artists/Works	**Pierre Auguste Renoir** (French, 1841–1919); *Le Bal du moulin de la Galette* (1876). Renoir's paintings captured people in everyday scenes. **Claude Monet** (French, 1840—1926); *Gladioli* (1876), a tranquil garden scene effectively using light and colors. Artists favored outdoor scenes for their natural light. **Edgar Degas** (French, 1834–1917); *La classe de danse* (The Dance Class), 1873–1874; celebrated Parisian life, from laundresses to cabaret singers to ballet dancers.

Postimpressionism/Expressionism

Postimpressionism (Expressionism)	
Goals	• To carry the emphasis on light and color even further than the Impressionists. • To experiment with bright colors and sharp brush lines to focus on imagination.
Artists/Works	**Paul Cézanne** (French, 1839–1906) *Still Life with a Curtain* (1895); bridge between the late nineteenth and twentieth centuries. His analytical approach would later influence cubism. **Vincent van Gogh** (Dutch, 1853–1890) *The Starry Night* (1889). Bright colors were a chief symbol of his expressionism. The sky was depicted as an overwhelming display of fireworks and moving vision of his mind's eye. **Paul Gauguin** (French, 1848–1903); *Fatata te Miti* (By the Sea) (1892). Stockbroker-turned-artist Gauguin experimented with Polynesian forms, colors, and legends; painted during his first trip to Tahiti.

New Ideas in Medicine and Science

The late nineteenth century also brought about advances in medicine and science. The following table summarizes some key changes.

New Ideas in Medicine and Science		
Name	**Major Ideas**	**Results**
Joseph Lister (British, 1827–1912)	Infections connected to filthy conditions; he insisted that staff keep hospital clean.	Doctors began to use sterilized medical instruments; European and American hospitals developed a standard of cleanliness.
Louis Pasteur (French, 1822–1895)	Germ theory—connection between microbes and disease	Developed vaccines against rabies, as well as the process of pasteurization, which kills diseases carrying bacteria in milk.
Dmitri Mendeleev (Russian, 1834–1907)	Organized all known elements arranged in order by weight—lightest to heaviest	Periodic table still used by scientists today.
Marie Curie (Polish/French, 1867–1934) **Pierre Curie** (French, 1859–1906)	Studied radioactivity	In 1910, four years after the death of her husband, Marie Curie isolated radium. In 1911, she won the Nobel Prize in Chemistry for the discovery of radium and polonium.

Women and the Struggle for Voting

By the 1890s, several industrial countries had universal male suffrage. However, no countries allowed women to vote. Since the 1840s in the United States, women such as **Susan B. Anthony** (1820–1906) and **Elizabeth Cady Stanton** (1815–1902) had organized campaigns for women's rights. In Great Britain, there was a split over the question of *suffrage* (voting rights) for women. Both men and women thought that women's suffrage was too radical a break with the past. Some claimed women did not have the mental ability to be involved in politics. **Queen Victoria** (1819–1901) called the struggle for suffrage wicked. Women also disagreed on how to achieve it.

In 1903, **Emmeline Pankhurst** (1858–1928) of Great Britain formed the Women's Social and Political Union (WSPU). The WSPU believed that after years of peaceful protest only aggressive or militant action would bring victory. The term *suffragette* was applied to the radical members of the WSPU. Besides peaceful demonstrations, many of these suffragettes heckled speakers in Parliament, cut telegraph wires, smashed windows, and burned public buildings. Pankhurst and her daughters Christabel (1880–1958) and Sylvia (1882–1960) were arrested and jailed many times. In jail, the Pankhursts went on hunger strikes to dramatize their cause. In June 1913, one radical suffragist died when she threw herself in front of the king's horse at the English Derby.

In France, **Jeanne-Elizabeth Schmahl** (1846–1915) founded in 1909 the French Union for Women's Suffrage. She rejected the militant tactics of the English movement and favored legal protests. French women did not gain the right to vote until after World War II. When Great Britain entered World War I, Pankhurst suspended her activities. When the war ended in 1918, Parliament granted the right to vote to women over the age of 30. In 1928, the required age was lowered to 21, making the voting age for both sexes the same.

Chronology of the Age of Imperialism

1763	End of Seven Years' War; Great Britain gains control of India.
1830	France occupies Algeria.
1839	The First Opium War begins.
1842	The First Opium War ends with the Treaty of Nanking.
1849	Gustave Courbet paints *The Stone Breakers*.
1850	Jean François Millet paints *The Sower*.
1850	The Taiping Rebellion in China begins; Chinese civil war against the Manchu rulers (Qing Dynasty); millions are killed.
1851	Great Exhibition in London celebrates the technological achievements of Great Britain.
1853	Commodore Perry opens up trade with Japan.
1857	The Sepoy Mutiny against British rule in India takes place.
1858	India comes under direct rule by Great Britain.
1869	Suez Canal completed.
1870	Cecil Rhodes arrives in Cape Town, South Africa.
1872	Thomas Cook organizes his first trip around the world. It takes 222 days.
1872	Claude Monet paints *Impression, Sunrise*.
1874	Edgar Degas paints *The Dance Class*.
1875	Great Britain gains control of the Suez Canal and begins to establish a protectorate over Egypt (in 1882).
1882	British land troops in Egypt.
1884–1885	International Berlin Conference on meets to establish guidelines for European imperialism in Africa.
1885	Germany controls German East Africa.
1886	British take over Burma.
1889	Vincent van Gogh paints *The Starry Night*.
1892	Pierre Auguste Renoir paints *Girls at the Piano*.
1897	Paul Gauguin paints *Where Do We Come From? What Are We? Where Are We Going?*
1897	First Zionist Conference meets in Basel, Switzerland.
1899–1901	The Boxer Rebellion in China against Westerners takes place.
1899	Open Door Policy is proposed by United States for China.
1899–1902	Boer War; British crush rebellion by Dutch farmers in South Africa.
1904–1905	Russo-Japanese War; Japan takes Korea and Port Arthur from Russia.
1910	Union of South Africa is formed.
1911–1912	Manchu Dynasty overthrown; Dr. Sun Yat-Sen is named president of Chinese Republic.

Sample Multiple-Choice Questions

1. Which of the following countries was not involved in the effort to secure colonies in Africa, Asia, and the Middle East at the end of the nineteenth century?

   A. Germany
   B. Belgium
   C. Italy
   D. Austria
   E. England

2. Which statement best expresses the motive for nineteenth-century European imperialism?

   A. Living space was needed for the excess population in Western Europe.
   B. European leaders believed imperialism was an effective method for reducing the number of wars.
   C. European nations would benefit from some aspects of the conquered nation's culture.
   D. Imperialism would benefit the economies of the colonial powers.
   E. European nations wanted democratic governments throughout the world.

3. Bismarck organized the Berlin Conference in 1884–85 to

   A. establish rules for dividing up Africa among the European countries.
   B. limit Russian expansion on the continent.
   C. work with the Africans to seek trade agreements.
   D. prevent Belgium from taking over the Congo.
   E. stop the spread of United States influence in Africa.

4. During the 1900s, Emmeline Pankhurst was associated with

   A. improvement in education.
   B. the Romantic literary movement.
   C. the advocation of cleanliness in hospitals.
   D. a radical struggle for women's suffrage.
   E. support for overseas expansion.

5. The nineteenth-century phrase, "the white man's burden," reflects the idea that

   A. Asians and Africans were equal to Europeans.
   B. Asians and Africans would be grateful for European help.
   C. imperialism was opposed by most Europeans.
   D. Europeans had a responsibility to improve the lives of their colonial people.
   E. democracy was the best form of government for Asia and Africa.

6. "As many more individuals of each species are born than can possibly survive; and as consequently, there is a frequently recurring struggle for existence, it follows that any being, if it vary however slightly in any manner profitable to itself, under the complex and sometimes varying conditions of life, will have a better chance of surviving, and thus be naturally selected. From the strong principle of inheritance, any selected variety will tend to propagate its new and modified form."

   The author of the above passage is

   A. Charles Darwin.
   B. Herbert Spencer.
   C. Karl Marx.
   D. Ivan Pavlov.
   E. Gregor Mendel.

7. Which of the following was a result of the Sepoy Mutiny or rebellion in 1857?

   A. The British East India Company raised taxes.
   B. India declared its independence.
   C. India adapted Christianity.
   D. The British East India Company took direct control of India.
   E. The British government ended the rule of the British East India Company.

8. Which statement best describes an effect of the Opium Wars on China?

   A. The British expelled all Chinese from Hong Kong.
   B. The British victory led to spheres of influence in China.
   C. The British ended the importing of opium into China.
   D. The British established a parliamentary democracy in China.
   E. Chinese isolation increased.

9. The Boxer Rebellion of the early twentieth century was an attempt to

   A. eliminate poverty among the Chinese peasants.
   B. bring Western-style democracy to China.
   C. restore trade between China and European nations.
   D. introduce communism.
   E. remove foreign influences from China.

10. A major goal of the Meiji Restoration was to focus on

    A. isolating Japan from the influence of foreign ideas.
    B. existing peacefully with their Asian neighbors.
    C. increasing the emperor's power by returning Japan to a feudal political system.
    D. modernizing Japan's economy to compete with Western nations.
    E. encouraging European powers to open up trading rights in China.

Multiple-Choice Questions: Answers and Explanations

1. **D.** Austria did not take an active role in the struggle for colonies. Germany, Belgium, Italy, and England established colonies in Africa, Asia, and the Middle East.

2. **D.** The statement that best expressed the motive for nineteenth-century European imperialism is that imperialism would benefit the economies of the colonial powers. During the Age of Imperialism, a global economy developed. From the industrialized European nations' mass-produced goods, investment capital was directed to the colonies. In return, the people of Asia and Africa provided natural resources and cheap labor. Rubber, copper, and gold came from Africa, cotton and tin from southwest Asia. These raw materials spurred the growth of European industries and financial markets. The colonies also provided new markets for the finished products of the Industrial Revolution. Tools, weapons, and clothing flowed out of the factories and back to the colonies, whose raw materials had made them possible. Although imperialists argued that living space was needed for the excess population of Europe, no European country after 1870 acquired any colony to which European families wished to move in large numbers. The millions who left in the late nineteenth century persisted in heading for the Americas, where there were no European colonies.

   Imperialism was not an effective method of reducing the number of wars. In 1896, Ethiopia defeated Italy in its attempt to conquer the region. In 1898, Great Britain and France almost went to war over the Sudan in Africa. In 1905, Germany and France clashed over Morocco. European countries believed that Western civilizations were superior to the civilizations of colonial people. Colonial officials rejected the cultures of the conquered peoples and tried to impose Western customs and traditions on the colonies. European countries did not establish democratic governments in Asia and Africa, but instead ruled directly or indirectly through local rulers without the consent of the people.

3. **A.** The Berlin Conference established ground rules for dividing up Africa among the European nations. In 1884–1885, European leaders met in Berlin to avoid conflicts among themselves. They agreed that European powers could not claim any part of Africa unless they set up a government office there. Europeans were also forced to send officials who exerted their power over local rulers. Leopold II, king of Belgium, wanted the Berlin Conference to recognize Belgium's control of the Congo Free State. Russia was not one of the European countries involved in the division of Africa. The Europeans did not invite any Africans to the Berlin Conference. Africans were not given any role in how Europe divided up the continent. The United States was never interested in extending its influence in Africa. The United States' area of imperial control was in Latin America and the Caribbean.

4. **D.** Emmeline Pankhurst was a radical in the efforts of women to gain the right to vote. As the leader of the Women's Social and Political Union in the early 1900s, she used militant methods, such as breaking windows and committing arson, to help women fight for the right to vote. Some resented her aggressive methods, but Emmeline Pankhurst believed that only extreme measures would help women achieve their goal. She is not associated with any literary, health, or artistic movement in European history.

5. **D.** "The White Man's Burden" reflects the idea that Europeans had a responsibility to improve the lives of their colonial people. In the 1890s, Rudyard Kipling's poem expressed the belief that Europeans had a sacred civilizing mission to bring the benefits of Western society to the impoverished people of the regions that they colonized. Kipling's poem encouraged Europeans to give unselfish service in distant lands. European civilization had reached unprecedented heights and they had unique benefits to bestow on all less advanced people. The phrase, "the white man's burden," was based on the perceived inferiority of Asians and Africans. It never considered the gratitude of Asians and Africans for Europe's help. It was expected that these areas would openly embrace Western civilization. This attitude permeated imperialism and there was never the belief that democracy should be the form of government in Asia and Africa. Imperialism was based on one country conquering a weaker one.

6. **A.** Charles Darwin is the author of this passage. In his book *On the Origins of Species by Means of Natural Selection* (1859) Darwin maintains that according to the idea of natural selection the populations that tend to survive are those that are the fittest or best adapted to their environment. The surviving members of a species produce offspring that share their advantage. Over generations, the species may change. In this way new species evolve. Darwin's idea of change through natural selection came to be called the Theory of Evolution. Herbert Spencer was the first to use the term "survival of the fittest" and is associated with Social Darwinism. Karl Marx is considered the father of Communism. Ivan Pavlov was a nineteenth-century Russian biologist who broke new ground in the social science of psychology. Gregor Mendel was a nineteenth-century German scientist who is considered to be the founder of the study of genetics.

7. **E.** The Sepoy Mutiny or Rebellion resulted in the British government ruling India directly as a colony. The British controlled India through the British East India Company until 1857. The British, who crushed the Sepoy Native Indian Troops, changed their policy after 1857. The government ended the rule of the British East India Company in 1858 and assumed control of the colony, ruling British India as a colony and ruling the native states indirectly as protectorates through British advisors. The British East India Company did not raise taxes since it did not control India after 1858. India did not achieve independence until after World War II. Hindu, not Christianity, is the major religion of India.

8. **B.** British victory in the Opium Wars led to spheres of influence in China. In 1839, when the Chinese tried to outlaw the opium trade, the British refused, and continued to import the drug. This led to the Opium Wars. The Chinese were easily defeated and signed the Treaty of Nanking (1842). The British annexed Hong Kong and secured the right to trade at four Chinese ports in addition to Canton. These trading ports became spheres of influence in which European nations secured exclusive trading privileges. After 1870, France, Germany, and Russia gained spheres of influence in China. These spheres of influence opened up China to trade rather than isolating it. The British remained in control of Hong Kong until 1997 and did not establish democracy in China.

9. **E.** The Boxer Rebellion of the early twentieth century was an attempt to remove foreign influences from China. In the 1890s, anti-foreign feelings were high in China because many Chinese resented the growing influence of foreign powers such as Great Britain, France, and Germany. In 1899, the Chinese formed a secret society called the Boxers (or Society of Righteous and Harmonious Fists), whose goal was to remove the foreigners who were destroying their lands with new technology such as telegraphs and machinery. The Boxers did not want any program to deal with poverty nor to promote democracy in China. They wanted to end trade with European nations. The Boxers were not Communists.

10. **D.** During the Meiji Restoration beginning in 1867, Japan's leaders focused on modernizing Japan's economy in order to compete with Western nations. Japan reversed its policy of isolation, ended feudalism, and began to modernize by borrowing from the Western powers. The goal of the Meiji leader, or enlightened ruler, was to make Japan a strong military and industrial power. Japanese leaders sent students abroad to Western countries to learn about their form of government, economies, technology, and customs. The government also brought foreign experts to Japan to improve industry. The Japanese adopted a constitution based on the model of Prussia with the emperor as the head. The new government was not intended to bring democracy, but to unite Japan and make it equal to Western powers. The Meiji Restoration did not isolate Japan from the influence of foreign ideas. The Japanese leaders borrowed Western ideas and adapted them to fit the needs of Japanese society. The Japanese introduced Western business methods but encouraged cooperation rather than competition among companies. Japan's modernization contributed to its rise as an imperial country. In 1895, the Japanese attacked and defeated China in the Sino-Japanese War. In 1904–1905, Japan clashed with Russia and defeated the Russians. In 1910, Japan annexed Korea.

World War I (1914–1918)

At the beginning of the twentieth century, the future of Europe appeared bright. European culture and values dominated the known world. After 100 years of rapid advances in science and technology, there was the belief that unlimited progress and growth would also lead to a future in which even war would be eliminated as a solution to problems in the world. Beneath the surface, however, there were forces that were threatening this optimistic view of the future—the alliance system, nationalism lurking in the Balkans, imperialism creating rivalries in Africa, and the arms race. In August 1914, these forces combined to start World War I, shattering the dreams of a new future and marking the beginning of Europe's decline in the twentieth century. World War I destroyed the Austro-Hungarian Empire, the German Empire, the Ottoman Empire, and the Russian Empire. World War I, also known as the **Great War,** contributed to the decline of France and Great Britain as their economies and populations were decimated by the horrors of this war. The soldiers who fought in the trenches in France and Germany became part of a lost generation who had little hope for the future.

World War I was a different type of war because it was fought on the European home front as well as on the battlefield. The civilian population was forced to make sacrifices, such as "meatless Mondays," and women entered the work force to replace men who had gone to the battlefield. Industrialization and technology also changed the methods of warfare. Nations developed more destructive weapons, such as mounted machine guns and poison gas, which resulted in the deaths of millions.

World War I also was a turning point in history. By 1919, the world of 1914 lay in ruins and the map of Europe had changed to reflect the rise of national states in Czechoslovakia and Yugoslavia. World War I ended the Russian Empire and led to the rise of communism. Fascism in Italy and Nazism in Germany developed in opposition to communism, as well as dissatisfaction with the Versailles Peace Treaty. The discontent of Germany and Italy, Russia's exclusion from the peace talks, and the resentment over the establishment of a Polish nation, as well as Japan's protesting the refusal of Western nations to recognize its claim over China, all led to anger and bitterness for the next twenty years. These feelings contributed to World War II in 1939.

The Underlying Causes of World War I

The Alliance System

The Franco-Prussian War and the establishment of the German Empire opened up a new era of international relations. Bismarck, in a short period from 1861 to 1871, had turned Germany into one of the most powerful nations in Europe. After France's humiliating defeat in the Franco-Prussian War and the loss of Alsace-Lorraine, Bismarck wanted to keep France from regaining these lost provinces or from exercising *revanche* (revenge) on victorious Germany. He also wanted to diplomatically isolate France and keep the Austro-Hungarian Empire and Russia on friendly terms with Germany in order to avoid being dragged into a great war between the two rival empires. To achieve these goals, Bismarck created a system of alliances. As a result, Europe was divided into two rival blocs. The alliance system consisted of the following:

- **Three Emperors' League (Dreikaiserbund):** This included Germany, Russia, and Austria-Hungary. The League established the principle of cooperation among the three powers in any further division of the Ottoman Empire. The League was also designed to neutralize the tension between Austria-Hungary and Russia. The alliance only lasted from 1881 to 1887. In 1887, Russia declined to renew the alliance because of tensions with Austria-Hungary over the Balkans.

- **Dual Alliance:** This alliance of 1879 was created between Germany and Austria-Hungary in order to isolate France.

- **Triple Alliance:** This alliance of 1882 included Austria-Hungary, Germany, and Italy. Italy was angry with France for preventing Italy from seizing Tunisia. The biggest weakness of the Triple Alliance was Italy's past history of animosity toward Austria and desire for *Italia Irredenta* (unredeemed territories), where Italians lived—such as Trieste and Fiume—that were still under Austrian control.

- **Reinsurance Treaty:** This secret treaty of 1887 was between Germany and Russia. Russia and Austria-Hungary were rivals over the Balkans. Bismarck wanted to be allied with both powers at the same time, in case any incidents developed. In 1890, the treaty ended and Germany chose not to renew it.

The following alliances were created in reaction to German alliances or actions.

- **Franco-Russian Alliance (1894):** The opportunity for an agreement between France and Russia arose in the wake of Germany's decision to terminate the Reinsurance Treaty with Russia in 1890. An alliance with Russia was most attractive to France, considering Bismarck's success in isolating France; while for Russia, the recent renewal of the Triple Alliance prompted consideration of Russia's need for capital for development as well as French military assistance in weapons procurement. France was also eager to check Germany's power and Russia needed an ally for its ambitions in the Balkans.

- **Entente Cordial:** Fearful of Germany's growing industrial and military strength, and the building of a powerful German navy, Great Britain negotiated an unwritten military understanding with France in 1904. The alignment of Great Britain and France, her former adversary, was regarded as a diplomatic revolution. Great Britain's decision to end its splendid isolation was due primarily to Germany's colonial activity and her large military buildup, which created fear that Germany was becoming too dominant in Europe.

- **Triple Entente:** With French support, the British signed an agreement with Russia in 1907 that settled Russo-British quarrels over imperial influence in Central Asia and Persia and opened the door for greater cooperation. The Triple Entente was an informal but powerful association of Britain, France, and Russia, rather than an alliance, because Britain refused to make formal military commitments. Although the Triple Entente did not bind Britain to fight alongside France and Russia, it did ensure that Britain would not fight against them.

By 1907 two rival camps existed in Europe. The Triple Alliance—consisting of Germany, Austria-Hungary, and Italy. On the other side was the Triple Entente—Great Britain, France and Russia. A dispute between any of the two powers could set off a chain reaction that might draw the entire continent into a war.

Nationalism

The excessive nationalism preceding World War I created jealousy and hatred among the European nations. In France, national pride was hurt by the loss of Alsace-Lorraine in the Franco-Prussian War and the French considered Germany their natural enemy. Other countries wanted to extend their territories to include people of their race or background. Serbia, for instance, wanted to annex Bosnia-Herzegovina. Subject nationalities of Czechs, Yugoslavs, and Poles sought independence. This sort of national feeling contributed to tension on the European continent. In Eastern Europe, Russia, as the largest Slavic country, defended the rights of people of similar backgrounds. This policy was known as **Pan-Slavism.** For example, by 1914, Russia was ready to support Serbia, its Slavic brother, against any threats.

Economics

Economic rivalries created competition between Great Britain and Germany. Great Britain felt threatened by Germany's economic growth. By 1900, German factories were out-producing British ones and Germany was challenging Great Britain in the world markets.

Imperialism

The European imperialist countries—such as Great Britain, France, and Germany—competed for territory, markets, and resources in Asia and Africa. This competition led to friction. Great Britain resented Germany for blocking their plan for a Cape to Cairo railway. Germany and Great Britain, however, acted to defeat Russia's efforts to acquire the Dardanelles, and Germany wanted to prevent the French from gaining Morocco.

Militarism

To protect their national and imperialist interests, Great Britain and Germany expanded their military forces. When Germany began to acquire colonies, Kaiser Wilhelm II began to build up the German navy. Admiral **Alfred von Tirpitz** (1849–1930) of Germany saw a large navy as the legitimate mark of a great power and as a source of pride and patriotism. The British, however, saw the German naval buildup as a challenge and a threat to British security and began to increase their military spending. The cycle of paranoia led to an arms race.

International Crises

The European powers before World War I confronted each other in a series of diplomatic clashes, each of which could have resulted in war:

- **First Moroccan Crisis of 1905:** On a visit to Morocco, a territory under French influence, Kaiser Wilhelm II protested Morocco's French domination. Testing the strength of the Entente Cordial of 1904 between the French and the British, Wilhelm II advocated Moroccan independence and sent a warship to the country. He then demanded a conference on Morocco, which took place at Algeciras in Spain in 1906. The conference recognized the special interest of France in Morocco, but reaffirmed Moroccan independence. France was supported by Great Britain, Italy, and the United States, who under President Theodore Roosevelt had organized the conference.

- **Second Moroccan Crisis of 1911:** Germany sent a gunboat, the *Panther,* to Agadir to protest the French occupation of the region. Germany compromised when it realized that Great Britain was supporting France. France was allowed to establish a protectorate in Morocco and, in return, Germany received some land in Equatorial Africa, namely parts of the French Congo.

The Moroccan crises were setbacks for Germany but drew France and Great Britain into a closer alliance, as their national interests seemed to be the same—to limit German power.

- **Balkans Crisis of 1908:** Both Serbia and the Austro-Hungarian Empire wanted to expand in the Balkans. When Austria annexed Bosnia-Herzegovina in 1908, Serbia protested and Russia sided with Serbia. The crisis was checked when Germany joined Austria's cause and balanced the Russian threat.

- **Balkan Crises of 1912–1913:** As a result of the Balkan War of 1912 with the Ottoman Empire, four Balkan states—Serbia, Montenegro, Bulgaria, and Greece—seized territory from the Ottoman Empire. Serbia's dispute with Bulgaria over the spoils of war led to the Second Balkan War. Bulgaria was defeated and Serbia, backed by Russia, appeared to have won an outlet to the Adriatic Sea. Austria, with the backing of Germany and Italy, intervened and forced the creation of Albania out of the former Ottoman lands, thereby blocking Serbia's ambitions. The Balkan crises of 1912 and 1913 brought Russia and Serbia closer together and intensified the animosity of Russia and Serbia for the Austro-Hungarian Empire.

These crises, combined with the underlying problems created by the alliance system, excessive nationalism, economic competition, imperialistic rivalries, and the arms race, created an international atmosphere that could erupt into war with a simple spark. The spark occurred in the Balkans.

The Immediate Cause of World War I

By 1914, the Balkans was a powder keg of nationalistic hatred and imperialistic rivalries. On June 28, 1914, Archduke Ferdinand, heir to the throne of Austria, and his wife Sophie, were assassinated on their fourteenth wedding anniversary when they were visiting Sarajevo, the capital of Bosnia. The assassin was a Serbian patriot; most people outside of Serbia consider him a terrorist named **Gavrilo Princip,** who was a member of a secret group known as the Black Hand. The goal of the group was to organize the southern Slavic people into a new single nation. Austria believed that Serbian officials aided the plot and were angered when it became known that Serbian officials were aware of the plot but did not warn them about it. Austria was determined to punish Serbia. The assassinations set off a chain reaction during the months of July and August that plunged Europe into a major war. The following list describes the chain of events:

- **July 23:** Fortified in its demands by the blank check of support given by Kaiser Wilhelm II of Germany on July 6, 1914, Austria presented to Serbia a harsh 48-hour unconditional ultimatum demanding that Serbia stop anti-Austrian propaganda and punish any Serbian official involved in the murder plot. Austria also wanted to join Serbia in investigating the assassination. Slavic Russia, the big brother to Serbia, encouraged her to stand tough against Austrian demands. Russia turned to France, which promised to support it against Germany and Austria. The alliance system, designed to preserve peace, had turned the assassinations from what might have been a local war into a conflict that would engulf the Great Powers. On July 28, 1914, Austria went to war against Serbia; Russia began mobilizing for war beginning on July 30, 1914.
- **August 1, 1914:** Germany declared war on Russia after Russia refused Germany's request to stop mobilization.
- **August 3, 1914:** Germany declared war on France. The German plan to attack France quickly could succeed only by German troops crossing through Belgium. Germany asked Belgium for permission to cross through the country. Belgium refused. However, Germany invaded anyway, violating the Treaty of 1839, which had guaranteed Belgium's neutrality by all the European great powers, including Prussia.
- **August 4, 1914:** Great Britain joined France and declared war on Germany.
- **August 6, 1914:** Austria declared war on Russia.

World War I had begun, involving the entire European continent in war for the first time since the Napoleonic conflict of the nineteenth century. European nations entered the war with enthusiasm and the hope that it would be a quick war. The common mood was, "The boys will be home by Christmas." British Prime Minister Edmund Grey was less optimistic, noting that "lamps are going out all over Europe. We shall never see them lit again in our lifetime." Grey believed that the war would permanently end the years of relative peace and prosperity that had existed in Europe since the end of the Congress of Vienna in 1815.

Although the Treaty of Versailles was later to blame Germany for the war, historians agree that all the nations of Europe bore responsibility for the events of August. The underlying causes of World War I can be attributed to the alliance system, aggressive nationalism, imperialism, and economic competition.

The Course of the War

World War I divided Europe into two camps:

- **Central Powers:** Germany, the Austro-Hungarian Empire, and the Ottoman Empire. Bulgaria joined in 1915 to secure revenge against Serbia.
- **Allies:** Great Britain, France, Russia, Serbia, Belgium, and more than 25 other nations. Japan joined in 1914 to acquire land in the Pacific, and Italy joined in 1915 with the promise of gaining territory from Austria, overseas territories from Germany, and the Ottoman Empire. Italy had remained neutral on the grounds that Germany had provoked the war and violated the defensive nature of the Triple Alliance. In 1917, the United States became a member of the Allies due to Germany's unrestricted submarine warfare.

German Strategy

Count Alfred von Schlieffen (1833–1913) was chief of the general German staff from 1901 to 1905. The **Schlieffen Plan,** developed in 1905, was designed to prevent Germany from needing to conduct a two-front war. The plan was to quickly sweep through northern France, through Belgium in the west, and then turn to Russia in the east. The plan was to knock out France within six weeks as in the Franco-Prussian War and then transport troops to the eastern front to help the Austrians against the Russians.

Western Front

By the first week of September, the Germans were within 30 miles of Paris, forcing government leaders to flee the city. However, the spirited defense of the Belgians, the more rapid mobilization of the Russians, and some unexpected victories in eastern Prussia by the Russian forces, forced Germany to revise its plan and send troops to the eastern front after all. At the Battle of the Marne River from September 5 to 9, the French fought heroically under the leadership of General Joseph Jacques Joffre and were reinforced by over 100,000 British troops. The French even recruited Paris taxies to bring reserve troops to the front. Germany fell back and Paris was saved.

Europe's hope for a quick war deteriorated into trench warfare as both sides dug in for the winter. At first, the trenches were built for a short amount of time, but as the stalemate continued, the Allies and Central Powers created a vast system of trenches that stretched from the Swiss frontier to the English Channel. Life in the trenches was not glamorous, as soldiers roasted in the summer and froze in the winter. Sanitary conditions were horrible; soldiers shared their food with rats and their beds with lice. Between the two trenches, there was a "no man's land" and troops occasionally were sent over the top to attack the enemy trenches. The casualties were staggering. The British lost 60,000 men per day and a total of 400,000 men at the Battle of the Somme in 1916. At Verdun, both sides lost over 700,000 men and in 1917, at Passchendaele, the British lost 250,000 men for five square miles of the West Flanders region of Belgium. Erich Remarque's great novel *All Quiet on the Western Front* (1929) described the horrors of war on the western front.

Eastern Front

The eastern front did not get bogged down in trenches as in the west, and the war was more mobile because battle lines covered much larger areas. In the beginning, the Russians fought well and pushed into east Germany, but General Paul von Hindenburg and Erich Ludendorff defeated the Russians at the Battle of Tannenberg. The Russians lost approx. 78,000 men and about 98,000 were captured in the fall of 1914, and by 1915, over 2.5 million Russian soldiers had been killed, wounded, or taken prisoner. These losses, combined with poor leadership of the government and the lack of food for soldiers and civilians, caused internal problems that led to the overthrow of Czar Nicholas in March 1917, and later the Communist Revolution in November 1917. The Communists, who had attracted support by promising an end to the war, withdrew from the war in 1918 and signed the Treaty of Brest-Litovsk, which gave away large territorial concessions to Germany. (The Communist Revolution is discussed in the following chapter.)

Southern Front

In southeastern Europe, the British attacked the Ottoman Empire. In 1915, Winston Churchill, the first Lord of the Admiralty, organized the **Gallipoli Campaign,** which was designed to strike at the Germans and Austrians through the Dardanelles and the Balkans. Churchill wanted to provide Russian troops with supplies via the Black Sea. The campaign was a failure and Churchill resigned (during World War II, Churchill would also advocate this plan). In 1918, an Allied force won back much of the Balkans and an Italian offensive compelled the surrender of the Austro-Hungarian Empire.

War in the Colonies and at Sea

Warfare in the colonial possessions went well for the Allies, who seized German possessions in Africa. Japan seized German outposts in China and the Pacific. It also tried to impose a protectorate over China. With Arab help, the British defeated the Ottoman Empire. The British success in Palestine was followed by the **Balfour Declaration** of 1917, which called for the creation of a Jewish state. In May 1915, German submarines sank the *Lusitania,* a British liner, claiming that it was carrying munitions—a claim that later was substantiated after WWII. This attack resulted in the death of 1,198 people, of which 128 were Americans. In 1915, President Woodrow Wilson's threat to break off diplomatic relations with Germany forced Germany to promise to stop sinking neutral ships without warning.

The British naval strength was supreme; Britain effectively blockaded Germany and kept control of the Atlantic sea lanes. From May 31 to June 1, 1916, Germany tried to break the blockade at the **Battle of Jutland.** This battle, fought between the British and German fleets, involved over 250 ships and ended in a draw. It was the last great battle to be fought exclusively by surface ships. Afterwards, Germany concentrated on the use of the U-boat (see the following section, "New Ways of Waging War"). Germany's use of submarine warfare inflicted great damages on the Allies but failed to break the blockade.

New Ways of Waging War

World War I is considered to be the first truly technological war. New weapons—such as the machine gun, larger artillery, armed tanks, poison gas, and the airplane—and new systems of communication added greatly to the destructiveness of the war. The machine gun, which had been greatly improved by World War I, provided a continuous stream of bullets that wiped out waves of attackers. This made it difficult for armed forces to advance and helped to create a stalemate. One light machine gun weighing 36 pounds (16.3 kg)—the **Lewis Gun** developed by American Colonel **Isaac Lewis** (1858–1931) in 1911—featured a revolving magazine that held forty-seven cartridges. By means of an adjustable clock-type recoil spring, the gun's firing rate could be regulated, ranging from 500 to 600 rounds per minute. The Germans' nickname for the Lewis Gun was "the Belgian Rattlesnake"; when the U.S. military did not buy his design, Lewis moved to Belgium, mass-produced his guns in Liege and sold them to the British and French military. Larger artillery could shell enemy lines from 15 miles away. In 1918, the Germans were shelling Paris from 70 miles away. One of the better improvements was a system called "sound ranging" for artillery, which could determine the exact location of enemy batteries and then accurately position guns for the areas before a battle.

Also part of the new warfare was the **armored tank** that moved on chained tracks, enabling it to cross many kinds of terrain. There is some doubt about the origin of the word *tank*; it is commonly accepted that it derived from the term "water carrier." The innocent name "tank" was initially given to divert any attention from the new war project. In September 1916, 49 tanks were introduced by the British at the Battle of the Somme. The early tanks were slow and clumsy. However, they eventually improved and aided the Allies in their war efforts. Poison gas, which destroyed the lungs of soldiers and left victims in agony for days and weeks, was probably the most feared of all weapons used in World War I. The French were the first to use it in 1914 in their unsuccessful attempt to stop the German army advance through Belgium. However, it was at the Second Battle of Ypres in April 1915 that the Germans used poison gas on a large scale on the western front. Although the eventual use of the gas mask mitigated the effects of this deadly weapon, it showed how modern warfare had become deadly and inhuman.

The Germans were the first to use submarines as serious fighting machines against merchant ships. German U-boats numbered only about 38 at the beginning of the war, and achieved notable success against British warships, but because of the reactions of neutral countries (especially the United States) Germany was reluctant to adapt a policy of unrestricted submarine warfare against merchant ships.

In December 1903, Orville and Wilbur Wright successfully flew a powered airplane. The Wright brothers offered their design to the United States War Department as well as other governments and individuals in Europe. They were repeatedly turned down. By 1911, the United States and other European countries began to realize that there was money in the aviation business. With the outbreak of World War I, some believed that the plane could offer an advantage. At first, airplanes were sent out over enemy positions to spot enemy formations and troop movements. The pilots independently armed themselves with pistols and sometimes rifles to shoot at an enemy plane. They also began to carry small bombs to drop over the side of their planes into enemy positions. Bombing raids were conducted at all times.

During the war, machine guns were mounted on planes so that these planes could fight each other in combat battles, which were known as "dog fights." World War I planes came in three varieties: single-wing (mono-planes), double-wing (bi-planes), and triple-wing (tri-planes). The more wings a plane had, the more mobility and stability it had, making it easier for the plane to evade gunfire or to better maneuver in a dog fight. The tri-plane was considered the favorite of the German flying ace, **Manfred von Richthofen,** better known as the Red Fox or the Red Baron. He is credited with shooting down 85 Allied planes. Planes were also used for moving supplies and for aerial photography during attacks in order to map positions.

Hot air balloons were still used during World War I. Many were used on the western front as observers because they were cheaper than planes. The development of fighter planes made it more dangerous to use them; subsequently, the hot air balloons became less effective. Dirigible bombers, such as **Zeppelins** named after Count **Ferdinand von Zeppelin** (1838–1917), were also used. They were extremely vulnerable to ground fire but could level buildings in seconds. Fast fighter planes and strong anti-artillery made it hard for Zeppelins to bomb in the daytime; thus, they would usually leave Germany at dusk and arrive over England by the cover of night to bomb. It is estimated that there were over 1,500 casualties due to these bombings.

Communication systems significantly improved during World War I. Wireless radios enabled different groups on the battlefield to communicate quickly without requiring men as messengers. The radio system was used to transmit messages from relay stations to main headquarters during the war.

War on the Home Front

World War I was the first war in which the entire population of a country participated in the war effort. Once the hope for a quick war ended, government leaders realized that they had to mobilize all their resources. Total war meant economic planning, rationing, wage and price controls, and restricting the freedom of labor. The role of women changed greatly as many women started to work in factories. By 1917, women comprised 43 percent of the labor force in Russia. The number of women driving buses and streetcars increased tenfold in Great Britain. Believing women would lower the wages, male-dominated professions were initially hostile towards women moving into their occupations. Government pressure and the principle of equal pay for equal work overcame these objections. As a result of the women's war efforts, Great Britain, Germany, and Austria granted women the right to vote immediately after the war. Children also participated through food drives and by collecting material that would help the war effort. The governments in all countries also used wartime propaganda to maintain popular support of the war and control popular opinion. They censored the news, controlled the arts, and created posters and movies to promote patriotism and arouse hatred towards the enemy.

Concluding the War

The year 1917 was a turning point in the war. In early 1917, the British had intercepted and decoded a message from the German Foreign Minister Arthur Zimmermann to the German Ambassador in Washington D.C. who forwarded it to the German ambassador in Mexico. The telegram promised that in return for Mexico's support, Germany would help Mexico win back Texas, Arizona, and New Mexico (the territories lost in the 1840s to the United States). The British revealed the **Zimmermann Telegram** to the American government. On March 1, 1917, the note was published in American newspapers and intensified anti-German feelings in the United States. In 1917, with Russia on the verge of defeat, Germany decided to resume its unrestricted submarine warfare.

On April 6, 1917, a month after the Russian Revolution, the United States entered the war. Germany gambled that it could gain quick victories before the impact of American troops could make a difference. The United States' entry made a difference, however. In 1918, the American Expeditionary Force of 2 million men led by General **John J. Pershing** helped to stem the tide at **Château-Thierry** and the **Argonne Forest.** By autumn, Bulgaria and the Ottoman Empire sued for peace, and the Austro-Hungarian government collapsed as subject nationalities revolted and splintered the empire into different national states. Revolutions also broke out across Germany. The military leaders informed the Kaiser that the war was lost and advised him to step down as the czar had done. Wilhelm II fled to Holland in early November, leading to the creation of a provisional republican government that agreed to negotiations based on U.S. President Woodrow Wilson's **Fourteen Points.** At 11 A.M., on the 11th day of November, 1918, Germany signed the armistice to end World War I.

The Treaty of Versailles

In January 1918, Woodrow Wilson, in a speech before Congress, outlined what he considered to be the war aims of the Allies. These Fourteen Points contained the ideals of "A Peace Without Victory." The most important of these Fourteen Points were the following:

- End of secret diplomacy
- Freedom of the seas
- Arms reductions
- Free trade
- National self-determination
- The creation of an international peace organization called the **League of Nations**

In January 1919, representatives of the countries known as the "Big Four" met at Versailles and each had different objectives:

- **David Lloyd George** of Great Britain sought to preserve its empire and maintain its industrial and naval supremacy.
- **Georges Clemenceau** of France sought revenge for the lost provinces of Alsace and Lorraine and wanted to insure France against future German invasions.
- **Vittorio Orlando** of Italy wanted to gain *Italia Irredenta,* unredeemed territories from Austria, and colonies in Africa and the Middle East.
- **Woodrow Wilson,** President of the United States, sought a just peace based on creating a League of Nations.

Russia and the Central Powers, as well as Japan, were excluded from the conference. Representatives of Italy walked out of the conference when the treaty did not meet their demands. The conflicting desires of the Allies led to a deadlock. France and Great Britain, who had suffered devastating economic losses and the loss of human life, thought that Wilson's approach was unrealistic. They were more interested in making sure that Germany never threatened the security of Europe again. Wilson, who was obsessed with the League of Nations, was willing to compromise on most issues to achieve his goal. The Versailles Treaty was far from the ideal originally requested by Wilson.

Provisions of the Versailles Treaty

- Article 231: Germany accepted sole responsibility for the war (War Guilt Clause).
- Germany was required to pay all the costs of the war, including civilian damages, such as the destruction done to the infrastructure of Allied countries, particularly France and Belgium, as well as pensions to widows. The total cost was expected to be $132 billion over thirty years.
- Germany's overseas colonies were distributed among the Allies. Parts of her territory were ceded to other nations: Alsace-Lorraine to France; northern Schleswig to Denmark; and west Prussia to Poland. France also gained control of the Saar coal mines as reparations. The Saar basin was to be occupied for 15 years by the major powers, after which the people of this area could vote on which country they wanted to join.
- The German army and navy was reduced to 100,000 and 15,000 men, respectively. Germany was forbidden from having armed aircraft.
- The Rhineland, a 30-mile strip of land in western Germany, had to be demilitarized and subjected to occupation by the Allies for 15 years. Other treaties were signed in 1919 with Austria, Hungary, Bulgaria, and Turkey that redrew the boundaries of Europe in the following ways:
  - Austria was obliged to recognize the independence of Czechoslovakia (combining the lands of the Czechs and Slovaks), which was inhabited by a large number of Germans.
  - Austria and Hungary became independent national states.
  - Poland became independent for the first time in the century.
  - Yugoslavia was created in the Balkans and dominated by the Serbs.

There were other treaties as well. These treaties, like the Versailles Treaty, were named after suburbs in Paris:

- The **Treaty of Trianon** (June 1920). Hungary lost about 70 percent of its territory to Romania, Yugoslavia, and Czechoslovakia and one third of its native Magyar population.
- The **Treaty of Neuilly** (November 1919). Bulgaria lost territory to Yugoslavia, Romania, and Greece.

- The **Treaty of Sèvres** (August 1920), provided for the following:
  - The liquidation of the Ottoman Empire by abolishing Turkish control in the Middle East, Mesopotamia (Iraq), Palestine (including Transjordan, which became a British mandate), and Lebanon (which became a French mandate).
  - The Ottoman Empire losing its non-Turkish territories, the Dardanelles, and the surrounding areas, which became internationalized and demilitarized. Turkey never recognized the Treaty of Sèvres. Although the treaty was accepted by the Sultan of Istanbul, it was rejected by the rival nationalist government of Kemal Ataturk who eventually signed the **Treaty of Lausanne** (1923), which nullified the Treaty of Sevres.

European leaders applied the principles of nationalism only to Europe. Despite the contributions of colonial soldiers who fought alongside European soldiers, the leaders at the Versailles Conference ignored Wilson's hope for self-determination for all people. France and Great Britain created systems of mandates over the former areas controlled by the Ottoman Empire. These mandates were to be held until these areas could stand alone. In actuality, they became European colonies. From Africa to the Middle East, colonized people believed that European leaders had betrayed them.

Impact of the War

The Versailles Treaty, which was the most important peace settlement that ended World War I, never really solved the problems that led to World War I. The United States rejected the treaty and did not join the League of Nations, which was established by 1920. France felt isolated when Great Britain backed out of a defensive alliance with her. Italy was angry because it did not get all the land that it was promised in its secret treaty with the Allies. Japan was upset that the West refused to recognize its claims in China. Russia was angry because it had been excluded from the conference and Poland and the Baltic states were carved out of its empire. Finally, Germany was angry because it thought that it was treated too harshly and was forced to sign the treaty. "Germany was stabbed in the back at Versailles" would be the rallying cry for the Nazi's rise to power.

World War I exacted a further toll upon Europe:

- 10 million soldiers were dead and 20 million were wounded. It cost $332 billion for war costs and property damages.
- The Ottoman Empire was destroyed and the Hohenzollern Dynasty of Germany, the Hapsburg Dynasty of the Austro-Hungarian Empire, and the Romanov Dynasty of Russia collapsed.
- Communism was established in Russia.
- The economies of Europe were weakened. Paying for the war brought heavy taxation and lower standards of living for the people of Europe. The United States emerged as a leading world power. America became a creditor nation from which the European nations borrowed in order to survive the devastation of the war.
- Psychologically, a generation was haunted by the horrors of the war and committed to never going to war again.
- World War I, which was called "the war to end all wars," created the seeds that would plunge Europe into another major war within twenty years.

Chronology of World War I

1879	Bismarck forms an alliance between Germany and the Austro-Hungarian Empire.
1882	Triple Alliance forms with Germany, the Austro-Hungarian Empire, and Italy.
1891	Germany begins to modernize its navy.
1894	Franco-Russian Alliance is formed.
1901	Guglielmo Marconi transmits telegraphic radio messages from Cornwall to Newfoundland.
1902	Great Britain enters into a military alliance with Japan.
1903	Orville and Wilbur Wright successfully fly a powered airplane.
1904	Entente Cordiale is formed between Great Britain and France in response to the Triple Alliance.
1905	Revolution erupts in Russia; Albert Einstein formulates the theory of relativity.
1906	Algeciras Conference—Great Britain and Italy support France's claim to Morocco against Germany's demand that Morocco be independent. This is a diplomatic defeat for Germany.
1907	Triple Entente is completed; military alliance formed among Great Britain, Russia, and France.
1911	Second Moroccan Crisis—Germany challenges French control of Morocco. Germany is forced to compromise.
1912	*S.S. Titanic* sinks on its maiden voyage; Second Balkan War begins (1912–1913).
June 28, 1914	Assassination of Archduke Ferdinand, heir to the throne of the Austro-Hungarian Empire.
July 28, 1914	The Austro-Hungarian Empire declares war on Serbia.
Aug. 1, 1914	In response to Russian mobilization, Germany declares war on Russia.
Aug. 3, 1914	Germany declares war on France.
Aug. 4, 1914	Great Britain declares war on Germany after Germany violates Belgium's neutrality.
Aug. 8, 1914	Japan enters the war against Germany.
Sept. 5–9, 1914	German advance in the west is stopped at the Battle of the Marne; Ottoman Empire and Bulgaria join forces with Germany.
Apr. 25, 1915	British and French troops attack the Ottoman Empire at Gallipoli.
Apr. 26, 1915	Italy joins the Allies in the secret Treaty of London and is promised colonies in Africa and the Middle East.
May 7, 1915	German submarine sinks the *Lusitania*, resulting in the loss of 139 American lives.
Feb.–Dec., 1916	Battle of Verdun; over 700,000 men are lost.
July–Nov., 1916	Battle of the Somme fails to achieve major breakthrough for the Allies; the British use tanks for the first time.
1917	Sigmund Freud's *A General Introduction to Psychoanalysis* is published; Zimmermann Telegram brings the United States closer to war with Germany.
Mar., 1917	Russian Revolution leads to the abdication of Czar Nicholas II. on March 15, 1917.
Apr. 6, 1917	United States declares war on Germany.
Nov. 6, 1917	Bolsheviks seize power in Petrograd.
Jan., 1918	President Woodrow Wilson issues his Fourteen Points, a framework for peace.
Mar. 3, 1918	Bolsheviks accept German peace terms at Brest-Litovsk.
Sept.-Oct., 1918	Allied offensive at Argonne breaks Germany's resistance.
Nov. 9, 1918	Kaiser Wilhelm II abdicates German throne and flees to Holland.
Nov. 11, 1918	Armistice ends the fighting along the western front; Austrian Emperor Charles I steps down.
Jan., 1919	The Versailles Peace Conference.
June, 1919	Versailles Treaty signed, imposing harsh settlement on Germany.

Sample Multiple-Choice Questions

1. Bismarck's alliance system was designed to

   A. promote relations with Great Britain.

   B. provide an opportunity for Germany to expand its borders.

   C. restrain Russia and the Austro-Hungarian Empire and isolate France.

   D. weaken the influence of the Ottoman Turks in the Balkans.

   E. encourage relations with France.

2. All of the following are usually considered the causes of World War I EXCEPT

   A. nationalism.

   B. rivalry over colonies in Africa and Asia.

   C. the arms race between Germany and Great Britain.

   D. rival alliances.

   E. Japanese aggression in the Pacific.

3. The Schlieffen Plan was designed to

   A. prevent Great Britain from helping France.

   B. rely on a slow defensive.

   C. achieve a quick victory over France.

   D. require Germany to defeat Russia quickly.

   E. require the use of Austro-Hungarian forces on the western front.

4. Which of the following new nations were created from the Austro-Hungarian empire as a result of the Versailles Treaty?

   A. Poland and Greece

   B. Czechoslovakia and Bulgaria

   C. Austria and Italy

   D. Yugoslavia and Poland

   E. Poland and Italy

5. Which of the following was characteristic of war on the western front?

   A. The use of airplanes allowed most of the fighting to be done in the sky.

   B. A number of inconclusive battles fought in trenches spread across the area.

   C. A propaganda war with little actual fighting took place.

   D. The terrain made it difficult to assemble large armies.

   E. A large-scale use of tanks occurred.

6. Women in World War I

   A. contributed little to the war effort.

   B. lost their economic position.

   C. made economic gains but few political gains.

   D. had very little change from their traditional roles during peacetime.

   E. maintained their nations' economies.

7. Which of the following nations did not gain independence after World War I?

   A. Poland

   B. Czechoslovakia

   C. Hungary

   D. Yugoslavia

   E. Bulgaria

8. All of the following are part of Wilson's Fourteen Points EXCEPT

   A. freedom of the seas.

   B. free trade.

   C. the end of secret treaties.

   D. aid to rebuild Germany and the Austro-Hungarian Empire.

   E. reduction of the arms race.

9. "... we shall fight for the things which have always been nearest our hearts, for democracy, for the right of those who submit to authority to have a voice in their own governments, for the rights and liberties of small nations, for a universal domination of rights by such a concert of free peoples as shall bring peace and safety to all nations and make the world itself at last free. ..." –President Woodrow Wilson

This statement by President Wilson is directly advocating the idea of

A. disarmament.
B. national self-determination.
C. territorial readjustments.
D. balance of power.
E. freedom of the seas.

10. Article 231 of the Versailles Treaty

A. contained the war guilt clause blaming Germany for World War I.
B. established the League of Nations.
C. ended the arms race.
D. divided Germany's colonies among the Allies.
E. returned Alsace-Lorraine to France.

Multiple-Choice Questions: Answers and Explanations

1. **C.** Bismarck's alliance system was designed to restrain Russia and isolate France. The rival aspirations of Austria and Russia in the Balkans were a major threat to peace. Bismarck was concerned that Germany would become involved if hostilities erupted. Bismarck also feared France's desire for revenge after her defeat in the Franco-Prussian War. These alliances were not formed for the purpose of promoting relations with Great Britain. In 1871, after Germany was united, Bismarck declared Germany to be satisfied. His alliances were not directly related to the weakening of the Ottoman Empire. The Ottoman Empire eventually became an ally of Germany. Bismarck's diplomacy promoted the isolation of a hostile France.

2. **E.** Japanese aggression in the Pacific is not considered a cause of World War I. Nationalism in the Balkans, rivalry over colonial possessions in Africa and Asia, the arms race between Germany and Great Britain, and the system of alliances are considered underlying causes that led to World War I.

3. **C.** The Schlieffen Plan was developed for a quick victory over France. The Schlieffen Plan called for defeating France first with a lightning attack through neutral Belgium before turning on Russia. The Germans thought that France could be defeated in six weeks. It was expected that Russia would take at least six weeks to fully mobilize before she could attack Germany. The Schlieffen Plan was directed at France and not at Great Britain. It relied on a quick offensive victory, not a slow defensive strategy. It was drawn up for a quick victory over France, not Russia, and did not include any Austro-Hungarian troops being used on the western front.

4. **D.** The Versailles Treaty resulted in the formation of several new nations. Yugoslavia was a new kingdom that was based on an expanding Serbia. Poland gained her independence after 100 years of foreign rule. Czechoslovakia rose out of the Austro-Hungarian Empire, but Bulgaria became independent in 1908. Greece and Italy had become independent in the nineteenth century.

5. **B.** A number of inconclusive battles fought in trenches across the area was characteristic of war on the western front. After the French stopped the German offensive at the Battle of the Marne in September 1914, the two opposing armies dug into the ground for trench warfare. The western front became deadlocked. Between the opposing trenches lay "no man's land," in which two armies fought over a few hundred yards and lost them without gaining a significant victory. In 1915, the British and French offensive never gained more than three miles of land from the enemy. At the Battle of the Somme in 1916, close to one-half million men lost their lives for 6 square miles. Zeppelins were used mainly for observations and later for small-scale bombing. The high casualty rate on the western front demonstrated that there were a number of costly battles. The government used propaganda to convince the home front that their cause was just. The terrain did not stop the Allies and Central Powers from assembling large armies. Tanks were not used often because they were slow and clumsy.

6. **E.** Women kept their nations' economies going during World War I. In every country, a large number of women left their homes and domestic service to work in industry, transportation, and offices. Women worked in war industries and manufacturing. They also built tanks, plowed fields, paved streets, and ran hospitals. When a food shortage occurred, British women went to the fields to grow their own food.

7. **E.** Bulgaria was part of the Ottoman Empire until 1878. In 1878, Russia forced the Ottoman Empire to give Bulgaria its autonomy as the Third Bulgarian State. It gained full independence in 1908. After World War I, Poland gained its independence after 100 years of foreign rule; Czechoslovakia and Hungary rose out of the old Austro-Hungarian state; and Yugoslavia was created in the Balkans with Serbian domination.

8. **D.** Wilson's Fourteen Points did not provide economic aid to rebuild Germany and the Austro-Hungarian Empire. Wilson's Fourteen Points provided a framework for peace that was directed at eliminating the causes of the war and not restructuring the defeated nations. Freedom of the seas, free trade, the end of secret treaties, and the reduction of the arms race were included in Wilson's Fourteen Points in the hope that "a just peace would be established to end all wars."

9. **B.** This statement by President Woodrow Wilson of the United States is directly advocating the idea of national self-determination. Self-determination means allowing people to decide for themselves under which government they wish to live. In January 1918, President Wilson issued the Fourteen Points, a plan for resolving World War I and preventing future wars. Seven of these points were specific suggestions for changing borders and creating new nations. The guiding idea behind these points was self-determination regarding the right of any national group to set up an independent state. The principle of self-determination resulted in a band of new nations emerging where the German, Austrian, and Russian empires had once ruled. These nations included the Baltic states of Estonia, Lithuania, and Latvia. Poland regained independence after more than 100 years of foreign rule. Three new republics, Czechoslovakia, Austria, and Hungary, rose out of the old Hapsburg Empire. In the Balkans, the new Slavic state of Yugoslavia became an independent nation, dominated by the Serbs. Disarmament means the reduction or limiting of national armies and navies. Territorial readjustments refer to the alignment of territories based on the interests of the nations who are strong enough to achieve their objectives. Balance of power is a policy designed to prevent any one nation from becoming too economically or militarily powerful. Freedom of the seas addresses the rights of neutral nations to trade with nations during wartime.

10. **A.** Article 231 of the Versailles Treaty contained the war guilt clause blaming Germany for World War I. The war guilt clause also held Germany responsible for all damages that it caused to the Allied nations. Article 231 did not establish the League of Nations. The Versailles Treaty required only Germany to limit its army to 100,000 soldiers. Article 231, moreover, did not deal with the issue of German colonies or the return of Alsace-Lorraine to France.

Europe in Crisis (1917–1939)

In Russia, World War I provided the spark that ignited conditions that had been simmering for decades. The Russian Czar Nicholas II, who had led Russia into World War I in 1914 with the enthusiastic support of the people, would become the target of their anger and frustration. By 1915, Russia's staggering casualties, her inability to provide the basic necessities for her people, and Nicholas' lack of leadership sparked a revolution that ended the 300-year-old dynasty of the Romanov family and—like the French Revolution of 1789—had a major effect on the world.

In 1917, Russia underwent two revolutions. In March 1917 continued disasters on the battlefield and riots in Petrograd over food and fuel shortages led to the collapse of the monarchy and the establishment of a republic. However, the insistence of the new provisional government on continuing to fight an unpopular war and its failure to provide food for the people enabled the Bolshevik Party to overthrow the government and set up a communist dictatorship. The Communist Revolution turned out to be the political fireball that would threaten all the other countries of Europe and influence world politics throughout the twentieth century. Disillusionment with the outcome of World War I created anxiety among people as scientists, psychologists, philosophers, writers, and artists began to question the moral foundations of Western society. The Great Depression contributed to doubts about the ability of Western democracy to deal with these issues.

The fear of communism also contributed to the rise of fascism in Italy and National Socialism (commonly known as Nazism) in Germany. Communists in Russia, fascists in Italy, and National Socialists followed a **totalitarian** form of government that was unique in the history of the world: a state-established, single-party dictatorship that used technology and communication to control the political, social, intellectual, and cultural components of its citizens' lives. The rise of totalitarian dictatorships presented a serious challenge to Western democracy.

As the dictators in Italy and Germany and the militarists in Japan pursued aggressive actions in their quest for empires, many European leaders, haunted by the memories of World War I, tried to avoid war through the policy of appeasement. However, appeasement only heightened the demands of the aggressors, and led to World War II in 1939, which proved to be more horrendous than anyone could have imagined.

The Russian Revolution

Czar **Nicholas II** (who reigned from 1894 to 1917) failed to understand the urgency of the problems created by industrialization, the rising influence of the middle class, and the anger of the exploited peasants and the **proletariat,** or working class. Because of these issues, political parties sprang up to meet the needs of various societal groups. The following groups were active at various times throughout the Russian Revolution.

Date Founded	Party	Beliefs and Significance
1898	SDs (Social Democrats), also known as the Russian Social Democratic Labor Party	Workers who wanted to remove the czar through strikes and mass action. They preached the revolutionary doctrines of Karl Marx (1818–1883). In 1903, at the Second National Congress, the SDs split into two factions that became known as the Bolsheviks and Mensheviks.
1903	Bolsheviks	**Vladimir Lenin** (1870–1924) was the founder and the leader of the Bolsheviks and favored a small, disciplined party of professional revolutionaries. He believed that a radical revolution was necessary to destroy capitalism. However, Marx had predicted that a communist revolution was inevitable only in industrial societies, such as those in Western Europe and the United States. Lenin thought that Marxism could occur in an agrarian Russia, if it were led by an intellectual elite. The Bolshevik Party became the Communist Party in 1918.

continued

Date Founded	Party	Beliefs and Significance
1903	Mensheviks	**Georgi Plekhanov** (1857–1918) was a Menshevik supporter who wanted a loosely organized, mass-party membership and believed that a bourgeoisie revolution must occur in Russia before it could move toward socialism. Plekhanov would support Russia's participation in World War I. In 1921, the Communist Party suppressed the Mensheviks.
1901–1922	SRs (Social Revolutionaries)	**Viktor Chernov** (1873–1952) was the party leader. His program called for the socialization of land, which was to be distributed among the peasants on the basis of need. In 1917, the party won a majority in the short-lived Constituent Assembly, which was disbanded by the Bolsheviks.
1905–1918	K-Ds (Kadets), the Constitutional Democratic Party	**Pavel Miliukov** (1859–1943), a famous Russian historian, was the founder of the Constitutional Democratic Party. This party was a middle-class group that supported a program of a liberal, constitutional monarchy with a liberal assembly. In 1906, the Kadets won a majority in the Duma. After 1907, the Kadets became fearful of the Social Revolutionaries and supported gradual constitutional change. Miliukov became foreign minister in the provisional government after the overthrow of the czar in March 1917. The Kadets were banned by the Bolsheviks in 1918.
1905	Octobrists	The Octobrists were led by **Alexander Guchkov** (1862–1936). The goal of the party was to help the government implement the October Manifesto. The Octobrists won the greatest number of seats during the Third Duma (1907–1912). In 1915, they joined the Constitutional Democratic Party, advocating a comprehensive program of reform. Guchkov became Minister of War in the provisional government.

Russo-Japanese War (1904–1905)

War broke out between Russia and Japan after the interests of the two nations conflicted over Korea and Manchuria. Nicholas entered the war with the hope that a call to fight for the Fatherland and faith in the czar would stem the unrest in his nation and lead to a quick victory. Despite its efforts, Russia suffered a humiliating defeat and was forced to sign the **Treaty of Portsmouth** (1905). Russia ceded the southern half of the Sakhalin Islands to Japan, surrendered its rights to Manchuria, and acknowledged Japan's special interest in Korea.

Russian Revolution of 1905

As the disasters of the war spread to the home front, evidence of government corruption and inefficiencies became public. Workers demanded shorter hours. Liberals called for reforms in government and for a constitution.

On Sunday, January 22, 1905, **Father Georgy Gapon,** a Russian Orthodox priest, organized a march of 200,000 unarmed workers to present a petition to the czar at the Winter Palace in St. Petersburg. The workers wanted an eight-hour workday, a representative assembly, the right to strike, and other liberal reforms. When the procession of workers reached the Winter Palace, it was attacked by soldiers who fired on the crowd. Over 100 workers were killed and some 300 were wounded. This incident, known as **Bloody Sunday,** led to a series of demonstrations and scattered uprisings across the nation. Universities closed down when student bodies staged a nationwide strike in response to the lack of civil liberties. Lawyers, doctors, engineers, and other middle-class workers established the Union of Unions and demanded a Constituent Assembly. Industrial workers all over Russia went on strike and in October 1905, the striking railroad workers paralyzed the nation. In St. Petersburg, the workers established **soviets,** or revolutionary councils that had first begun as strike committees but developed into elective bodies by the town workers. Over the next few months, Soviets of Workers' Deputies were established in over 50 different towns.

The Liberals in the **Zemstvos** (the provincial councils elected by the landowners and peasants which had been established by Czar Alexander II in 1864 as part of his land reforms) forced Nicholas II to make changes. In

October 1905, the czar issued the **October Manifesto,** promising to pass a new constitution that guaranteed certain civil rights and liberties, and created a lawmaking body, the **Duma,** elected by universal male suffrage. The Manifesto won over the moderates. However, many workers boycotted the election because they distrusted the czar and his supporters. Joined by the soldiers returning from the Russo-Japanese War, the workers denounced the Manifesto. In 1906, the first Duma met, but its powers were limited because it lacked control over finances and foreign affairs and was subject to dismissal by the czar. In 1906, at their first meeting, the members of the Duma put forth a series of demands including the release of political prisoners, trade union rights, and land reforms. Nicholas II rejected these proposals and dissolved the Duma.

Nicholas II appointed **Peter Stolypin,** a conservative minister who tried to restore order through arrests, *pogroms* (organized violence against the Jews), and executions. Alexander III had started these pogroms in 1881 as a way to establish a uniform Russian culture. However, Stolypin realized that Russia needed reforms as well as repressive measures. He introduced land reforms, strengthened the Zemstvos, abolished all debts on the land, permitted peasants to abolish the *mirs* (land village communities), and transferred land titles to the peasants. This led to the rise of a wealthy class of peasants, the **Kulaks.** Stolypin tried to improve education but was assassinated in 1911 by conservatives who thought that his reforms were too radical. The Duma met several times during these years (1911–1917) but the restriction of suffrage to the upper class limited its power and it became similar to a debating society.

World War I

World War I, like the Crimean and Russo-Japanese wars, quickly exhausted Russian resources. The transportation system was unable to provide soldiers with the food and supplies necessary to fight the war. As casualties mounted and reports circulated abut the poor leadership of the Russian generals, the public began to call for a new government led by the Duma and not the czar. Meanwhile, Nicholas II decided to personally join the army on the battlefront to lead the war effort—a mistake because he was not a military man. The fortunes of the military continued to decline as casualties rose and economic conditions worsened. In his absence, the czar put **Alexandra,** his wife, in charge of domestic affairs—another mistake as the Russians distrusted her because she was German-born and had little knowledge of how to run a government. Alexandra fell under the influence of mystic monk **Grigori Rasputin** (1869–1916), who convinced her that he had the power to stop the bleeding of her son, Alexis, a hemophiliac. By 1916, Rasputin had used his influence over Alexandra to control who would and who would not be appointed to government. Rumors spread that Alexandra and Rasputin were lovers and stories about profiteering and corruption in government over supplies for the military hurt the government even more. In December 1916, Rasputin was assassinated by a group of palace nobles who wanted to restore prestige to the throne. Nevertheless, the czar continued to resist any efforts at reform.

The March and November Revolutions

In Russia, the March and November revolutions are known as the February and October revolutions. At the time, Russia was still using the Julian Calendar, which was thirteen days behind the Western or Gregorian Calendar used in Western Europe. In 1918, Russia adapted the Western Calendar. The following list contains the sequence of events using the dates of the Western Calendar:

- **March 8–12, 1917:** Food riots and strikes break out in Petrograd (St. Petersburg). Nicholas sends troops to suppress the revolt but the troops refuse to fire on the crowd.
- **March 12, 1917:** The Duma, after being dismissed by the czar, sets up a provisional government or temporary government headed by the moderate Prince Georgy Lvov. The provisional government supports reforms such as freedom of speech and religion, the right to unionize, and other liberal programs.
- **March 15, 1917:** The czar abdicates.
- **March 17, 1917:** A republic is proclaimed. **Vladimir Lenin** (1870–1924), whose real name is Vladimir Ilyich Ulyanov, declares Russia the freest country in the world.
- **April 16, 1917:** Lenin, who had been exiled to Switzerland, is shipped back to Russia by the Germans in a sealed train. The Germans believe that Lenin will fight for peace immediately. After his arrival, Lenin begins to attract support with the slogans, "All land to the peasants," "Stop the war," and "All power to the Soviets."

- **May 17, 1917:** A reorganized government is formed that includes the socialist, **Alexander Kerensky** (1881–1970). Kerensky tours the eastern front where he appeals to the soldiers to continue fighting. Encouraged by the Bolsheviks who oppose the war, there are demonstrations against Kerensky in Petrograd. The provisional government, however, is not in tune with the desires of the Russian people and insists that the country's national duty is to continue involvement in World War I.

  From the beginning, the provisional government finds that its biggest problem is having to share power with the **Petrograd Soviet of Workers' and Soldiers' Deputies,** a council of workers and soldiers. The Soviets issue **Order No. 1,** stripping officers of their authority and placing power in the hands of a committee of soldiers. Army discipline breaks down and massive desertion and chaos spread over the country.

- **July, 1917:** Lenin fails in an attempt to overthrow the government and is forced to go into hiding; other Bolshevik leaders are thrown into jail. Events begin to turn in favor of the Soviets. Lvov retires and Kerensky replaces him on July 17, 1917. Kerensky appoints General **Lavr Kornilov** (1870–1918) as supreme commander of the Russian army; however, Kornilov and Kerensky soon disagree over military policy. To Kornilov, Kerensky is weak and unable to restore order and stability to the country and to the military. Kornilov also wants to restore the death penalty for soldiers. Lenin returns from Finland and works closely with spellbinding orator **Leon Trotsky** (born Lev Bronstein, 1879–1940). During his exile from Russia for his opposition to the czar, Trotsky lived in the Bronx at the beginning of 1917 and then returned to Russia in May 1917 and joined the Bolshevik party.

- **September/October 1917:** Kerensky dismisses Kornilov from office when they are unable to resolve their differences. In retaliation, Kornilov orders troops to seize control of the government in Petrograd. Kerensky appeals to the Petrograd Soviet for support. The Petrograd soldiers free the Bolsheviks from prison to help them prepare the city for attack. The Bolsheviks, led by Lenin and Trotsky, agree to support Kerensky in defense of the city. Within a few days, the Bolsheviks recruit over 25,000 men. When Kornilov's troops refuse to attack Petrograd, the coup fails. Kornilov is arrested but escapes. (Later he becomes commander of the White Army during the Civil War in Russia.) Kerensky now becomes the supreme commander. As soon as the Petrograd soldiers are behind the Bolsheviks and Trotsky becomes head of the Petrograd Soviet, Russia is ripe for revolution. With Trotsky as the head of the Petrograd Soviet and with Lenin and the Bolsheviks able to control a militia of over 25,000 men, Kerensky is unable to reassert his authority.

- **November 6, 1917:** Bolshevik soldiers, led by Trotsky, storm the Winter Palace and other key centers in Petrograd. Kerensky escapes and lives briefly in Finland, England, and France before going to the United States in 1940 when the Germans overrun France. He spends much of his time in the States teaching at the Hoover Institute at Stanford University. He dies in 1970. In Moscow and other vital areas, the Bolsheviks succeed in taking over and establishing control.

- **November 7, 1917:** The Russian Soviet Federative Socialist Republic is established with Lenin as the head of state. Trotsky is appointed People's Commissar for Foreign Affairs and **Joseph Stalin** (1879–1953), whose real name is Josef Dzhugashvili, is made the People's Commissar of Nationalities.

The Bolsheviks were successful in winning the revolution because Lenin and Trotsky were superior leaders who provided solutions to the anarchy that existed in Russia. Unlike the provisional government, they also appealed to the peasants, the industrial workers, and the soldiers exhausted by war, with their slogan, "Peace, Land, and Bread."

Soviet Russia from 1918 to 1928

Lenin used the motto, "Promises are like pie crust, made to be broken," as a guide in organizing his government. An immediate problem for Lenin was the Constituent Assembly. The provisional government had finally scheduled elections for November 25, 1917, under universal male suffrage. Thirty-six million people voted and the results were a stunning blow to the Bolshevik Party, which received only one-fourth of the votes, with the majority going to the Social Revolutionaries. Lenin had no intention of giving up power to the freely elected Constituent Assembly. The Assembly met in January, 1918, but after two days, Lenin ordered the soldiers to disburse it. This was Lenin's first step in the process of setting up a one-party dictatorship.

In March of 1918, Russia withdrew from World War I by signing the **Treaty of Brest-Litovsk** and ceding Latvia, Lithuania, Estonia, Russian Poland, and the Ukraine to Germany. Of course, much of this treaty was torn up after Germany surrendered and signed the armistice in November 1918. Russia had lost about one-third of its population in the war.

Civil War in Russia (1918–1921)

Opposition to Lenin's government began to develop. Officers of the old army, joined by the Kulaks or well-to-do peasants (**Whites**) and most other Russian political parties, organized resistance to the Bolsheviks (**Reds**). The Whites wanted self-rule rather than a Bolshevik dictatorship. A small Allied mission was sent by the British, French, and Americans to help the Whites. In the spring of 1918, the Allies landed near Archangel in northern Russia. Although they remained there until the end of 1919, their mission was unsuccessful, as the Whites could never really unite. To protect the revolution, the Reds acted ruthlessly, assassinating Czar Nicholas II and his family, defeating all threats, and thus winning the Civil War. The Red Army was successful because Trotsky was a superb military organizer who reformed the military into an efficient fighting force. The Reds also had a well-defined political program and—under the guise of **War Communism**—Lenin nationalized all major industries, which contributed to a total war effort; the state also forcibly requisitioned grain and shipped it from the country-side to feed the army and the workers in the cities. Lenin also used the **Cheka,** or the **Commission for Combating Counter-Revolution and Sabotage,** as a secret police force to control all dissent within Russia through the use of terror. Finally, the Reds appealed to Russian nationalism to counteract foreign aid to the Whites. The Whites also failed because their political program was vaguely conservative and did not unite all the foes of the Reds under a democratic banner. White leaders refused to call for a democratic republic and a federation of nationalities that could have helped their cause against the Reds. By 1920, the Bolsheviks had firmly established control of Russia. In 1922, Russia became officially known as the **Union of Soviet Socialist Republics (U.S.S.R.),** containing four republics: the Russian Soviet Federative Socialist Republic (SFSR), the Ukrainian Soviet Socialist Republic (SSR), the Byelorussian SSR, and the Transcaucasian SFSR (combining the territories of Georgia, Azerbaijan, and Armenia).

Russia's New Economic Policy

The Civil War in Russia had caused the deaths of millions, and the famine of 1921–1922 claimed additional millions. In March 1921, a major rebellion broke out in Kronstadt, a naval base near Petrograd that had been a stronghold of Bolshevism. The sailors were angry at the lack of political freedom and the failure of War Communism to provide enough food for the population. Lenin, with Trotsky's support, quickly crushed the rebellion. The Kronstadt rebellion was the first major internal uprising against Soviet rule in Russia since the end of the Civil War. Lenin realized that he needed to readjust his economic policies. In 1921, he introduced the **New Economic Policy (NEP)** to replace War Communism. Under this system, the peasants were allowed to sell surplus crops on the open market and private owners were allowed to operate retail stores for profit. The major industries still remained under government control. The NEP, a temporary retreat from communism, revived the economy. By 1927, agricultural and industrial production had reached pre-World War I levels.

Trotsky, leader of the Left Opposition, was critical of the NEP because he believed that communism had to become a worldwide revolution in order to survive and wanted to return to the state control of War Communism. **Nikolai Bukharin** (1888–1938), leader of the Right Opposition, wanted to extend the NEP and restore even more private enterprise. He supported building communism within the Soviet state. Neither of these men would pick up the mantel of leadership after Lenin's death.

The Rise of Stalin

Lenin suffered two strokes in 1922 and one more in March of 1923. He died in 1924 at the age of 54, leaving Trotsky and Stalin as the chief contenders for power. Stalin, a Georgian who had joined the Communist Party in 1902, was not interested in an ideological debate but wanted to gain power for himself. As the first General Secretary of the Communist Party, he was able to establish power within the Soviet system. Trotsky was a brilliant theorist, who had engineered the success of the Red Army in the Civil War but his theory of worldwide or permanent revolution did not appeal to the Soviet people. Stalin, with his theory of "Socialism in one country," believed that Russia with its vast resources could build itself up as a socialist country alone, without support from the outside and with no need for a worldwide revolution. This theory was more attractive to people, as it made revolution seem distant, and the need to make the Soviet Union better was a more realistic goal. In 1927, Stalin expelled Trotsky from the party and sent him to Central Asia. Trotsky eventually fled to the West, but was assassinated in Mexico on orders from Stalin. Stalin, who had used Bukharin to oust Trotsky from power, expelled him from the party in 1929, which left Stalin in undisputed control of the Soviet Union.

In 1928, Stalin introduced his first **Five-Year Plan** of centralized government, intending to increase industrial and agricultural production in order to transform the Soviet Union into an industrial giant. His plan was to increase the production of heavy industry, such as coal and steel, in order to produce weapons that would strengthen the country militarily. Stalin appealed to the nationalism of the people by promising that his Five-Year Plan would enable Russia to catch up with Western countries. Stalin financed this plan by means of the **collectivization** of the farmers (forcible consolidation of individual farms into state-controlled enterprises), waging a preventive war against the Kulaks to bring them and their land under state control. The collectivization of the farms was an agricultural disaster and a human tragedy. Peasants were shot on sight if they refused to join the collective farms. Millions of peasants and Kulaks died because of Stalin's brutal policy. By 1935, 95 percent of Russian farms had become collective. There were two different types of collective farms:

- **kolkhoz:** This was a collective farm that was owned and operated by its members, who were forced to deliver a large part of their crop to the state at prices fixed by the state. Sometimes the prices were so low that the peasants earned little from their work. The only benefit was that each family was allowed to cultivate a small plot for their own use. From this plot, they could sell any surplus crops on the open market.
- **sovkhoz:** This was a larger farm than the kolkhoz, where the peasants were simply employees and paid a straight salary.

The government also set up hundreds of Machine and Tractor Stations throughout the country. Collectivization helped to make it easier for the government to control the people. It was also a political victory for Stalin and the Communist Party, as peasants were eliminated as a potential threat and the state was able to control and regulate farms, thus taking what it needed for its industrial program.

From 1934 to 1938, Stalin also directed a series of **purge** trials, which consisted of trumped-up or false accusations, mock trials, and then suicides or executions. Stalin's **Reign of Terror** resulted in the deaths of those who were important in the founding of the revolution, as well as high military officers and others who were not loyal to him. Stalin intertwined terror within the state and it is estimated that he ordered the deaths of over 15 million people. By 1938, Stalin's cruel and brutal methods had enabled him to establish complete control over Russia and transformed the Soviet Union into an industrial giant. However, Stalin's cruelty had created fear and terror throughout the nation.

Western Democracies (1920–1929)

Great Britain, like other European countries, emerged from World War I with a set of unique problems: Its overseas trade was destroyed, the nation was deeply in debt, and its factories were outdated. In 1920, over 2 million people were unemployed, with unemployment averaging about 12 percent annually until the Great Depression began in 1929.

The **Labour Party** surpassed the **Liberal Party** in strength. Labour leaders gained support by promising social legislation. The middle class backed the **Conservative Party,** which held power during most of the decade. In 1923, the Labour Party reigned briefly under the leadership of **Ramsay MacDonald,** whose government failed because of his efforts to establish formal ties with the Soviet Union. From 1924 to 1929, **Stanley Baldwin** and the Conservative Party ruled as the fear of communism and a general strike by miners contributed to a drift toward the right. The Conservative government introduced protective tariffs, with the result that other nations retaliated with protective tariffs against British goods. Agricultural production faced competition from increased production abroad. The Great Depression of 1929 resulted in a series of coalition governments with leadership from all three parties. Ramsay MacDonald, who was the leader of the Labour Party, resigned in 1935 because of ill health. He was replaced by conservatives Stanley Baldwin and later **Neville Chamberlain** in 1937, who ruled until the start of World War II.

Political Parties Active in Great Britain in the 1920s and 1930s		
Party	**Leaders**	**Beliefs**
Conservative Party	**Stanley Baldwin** (1867–1947; in office 1923–24, 1924–29, 1935–37)	Conservatives were called Tories before the 1832 suffrage bill.
	Neville Chamberlain (1869–1940; in office 1937–40)	Supported high tariffs and social reform, as the number of unemployed began to rise in the 1930s.
		Drew support from the upper-middle class, industrialists, and prosperous farmers.
		Supported free enterprise.
Labour Party	**Ramsay MacDonald** (1866–1937; in office 1924, 1929–31, 1931–35)	Favored nationalization of major industries.
		Urged the expansion of the welfare program.
		Supporters were workers, small farmers, and shopkeepers.
Liberal Party	**Lloyd George** (1863–1945; in office 1916–22)	Formerly the Whig Party.
		Lost upper-class support to the Conservatives and lower-class support to the Labour Party.
		Became a minority party after 1922.

Empire Affairs

By the 1920s, the British Empire covered one-fourth of the world. The British had colonies in Asia, Africa, North America (Canada), South America, the West Indies, and Australasia (Australia and New Zealand). Britain enacted the **Statute of Westminster** in 1931, which set up the **Commonwealth of Nations** that granted self-rule to the colonies of Canada, Australia, New Zealand, and South Africa. These nations were linked together by economic and cultural ties, but each member of the Commonwealth pursued its own course. They had supported Great Britain during World War I and were all part of the British Imperial War Cabinet that had helped set up war policy. By 1931, these nations had become vital trading partners with Great Britain. However, Great Britain was not willing to allow freedom for colonies in the other areas that they controlled because Great Britain, like other Western countries, did not believe that these colonies were ready for self-government.

The greatest opposition to colonial rule came from India, where **Mohandas Gandhi** (1869–1948) proposed a policy of non-violent and passive resistance to British rule and actions. Despite challenges from nationalist groups, the British Empire would still stretch around the world and be a source of wealth and pride.

The British still faced the Irish Question, which was the Irish demand for self-rule (or **home rule**). Throughout the 1800s, the Irish demand for home rule intensified. The British refused to consider the question because of the concern for Ireland's Protestants. In the 1600s, English and Scottish Protestant settlers had colonized Ireland and took possession of the best lands primarily in the North, which became known as **Ulster.** Irish Protestants were fearful that they would be a minority in an independent, Catholic country. Finally, Parliament passed the Home Rule Act in 1914, but it was put on hold when World War I began. Irish militants refused to wait and launched the **Easter Rising** in 1916, but the British quickly crushed it. From 1919 until 1922, the **Irish Republican Army** (IRA) waged savage guerrilla warfare until moderate leaders in Ireland and England worked out a compromise. Most of Ireland was free and became known as the **Irish Free State** or **Éire.** The six northern Protestant counties (Ulster) remained under British rule. The compromise ended the immediate violence, but many nationalists and the IRA never accepted this division. The problems of Northern Ireland would remain an unresolved issue throughout the twentieth century.

France (1919–1929)

Like Great Britain, France suffered enormous casualties in the war, including a severe loss of its young population and the destruction of nearly one-quarter of its manufacturing industries and agriculture. France had borrowed a great deal of money during the war and relied heavily on German reparations to help spur its economy. The inability of Germany to make these repayments created a financial crisis that led to the steady decline of the franc. In January 1923, **Raymond Poincaré** (1860–1934), the French prime minister, sent troops into the Ruhr Valley to obtain payments when Germany defaulted on its loans. The French invasion led to a wave of patriotism in Germany and the government ordered the people of the Ruhr Valley to stop working and passively resist the French occupation. Poincaré's action was criticized by the British and the United States. By the summer of 1923, a compromise was reached when a moderate German government, under **Gustav Stresemann** (1878–1929), assumed leadership. The Germans called off the passive resistance and agreed to pay off the reparations, but asked for a reevaluation of Germany's ability to pay.

Throughout the 1920s, political divisions and financial problems plagued the French government, which was ruled by a coalition of parties from conservatives to communists who competed for power. France's chief foreign-policy concern was securing its borders against Germany. To prevent a future invasion, France constructed the **Maginot Line,** a series of concrete fortifications along its western boundaries; it also sought security by building buffer states (making treaties with other countries) around Germany, including the U.S.S.R. In the **Locarno Pact** (1925), Germany promised to accept as permanent its western boundaries with Belgium and France, as well as guaranteeing that the Rhineland remain demilitarized. In 1928, the **Kellogg-Briand Pact** was signed by France—and later, 64 other nations—outlawing war as an instrument of foreign policy.

A Culture in Conflict

The horrors of World War I shattered the values and beliefs that had guided Western society since the Age of Enlightenment. People generally became less optimistic and had less faith in rational thinking. There was a rejection of accepted beliefs and the power of the rational mind to understand society. The writer **Gertrude Stein** (1874–1946) referred to many of her fellow American expatriates, who consisted of painters and artists, as the "Lost Generation." They had fought in World War I and rejected the Victorian Age's moral values, which had been destroyed by the carnage and suffering created by the war. Scientists, psychologists, philosophers, and writers began to propose new ideas to address the issue that human beings were violent and capable of irrational and destructive behavior. Although some of these ideas had their origins in the late-nineteenth century, they became more prevalent in the 1920s and 1930s.

Physics

By the late 1890s, scientists expressed reservations that a mechanical model and absolute time and space described the world. German physicists and contemporaries Max Planck and Albert Einstein vigorously challenged this approach. **Max Planck** (1858–1947) is considered the founder of quantum theory, which states that all energy is made up of discrete packets or quanta and is not a continuous stream. Planck's work with subatomic energy and his discovery called into question the old view of atoms as stable, basic building blocks of nature.

Albert Einstein (1879–1955) proposed the **theory of relativity,** in which he postulated that the measurement of space and time were not absolute and were relative to the viewpoint or position of the observer. **Relative motion** is the key to Einstein's ideas, which had implications not only for science but for how people viewed the universe. His ideas raised questions about the Newtonian perspective of a world operating according to absolute laws of motion and gravity. His theory of relativity expressed by the equation $E = mc^2$ (energy = mass × the speed of light squared) showed that large amounts of energy could be released from a small amount of matter. The atomic bomb would illustrate this principle. In 1935 Einstein immigrated to the United Sates because of the National Socialists' rise to power.

Psychology

Sigmund Freud (1856–1939) was an Austrian physician who challenged faith in reason. Prior to Freud, scholars assumed that the conscious mind processed experiences in a rational and logical way. In *The Interpretation of Dreams* (1900), Freud said that the key to understanding the mind is the irrational unconscious (the **id**), which is driven by sexual aggression and pleasure-seeking desires. Human behavior is a compromise between the id and the **ego,** the rationalizing conscious that meditates what a person can do, and the ingrained moral values of society (the **superego**), which checks or represses our powerful urges. Tension between repressed drives and social norms causes psychological illness. Freud was a pioneer in the field of **psychoanalysis,** the study of how the mind works and how to treat mental disorders.

Philosophy

The following men attacked traditional beliefs in rational human behavior and Western society.

Philosophers	Main Ideas
Friedrick Nietzche (German; 1844–1900)	Western civilization is in decline because Christianity embodied a slave morality that glorified weakness. A few superior individuals or a superman need to become the leader of these inferior people. Hitler used Nietzche's ideas to support the use of brute force to glorify war.
Henri Bergson (French; 1859–1941)	Immediate intuition and experiences are as important as rational and scientific thinking.
George Sorel (French Socialist; 1847–1922)	Rejected democracy. Argued that socialism would succeed through great violent strikes of all working people.
Soren Kierkegaard (Danish; 1813–1855)	Like Nietzche, condemned Christianity. Established the foundation for existentialism.
Jean Paul Sartre (French; 1905–1980)	Popularized existentialism, a belief that individuals can overcome the meaninglessness of life by self-affirmation of one's own values and beliefs. Ideas important in France after World War II because they promoted positive action in a period of hopelessness.

The New Literature

The horrors of World War I and the influence of Freudianism, which focused on the irrationality of the human experience, affected writers of the 1920s and 1930s.

- **T. S. Eliot** (1888–1965), an American living in England, wrote *The Waste Land* (1922), which depicted the modern world drained of hope and faith.

- **Oswald Spengler** (1880–1936), a German writer, in *The Decline of the West* (1918), and Czech-born writer **Franz Kafka** (1883–1924), in *The Trial* (1925), predicted a dystopian future.

- English writer **Virginia Woolf** (1882–1941) and Irish novelist **James Joyce** (1882–1941) adapted the "stream of consciousness" style of writing, probing and examining a character's random thoughts and feelings that bubbled up without logic or order. Woolf's *Mrs. Dalloway* and Joyce's *Ulysses* explore the inner thoughts of the characters as they go through the daily routines of life. In *Ulysses,* Joyce breaks with normal sentence structure and vocabulary in order to mirror the workings of the human mind.

Rebellion in Art /Music

In 1903, Spanish artist **Pablo Picasso** (1881–1973) founded **cubism**. Cubism is based on the following concepts:

- Transformation of natural shapes into geometric forms.
- Breaking three-dimensional objects into complex patterns of angles and planes.
- Focusing on moods rather than nature or objects.

Dadaism originated in Switzerland in the First World War and was popular in the 1920s. It was a movement using art forms as a weapon against prevailing standards in art. The term "Dada," indicated the loss of meaning in existing culture. Artists noted that established societal values had become meaningless due to the horrors of World War I. Two important artists were German-French sculptor, painter, and abstract artist **Hans Arp** (1887–1966) and German painter and sculptor **Max Ernst** (1891–1976). Harp's work entitled *Collage with Squares Arranged According to the Laws of Chance* (1917) and Ernst's painting, *The Virgin Chastises the Infant Jesus Before Three Witnesses* (1926) were intended to shock and disturb followers of traditional art.

Surrealism was influenced by Freud and cubism. Surrealists attempted to portray the workings of the unconscious. Spanish artist **Salvador Dalí's** (1904–1989) famous painting *The Persistence of Memory* (1931) portrays a dream where there is no certitude, not even time.

Developments in music also broke with traditional convention. The ballet, *The Rite of Spring,* by Igor Stravinsky (1882–1971) resulted in a riot when it was first performed in Paris in 1913 by Sergei Diaghilev's famous Russian ballet company, the Ballet Russe. Stravinsky's pulsating music and the earthy performances of the dancers were considered shocking and almost pornographic.

Architecture

Functionalism became the dominant trend, emphasizing efficiency and cleanliness instead of ornamentation. **Frank Lloyd Wright** (1867–1959), an American architect, was the founder of functionalism. **Walter Gropius** (1883–1969) was the founder of the Bauhaus school of architecture which was a major proponent of functionalism and industrial form in Germany. Another leader of the Bauhaus school was **Miles van der Rohe** (1886–1969) who became director of the school from 1930 until 1933 and eventually immigrated to the United States in 1937 under pressure from the Nazi regime. He settled in Chicago where his classic Lake Shore Apartments, built between 1948 and 1951, symbolized modern architecture after World War II.

Mass Media

The general public embraced movies, radio, and advertising in the 1920s and 1930s. Radio, which had become possible due to Guglielmo Marconi's development of wireless communication, was common in most households. By the late 1930s, three out of four houses in Britain and Germany had a radio. Adolf Hitler and other dictators used the radio for political propaganda.

Movies became a source of entertainment and were very powerful tools of indoctrination. In the 1920s, **Sergei Eisenstein** (1898–1948) brilliantly dramatized the communists' view of history. In Germany, Hitler turned to the filmmaker **Leni Riefenstahl** (1902–2003) to make documentary propaganda. Her film, *Triumph of the Will,* depicts the joyful crowds and mass procession of Nazi followers welcoming Hitler at Nuremberg in 1934. The new media was becoming a potentially dangerous instrument of political manipulation.

The Great Depression

The Great Depression did not begin with the **Wall Street Crash** of October 1929; its beginnings were much earlier. Despite their popular image, the Roaring Twenties were not as glamorous as they appeared. Beneath the economic boom, there were serious problems. People were overextended on credit and speculators had invested heavily in the market with the hope of a good return to offset their borrowing. The United States led the world in industrial and agricultural output, and the availability of their loans helped to finance the European recovery. In 1924, the United States developed the **Dawes Plan,** which provided a solution for the reparation problem by lending money to Germany so it could pay France and Great Britain. In turn, France and Great Britain could pay back loans to the United States that they had taken out during World War I. In 1929, the **Young Plan** further reduced German reparation. The economies of the United States and Europe were so intertwined that when the market crashed in the United States in 1929, it had a worldwide effect.

As the United States economy faltered, American banks began to recall their loans, which had a dramatic effect on the European economies. The financial crisis led to a decline in production in the United States. Countries began to raise tariffs to protect their industries, which led to further decline. In 1931, the Creditanstalt, the most important bank in Austria, collapsed, and banks throughout Germany and Eastern Europe also began to collapse. By 1932, the economies of Europe were only producing at one-half of their 1929 level. In the United States, one-fourth of the population was unemployed. **Franklin D. Roosevelt** (American president from 1933–1945) proposed the **New Deal**, whose goal was to preserve capitalism through reform. He introduced social legislation including **Social Security** (a government program designed to provide basic income for those who have retired), and attacked the problem of mass unemployment by using federal government funds to support public works projects. Roosevelt supported the ideas of the English economist, **John Maynard Keynes** (1883–1946), who urged that the government prime the pump, or spend during the Depression in order to get the economy going again. Although the New Deal helped the United States, it failed to pull the United States out of the Depression until war threatened Europe in 1939.

Great Britain

During the Great Depression, Great Britain did not follow Keynes' program. The national government (a coalition of Labourites and Conservatives) followed orthodox economics by trying to balance the budget, going off the gold standard, and concentrating on the national markets. By 1937, production had grown by 27 percent, but Britain, like the United States, did not come out of the Depression until the advent of World War II.

France

Because France was less industrialized and more isolated from the world community, it experienced the effects of the Great Depression later. Still, a steady economic downturn did occur through 1935, adding to an unstable political climate. In 1933, five coalition governments were formed and fell in rapid succession. In 1934, fascists rioted and threatened to overthrow the republic. In 1936, the communists, socialists, and radicals formed an alliance—the **Popular Front**—and united behind **Léon Blum** (1872–1950). Inspired by Franklin D. Roosevelt's New Deal, he encouraged social reform, complete with paid vacations and 40-hour work-weeks. The radical elements were not satisfied, however, and the wealthy began to sneak money out of the country. Blum was forced to resign in 1937 and was replaced by the conservative **Édouard Daladier** (1884–1970), who overturned Blum's reforms.

The Rise of Totalitarianism

The democratic countries of Great Britain and France muddled through the Depression. They survived, but neither country had strong enough leadership to meet the challenge. The void of democratic leadership on the European continent convinced many Europeans that dictatorships could provide hope for the future, especially as the Soviet Union had been one of the countries least affected by the economic crisis.

The post–World War I period gave rise to fascism in Italy and National Socialism in Germany. The roots of fascism and Nazism were found in racism, extreme nationalism, an emphasis on violence, and the glorification of war as the highest virtue in society. The economic, political, and social conditions of post–World War I contributed to the rise of each of these political movements, both of them forms of **totalitarianism**—a movement that stresses that the individual is less important than the state and the goals of the state are never subordinate to those of the individual. Fascism rose first in Italy in 1922 because of the dissatisfaction created by World War I. Nazism in Germany arose due to the problems created by World War I and the chaos caused by the Great Depression. Following is a chart highlighting the major characteristics of Mussolini's fascist Italy and Hitler's Nazi Germany:

Mussolini's Fascist Italy and Hitler's Nazi Germany		
Leader	**Benito Mussolini—"Il Duce" (Fascism)**	**Adolf Hitler—"Der Führer"—National Socialist Party (Nazism)**
Date	1922–1945	1933–1945
Country	Italy	Germany
Basic ideas	Attacked democracy and supported dictatorship. Opposed goals of Marxism. Advocated extreme nationalism. Wanted to restore the greatness of the Roman Empire. Glorified violence in war. Slogan: "Believe, Fight, and Obey".	Attacked democracy and supported dictatorship. Opposed goals of Marxism. Advocated extreme nationalism, uniting all German people. Advocated a belief in Aryan supremacy. Promoted anti-Semitism—believed Germany was the Master Race and the Jewish people Germany's greatest enemy.
Reasons for popular appeal	Economic distress—inflation drove up prices and widespread unemployment. Fear of communism, where workers seize factories and peasants seize lands. Landowners and industrialists supported fascists who promised to fight socialists and communism. Appealed to nationalism—nationalists and militarists were unhappy with Italy's failure to gain territories from the Paris Peace Conference. Weak government—no political party dominated the government, which was unable to maintain law and order and deal with the threat of fascism. Leadership of Mussolini, who was a socialist, but became ultra-nationalist in World War I. In 1919, he organized veterans and discontented Italians into the Fascist Party; he was a fiery speaker who promised to end corruption and replace turmoil with order.	Economic distress—inflation spiraled out of control (a loaf of bread cost 10,000 Marks); the government printed huge quantities of paper money to pay off its war debt; the Great Depression caused havoc (6 million Germans out of work). The unemployment rate was at 43 percent. Hitler promised work and bread for the people. Fear of communism—by 1930, communists polled over six million votes; conservatives feared a communist takeover. Appealed to nationalism—Germans of all classes refused to accept the Versailles Treaty; they hated the War Guilt Clause with its heavy reparation payment; many accused Marxists and Jews of stabbing Germany in the back; the Nazis exploited nationalism. Weak government—in 1919, a new German Republic was established in the city of Weimar; the Weimar Republic. Parliamentary democracy had no single dominant party; they were unable to deal with the country's pressing problems. Leadership of Hitler—born in Austria, and an unsuccessful artist, he was wounded in World War I; he was shocked by the Versailles Treaty; he founded the National Socialist Party in 1920; the Munich Beer Hall Putsch (coup) failed (1923); while in jail, Hitler wrote **Mein Kampf** (My Struggle), outlining the goals of Nazism. He was a charismatic orator who promised to restore the greatness of Germany.

Leader	Benito Mussolini—"Il Duce" (Fascism)	Adolf Hitler—"Der Führer"—National Socialist Party (Nazism)
Steps to power	Mussolini formed the *Fasci italiani di combattimento* (the Union of Combat), which used violence to gain power. The *Squadristi* (Black Shirts) were created to break up socialist rallies and eliminate opponents. May 1921—Mussolini's Fascist Party gained 35 seats in the General Election. October 1922—The fascists marched on Rome, and King Victor Emmanuel II appointed Mussolini as Premier.	Hitler organized Storm Troopers (SA, Brown Shirts), his personal army to fight communists. Election of 1930—the Nazi Party gained 107 seats in the parliamentary elections, a step up from 12 in 1928. Hitler promised to deal with problems created by the Great Depression. January 20, 1933—President von Hindenburg, a military hero of World War I, appointed Hitler as Chancellor. February 1933—the Reichstag Fire was blamed on the Communist Party. Hitler suspended all civil liberties. The Nazi Party failed to gain a majority in the national elections—44 percent of the vote. Hitler banned all parties. The Reichstag passed the Enabling Act, giving Hitler absolute power for four years. June 30, 1934—Night of the Long Knives—Hitler's SS arrested and put to death Ernst Rohm, leader of the Brown Shirts, and 1,000 of his troops.
Features of government	Economic—a corporate state representing business, labor, and government; the Fascist Party controlled industry, agriculture, and trade; workers were forbidden to strike; private ownership was permitted but strictly regulated; this was a model for New Deal laws in the United States. Social policy—women were encouraged to have large families; women were valued as wives, not workers; Mussolini was glorified as a father figure.	**Heinrich Himmler** (1900–1945), head of the **Gestapo,** or Secret Police—suppressed all opposition. Economic—the Nazi Party brought business and labor under government control; the state controlled prices, production, and profits; workers were not allowed to strike. Social policy—**Joseph Goebbels** (1897–1945) used propaganda—the Big Lie Technique—to glorify Hitler. Nineteenth-century composer Richard Wagner's music reinforced the heroism of Nazism. Women were offered bonuses for purebred Aryan children. Restriction of Catholic churches. All Protestant churches were united into one single state religion; Jews were blamed for all of Germany's problems; steps were taken to drive Jews out of Germany.
Results	Reduced unemployment. Sponsored public works—the Pontine Marshes, south of Rome, were drained and restored to agricultural uses. Settled dispute with the Vatican: the Lateran Treaty (1929), recognized the pope as the sovereign of Vatican City. Pope Pius XII recognized fascism as legitimate.	Public Works Program led to economic recovery. This renewed Germany's power through the rebuilding of the armed forces. The Berlin Olympics (1936) restored national pride.
Failings	Destroyed democracy. Living standards were still low compared to Western Europe. Efforts to restore Italian greatness led to their defeat in World War II. Many postwar problems.	Destroyed democracy. Super nationalism and militarism led to the massive destruction during World War II. A policy of anti-Semitism/genocide led to the deaths of millions of people.

Failure of Appeasement

The challenge to world peace followed a set pattern during the 1930s. Dictators and militarists in Italy, Germany, and Japan took aggressive actions, which other European countries met with the policy of appeasement—capitulating to the aggressors' demands in order to avoid war. France was demoralized from World War I and Great Britain believed that Hitler was justified in violating the Versailles Treaty because it was too harsh. Both countries also believed that Nazism was a better alternative than the specter of communism spreading over Europe. Adopting an appeasement policy also was necessitated by the Great Depression, which had drained the strength of the Western democracies. The United States, which had rejected the Versailles Treaty in 1920, passed a series of neutrality acts in the 1930s that were intended to prevent American involvement in a European conflict, but not to prevent a war. In Japan, the economic disasters of the Great Depression and the rise of militarists and ultranationalists led to the demand for expansion. Militarists argued that only by foreign conquests would Japan gain respect as a great nation as well as gain the necessary resources to help meet the nation's economic needs.

The actions of Japan, Germany, and Italy from 1931 to 1939 and the subsequent responses of other European powers demonstrated the failure of the appeasement policy. The following list shows the steps leading to the failure of appeasement:

- **1931–32:** Japan invades Manchuria. The League of Nations fails to halt the aggressors and reveals its weaknesses.
- **1933:** Hitler pulls Germany out of the League of Nations.
- **1935:** Hitler begins to remilitarize in violation of the Versailles Treaty. France and Great Britain do nothing to stop him.
- **1935:** Italy invades Ethiopia. The League of Nations puts an embargo on Italy. All goods are banned except for oil. Emperor Haile Selassie of Ethiopia protests to the League of Nations but nothing is done.
- **1936:** Hitler occupies the Rhineland in defiance of the Versailles Treaty. Hitler's generals warn him of Germany's military being unprepared in the event of a British military reaction. The other European nations continue to do nothing.
- **1936:** Hitler and Mussolini form the **Rome-Berlin Axis.** It was a treaty of friendship between the two dictators.
- **1936: General Francisco Franco** (1892–1975) and his fascist supporters begin a revolt against the legally elected leftist government of Spain. This revolt touches off a bloody civil war. Conservatives support Franco's forces, the Nationalists. The Loyalists include communists, socialists, and supporters of democracy. Great Britain, France, and the United States remain neutral and place an embargo on weapons so that war cannot spread. Hitler and Mussolini aid Franco. The Soviet Union becomes involved by supplying the republican (Loyalist) government with weapons and military advisors. The Nazis use Spain to test their new weapons and methods, such as carpet-bombing and Blitzkrieg warfare (see the following chapter for more on Blitzkrieg warfare).
- **1936–1940:** Germany, Japan, and Italy sign the **Anti-Comintern Pact** in 1936 to oppose the spread of communism. In 1940, Japan joins Italy and Germany in the **Rome-Berlin Tokyo Axis.** In 1937 Japan launches a full-scale invasion of China. The Chinese resist Japanese aggression. The United States and other European countries do very little.
- **April 1937:** German bombers attack the market square in the city of Guernica, Spain, killing over 1,600 people—an event later memorialized by Spanish artist Pablo Picasso, in his cubist masterpiece, *Guernica,* symbolizing the violent consequences of war. (*Note:* Picasso willed this painting to the Spanish people only when the nation became a republic. Franco, with the aid of the Nazis, took over in March 1939. After Franco's death in 1975, Spain received the painting.)
- **1938:** Hitler invades Austria on the grounds that all German-speaking people belong together (*Anschluss*). *Anschluss* violates Article 80 of the Versailles treaty that forced Germany to acknowledge the independence of Austria. The Western powers continue to do nothing.

- **September 1938:** Hitler demands the **Sudetenland,** a German-speaking region of Czechoslovakia, bordering Germany. Hitler's Chief of General Staff, **Franz Halder** (1884–1972) plots a coup against him to avoid a war, in the event that Britain and France fight over the issue. The Soviet Union expresses a willingness to unite with France and Britain to defend the Czechs. At Mussolini's suggestion, a conference is held at Munich. **Neville Chamberlain,** who became prime minister of England in 1937, believes it is silly to get involved in quarrels with people "whom we know nothing about." Chamberlain meets with Daladier (prime minister of France), Mussolini, and Hitler. Czech President **Eduard Benes** (1884–1948) is not invited. The Munich Conference cedes the Sudetenland to Germany, which marks the apex of appeasement. Chamberlain returns to London and is met by a huge crowd proclaiming, "There will be peace in our time."

- **March 10–16, 1939:** Hitler takes all of Czechoslovakia. Mussolini invades Albania. Hitler demands the return of Danzig and the Polish Corridor, on the grounds that these areas were inhabited by German-speaking people. Hitler justifies these demands on the belief of *Lebensraum,* or living space for the German people.

- **August, 1939:** Hitler signs the **Non-Aggression Pact** with Stalin, in which they agree not to fight each other. This protects Germany against a two-front war, as in World War I. The pact also paves the way for Hitler's invasion of Poland. Russia receives Eastern Poland in the deal.

Chronology of Europe in Crisis

1894	Nicholas II becomes Czar.
1895	Lenin arrested and sent to Siberia; he emigrates to the West in 1900, spending most of the next 17 years in Switzerland.
1900	Sigmund Freud writes *The Interpretation of Dreams*.
1904	Russo-Japanese War begins.
1905	Bloody Sunday Massacre in St. Petersburg; October Manifesto establishes a constitutional monarchy and institution of the Duma, a representative assembly.
1907	Pablo Picasso paints his first cubist work, *Les Demoiselles d'Avignon*.
1913	Igor Stravinsky's ballet, *The Rite of Spring*, is first performed in Paris, causing a riot.
1914	Outbreak of World War I.
1916	Rasputin assassinated.
March 15, 1917	Czar Nicholas II abdicates.
March 17, 1917	Republic proclaimed in Russia.
April 16, 1917	Lenin arrives in Russia.
July 1917	Bolsheviks' attempted coup fails; Lenin flees to Finland; Trotsky is arrested.
November 6–7, 1917	Bolsheviks seize power.
March 1918	Treaty of Brest-Litovsk formally ends Russian involvement in World War I.
1918–1921	Civil War takes place in Russia.
1919	Adolf Hitler joins the German Workers' Party, which later becomes the National Socialist German Workers' Party; Benito Mussolini organizes the Black Shirts.
1919	Weimar Republic proclaimed in Germany.
1921	Lenin introduces his New Economic Plan.
1922	Virginia Woolf publishes *Jacob's Room*.
1922	Treaty of Rapallo signed by Germany and the U.S.S.R. Germany is the first country to recognize the Soviet Union.
October 28, 1922	Mussolini's March on Rome.
January 1923	Massive inflation in Germany.
August 11, 1923	Unsuccessful Munich Beer Hall Putsch led by Hitler; Hitler spends eight months in jail, where he writes *Mein Kampf*.
1924	Lenin dies, leading to a struggle for power between Trotsky and Stalin.
1925	Franz Kafka publishes *The Trial*; the Locarno Pact is signed, in which Western European allies recognize a post-World War I settlement in return for normalizing relations with the Weimar Republic.
1928	Stalin begins the first Five-Year Plan and collectivization of land among Kulaks.
1929	Mussolini signs the Lateran Pact with the Vatican; cessation of American loans to Europe because of the Wall Street Crash.
1930	Hitler and the National Socialist Party win 107 seats in the Reichstag elections.
1931	Japan invades Manchuria, part of China.
January 1933	President von Hindenburg accepts a cabinet with Hitler as chancellor.
October 1933	Germany withdraws from the League of Nations.
1933–1938	Stalin's Purge Trials take place.
1934	Death of President Hindenburg; Hitler becomes president but retains the title, "Der Führer."
1934	Leni Riefenstahl produces *Triumph of the Will*, a documentary film on the Nuremberg Nazi rally.

(continued)

1935	Hitler passes the Nuremberg Laws, depriving Jews of their citizenship; Germany begins to rearm; Mussolini attacks Ethiopia.
1936–1939	Spanish Civil War; Hitler and Mussolini support General Franco, a Fascist; Franco wins and stays in power until his death in 1975.
1936	Formation of Rome-Berlin Axis.
1937	Pablo Picasso paints *Guernica*.
1938	Munich Conference.
1939	Nazi-Soviet Non-Aggression Pact is signed.
September 1939	Germany invades Poland.

Sample Multiple-Choice Questions

1. One characteristic of a totalitarian state is that

   A.   minority groups are granted many civil liberties.

   B.   several political parties run the economic system.

   C.   citizens are encouraged to criticize the government.

   D.   the government controls and censors the media.

   E.   artists and musicians experience artistic freedom.

2. Which statement best describes the relationship between World War I and the Russian Revolution?

   A.   World War I postponed the Russian Revolution by restoring confidence in the czar.

   B.   The Russian Revolution inspired the Russian people to win World War I.

   C.   World War I gave the czar's army the needed experience to suppress the Russian Revolution.

   D.   Opposition forces cooperated to fight the Germans.

   E.   World War I created conditions within Russia that helped trigger a revolution.

3. "... The organization of the revolutionaries must consist first, foremost, and mainly of people who make revolutionary activity their profession.... Such an organization must of necessity be not too extensive and as secret as possible ..."

   This quotation expresses Lenin's idea to

   A.   defeat Germany in World War I.

   B.   establish democracy in Russia.

   C.   maintain communist power in Western Europe.

   D.   overthrow the Russian government.

   E.   establish diplomatic relations with the United States.

4. Which of the following had the least influence on European intellectual thought after World War I?

   A.   The ideals of the Enlightenment and Newton's view of the universe

   B.   The existential works of Jean Paul Sartre

   C.   The writings of Sigmund Freud

   D.   The scientific ideas of Albert Einstein and Max Planck

   E.   The literary works of Virginia Woolf and James Joyce

5. What was the major goal of Joseph Stalin's Five-Year Plans in the Soviet Union?

   A.   Encouragement of rapid industrialization

   B.   Support for capitalism

   C.   Improvement of literacy rates

   D.   Inclusion of peasants in the decision-making process

   E.   Programs to westernize, educate, and enlighten the population

6. Which of the following did not contribute to Mussolini's rise to power?

   A.   Peasant unrest in the countryside of Italy from 1919 until 1922

   B.   Severe unemployment after the war

   C.   The Nationalists' demand that Italy should receive more territory from the Versailles Treaty

   D.   Support of strong, wealthy landowners and industrialists

   E.   Close cooperation with the Communist Party

7. Mussolini's Corporate State provided

   A.   a *laissez-faire* approach to business.

   B.   the abolition of private ownership of business.

   C.   limits on profits but not on wages.

   D.   prohibition of strikes by labor.

   E.   encouragement of women to work in factories.

8. The belief that Germany and Austria should be united is known as:

   A. *Lebensraum.*
   B. *Anschluss.*
   C. Axis powers.
   D. Anti-Comintern Pact.
   E. Danzig Corridor.

9. Which situation contributed to Adolf Hitler's rise to power in Germany after World War I?

   A. Support of Hitler's radical policies by the Social Democrats in the Reichstag
   B. Strong feelings of nationalism created by disappointment with the Versailles Treaty and the economic problems of the country
   C. Refusal by the League of Nations to admit Germany as a member
   D. Violence and terrorism promoted by Germany's former enemies
   E. Rapid growth of the economy, leading to the rise of a middle class

10. A cartoon from the 1930s shows two "nursemaids" (one representing Neville Chamberlain of Britain, the other representing Europe) tip-toeing past a cradle in which lies the "baby" (Hitler), sucking on a bottle upon which are the words "Munich Agreement" and clutching a cloth bundle upon which is written "added concessions." The caption states, "Shh-hh! He'll be quiet now—maybe!" Which policy did the "nursemaids" use to keep the "baby" quiet?

    A. Militarism
    B. Isolationism
    C. Imperialism
    D. Appeasement
    E. Collective security

Multiple-Choice Questions: Answers and Explanations

1. **D.** One characteristic of a totalitarian state is that the government controls and censors the media; it controls all aspects of a citizen's life through a one-party dictatorship. Dictators like Mussolini of Italy, Hitler of Germany, and Lenin and Stalin of Russia suppressed rival parties and controlled the press. Critics were thrown in jail. Mussolini's Black Shirts assaulted and used terror against those who spoke against him. Hitler used the Gestapo, his secret police, to suppress all opposition; newspapers, radio, and films had to praise the virtues of Nazism. In Russia, Stalin controlled all artistic and cultural activities through the Communist Party. Totalitarian government suppresses civil liberties such as freedom of the press and speech and has little regard for minority groups. In a totalitarian state, the government bans all political parties. Dictators like Hitler and Mussolini allowed only the Nazi or Fascist Party to exist. Totalitarian leaders used their secret police to jail anyone who criticized the government. Stalin's secret police, the Cheka, renamed NKVD in 1934, killed all enemies of the state. There is no tolerance for creative artists or musicians in a totalitarian state.

2. **E.** World War I created conditions in Russia that helped trigger the Bolshevik Revolution. Russia was not ready to fight a war. Russian soldiers lacked adequate supplies and weapons. By 1915, soldiers had no ammunition, rifles, or medical care. In 1915, Russian casualties reached almost two million. In March 1917, workers led food riots all across Russia. In St. Petersburg, when soldiers refused to fire upon the striking workers, Nicholas II, czar of Russia, was forced to give up his throne and the leaders of the Duma, the Russian Parliament, set up a republic. The decision to continue the war, and an inability to provide food, resulted in the loss of support for the new government among the people. Lenin, who had been in exile when the March revolution broke out, was sneaked into the country by the Germans, who used him to undermine the support of the provisional government. In November 1917, the Bolsheviks seized control of the government. The decision of the czar to take personal charge of the war proved to be a blunder because the army continued to fight poorly. Opposing forces did not cooperate to fight foreign invaders. The czar's army during World War I lost confidence in Russia's military leadership, and deserted. The Russian Revolution led to the withdrawal of Russia from the war. In March 1918, the Bolsheviks signed the Treaty of Brest-Litovsk with Germany. The harsh treaty ended Russia's participation in the war.

3. **D.** This quotation expresses Lenin's plan to overthrow the Russian government. Lenin believed that in order for Marxism to succeed in Russia, a revolutionary elite was needed. Marx claimed that revolution was only possible in an industrial country; however, Lenin believed that this elite or vanguard of the proletariat could start a revolution in an agrarian country and would exercise control until the state withered away. Lenin did not plan to defeat Germany but instead wanted peace to gain support for his government. He did not establish democracy or have any plan to spread communism in Western Europe. Russia was the only communist state in Europe in 1917. The United States would not recognize the Soviet Union until 1933, nine years after Lenin's death.

4. **A.** The European intellectual and literary community rejected the Enlightenment movement and Isaac Newton's law of a structured universe based on rationality and order. They also rejected the belief in progress and the optimism that the future will be better, both of which stemmed from the Enlightenment movement. Sartre, Freud, Einstein, and Planck believed that there was no order in the meaning of life and no specific pattern in which society developed.

5. **A.** The major goal of Joseph Stalin's Five-Year Plans was to encourage rapid industrialization of the Soviet Union and turn it into an industrial giant. The Plans emphasized expanding industries such as iron and steel, chemicals, electric power generation, and machinery production in order to produce weapons and strengthen the country militarily. The Five-Year Plans set up a command economy, which rejected private enterprise, or capitalism.

6. **E.** Mussolini opposed the goals of a socialist or communist economy, condemning the communist Marxist ideology that belittled nationalism and urged international working-class unity. Mussolini's view was that only fascism could save Italy from the evils of communism. Backed by wealthy industrialists and landowners, Mussolini rose to power because peasants had begun to seize lands and factories, and fascism answered a need for order. Widespread unemployment among war veterans and frustration among nationalists that Italy had not received its just amount of territory also helped Mussolini.

7. **D.** Mussolini's Corporate State prohibited strikes by labor, but organized industry and labor into a small number of fascist-led associations that strictly controlled Italian workers, set wages, hours, and working conditions, and regulated profits. Although it rejected *laissez-faire,* the Corporate State did not abolish private enterprise, allowing industries to remain under private ownership but watching them closely. Women were encouraged to be housewives and not workers.

8. **B.** *Anschluss* is the belief that all German-speaking people belong together. *Anschluss* violated the World War I Treaty of St.Germain, which had made Austria an independent country. In 1938 Hitler invaded Austria. *Lebensraum,* or living space, was used by Hitler to justify Germany's expansion in the 1930s. Axis powers refer to alliances between Germany, Italy, and Japan. The Anti-Comintern Pact was signed by Germany, Italy, and Japan to oppose communism. The Danzig Corridor consisted of areas that Hitler demanded from Poland on the grounds that German-speaking people lived there.

9. **B.** The strong sense of nationalism created by the anger at the Versailles Treaty and the economic conditions at the end of World War I (widespread unemployment and inflation that destroyed the life savings of many people) led to Hitler's rise to power. Many Germans blamed the Treaty of Versailles for the country's troubles and condemned the Weimar Republic as a foreign system forced on the country by the victors. In their eyes, Germany's economic problems stemmed from the loss of its European territories and overseas colonies, and reparation payments of $132 billion. Germany's rampant inflation in the early 1920s, when 4 trillion marks were equivalent to one dollar, added to the unrest. Although the economy was revived in the mid-1920s, the Great Depression destroyed any hope of recovery. In the 1930s, Germany turned to Adolf Hitler and the Nazi Party because Hitler claimed that Germany had not lost the war, but had been stabbed in the back at Versailles. He promised to solve the economic chaos and restore Germany's greatness, convincing them that they were the Master Race.

10. **D.** Appeasement was the policy adopted by England and France in the 1930s, in which the two countries gave in to the demands of Hitler and Mussolini in order to avoid war. Militarism is a policy that supports aggressive military preparedness. Isolationism is a policy that promotes non-involvement in foreign affairs. Imperialism or colonialism supports the extension of stronger nations over weaker ones. Collective security is a policy of international cooperation to promote peace.

World War II (1939–1945)

When World War II began in 1939, there was little enthusiasm, not even a noble slogan about the glory of war. Many saw the war as a continuation of the problems created in World War I. Dissatisfaction with the Versailles Treaty, the War Guilt Clause, the question of protection, problems created by new nationalist states, and the failure of collective security all contributed to the start of World War II. The **Axis powers** (Germany, Italy, and later Japan; so named when, in 1936, the Italian leader Benito Mussolini gave a speech in which he referred to a vertical line between Rome and Berlin as "an axis around which all European states" could collaborate.) pursued aggressive actions to redress perceived inequities that arose out of World War I. This treaty of friendship between Germany and Italy was later extended to Japan by the **Tripartite Treaty of 1940.** At first, democratic nations, such as the United States, England, and France, chose to follow a policy of appeasement. But when that course of action failed to stop Germany from invading Poland, World War II began. Unlike World War I, which was fought primarily in Europe, World War II was truly a global war in that it was fought in all the major areas of the world, except for the Americas. Initially, the Axis powers were victorious, but the entry of the United States and the failure of the German invasion of the Soviet Union changed the tide in favor of the Allies—England, France, the United States, and the Soviet Union.

The war was one of the most devastating conflicts in history. New mechanized warfare and advanced technology made it even more destructive than World War I. Civilian populations felt the war's full effects: Saturation bombing, or fire bombing, was used on cities such as Dresden and Hamburg, in Germany. The use of the atomic bomb over Hiroshima and Nagasaki in Japan (World War II ushered in the Atomic Age) demonstrated the horrors of nuclear war and modern technology. The war brought massive devastation, as well as an enormous loss of life and property. Over 75 million people were killed worldwide and civilian deaths reached record numbers. Germany's defeat also exposed the horrors of the Nazis' policy of genocide that had led to the Holocaust and the deaths of millions of people.

World War II accelerated the decline of Britain and France as major powers, and the United States and Russia emerged as the two superpowers. Although allies in the war, the United States and Russia were strange bedfellows. The fear of the spread of communism eventually led to the ideological conflict of the Cold War that dominated international relations for the latter half of the twentieth century.

Outbreak of World War II (1939–1941)

Hitler's Empire

Poland

On September 1, 1939, Germany invaded Poland. On September 3, Britain and France finally decided to honor their agreement to defend Poland, and declared war on Germany. The Germans believed that they had a strategy to end the fighting in a short time. Their method was called **Blitzkrieg,** or "lightning war," and involved the use of tanks, airplanes, and trucks. By October, Hitler's armies had crushed Poland. Germany soon annexed western Poland. As agreed in the **Non-Aggression Pact of 1939,** Russia seized the eastern half of Poland as well as the Baltic countries. In November, Russia seized parts of Finland, which put up a valiant but unsuccessful resistance.

October 1939–March 1940

This was a time of **Sitzkrieg**, or "phony war." Hitler consolidated his gains in Poland and equipped his military in preparation for the coming attack against Europe. The French remained behind the **Maginot Line** and Britain sent troops there to wait for the expected attack. The Maginot Line was a series of concrete fortifications that extended 200 miles along the French border with Germany.

Conquest of Denmark and Norway

In April of 1940, Blitzkreig struck again. Germany invaded Norway and Denmark in order to secure a supply of iron ore. Both of these countries failed to withstand the German invasion and fell within days.

Defeat of France (1940)

In May, the German army invaded northern France by going through neutral Holland and Belgium. Within weeks, Germany defeated these countries. The Germans had managed to bypass the Maginot Line (which did not extend into the Belgian frontier), split the Franco-British forces, and trap the entire British army on the beaches of Dunkirk. In a desperate gamble to triumph over the Germans, the British sent every available naval vessel, even pleasure ships, across the English Channel to rescue the troops. The **Miracle of Dunkirk** resulted in the ferrying of over 300,000 troops to safety.

Meanwhile, Mussolini, sensing an easy victory, declared war on France and proceeded to attack from the south in June.

On June 22, 1940, German forces captured Paris. The Germans soon occupied all of northern France. In the south, a puppet state called the **Vichy Government** was established, headed by **Marshall Petain** (1856–1951). Not willing to accept defeat, French resistance forces, led by **Charles de Gaulle** (1890–1970), escaped to England where they worked to liberate their homeland; throughout the remainder of the war, the Vichy Government faced many battles with de Gaulle's resistance forces. The swiftness of the German victories caught the world by surprise. Most nations expected a conflict involving trench warfare, as was the case in World War I, where the war reached a stalemate and there were no quick victories. By 1940, Hitler ruled over all of continental Europe. Like Napoleon, he dominated the continent, with the exception of Britain. Italy was his ally, while the Soviet Union remained neutral.

Battle of Britain

Hitler hoped that Britain would recognize that it was standing alone and ask for peace. However, **Winston Churchill** (prime minister from 1940 to 1945 and 1951 to 1955), who succeeded Neville Chamberlain as prime minister in May 1940, refused to surrender. Churchill inspired the nation with his plea that he had nothing to offer but "blood, toil, tears, and sweat." When faced with this defiance, Hitler attacked.

On August 15, the German **Luftwaffe** (air force) began to bomb Britain in preparation for an invasion across the English Channel. Up to 1,000 planes attacked British airfields and key factories. The British Royal Air Force was able to defend itself and its country against these attacks with the help of radar that detected incoming planes. Losses were heavy on both sides. Following the advice of the leader of the Luftwaffe, **Hermann Goering** (1893–1946), Hitler ordered the bombing of British cities, hoping to weaken British morale. From August 1940 until June 1941, London and other cities were attacked through the night until dawn. Despite heavy British losses, this new plan turned out to be a mistake on the part of Germany. As a result of the increased bombing of civilian sites, Britain boosted its military production, and its anti-aircraft defense improved with the help of radar. By June 1941, Hitler abandoned his efforts to invade England in favor of a new campaign in Eastern Europe, specifically Russia.

Critical Turning Points in the War

Invasion of Russia

On June 22, 1941, Hitler launched a major attack against Russia called **Operation Barbarossa** after the German king who had participated in the First Crusade during the eleventh century. The goal of the Russian invasion was to gain control of the Ukraine's vast wheat fields and the Caucasus's oil fields. Hitler ordered a massive Blitzkrieg with an army of three million men along a 2,000-mile border, catching Stalin by surprise. By October 1941, German troops had surrounded Leningrad, which was within 25 miles of Moscow, and had conquered most of the Ukraine. Hitler's propaganda machine proclaimed the war to be over, but it was mistaken. Russia did not collapse; instead, history repeated itself. Like Napoleon's forces, the German invaders were not prepared for the cold Russian winter. Germans, in summer uniform, froze to death as the temperature plunged to –20° Fahrenheit. Their fuel and oil froze as trucks and weapons became useless. At the **Siege of Leningrad,** which lasted 900 days, the Russians fought valiantly. More than 1.5 million citizens died during this siege and some inhabitants even resorted to cannibalism to survive. Hitler's failure to conquer Russia drained Germany's resources and caused him to have to fight two fronts simultaneously, which ultimately contributed to Germany's defeat.

Entry of the United States

Although the United States had declared its neutrality in 1939, President Franklin D. Roosevelt realized that a German victory would be a threat to the nation's interests. He worked closely with Churchill to provide support during the Battle of Britain. In 1940, President Roosevelt traded 50 old destroyers to Britain in exchange for military bases in Newfoundland and the Caribbean.

In March 1941, Congress approved the **Lend-Lease Act,** which allowed the president to lend or sell war materials to any country that he deemed vital to that country's defense. Roosevelt declared that the United States would become the arsenal of democracy. The Lend-Lease Act created a British-Soviet-U.S. economic alliance, providing the groundwork for the establishment of the **Big Three,** as these countries were later known. Hitler proclaimed the Lend-Lease Act an economic declaration of war and began attacking American merchant ships.

In **August 1941,** Roosevelt and Churchill signed the **Atlantic Charter,** a broad set of peace principles, such as freedom from fear and want, and belief in **national sovereignty**—the right of all people to choose their own form of government. The Atlantic Charter was very similar to Wilson's Fourteen Points and a permanent system of general security, which laid the foundation for the United Nations. Meanwhile, the United States had taken economic steps to stop Japanese aggression in Asia. When Japan advanced into French Indo-China and the Dutch East Indies (present-day Indonesia), the United States banned the sale of oil to Japan. This move angered the Japanese. In retaliation, on **December 7, 1941,** the Japanese launched a surprise attack upon the United States military base at **Pearl Harbor,** Hawaii. Close to 2,500 Americans were killed. On December 8, 1941, the United States and Britain declared war on Japan. Soon after, on **December 11, 1941,** Germany and Italy declared war on the United States. The conflict became a global war involving all the major powers. The American entry into the war was crucial because the U.S. aid to the Allies—along with the heroic support of the British and Soviet people and the assistance of the resistance groups in Europe—contributed eventually to an Allied victory.

The Road to Victory (1942–1945)

Churchill convinced Roosevelt that the focus of the war should be to defeat Germany first and then concentrate on Japan. Here are the highlights of the war following the entry of the United States:

- **May 1942:** In North Africa, the British, under the command of General **Bernard Montgomery** (1887–1976), defeated German and Italian forces led by the brilliant General **Erwin Rommel** (1891–1944), known as the Desert Fox, at El Alamein, only seventy miles from Alexandria, Egypt. Rommel's defeat prevented the Germans from taking control of the Suez Canal. The Suez Canal was the key for reaching the oil fields of the Middle East. In November 1942, American General **Dwight D. Eisenhower** (1890–1969) took command of joint Anglo-American forces in Morocco and Algiers. Combining with Montgomery's forces, they destroyed Rommel's army.

- **May–June 1942:** The United States defeated the Japanese at the **Battle of the Coral Sea** and later Midway. American victories stopped the Japanese advance in the Pacific and prevented another attack on Hawaii. The **Battle of Midway** established American naval superiority in the Pacific.

- **August 1942:** Under the command of General **Douglas MacArthur** (1880–1964), the American marines launched their first offensive at **Guadalcanal** in the Solomon Islands. The attack was the beginning of an island-hopping strategy, the goal of which was to capture strategic Japanese-held islands and bypass others. These islands would serve as stepping-stones for a direct invasion of Japan.

- **August 1942–February 1943:** The **Battle of Stalingrad** began in August and—following a six-month struggle that involved house-to-house fighting—the Soviet forces defeated Germany. By January 1943, the Germans had lost over 300,000 men. The Battle of Stalingrad was the turning point in the war because the Russians had struck a deadly blow to Hitler's war machine and seized large quantities of German military equipment. The Russian forces took the offensive and slowly began to drive the Germans out of the Soviet Union.

- **January 1943:** Roosevelt and Churchill met at **Casablanca** and agreed to launch an invasion of Sicily and Italy and to fight until the Axis powers surrendered unconditionally. Roosevelt called this meeting the "Unconditional Surrender Conference." The reason for the announcement of unconditional surrender was to reassure Russia, which was fearful that the Allies might sign a separate treaty with Hitler. Russia was also suspicious about the failure of the Allies to establish a genuine second front through France. The Russians had suffered enormous losses on the Eastern Front and claimed that a second front would divert German forces from Russia.

- **July 1943–August 1944:** The Allies, under General Montgomery and American General **George Patton** (1885–1945), invaded Sicily and then mainland Italy. Mussolini resigned and Italy surrendered. In September, however, German troops returned Mussolini to power. The Allies faced German resistance for the next 18 months until Germany was defeated.

- **November 28–December 1, 1943:** The leaders of the Big Three (Churchill, Stalin, and Roosevelt) met in **Teheran,** Iran, for the first time. They agreed on postwar occupation of Germany, demilitarization of Germany, and the creation of an international peace organization. Churchill and Roosevelt promised to open a second front of warfare through France. This decision to invade Hitler via France meant that the American, British, and Russian troops would meet along a north-south line in Germany and that only Russia would liberate Eastern Europe—a strategy that had a profound impact upon post–World War II Europe.

- **Invasion of Normandy (D-Day), June 6, 1944:** Eisenhower directed the largest amphibious assault of the war on the beaches of Normandy in France. This established the second front; by August, Paris had been liberated, and by the end of 1944 all of France had been liberated. The next goal was Germany. Hitler was under attack on the Eastern and Western Fronts.

- **Battle of the Bulge, December 1944:** Germany launched a last-grasp counterattack in Belgium through the Argonne Forest. It slowed the Allied advance but the Allies continued to press forward toward Germany.

- **January 1945:** The Russian forces marched westward through Poland.

- **February 1945:** The Allied firebombing of Dresden killed over 135,000 people.

- The Big Three leaders met at Yalta in southern Russia on the Black Sea from February 4 to February 11. The **Yalta Conference** drew up the structure of postwar Europe. They agreed that Germany would be divided into four zones of occupation. Stalin agreed to hold free elections in Eastern Europe and declare war against Japan in return for land from Japan that had been lost in the Russo-Japanese War. The Big Three leaders also agreed to the veto system of voting in the Security Council of the United Nations. The Yalta Conference would be a source of controversy in the future because the concessions worked out over the status of the countries in Eastern Europe eventually broke down and became a source of friction between the United States and Russia.

- **March 1945:** The American firebombing of Tokyo killed more than 80,000 Japanese. The **Battle of Iwo Jima** ended after a vicious struggle, leaving 26,000 Americans dead.

- **April 1945:** Japan was defeated at the **Battle of Okinawa.** The Allies moved closer to Japan.

- Mussolini attempted to escape Italy but was caught and killed on April 28, and on April 30, Hitler and his mistress Eva Braun (1912–1945), whom he had married the day before on April 29, committed suicide in a Berlin bunker.

- **May 8, 1945 (VE Day):** The war in Europe ended.

- **July/August 1945:** Churchill (after July 28, Clement Attlee, the new British prime minister, took his place), Stalin, and President **Harry Truman** (1884–1972) attended the **Potsdam Conference** in Germany. The conference addressed the issues of postwar Germany and free elections in Eastern Europe. Truman demanded that Stalin carry out free elections in the countries of Eastern Europe. Stalin refused and the sown seeds of distrust would severely hamper the friendship between the United States and Russia as the war drew to an end.

- **August 6, 1945:** The United States dropped an atomic bomb on **Hiroshima** and over 130,000 people were killed and 90 percent of the city was destroyed.

- **August 8, 1945:** The United States dropped an atomic bomb on **Nagasaki,** resulting in the deaths of 75,000 people. Russia declared war on Japan and invaded Manchuria.
- **September 2, 1945 (VJ Day):** Japan surrendered.

The Holocaust

The efforts of Hitler and the Nazis to destroy all the Jews of Europe are known as the **Holocaust.** In his policy of anti-Semitism, Hitler set out to drive Jews from Germany. In 1935, the **Nuremberg Laws** placed severe restrictions on the Jewish people. They were prohibited from marrying non-Jews, denied citizenship, forced to wear a yellow Star of David, and prohibited from attending or teaching at German schools or universities.

On November 9, 1938, the **Kristallnacht** (Night of Broken Glass) riots took place. Nazi-led mobs attacked Jewish synagogues, businesses, and homes. The night of violence initiated a period of intense persecution for the Jews in which over 91 Jews were killed and 30,000 Jews were rounded up and later sent to concentration camps.

By 1939, German Jews had lost all their civil rights, and after the fall of Warsaw, the Nazis began deporting them to Poland. Jews from all over Europe were moved into ghettos surrounded by barbed wire, forced to wear the Star of David, and used as slave labor. In January 1942, German leaders met at Wannsee, a suburb of Berlin to carry out **the Final Solution of the Jewish Question**—the murder of every Jew. Jews in all parts of Hitler's empire were systematically arrested and shipped like cattle to concentration camps or death camps. A **death camp** was a concentration camp with special apparatus for systematic murder. All of them were located in Poland. Victims were sent to "shower" rooms that were really gas chambers. Special camp workers stripped victims of their gold teeth or hair. Bodies were cremated while bones were crushed for fertilizer. The most infamous of these death camps was at **Auschwitz** in Poland, where 12,000 Jews were killed each day, close to 1 million in total.

When the war finally came to an end, over 6 million Jews had been killed, as well as millions of homosexuals, gypsies, communists, and Slavs. The ultimate monstrosity of the Nazi policy of genocide had contributed to the death of millions of people. Although they were aware of the Nazi concentration and death camps during the war, when the Allies discovered the full extent of these atrocities, they agreed that Axis leaders should be tried for "crimes against humanity." On November 21, 1945, the **Nuremberg Trials** began and lasted until October 1, 1946. An international military tribunal put Nazi war criminals on trial. A total of 177 Germans and Austrians were tried and 142 were found guilty. Some top Nazis received death sentences. Similar war crime trials were held in Japan and Italy. These trials showed that political and military leaders had to be held responsible and accountable for their actions in wartime.

Impact of World War II

The human losses in World War II were staggering. The Soviet Union alone lost 28 million people. Throughout Europe and Asia, parts of many cities were in ruins. Heavy bombings had destroyed major cities such as Hamburg and Dresden in Germany, and both European and Asian nations faced the difficult problems of economic recovery.

Britain and France's colonial powers declined and they were forced to gradually relinquish their empires. Their colonies in the Americas, Asia, and Africa, embraced nationalism and rejected the remnants of European imperialism.

Building on the foundation of the League of Nations, the Allies established the **United Nations** as an international organization to secure peace. In April 1945, representatives from 50 nations met in San Francisco to draft the charter for the United Nations. Unlike 1920 when the United States rejected the League of Nations, the United States became a member of the United Nations and the headquarters were set up in New York. The United States and Russia emerged as the two superpowers. The two countries had cooperated with each other to defeat Nazi Germany but by 1945, the alliance was slowly disintegrating. Conflicting ideologies (democracy and communism) and mutual distrust between the Allies and Russians eventually led to the **Cold War.** The Cold War became the driving force that determined events for over 45 years afterwards.

Chronology of World War II

September 1, 1939	World War II begins; Germany invades Poland
1940	Germany conquers Norway, Denmark, the Netherlands, Luxembourg, and France Battle of Britain
1941	United States adopts Lend-Lease Act Germany invades Russia Soviet Union signs a non-aggression pact with Japan Japan bombs Pearl Harbor
1942	Battle of Midway Battle of Stalingrad—German offensive stopped
1943	Casablanca Conference Allied forces take Sicily Teheran Conference—First meeting of Big Three
1944	D-Day, June 6, at Normandy
1945	Yalta Conference VE Day, May 8, Germany surrenders Potsdam Conference—First meeting of Stalin and Truman August 6—Atomic bomb dropped on Hiroshima; August 8—Nagasaki September 2—VJ Day—Japanese surrender

Sample Multiple-Choice Questions

1. The Atlantic Charter of 1941 was important to colonial people because

   A. Great Britain promised to end its colonial rule in Asia and Africa.
   B. they believed it gave them the right to govern themselves.
   C. all European countries promised economic aid to their former colonies.
   D. the United States pledged to support the colonial struggle for freedom.
   E. it allowed all colonial governments to become part of the United Nations.

2. The turning point of the war in North Africa was the British victory over German forces at

   A. the Coral Sea.
   B. Midway.
   C. Stalingrad.
   D. El Alamein.
   E. Leningrad.

3. One of the main reasons for Hitler's invasion of Russia was

   A. to prevent the Japanese from taking territory from Russia in Asia.
   B. to gain control of the wheat fields in the Ukraine, which could provide additional food for the German war effort.
   C. because he feared a Russian invasion of Germany.
   D. to establish military bases in Russia.
   E. to liberate the Russian people from Bolshevism.

4. *Sitzkrieg* refers to

   A. a phony war from October 1939 to March 1940.
   B. the defeat of Poland.
   C. a German counter-attack at Battle of the Bulge.
   D. a German invasion of Russia.
   E. the Battle of Britain.

5. Prior to June 1944, what country carried the bulk of the land war against Germany?

   A. Britain
   B. The United States
   C. The Soviet Union
   D. France
   E. The French Resistance Movement

6. All of the following were a result of the Teheran Conference EXCEPT

   A. a second front through France.
   B. postwar occupation of Germany.
   C. the demilitarization of Germany.
   D. the first meeting of the Big Three.
   E. a demand for unconditional surrender of the Axis powers.

7. Which is considered the turning point of the war on the Eastern Front?

   A. The Battle of Leningrad
   B. The Battle of Stalingrad
   C. Brest-Litovsk
   D. The Battle of El Alamein
   E. The bombing of Dresden

8. Why did the wartime cooperation between the Soviet Union and the Western powers break down at Potsdam?

   A. The Western powers refused to acknowledge the division of Germany.
   B. Stalin demanded more territory from Japan.
   C. Stalin refused to carry out free elections in Eastern Europe.
   D. Churchill insisted that Germany be blamed solely for the war.
   E. The Soviet Union refused to join the United Nations.

9. At the Yalta Conference, the Soviet Union agreed to

   A. the creation of the United Nations.
   B. free elections in Eastern Europe.
   C. share atomic secrets with other nations.
   D. the joint invasion of Japan.
   E. no separate peace treaties with the Axis powers.

10. The Nuremberg Trials of 1945/1946 established the principle of

    A. collective guilt.
    B. war crimes being justified under extreme circumstances.
    C. national leaders being held personally responsible for crimes against humanity.
    D. individuals who followed the orders of their superiors not being held accountable.
    E. genocide.

Multiple-Choice Questions: Answers and Explanations

1. **B.** The Atlantic Charter was signed on August 14, 1941, and outlined the principles of freedom and economic development to ensure peace. Churchill was reluctant to sign the Atlantic Charter because it contained the provision that people could choose their own government. Churchill believed that Roosevelt was trying to do away with the British Empire. At the signing, Roosevelt became a hero to oppressed people all over the world for his opposition to the imperialist policies of the British, French, and Dutch. Colonial people believed that the Atlantic Charter gave them the right to self-government. It was reported that within a few days of the signing of the Atlantic Charter, Churchill received reports that the Burmese people would call for independence from Britain after the war. This same spirit was expressed by other colonial people living in Egypt and other parts of Africa. The Atlantic Charter did not provide for economic aid to former colonial countries nor would the United States promise to support the struggle for freedom or allow former colonial governments to become part of the United Nations.

2. **D.** The British army defeated the German army at El Alamein, which is 70 miles from Alexandria, Egypt. This battle protected Britain's Suez Canal, the lifeline of the British Empire. The Coral Sea and Midway were naval battles fought by the United States Navy against Japan. Stalingrad and Leningrad were the sites of battles on the Russian front.

3. **B.** Hitler embarked on Operation Barbarossa because he realized that the potential wealth of the raw materials in the Ural Mountains, the vast forests of Siberia, and the tremendous wheat fields in the Ukraine would enable Germany to dominate Europe and carry out the war against England and other countries. Hitler did not fear Japanese expansion in Asia nor did he fear a Russian invasion. Russia was surprised by the German invasion; Stalin had refused to believe that Hitler would violate the non-aggression pact. Hitler wanted to destroy Stalin but never intended to liberate the Russian people from the yoke of communism.

4. **A.** *Sitzkrieg* refers to the phony war from October 1939 to March 1940 where there was little fighting after the German invasion of Poland. The defeat of Poland in four weeks demonstrated the effectiveness of *Blitzkrieg* (Lightning War). In June 1941, the Germans invaded Russia with over 3 million men and expected that their invasion would be over by the winter. German forces were repelled at the Battle of the Bulge. The Battle of Britain resulted in the failure of German air power to defeat the British.

5. **C.** The Soviet Union carried the bulk of the land war against Germany. France was knocked out of the war in 1940 and Britain was never a land power. The Soviet Union bore the brunt of the war effort until the establishment of the second front in June 1944. The United States did not bear the brunt until D-Day. The French Resistance Movement had very little impact on the war effort against Germany.

6. **E.** The Teheran Conference did not demand the unconditional surrender of the Axis powers. Churchill and Roosevelt had met in January 1943 at Casablanca and agreed upon a policy of unconditional surrender. The Teheran Conference addressed the issue of the second front, demilitarization of Germany, and postwar occupation of Germany. It was also the first time that Stalin, Churchill, and Roosevelt met.

7. **B.** The Battle of Stalingrad marked the turning point of the war on the Eastern Front. The Battle of Stalingrad stopped the German advances in the south and turned the tide of the battle. Leningrad was besieged for 900 days. It is a heroic tale but did not represent a turning point on the Eastern Front. Brest-Litovsk was the site of the peace negotiations between Germany and the Bolsheviks that ended Russia's participation in World War I. The Battle of El Alamein marked the turning point in North Africa. The bombing of Dresden in Germany dealt with Allied efforts in 1945 to defeat Germany. It was not an area of conflict on the Eastern Front.

8. **C.** Stalin's refusal to carry out free elections in Eastern Europe led to a breakdown of wartime cooperation between the Soviet Union and the Western powers at Potsdam. President Truman, who had succeeded Franklin D. Roosevelt, insisted that Stalin carry out his pledge of free elections that he had agreed to at the Yalta Conference. Stalin's refusal laid the groundwork for the beginning of the Cold War. The Allied powers had agreed to the postwar occupation of Germany. Stalin did not demand more territory from Japan nor did he refuse to join the United Nations. None of the Allied nations wanted to blame Germany solely for the war. They wanted to avoid the mistakes of the Versailles Treaty.

9. **B.** At Yalta, the Soviet Union agreed to free elections in Eastern Europe. Stalin was determined to create a buffer zone against Germany and wanted to decide the fate of Eastern Europe himself. Churchill and Roosevelt agreed to the compromise because they could not really stop Stalin and were unwilling to go to war over Eastern Europe. The Allied nations had pledged to create a United Nations in 1941. The Soviet Union agreed to declare war on Japan but there was no discussion of a joint invasion. The Allied nations did not share atomic secrets with each other. Stalin was never informed that the United States was developing the atomic bomb. The Casablanca Conference declared that there would be no separate treaties with the Axis powers.

10. **C.** The Nuremberg Trials established the principle that Axis leaders should be tried for crimes against humanity. At the end of World War I, nothing was done to punish those leaders who were responsible for the war. At the Nuremberg Trials, Nazi war criminals were put on trial and 142 were found guilty. These trials were held for leading industrialists, military commanders, and others involved in the Final Solution. The Nuremberg Trials did not deal with genocide or collective war guilt. The Nuremberg tribunal rejected the idea that war crimes can be justified or that soldiers must blindly follow the orders of their leaders when they realize those orders are immoral.

The Cold War (1947–1980)

After the defeat of Germany, the Grand Alliance (Big Three) of the United States, Britain, and the Soviet Union failed to hold together. Once again, Europe became the battleground of a new war—the Cold War. The origins of the Cold War stemmed from the ideological differences between the United States and the Soviet Union, and disputes over Eastern Europe. By 1950, the Iron Curtain was in place and Western and Eastern Europe were going their separate ways. Despite efforts to coexist with the West after the death of Stalin in 1953, the Soviet Union maintained a firm grip on Eastern Europe and crushed any efforts at freedom by these satellite countries, establishing an empire in Eastern Europe that served as a buffer against any attacks. The split between the Soviet and Western Blocs influenced policies in other parts of the world, and the tensions of the Cold War led to the creation of a nuclear weapons system that cost billions of dollars and raised the fear of nuclear disaster.

Battered Europe recovered quickly and successfully with the aid of the Marshall Plan and economic cooperation among Western European nations regulating the coal, iron, and steel industries. The European economic miracle was also made possible because European nations coordinated the distribution of American aid so that barriers to European trade were quickly dropped. By the 1970s, a revitalized West Germany sought to bring about reconciliation between Eastern and Western Europe. These efforts achieved some success.

The devastating effects of World War II also contributed to the decline of European empires. England and France were too weak to hold on to their colonies in Asia, Africa, and the Middle East. The changes that affected Europe's growth and the decline of her imperial empires foreshadowed the winds of change that swept across Europe in the 1980s and ultimately led to the end of the Cold War and the collapse of Communism in Europe.

The Cold War and Communism after World War II

The United States and the Soviet Union had cooperated to defeat the Axis powers in World War II. However, conflicting ideology and mutual distrust led to the **Cold War,** a continuing state of tension and hostility between the two superpowers.

The uneasy relationship between the United States and the Soviet Union was based on philosophical differences: The United States was a democratic capitalist country and the Soviet Union was a totalitarian communist state. At first, the focus of the Cold War was on Eastern Europe, whose territories the Soviet Union occupied. Stalin had forced pro-Soviet communist governments onto the Eastern European countries of Poland, Czechoslovakia, Hungary, Romania, and Bulgaria. The Red Army had overrun these countries on their march towards Berlin. Thus these countries became Soviet satellites and served as a defensive shield for the Soviet Union. Yugoslavia, however, did not fall under Soviet control. Although Josip Broz, known as **Marshal Tito** (1882–1980), was a communist ruler, he defied Stalin and pursued nationalist policies. Tito was able to act independently because Soviet troops did not occupy Yugoslavia and the country did not border on the Soviet Union.

The Western powers feared the spread of communism. In a 1946 speech at Fulton, Missouri, Winston Churchill proclaimed that an **"Iron Curtain"** had descended over Eastern Europe. Churchill's Iron Curtain speech became a symbol for the growing fear of communism as well as the division of Europe into the Soviet-dominated countries of Eastern Europe and the Western Bloc of democratic countries led by the United States. The Cold War rivalry divided Europe and led to crises around the world. Although the two superpowers never fought each other outright, they were involved in small-scale fighting by supporting opposite sides.

Greece and Turkey

In 1947, the government of Greece was in serious danger of being overthrown by the Greek communists. If Greece fell, Turkey could also be in danger of becoming a Soviet puppet state. Britain informed the United States that it was unable to help Greece, and the United States accepted the challenge. In February of 1947, President

Truman asked Congress for $400 million in American military aid for Greece and Turkey. The **Truman Doctrine** was the opening shot in the Cold War, asserting that the United States would support "free peoples who are resisting attempted subjugation by armed minorities or by outside pressures"—in other words, any country that rejected or resisted communism. The United States declared that its goal was to contain communism or limit communism to the areas already under Soviet control. United States aid helped to keep Greece and Turkey from falling under communist control.

Berlin Blockade (1948–1949) and the Two Germanys

At the end of World War II, Germany was divided into four zones of occupation. Berlin was also divided into four zones: American, British, French, and Soviet. In 1948, the Soviet Union announced that the Allies could no longer use the land routes to Berlin that passed through the Soviet zone of occupation. This was because Stalin was angry that the West did not agree with him on a German unification plan and that the three Western Allies (Britain, France, and the United States) had decided to unite their zones of occupation. He was also upset about currency reform (the introduction of new currency for the Western zones) that foreshadowed the creation of West Germany. To thwart the blockade, the Western powers resorted to an airlift. The **Berlin Airlift** lasted for almost a year (321 days) as the United States flew in supplies of food and other necessities on a daily basis. In 1949, the Soviet Union lifted the blockade. In May 1949 the three Western allies formed the Federal Republic of Germany with the city of Bonn as its capital and the Soviet zone became known as German Democratic Republic with East Berlin as its capital. They became informally known as West Germany and East Germany.

North Atlantic Treaty Organization (1949)

The threat of the Soviet Union and its bloc of Communist states to the security of Western Europe led to the formation of the **North Atlantic Treaty Organization (NATO)** in 1949. NATO was a military defensive alliance formed by the United States, Canada, and ten Western European countries to help each other if any one of the nations were attacked. In 1952, Greece and Turkey were admitted, and in 1955, West Germany (Federal Republic of Germany) became a member. The Soviet Union responded in 1955 by forming its own military alliance, the **Warsaw Pact,** consisting of the U.S.S.R. and seven satellites in Eastern Europe.

Birth of the Nuclear Race

In 1949, the same year that NATO was formed, the Soviet Union tested its first atomic bomb. The United States no longer had a nuclear monopoly. In 1952, the United States announced that it had developed a hydrogen bomb, or H-bomb, a thousand times more destructive than the atomic bomb. In 1953, the Soviet Union announced that it, too, had tested an H-bomb. The nuclear race continued throughout the Cold War.

Victory in China

In 1949, after decades of civil war, the Communists under **Mao Tse-tung** (1893–1976) defeated the Nationalist forces of **Chiang Kai-Shek** (1887–1975), despite the economic and military aid given to the Nationalists by the United States. The Communists were successful because of the support of the Soviet Union, Mao's promise of land to the peasants, and corruption within the Nationalist forces. In 1949, Kai-Shek fled to Taiwan, an island off the Chinese coast. Throughout the 1950s and '60s, the United States recognized the Nationalist government as the legitimate government and refused to recognize Mao's Communist government.

Korean War (1950–1953)

At the end of World War II, Korea was divided at the **38th Parallel** into the South, which was controlled by the United States, and the Soviet zone in the North. The Cold War intensified as Stalin backed the North Korean invasion of South Korea on June 25, 1950. The United Nations Security Council (which met in Lake Success, Long Island, but without Soviet representatives, who were voluntarily absent) sponsored a resolution calling on North Korea to withdraw. When the request was ignored, the United Nations asked member nations to provide military aid and contribute troops. The majority of the military support came from the United States. In 1951, a cease-fire was discussed, but talks dragged on for the next two years. In 1953, an armistice was signed that still left Korea a divided country at the 38th Parallel.

Death of Stalin/De-Stalinization

In 1953, Stalin's death started a bitter struggle for power in the Soviet Union. **Georgy Malenkov** (1903–1988) served as Premier, but party leaders exercised control behind the scenes. This so-called **Troika** consisted of **Lavrenti Beria** (1899–1953), head of the Secret Police, and **Vyacheslav Molotov** (1889–1986), the Foreign Minister, who were determined that no one should dominate any regime in the way that Stalin had. However, Beria was soon arrested and executed. Malenkov was ousted after two years and replaced by **Nikolai Bulganin** (1895–1975), who was a mere figurehead. Molotov was demoted to a lower position and disappeared from public life. **Nikita Khrushchev** (1894–1971) emerged as the new party leader by 1958.

Khrushchev pursued a policy of de-Stalinization and, in 1956, at the 20th Congress of the Communist Party, attacked the abuses of power that had taken place during Stalin's long years as the party leader. Assaulting Stalin's cult of personality, and claiming that Stalin had not followed the policies of Marxism and Leninism, Khrushchev initiated a "thaw in the Cold War" and called for peaceful coexistence. Under Khrushchev, Communist goals did not change, but a policy of liberalization began. Soviet economic life improved and greater intellectual freedom was allowed. (Soviet novelist Boris Pasternak was not allowed to accept the Nobel Prize in Literature in 1958, however). Peaceful coexistence led to a relaxation of tension with the West. In 1955 representatives from Britain, France, and the United States met with Soviet representatives at the **Geneva Summit.** They discussed East-West relations in a friendly atmosphere but were unable to resolve their differences.

Uprisings in Poland and Hungary (1956)

Khrushchev's anti-Stalin campaign led to Nationalist revolts in Poland and Hungary. Workers in Poland went on strike for better working conditions and greater independence. **Wladyslaw Gomulka** (1905–1982), who had recently been released as a political prisoner, managed to win greater concessions for Poland while calming anti-Soviet feelings.

In Hungary, people revolted and demanded that the Soviet troops leave. **Imre Nagy** (1896–1958), a liberal Communist reformer, became president and declared Hungary's neutrality and withdrew from the Warsaw Pact. Khrushchev sent in a large army with tanks and crushed the rebellion. The Soviets deposed Nagy and installed a puppet regime under **János Kádár** (1912–1989).

U-2 Incident/Summit Meeting

In 1959, when Khrushchev came to the United States, visited Disneyland, and appeared on American television, the Cold War tensions seemed to be diminishing. However, this hope ended quickly. In June 1960, prior to the Paris Summit Conference, the Soviet Union shot down an unarmed American U-2 reconnaissance, or spy plane, piloted by Francis Gary Powers, deep inside Soviet territory. In Paris, Khrushchev demanded an apology from the United States for the plane's presence; when President Eisenhower refused to apologize, the summit ended. Subsequently, the crisis in Berlin and Cuba added to Cold War tensions. However, Eisenhower did admit that the plane was spying and agreed to suspend flights over the Soviet Union.

Berlin Wall

In August of 1961, shortly after John F. Kennedy was elected president, Khrushchev ordered the construction of the **Berlin Wall,** which was built by the East Germans. The wall was made of concrete blocks and barbed wire and extended along the border between East and West Berlin, sealing off East Berlin in violation of existing agreements. It is estimated that about 171 people were killed or died trying to escape the Berlin Wall and that around 5,000 were successful in escaping. The Berlin Wall became an ugly symbol of the Cold War and the failure of the communist system.

Cuban Missile Crisis

In 1959, **Fidel Castro** (b. 1926) had overthrown the corrupt Cuban government of **Fulgencio Batista** (1901–1973), while promising to restore democracy. In 1961, he proclaimed Cuba to be a communist state and began receiving support from the Soviet Union. In 1962, Khrushchev ordered missiles with nuclear warheads installed in Cuba, and President Kennedy announced a naval blockade of Cuba. During 13 tense days in October, the **Cuban Missile Crisis** was defused. The Soviets agreed to remove the missiles, and in return the United States promised not to invade Cuba. Party conservatives blamed Khrushchev for his de-Stalinization program, the split between China and the Soviet Union, the Cuban fiasco, and the failure to improve agricultural and industrial production. In October of 1964, Khrushchev was forced into retirement and replaced by **Leonid Brezhnev** (1906–1982).

The Brezhnev Era (1964–1982)

Next to Stalin, Leonid Brezhnev ruled the Soviet Union longer than any other leader. Brezhnev and his supporters stressed the ties with the Stalinist era by focusing on his good points and ignoring his crimes. Brezhnev strengthened the Soviet bureaucracy as well as the KGB (Committee of State Security)—formed in 1954; its mission was to defend the Soviet government from its enemies at home and abroad. The KGB suppressed dissidents who spoke out against the government at home and in the satellite countries. The Soviets also invested in a large military buildup and were determined to never again suffer a humiliating defeat, as happened in the Cuban Missile Crisis. Yet Brezhnev proceeded cautiously in the mid-1960s and sought to avoid confrontation with the West. He was determined, however, to protect Soviet interests.

Brezhnev Doctrine (1968)

In 1968, **Alexander Dubček** (1921–1992) became head of the Czechoslovakia Communist Party and began a series of reforms known as the **Prague Spring** reforms, which sought to make communism more humanistic. He lifted censorship, permitted non-communists to form political groups, and wanted to trade with the West, but still remain true to communist ideals. Brezhnev viewed these reforms as a capitalistic threat to the socialist ideologies of communism and, in August of 1968, sent over 500,000 Soviet and Eastern European troops to occupy Czechoslovakia. In the **Brezhnev Doctrine,** he defended the Soviet military invasion of Czechoslovakia, saying in effect, that antisocialist elements in a single socialist country can compromise the entire socialist system, and thus other socialist countries have the right to intervene militarily if they see the need to do so.

The Brezhnev Doctrine was seriously tested in Poland. Throughout the 1970s, Poland had suffered economic hardship and Polish workers had rioted in 1970 and 1976 against increased food prices. In 1980, scattered strikes spread across Poland to protest the rise in meat prices. **Lech Walesa** (b. 1943), an electrician at the Gdansk shipyards, organized **Solidarity,** an independent trade union that called for political, industrial, and economic changes. Solidarity had the support of millions of workers, intellectuals, and the Catholic Church. In 1978, **Karol Wojtyla,** (1920–2005) the former archbishop of Krakow, Poland, was elected Pope **John Paul II,** the first Polish pope. He supported the struggle for the rights of people across the world, especially in his native country. Solidarity created concern in the Soviet Union, as well as in other Soviet Bloc nations. However, still facing criticism from its invasion of Afghanistan in 1979, the Soviets played a waiting game. When Solidarity began to lose its cohesiveness, the Polish Communist leadership declared martial law and arrested Walesa and other leaders. Solidarity went underground and fought with great popular support, paving the way for greater changes in the Soviet Union and Eastern Europe during the latter half of the 1980s.

Détente

During the 1970s, a spirit of *détente* developed in the Cold War. **Détente** means a progressive relaxation of tension, and involved the following events:

- **1972:** President Richard Nixon visited Moscow. The United States and the Soviet Union signed significant accords on space flights, health, and trading agreements. These accords included an agreement on joint space flight, cooperation in medical, science, and public health, and the end of the prohibition of shipping of American goods to the Soviet Union. They also signed the **SALT I Accord (Strategic Arms Limitation Talks)**, which was designed to limit the spread of nuclear weapons. Limits were set on both long-range missiles (intercontinental ballistics missiles) and defensive missiles.
- **1973:** Brezhnev visited the United States and spoke to the American people via television.
- **1975:** The United States, Canada, and 33 European nations met at Helsinki, Finland to sign the **Helsinki Pact.** The European countries formally agreed to recognize Soviet territorial gains in Europe, the division of Germany into two nations, and Soviet domination of Eastern Europe. The Soviet Union, the United States, and the other European nations also agreed to further the cause of human rights.

The spirit of détente came to an end with the Soviet invasion of Afghanistan in 1979. The Soviets invaded Afghanistan in order to keep Afghanistan's Communist government in power, again using the Brezhnev Doctrine to justify the invasion. Many in the West were convinced that the Soviets were violating the spirit of détente. The Afghanistan invasion drained the Soviet economy and morale at home.

By the time of Brezhnev's death in 1982, the Soviet Union faced many serious problems. The centralized economy was still inefficient and unable to produce enough food to feed the people, so the Soviet Union had to import grain from the capitalist nations. The Soviet bureaucracy had little understanding of how the centralized economy had failed the people. Within the next few years, sweeping changes dramatically altered the future of Communism in the Soviet Union.

Political and Economic Recovery in Europe

World War II left Europe with a devastated infrastructure and in a weakened economic condition. In 1947, United States Secretary of State **George Marshall** (1880–1959) offered economic aid to all European countries. The **Marshall Plan,** officially known as the European Recovery Program, provided over $13 billion in aid for foodstuff, machinery, and raw materials. The goal of the program was to achieve recovery, not relief, and to lessen the dangers of communism. Stalin forbade Eastern European countries to accept this aid and promised that the Soviet Union would help them instead.

As the Marshall Plan aid poured in, the battered economies of Western Europe began to improve. They rebuilt factories, farms, and transportation systems destroyed in the war. The close cooperation among European nations as required by the Marshall Plan also promoted economic growth. In 1950, French statesman **Jean Monnet** (1888–1979) and Foreign Minister **Robert Schuman** (1886–1963) proposed an economic union of Western European nations to integrate all European coal and steel production. In 1951, France, West Germany, Belgium, Italy, the Netherlands, and Luxembourg accepted this idea. They set up the **European Coal and Steel Community (ECSC).** By 1958, coal and steel moved freely among these six nations.

In 1957, these same six nations that formed the ECSC established the **European Economic Community (EC) or** the **Common Market.** The goal of the organization was the reduction of all tariffs among the six countries and the inclusion of free movement of capital and economic policies and institutions. By 1973, Britain, Denmark, and Ireland joined. The Common Market was a great success. In the 1980s, the Common Market expanded to include Greece (1981) and Spain and Portugal (1986); it became known as the **European Union** in 1993. This union benefited Western Europe in several ways. By promoting economic cooperation among individual European nations, it reduced the threat of conflict. It also enabled Western Europe to compete for world markets with North America and East Asia.

West Germany

West Germany led the economic miracle. A free market economy with a social welfare network brought economic growth to West Germany. Politically, Germany evolved into a stable democracy. The United States worked closely with the **Christian Democratic Union** (heirs to the old Catholic Centre Party, which had been organized in the 1870s to defend Catholic interests) to ensure that West Germany became an integral part of the Western alliance. From 1949 to 1963, **Konrad Adenauer** (1876–1967) provided strong leadership that helped to revive West Germany. At the age of 73, Adenauer ("Der Alte"—the old one) worked to rebuild the German economy by using the influx of refugees from Eastern Europe as a valuable labor resource in building up the country. Under his leadership, West Germany rebuilt their factories, cities, and trade. By the mid-1950s, industrial production surpassed prewar German levels, and by the 1960s, West Germany had become one of the leading economies in Western Europe. In April 1963, **Ludwig Erhard** (1897–1977), who had been Adenauer's economic minister, succeeded him. Under Erhard's leadership, the economy suffered a temporary recession. In 1969, **Willy Brandt** (1913–1992), leader of the **Social Democratic Party** and former Mayor of West Berlin, became chancellor. Brandt was the first Socialist chancellor in 40 years and began his policy of **"Ostpolitik,"** or Eastern Policy, seeking reconciliation between East and West Germany. He signed treaties with the Soviet Union, Poland, and Czechoslovakia, and also signed a treaty of mutual recognition with East Germany. Although Brandt's long-term goal of German unification would take another twenty years, he was awarded the Nobel Peace Prize in 1971 for his efforts to improve relations with Eastern Europe and East Germany. However, in 1974, Brandt resigned because a close personal aide on his staff confessed that he was an East German spy. In that same year, the Socialist Democrats chose **Helmut Schmidt** (b. 1918) as successor. Poor economic conditions in addition to an attack by the Greens, a loose coalition of environmentalists, pulled strength away from the Socialists and ended Schmidt's rule in 1982. **Helmut Kohl** (b. 1930), a conservative Christian Democrat, became chancellor of West Germany until 1990 and of the reunited Germany from 1990 to 1998. His sixteen-year tenure was the longest of any chancellor since Otto von Bismarck.

Great Britain

World War II battered Great Britain's economy. In 1945, the **Labour Party** under **Clement Attlee** (1883–1967) assumed power and began to transform Great Britain into a welfare state, nationalizing industries and expanding social programs to include social security and national health insurance. The National Health Service granted every citizen the right to free medical, dental, hospital, and nursing care. The Labour government was succeeded by three conservative governments: Churchill from 1951 to 1955, **Anthony Eden** (1897–1977) from 1955 to 1957, and **Harold Macmillan** (1894–1986) from 1957 to 1963. These conservative leaders restored some private enterprise to the iron and steel industries, introduced some fees for national health, and accepted the basic outline of the welfare state. Labour returned to power under **Harold Wilson** (1916–1995) from 1964 to 1970, restoring free medical service from cradle to grave, as well as state-funded universities and public housing programs.

Throughout the 1970s, power shifted between the Conservative and Labour Parties. Inflation, created by the Arab oil embargoes of 1973 and 1979, caused problems for England. Labor productivity was low. The pound was devalued in 1976 and frequent strikes hurt the economy. In 1979, **Margaret Thatcher** (b. 1925), a Conservative, became Britain's first female prime minister and served three consecutive terms in office. As prime minister, she advocated privatization of state-owned industries, curbing the power of the trade unions, cutting the size of the government bureaucracy, trimming welfare services, and lowering taxes, especially for the rich. Thatcher's policies succeeded in reducing inflation but unemployment dramatically increased. Thatcher was controversial and due to her strong standards and her leadership style, she became known as the "Iron Lady"—adapting as her political mantra a nickname the Soviet communists had coined as an insult. Her famous statement, "the lady's not for turning," refers to her refusal to back down on key issues. Thatcher and American President **Ronald Reagan** (1911–2004) became close friends because of their strong distrust of communism and their firm belief in the private market system. Next to Winston Churchill, Thatcher was the longest-serving British Prime Minister in more than 150 years. Her efforts to introduce market principles into the National Health Service and the educational system as well as her opposition to any closer integration with Europe led to divisions within the Conservative Party. The British film, and later play, *Billy Elliot,* provides a view of how Thatcher broke the power of coal miners during the strike of 1984-85. The closing of many of these mines created a national controversy. Victory in the **Falklands War** against Argentina in 1982 and divided opposition helped Thatcher win a landslide victory in 1983. She narrowly escaped death in 1984 when the IRA planted a bomb at a Conservative political convention. In November 1990, she agreed to resign and was succeeded by **John Major** (b. 1943). Major was the leader of the Conservative Party until 1997. He followed most of Thatcher's policies but was a greater advocate of European integration.

France

At the end of World War II, France was a weak country. The **French Fourth Republic**, set up at the end of World War II, suffered from the same weaknesses as the Third Republic: a weak executive and a strong legislature comprised of too many political parties—a combination that led to multiparty coalitions and frequent changes in government. In 1958, the threat of civil war in the North African colony of Algeria resulted in the downfall of the Fourth Republic. In 1958, **Charles de Gaulle** (1890–1970) was called out of retirement to head an emergency government. The National Assembly voted to give de Gaulle complete power for six months to draw up a new constitution for the country. That same year, de Gaulle set up the **French Fifth Republic,** which was accepted by an overwhelming majority. Its constitution provided for a much stronger presidential office with the power to dissolve the legislature, submit popular issues to the people, and assume emergency power whenever necessary. De Gaulle became the first president of the Fifth Republic. Through de Gaulle's efforts, French prestige and power were restored and stability returned to the country. In July 1962, de Gaulle solved the Algerian issue by granting the colony its independence.

In his foreign policy, de Gaulle tried to make France an independent force in world affairs. His strongly nationalistic policies angered the United States and Great Britain. In 1963, he opposed British entry into the Common Market. In 1966, he decided to withdraw all French troops from NATO and demanded that all NATO bases and headquarters be removed from French soil. He even advocated the building of an independent French nuclear force. In 1965, de Gaulle had been reelected to a second term. However, by 1968, concern over inflation and housing as well as his expenditures on nuclear policies rather than on education, led to student revolts and strikes by 10 million workers. De Gaulle survived politically by promising educational reforms and wage increases. In April 1969, de Gaulle demanded a referendum to support a new constitution that would reduce the power of the Senate. His proposal for changes was rejected and he was forced to resign. De Gaulle's successors, **Georges Pompidou** (1911–1974), president from 1969–1974 and **Valéry Giscard d'Estaing** (b. 1926), who was president from 1974 to 1981, continued to follow an independent foreign policy. However, France did finally agree to British entry into the Common Market. Like the rest of Europe, the economic recession of the 1970s and early 1980s hurt the country's prosperity. The French Socialist **François Mitterrand** (1916–1996), who was president from 1981 to 1995, tried to revive the economy by nationalizing private companies and banks and increasing wages and other social benefits. However, the economic crisis deepened and Mitterrand was forced to cut social programs and taxes. Mitterrand was able to control inflation but unemployment increased. France continued to face economic problems during the 1980s and early 1990s.

Italy

At the end of World War II, Italy rejected and removed the monarchy, which had been associated with fascism, and set up a republic. Postwar Italy was economically divided into two regions: the prosperous and industrial north and the rural south, which was primarily agricultural. Politically, Italy had a multiparty system like France, and the Christian Democrats, who were allied with the Catholic Church, dominated the national scene. The leading figure in post-Fascist Italy was **Alcide De Gasperi** (1881–1954), who provided strength and stability for seven formative years. In the 1948 election, De Gasperi, supported by the United States and the Vatican, won a major victory over the Communists who were bidding for power. As in France, Italy's Communist Party was strong, but never won enough votes to form a majority government. After 1948, the Christian Democrats would govern the country, but without the majority that they had won in 1948. Financial scandals and political corruption hurt the national parties. Yet, the alliance of the Catholic Church and the Christian Democrats supplied national unity to Italian politics by providing prime ministers with a coalition government.

Despite these problems, Italy developed economically, and by the 1970s had advanced into one of the ten industrial powers. However, as in other European countries, the Arab oil embargo adversely affected the economy, which was more dependent on oil imports than other industrialized countries. By 1973, Italy's inflation rate was

25 percent, and was still 16 percent in the early 1980s; her unemployment rate was high and the lira had dropped in value. Italy also suffered from terrorism, and the 1978 assassination of **Aldo Moro** (1916–1978), a respected Christian Democrat and former prime minister, by a radical group known as the **Red Brigades,** added to the difficulties of the Italian government. However, in January 1983 about 25 members of the Red Brigades were sentenced to life imprisonment in connection with Moro's kidnapping and murder. By 1986, internal security had improved. A major effort against organized crime was under way by the mid 1980s: over 1,000 suspects were convicted in trials against the Camorra in Naples and the Mafia in Sicily. Although there have been 48 coalition governments in Italy from 1945 to 1988, Italy has remained a stable country.

The End of Colonialism

The post–World War II era marked the final collapse of European imperialism. Winston Churchill had hoped to maintain control of the vast holdings of the British Empire, but Britain was militarily too weak to defend its possessions. The Cold War also undermined British imperialism, as the United States supported the right of people to self-determination, and so did the Soviet Union. The demise of the empire began in 1947, when India, "the jewel in the crown," declared its independence. This began a chain reaction. In 1948, the British withdrew from Palestine and left to the United Nations the task of determining the area's future. The Jewish state of Israel was created out of part of British-controlled Palestine.

The Arab nations of Egypt, Iraq, Jordan, Lebanon, Saudi Arabia and Syria refused to accept (and have still not accepted) the state of Israel and immediately attacked it. The Israeli army defeated these nations but the issue of a Palestinian state was still not resolved. Wars broke out in 1956, 1967, and 1973. In Egypt, Gamal Abdel Nasser (1918–1970) nationalized the Suez Canal in 1956, ending British control. Britain, France, and Israel invaded, but the United States and the Soviet Union immediately condemned the attack. Working through the United Nations, they secured the withdrawal of the invading forces and stationed a United Nations Emergency Force on the Egyptian border. The negative response by the United States and the Soviet Union was a reminder to Britain that the "sun was setting on the British Empire." By 1957, Ghana declared its independence and the rest of the British African Empire declared its independence without any major upheavals.

The Dutch and French did not relinquish their control over the colonies as readily as Britain. During World War II, the Dutch colonies fell under Japanese control. After the war, Indonesian Nationalists set up a republic. The Dutch tried to restore control, but the United Nations Security Council secured a cease-fire, and in 1949 granted independence to Indonesia. France also struggled to maintain its empire in **Indochina** (Vietnam, Cambodia, and Laos). After World War II, the French promised partial independence, but their offer was rejected. Led by Nationalist **Ho Chi Minh** (1890–1969), the Vietnamese, who had fought against the Japanese in World War II, waged an eight-year struggle for freedom. In 1954, France lost Vietnam. The **Geneva Accord** recognized the independence of Cambodia and Laos and divided Vietnam into the North (backed by the Communists) and the South (supported by the United States). Despite massive American aid to South Vietnam and the commitment of about 500,000 troops in the 1960s, South Vietnam could not defeat the North Vietnamese. In 1968 the guerrilla forces (Viet Cong) launched a massive attack on American and South Vietnam forces. Although this assault which took place during the Tet or Vietnamese New Year did not capture any major cities, it convinced Americans that the war was not going well. Growing antiwar sentiment eventually forced the United States to withdraw in 1973. In 1975 North Vietnam captured Saigon, the capital of the south and the country was united. By 1956, the French had also ended their colonial rule over Morocco and Tunisia. The struggle over Algeria was different, as the French had controlled Algeria since 1830 and French settlers and the French military opposed Algeria's independence. Civil war threatened the country over this issue. In 1958, Charles de Gaulle took over the government and in 1962 made peace with Algeria and granted her independence. Within two decades of the conclusion of World War II, the colonial empires of the Western countries had been dismantled.

Chronology of the Cold War

1945	Potsdam Conference—Truman and Stalin disagree over the Yalta Conference on Eastern Europe.
1946	Churchill gives his "Iron Curtain" speech.
1947	India becomes independent. The Truman Doctrine and the Marshall Plan are announced.
1948	The Berlin Blockade begins. The Berlin Airlift lasts for 321 days. Marshal Tito breaks with the U.S.S.R. State of Israel is created.
1949	The Berlin Blockade ends. NATO is formed. Chinese Communists defeat the Nationalists. The Federal Republic of Germany and the German Democratic Republic are created. The Soviet Union tests an atomic bomb.
1950	The Korean War begins.
1952	Greece and Turkey join NATO. The United States tests the H-bomb.
1953	Joseph Stalin dies.
1954	In Vietnam, Ho Chi Minh defeats the French at Dien Bien Phu.
1955	The Warsaw Pact is formed.
1956	Khrushchev begins de-Stalinization. Uprisings occur in Poland and Hungary. Suez Canal Crisis takes place.
1957	The European Common Market is formed. The U.S.S.R. launches Sputnik I and Sputnik II—the first earth satellites.
1960	Belgian Congo becomes free.
1961	The Berlin Wall is built.
1962	John Glenn orbits the earth. The Cuban Missile Crisis occurs.
1963	Dr. Michael Ellis DeBakey demonstrates the first use of an artificial heart.
1964	Leonid Brezhnev becomes General Secretary of the Communist Party of the Soviet Union.
1967	South African cardiac surgeon Christian Barnard performs the first successful heart transplant.
1968	Tet Offensive takes place in Vietnam. The Prague Spring begins in Czechoslovakia.
1969	Apollo 11 lands on the moon.
1970	Egyptian leader Gamal Abdel Nasser dies.
1972	President Nixon visits Moscow, signs SALT I treaty, limiting anti-ballistic missile systems.
1973	Oil crisis affects the world.
1978	Pope John Paul II elected as the first Polish pope.
1979	Margaret Thatcher leads Conservative Party to victory. The Soviets invade Afghanistan. The United States imposes a grain embargo on the Soviet Union.
1980	Solidarity is formed in Poland.
1981	François Mitterrand is elected President of France.

Sample Multiple-Choice Questions

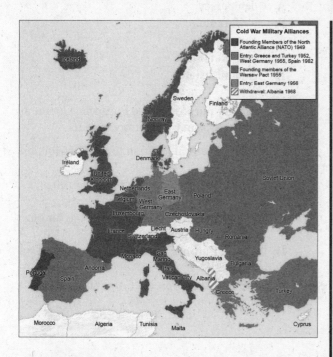

1. This map best represents the division of Europe that led to the

   A. Crimean War.
   B. formation of the Common Market.
   C. creation of NATO and the Warsaw Pact.
   D. Triple Alliance and Triple Entente.
   E. establishment of the League of Nations.

2. Khrushchev's de-Stalinization speech had the following effects on the communist world:

   A. Democratic elections in satellite nations controlled by the Soviet Union
   B. Uprisings in Yugoslavia against Marshal Tito's government
   C. Revolts in Poland and Hungary
   D. A dialogue established between the Soviet Union and the Catholic Church
   E. Boris Pasternak's 1958 acceptance of the Nobel Prize in Literature

3. The revolt in Hungary (1956), the demonstrations in Czechoslovakia (1968), and the formation of Solidarity in Poland (1980s) are similar in that they

   A. were movements to restore the power of the aristocracy.
   B. were tolerated by the Communist leaders, who accepted the need for change.
   C. represented a challenge to Communist leadership.
   D. represented attempts to rid these countries of Western ideas and influence.
   E. were attempts by the Communists to provide humanitarian aid.

4. Which of the following leaders is associated with the Prague Spring of 1968?

   A. Lech Walesa
   B. Alexander Dubček
   C. Wladyslaw Gomulka
   D. Imre Nagy
   E. Václav Havel

5. Which was one of the causes of the Cold War between the United States and the U.S.S.R. after World War II?

   A. The struggle for colonies in Africa
   B. The Soviet Union's support of Fidel Castro
   C. Rivalry in Asia
   D. Ideological differences
   E. The United States' support of dissidents within the Soviet Union

6. Which had the greatest impact on ending the Summit meeting of 1960?

   A. Fidel Castro's announcement that he was a communist
   B. The claim that the United States promoted revolution in Hungary and Poland
   C. An American U-2 spy plane being shot down by the Soviet Union
   D. The construction of the Berlin Wall
   E. Refusal of the United States to abandon military bases in Western Europe

7. Nikita Khrushchev introduced the policy of

    A. peaceful coexistence.
    B. *détente.*
    C. *perestroika.*
    D. *glasnost.*
    E. Spirit of Glassboro.

8. The most significant occurrence in Africa since 1950 has been the

    A. decrease in the birth rate.
    B. decline of European colonialism.
    C. unification of East African nations.
    D. establishment of communist regimes in most nations.
    E. establishment of industrial economies.

9. The Labour Party which controlled the English government after World War II introduced a

    A. democracy.
    B. welfare state.
    C. communist state.
    D. corporate state.
    E. capitalist state.

10. The primary purpose of the European Common Market (European Community) was to

    A. create a central location for the distribution of goods.
    B. force Eastern European nations to change their trading partners.
    C. establish a tariff-free flow of goods among member nations.
    D. reduce European dependence on foreign oil reserves.
    E. promote a one-product economy.

Multiple-Choice Questions: Answers and Explanations

1. **C.** The map represents Europe at the beginning of the Cold War during which NATO was formed (1949). Consisting of Western European countries and the United States, NATO was a defensive alliance against communism. The Warsaw Pact (1955) consisted of the U.S.S.R. and seven satellite nations in Eastern Europe. The Crimean War was fought in 1854 and involved Russia, Great Britain, and France. The Triple Alliance and Triple Entente were formed in the late 1890s and early twentieth century. The League of Nations was created in 1920.

2. **C.** Revolts broke out in Poland and Hungary. Khrushchev's policy of de-Stalinization and his speech before the 20th Congress, attacking Stalin's cult of personality, led to a thaw in relations with the Western countries, and Poland and Hungary perceived Khrushchev's policy of liberalization as a mandate for change. Workers in Poland went on strike for better working conditions. In Hungary, the people demanded that Soviet troops leave. In 1956, Khrushchev sent the Soviet army to crush the Hungarian revolt. Khrushchev's policy led to a relaxation of tension and not to democratic elections or revolts in Yugoslavia. There was no improvement in relations with the Catholic Church. The Russian author, Boris Pasternak, received the Nobel Prize in Literature but was not allowed to travel to Sweden to accept it.

3. **C.** The revolt in Hungary, the demonstrations in Czechoslovakia, and the formation of Solidarity in Poland are similar in that they represented a challenge to Communist leadership. In Hungary, Imre Nagy was a liberal Communist who wanted to withdraw from the Warsaw Pact. In Czechoslovakia, Alexander Dubček wanted to liberalize his Communist regime, and Solidarity was formed to promote political and social changes. In Hungary and Czechoslovakia, the Soviet Union sent in troops. In Poland, the Communists declared martial law and arrested Solidarity leaders. These movements were designed to change Communism, not restore the power of the aristocracy. These movements were not tolerated by the Communists nor were they attempts to provide humanitarian aid. These movements were interested in promoting Western ideas of democracy and not an attempt to rid their countries of Western influence.

4. **B.** Alexander Dubček began the series of reforms known as the Prague Spring reform. He wanted to bring about more humanistic socialism such as lifting censorship and trading with the West. The reform movement was crushed. Lech Walesa was the leader of the Polish Solidarity movement. Walesa was an electrician at the Gdansk shipyard who organized Solidarity, an independent trade union. In 1990, he was elected president of the Republic of Poland after the fall of Communism. Wladyslaw Gomulka was part of the Polish uprising in 1956. Imre Nagy was the Hungarian leader who opposed the Soviet Union in 1956. Václav Havel was a playwright who was elected President of Czechoslovakia in 1989 and the first President of the Czech Republic in 1993.

5. **D.** Ideological differences were one basic cause of the Cold War between the United States and the U.S.S.R. after World War II. The United States' political system is based on democracy, capitalism, and the importance of the individual. Both the United States and the U.S.S.R. supported self-determination in Africa to end Western imperialism. They disagreed on which form of government they would follow. Soviet support of Fidel Castro began in the 1950s. Rivalry in Asia existed among the United States, Soviet Union, and China. The United States' support of dissidents within the Soviet Union was an ideological outgrowth of a difference between communism and democracy.

6. **C.** On May 1, 1960, the Soviets shot down a CIA spy plane and captured the pilot, Francis Gary Powers. The United States first issued public denials, but President Eisenhower was later forced to admit the plane had been spying on the Soviet Union. On May 16, Soviet leader Nikita Khrushchev lashed out at President Eisenhower at the Paris summit meeting between the two heads of state. Khrushchev's outburst angered Eisenhower and doomed any chances for successful negotiations at the summit. The summit meeting officially adjourned the next day with no further meetings between the two men. Eisenhower's planned trip to Moscow in June was cancelled. Castro's announcement that he was a communist and the construction of the Berlin Wall in 1961 did not affect the Paris summit meeting, but added to the Cold War tensions during the Kennedy administration. The uprisings in Poland and Hungary had occurred in 1956. The issue of military bases in Western Europe was not discussed at the Paris summit meeting.

7. **A.** Nikita Khrushchev introduced a policy of peaceful coexistence after the death of Joseph Stalin in 1953. Although Khrushchev believed that the Soviet Union would eventually bury the United States, he sought nonviolent ways to compete and coexist with non-communist nations. He introduced a relaxation of tensions, or a thaw with the United States. Yet by 1961, he built the Berlin Wall and brought the United States to the brink of war in the Cuban Missile Crisis. *Détente* is associated with the Brezhnev regime. Mikhail Gorbachev introduced *perestroika* and *glasnost*. The Spirit of Glassboro was a meeting between United States and Soviet leaders held in New Jersey in 1967, which produced nothing of substance.

8. **B.** The decline of European colonialism is the most significant occurrence in Africa since 1950. At the end of World War II, most of Africa was under European rule. By 1959, the following nations were independent: Libya, Egypt, Ethiopia, Liberia, and the Union of South Africa. Since 1959, more than 40 nations have gained their independence. The population in Africa has been increasing despite the AIDS epidemic. There has been no unification of East African nations. Communism is no longer a threat to the African continent. Despite its vast resources, most of Africa has not been industrialized.

9. **B.** The Labour Party introduced the welfare state after World War II. Clement Attlee, the Labour Prime Minister who succeeded Winston Churchill in 1945, transformed Britain into a welfare state. The Labour Party introduced social programs that provided public housing and established old-age pensions, unemployment insurance, and the creation of a National Health Service, or free medical care. The Conservatives, under Margaret Thatcher in 1979, began to roll back the welfare state. England has had a parliamentary-type democracy since 1689. It has never followed a communist or corporate form of government. The Labour Party nationalized the Bank of England but did not introduce communism to England.

10. **C.** The primary purpose of the European Common Market was to establish a tariff-free flow of goods among member nations. In 1957, the European Common Market was formed by six industrialized Western nations to expand trade by ending tariffs and allowing capital and labor to move freely across the borders of these European nations. The Common Market was a trade agreement, not a distribution center for goods. It was only for Western industrialized countries. The Common Market did not reduce dependence on foreign oil reserves as the Arab Embargo of the 1970s demonstrated. The Common Market was for industrialized and diversified economies.

Contemporary Europe

From 1945 until the 1980s, the problems created by the Cold War loomed over Europe. Under its shadow, however, Western Europe and the United States experienced remarkable economic growth. The Soviet Union and communist Eastern Europe, under the iron hand of Stalin, also rebuilt. However, economic growth slowed and stagnated in the 1970s, as the Soviet economy was unable to meet the needs for both military spending and consumer goods. In 1985, Mikhail Gorbachev became the leader of the Soviet Union and sought some reforms in both the Soviet Union and the Communist Bloc. Gorbachev began to restructure the Soviet economy and instituted political changes that would allow for greater openness in Soviet society. He also encouraged reforms in Eastern Europe. His policies contributed to the collapse of communism in Eastern Europe and the breakup of the Soviet Union.

The year 1989, like 1789 (the French Revolution), was a remarkable year in European history. Freedom swept across Eastern Europe, and communist-led regimes collapsed peacefully in Poland, Hungary, Czechoslovakia, Bulgaria, and Albania. The collapse of the Berlin Wall in 1989 and the unification of Germany in 1990 symbolized the decline of the Soviet satellite system that had dominated Europe for a half-century. Gorbachev's policies also affected minorities within the multinational Soviet Empire. By 1991, the Baltic states had regained their independence. By the end of 1991, other Soviet republics declared their independence and Boris Yeltsin became president of the Russian Federation. After 74 years, communism ceased to exist in Russia.

The collapse of communism in Europe also unleashed ethnic tensions in Eastern Europe that had been suppressed for many years. The Soviet domination of Eastern Europe had been based on absolute control without any regard for the different ethnic groups. In 1991, ethnic conflicts tore Yugoslavia apart in a long and tragic civil war. The conflict led to ethnic cleansing and tested the ability of Europe to deal with post–Cold War problems.

The problem of ethnic nationalism and violence in the 1990s became part of a global pattern of violence and conflicts. The efforts of Basque separatists in northern Spain to gain independence from the Spanish government through assassinations and car bombings, as well as the continued violence in Northern Ireland between Protestants and Catholics, demonstrated the scope of the growing problem of terrorism. On September 11, 2001, the terrorist attacks on the Twin Towers of the World Trade Center in New York and the Pentagon outside of Washington, D.C., revealed the global dimensions of terrorism.

The latter half of the twentieth century brought economic changes as well as social changes to Europe. Economic changes in Western Europe during the Cold War era affected European society. The family and the role of women underwent a change as the divorce rate increased and the birth rate decreased. European society was also becoming more diverse as immigrants from foreign countries settled in Europe and provided a cheap source of labor for the booming economy. During the economic recession of the 1970s, Europe began to resent the newcomers. They were blamed for high unemployment and there was fear that the high birth rate of these newcomers from Africa, Asia, as well as the immigrants the countries of Eastern Europe and Yugoslavia threatened the values of Western European society.

Throughout the 1980s and '90s, Europe continued to promote economic unity to ensure its economic growth. The dream of a United States of Europe became a reality with the introduction of a new European currency (the *euro*) at the beginning of the twenty-first century and the enlargement of the European Union in the ensuing years.

The Collapse of Communism in the Soviet Union and Eastern Europe

The 18-year rule of Leonid Brezhnev brought security for the Soviet bureaucracy. Government censors carefully controlled what writers could publish. Brezhnev rigorously cracked down on those who spoke out against the government. The secret police, the KGB, arrested many dissidents including Alexander Solzhenitsyn, the winner of the 1970 Noble Peace Prize and expelled him from the Soviet Union in 1970. The system protected the elite but was apathetic toward the masses. The state could produce impressive results when it poured resources into major projects such as the development of new weapons and the space race; however, Soviet consumer products such as shoes, suits, and television sets, were inferior to those made in the West. People spent hours waiting in line to buy food and goods. Economic efficiency and personal initiatives were discouraged.

The Soviet Union's invasion of Afghanistan drained the Soviet economy and provoked a moral crisis similar to that created by the Vietnam War in the United States. The Soviet Union had invaded Afghanistan in 1979 and killed the Afghani president Hafizullah Amin (1929–1979) and installed Babrak Karmal (1929–1996) who served as president until 1986. The Soviet Union became bogged down in a no-win situation against determined Afghan fighters. In 1982, Brezhnev's successor, **Yuri Andropov** (1914–1984), Chief of the KGB, tried to introduce some moderate reforms in the Soviet Union. He sought to improve economic performance by providing factory managers with material incentives, and campaigned against worker absenteeism and high-level corruption. At 72, **Konstantin Chernenko** (1911–1985), who replaced Andropov after his sudden death in 1984, made no significant changes before dying in 1985. In 1985, the worsening economic conditions and the failure of old-line Soviet leadership led to the selection of **Mikhail Gorbachev** (b. 1931) as the new president of the Soviet Union. Gorbachev was an energetic individual who was determined to reform inefficiencies in the government and the economy. Gorbachev's reforms, however, unleashed waves of change that he was unable to control and resulted in the collapse of the Soviet Empire and communism in Eastern Europe.

The cornerstone of his program was *perestroika* or economic restructuring. His program called for less government planning, and more power to local factory managers to make production decisions. The program also allowed some Soviet citizens to operate small retail businesses. Farmers were given permission to grow some food that could be sold on the free market. (Gorbachev's policy of perestroika was similar in some respects to Lenin's New Economic Policy of 1921. Lenin's program also allowed some capitalist ventures. While the state controlled the major industries, small private businesses were allowed to open for profit. Peasants were also allowed to hold on to small plots of land to sell their surplus crops.) Initial economic reforms were difficult to implement. The reforms were denounced by old-line communists and bureaucrats whose jobs were threatened. Radicals and democrats urged a more rapid move to a free market economy. The economy and the people were unprepared for these changes, however, and the economy stalled in its progression from central planning to a free market. Shortages grew worse and prices soared. By 1990, Gorbachev's economic initiatives had achieved very little success.

Gorbachev believed that economic reforms could not occur without a free flow of ideas and information. As part of his reform program, he introduced a policy of *glasnost* or openness in Soviet society. He encouraged citizens to openly discuss the strengths and weaknesses of the Soviet Union. Reporters actively investigated social problems and openly criticized the government. Censorship ended and free speech was promoted. Attacks on the crimes of the Stalin era appeared often in Soviet plays and newspapers, and the works of writers who had been banned for many years were made available. The government also allowed churches to open. Political reforms were also revolutionary. In 1987, the principle of a two-candidate election was introduced. However, only Communist Party members were allowed on the ballot. In the past, voters had merely approved candidates who were hand-picked by the Communist Party. Now voters could choose from a list of Communist candidates for each office. In 1988, a new constitution was adopted, calling for the election of a new legislative body. In 1989, the Soviet Union held its first elections with modified choices since 1917. In some areas where the Communist Party leaders ran unopposed, the people were so angry that they crossed off the ballots the names of party leaders and wrote in local candidates. By 1990, Gorbachev was forced to admit non-Communist parties into the political process. Gorbachev attempted to consolidate his power by creating a new state presidency and in March 1990 became the Soviet Union's first president.

In foreign affairs, Gorbachev withdrew troops from Afghanistan in 1989 and refused to accept the Brezhnev Doctrine, which claimed that the Soviet Union had the right to intervene in any communist country under its control. In 1989, Gorbachev's reforms unleashed a wave of peaceful revolutions throughout Eastern Europe that overturned the existing communist government in those countries and ended Soviet domination in Eastern Europe.

In Poland, the Communist government legalized **Solidarity,** an independent trade union, and held free democratic elections for the first time in over 50 years. On June 4, 1989, Solidarity candidates, who had outpolled Communist Party members, became the first freely elected opposition in a communist country. In 1990, **Lech Walesa** (b. 1943) was elected president of the Republic of Poland.

Democracy spread to other Soviet satellite countries as well. In Czechoslovakia, communism ended in December of 1989. Massive street demonstrations led by students and intellectuals led to the ouster of the Communist leaders within ten days. This non-violent revolution became known as the "Velvet Revolution." **Václav Havel** (b. 1936), a dissident playwright, was chief spokesman of the revolution and was elected president in 1989. He would be Czechoslovakia's last president and the first president of the new **Czech Republic** (1993–2003), when Czechoslovakia peacefully split into the Czech Republic and the Slovak Republic, or Slovakia. Poland, the Czech Republic, Slovakia, and Hungary were the most successful in making the transition from communism to democracy. In 1997, Poland, the Czech Republic, and Hungary were asked to join NATO as a way of becoming fully integrated into Western society after years of communist domination. Despite Russia's objection, NATO officially admitted these countries into the alliance in March 1999. In Bulgaria, the Communist leadership stepped down without putting up any resistance. In Hungary, the Communist Party was broken up and free elections were held in 1990. The Hungarians also tore down the barbed wire "Iron Curtain" that separated Austria and Hungary, and opened their borders to refugees from East Germany.

In East Germany, the communist government was forced to open its borders and in November of 1989, joyous Germans from both sides tore down the Berlin Wall, which had divided the nation for almost 30 years. During the first week alone, over 2 million East Germans poured into West Germany. The Communist leaders were arrested, and elections, which were won by the conservative pro-unification Christian Democrats, were held in March of 1990. By October 1990, Germany was united and Helmut Kohl, the leader of the Christian Democrats, became the country's first chancellor of the newly united Germany. Kohl was skillful in assuring the United States, other European countries, and the Soviet Union that they need not fear a reunified Germany. In July 1990, Kohl, in a historic agreement with the Soviet Union, affirmed their peaceful intentions, recognized the pre-1945 borders, and pledged that a united Germany would not own anti-ballistic missile systems. On October 3, 1990, East and West Germany formally became a single nation.

Communism experienced a violent end in Romania. **Nicolae Ceausescu** (1918–1989), the Communist dictator, ordered his security forces to slaughter thousands of protesters, thereby sparking an armed uprising. After Ceausescu's forces were defeated, he and his wife were captured and put to death by a military tribunal. A provisional government emerged to govern the country. In May 1990, elections were won by the National Salvation Front, whose formerly Communist leaders called for a gradual and controlled transition to a free market economy.

In November of 1990, Gorbachev sought to end Soviet deficits through military cuts. Twenty-two members of NATO and the Warsaw Pact met in Paris to sign the Treaty on Conventional Armed Forces in Europe (CFE), a general peace treaty that officially ended the Cold War. They agreed to scale down their conventional armed forces. The CFE called for equal ceilings in NATO and the Warsaw Pact land-based forces from the Atlantic to the Urals. However, it excluded naval forces and American–based ground and air forces earmarked for NATO. The treaty expired in 1995. The United States, the Soviet Union, and the nations of Western Europe also signed the Charter of Paris for a New Europe, declaring that relations in Europe would be founded on respect and cooperation. Meanwhile, Gorbachev continued to face problems at home. Ethnic tensions brewed beneath the surface of Russian society. Unrest spread across the country. Riots broke out in the Soviet Republics in Central Asia. The first real challenges came from Lithuania, which declared its independence in March 1990. In January 1991, Soviet troops attacked civilians in the Lithuanian capital and killed 14 and wounded more than 150 civilians. The Soviet's strong response to the revolt undermined moderate and Western support for Gorbachev. The continued lack of economic progress and the unrest within the country undermined his support. More people were looking to **Boris Yeltsin** (1931–2007), for leadership. First appointed chairman of the Supreme Soviet of the Soviet Federative Socialist Republic (SFSR) in 1990 and then elected president of the Russian Federation in May 1991, Yeltsin declared Russia's independence from the Soviet Union. The rivalry between Gorbachev and Yeltsin added to the unstable conditions within the country. Meanwhile, in a last-gasp effort, Soviet conservatives who were defeated at the Communist Party Congress in July 1990, kidnapped Gorbachev, who was on vacation, and tried to seize power in August of 1991. The coup failed in the face of popular opposition and Yeltsin's defiant stand. Gorbachev was returned to power as the head of the Soviet Union. In the conservatives' efforts to restore Communist Party power and to preserve the empire, they destroyed communism. Anti-communist revolutions swept across the nation as each republic declared its freedom and independence. Gorbachev resigned as president. On December 21, 1991, the **Commonwealth of Independent States** (CIS) was formed. The formation of the CIS marked the end of the Soviet Union. On December 25, 1991, when Gorbachev resigned as president, the Soviet Union ceased to exist.

The CIS consists of 11 of the 15 republics that formed the old Soviet Union. This loose confederation consists of separate national economies, each with its own goals and policies. The collapse of the Soviet Union ended its role as a superpower and led to economic hardships. After the breakup, Boris Yeltsin, the president of Russia, the largest republic, assumed leadership. His efforts to privatize the economy (known as "shock therapy") were disappointing. Prices skyrocketed, production fell 20 percent, and runaway inflation that averaged about 800 percent left a few rich and many poor. The quality of public services and health care suffered and the social safety net that Communism had provided was lost. The average Russian male life expectancy dropped from 69 years in 1991 to 59 in 2005. Yeltsin, displaying erratic behavior and suffering from illness, did not provide stable leadership. In September 1993, Yeltsin suspended Parliament, which responded by beginning impeachment proceedings against him. On October 4, 1993, after pro-Parliament rioters rampaged through Moscow, Yeltsin ordered tanks to attack the parliament building and crushed the revolt. In 1994, Yeltsin was also forced to deal with the secessionist revolt that erupted in Chechnya, a largely Muslim area in the oil-rich Caucasus region in southwestern Russia. Chechnya had declared its independence in 1991, but Yeltsin denied the region's right to secede. In 1994, he ordered 40,000 troops to invade Chechnya to restore order. The war was unpopular and he was forced in the midst of his reelection campaign in 1996 to accept a face-saving truce. Yeltsin won reelection in 1996, but continued to face opposition in the Russian Parliament. Despite economic aid from the West and the International Monetary Fund, Russia's economic conditions did not improve. In 1998, Russia defaulted on its debt payment. In the face of these problems, Yeltsin resigned in December 1999 and made **Vladimir Putin** (b. 1952), regarded as intelligent, tough, and a hard worker, acting president.

In March of 2000, Putin was elected president, a position he held until 2008. Under Putin, Russia became more authoritarian than democratic. He quickly sought to reassert the central government's authority over the various republics and put significant restrictions on media freedom. After the terrorist attacks on the United States on September 11, 2001, Putin extended cooperation with the United States and used the global war on terror to resume the war against Chechnyan separatists and to destroy opposition to Russian domination. Chechnya, however, is still an ongoing problem. Putin also promoted changes that allowed him to appoint provincial governors, which increased the central government's control over the country under the guise of fighting terrorism. There are now 79 regions in Russia. Putin created 7 super-regions to control them; each super-region is headed by a presidential appointee; thus, Putin effectively destroyed federalism in Russia.

Under Putin, the Russian government also came to dominate the economy, extending governmental control over Russian oil and gas and increasing the use of economic retaliation against nations that clashed politically with Russia. Unlike Yeltsin, Putin was very popular with the Russian people and was easily reelected in March 2004. Part of Putin's high approval rating was because the worldwide increase in oil prices improved the standard of living for a majority of the Russian people. The Russian people also supported his efforts to restore the country's military prowess. Putin's efforts to limit the expansion of NATO and his opposition to setting up missile sites in the areas of former Russian satellite countries in Europe was also popular with the people. Relations and rhetoric with the West, especially the United States, currently appear to resemble that of the Cold War era. In 2008, Putin's second term ended and his handpicked successor, **Dmitry Medvedev** (b. 1965), was elected president in March 2008. Putin became prime minister again and chairman of the United Russia Party when Medvedev assumed the presidency in May 2008. The question of whether Putin will run again for the presidency in 2012 and who really controls Russia today is a major political uncertainty facing the nation. Democracy faces a difficult future in Russia.

Ethnic Tensions in Eastern Europe

The Communist government had suppressed and controlled ethnic divisions in the multinational states of Eastern Europe; however, with the collapse of communism, these tensions resurfaced. In the case of Czechoslovakia, these tensions were resolved peacefully. On January 1, 1993, the Czechoslovakian Federation was dissolved and two separate, independent countries were established—the Czech Republic and the Slovak Republic.

The most tragic of ethnic conflicts occurred in the multinational state of Yugoslavia. Until Marshall Tito's death in 1980, Yugoslavia's many ethnic groups were kept in check; after his death, however, Yugoslavia fell into regional and ethnic chaos combined with economic decline. The revolutions of 1989 accelerated the breakup. Serbian President **Slobodan Milosevic** (1941–2006) wanted to take land from other republics and create a greater Serbia. In 1991, Slovenia and Croatia declared their independence. Milosevic responded by attacking Slovenia. Slovenia was able to repulse the Serbian attack but Milosevic's forces were able to take over about 30 percent of Croatia. In 1992, the civil war spread to Bosnia-Herzegovina, when Bosnia declared its independence. The Bosnian Serbs, who represented about 30 percent of the population, refused to live under the more numerous Bosnian Muslims. With the support of Milosevic, the Serbs began a policy of ethnic cleansing—the forcible removal of non-Serbian groups from areas that they controlled. Ethnic cleansing recalled the horrors of the Nazi Holocaust as thousands of Bosnian Muslim villages were destroyed. Civilians were tortured and refugees were herded into United Nations refugee camps. The scenes of cruelty and horror shocked the Western world. When the Bosnian Serbs overran the Muslim city of Gorazde—which the United Nations had declared a safe area— and caused the deaths of several thousand civilians, the world had seen enough. Under the direction of NATO, Serbian military targets were bombed and the Croatian Army drove the Serbs from Croatia. In November of 1995, under a United States–sponsored peace meeting at Wright-Patterson Airbase in Dayton, Ohio, Bosnia was divided along religious and ethnic lines. Troops from NATO patrolled Bosnia to keep the peace.

Kosovo was another center of conflict in Yugoslavia. In 1990, Milosevic abolished self-rule in the Serbian province of Kosovo, where Albanian-speaking Muslims constituted the overwhelming majority and the Serbs were a small minority. Kosovo was significant for the Serbs because they considered it the birthplace of their liberty that evolved out of their defeat by the Ottoman Turks at the Battle of Kosovo in 1389. Although the Serbs were defeated, the battle came to be seen a symbol of Serbian patriotism and desire for independence from the Ottoman Turks. The Albanian Muslims, who lived in Kosovo and had hopes for self-rule from the Dayton Agreement, gained nothing. In 1998, militants formed the **Kosovo Liberation Army** (KLA) and began to fight for independence.

In the summer of 1998, Milosevic ordered an offensive against the KLA that displaced over 250,000 people within Kosovo. By January of 1999, the Western powers, led by the United States, were threatening air attacks if Milosevic did not withdraw from Kosovo and accept self-government. When Milosevic refused, NATO began heavy bombing on March 24, 1999. The aerial bombing lasted for two and one-half months, resulting in the withdrawal of Serbian troops from Kosovo. The aerial bombing of Kosovo was the first time that the NATO alliance was used to attack another sovereign nation. Milosevic's debacle in Kosovo eventually led to a loss of political power. In 2000, Milosevic was forced to call for new elections and lost to **Vojislav Kostunica** (b. 1944). Milosevic did not go quietly, only relinquishing power when massive street demonstrations demanded that he carry out the mandate of the people. In 2001, Milosevic was sent to The Hague, the Netherlands, to stand trial for war crimes. In 2006, he was found dead in his cell.

After nine years of being administered by the United Nations, Kosovo declared its independence from Serbia in February, 2008. It was the seventh state to emerge from the former Yugoslavia. Serbia and Russia condemned the declaration of independence as illegal. Russia claimed that it threatened to touch off a new conflict in the Balkans. However, despite the fear of an outbreak of serious violence and the flood of minority Serbian Kosovars fleeing their homes, this did not occur.

Recent Political Changes

Germany

The continuing problem of high unemployment created by the newly reunified Germany contributed to the election of the Social Democratic Party under the leadership of **Gerhard Schroder** (b. 1944). He won the election by promising to create a "New Middle" in German politics. He also promised more jobs and during his first term, the number of unemployed dropped, but then rose to much the same level that he had inherited from Helmut Kohl. In February 2005, the German jobless rate rose above 5 million. Schroder was narrowly reelected in 2002, which was partially attributed to his opposition to the pending United States-led intervention in Iraq. In 2003, he introduced a series of reforms that combined tax cuts and changes to the welfare state. His package of benefit cuts for the long-term unemployed that was implemented in January 2005 was unpopular with his core supporters of Social Democrats who feared that Schroder was dismantling the welfare state. In May 2005, his party lost power in one of its traditional strongholds, which prompted Schroder to deliberately engineer a no-confidence vote in Parliament, thus paving the way for national elections in September 2005. In November 2005, **Angela Merkel** (b. 1954) of the Christian Democratic Union (CDU)—born in Communist East Germany and a researcher in the field of physics—became the first female chancellor of Germany. Because no one party received a majority of seats in the Bundestag, the German Parliament, she formed a grand coalition comprised of the Social Democratic Party, the Christian Social Union, and her own CDU. She has been following a pro-free market reform agenda and has made serious efforts to overhaul the government health care system. She has pushed through a later retirement age and raised payments to new parents, increasing Germany's birth rate. Merkel's reforms are sparking an economic rebound, with the unemployment rate falling. She has continued to remain popular with the voters resulting in her reelection in 2009. *Forbes Magazine* selected her number one in a list of the "100 Most Powerful Women in the World." How she fares in the future will depend on how successfully she addresses the ongoing economic crisis facing Germany.

Great Britain

In 1997, **Tony Blair** (b. 1953), at the age of 44, became Great Britain's youngest prime minister of the twentieth century. Blair, who had become the leader of the Labour Party in 1994, replaced John Major, after eighteen years of Conservative Party rule over the British government. Blair was often compared to American President Bill Clinton, who was 46 when he took office in 1993. Blair changed the Labour Party from a socialist labor union-based political party to a centrist free enterprise party. He referred to the party as "New Labour." Blair sought to improve England's social services by increasing public spending on health and education. He also introduced a national minimum wage, tuition fees for higher education, and greater regional control by establishing the Scottish Parliament and the National Assembly for Wales. He was also a full supporter of Britain's induction into the European Community. Blair is the longest Labour PM ever, leading the Labour Party to three consecutive general election victories from 1997 to 2005. Blair's popularity, as well as that of the Labour Party, suffered as a result of his decision to support the war in Iraq. In May 2007, Blair resigned as leader of the Labour Party. He was succeeded as Labour Party leader and as Prime Minister by **Gordon Brown** (b. 1951), who had served as Chancellor of the Exchequer for many years under Blair. The sagging economy, rising unemployment, and faltering home prices have done little to help improve the popularity of either the Labour Party or Gordon Brown.

France

In 1995, **Jacques Chirac** (b. 1932), the Gaullist mayor of Paris, was elected president of France. Chirac was the second-longest-serving president of France (12 years) behind François Mitterrand. Chirac was elected on the platform of tax cuts, job programs, and addressing the issue of labor strikes and racism. He was reelected in 2002, but his second term was dominated by major student protests in 2005, which led to civil unrest in the autumn of 2005 following the deaths of two young Muslim boys in the Paris suburb of Aulnay-sous-Bois. Chirac also came under attack for charges of corruption when he had been mayor of Paris, with claims of lavish spending of the city's money on family groceries at the rate of thousands of dollars a week. However, in foreign policy, the French people approved of his opposition to the American-led invasion of Iraq in 2003. In 2007, Chirac announced that he would not run for a third term. Conservative **Nicholas Sarkozy** (b. 1955) became the president when he defeated Socialist Party candidate **Ségolène Royal** (b. 1953) in a runoff election. The son of a Hungarian immigrant, Sarkozy was elected on the promise to transform the country, restore its self-respect, and reinvigorate ties with the United States and the rest of Europe, as well as implement a stricter immigration policy. His election signaled a shift to the right in French politics, and only time will tell if his victory will herald a major transition for French society.

Italy

Revelations of corruption and scandals involving senior politicians, members of the government administration, and business leaders rocked Italy in the early 1990s. The scandals discredited the major parties, which had governed Italy since 1948. In 1994, **Silvio Berlusconi** (b. 1936), founder of the **Forza Italia** ("Forward Italy") party, emerged as prime minister. Berlusconi, a conservative, successful Italian businessman who controlled most of the major media stations in Italy outside of government controls, was a newcomer to Italian politics. Berlusconi's government became victim to charges of government corruption and he was forced to resign. In 1996, **Romano Prodi** (b. 1939), an economics professor and a member of the Olive Tree party, became prime minister. His government failed because of a no-confidence vote over the budgetary cuts. Berlusconi emerged as prime minister in 2001, but his support for U.S. President Bush and the wars in Iraq and Afghanistan led to his defeat in 2006 (Berlusconi actually received more votes than Prodi, but due to electoral changes he lost, similar to Al Gore's presidential loss in 2000), and Prodi assumed the position of prime minister for the second time in May of that year. However, Berlusconi's victory in the 2008 general election paved the way for his third mandate as prime minister. As of May, he is the longest-serving current leader of one of the **Group of Eight** (G8) nations. *Note:* The G-8 was founded in 1975 as the G-6 by France. It contains the most powerful economies in the world and it is a forum to discuss mostly economic topics. It contains the U.S., France, Germany, Great Britain, Italy, and Japan. In 1976 Canada was added and in 1997, Russia. Recently there has been support to add China, India, Brazil, Mexico, and South Africa.

Economic and Social Changes

The postwar recovery of Europe was a remarkable achievement but it had been a rocky road. By the 1960s, the European Common Market had revitalized Europe. The West German economy was booming and lagged behind only the United States and Japan. The European economy took a hit in the 1970s with the oil crisis and the high cost of energy. It also suffered from the worst economic decline since the 1930s as unemployment threatened to slow economic growth.

The postwar boom of Europe was fueled by cheap oil. In 1973, the Arab-led **Organization of the Petroleum Exporting Countries (OPEC)** instituted an oil embargo against those countries that supported Israel in the Yom Kippur War with the Arabs. This embargo and the subsequent embargo in 1979 disrupted the economies which were dependent on oil and led to massive increases in oil prices that plunged the world into the worst economic decline since the 1930s. The crisis hit Western Europe harder because 70 percent of its oil came from the Middle East. European optimism, which was so prevalent in previous decades, seemed to have faded away.

During the 1970s and '80s, the governments of Western Europe raised taxes, cut social services, and returned some nationalized industries to private ownership. Europe also tried to reduce its dependency on foreign oil. Western European countries turned toward alternative energy sources, including coal and nuclear power. In France, close to 78 percent of the electrical power would be generated by nuclear reactors.

As the economy began to recover in the 1980s, the hope for European unity revived. In 1987, the **Single European Act** laid down a legal framework for establishing a free market of labor, capital, and service to enable the free flow of goods. In December 1991, 12 Western European nations, committed to creating European political unity similar to a "United States of Europe," negotiated the **Maastricht Treaty** (formerly the Treaty on European Union), which was signed on February 7, 1992, at Maastricht in the Netherlands. One goal of the participating nations was to create economic and political integration by establishing a common currency, a single passport, and a common banking system. The treaty also established a structure that introduced cooperation in law enforcement, criminal justice, judicial matters, and asylum and immigration.

There was some opposition toward European unity because many nationalists believed that unity would destroy their unique identity. Others were fearful that monetary unions required governments to meet stringent fiscal standards, which would drastically reduce their countries' social and health benefits. In January 2002, the European Union nations officially began circulating the **euro,** which has become the common currency of all the participating nations that have accepted it. The introduction of the euro and its successful acceptance brought many new members to the EU. In May 2004, ten new members, primarily from the former Eastern Bloc, joined the EU. These ten new members are Cyprus, the Czech Republic, Slovakia, Slovenia, Latvia, Lithuania, Estonia, Hungary, Malta, and Poland. Bulgaria and Rumania joined in 2007. Despite these achievements, the EU faces uncertainty. Whether or not Turkey should become a member has been unresolved since the 1980s. There is a question of whether Turkey is Muslim or European, and whether Turkey's stand on human rights violates the spirit of the European community. A proposed EU constitution that was scheduled to go into effect in 2007 and needed the approval of all states was rejected by France and Holland in 2005 in a national vote. The treaty was rewritten and called the Lisbon Treaty; it passed all the member states and went into effect in December 2009. It created among other things a permanent European presidency and increased the powers of the European parliament.

Lifestyle Changes

The economic changes within Europe during the second half of the twentieth century have dramatically affected European society. The standard of living rose throughout the 1950s, '60s, and '70s. In the mid-twentieth century, food and drink cost roughly two-thirds of the average family income in Europe. By the mid-1960s, it took about one-third to two-fifths of the family income. This translated into more money being available for consumer goods. The rising standard of living and the spread of standardized goods helped to reduce the gap between the rich and the poor in Western society, the result of which was that European society became more democratic. Old class lines based on birth and wealth blurred as large numbers of people moved from the rural areas into the cities. The demands of the growing economy broke down rigid class divisions as the requirements for jobs were based on skill, not wealth. European governments also reduced class tension with social programs to help families meet their basic needs. Most European governments gave maternity grants and built public housing for low-income families and individuals. Educational opportunities increased the literacy rate. These steps provided a safety net to ensure the well-being of individuals.

The economic prosperity of the post-World War II era and the cohorts of baby boomers born after the war helped contribute to a distinctive and international youth culture. The Teddy Boy movement emerged in the 1950s as England was coming to the end of its post war austerity. The Teddy Boy movement was typified by young men wearing clothes inspired by the style of the Edwardian period between 1901 and 1910: long jackets with velvet collars, bright ankle socks, and slim ties. Their hair was long and greased. Teddy Girls wore ponytails, toreador pants and low cut tops to make themselves look less prissy. The Teddy Boy and Girl subculture started in London, spread across England, and became strongly associated with the American rock-and-roll music of the period. However, it was the young people in the United States that took the lead in creating a distinctly teenage or youth market subculture. Rock music helped to connect this subculture, and in the 1960s the Beatles thrilled millions of young people on both sides of the Atlantic, often to the dismay of their parents. Like Elvis, the Beatles' lyrics suggested personal and sexual freedom that older people found disturbing. The youth culture rebellion against the status quo was reflected in the lyrics of rock music and the use of illegal drugs and a rejection of traditional, social norms like marriage. The youth culture fused with the counterculture in opposition to the established order of the 1960s. Students embraced romanticism and the idealism of a simple society and rejected the materialism and consumer-centered ideas of Western society. This revolutionary idealism encouraged anti-war protesters in the United States and intensified student radicalism in Europe. Following the American example, European students challenged their universities' rigid educational policies. The most far-reaching of these revolts occurred in France in 1968. The student rebellions of 1968 signaled the end to an era that was more conservative and a return to an era of uncertainty and conflict in the 1970s and '80s.

These economic and social changes affected the lives of European women. A growing number of women worked outside the home, and as their incomes and standards of living improved, family life began to change. Many women began to realize that the interruption of their careers to care for small children led to lower wages. This attitude led to a decline in the birth rate. Family stability, moreover, declined as divorce rates rose. The economic malaise that engulfed Europe during the 1970s and '80s directly affected the number of women in the workforce. More women were now required to work in order to maintain the family's standard of living that had been improving since the end of World War II. These developments added to the demographic and societal changes in Europe.

Beginning in the 1970s, efforts were made to ensure legal and economic equality for European women. One influential writer was **Simone de Beauvoir** (1908–1986). Her book, *The Second Sex* (1949), was one of the earliest attempts to address human history from a feminist perspective. She argued that women could only become free by way of courageous actions and self-assertive creativity. The book is considered to be a pillar of feminist thought in the twentieth century. The women's movement gained new rights for women. In Italy, prewar restrictions of divorce and abortion for women by Mussolini and the Catholic Church were removed.

Demographic Changes

As the Western European countries of Belgium, France, and Germany began to recover after World War II, they initially attracted immigrants from Italy and Spain. In the 1960s, Western European countries also began to import laborers from Muslim nations. Also at this time, West Germany set up a Turkish "guest worker" program on a temporary basis, but most of the guest workers remained and settled in cities. In the aftermath of decolonization, immigrants from India, Pakistan, Bangladesh, and East Africa were attracted to Great Britain and many immigrants from North Africa and Southeast Asia settled in France. A small percentage of these immigrants settled in Italy, Spain, Denmark, and the Netherlands. A majority of these immigrants were Muslims. As a result of the collapse of the Soviet Union in the late 1980s and the civil war in Yugoslavia in the 1990s, thousands of refugees also began to migrate to Western Europe.

The continuing streams of immigrant groups that have migrated to Europe have begun to alter the homogeneity of the European continent. In the middle of the twentieth century, there were small numbers of Muslims living in Western Europe. At the beginning of the twenty-first century, there are between 15 and 17 million Muslims in Western Europe, including approximately 3.6 million in France, 4 million in Germany, and 1.6 million in Britain. Islam is now the second-largest religion in Europe and one of the largest mosques in Europe is in Rome, the very heart of Christendom. The high fertility rate among these Muslim immigrants is also perceived by many Europeans as a threat that they will become a minority in their own society. In the Netherlands, for instance (long considered the most tolerant of European nations), new arrivals must learn to speak Dutch and take classes on Dutch societal values. In parts of Rotterdam, 24 percent of the city's population can trace their origins outside of Holland and Amsterdam.

Some Europeans claim that Muslims are creating a parallel society. These concerns have led to the rise of extremist groups like neo-Nazis in Germany and skinheads in Great Britain, who have resorted to violent actions against immigrants. Political parties, like the Freedom Party of Austria led by Heinz-Christian Strache and the Front National led by Jean-Marie Le Pen in France, have called for tighter restrictions on immigration. In France the government passed a law banning Islamic head scarves in public schools beginning in 2005. In 2009, Switzerland voted to include in their constitution a law banning the construction of minarets, which are the prayer towers of the mosques. These steps have contributed to tension between the European and Muslim populations.

In the beginning of the twenty-first century, the European Union has become a powerful economic force. With less than 7 percent of the world's population (490 million people), it is the world's largest trading bloc and generates about 30 percent of the gross world product. Europe has a promising future but there are questions that need to be answered: Should the EU be exclusively comprised of Christian nations or should it include Muslim countries like Turkey? Should the EU develop its own military army that can be used to address international crises? How should the EU deal with its declining birth rate and its critical need for labor? How will the EU deal with immigration and the development of a multicultural European society? How Europe addresses these concerns will affect the continent and the world.

Chronology of Contemporary Europe

1982	Death of Brezhnev; Yuri Andropov becomes leader of the Soviet Union; Helmut Kohl becomes West Germany's chancellor.
1983	Compact disc is introduced.
1984	Yuri Andropov dies; Apple Macintosh is launched.
1985	Mikhail Gorbachev succeeds Konstantin Chernenko as leader of Russia.
1986	United States President Ronald Reagan meets with Gorbachev.
1987	Single European Act–a legal framework establishing a free market of labor and capital.
1989	Soviet troops withdraw from Afghanistan.
1989	Revolutionary movements throughout Eastern Europe lead to the end of communism.
March 1990	Pro-democratic groups achieve gains in Russia, the Ukraine, and Byelorussia. Lithuania declares its independence, followed by Latvia (May 4).
October 1990	Gorbachev wins the Nobel Peace Prize.
October 1990	German unification takes place.
August 1991	Gorbachev survives a coup by Soviet hard-liners.
December 1991	Soviet Union ceases to exist and the Commonwealth of Independent States (CIS) replaces it.
1992	Croatian and Serbian forces fight over the division of Bosnia. Slobodan Milosevic implements ethnic cleansing. The Maastricht Treaty is signed, promoting further economic integration within the European Community.
1993	Boris Yeltsin emerges as the dominant leader with the new CIS.
1994	The UN unsuccessfully tries to mediate the Bosnian controversy.
1997	Tony Blair becomes Prime Minister of Great Britain.
1998	Serbian forces begin an aggressive campaign against ethnic Albanians.
1999	NATO troops bomb Serbian forces in Kosovo, and Milosevic is forced to withdraw.
2000	Vladimir Putin replaces Yeltsin as president of Russia. Vojislav Kostunica defeats Milosevic in Serbian election.
2001	Terrorist attack on World Trade Center in New York.
2002	The euro is introduced.
2003	The United States invades Iraq.
2004	European Union expands to include nations from Eastern Europe.
2005	Pope John Paul II dies. Angela Merkel becomes first female Chancellor of Germany.
2005	Suicide bomb attack on London transport system.
2007	Nicholas Sarkozy becomes president of France.

Sample Multiple-Choice Questions

1. All of the following were characteristics of life during the Brezhnev era EXCEPT
   A. low productivity by Soviet industry.
   B. lack of artistic freedom.
   C. strict government control by the Soviet bureaucracy.
   D. lack of consumer goods.
   E. victory in the war against Afghanistan.

2. Which of the following succeeded Brezhnev as leader of the Soviet Union?
   A. Konstantin Chernenko
   B. Yuri Andropov
   C. Mikhail Gorbachev
   D. Vladimir Putin
   E. Boris Yeltsin

3. Gorbachev's plan of *perestroika* was similar to
   A. Lenin's policy of War Communism.
   B. Stalin's policy of Collectivization.
   C. Lenin's New Economic Policy.
   D. Stalin's Five-Year Plan.
   E. Khrushchev's policy of Improved Farm Production.

4. Since the collapse of the Soviet Union, what has been a major source of difficulty in Eastern and Central Europe and its former republics?
   A. Failure to establish a market economy
   B. Ethnic violence has broken out in some regions
   C. Efforts of the Chinese to expand their influence in these areas
   D. Unwillingness of industrial leaders to invest in these areas
   E. Decline of living standards of people in these areas

5. Which of the following countries did not experience a peaceful exchange of power during the revolutions in Eastern Europe in 1989?
   A. Poland
   B. East Germany
   C. Hungary
   D. Czechoslovakia
   E. Romania

6. Which of the following officially ended the Cold War?
   A. Unification of Germany in 1990
   B. The demise of the Soviet Union in 1991
   C. The revolutions in Eastern Europe during 1989 that ended Soviet domination in the region
   D. The CFE Agreement of November 1990
   E. Destruction of the Berlin Wall

7. Which of the following is the least accurate statement about immigrants to Western Europe since 1960?
   A. A majority of them have been Muslims.
   B. The decolonization of the British and French fostered immigration to the European continent.
   C. Most of the immigrants have settled in cities.
   D. Most of the Muslim immigrants have become assimilated within the different European countries.
   E. They have provided the manpower for the poorly paid jobs that Europeans do not want to do.

8. The main purpose of the Maastricht Treaty was to

   A. negotiate a reduction in tariffs with the United States.

   B. open up the European Union to Russia.

   C. establish unified military forces to be used with NATO.

   D. create a common currency system and a central banking system for the European Union.

   E. adapt a common immigration policy among the European Union countries.

9. Which of the following men was elected the first president of Poland in 1990?

   A. Lech Walesa

   B. Václav Havel

   C. Nicolae Ceausescu

   D. Vladimir Putin

   E. Vojislav Kostunica

10. A major problem facing the European Union is

   A. the failure of many countries to accept the EU.

   B. unwillingness of the original members of the EU to accept new members into their group.

   C. disagreements over a common banking system.

   D. hesitancy to accept Turkey into the EU because it is a Muslim nation, has a poor human rights policy, and is economically undeveloped.

   E. disagreement on where to establish a permanent headquarters for the EU.

Multiple-Choice Questions: Answers and Explanations

1. **E.** During Brezhnev's regime, the Soviet Union was not able to gain victory in Afghanistan. Brezhnev ordered troops into Afghanistan in December 1979 to preserve communist rule, and airlifted special troops to Kabul, the capital. The Soviets occupied Afghanistan with 100,000 men. The war in Afghanistan dragged on until 1989, when Gorbachev withdrew the Soviet troops. The Afghanistan war was not popular at home, and Soviet losses destroyed the morale of the country. During Brezhnev's 18-year rule, the Soviet economy lagged behind the West and consumer goods were not readily available. Brezhnev could not fulfill the basic needs of the people. People spent hours in line waiting to buy food and other goods. Soviet goods were also inferior to those of the West. During the Brezhnev regime, the government controlled artistic expression and the Soviet bureaucracy controlled every aspect of the lives of the people.

2. **B.** Yuri Andropov succeeded Brezhnev as leader of the Soviet Union in 1982. He died in 1984 and was succeeded by Konstantin Chernenko, who ruled until 1985. Mikhail Gorbachev ruled from 1985 to 1991. Boris Yeltsin ruled from 1991 to 1999. Vladimir Putin was elected in 2000.

3. **C.** Gorbachev's policy of *perestroika* was similar to Lenin's New Economic Policy (NEP). Perestroika was designed to restructure the Soviet economy by permitting some private enterprise and allowing farmers to sell in the free market. Lenin introduced the NEP in 1921 to restore Russia's economic health. This plan allowed for some enterprises to be privately owned and also allowed farmers some economic freedom. Like perestroika, the NEP promoted foreign investments in the Soviet Union. Perestroika and the NEP were designed to promote the market economy under the umbrella of a command economy. Lenin's policy of War Communism, Stalin's policy of Collectivization and his Five-Year Plan, and Khrushchev's policy of Improved Farm Production were designed to continue the command economy without the private enterprise system.

4. **B.** The collapse of communism resulted in the resurgence of ethnic tensions in Eastern Europe. The greatest tensions arose in the multinational state of Yugoslavia. Civil war divided the country from 1991 until late 1999. The ongoing problems in Chechnya also presented problems for Russia. The transition from a command economy to a market economy has been difficult for many of these former communist countries but they are making progress. The decline of living standards and the unwillingness of industrial leaders to invest were tied to the uncertain economic conditions created by civil unrest. The Chinese had no influence in these regions.

5. **E.** Romania did not have a peaceful exchange of power during the revolutions that swept across Eastern Europe in 1989. The iron-fisted Romanian dictator, Nicolae Ceausescu, refused to support change and ordered security forces to smash the protests. His decision to slaughter thousands provoked an armed uprising. Ceausescu and his wife were captured and executed by a military court. In Poland, East Germany, Hungary, and Czechoslovakia, there was little or no violence during the transfer of power.

6. **D.** The CFE Treaty of November 1990 officially ended the Cold War. In this treaty, the United States, the Soviet Union, the 22 members of NATO, and the Warsaw Pact nations agreed to reduce the number of conventional forces in Europe and respect the existing postwar borders. This accord was a result of the revolution that ended communist leadership in Eastern Europe. The destruction of the Berlin Wall and the unification of Germany contributed to the CFE Treaty. The demise of the Soviet Union symbolized the failure of communism, not the Cold War.

7. **D.** Since September 11, 2001, there has been an intense debate on how to integrate Muslims into European society. Islam is the second-largest religion in Western Europe and there are over 20 million Muslims living in Europe. Many Europeans feel that Muslims live in separate, parallel societies and resist calls to assimilate into the culture of their new home. Poverty and rampant unemployment distance Muslim youths from the mainstream life of their adopted homeland. This alienation is also fueled by some radical Islamic groups that do not allow Muslim youths to integrate into Western society. The unrest in the Paris suburb of Aulnay-sous-Bois in 2005 reflected the frustration of many Muslims living in the area. Although a majority of immigrants to Western Europe are Muslims, live in major cities, and do the jobs that Europeans choose not to do, they have not been readily accepted by the Europeans who are critical of Muslims benefitting from Europe's generous welfare system. For example, in Denmark half of the welfare state spending is spent on Muslims who comprise only 2 percent of the population.

8. **D.** One of the purposes of the Maastricht Treaty was to create a common currency system and central banking system for the European Community. In November 1991, 12 European nations met at Maastricht, a Dutch city, and agreed to promote economic and political integration. In January of 2002, the European Union officially began circulating the euro. The Maastricht Treaty did not deal with tariff reduction with the United States nor was there any provision for unified military forces. The European Union has begun to try to deal with the influx of immigration (legal and illegal) from Eastern Europe and Third World countries.

9. **A.** Lech Walesa was elected president of Poland in 1990. Havel was elected president of Czechoslovakia in 1989. Ceausescu was the Communist leader of Romania, whose government was overthrown in 1989 and who was put to death. Putin is the present leader of the Soviet Union. Kostunica was elected president of Serbia in 2000.

10. **D.** Turkey's application to the European Union was made in April 1987. Proponents argue that Turkey's large economy and strategic location will enhance the European position in the world. However, some European nations, in particular France, are fearful that Turkey's admission might lead to demands for accession by Morocco, another Muslim nation. In January 2007, Nicholas Sarkozy, leader of France, insisted that Turkey has no place inside the European Union. Austria is fearful of another wave of Muslim immigration, citing the poor integration of its existing Muslim minority. European Union members have also expressed reservations about Turkey's human rights record. Amnesty International has reported the persistence of such practices as arbitrary arrests, torture, and censorship. European Union members are concerned that Turkey has not fully accepted Western values and ideals in their society. Others worry that Turkey's large and rapidly growing population and low average income would make integration into the EU difficult. The euro and the central banking system have been readily accepted by member nations and in the world community. The original members of the European Union numbered six in 1951 and they have expanded to 27 members as of 2009. There is little disagreement that Brussels should remain the permanent headquarters of the European Union.

PART II

AP EUROPEAN HISTORY PRACTICE EXAMS

Answer Sheet for Sample Practice Exam I

Remove this sheet and use it to mark your answers for the multiple-choice section of Sample Practice Exam I.

1 Ⓐ Ⓑ Ⓒ Ⓓ Ⓔ	21 Ⓐ Ⓑ Ⓒ Ⓓ Ⓔ	41 Ⓐ Ⓑ Ⓒ Ⓓ Ⓔ	61 Ⓐ Ⓑ Ⓒ Ⓓ Ⓔ
2 Ⓐ Ⓑ Ⓒ Ⓓ Ⓔ	22 Ⓐ Ⓑ Ⓒ Ⓓ Ⓔ	42 Ⓐ Ⓑ Ⓒ Ⓓ Ⓔ	62 Ⓐ Ⓑ Ⓒ Ⓓ Ⓔ
3 Ⓐ Ⓑ Ⓒ Ⓓ Ⓔ	23 Ⓐ Ⓑ Ⓒ Ⓓ Ⓔ	43 Ⓐ Ⓑ Ⓒ Ⓓ Ⓔ	63 Ⓐ Ⓑ Ⓒ Ⓓ Ⓔ
4 Ⓐ Ⓑ Ⓒ Ⓓ Ⓔ	24 Ⓐ Ⓑ Ⓒ Ⓓ Ⓔ	44 Ⓐ Ⓑ Ⓒ Ⓓ Ⓔ	64 Ⓐ Ⓑ Ⓒ Ⓓ Ⓔ
5 Ⓐ Ⓑ Ⓒ Ⓓ Ⓔ	25 Ⓐ Ⓑ Ⓒ Ⓓ Ⓔ	45 Ⓐ Ⓑ Ⓒ Ⓓ Ⓔ	65 Ⓐ Ⓑ Ⓒ Ⓓ Ⓔ
6 Ⓐ Ⓑ Ⓒ Ⓓ Ⓔ	26 Ⓐ Ⓑ Ⓒ Ⓓ Ⓔ	46 Ⓐ Ⓑ Ⓒ Ⓓ Ⓔ	66 Ⓐ Ⓑ Ⓒ Ⓓ Ⓔ
7 Ⓐ Ⓑ Ⓒ Ⓓ Ⓔ	27 Ⓐ Ⓑ Ⓒ Ⓓ Ⓔ	47 Ⓐ Ⓑ Ⓒ Ⓓ Ⓔ	67 Ⓐ Ⓑ Ⓒ Ⓓ Ⓔ
8 Ⓐ Ⓑ Ⓒ Ⓓ Ⓔ	28 Ⓐ Ⓑ Ⓒ Ⓓ Ⓔ	48 Ⓐ Ⓑ Ⓒ Ⓓ Ⓔ	68 Ⓐ Ⓑ Ⓒ Ⓓ Ⓔ
9 Ⓐ Ⓑ Ⓒ Ⓓ Ⓔ	29 Ⓐ Ⓑ Ⓒ Ⓓ Ⓔ	49 Ⓐ Ⓑ Ⓒ Ⓓ Ⓔ	69 Ⓐ Ⓑ Ⓒ Ⓓ Ⓔ
10 Ⓐ Ⓑ Ⓒ Ⓓ Ⓔ	30 Ⓐ Ⓑ Ⓒ Ⓓ Ⓔ	50 Ⓐ Ⓑ Ⓒ Ⓓ Ⓔ	70 Ⓐ Ⓑ Ⓒ Ⓓ Ⓔ
11 Ⓐ Ⓑ Ⓒ Ⓓ Ⓔ	31 Ⓐ Ⓑ Ⓒ Ⓓ Ⓔ	51 Ⓐ Ⓑ Ⓒ Ⓓ Ⓔ	71 Ⓐ Ⓑ Ⓒ Ⓓ Ⓔ
12 Ⓐ Ⓑ Ⓒ Ⓓ Ⓔ	32 Ⓐ Ⓑ Ⓒ Ⓓ Ⓔ	52 Ⓐ Ⓑ Ⓒ Ⓓ Ⓔ	72 Ⓐ Ⓑ Ⓒ Ⓓ Ⓔ
13 Ⓐ Ⓑ Ⓒ Ⓓ Ⓔ	33 Ⓐ Ⓑ Ⓒ Ⓓ Ⓔ	53 Ⓐ Ⓑ Ⓒ Ⓓ Ⓔ	73 Ⓐ Ⓑ Ⓒ Ⓓ Ⓔ
14 Ⓐ Ⓑ Ⓒ Ⓓ Ⓔ	34 Ⓐ Ⓑ Ⓒ Ⓓ Ⓔ	54 Ⓐ Ⓑ Ⓒ Ⓓ Ⓔ	74 Ⓐ Ⓑ Ⓒ Ⓓ Ⓔ
15 Ⓐ Ⓑ Ⓒ Ⓓ Ⓔ	35 Ⓐ Ⓑ Ⓒ Ⓓ Ⓔ	55 Ⓐ Ⓑ Ⓒ Ⓓ Ⓔ	75 Ⓐ Ⓑ Ⓒ Ⓓ Ⓔ
16 Ⓐ Ⓑ Ⓒ Ⓓ Ⓔ	36 Ⓐ Ⓑ Ⓒ Ⓓ Ⓔ	56 Ⓐ Ⓑ Ⓒ Ⓓ Ⓔ	76 Ⓐ Ⓑ Ⓒ Ⓓ Ⓔ
17 Ⓐ Ⓑ Ⓒ Ⓓ Ⓔ	37 Ⓐ Ⓑ Ⓒ Ⓓ Ⓔ	57 Ⓐ Ⓑ Ⓒ Ⓓ Ⓔ	77 Ⓐ Ⓑ Ⓒ Ⓓ Ⓔ
18 Ⓐ Ⓑ Ⓒ Ⓓ Ⓔ	38 Ⓐ Ⓑ Ⓒ Ⓓ Ⓔ	58 Ⓐ Ⓑ Ⓒ Ⓓ Ⓔ	78 Ⓐ Ⓑ Ⓒ Ⓓ Ⓔ
19 Ⓐ Ⓑ Ⓒ Ⓓ Ⓔ	39 Ⓐ Ⓑ Ⓒ Ⓓ Ⓔ	59 Ⓐ Ⓑ Ⓒ Ⓓ Ⓔ	79 Ⓐ Ⓑ Ⓒ Ⓓ Ⓔ
20 Ⓐ Ⓑ Ⓒ Ⓓ Ⓔ	40 Ⓐ Ⓑ Ⓒ Ⓓ Ⓔ	60 Ⓐ Ⓑ Ⓒ Ⓓ Ⓔ	80 Ⓐ Ⓑ Ⓒ Ⓓ Ⓔ

CUT HERE

CUT HERE

Section I: Multiple-Choice Questions

Time: 55 minutes
80 Questions
Percent of total grade = 50%

Directions: Each of the questions or incomplete statements below is followed by five suggested answers or completions. Select the one that is best in each case and then fill in the corresponding oval on the answer sheet.

1. The following were all underlying causes of World War I EXCEPT

   A. various alliances between certain countries.
   B. excessive nationalism in Europe.
   C. the expansion of armies.
   D. the desire of certain countries to spread democracy.
   E. an increase in imperialistic competition among Great Britain, France, and Germany.

2. Humanism focused on

   A. the role of God in an individual's life.
   B. the importance of the afterlife.
   C. worldly and secular themes and the importance of the individual.
   D. the use of Latin in education.
   E. improving the status of women in society.

3. "O my brothers, love your country. There is no true country without a uniform law. . . . And, . . . it is necessary that all should contribute to the making of them. Do not accept any other formula. . . . So long as a single [one] of your brothers is not represented by his own vote, you have not got a country."

   Which of the following would most likely accept the ideas in this passage?

   A. Giuseppe Mazzini
   B. Camillo Cavour
   C. Victor Emmanuel II
   D. Pope Pius IX
   E. Vincenzo Gioberti

4. Which of the following statements best describes France in the early eighteenth century?

   A. France was the cultural and intellectual center of Europe.
   B. Other European nations considered France a weak and ineffective nation.
   C. France had been successful in asserting its superiority over England, its chief rival.
   D. The French system of government was among the most innovative in Europe.
   E. The French government was becoming more democratic.

5. Which statement constitutes a major decision reached at the Casablanca Conference?

   A. The United States and England agreed to invade Germany through the soft belly of Europe (Italy).
   B. Germany was ordered to surrender unconditionally.
   C. Meetings were scheduled for the development of the atomic bomb.
   D. Decisions were made as to how to divide Germany at the end of the war.
   E. A program on how to rebuild Europe was discussed.

6. Martin Luther believed salvation comes to an individual

   A. with the help of the clergy.
   B. by living a monastic life.
   C. with the intervention of a priest.
   D. by faith alone.
   E. by performing good works.

7. The main characteristic of the Enlightenment was

   A. a rejection of traditional authority and a belief that all faith should reside in God.
   B. the belief that reason and logical thinking could discover the laws that govern the universe.
   C. the belief that man is born evil and there is little hope for future progress.
   D. that the best government is based on the Divine Right theory of government.
   E. a belief that traditional values combined with progress would improve society.

8. The fall of communism in countries such as Poland, Hungary, Czechoslovakia, Bulgaria, and Albania was characterized by

   A. a series of long wars with many casualties.
   B. a peaceful transition.
   C. treaties signed by each of these countries.
   D. intervention by the United States.
   E. civil war in these countries.

9. All of the following factors contributed to the rise of absolute rulers in Europe in the fifteenth century EXCEPT

   A. the need for a direct trade route to East Asia.
   B. a series of wars between the Italian city-states.
   C. the need for capital to finance explorations.
   D. Asian and Italian monopolies on existing trade routes.
   E. the awakening spirit of nationalism.

10. In which country was the Carbonari first organized?

    A. Italy
    B. Portugal
    C. Britain
    D. Russia
    E. Prussia

11. "Take up the White Man's burden—Send forth the best ye breed—Go bind your sons to exile— To serve your captives' need . . ."

    Which idea does the author of this passage support?

    A. Imperialism
    B. Nationalism
    C. Socialism
    D. Fascism
    E. Totalitarianism

12. Which was a key demand of the Chartists?

    A. Compulsory workmen's compensation
    B. Nationalizing key industries
    C. A protective tariff against imported goods
    D. Universal male suffrage
    E. Granting women the right to vote

13. Which of the following was a consequence of the Russo-Japanese War?

    A. Communists became part of the government.
    B. Nicholas II reformed the military.
    C. Nicholas II shared power with the Duma.
    D. Nicholas II signed the October Manifesto establishing a Duma.
    E. Nicholas II granted the Duma greater control over Russia's financial and foreign affairs.

14. Churchill's "Iron Curtain" speech was

    A. Britain's detailed military plan of attack against the Soviet Union.
    B. an attempt to persuade the Eastern European nations to join the Western Bloc.
    C. a symbol of the growing fear of communism and the division between the Soviet-dominated states and the Western Bloc.
    D. a rebuke of the United States for its leniency towards communism.
    E. a plea to Russia and the United States to attempt compromise.

15. Which of the following men did NOT support the unification of Italy?

    A. Bismarck
    B. Pope Pius IX
    C. Victor Emmanuel II
    D. Napoleon III
    E. The Duke of Parma

16. What was the main goal of Operation Barbarossa?

    A. To punish Stalin for providing help against Great Britain
    B. To prevent an attack by the Soviet Union
    C. To gain control of the wheat fields of the Ukraine and the oil fields of the Caucasus
    D. To establish a Nazi puppet state in Leningrad
    E. To secure a water outlet to the east

17. What role did the Duke of Sully play in the rise of absolutism in France?

    A. As minister to Henry IV, he was instrumental in helping the monarch consolidate his power.
    B. He led the people of France in a revolution that, by suppressing the monarch, was able to demonstrate its strength.
    C. He was largely responsible for improving relations between the monarch and the Catholic Church.
    D. He advised Henry IV as to whom he should choose as an heir.
    E. He was a diplomat who maintained positive relations with other European nations.

18. The group of workers in the nineteenth century who opposed industrialization and smashed the machines were

    A. Chartists.
    B. Utopian Socialists.
    C. Marxists.
    D. Capitalists.
    E. Luddites.

19. All of the following were Renaissance humanists EXCEPT

    A. Francesco Petrarca.
    B. Giovanni Boccaccio.
    C. Johannes Gutenberg.
    D. Baldassare Castiglione.
    E. Pico della Mirandola.

20. "I think therefore I am" expresses the philosophy of

    A. Voltaire.
    B. Rousseau.
    C. Francis Bacon.
    D. René Descartes.
    E. John Locke.

21. Which was NOT part of Hitler's platform?

    A. Aryan supremacy
    B. Exaggerated nationalism
    C. Establishing an alliance with the Soviet Union
    D. A public works program to reduce unemployment
    E. Remilitarizing the German army and navy

22. The major result of the Balkan Crisis of 1912–1913 was that

    A. an alliance was formed between Bulgaria and the Ottoman Empire.
    B. France gained control of the Balkan region.
    C. hostility was created toward Austria-Hungary in Serbia and Russia.
    D. those living in Serbia and Austria-Hungary were granted political freedom.
    E. a peace agreement was reached between the Balkan League and the Ottoman Empire.

23. In what way did the Thermidorian Reaction affect the French Revolution?

    A. The Civil Constitution of the clergy was adopted.
    B. It ended the Reign of Terror.
    C. European nations invaded France to restore Louis XVI and Marie Antoinette to the throne.
    D. The National Assembly established a limited monarchy.
    E. Napoleon was invited to take over the government and restore order.

24. Which of the following statements would Ulrich Zwingli believe but Martin Luther reject?

    A. Priests should not have to remain celibate.
    B. People should not worship saints.
    C. The Bible is the true Christian authority.
    D. People should deny all sacraments.
    E. The abuses committed by the Roman Catholic Church are intolerable.

25. All of the following contributed to the New Imperialism of the late-nineteenth century EXCEPT

    A. Western European nations viewed colonies as a market for manufactured goods.
    B. colonies provided raw materials for Western European nations.
    C. some Europeans viewed colonies as an area in which to spread Christianity.
    D. there was a desire to spread democracy.
    E. owning colonies was a sign of military power.

26. All are symbols of the Age of Metternich EXCEPT

    A. the Concert of Europe.
    B. the Carlsbad Decree.
    C. the Six Acts.
    D. the July Ordinances.
    E. the Boulanger Affair.

27. Which of the following men created guidelines for how a ruler could govern successfully?

    A. Thomas More
    B. Desiderius Erasmus
    C. Niccolo Machiavelli
    D. Montaigne
    E. Lorenzo Valla

28. Which of the following was NOT a part of *The Declaration of the Rights of Man and of the Citizen?*

    A. Men are born free and equal before the law.
    B. Men are guaranteed freedom of speech, religion, and due process before the law.
    C. Taxes have to be paid according to the ability to pay.
    D. The right to rule rests not only on the king, but also on the general rule of the people.
    E. Feudalism is officially abolished.

29. Which of the following events helped to strengthen the supremacy of the Catholic Church?

    A. The Great Schism
    B. The Babylonian captivity
    C. The sale of indulgences
    D. The Council of Trent
    E. The Peace of Augsburg

30. Which of the following men was NOT an inventor during the early days of the Industrial Revolution?

    A. Thomas Malthus
    B. Eli Whitney
    C. Richard Arkwright
    D. Edmund Cartwright
    E. James Watt

31. The Yalta Conference has been a source of controversy because

    A. it was the first meeting between Stalin and Truman.
    B. Stalin refused to support the United States' war effort against Japan.
    C. Stalin disagreed over where the United Nations headquarters should be located.
    D. of the status of free elections in the countries of Eastern Europe that were liberated by the Soviet Union.
    E. the British received territory in Africa and the Middle East.

32. *The Massacre of Chios* by Eugène Delacroix glorified which of the following?

    A. The Revolution of 1848
    B. The Greek struggle for independence against the Ottoman Turks
    C. Revolutions in Spain and Sardinia in 1830
    D. The election of Louis Napoleon in 1848
    E. The success of the revolutions of Latin America in the 1830s

33. The Schlieffen Plan was

    A. Germany's strategy on how to avoid a prolonged two-front war.
    B. Russia's plan to attack Germany's partner, Austria-Hungary.
    C. Germany's response to the Balkan crisis.
    D. Serbia's declaration of war against Austria.
    E. Russia's preparation for war against Serbia.

34. The rule of James I created hostility in England because

    A. James refused to reform the Church of England.
    B. The people of England wanted James to be more involved in foreign affairs so that England could assert her superiority over Europe.
    C. The people of England believed that James was not a strong enough leader.
    D. James unfairly taxed the peasants.
    E. James agreed to an alliance with France without consulting with Parliament.

35. In the Crimean War, Cavour's major goal was

    A. to become an ally of Russia.
    B. to secure trading rights from Russia.
    C. to bring the question of Italian unification to the Peace Conference.
    D. to acquire territories from England.
    E. to convince Austria that Italian unification was a just cause.

36. "Fascism is a religion. The twentieth century will be known in history as the century of Fascism."

    This statement is most closely attributed to

    A. Francisco Franco.
    B. Benito Mussolini.
    C. Juan Peron.
    D. Adolf Hitler.
    E. Alexander Kerensky.

37. Which of the following individuals would NOT be considered part of the Scientific Revolution?

    A. Francis Bacon
    B. Baron de Montesquieu
    C. René Descartes
    D. Galileo Galilei
    E. Nicholas Copernicus

38. All of the following countries were involved in the "Scramble for Africa" in the late nineteenth century, EXCEPT

    A. Italy.
    B. France.
    C. Britain.
    D. Austria-Hungary.
    E. Portugal.

39. All of the following are associated with the June Days in Paris in 1848 EXCEPT

    A. class warfare among middle-class peasants and the workers.
    B. the selection of Louis Napoleon as president in 1848.
    C. establishment of national workshops.
    D. abdication of King Louis-Philippe.
    E. intervention by the Concert of Europe to prevent the spread of the revolution.

40. Which of the following countries did NOT acquire territory from China in the late-nineteenth century?

    A. Britain
    B. Japan
    C. Russia
    D. Germany
    E. The United States

41. Which of the following groups became the spiritual soldiers of the Counter Reformation?

    A. Lutherans
    B. Jesuits
    C. Calvinists
    D. Baptists
    E. Anglicans

42. Mary Wollstonecraft is best known for

    A. writing the *Declaration of the Rights of Woman and the Female Citizen*.
    B. writing the *Civil Constitution of the Clergy*.
    C. writing *A Vindication of the Rights of Woman*.
    D. writing a series of pamphlets that spread the ideas of the revolution to the lower classes.
    E. leading the royal family back to Paris when they had tried to flee the city.

43. Which is the best description of the Nuremberg Trials?

    A. Trials of army officers who plotted against Hitler
    B. Trials of business leaders who supported the Nazi Party
    C. Trials of Nazi and Austrian war criminals
    D. Mass purges of peasants in the Soviet Union
    E. Trials against German, Italian, and Japanese war criminals

44. Which of the following is NOT associated with Joseph Stalin's efforts to promote communism?

    A. The belief in the idea of socialism in one country
    B. Establishment of the kolkhoz collectives
    C. Purge Trials of 1934–1938
    D. Active support of Mao Tse-tung's Communist Party in China against the Nationalists
    E. Expulsion of Nikolai Bukharin from the Communist Party in 1929

45. "Off with the beard!" A Russian cartoon from the late 1700s to early 1800s shows a barber cutting off a Russian nobleman's beard with a pair of scissors. What does this cartoon symbolize?

    A. Catherine the Great's efforts to control the nobles
    B. Europe's efforts to become sanitary
    C. Efforts of the Russian Orthodox Church to enforce a strict way for nobles to appear in public
    D. Peter the Great's efforts to Westernize Russia by making nobles adapt to a Western style of dress
    E. A rite of passage of the Russian Orthodox religion

46. The city most influential in introducing intellectual and cultural ideas of the Renaissance was

    A. Paris.
    B. Florence.
    C. Venice.
    D. London.
    E. Rome.

47. Karl Marx and Friedrich Engels, in *The Communist Manifesto*, claimed that

    A. a communist revolution would first come to an agricultural country.
    B. there would be a worldwide revolution to end the abuses of capitalism.
    C. workers of communism would share in running the state economy.
    D. capitalism could be reformed.
    E. the proletariat would be the only class to survive the communist revolution.

48. "Kings are God's lieutenants on earth."

    The above quotation represents which type of government?

    A. Direct democracy
    B. Totalitarianism
    C. Republic
    D. Rule by Divine Right
    E. Limited monarchy

49. This Soviet propaganda poster represents a government program known as

    A. War Communism.
    B. the Five-Year Plan.
    C. New Economic Policy.
    D. *perestroika.*
    E. a *kolkhoz.*

50. What enabled Great Britain to dominate India from 1763 to 1947?

    A. British respect for Hindu customs
    B. Closer cooperation between Muslims and Hindus living in India
    C. British support of home rule
    D. Differences in languages and religion created divisions within the population of India
    E. British social reforms

51. "Each of us puts his person and all his power in common under the supreme direction of the general will, and . . . whoever refused to obey the general will shall be compelled to do so."

    The ideas contained in this passage best represent the views of

    A. Thomas Hobbes.
    B. Jean Jacques Rousseau.
    C. John Locke.
    D. Voltaire.
    E. Montesquieu.

52. A major problem of the Weimar Republic was

    A. that it was primarily a two-party system.
    B. that there was no provision for women's suffrage.
    C. that the right of workers to unionize was prohibited by law.
    D. the inability to effectively solve Germany's economic problems.
    E. that government nationalized all the industries.

53. A major result of Bismarck's *Kulturkampf* in Germany was that

    A. the Catholic Church was allowed to establish a separate school without government supervision.
    B. the state discontinued the requirement that everyone be married before a civil authority.
    C. the Jesuits began to open up more schools in Germany.
    D. the Catholic Center Party gained strength.
    E. the state provided funds for Catholic education.

54. Which of the following was NOT a result of England's Glorious Revolution?

    A. The Divine Right theory ended in England.
    B. Parliament asserted its supremacy over the monarchy.
    C. England adopted both Catholicism and Anglicanism as its official religions.
    D. Parliament passed the Bill of Rights.
    E. It was the first step toward a constitutional monarchy.

55. Article 231 of the Versailles Treaty resulted in

    A.   Germany taking sole responsibility for the war.
    B.   establishment of the League of Nations.
    C.   creation of the new nation of Poland.
    D.   denunciation of all secret treaties.
    E.   demilitarization of Germany.

56. "I will not accept the crown from the gutter," was a statement uttered in 1849 by

    A.   Friedrich Wilhelm IV, King of Prussia.
    B.   Louis-Philippe, King of France.
    C.   Ferdinand I, King of Austria.
    D.   Alexander I, Czar of Russia.
    E.   Victor Emmanuel II, King of Sardinia.

57. "Labour, like all other things which are purchased and sold, . . . has its natural market price. That price which is necessary to enable the labourers . . . to subsist and to perpetuate their race."

    This passage is associated with

    A.   David Ricardo, *On the Principles of Political Economy and Taxation*.
    B.   Thomas Malthus, *The Principle of Population*.
    C.   Herbert Spencer, *Principles of Sociology*.
    D.   Adam Smith, *The Wealth of Nations*.
    E.   John Stuart Mill, *On Liberty*.

58. The Civil Constitution of the Clergy resulted in the

    A.   end of absolute monarchy in France.
    B.   Church's subjection to state control.
    C.   strengthening of the power of the papacy.
    D.   beheading of Marie Antoinette.
    E.   restoration of the French absolute monarchy.

59. Henry Tudor's (Henry VII) most famous accomplishment was

    A.   constructing the Versailles Palace in France.
    B.   helping to give rise to the bourgeoisie class.
    C.   establishing the Star Chamber in England.
    D.   helping the House of York in the War of the Roses.
    E.   becoming a patron of the arts.

60. The Conservative Party in Great Britain during the 1920s was led by

    A.   Winston Churchill.
    B.   Stanley Baldwin.
    C.   Arthur Balfour.
    D.   Neville Chamberlain.
    E.   Lloyd George.

61. Nicholas I, who ruled as Czar of Russia from 1825 to 1855, supported

    A.   modernization of Russia.
    B.   a liberal constitution for the government.
    C.   emancipation of the serfs.
    D.   orthodoxy, autocracy, and nationalism.
    E.   a policy of tolerance towards non-Russians living in the empire.

62. The Meiji Restoration in Japan was characterized by

    A.   a return to isolation.
    B.   the adaptation of democracy.
    C.   a return to feudalism.
    D.   the abolition of the position of the emperor.
    E.   the modernization and reform of Japan in order for it to compete with Western powers.

63. The Romantic poetry of William Wordsworth and William Blake was a reaction against

    A.   nationalism.
    B.   the horrors of the Industrial Revolution and the scientific rationalism of the Enlightenment.
    C.   democracy.
    D.   the growing influence of the Catholic Church.
    E.   the growth of labor unions.

64. Under Joseph Stalin, the Soviet Union emphasized a Command Economy and a series of Five-Year Plans to primarily

    A.   make consumer goods more affordable.
    B.   encourage farmers to sell more goods on the retail markets.
    C.   increase its industrial output by developing heavy industry.
    D.   expand exports to the Western countries.
    E.   create demand for more imported goods.

65. Which was NOT a major characteristic of the Scientific Revolution of the seventeenth century?

   A. Growth of a learned society, such as the Royal Society of London
   B. A general acceptance of Aristotle's theories
   C. A widespread growth of knowledge among the general population
   D. Development of a modern scientific method that stressed reason over tradition
   E. The uncovering of much knowledge about the physical world

66. *Guernica*, the painting by Pablo Picasso, was inspired by

   A. the Spanish Civil War (1936–1939).
   B. Hitler's rise to power.
   C. Mussolini's rise to power.
   D. Italy's invasion of Ethiopia.
   E. the Nazi-Soviet Non-Aggression Pact.

67. All of the following countries came into existence after World War I EXCEPT

   A. Albania.
   B. Finland.
   C. Czechoslovakia.
   D. Yugoslavia.
   E. Estonia.

68. As a result of the Napoleonic Code, women in France

   A. were able to play an active role in the government.
   B. were unfairly held in prisons.
   C. were able to vote.
   D. were able to own property.
   E. were given few or no rights.

69. All of the following are results of the Franco-Prussian War EXCEPT

   A. Bismarck's policy of Blood and Iron had been successful.
   B. the Second German Empire was created.
   C. France's influence in Europe dating from Louis XIV had ended.
   D. England feared that Germany would upset the balance of power in Europe.
   E. Bismarck's policy became more lenient toward France.

70. Which of the following is NOT considered an important literary or artistic figure in the School of Realism?

   A. Gustave Courbet
   B. Émile Zola
   C. George Eliot
   D. Emmeline Pankhurst
   E. Gustave Flaubert

71. The Tanzimat reforms of the nineteenth century in the Ottoman Empire sought to achieve all of the following EXCEPT

   A. equality before the law for Jews, Christians, and Muslims.
   B. modernization of the economy.
   C. reform of the military.
   D. establishment of democracy.
   E. a halt to the growth of nationalism in the empire.

72. During the fifteenth century, Ferdinand and Isabella made Spain

   A. a place where people of all religions could reside.
   B. a strong royal monarchy by using the Church and consolidating royal authority.
   C. more isolated from the rest of Europe.
   D. less unified than it had been in the medieval ages.
   E. a place where aristocratic power was most powerful.

73. "Woman is born free and lives equal to man in her rights. Social distinctions can be based only on the common utility." The author of this excerpt is

   A. Olympe de Gouges.
   B. Claudine Alexandrine Guerin de Tencin
   C. Marie-Thérèse Geoffrin.
   D. Catherine the Great.
   E. Maria Theresa.

74. Napoleon's Continental System was

   A. a successful means of defeating Great Britain.
   B. a series of military attacks against Austria.
   C. economic warfare against Great Britain.
   D. a jobs program for France.
   E. an improved system of public schools.

75. All of the following were members of the Quadruple Alliance EXCEPT

   A. Prussia.
   B. Russia.
   C. Great Britain.
   D. Spain.
   E. Austria.

76. All of the following were characteristics of Gorbachev's *perestroika* EXCEPT

   A. there was less government planning.
   B. local factory managers received more power.
   C. Soviet citizens could operate small retail businesses.
   D. nuclear weapons were disarmed.
   E. farmers were able to sell some of their goods on the free market.

77. All of the following were a major result of the Industrial Revolution EXCEPT

   A. establishment of the Royal Society of London to encourage research.
   B. the growth of capitalism.
   C. an increase in the standard of living.
   D. the rise of the middle and working classes.
   E. the growth of cities.

78. The July Revolution of 1830 led to the downfall of the regime of

   A. Charles X.
   B. Louis XVIII.
   C. Louis Napoleon.
   D. Talleyrand.
   E. Alphonse de Lamartine.

79. The Dual Monarchy referred to

   A. the Kingdom of the Two Sicilies.
   B. Austria-Hungary.
   C. the United Kingdom of Great Britain and Ireland.
   D. Piedmont-Sardinia.
   E. the Papal States.

80. Which of the following statements was the result of World War I?

   A. Russia became a dominant power, replacing Germany.
   B. Germany became a democratic republic.
   C. The Ottoman Empire expanded its territories.
   D. Germany underwent an economic revival.
   E. The United States recognized the Soviet Union as the legitimate government of the country.

Section II: Part A—Document-Based Questions

Suggested writing time—45 minutes
Percent of Section II score—45%

Directions: The following question is based on the accompanying Documents 1 through 10. (Some of the documents have been edited for the purpose of this exercise.) This question is designed to test your ability to work with historical documents. As you analyze the documents, take into account both the sources of the documents and the authors' points of view. Write an essay on the following topic that integrates your analysis of the documents. Do not simply summarize the documents individually. You may refer to relevant historical facts and developments not mentioned in the documents.

1. Discuss and analyze the causes of the New Imperialism.

   Historical Background: By the early part of the nineteenth century, it appeared that the countries of Europe had lost interest in building overseas empires. However, the last third of the nineteenth century saw a new scramble for colonies. Britain, France, Germany, Belgium, Italy, and Portugal engaged in a race to annex the undeveloped areas of the world. By 1914, one-third of the world's people were under colonial control, with the countries of Europe holding the lion's share.

Document 1

All great nations in the fullness of their strength have desired to set their mark upon barbarian lands. All over the globe today we see the peoples of Europe creating a mighty aristocracy of the white races. Those who take no share in this great rivalry will play a pitiable part in time to come. . . . It is a sound and normal trait in a civilized nation to avert the existing dangers of over-population by colonization on a large scale. This puts no check upon nature, and . . . augments the national strength of the mother country at the same time.

Source: Heinrich von Treitschke, *Politics*, 1897.

Document 2

No one in France . . . doubts the benefits of colonization and the advantages which it offers both to the country which undertakes it and to that which receives it. Everyone agrees that colonies offer markets for raw materials, the means of production, the products lacking to the mother-country; that they open markets to all the commerce and all the industries of an old country, by the wants, by the new needs of the people with whom they are in relation. . . .

Source: The French Society of Colonial and Maritime Studies, 1876. A. Murphy, *The Ideology of French Imperialism*, Catholic University of America Press, 1948.

Document 3

Take up the White Man's burden —
        Send forth the best ye breed —
Go bind your sons to exile
        To serve your captives' need;
To wait in heavy harness
        On fluttered folk and wild —
Your new-caught, sullen peoples,
        Half devil and half child.

Source: Rudyard Kipling, "The White Man's Burden," 1899.

Document 4

In the area of economics, I am placing before you . . . the need for outlets. Why? Because next door Germany is setting up trade barriers; because across the ocean the United States of America have become protectionists . . .; because not only are those great markets shrinking . . . but these great states are beginning to pour into our own markets products not seen there before. . . . We must say openly that indeed the higher races have a right over the lower races. . . . They have the duty to civilize the inferior races . . . I say that French colonial policy, the policy of colonial expansion . . . was inspired by the fact that a navy such as ours cannot do without safe harbors, defenses, supply centers on the high seas . . . At present, as you know, a warship . . . cannot carry more than two weeks' supply of coal. . . . Hence the need to have places of supply, shelters, ports for defense and provisioning . . . .

Source: Jules Ferry, "Speech Before the French Chamber of Deputies," March 28, 1884.

Document 5

We . . . must recognize that in order that we may have more employment to give we must create more demand. Give me the demand for more goods and then I will undertake to give plenty of employment in making the goods; and the only thing, in my opinion, that the government can do in order to meet this great difficulty . . . , is so to arrange its policy that . . . new markets shall be created, and that old markets shall be effectually developed. . . . For these reasons, . . . I would never lose the hold which we now have over our great Indian dependency, by far the greatest and most valuable of all the customers we have or ever shall have in this country. For the same reasons I approve of the continued occupation of Egypt, and for the same reasons I have urged upon this government, and upon previous governments, the necessity for using every legitimate opportunity to extend our influence and control in that great African continent which is now being opened up to civilization and to commerce.

Source: Joseph Chamberlain, British Secretary of State for the Colonies, 1893. *The Imperialism Reader*, edited by Richard M. Brace, Van Nostrand Company, Inc., 1962.

Document 6

In spite of the fact that we have no such fleet as we should have, we have conquered for ourselves a place in the sun. It will now be my task to see to it that this place in the sun shall remain our undisputed possession, in order that the sun's rays may fall fruitfully upon our activity and trade in foreign parts, that our industry and agriculture may develop within the state and our sailing sports upon the water for our future lies upon the water. The more Germans go out upon the water, whether it be in races or regattas, whether it be in journeys across the ocean, or in the service of the battle flag, so much the better it will be for us.

Source: Kaiser Wilhelm II of Germany: Speech to the North German Regatta Association, 1901.

Document 7

It seems to me that God, with infinite wisdom and skill, is training the Anglo-Saxon race for an hour sure to come in the world's future . . . The unoccupied arable lands of the earth are limited, and will soon be taken . . . Then will the world center upon a new stage of its history—the final competition of races, for which the Anglo-Saxon is being schooled. . . . Then this race of unequalled energy . . . the representative, let us hope, of the largest liberty, the purest Christianity, the highest civilization . . . will spread itself over the earth. . . . And can any one doubt that the result of this competition of races will be the "survival of the fittest"?

Source: Josiah Strong (American Protestant Minister), *Our Country: Its Possible Future and Its Present Crisis,* 1885.

Document 8

I contend that we (Britons) are the finest race in the world, and the more of the world we inhabit, the better it is for the human race. . . . It is our duty to seize every opportunity of acquiring more territory and we should keep this one idea steadily before our eyes that more territory simply means more of the Anglo-Saxon race, more of the best, the most human, most honourable race the world possesses.

Source: Cecil Rhodes (a British Imperialist), *Confessions of Faith*, 1877.

Document 9

. . . In order to keep your forty millions here from eating each other for lack of other victuals, we beyond the seas must keep open as much of the surface of this planet as we can for the overflow of your population to inhabit and . . . create markets where you can dispose of the produce of your factories and of your mines. The Empire, I am always telling you, is a bread-and-butter question. If you have not to be cannibals, you have got to be Imperialists."

Source: W. T. Stead (an English journalist), *The History of the Mystery*, 1897.

Document 10

. . . Imperialism is often confused with commerce or with the opening of commercial markets. . . . Imperialism means something quite different from the sale of purchase of commodities. It entails a profound action on a people and a territory, providing the inhabitants with some education and regular justice, teaching them the division of labour and the uses of capital when they are ignorant of these things. It opens an area not only to the merchandise of the mother country, but to its capital and its savings, to its engineers, to its overseers, to its emigrants. . . . Such a transformation of a barbarian country cannot be accomplished by simple commercial relations.

Source: Paul Leroy-Beaulieu (a French imperialist) 1891; Ref.: S. Pollard et al, *Documents of European Economic History*, Vol. 2, Edward Arnold, 1968.

Section II: Part B—Thematic Essays

(Suggested planning and writing time—70 minutes)
Percent of Section II score—55%

Directions: You are to answer TWO questions, one from each group of three questions below. Make your selections carefully, choosing the questions that you are best prepared to answer thoroughly in the time permitted. You should spend 5 minutes organizing or outlining each essay. In writing your essays, use specific examples to support your answer. If time permits when you finish writing, check your work. Be certain to number your answers as the questions are numbered below.

Group 1

Choose ONE question from this group. The suggested writing time for this question is 30 minutes. You are advised to spend 5 minutes planning your answer in the area below.

1. Compare and contrast the religious ideas of Martin Luther and John Calvin.

2. Discuss and analyze the ideas of John Locke and Jean Jacques Rousseau.

3. Discuss and assess the success of Peter the Great (who reigned from 1682 to 1725) in trying to modernize Russia.

Group 2

Choose ONE question from this group. The suggested writing time for this question is 30 minutes. You are advised to spend 5 minutes planning your answer in the area below.

1. Historians have claimed that the Versailles Treaty laid the seeds of distrust that caused World War II. Evaluate to what extent this statement is accurate.

2. Discuss and analyze the causes of the Cold War.

3. Karl Marx wrote that all of history was a class struggle. Discuss and analyze Marx's view of historical development.

Answer Key for Practice Exam I

Section I: Multiple-Choice Questions

1. D	28. E	55. A
2. C	29. D	56. A
3. A	30. A	57. A
4. A	31. D	58. B
5. B	32. B	59. C
6. D	33. A	60. B
7. B	34. A	61. D
8. B	35. C	62. E
9. B	36. B	63. B
10. A	37. B	64. C
11. A	38. D	65. C
12. D	39. E	66. A
13. D	40. E	67. A
14. C	41. B	68. E
15. B	42. C	69. E
16. C	43. C	70. D
17. A	44. D	71. D
18. E	45. D	72. B
19. C	46. B	73. A
20. D	47. B	74. C
21. C	48. D	75. D
22. C	49. B	76. D
23. B	50. D	77. A
24. D	51. B	78. A
25. D	52. D	79. B
26. E	53. D	80. B
27. C	54. C	

Section II: Free-Response Essays

Student essays and analysis appear beginning on page 271.

Answers and Explanations for Practice Exam I

Section I: Multiple-Choice Questions

1. **D.** The desire of certain countries to spread democracy was not an underlying cause of World War I. The Alliance System dividing Europe into armed camps between the Triple Alliance and the Triple Entente raised tensions. The excessive nationalism of minority groups in the Balkans divided the Austro-Hungarian Empire and Russia. The buildup of armed forces in Germany and England as well as the rivalry in Africa over colonies created the causes that led to World War I. The European countries wanted to protect the balance of power and not spread political ideology.

2. **C.** Humanism focused on worldly and secular themes and the importance of the individual. Humanism was a literary movement that began in Italy during the fourteenth century and stressed that secular subjects were just as important as religious themes. Humanists believed that man had unlimited potential and glorified his abilities; they idealized the importance of God and the afterlife, but that was not their main focus. Many Humanists stressed the use of the vernacular, not Latin, and made little effort to focus on the status of women in society.

3. **A.** Giuseppe Mazzini supported the idea stated in this passage. Mazzini was the founder of Young Italy, a nationalist organization that wanted to unite Italy by expelling Austria from Italy. He favored a democratic republican government for Italy. Cavour, prime minister of Piedmont-Sardinia, favored a constitutional monarchy with Victor Emmanuel II as king. Pope Pius IX opposed unification of Italy. Vincenzo Gioberti wanted a united Italy with a confederation type of government.

4. **A.** In the early eighteenth century, France was the cultural center of Europe and it was the home of the Enlightenment. French was the international language, and France was the most populous nation with 25.5 million people. French exports were greater than those of Great Britain. Although France was not considered a weak nation, it had never been successful in defeating Great Britain during the long reign of Louis XIV. The French government was not innovative, and still functioned as a medieval society, referred to as the Old Regime. The French government was an absolute monarchy and little effort was made to become more democratic until the French Revolution in 1789.

5. **B.** In January 1943, Roosevelt and Churchill met at Casablanca, where they agreed to demand the unconditional surrender of the Axis countries. They made this public announcement because Stalin was fearful that the Allies would sign a separate treaty with Germany. Roosevelt and Churchill also agreed to launch an invasion of Italy through Sicily. They knew that Stalin wanted a second front in Europe against France to take the pressure off Russia, which Stalin felt was carrying the brunt of the war. The other answer choices are wrong for the following reasons: Roosevelt and Churchill did not agree to invade Germany; Russia was never informed at any of the conferences about the United States' development of the atomic bomb; Churchill, Stalin, and Roosevelt discussed the division of Germany at the Teheran and Yalta Conferences, not in Casablanca; and there was never any discussion on a rebuilding program at any of these conferences.

6. **D.** Martin Luther believed that salvation was achieved by faith alone. He considered the Bible the final authority and he urged each individual to read and interpret it. Luther rejected the intervention of saints, priests, the monastic life, and good works. He believed that each person should serve God in his or her own way.

7. **B.** A major characteristic of the Enlightenment was a belief that man—through reason and logical thinking—could discover the laws that govern the universe and that all laws of society and human nature could be explained by using rationality. Enlightenment thinkers rejected authority, and put faith in reason, not in God. They were optimists and rejected the Divine Right theory. They justified absolute rule by asserting that the king ruled because he ruled in the people's interest. The Enlightenment also valued progress over traditional values.

8. **B.** The fall of communism in Poland, Hungary, Czechoslovakia, Bulgaria, and Albania was characterized by a peaceful transition and peaceful free elections, which took place between 1989 and 1991. These countries did not sign treaties with each other nor did the United States intervene. Civil war did not break out in any of these countries with the exception of Romania, which suffered both political violence and casualties.

9. **B.** A series of wars between the Italian city-states did not contribute to the rise of absolute rulers in Europe in the fifteenth century. Divided into many different republics such as Florence, Venice, and Genoa, Italy was subjected to invasion throughout the fifteenth and sixteenth centuries. The need for direct trade routes to Asia and the need for capital in order to break the Asian and Italian monopolies forced countries to centralize power in a king or queen, leading to national states or absolute monarchies. The awakening spirit of nationalism also helped increase the power of the rulers as a rallying point.

10. **A.** The Carbonari was a secret society that was first organized in Italy in the early nineteenth century and also flourished in Spain and France. Carbonari in Italian means "charcoal burners." The society originated in the Kingdom of Naples in the 1800s and drew its members from all stations in life, particularly the army. The Carbonari was a closely organized society that advocated political freedom for the Italians against Austrian control of Italy. The Carbonari was partially responsible for uprisings in Naples in 1820, Spain in 1820, and Piedmonte in 1821. After 1830, the Carbonari disappeared and most of its members joined the Young Italy Society. The Carbonari did not exist in Britain, Portugal, Russia, or Prussia.

11. **A.** Imperialism is the idea supported by Rudyard Kipling, the author of the passage. Kipling, like other Europeans, believed that it was the obligation of the Europeans to spread civilization to the uncivilized. The belief in the superiority of European civilization led to imperialism, and missionaries believed that European control would help spread religion. Nationalism is a belief that each group of people is entitled to its own nation or government. Socialism is a system in which the government owns and operates all essential means of production, distribution, and exchange of goods. Fascism is a totalitarian system of government that glorifies the nation over the individual.

12. **D.** A key demand of the Chartists in Great Britain was universal male suffrage. In the People's Charter of 1838, from which the movement derived its name, city workers wanted to extend the franchise (voting rights); the 1838 Charter failed to achieve the Chartists' goals but eventually all of their demands, such as secret ballots, were passed by the beginning of the twentieth century. The Chartists were opposed to giving women the right to vote and their platform focused upon political reform, not social changes such as workmen's compensation, nationalizing key industries, and protective tariffs.

13. **D.** One consequence of the Russo-Japanese War was that Nicholas II signed the October Manifesto establishing a Duma. Russia's defeat in the Russo-Japanese War led to widespread demand for reforms. When the czar's army fired on the crowds that demonstrated at the Winter Palace in St. Petersburg for shorter working hours and more representatives in government (an event that became known as Bloody Sunday), the czar was forced to sign the October Manifesto, which guaranteed civil liberties and provided for the creation of a lawmaking body, the Duma, elected by universal male suffrage. However, the Duma had little control over Russia's finances and foreign affairs. In 1906, Nicholas II dissolved the Duma and by the beginning of World War I, the Duma was like a debating society with little power. Nicholas II did not reform the military because he depended upon it for support. The Communists were not a major political influence in 1905 and would not gain many followers until World War I. Nicholas II did not really believe in sharing power with the Duma. The Duma could debate and pass laws, but the czar had the final power of veto.

14. **C.** Churchill's "Iron Curtain" speech, given in Fulton, Missouri, in 1946, was a symbol of the growing fear and division between the Soviet-dominated states and the Western Bloc. It proclaimed that an "iron curtain" had descended over Eastern Europe and that Europe was divided between those who were controlled by the Soviet Union and those who followed the West led by the United States. This symbolic iron curtain divided Europe for 43 years until communism collapsed in 1989. Churchill's speech was

designed to create an awareness of the dangers of communism; it was not a military plan, nor was it intended to persuade Eastern European countries to join the Western Bloc; furthermore, it was not a rebuke to the United States or a plea for compromise.

15. **B.** Pope Pius IX did not support Italian unification; he opposed the unification of Italy because he was afraid that it would end his temporal (civil) rule over the Papal States. Bismarck supported Italian unification as a way to weaken Austrian influence and gain an ally in Prussia in the struggle for independence. Victor Emmanuel II was king of Piedmont-Sardinia, and would become the first king of a united Italy in 1861. Napoleon III supported Italian unification because by fighting reactionary Austrians, he would pacify the French liberals, whom he was suppressing. The Duchy of Parma voted for annexation to Sardinia after the people of Parma drove out the Austrians in 1860.

16. **C.** The main goal of Operation Barbarossa was to gain control of the wheat fields of the Ukraine and the oil fields of the Caucasus. By 1941, Hitler realized that he would be unable to defeat Great Britain and needed the wheat from the Ukraine and the oil from the Caucasus to enable him to carry on the war. Hitler did not necessarily want to establish a puppet state in Leningrad; he needed the resources of Russia, however. Conquering Russia would provide Germany with a land empire, not a water outlet.

17. **A.** The Duke of Sully was instrumental in helping Henry IV to consolidate his power. Sully was a financial genius who reduced the debt by reforming the tax system. He constructed roads that improved transportation and promoted economic prosperity; he also strengthened the power of the monarchs by limiting the power of the nobles over the parliament. Sully did not lead a revolution in France nor did he have any control over who would be the heir to Henry IV. Henry IV and Sully's relationship with other European nations did not contribute to absolutism in France, and Henry IV and Sully had established peace with the Church when the king converted to Catholicism.

18. **E.** The Luddites were a group of nineteenth-century handicraft workers in northern England who opposed industrialization and smashed machinery, believing that the new machines were putting them out of work. Chartists were reformers in Great Britain who wanted to extend the franchise to city workers. Utopian Socialists and Marxists wanted to destroy the capitalist system by creating an ideal society or establishing communism. Capitalists were the factory owners.

19. **C.** Johannes Gutenberg was a German who invented movable print type in 1450, which increased the output of books. Francesco Petrarca, Giovanni Boccaccio, Baldassare Castiglione, and Pico della Mirandola were all Italian humanist writers of the Renaissance.

20. **D.** René Descartes expressed the view, "I think, therefore I am." Descartes was a French mathematician and philosopher who stressed inductive reasoning. His famous quote proved his belief in his own existence. Descartes' ideas promoted the Scientific Revolution. Voltaire and Rousseau were philosophers who attacked the abuses of society in order to change unjust conditions; Francis Bacon was an Englishman who promoted the scientific method, and John Locke was an English philosopher who wrote *Two Treatises of Government*, defending the Glorious Revolution in England.

21. **C.** Hitler's platform did not include establishing an alliance with the Soviet Union. By 1930, the Communists polled over six million votes and German Conservatives feared a Communist revolution. Hitler blamed the Communists for the Reichstag fire in February 1933, and he and the Nazi Party promised to fight communism. Hitler's platform appealed to Aryan supremacy and his National Socialist Party provided an extensive public works program to help the country out of the depression. Hitler also promised to remilitarize the army and navy as a way to show the Nazi Party's disdain for the Versailles Treaty.

22. **C.** The Balkan Crisis of 1912–13 created hostility in Serbia and Russia toward Austria-Hungary. In 1912, Serbia's dispute with Bulgaria over the spoils of war after they had joined together to defeat the Ottoman Empire led to Russia backing Serbia but Austria (supported by Germany) denying Serbia's goal of getting an outlet on the Adriatic Sea. Austria's approach reflected her fear of Russian influence in the Balkans and the greater fear that it would cause unrest among Serbians and other Slavic people in the Austro-Hungarian Empire. The Balkan Crisis did not result in political freedom for Serbians living in the Austro-Hungarian

Empire; Austria continued to exercise control of the Serbians in order to dominate the many other ethnic groups living in its multinational empire. There was no alliance between Bulgaria and the Ottoman Empire; Bulgaria had defeated the Ottoman Empire in 1912. France was not involved in the Balkan Crisis of 1912–13.

23. **B.** On July 28, 1794, Robespierre, who is associated with the Reign of Terror, was guillotined. His death ended the Reign of Terror and began the Thermidorian Reaction, in which the moderates gained control of the government. Moderates ended the role of the Committee of Public Safety and established a constitution which was controlled by the middle class and men who owned property. The new government, known as The National Convention, closed the Jacobin clubs. The government also freed those citizens who were considered enemies during the Reign of Terror. The National Assembly passed the Civil Constitution of the Clergy in 1790. Louis XVI and Marie Antoinette were executed in 1793. Napoleon did not come to power until 1799.

24. **D.** Martin Luther would reject Ulrich Zwingli's statement denying all sacraments. Luther, unlike Zwingli, believed in the sacraments of Baptism, Communion, and Penance. Zwingli denied all seven sacraments. Both accepted no celibacy for the priests, opposed the worshipping of saints, and regarded the Bible as the final authority.

25. **D.** The desire to spread democracy was not a factor that contributed to the New Imperialism. Instead, the New Imperialism was promoted by the Industrial Revolution. Colonies were considered a market for the manufacture of goods and a source of raw materials. Missionaries saw colonies as a way to spread Christianity to those who they believed had no religion. Many nations saw colonies as a symbol that their country had achieved a "place in the sun" as a military power.

26. **E.** The Boulanger Affair occurred from 1886 to 1889, 38 years after the Age of Metternich (1848). Boulanger was a general who favored the monarchy, and who tried to seize control of the Third Republic but failed. The Concert of Europe, the Carlsbad Decree in Austria, the Six Acts in England, and the July Ordinances in France were efforts to control the spread of democracy and nationalism. These terms are associated with the Age of Metternich.

27. **C.** Niccolo Machiavelli wrote *The Prince* in 1513 to provide guidelines for rulers who wanted to be successful. The book focused on how a ruler could maintain power by adapting the slogan, "the end justifies the means." Machiavelli's ideal ruler had to be both a fox and a lion. Erasmus was a Dutch humanist who criticized the abuses of the Church. Thomas More was an Englishman who wrote *Utopia*. Montaigne was a French writer and Lorenzo Valla was an Italian humanist.

28. **E.** *The Declaration of the Rights of Man and of the Citizen* in France did not abolish feudalism. It was based on the principles of Enlightenment and the American Declaration of Independence. The National Assembly, formed on August 4, 1789, ended feudalism by abolishing all special privileges of the nobles, such as their exemption from taxes. *The Declaration of the Rights of Man and of the Citizen* established equality before the law, civil liberties, and equitable distribution of taxation. It also limited the power of the monarchy.

29. **D.** The Council of Trent (1545–1563) strengthened the supremacy of the Catholic Church, reaffirming the dogma of the Church and contributing to the Catholic Church's efforts to combat Protestantism. It reestablished the power of the Church by eliminating abuses such as simony and the sale of indulgences, which many people, including Luther, thought were corrupting the Church. The Jesuits became the spiritual leaders of the Council of Trent or Counter Reformation. The Great Schism and the Babylonian captivity undermined the power of the papacy by quarreling over who should be pope. The Peace of Augsburg allowed the king to decide the religion of his people.

30. **A.** Thomas Malthus was not an inventor. He was an economist who believed that the population growth was increasing faster than the food supply. All of the other men were inventors: Eli Whitney—cotton gin; Richard Arkwright—water frame; Edmund Cartwright—power loom; James Watt—steam engine.

31. **D.** The Yalta Conference, held in February 1945, was a source of controversy during the Cold War because of the status of free elections in the countries of Eastern Europe that were liberated by the Soviet Union.

Roosevelt made concessions to Stalin by agreeing to allow him to hold free elections in the areas he controlled. Stalin gave a verbal agreement to allow elections but he rejected the suggestion of international supervision of these elections. Stalin's violation of the promise of self-determination for these countries became a source of friction between the United States and Russia, which contributed to the Cold War. The Teheran Conference was the first meeting of the Big Three. At Yalta, Stalin did agree to support the United States' declaration of war against Japan and there was no disagreement about the location of the United Nations headquarters. The status of British territory in Africa and the Middle East was not an issue at Yalta.

32. **B.** *The Massacre of Chios* by Eugène Delacroix glorified the Greek struggle for independence against the Ottoman Empire. The Greek struggle for freedom won the enthusiastic support of liberal nationalists and romantics such as Delacroix. He was the founder of the Romantic School of Painting. His painting illustrates the idealistic conception of the revolutionaries who are being oppressed by the Turks. Delacroix never painted any works of any revolutions in Spain, Sardinia, or Latin America. He also never painted the election of Louis Napoleon in 1848.

33. **A.** The Schlieffen Plan was Germany's strategy on how to avoid a prolonged two-front war. Under the Schlieffen Plan, German forces would sweep through France via Belgium and then turn to defeat Russia in the East. The plan was to defeat France within six weeks and then to transport troops to the eastern front to help the Austrians against the Russians. The plan did not consider any Russian action against Austria-Hungary nor was Serbia or the Balkans part of the strategy. The Schlieffen Plan was based on the premise that the Russian army would be slow to mobilize and thus give Germany enough time to defeat France quickly.

34. **A.** The rule of James I created hostility in England because he refused to reform the Church of England. James I antagonized the Puritans, a powerful Calvinist sect that considered the Church of England, or Anglicanism, too close to Catholicism and tried to change Anglican practices. The criticism of his foreign policy was that it was too pro-Catholic, not about England's involvement. James I angered people because he tried to rule by divine right. He created resentment because he tried to raise taxes without the consent of Parliament, which was mainly middle class, not peasants. James I did not have an alliance with Spain, but was friendly toward Spain.

35. **C.** Cavour's major goal in the Crimean War was to raise the issue of Italian unification at the Peace Conference. Cavour took Piedmont into the war against Russia with the hope of winning a place at the peace table in order to address the issue of Italian unification. Cavour did not become an ally of Russia nor did he receive trading rights and territories from England. He entered the war on the side of England and France and his goal was to unify Italy. Cavour realized that Austria would never agree to unification unless Piedmont-Sardinia received the support from other European powers such as France, Prussia, and England.

36. **B.** This statement is associated with Benito Mussolini. Mussolini was the Italian leader who led the National Fascist Party from 1922 to 1945 and is considered the founder of Italian fascism. Adolf Hitler of Germany and Francisco Franco of Spain implemented a form of fascism in their countries. Hitler ruled from 1933 to 1945 and his form of fascism became known as Nazism. In Spain, Franco was supported by both Mussolini and Hitler in the civil war against the communists in Spain during the 1930s. Juan Peron, dictator of Argentina, considered Italian leader Benito Mussolini one of the greatest leaders of the twentieth century. Peron was leader of Argentina from 1946–1955 and returned from exile to lead Argentina in 1973 before his death in 1974. Alexander Kerensky served as Prime Minister of the Russian Provisional Government from July to October 1917.

37. **B.** Baron de Montesquieu should not be considered as part of the Scientific Revolution because he was a philosopher who wrote *The Spirit of Laws,* which describes how power of the government should be limited. Francis Bacon, René Descartes, Galileo Galilei, and Nicholas Copernicus all made important contributions to the Scientific Revolution.

38. **D.** Austria-Hungary never became involved in the partition of Africa during the period from 1870 to 1914. Italy, France, Portugal, and Great Britain all had colonies in Africa.

39. **E.** The Concert of Europe never intervened to prevent the spread of revolution in Paris in June of 1848; it had disbanded by that time. By 1820, England had withdrawn and Metternich was forced to flee Austria during its 1848 revolution. The June Days led to the abdication of Louis-Philippe and the establishment of the Second French Republic with Louis Napoleon elected president. During the June Days in Paris, class warfare broke out among the workers, the peasants, and the middle class, who feared the radical Socialist demands and thought the national workshops were a waste of money.

40. **E.** The United States never acquired any territory in China in the nineteenth century. The United States was interested in trading with China. The United States believed that the European division of China would threaten the ability of the United States to openly trade with China. In 1900, the United States issued the Open Door Policy, which proposed that all nations be allowed to trade freely with China. Great Britain gained control of Hong Kong and areas near the Yangtze River. Japan gained control of Southern Manchuria after the Russo-Japanese War. Russia extended influence over Manchuria. Germany acquired a sphere of influence in northeastern China over the Shantung Peninsula.

41. **B.** The Jesuits were the spiritual soldiers of the Counter Reformation. Founded by Ignatius Loyola, a former Spanish soldier and nobleman, the Jesuits were organized along military lines and were trained in education and philosophy. They revived the Inquisition to suppress heresy and reassert the dominance of Catholicism. Lutherans, Calvinists, Baptists, and Anglicans were Protestant sects that broke away from the Catholic Church.

42. **C.** Mary Wollstonecraft is best known for writing *A Vindication of the Rights of Woman* (1792). In this book, she argued that women were not naturally inferior to men. She ridiculed prevailing notions about women as helpless, charming adornments in the household. Her book was written as the first response to Edmund Burke's *Reflections on the Revolution in France*. Mary Wollstonecraft was a British writer and was not involved in any of the events connected with the French Revolution. Olympe de Gouges wrote the *Declaration of the Rights of Woman and the Female Citizen*.

43. **C.** The Nuremberg Trials began in Nuremberg, Germany in November 1945 and lasted until October 1946. The purpose of this international tribunal of 23 nations was to specifically put on trial 177 Germans and Austrians for crimes against humanity; 142 were found guilty. Italian and Japanese war criminals were tried in their own countries. The Nuremberg Trials were not concerned with the plot to assassinate Hitler or the role of business leaders in Nazi Germany. The trials did not deal with the purges in the Soviet Union.

44. **D.** Stalin never actively supported Mao's Chinese Communist Party. In 1921, the Soviet Union began supporting the Chinese Nationalist Party and encouraged the Communist Party of China to sign a treaty with the Nationalist government. Stalin did not embrace Mao's revolutionary movement. During the civil war between the Nationalists and the Chinese Communist Party, Stalin was intent on waiting to see if the Communists, who had elected Mao Tse-tung leader of the party in 1935, would prove to be an effective force. He doubted the ability of Maoist peasants to defeat Chiang Kai-Shek's Nationalist Party. He also feared a potential threat from China as a rival communist power if they defeated the Nationalists. In August 1945, Stalin signed a treaty of friendship with Chiang Kai-Shek in order to get territorial concessions in the Far East. In the end, Stalin failed to take into account Mao's leadership ability. Stalin was eventually forced to support Mao in 1949 after the Communists proclaimed the People's Republic of China. Stalin promoted the idea of socialism in one country before exporting the revolution. The use of the kolkhoz collectives helped Stalin to promote the collectivization of the farmers. Stalin used the Purge Trials from 1934 to 1938 to eliminate all his rivals. Bukharin, who supported Stalin's efforts to oust Trotsky from power, was expelled from the party in 1929.

45. **D.** This cartoon represents Peter the Great's efforts to Westernize Russia by making nobles adapt to a Western style of dress. He was determined to introduce new techniques and ideas from Western Europe to make Russia stronger. Peter wanted to replace the old-fashioned robes of the Russian noblemen and also insisted that they shave their beards. During his reign from 1682 to 1725, Peter brought technical experts, teachers, and soldiers to help Russia achieve his goal of modernization. The cartoon doesn't symbolize any of the other choices.

46. **B.** Florence was the intellectual and cultural center of the Renaissance. Florence's Medici family, who had become wealthy from trading and banking, became patrons of the arts and were instrumental in luring people of talent to the city. Although Venice was a major trading center, it never became a cultural center in Italy; likewise, Rome was the center of the Catholic Church but not an intellectual and cultural center. Paris and London did not become cultural and intellectual centers until the seventeenth and eighteenth centuries.

47. **B.** Karl Marx and Friedrich Engels, in *The Communist Manifesto,* claimed that there would be a worldwide revolution to end the abuses of capitalism. They believed that history was a class struggle between the haves and the have-nots, and that in the last stage of this struggle, the proletariat would rise and overthrow capitalism. They also believed that communism would only come to industrial nations like Great Britain or the United States, not agricultural countries. Under pure communism, *The Communist Manifesto* states, there would be no state, and society would be classless. Revolution against capitalism was inevitable because the workers were too oppressed and capitalism was doomed to extinction, not reform.

48. **D.** This quotation represents a government ruled by Divine Right. Divine Right is a belief that kings or queens receive all power from God to rule directly. Direct democracy, totalitarianism, republics, and limited monarchies do not claim that God is their source of political power.

49. **B.** This poster refers to the Soviet Five-Year Plan, which was introduced by Stalin to lay the foundation for industrialization. This poster from the 1930s translates to "We will turn the Five-Year Plan into a four-year one." This plan enabled Russia to focus on improving production in iron, steel, and coal over consumer goods. Stalin, who introduced a series of Five-Year Plans from the late 1920s to the beginning of the 1950s, hoped that these plans would ensure the growth of a strong military. Lenin introduced War Communism in 1918, which nationalized all the major industries. In 1921 Lenin replaced War Communism with the New Economic Policy, which allowed some private enterprise. *Perestroika* was an economic policy introduced by Mikhail Gorbachev in 1980 to restructure the Soviet economy. A *kolkhoz* was a collective farm; Stalin introduced these in the 1930s to improve agricultural production.

50. **D.** The people of India were divided linguistically among more than a dozen main languages and over 200 dialects. The differences between Hindus and Muslims also divided the population. In addition, India was divided into many independent states, each headed by its own prince. Britain used the principle of "divide and conquer." The British did not respect Hindu customs. They outlawed the practice of suttee and other customs which they considered barbaric. There was little cooperation between Muslims and Hindus living in India. Mohammed Ali Jinnah founded the Muslim League in order to protect the rights of Muslims living in India. The British did not support home rule and British social reforms were not enough for India's needs.

51. **B.** The ideas contained in this passage best represent the views of Jean Jacques Rousseau. Rousseau wrote *The Social Contract* in which he stated that people create a government to protect each other from the inequalities that arise in society. The people submit to the general will, or the will of the majority, and this general will is supreme. Government enforces the general will as an absolute power or unlimited power. Rousseau believed that if a government failed, the people had the right to overthrow it. However, dictatorships used Rousseau's concept of general will to justify their governments. Thomas Hobbes, who wrote *The Leviathan,* defended royal absolutism and claimed that the people do not have the right to change the government. John Locke, Voltaire, and Montesquieu admired the British system of government. John Locke's *Two Treatises of Government* provided for a government based on a social contract, but Locke was more concerned with individual rights and limits on the power of the government.

52. **D.** A major problem of the Weimar Republic was its inability to effectively solve Germany's economic problems. Until 1923, the Weimar Republic, instead of raising taxes, printed excessive quantities of paper money. This policy led to spiraling inflation where a loaf of bread cost 10,000 marks. The inflation hurt the middle class as savings and pensions became worthless. The Great Depression of 1929 created more havoc, putting over six million Germans out of work, adding to the perception that the Weimar Republic could not solve the nation's economic problems. The Weimar Republic included many different parties, such as Communist, Socialist, Democratic, National-Socialist (Nazis), and a variety of minor parties. The Nazis gained a strong following by promising to improve the economy. In the Weimar Republic, women were allowed to vote and workers could unionize, but no industries were nationalized.

53. **D.** A major result of Bismarck's *Kulturkampf* in Germany was that the Catholic Center Party gained strength. In 1872, Bismarck launched his *Kulturkampf*, or battle for civilization, in which he required Catholics to put their allegiance to the state before the Church. His attack on the Church rallied its members, enabling the Catholic Center Party to gain strength in the Reichstag. A realist, Bismarck saw his mistake and made peace with the Church. Bismarck's *Kulturkampf* required that the state had the right to supervise Catholic education and they could not set up separate schools. The state required, and did not discontinue, the practice that everyone be married before a civil authority. Bismarck expelled the Jesuits from Germany.

54. **C.** As a result of the Glorious Revolution, England did not adopt both Catholicism and Anglicanism as her official religions. The Glorious Revolution, however, resulted in the passage of the Bill of Rights, which required all English rulers to be Anglicans. The Toleration Act of 1689 granted freedom of worship to Protestants who were dissenters from the Church of England but not to Catholics and Quakers. The Bill of Rights of 1689 ensured the supremacy of Parliament over the monarchy, ended the Divine Right Theory, and laid the foundation for a constitutional monarchy in England.

55. **A.** Article 231 of the Versailles Treaty resulted in Germany taking sole responsibility for the war. Germany was also required to pay all war costs, including civilian damages, and pensions to French war widows in the Allied countries. The establishment of the League of Nations, the creation of Poland, and the demilitarization of Germany are all contained in the Versailles Treaty but not in Article 231. The Versailles Treaty did not have a provision for denouncing all secret treaties.

56. **A.** Friedrich Wilhelm IV, King of Prussia, made this statement in 1849 when the Frankfurt Assembly offered him the crown of a united Germany. Wilhelm was fearful that acceptance of the crown might lead to war with Austria. The king's refusal ended the Frankfurt Assembly, which had prepared a liberal constitution for a united Germany. None of the other monarchs were associated with the events of the Frankfurt Assembly.

57. **A.** This passage is associated with David Ricardo's *On the Principles of Political Economy and Taxation*. Ricardo's main point was that labor was guided by the "iron hand" of wages, which included the belief that large families led to an increased supply of labor that lowered wages and raised unemployment. Malthus wrote about the fear of overpopulation. Spencer, a nineteenth-century English philosopher, wrote *Principles of Sociology*. In this work, Spencer pointed out that the role of the state was to maintain a balance between freedom and justice. Smith wrote about the invisible hand of capitalism, and Mill supported freedom for the individual but feared unrestrained freedom.

58. **B.** The Civil Constitution of the Clergy resulted in the Church's subjection to state control, declaring that the Catholic Church was independent from the pope and that the Catholic clergy was to be paid by the people. All members of the clergy had to swear allegiance to the government. The Civil Constitution was a religious measure to control the Catholic clergy and to reduce the influence of the papacy in France; it did not address the issue of restoring the French absolute monarchy. The National Convention ended absolute monarchy in France in 1793 and was responsible for the beheading of Marie Antoinette.

59. **C.** Henry Tudor's (Henry VII) most famous accomplishment was establishing the Star Chamber in England. Henry VII used the Star Chamber to prevent aristocratic interference in the administration of justice. This procedure helped to promote stability and halted the period of anarchy that existed during the Hundred Years' War. Louis XIV constructed the Versailles Palace. There was no rising bourgeoisie class in England nor was Henry VII a strong supporter of the arts. Henry VII opposed the House of York.

60. **B.** Stanley Baldwin was the leader of the Conservative Party in Great Britain during the 1920s, holding power from 1924 to 1929. Neville Chamberlain was the Conservative prime minister in 1937 and was replaced by Winston Churchill, another Conservative leader, at the beginning of World War II. Lloyd George was a liberal who led Britain to victory in World War I. Arthur Balfour was a British government official who gave support to the Zionist movement for the establishment of a homeland for the Jewish people in Palestine.

61. **D.** Czar Nicholas I supported orthodoxy (the strong connection between church and government), autocracy (absolute power of the czar), and nationalism (evidenced by suppressing non-Russians within the empire). Russia was the only country not affected by the revolutions of 1848. Nicholas I was a conservative who opposed modernization for fear it would undermine the state, and he had little use for a liberal constitution. Alexander II, not Nicholas I, emancipated the serfs.

62. **E.** The Meiji Restoration in Japan (1868–1912) was characterized by the modernization and reform of Japan in order for it to compete with Western powers. It revised Japan's policy of isolation, ended feudalism, and developed its military and industrial power. Japanese leaders sent students abroad to Western countries to learn about their form of government, economics, technology, and customs. The Japanese adapted a constitution based on the model of Prussia with the emperor as its head. The Meiji government also established a banking system and modern shipyards and built up a modern army based on a draft. The Meiji Restoration did not introduce democracy and did not abolish the position of the emperor.

63. **B.** The Romantic poetry of William Wordsworth and William Blake was a reaction against the horrors of the Industrial Revolution and the scientific rationalism of the Enlightenment. Wordsworth and Blake criticized the Industrial Revolution. Blake called the early factories satanic mills and protested the hard life of the London poor. Wordsworth lamented the destruction of the rural villages and attacked the factories for their pollution of land and water. The Romantic poets did not reject nationalism or democracy, nor did they write in reaction to the growth of labor unions in England or the growing influence of the Catholic Church, which was not a dominant force in England in the nineteenth century.

64. **C.** The goal of Joseph Stalin's Command Economy and a series of Five-Year Plans was to increase the Soviet Union's industrial output by developing heavy industry, such as iron, steel, aluminum, and machinery, to produce weapons to strengthen the country militarily. The Five-Year Plans gave low priority to consumer goods and provided for collectivization of farms. They were not concerned with expanding exports to the West, or the importing of goods.

65. **C.** The Scientific Revolution did not result in the widespread growth of knowledge among the general population. Instead, it was primarily an intellectual revolution that did not affect the daily lives of the people until the nineteenth century with the growth of the Industrial Revolution. Through scientific methods, the Scientific Revolution challenged and rejected Aristotle's theories. The Scientific Revolution helped to uncover knowledge about the physical world as the Royal Society of England and other learned societies promoted scientific research.

66. **A.** The painting of *Guernica* by Pablo Picasso was inspired by the Spanish Civil War (1936–1939). The Spanish Civil War involved a struggle between the Loyalists (communists, democrats, and republicans) and the Spanish Fascists led by General Francisco Franco and aided by Hitler and Mussolini. The Soviet Union supported the Loyalists. In 1937, German bombers attacked the market square in the city of Guernica, killing over 1,600 people. Picasso's painting, which is over 11 feet tall and 25 feet wide, became the symbol of the brutality of the war. Picasso's painting was not inspired by any of the other events such as Hitler or Mussolini's rise to power, the invasion of Ethiopia, or the Nazi-Soviet Non-Aggression Pact.

67. **A.** Albania was created as a result of the Balkan Crisis of 1912–1913. Austria, with the backing of Germany, created Albania out of land belonging to the former Ottoman Empire to block Serbia's ambition to gain an outlet to the Adriatic Sea. Finland, Czechoslovakia, Yugoslavia, and Estonia were all new nations created at the Versailles Conference and carved out of the Austro-Hungarian and Russian Empires.

68. **E.** The Napoleonic Code established a uniform legal system to replace an outdated medieval system, but women lost rights. Although the Napoleonic Code reversed the Revolutionary reforms of sharing inheritances among all heirs and even declared equal inheritance rights for illegitimate offspring, it reaffirmed the traditional rights of male householders. A wife could not buy or sell property without her husband's approval. Napoleon saw the role of women as chiefly bearing and rearing children. Women were not unfairly imprisoned and the Napoleonic Code never provided for their political or economic equality.

69. **E.** Bismarck's policy did not become more lenient toward France as a result of the Franco-Prussian War. In fact, in his drive to defeat France during the Franco-Prussian War, Bismarck had brought Paris to submission by starving the city for over five months. In the Treaty of Frankfurt in 1871, he demanded that France pay a war indemnity of five billion gold francs and forced France to cede the border regions of Alsace and Lorraine. The French never reconciled themselves to the loss of these two border provinces. Bismarck's policy of Blood and Iron was successful in uniting Germany by defeating two major powers, Austria and France. The Second German Empire was created in 1871 when Wilhelm I was crowned German emperor. France had been the most dominant power on the continent since the early 1700s, but the new German Empire replaced France in that regard. Germany's victory frightened Great Britain, which had followed a policy of isolation by trying to prevent any one country from dominating the continent. The fear of German dominance influenced Britain's foreign policy as well as that of France and Russia.

70. **D.** Emmeline Pankhurst (1858–1928) was an English political activist and leader of the British suffragette movement. She founded the Women's Social and Political Union in 1903, whose goals were to gain suffrage (or the right to vote for women) as well as social reform. Gustave Courbet was a French artist who belonged to the school of painting known as Realism. Émile Zola, George Eliot (Mary Ann Evans), and Gustave Flaubert are considered to be realistic writers of the nineteenth century.

71. **D.** The Tanzimat reformers wanted to reform the crumbling empire on the European model but they did not support a democratic form of government. They wanted to create equality before the law for all religions but still wanted Islam to be the dominant religion. Tanzimat reformers also realized that the sultan had to modernize his army and economy in order to survive. Finally, their multinational empire would only survive if they stemmed the growth of nationalism, which would prove difficult to achieve.

72. **B.** Ferdinand and Isabella made Spain a strong royal monarchy by using the Church and consolidating royal authority. They strengthened royal authority by using the *hermandades* or local police to enforce royal justice; they also revived the Inquisition to help consolidate their power. Ferdinand and Isabella expelled the Jews and drove the Moors from Spain. These rulers did not isolate themselves from Europe. They unified Spain and controlled the power of the aristocracy.

73. **A.** Olympe de Gouges (1745–1793) wrote these words in *Declaration of the Rights of Woman and the Female Citizen* (1791). De Gouges asserted that women should be guaranteed the same rights as men to own property and should be regarded as citizens. De Gouges was guillotined in 1793. Claudine Alexandrine Guerin de Tencin and Marie- Thérèse Geoffrin were important women during the Enlightenment who hosted salons in Paris promoting the ideas of the Enlightenment. Catherine the Great was ruler of Russia from 1762 to 1796. Marie Thérèse was ruler of Austria from 1740 to 1780. Both of these rulers are considered enlightened despots.

74. **C.** Napoleon's Continental System was economic warfare against Great Britain. Napoleon was unable to invade Great Britain and in 1812, Great Britain was the only country he did not control in Europe. The purpose of the Continental System was to prevent European nations from trading with the British. He hoped that by boycotting British goods, he would be able to bring Great Britain to its knees. The Continental System was not a jobs program, nor was it an educational program. Napoleon had defeated Austria when he implemented the Continental System.

75. **D.** Spain was never a member of the Quadruple Alliance. The Quadruple Alliance, or Concert of Europe, consisted of Austria, Prussia, Russia, and Great Britain. The purpose of the Alliance was to maintain the balance of power in Europe after the Congress of Vienna.

76. **D.** *Perestroika* was not designed to lead to nuclear disarmament. It was an economic program that involved less government planning by allowing some businesses and some farmers to operate on the free market system. *Perestroika* also allowed individuals greater power on the local economic level.

77. **A.** The Royal Society of London was established in the seventeenth century to encourage scientific research; it was not a result of the Industrial Revolution. The growth of capitalism, the increase in the standard of living, the rise of the middle and working classes, and the growth of cities were direct consequences of the Industrial Revolution.

78. **A.** The July Revolution of 1830 led to the downfall of the regime of Charles X. In 1830, the French drove out Charles X because he attempted to restore conditions similar to that of the Old Regime, limited the right to vote, and suspended the legislature. After three days of French rioting, Charles X abdicated and fled to England. Louis XVIII was king of France until 1824. Louis Napoleon, nephew of Napoleon Bonaparte, was elected president of the Second Republic in 1848. Talleyrand was a French government leader and Alphonse de Lamartine was a moderate liberal who led the government in 1848.

79. **B.** The Dual Monarchy referred to Austria-Hungary. In 1867, the Ausgleich, or Compromise of 1867, established the Dual Monarchy under which Austria and Hungary were separate states under the leadership of Francis Joseph I, who became emperor of Austria and king of Hungary. The Kingdom of the Two Sicilies and Piedmont-Sardinia were part of the united Italy. The Papal States were the territories controlled by the Vatican. Great Britain and Ireland were never part of the Dual Monarchy.

80. **B.** A result of World War I was that Germany became a democratic republic from 1919 to 1933. At the war's end, the German people revolted against Kaiser Wilhelm II and overthrew his autocratic regime. The republic's constitution was drawn up at the city of Weimar. The Weimar Republic provided for a president who was elected by the people. The president was in charge of the army and could dissolve the Reichstag. (The German Parliament) In case of an emergency, he could suspend civil rights. Russia, which became known as the Soviet Union after the communists formed the government, suffered from famine and civil war after World War I and did not become a dominant power until the end of World War II. As a result of World War I, the Ottoman Empire was broken up, and some of the territory was split between England and France. Another result of the war was that Germany suffered from runaway inflation. The United States did not recognize the Soviet Union until 1933.

Section II: Free-Response Essays

Part A: First Sample Student DBQ Essay

By 1815, most European countries had very little need for colonies. Adam Smith argued that the burdens of colonialism outweighed its alleged benefits. As late as 1868, Bismarck, chancellor of Germany, thought that there were no advantages to colonies and Benjamin Disraeli, prime minister of Great Britain, called colonies a "millstone around our necks." These attitudes would come to an abrupt end by the 1880s and Europe would enter the age of the "New Imperialism." Economic, political, and social factors were behind the birth of this "New Imperialism." In the years between the Congress of Vienna in 1815 and the New Imperialism of the 1880s, strong, centrally governed nation-states had emerged in Europe. The Industrial Revolution had sparked tremendous economic growth in Europe and Westerners had a renewed pride that they were a unique and gifted people. Inspired by this growth and renewed confidence, Europeans embarked on a path of aggressive nationalism that led to the New Imperialism. Economic motives were important factors in the extensions of the political empires of European countries. The Industrial Revolution created needs that spurred overseas expansion. Many manufacturers wanted access to natural resources and also wanted to expand their markets. W. T. Stead, an English journalist, saw colonies as a "bread and butter issue" that could serve to create markets and could also be a market for their goods that they produced (Doc. 9). Joseph Chamberlain, the British Secretary of State for the colonies, insisted that the only way the government could create more employment and demand was to open up new markets. He argued that Britain should not only continue its occupation of Egypt and India but should extend its influence over Africa (Doc. 5). The French Society of Colonial and Maritime Studies also agreed with Chamberlain's views. They believed that colonies not only provided raw materials but also provided benefits for the mother country (Doc. 2). The quest of new markets, however, was also influenced by the rapid industrialization of Germany, Belgium, and other nations, which were able to satisfy their own home markets and were beginning to protect their markets from imports by establishing tariff barriers. Jules Ferry, twice prime minister of France (1880–81; 1883–85), alluded to that fear when he pointed out that Germany and the United States were setting up trade barriers, creating a shrinking market for French goods (Doc. 4). Thus, government became responsive enough to undertake the conquest of undeveloped territories. Asia and Africa became a special attraction because these areas offered the raw material needed for the industrial factories of Europe including cotton, silk, vegetable oils, and rare minerals. The products of the tropics were also welcomed in Europe.

Other Europeans argued that colonies also benefited the mother country because they would relieve the problem of overpopulation. W. T. Stead believed that the only way to keep people in England from cannibalism was to relocate many of them in these overseas areas (Doc. 9). The German nationalist historian, Heinrich von Treitschke, argued that only by colonization on a large scale could a civilized country avoid the dangers of overpopulation (Doc. 1). However, Grover Clark, a historian in the 1930s, in a work entitled *The Balance Sheet of Imperialism,* claimed that most of the European population migrated to the traditional areas in North America and Australia rather than Asia and Africa because they did not offer the climatic or economic conditions necessary to attract large migrations of European settlers to these areas.

Closely connected to the economic motives were political and military issues. Many Europeans were convinced that colonies were essential to a great nation. Treitschke asserted that all great nations must extend their control over "barbarian land" or they would no longer be a great power in the future (Doc. 1). In a speech before the North German Regatta Association, Kaiser Wilhelm II reinforced Treitschke's view that Germany must expand overseas if she wants to continue to have her "place in the sun" (Doc. 6). In 1884–1885, Bismarck and Ferry called the Berlin Conference to lay down the basic rules for colonizing Africa so that no one European power would dominate the entire continent.

The belief in a "place in the sun" also was connected to military needs. Steam-powered merchant ships and naval vessels required bases around the world to take on coal and supplies. Ferry asserted that the French navy, which could not do without safe harbors and supply centers, inspired the policy of colonial expansion (Doc. 4). Many Westerners during the time were influenced by the ideas of the American naval historian, Alfred T. Mahan, who believed that a strong nation could only survive by expanding its naval power. Of course, a strong navy required that a country acquire coaling and fueling bases around the world.

Humanitarian and religious goals influenced many westerners. Rudyard Kipling, perhaps the most influential of the British writers, encouraged Europeans to "take up the White Man's Burden." The goal was to civilize these people and spread Western civilization (Doc. 3). The nineteenth-century French author, Paul Beaulieu, believed that imperialism "provides the inhabitants with some regular education and regular justice." He also claimed that the overall objective was to transform the barbarian countries (Doc. 10).

Behind the idea of a civilizing mission was the belief in the superiority of the West. Cecil Rhodes, the successful British Imperialist, argued that the more territory the British controlled, the better it was for the world since the Anglo-Saxon race was the most "honourable race" (Doc. 8). Ferry also believed that the superior races had a right over the lower races to spread civilization. Many Westerners had embraced the scientific ideas of Social Darwinism. In 1859, Charles Darwin had published *On the Origin of Species* about the survival of the fittest and and Social Darwinists like Herber Spencer applied it to the European race. Some people, such as Josiah Strong, an American Protestant missionary, argued "the Anglo-Saxons were superior and that in the competition for unoccupied land the fittest would survive (Doc. 7)." This meant that imperial conquests and destruction of the weaker races in Asia and Africa were nature's way of making society better by removing the weakest elements in society.

The emergence of the New Imperialism in Europe in the late 1800s was an outgrowth of the economic, political, and social development that had influenced the continent since the Congress of Vienna in 1814–1815. The economic thrust of robust industrial capitalism, the competitive pressure between the European nations, and the belief that Europeans were the superior race with an obligation to spread their civilization resulted in the transformation of the map in areas of the world such as Africa and Asia.

Reader's Comments on Part A: First Sample Student DBQ Essay

- Has a clear, well-developed thesis.
- The essay is well organized and the student makes use of all of the documents.
- The authorship and point of view of each document is identified, such as Chamberlain, Ferry, and so on.
- The outside information is relevant (Grover Clark) and clarifies and assesses the ideas in the document.
- The student effectively discusses and analyzes the causes of the New Imperialism.

Possible student score: 8–9

Part A: Second Sample Student DBQ Essay

The New Imperialism had several causes behind its development. During the nineteenth century, many changes were occurring in Europe. These changes spurred many countries to seek colonies. The reasons for Europeans' taking aggressive steps towards colonizing new lands were many. From these new attitudes about imperialism came a new era in Europe—the age of New Imperialism.

Colonies were seen as a major source of profit to the mother country (Doc. 5). If a country possessed a colony, many profitable consequences resulted. They allowed the country to reap benefits such as an increase in revenue or more access to natural resources to expand markets.

Some countries chose to colonize because they felt it was their natural right to do so. Countries felt that it was their duty to take over lands because they were much more civilized. Europeans saw colonization as a way to spread civilization. Because Europe was much more advanced in technology and the arts, they took colonization as an opportunity to bring their novel ideas to foreign countries, which they saw as less progressive (Doc. 3). Britain especially saw their race as superior (Doc. 8). Because of this superiority, they felt as if they had to spread their race.

Countries also got involved in imperialism for the simple fact of prestige and honor. Those countries that had a lot of colonies were seen as a major world power. A lot of benefits came with having colonies. A country looked better to the outside world if it controlled a great number of colonies. European leaders used their new colonies to enhance their status and give off a better impression.

New Imperialism was a profitable time for Europe. Taking over new colonies was the result of many reasons, such as wanting more natural resources and more prestige. Europe changed dramatically during this time.

Reader's Comments on Part A: Second Sample Student DBQ Essay

- The thesis statement is never made.
- Insufficient amount of documents listed.
- No supporting data when listing documents.
- Little or no outside relevant information.
- Conclusion is weak.

Possible student score: 1–3

Part B: First Sample Student Thematic Essay, Group 1–1

Martin Luther (1483–1564) and John Calvin (1509–1564) were in agreement that religious authority rested with the Bible and not the pope. The Bible was the final authority because each individual could read it and determine church practices and doctrine. There was no need for the pope or any higher authority. However, Luther and Calvin disagreed on how to interpret and apply the Scriptures to the community of believers. One of Luther's major doctrines was "justification by faith alone." From reading and pondering St. Paul's letter to the Romans (1:17) found in the New Testament, Luther concluded that what justifies a good man is not what the church knows as works (prayers, the sacraments, and indulgences) but faith alone. Luther rejected the church doctrine that good deeds were necessary for salvation. The Catholic Church, however, never really taught that indulgences or good works could compensate for the evils of sin. Luther believed that a man did not earn grace by good living; he did good because he possessed the grace of God.

Luther's faith in the Bible and the power of the individual to read and reflect on scriptures led to the conclusion that the church consisted of the entire community of Christian believers. Luther believed that every person should serve God in his or her individual calling. Medieval churchmen, however, had tended to identify the church with their clergy. Luther, like most Protestants, agreed that the clergy was unnecessary except to serve as pastors of a congregation.

There were two main differences between Calvin and Luther. Calvin had his own ideas about the power of God, the nature of human beings, and the power of the state. Luther had rejected St. Augustine's idea of predestination. Calvin in The Institutes of Christian Religion made predestination the cornerstone of his religious beliefs. Calvin believed that human beings did not have free will because that would take away from the power of God. Man could not actively work to achieve salvation. God decides (predetermines) at the beginning of time who would be saved and who would be damned. Those predestined for salvation could be identified by their virtuous lives. In time, the elect could be determined by their economic and material success.

Unlike Luther, Calvin did not believe that the church should be ruled by the state. Calvinists did not recognize the subordination of the church to the state or the right of any government, king, or parliament to lay down laws for religion. Calvin believed in setting up a theocratic government run by church leaders.

Luther and Calvin agreed on the basic issues of the authority of the pope and the role of the individual in the church. However, they disagreed on how to interpret the role of God and the individual in society.

Reader's Comments on Part B: First Sample Student Thematic Essay, Group 1–1

- Thesis is stated clearly and developed throughout the essay.
- Specifically accounts for the differences between Luther and Calvin.
- Supports thesis with specific information, with references to St. Paul, St. Augustine.
- Conclusion could be stronger.

Possible student score: 7–9 (more toward the lower end of the scale)

Part B: Second Sample Student Thematic Essay, Group 1–1

Martin Luther and John Calvin both brought new ideas about religion to their countries. They both definitely saw flaws in the Roman Catholic Church as it was. While they did agree on some major concepts, they did not see eye to eye on some issues.

Luther and Calvin both acknowledged that there was really no need for a pope in the church. They believed that real authority came from the Bible and not from what a priest said or did.

Luther, unlike Calvin, felt that the church should be run by the state. He also believed that an individual could interpret and reflect on the Bible in his/her own way. Luther also claimed that faith alone was good enough to achieve salvation.

Calvin did not believe in the church and state being separate. He hoped for a government ruled by the leaders of the church. The main idea behind Calvinism was the concept of predestination. Calvin did not feel that a person could do anything during his/her life to help achieve salvation. Luther did not believe in predestination.

Luther and Calvin were both pioneers in bringing about changes in how people practiced and viewed religion. They both were committed to correcting the flaws in the Roman Catholic Church. However, they failed to agree on certain ideas, which led to the creation of two different religions—Lutheranism and Calvinism.

Reader's Comments on Part B: Second Sample Student Thematic Essay, Group 1–1

- Thesis statement is poorly made.
- Organization is weak.
- No elaboration of differences, such as Luther's views on the state.
- Fails to analyze the importance of predestination.

Possible student score: 1–3

Part B: First Sample Student Thematic Essay, Group 1–2

John Locke and Jean Jacques Rousseau agreed about man and the state of nature and the meaning of the social contract but drew different conclusions from these basic areas of agreement. John Locke was a political thinker and Jean Jacques Rousseau was a social philosopher. Locke's *Two Treatises on Government* and Rousseau's *Social Contract* would influence political thinkers for many years. John Locke, who was born into an Anglican family with Puritan leanings, was forced to flee England during the reign of Charles II (1660–1685) for his liberal views. In 1689, after James II was overthrown, Locke returned to England. In 1690, he published the *Two Treatises on Government* to justify the English Parliament in the Glorious Revolution. Locke argued that James II had violated nature's law and deserved to be deposed. Locke asserted that men are born free in the state of nature where they are happy, free, and entitled to the natural right of life, liberty, and property. To protect these rights, men formed societies by a social contract and transferred to the government the obligation of safeguarding these rights. If the government, which was party to the compact, failed to live up to this contract, the people have a right to overthrow it. This is what happened in England in 1688 and James II deserved to be deposed.

Jean Jacques Rousseau (1712–1778) was born into a poor family and led a disorganized life and felt uncomfortable in the social world of the Enlightenment. His book *The Social Contract* was published in France in 1762. Rousseau began with Locke's ideas of the state of nature but he arrived at a different conclusion. He believed like Locke that man in the state of nature had certain rights. However, they disagreed after this. After people enter into a social contract to form a government, they give up all their rights to the control of the community and must submit to the general will. The general will is a kind of ideal representing what was best for the whole state, a will for the general good. If someone disagreed with the general will, it became necessary to "force a man to be free." The general will controls everything.

Locke and Rousseau began with the belief in the natural law and the state of nature but they reached different conclusions. Locke's ideas would influence the right of people to overthrow the government, and the right of revolution would echo throughout Europe and in the British colonies in America. Rousseau's ideas fanned the flame of revolution, but dictators have used his focus on the right of the community over the individual in order to justify their undemocratic governments.

Reader's Comments on Part B: First Sample Student Thematic Essay, Group 1–2

- Thesis is clearly stated but simplistic.
- Specifically points out the areas of agreement but also differences between Locke and Rousseau (general will; rights of individual versus community).
- Fails to evaluate the full implication of the general will.
- The conclusion is good.

Possible student score: 4–5

Part B: Second Sample Student Thematic Essay, Group 1–2

John Locke and Jean Jacques Rousseau were two political thinkers who promoted the belief in the social contract and the state of nature. Locke wrote at the time of the Glorious Revolution and Rousseau wrote during the French Revolution. Locke and Rousseau believed in a social contract in which people entered to establish a government. Locke believed that this social contract or compact insured that Great Britain's government would protect the rights of the people.

Rousseau believed that government was a contract but the community was more important than the person. This idea led to problems for future years. The question of what was the general will lead to problems about the meaning of the social contract. Locke's social contract led to democracy.

Both Locke and Rousseau agreed on a social contract but disagreed on how society should interpret it.

Reader's Comments on Part B: Second Sample Student Thematic Essay, Group 1–2

- There is no thesis statement.
- There is no real analysis of how Locke and Rousseau differ on the Social Contract.
- There are factual errors, such as that Rousseau did not write during the French Revolution. (He died in 1778.)
- The essay does not refer to the bodies of work of Locke and Rousseau.
- The essay is very superficial.

Possible student score: 1–3

Part B: First Sample Student Thematic Essay, Group 1–3

Peter the Great was one of Russia's most influential leaders. Throughout his 36-year rule, he strove to constantly ensure that Russia became more modern—thus, more Western. He also ceaselessly built up and reformed the Russian army. While many of Peter the Great's reforms had positive effects on Russia, when his reign ended in 1725, the state of Russia was still very uncertain, and was not fully modernized.

Although Peter the Great came to the Russian throne in 1682 at the age of ten, he did not take control of the government until seven years later. Peter was not well educated, but his immense curiosity played a role in how he ruled. In the late seventeenth century, Peter traveled to European cities to observe their political, social, and economical practices. He took back to Russia not only his observations on life in Western Europe, but also a group of scholars, soldiers, and noblemen whom he had recruited and gathered throughout his travels. He would use these people and his observations to modernize Russia.

One of Peter the Great's most sweeping reforms was that of the Russian army. Before Peter's reign, the army was feeble, with part-time soldiers who were unskilled in modern military techniques. To improve Russia's military, Peter required that all noblemen serve in the army, or in civil service. In recognition of the skilled nature of many Western armies, Peter set up schools and universities to teach his noble soldiers the correct military techniques. Peter established a standing, regular army of 200,000 men, mainly commoners, who were required to serve in the military.

In addition to changes to Russia's military, Peter the Great felt it necessary to centralize his power, and he did so by bringing all Russians—including the Orthodox Church—under his control. He insisted that all of Russia would follow the European calendar, with the New Year starting on January 1, rather than on September 1. In response to the practices he had observed while in Western Europe, Peter insisted that nobles shave their beards and dress in modern, Western-style clothing, in place of their old-fashioned robes and beards. Women were no longer required to veil their faces in public and were not required to seclude themselves in their houses. He invited women to his lavish parties, much to the disapproval of many citizens. In addition, Peter put an end to arranged marriages.

By the end of Peter the Great's reign, Russia had made great strides in many other areas. He increased the number of factories in Russia, and encouraged the exportation of Russian goods. Peter was responsible for making potatoes the staple crop of Russia. He simplified the Russian alphabet and developed Russia's system of education by forming academies to study mathematics, engineering, and science.

The greatest symbol of Peter's reign was the capital city of St. Petersburg. Located near the Baltic coast, St. Petersburg was a lavish city that was built mainly because Peter forced thousands of serfs to drain the swamps near the city. Many of these serfs died in the process, but after their work was done, Peter brought Italian architects and artisans to design a "Western" city.

Despite these numerous reforms and advances, Peter the Great was not entirely successful in modernizing Russia—for example, he failed to gain a warm water port that could remain open year round. During his 36-year rule, Peter and his army were constantly engaged in battle, yet Peter's territorial gains were minimal, at best. In general, Peter the Great did not leave a lasting legacy upon his death in 1725. Because he ruled primarily by fear tactics, many of his policies did not last after his death.

Peter the Great's biggest failure was his reliance on serfdom. The serfs who had helped to build his "window to the West" were actually holding Russia back from true modernization. As Peter continued to bring Western ideas into Russia, the divide between the poor and the educated elite widened. There was great hatred of Peter among those who were forced to work the land as serfs, as they saw no benefits to Peter's modernization. By clinging to a system of serfdom that had long been abolished in the rest of Europe, Peter the Great failed to fully modernize and Westernize Russia.

Reader's Comments on Part B: First Sample Student Thematic Essay, Group 1–3

- Information is organized and fully supports the thesis.
- Good factual information about Peter's efforts to improve the military life at the court. However, there is an error in the number of years that he ruled. (It should be 43, not 36.)
- Conclusion is detailed and analytical.

Possible student score: 8–9

Part B: Second Sample Student Thematic Essay, Group 1–3

Peter the Great ruled Russia from the late seventeenth century until the early eighteenth century. He tried to Westernize Russia through various economic and social reforms. He also built up the Russian military. His reforms were very successful and Russia became more like the other Western European nations due to Peter's reign.

Peter the Great wanted to make Russia as modern as other Western European nations. He studied other countries' political, economic, and social systems and used what he had learned in ruling Russia. His ultimate goal was to make Russia the most powerful and modern nation in Europe.

Peter improved Russia's economy by building more factories and trading with other countries. He also improved Russia's system of education. He treated women better, and invited them to parties at his castles. Peter forced men to shave their beards and made them dress the way people in the West were dressing. He tried to control all aspects of Russia, including religion. He did not let Russian Orthodox citizens practice their religion freely.

Peter greatly improved Russia's military. He made it more similar to armies in Western European countries, and he forced Russian noblemen to serve in the army. He also forced the peasants to serve in the army, so that Russia would have a full-time military. This was one way that he saw he could be more like Western European nations. He also taught the noblemen in his army how to fight properly.

Peter was a harsh leader. He relied on serfs to make many of his reforms. Serfs built Peter's capital city of St. Petersburg, and many of them died in the process. St. Petersburg was Peter the Great's vision of Westernization, and he achieved his goal at any cost, even if it meant the death of his citizens.

Peter's reforms were both good and bad for Russia. He did help to modernize Russia, although he treated the Russian peasants very poorly. This prevented Russia from being as modern a nation as possible.

Reader's Comments on Part B: Second Sample Student Thematic Essay, Group 1–3

- Thesis statement is weak.
- Factual information is weak, too general.
- Some information is inaccurate: Peter the Great did allow the Russians to practice their religion.
- Very superficial treatment.
- Conclusion is weak.

Possible student score: 2–3

Part B: First Sample Student Thematic Essay, Group 2–1

The Versailles Treaty that ended World War I provided a temporary truce between England and France for dominance on the European continent. On November 11, 1918, Germany had signed the Armistice with the Western powers based on the belief that President Woodrow Wilson's ideals of the Fourteen Points would be the basis of the negotiated peace treaty. When the new German government, the Weimar Republic, refused to sign the treaty because of its harshness, the Western leaders informed Germany that they had to sign it or be prepared to resume hostilities. The severe restriction of the Versailles Treaty led to the belief in Germany that the country had been "stabbed in the back." This slogan would provide the rallying cry for the Nazis' rise to power, whose main goal was to readdress the injustices of the Versailles Treaty.

The Versailles Treaty created bitterness among the German people. Germany resented Article 231, the War Guilt Clause, which required them to accept full responsibility for the war and pay the reparation costs that amounted to over $132 billion. The Germans also were angry that their military force was limited to 100,000 men, and Germany was stripped of its overseas colonies.

Adolf Hitler and the Nazis exploited this bitterness and focused on nationalists who refused to accept their defeat in World War I. Although Hitler and his National Socialist Party never received a majority of the votes, he was to portray the Weimar Republic as the government that had betrayed Germany. The economic condition of runaway inflation caused by the reparations debt imposed by the Versailles Treaty added to the discontent towards the Weimar Republic.

Hitler was also able to appeal to the extreme nationalists because he pointed out that the Versailles Treaty had removed valuable lands from the German Empire. Hitler struck a responsive chord with the German people when he demanded that the Sudetenland, a region of Czechoslovakia where German-speaking people lived, be returned. Germans were also angry that they had lost Danzig to Poland in the Versailles Treaty. Danzig, which had been an old German town, was given to Poland so that Poland could have an outlet to the sea, but it cut off the bulk of Germany from East Prussia.

Other countries also resented the Versailles Treaty. Italy had walked out of the conference because it did not get all the land it wanted. The United States rejected the treaty and the League of Nations' effectiveness was diminished. Japan was angry that the West refused to recognize its claims in China. Russia was angry because it had been excluded from the conference and lost the Baltic States. By the 1930s, England and France began to believe that the Versailles Treaty was unfair and that Hitler was correct in seeking to address the injustices. The Versailles Treaty did lay the seeds of distrust that led to World War II. The treaty was a factor that led to World War II, but the economic crisis created by the Great Depression and Adolf Hitler's ideas, leadership, and his ability to exploit these conditions also led to World War II.

Reader's Comments on Part B: First Sample Student Thematic Essay, Group 2–1

- Thesis is clearly stated.
- The essay addresses the specific criticisms of the Versailles Treaty.
- Uses good detail and linkage with Versailles and the German people.
- The section on Hitler is well developed.
- Could have developed the conclusion more.

Possible student score: 7–9

Part B: Second Sample Student Thematic Essay, Group 2–1

Many people believe that the Treaty of Versailles was one of the biggest reasons for World War II. The Treaty of Versailles ended World War I. It placed blame for the war on Germany, and made Germany pay other countries many billions of dollars. The people of Germany were very angry because of this, and they began to resent that the rest of Europe made them take all the blame for World War I. Germany felt that they had been unfairly blamed for the first World War.

The Treaty of Versailles also required that the Germans have a much smaller army than they did at the start of World War I. This part of the treaty was an attempt to try to stop something like World War I from happening again. Germany resented this clause of the treaty, and their resentment eventually led to World War II.

While the Treaty of Versailles did not start World War II, it played a big role because the Germans felt angry because of what they had been forced to accept. Adolf Hitler, the man behind the start of World War II, used the anger of the German people to rise to power. After World War I, Germany's economy was bad and it was hard for people to find jobs. People became more and more angry, and blamed their bad situation on the Treaty of Versailles, which had forced Germany to pay billions of dollars to other European nations.

The Treaty of Versailles, which ended World War I, played a major role in the cause of World War II. The German people were angry at having to accept complete blame for the war, and Adolf Hitler capitalized on this anger. His rule eventually led to World War II.

Reader's Comments on Part B: Second Sample Student Thematic Essay, Group 2–1

- Factual information is weak.
- No details about Hitler or the Great Depression.
- Very superficial.

Possible student score: 1–3

Part B: First Sample Student Thematic Essay, Group 2–2

At the end of World War II, most of Europe was in shambles and devastated from the war. However, out of this turmoil two super powers managed to emerge—the United States and the Soviet Union. These two countries were able to acquire enough economic resources and military might to dominate the world. Yet, with this new power came tense rivalry and a world becoming more and more divided. These tensions ultimately led to the Cold War.

The Cold War began some time after the end of World War II. It was a period of severe tension and hostility between the West and the Soviet Union without actual armed conflicts between the nations. The cause of this tension rested in the fact that Stalin in Eastern Europe had very different goals as compared to the Western powers.

As a result of seeing the horrors of the Nazi regime, the United States became an even bigger supporter of democracy. The Unites States believed that strengthening democracy would ensure tolerance and peace. Most Western Allies built new governments that focused on democratic constitutions to protect the rights of all citizens. The teaching of democratic principles was emphasized throughout the West.

Stalin, the leader of Russia at this time, had a different view about how to govern a country. He wanted Communism to spread throughout his country. Stalin also wished to protect Russia from any further invasions by the Germans. Stalin had his Red Army occupy lands in Eastern Europe. Stalin hoped that the West would accept this occupation.

However, Western leaders, such as Roosevelt and Churchill, did not agree to such a thing. They both rejected Stalin's view. Stalin chose to ignore the West's arguments and managed to install pro-Soviet Communist governments through out Eastern Europe. This was done by destroying all rival political parties and even assassinating democratic leaders.

These acts committed by Stalin further increased the tension between Eastern Europe and the West. Churchill claimed that an "Iron Curtain" had descended across the continent. This term expressed the growing fear of Communism, which led to greater tensions. The United States took a bigger stand on democracy. In 1947, President Truman wrote a policy that stated that the United States would support any people who were trying to resist outside pressures. This policy came to be known as the Truman Doctrine. He made it clear to Stalin and all of Eastern Europe that the U.S. would resist any sort of expansion of Communism no matter where or at what cost. This policy instilled more fear in the East and helped to further increase tensions. The Marshall Plan, which assisted democratic countries who were in economic need, further angered Stalin. Tensions over Germany led to the Berlin Blockade, which was resolved by a dramatic airlift that only added to the tensions between the West and the Soviet Union. In 1949, the creation of NATO, a defensive alliance against the spread of Communism, resulted in the formation of the Warsaw Pact by the Soviet bloc of nations. Tension between the United States and Russia was also escalated by the nuclear race. The arms race created the fear that nuclear warfare was a possibility and could destroy the world.

Both sides made many efforts to support their cause. The West, led by the United States, stood firm in its belief that democracy was the best government and that the spread of Communism had to be contained. The Soviet Union under Stalin was determined to ensure the supremacy of the Soviet Empire. These two opposing views led to the intense rivalry of the Cold War, which lasted for over 40 years.

Reader's Comments on Part B: First Sample Student Thematic Essay, Group 2–2

- The thesis statement is good.
- The essay is rich in detail but lacks analysis.
- Superficial treatment of the Iron Curtain, Truman Doctrine, and Marshall Plan.
- Conclusion is weak.

Possible student score: 5–7

Part B: Second Sample Student Thematic Essay, Group 2–2

There were many reasons why a Cold War existed between the West and the East after 1945. This war, which was called a Cold War because it did not involve any armed conflict between nations, led to over 40 years of severe tension between those countries that were democratic and those which were Communist.

The West, most especially the United States, believed that democracy was the best form of government. They did all that they could to spread democracy throughout the West. Stalin did not agree with the Western ideas. He felt that the best government was Communism. He spread this form of government through the East. Soon Europe was divided into the Eastern Soviet dominated region and the Western region.

Increasing tension forced both the East and the West to use all of their resources to further strengthen their side. The United States did not stay isolated but became a major world power in its support of democracy. Stalin grew more suspicious of the West, which caused the tension to mount even more. Stalin did all that he could to ensure that the East remains a strong Communist force.

The main reason behind the Cold War was the two opposing views held in the East and the West. The West supported democracy while the East claimed Communism was superior. This conflict led to severe tensions, which would last for more than 40 years and result in ongoing conflicts between the West and the East.

Reader's Comments on Part B: Second Sample Student Thematic Essay, Group 2–2

- Thesis statement is not clear.
- Few or no basic facts.
- Redundant sentence structure.
- Conclusion is poor.

Possible student score: 1–2

Part B: First Sample Student Thematic Essay, Group 2–3

Karl Marx (1818–1883) was a German writer and economist who is considered the Father of Communism. Marx wrote *The Communist Manifesto* in which he outlined his main political philosophy. Marx based his ideas in part on the teachings of the German philosopher Georg Wilhelm Friedrich Hegel, who taught that history was a dialectic that was constantly changing as new ideas came into conflict with one another.

Like Hegel, Marx believed that history was a constant conflict. However, Marx believed that economic conditions, not ideas, determined the course of history. The class that possessed the economic power controlled the government and institutions. Laws and social systems are all developed in accord with society's economic base. No ruling class has ever been willing to give up power. The only way to achieve change was through revolution. Thus, conflict between classes was inevitable. Marx asserts that history was a struggle between the "haves and have-nots." Marx pointed out that in ancient times, the conflict was between the patrician and the plebeian. In the Middle Ages the struggle was between the lord and the serf. In the present day of the industrial society, the struggle is between the capitalist and the proletariat. Marx believed that the industrial society of capitalism was only a temporary phase. As the backbone of capitalism, the proletariat was the true productive class. Marx predicted that workers (proletariat) would seize control of the government from the capitalists and build a society in which the people owned everything. Without private property there would be a classless society and the government would wither away. The last stage of history for Marx would be pure Communism in which the goal would be "from each according to his ability to each according to his needs." The Marx view of history leaves out the importance of nationalism and religion. In his appeal that "working men of all countries unite," Marx did not realize that nationalism was a major part of history. The destruction of the Berlin Wall in 1989 demonstrated that Germans were German first and then Communists. Furthermore, Marx was writing at a time when the gap between the working poor contrasted sharply with the wealthy industrialists. Marx's prediction about the workers was erroneous. By 1900, conditions in Western Europe had changed. Workers, through unions, began to improve their standards of living. Rather than overthrow the government, workers gained the right to vote and used it to correct some of the injustices. Finally, Marx's prediction about Communist revolutions occurring in an industrial country was also misguided. The Communist Revolution took place in an agricultural country which according to Marx was not ripe for revolution. The State did not wither away but became more powerful.

Although Marx's view of history as a class struggle was erroneous, his philosophy had powerful appeal to the people. Marx's belief that economics determine history was a scientific analysis of human events which guaranteed the rise of Communism and its conclusion. Like religion, which guaranteed paradise in the afterlife, Marx promised happiness on earth. Marx's appeal was that he made Communism into a material religion.

Reader's Comments on Part B: First Sample Student Thematic Essay, Group 2–3

- Thesis statement is not clear.
- Rich in facts, but misplaced information. Marx's economic ideas are contained in *Das Kapital* and reference to Hegel should be Wilhelm Friedrich Hegel.
- Good analysis of errors behind Marx's ideas.
- Conclusion is creative but needs greater analysis.

Possible student score: 7–8

Part B: Second Sample Student Thematic Essay, Group 2–3

Marx's view that all history was a class struggle helped to explain why society developed as it did in the past. In 1848, Karl Marx wrote *The Communist Manifesto* in response to the problems created by the Industrial Revolution. Marx believed that the difficult conditions that existed under capitalism made it inevitable that Communism would be successful. The problems of society were so bad that the worker thought he had no hope for the future. He worked 10–12 hours per day and there was no protection against accidents. Marx predicted that when the Communists gained control of society there would not be a division between workers and owners. A classless society would develop and the lack of goods would no longer create conflict.

In history, Marx predicted that there has always been a class struggle because the rich always seem to be getting richer by exploiting the poor. Under Communism, this exploitation would stop because there would no longer be any private property. Marx also predicted that there would be worldwide revolutions that would affect every country. Marx's prediction, however, never came true because Communism only came to Russia and China.

Reader's Comments on Part B: Second Sample Student Thematic Essay, Group 2–3

- Thesis statement is not clear.
- No analysis of facts such as the difficult conditions during the Industrial Revolution.
- Very general, no details.

Possible student score: 1–3

Answer Sheet for Sample Practice Exam II

Remove this sheet and use it to mark your answers for the multiple-choice section of Sample Practice Exam II.

CUT HERE

1 Ⓐ Ⓑ Ⓒ Ⓓ Ⓔ	21 Ⓐ Ⓑ Ⓒ Ⓓ Ⓔ	41 Ⓐ Ⓑ Ⓒ Ⓓ Ⓔ	61 Ⓐ Ⓑ Ⓒ Ⓓ Ⓔ
2 Ⓐ Ⓑ Ⓒ Ⓓ Ⓔ	22 Ⓐ Ⓑ Ⓒ Ⓓ Ⓔ	42 Ⓐ Ⓑ Ⓒ Ⓓ Ⓔ	62 Ⓐ Ⓑ Ⓒ Ⓓ Ⓔ
3 Ⓐ Ⓑ Ⓒ Ⓓ Ⓔ	23 Ⓐ Ⓑ Ⓒ Ⓓ Ⓔ	43 Ⓐ Ⓑ Ⓒ Ⓓ Ⓔ	63 Ⓐ Ⓑ Ⓒ Ⓓ Ⓔ
4 Ⓐ Ⓑ Ⓒ Ⓓ Ⓔ	24 Ⓐ Ⓑ Ⓒ Ⓓ Ⓔ	44 Ⓐ Ⓑ Ⓒ Ⓓ Ⓔ	64 Ⓐ Ⓑ Ⓒ Ⓓ Ⓔ
5 Ⓐ Ⓑ Ⓒ Ⓓ Ⓔ	25 Ⓐ Ⓑ Ⓒ Ⓓ Ⓔ	45 Ⓐ Ⓑ Ⓒ Ⓓ Ⓔ	65 Ⓐ Ⓑ Ⓒ Ⓓ Ⓔ
6 Ⓐ Ⓑ Ⓒ Ⓓ Ⓔ	26 Ⓐ Ⓑ Ⓒ Ⓓ Ⓔ	46 Ⓐ Ⓑ Ⓒ Ⓓ Ⓔ	66 Ⓐ Ⓑ Ⓒ Ⓓ Ⓔ
7 Ⓐ Ⓑ Ⓒ Ⓓ Ⓔ	27 Ⓐ Ⓑ Ⓒ Ⓓ Ⓔ	47 Ⓐ Ⓑ Ⓒ Ⓓ Ⓔ	67 Ⓐ Ⓑ Ⓒ Ⓓ Ⓔ
8 Ⓐ Ⓑ Ⓒ Ⓓ Ⓔ	28 Ⓐ Ⓑ Ⓒ Ⓓ Ⓔ	48 Ⓐ Ⓑ Ⓒ Ⓓ Ⓔ	68 Ⓐ Ⓑ Ⓒ Ⓓ Ⓔ
9 Ⓐ Ⓑ Ⓒ Ⓓ Ⓔ	29 Ⓐ Ⓑ Ⓒ Ⓓ Ⓔ	49 Ⓐ Ⓑ Ⓒ Ⓓ Ⓔ	69 Ⓐ Ⓑ Ⓒ Ⓓ Ⓔ
10 Ⓐ Ⓑ Ⓒ Ⓓ Ⓔ	30 Ⓐ Ⓑ Ⓒ Ⓓ Ⓔ	50 Ⓐ Ⓑ Ⓒ Ⓓ Ⓔ	70 Ⓐ Ⓑ Ⓒ Ⓓ Ⓔ
11 Ⓐ Ⓑ Ⓒ Ⓓ Ⓔ	31 Ⓐ Ⓑ Ⓒ Ⓓ Ⓔ	51 Ⓐ Ⓑ Ⓒ Ⓓ Ⓔ	71 Ⓐ Ⓑ Ⓒ Ⓓ Ⓔ
12 Ⓐ Ⓑ Ⓒ Ⓓ Ⓔ	32 Ⓐ Ⓑ Ⓒ Ⓓ Ⓔ	52 Ⓐ Ⓑ Ⓒ Ⓓ Ⓔ	72 Ⓐ Ⓑ Ⓒ Ⓓ Ⓔ
13 Ⓐ Ⓑ Ⓒ Ⓓ Ⓔ	33 Ⓐ Ⓑ Ⓒ Ⓓ Ⓔ	53 Ⓐ Ⓑ Ⓒ Ⓓ Ⓔ	73 Ⓐ Ⓑ Ⓒ Ⓓ Ⓔ
14 Ⓐ Ⓑ Ⓒ Ⓓ Ⓔ	34 Ⓐ Ⓑ Ⓒ Ⓓ Ⓔ	54 Ⓐ Ⓑ Ⓒ Ⓓ Ⓔ	74 Ⓐ Ⓑ Ⓒ Ⓓ Ⓔ
15 Ⓐ Ⓑ Ⓒ Ⓓ Ⓔ	35 Ⓐ Ⓑ Ⓒ Ⓓ Ⓔ	55 Ⓐ Ⓑ Ⓒ Ⓓ Ⓔ	75 Ⓐ Ⓑ Ⓒ Ⓓ Ⓔ
16 Ⓐ Ⓑ Ⓒ Ⓓ Ⓔ	36 Ⓐ Ⓑ Ⓒ Ⓓ Ⓔ	56 Ⓐ Ⓑ Ⓒ Ⓓ Ⓔ	76 Ⓐ Ⓑ Ⓒ Ⓓ Ⓔ
17 Ⓐ Ⓑ Ⓒ Ⓓ Ⓔ	37 Ⓐ Ⓑ Ⓒ Ⓓ Ⓔ	57 Ⓐ Ⓑ Ⓒ Ⓓ Ⓔ	77 Ⓐ Ⓑ Ⓒ Ⓓ Ⓔ
18 Ⓐ Ⓑ Ⓒ Ⓓ Ⓔ	38 Ⓐ Ⓑ Ⓒ Ⓓ Ⓔ	58 Ⓐ Ⓑ Ⓒ Ⓓ Ⓔ	78 Ⓐ Ⓑ Ⓒ Ⓓ Ⓔ
19 Ⓐ Ⓑ Ⓒ Ⓓ Ⓔ	39 Ⓐ Ⓑ Ⓒ Ⓓ Ⓔ	59 Ⓐ Ⓑ Ⓒ Ⓓ Ⓔ	79 Ⓐ Ⓑ Ⓒ Ⓓ Ⓔ
20 Ⓐ Ⓑ Ⓒ Ⓓ Ⓔ	40 Ⓐ Ⓑ Ⓒ Ⓓ Ⓔ	60 Ⓐ Ⓑ Ⓒ Ⓓ Ⓔ	80 Ⓐ Ⓑ Ⓒ Ⓓ Ⓔ

Section I: Multiple-Choice Questions

Time: 55 minutes
80 Questions
Percent of total grade = 50%

Directions: Each of the questions or incomplete statements below is followed by five suggested answers or completions. Select the one that is best in each case and then fill in the corresponding oval on the answer sheet.

1. *Détente* resulted in all of the following EXCEPT

   A. the signing of the SALT Accords.
   B. the Helsinki Pact.
   C. President Nixon's visit to Moscow.
   D. the revocation of the Brezhnev Doctrine.
   E. the Soviet invasion of Afghanistan.

2. The beginning of World War I was sparked by the assassination of

   A. Czar Nicholas II.
   B. Otto von Bismarck.
   C. Archduke Francis Ferdinand.
   D. Emperor Franz Joseph I.
   E. Kaiser Wilhelm II.

3. The Renaissance was different from the Middle Ages in all of the following ways EXCEPT

   A. studying of the civilizations of Greece and Rome was stressed.
   B. kings centralized the power of government.
   C. the secular world was emphasized.
   D. the individual was glorified.
   E. the Church was the dominant institution in society.

4. Which of the following statesmen insisted that Italy was only a "geographic expression"?

   A. Metternich
   B. Cavour
   C. Bismarck
   D. Louis Napoleon
   E. Napoleon I

5. *Lettres de cachet* were symbols of

   A. French toleration of differences.
   B. the absolutism of the French monarchy.
   C. France's economic supremacy.
   D. the bourgeoisie's attempts at revolting against the monarchy.
   E. a series of reforms that tried to improve peasant life in France.

6. The Final Solution refers to

   A. Hitler's plan to attack the Soviet Union.
   B. the Allied plan to begin the Second Front against Germany.
   C. the plan to exterminate Europe's Jewish population.
   D. the Allied plan to bomb Germany's cities.
   E. Hitler's decision to attack Poland.

7. The Protestant Reformation was similar to the Renaissance because

   A. it emphasized the importance of the individual, and faith in the ability of human reason.
   B. the influence of the Church increased.
   C. political rulers became less important.
   D. education focused on the classical texts of Greece and Rome.
   E. Florence flourished as the major intellectual and cultural center.

8. A common similarity between the Renaissance and the Enlightenment is that both

   A. promoted traditional values.
   B. supported democracy.
   C. encouraged a belief in the futility of life.
   D. produced major cultural changes.
   E. encouraged the importance of religion as a stabilizing force in society.

9. Which of the following nations was NOT a member of the original European Common Market?

 A. West Germany
 B. France
 C. Great Britain
 D. Italy
 E. Belgium

10. What was one of the main characteristics of English absolutism in the seventeenth century?

 A. English kings were successful in ruling without Parliament.
 B. Absolutism in England stressed the role of the Church.
 C. England's constitutional absolutism limited the power of the king.
 D. The English monarchy had the support of the Puritans.
 E. The Tudor and Stuart monarchs were popular with the people.

11. Louis Blanc promoted a program that included

 A. national workshops supported by the government.
 B. unions for workers.
 C. government seizure of all property belonging to individuals.
 D. a worldwide revolution.
 E. government support of unemployment insurance.

12. Which of the following countries never became a subject of imperialism?

 A. China
 B. India
 C. Japan
 D. Egypt
 E. Morocco

13. "When France sneezes, Europe catches a cold."

 What event would have caused Metternich to make this statement?

 A. The July Revolution of 1830 in France
 B. The election of Louis-Philippe as king of France
 C. The election of Louis Napoleon as president of the Second French Republic in 1848
 D. The forming of the Quadruple Alliance
 E. The Peterloo Massacre

14. The most important officials in the provisional government of Russia in 1917 were the

 A. Bolsheviks and Socialists.
 B. Socialists and Czarists.
 C. Mensheviks and Socialists.
 D. Bolsheviks and Liberals.
 E. Liberals and Socialists.

15. What factor contributed to Yugoslavia's success in not falling under Soviet control?

 A. Marshal Tito's aggressive military campaign
 B. Yugoslavia did not border the Soviet Union
 C. A treaty between the Soviet Union and Yugoslavia
 D. Military aid from the United States
 E. Protection from Britain

16. All of the following were problems faced by Russia in 1991 EXCEPT

 A. runaway inflation.
 B. ethnic tensions in many parts of Russia.
 C. decline in the quality of life.
 D. lack of stable leadership by Boris Yeltsin.
 E. fear of a military coup by former members of the Communist Party.

17. "The Sicilians are fighting against the enemies of Italy. It is the duty of every Italian to succor them . . . to arms. Let me put an end . . . to the miseries of so many centuries."

The author of this passage was

A. Giuseppe Garibaldi.
B. Giuseppe Mazzini.
C. Camillo Cavour.
D. Victor Emmanuel.
E. Napoleon III.

18. The terms, "White Man's Burden" and "Scramble for Africa," refer to a time period in history known as the

A. Age of Discovery.
B. Age of Imperialism.
C. Age of Nationalism.
D. Cold War Era.
E. Industrial Revolution.

19. Which of the following was a factor in the success of the Tudor monarchy in England?

A. They had no real authority and let Parliament make all government decisions.
B. Parliament was never consulted.
C. They acquired many colonies overseas in regions such as Asia and Africa.
D. They maintained peaceful relations with the Catholic Church.
E. The Tudors ruled absolutely while consulting with Parliament.

20. Which one of the following inventors is correctly associated with his invention during the Agricultural Revolution?

A. Jethro Tull—scientific breeding of animals
B. Robert Blackwell—self-cleaning steel plow
C. Charles Newbold—the reaper
D. Charles "Turnip" Townshend—crop rotation
E. John Deere—the seed drill

21. The Edict of Nantes in France granted religious freedom to the

A. Catholics.
B. Jews.
C. Huguenots.
D. Baptists.
E. Anglicans.

22. The greatest influence in spreading the ideas of the Renaissance from Italy to other parts of the world was

A. the wealth of the Medici family.
B. humanists traveling to other parts of Europe, preaching their ideas.
C. the invention of movable metal type and the printing press.
D. the patronage of painters in Italy.
E. the opening of new schools to teach Renaissance ideals.

23. Newton is considered the greatest figure of the Scientific Revolution because he

A. introduced Scientific Method.
B. established a school of astronomy.
C. established the existence of God as a daily presence in life.
D. developed mathematical laws to explain the orderly manner in which planets revolved around the sun.
E. introduced the laws of universal gravitation, which supported the medieval view of the universe.

24. After World War II, Soviet domination of Eastern Europe was most directly the result of

A. the United States' policy of isolationism.
B. growing democratic movements.
C. peace agreements supported by the United Nations.
D. Soviet military occupation of the region.
E. secret treaties between the Soviet Union and other Eastern European nations.

25. Which of the following had the greatest impact on the growth of employment in England between 1914 and 1918?

    A. Introduction of the assembly line in the production of manufactured goods
    B. An increase in factory and military jobs caused by World War I
    C. Development of economic opportunities in the British Empire
    D. Investments by American businesses in England
    E. The expansion of the British economy due to their investments in new industries in the United States

26. All of the following were results of World War I EXCEPT

    A. the Ottoman Empire was destroyed.
    B. communism was established in Russia.
    C. the economies of Europe were weakened.
    D. Russia emerged as a leading world power.
    E. the Hapsburgs of Austria-Hungary and the Romanov Dynasty of Russia collapsed.

27. Hitler's first violation of the Treaty of Versailles was his

    A. occupation of the Rhineland.
    B. remilitarization of Germany.
    C. invasion of Russia.
    D. signing of the agreement with Fascist Italy.
    E. annexation of Austria.

28. An immediate effect of the Declaration of Pillnitz was that

    A. the French received military support from other European nations.
    B. the French received financial support from other European nations.
    C. the people of Prussia and Austria began their own revolutions.
    D. France declared war on Austria.
    E. Austria and Prussia declared war on each other.

29. Which of the following problems did NOT contribute to the Protestant Reformation?

    A. Sales of indulgences by priests
    B. Simony
    C. The Great Schism
    D. Nepotism
    E. The rise of reform leaders John Wycliffe and Jan Hus

30. The Peace of Westphalia

    A. denied Lutherans religious freedom.
    B. increased the strength of the papacy.
    C. marked the end of the Thirty Years' War.
    D. revoked the Peace of Augsburg.
    E. weakened the strength of German princes.

31. This late-nineteenth-century cartoon best illustrates the principles of

Credit: The Granger Collection, New York.

A. imperialism.
B. nationalism.
C. ethnocentrism.
D. industrialism.
E. isolationism.

32. A major issue dividing the delegates at the Frankfurt Assembly of 1848 was

A. a disagreement over whether the Zollverein should be continued.
B. the need to address relations between a united Germany and France.
C. how to establish closer ties with Russia.
D. the status of Protestantism in Northern Germany and Catholicism in Southern Germany.
E. the struggle between those delegates who wanted to include the German-speaking province of Austria under German rule and those who wanted to exclude them.

33. Mikhail Gorbachev's reforms included *perestroika,* which refers to

A. the introduction of a police state in certain violent regions.
B. lowered price caps on agricultural goods.
C. economic restructuring that allowed some capitalist ventures.
D. rations for food, clothes, and other necessities.
E. free elections.

34. Northern Humanists interpreted the ideas of the Italian Renaissance by

    A. emphasizing Italian art.
    B. paying more attention to Biblical and early Christian themes.
    C. stressing more of a secular view.
    D. using vernacular language.
    E. supporting the study of poetry, history, astronomy, and music.

35. The statue of this Enlightenment figure in Warsaw, Poland represents

Credit: (User: Halibutt/GFDL)

    A. Johannes Kepler.
    B. Nicholas Copernicus.
    C. René Descartes.
    D. Tycho Brahe.
    E. Francis Bacon.

36. A major component of Calvinism was John Calvin's belief that

    A. man was born a sinner and God had already determined who was going to be saved and who was damned.
    B. priests were needed to interpret the Bible.
    C. saints were a symbol of worship.
    D. doing good deeds would help one's status in the afterlife.
    E. sacraments were essential.

37. The Industrial Revolution began in England because

    A. the country was rich in natural resources such as coal and iron ore.
    B. the English government encouraged migration from its colonies as a way to gain workers for the factories.
    C. France supplied the English government with additional workers for the factories in London.
    D. the English government controlled production.
    E. the English government's social policy created a positive work ethic among the workers.

38. Which was one of the effects of the Great Depression in Europe during the 1930s?

    A. It led to the rise of fascism in Italy.
    B. It contributed to widespread dissatisfaction with communism in Russia.
    C. It created the situation that attracted supporters for the Nazi Party.
    D. It renewed support in Great Britain and France for democracy.
    E. It led to a large-scale migration to the United States.

39. The riots in Manchester, England, after the Napoleonic War in 1819 led to

    A. the Peterloo Massacre.
    B. the Government Works Program for the poor.
    C. the abolition of property qualifications for voting.
    D. the Corn Laws.
    E. limiting the power of the House of Lords.

40. In the early 1990s, Czechoslovakia

    A. expanded its territory south into Bosnia-Herzegovina.
    B. peacefully divided into two independent nations.
    C. began stockpiling nuclear weapons.
    D. became the first nation to rejoin the Warsaw Pact.
    E. resisted a United Nations invasion of Slovakia.

41. As Louis XIV's finance minister, Jean-Baptiste Colbert helped to

    A. overthrow the French throne.
    B. ensure that every class received equal treatment under Louis XIV's rule.
    C. form a strong and peaceful relationship between the monarchy and the Church.
    D. advance France's prosperity by his economic policies.
    E. promote peace in Europe.

42. All of the following are associated with Bismarck and the unification of Germany EXCEPT

    A. Helmuth von Moltke.
    B. the Franco-Prussian War.
    C. the Austro-Prussian War.
    D. the Berlin Conference of 1884.
    E. the Danish War.

43. Jeanne-Elizabeth Schmahl is considered to be a leader of

    A. the Realism movement in art.
    B. the Suffrage movement in France.
    C. Classical music of the eighteenth century.
    D. the Suffrage movement in England.
    E. social reforms in Germany.

44. Who of the following is considered an Enlightened Despot ruler?

    A. Frederick the Great
    B. Louis XIV
    C. Alexander I
    D. James I
    E. Charles V

45. Which of the following authors is associated with the literary term known as the "stream of consciousness"?

    A. Ernest Hemingway
    B. James Joyce
    C. T. S. Eliot
    D. Erich Maria Remarque
    E. F. Scott Fitzgerald

46. In the early 1800s, English Parliament represented primarily the interests of the

    A. middle class.
    B. urban workers.
    C. landed aristocracy.
    D. Anglican Church.
    E. emerging capitalist owners.

47. Critics of the New Imperialism condemned it for all of the following reasons EXCEPT

    A. imperialism benefited only the special interest groups, such as the capitalists, rather than the nations.
    B. they rejected the Social Darwinism of imperialism.
    C. imperialism was benefiting the colonies at the expense of the economy of the mother country.
    D. imperialists disregarded the culture of the colonial people.
    E. imperialists had a double standard of liberty at home but dictatorship in the colonies.

48. How did Henry VIII make the Anglican Church different from the Roman Catholic Church?

    A. The king, not the pope, was the head of the Church.
    B. The sacraments were abolished.
    C. The Bible was no longer used in services.
    D. Priests did not perform worship services.
    E. Worship services were no longer held on Sundays.

49. All of the following were achievements of Napoleon EXCEPT

   A. the Napoleonic Code.
   B. peace with the Catholic Church.
   C. the annexation of parts of the Netherlands and Belgium to France.
   D. a strengthened role and status of women in France.
   E. a modernized financial system.

50. The Lateran Treaty (1929) between Mussolini and Pope Pius XII resulted in

   A. an agreement to fight communism.
   B. recognition of the pope as the sovereign of Vatican City.
   C. the abdication of the Italian king.
   D. the return of papal lands to the different local governments in Italy.
   E. a schedule for democratic elections for a parliamentary government.

51. Which of the following events was NOT associated with Nikita Khrushchev?

   A. De-Stalinization
   B. A period of liberalization in Russia
   C. Russia's presence at the Geneva Summit
   D. Revolutions in Poland and Hungary
   E. Formation of the North Atlantic Treaty Alliance (NATO)

52. Voltaire's statement, *"écrasez l'infâme"* ("crush the horrible things"), refers to

   A. the government of Louis XIV.
   B. the Catholic Church.
   C. the military.
   D. the middle class.
   E. the poor.

53. Which of the following statements summarizes one of the major themes of Machiavelli's *The Prince*?

   A. Loyalty to a city is a foolish diversion of human devotion.
   B. The end justifies the means.
   C. In diplomacy, honesty is the best policy.
   D. Only through prayer can a man achieve his full measure of virtue.
   E. Civilization reached its lowest point during the Roman Republic.

54. One of the results of the Sadler Committee of 1832 was that it led to

   A. the formation of minimum wage laws for workers.
   B. government recognition of unions.
   C. passage of legislation regulating the employment of children in factories.
   D. a demand for social legislation.
   E. nationalization of the iron and steel industry.

55. Which of the following did NOT happen after Charles I signed the Petition of Rights?

   A. Charles ruled for 11 years without Parliament.
   B. Calvinists in Scotland revolted against Charles' attempts to impose the Anglican religion on them.
   C. Charles was unable to levy taxes without Parliament's consent.
   D. The Long Parliament ruled for 20 years and passed laws that limited the power of the king.
   E. Charles requested money from Parliament for his military expedition against Spain.

56. Which of these men composed nine symphonies, the third of which was originally intended to honor Napoleon?

   A. Ludwig van Beethoven
   B. Nicolò Paganini
   C. Victor Hugo
   D. Igor Stravinsky
   E. Franz Liszt

57. Which of the following led to Britain's declaration of war on Germany in 1914?

   A. Austria's ultimatum to Serbia
   B. Germany's invasion of Belgium
   C. Germany's invasion of Russia
   D. Russia's support of Serbia
   E. Italy's decision to remain neutral

58. In which of the following ways did the Sepoy Mutiny affect India?

   A. Great Britain relinquished government control to the British East India Company.
   B. The British government assumed direct control of India.
   C. Islam and Hinduism became recognized as state religions.
   D. Parliamentary democracy was introduced in India.
   E. India gained its independence.

59. Which was NOT a major characteristic of the Scientific Revolution of the seventeenth century?

   A. Growth of a learned society, such as the Royal Society of London
   B. Challenging of medieval superstition and general acceptance of Aristotle's theories
   C. A widespread growth of knowledge among the general population
   D. Development of a modern scientific method that stressed reason over tradition
   E. The acquisition of knowledge about the physical world

60. The painting of *Guernica* by Pablo Picasso was inspired by

   A. the Spanish Civil War (1936–1939).
   B. Hitler's rise to power.
   C. Mussolini's support of the Spanish Fascists.
   D. Italy's invasion of Ethiopia.
   E. the Nazi-Soviet Non-Aggression Pact.

61. The *Ausgleich,* or Compromise of 1867, established all of the following EXCEPT

   A. a dual monarchy in Austria-Hungary.
   B. Francis Joseph I becoming emperor.
   C. each state having its own parliament.
   D. each half of the empire gaining control of its own nationalities.
   E. a uniform educational and monetary system.

62. What impact did the reign of Louis XIV have on the Huguenots?

   A. They enjoyed a long period of religious freedom.
   B. They eventually left France because Louis XIV destroyed their property and took away their civil rights.
   C. They were sent to France's colonies to work the land.
   D. They were forced to live in poor conditions and many died from disease.
   E. They became trusted advisers and provided wise counsel to Louis XIV.

63. The Allied . . . governments . . . affirm and Germany accepts responsibility for causing all the loss and damages to which the Allied . . . governments have been subjected . . . on them by the aggression of Germany.

   In which of the following documents would this passage be found?

   A. The Atlantic Charter
   B. The Treaty of Versailles
   C. The Charter of the League of Nations
   D. The Treaty of Frankfurt
   E. The Treaty of Westphalia

64. An important result of the Revolution of 1848 in France was

   A. the return of the Bourbon Dynasty.
   B. the establishment of National Workshops as a permanent government policy.
   C. the intervention by Austria to uphold peace.
   D. the return of Charles X from England.
   E. the election of Louis Napoleon.

65. Which of the following historians coined the term "Industrial Revolution?"

   A. Arnold Toynbee
   B. Saint-Simon
   C. Leopold von Ranke
   D. Max Weber
   E. Jacob Burckhardt

66. All of the following were a result of the Catholic or Counter Reformation EXCEPT

    A. the creation of the Index of Prohibited Books in Catholic countries.
    B. the revival of the medieval Inquisition, resulting in the deaths of heretics.
    C. condemnation of abuses within the Church, such as nepotism and simony.
    D. the resurgence of more religious art.
    E. the official abolishment of the sacraments.

67. By 1807, Napoleon's Grand Empire included all of the following countries EXCEPT

    A. Great Britain.
    B. Italy.
    C. Germany.
    D. the Netherlands.
    E. Spain.

68. Which was a major theme of Humanist writers?

    A. Glorifying the individual and worldly subjects
    B. The role of religion in one's life
    C. The importance of feudalism
    D. The damaging effects of educating people through poetry and astronomy
    E. Breaking away from the ideas of the classical writers of ancient Greece

69. What area was known as the "powder keg" of Europe at the beginning of the twentieth century?

    A. The Balkans
    B. The Russian Empire
    C. The German Empire
    D. The Ottoman Empire
    E. The Unified Italian States

70. During the Cold War, the United States and the Soviet Union were reluctant to become involved in direct conflict because

    A. neither country wanted to fight a war on their soil.
    B. there was potential for global nuclear destruction.
    C. both countries received pressure from nonaligned nations.
    D. the United Nations played a role in peacekeeping.
    E. there were increased tensions in the Middle East.

WONDER HOW LONG THE HONEYMOON WILL LAST?

©CORBIS

71. This cartoon symbolizes

    A. the Nazi-Soviet Non-Aggression Pact of 1939.
    B. the formation of the Pact of Steel.
    C. the Soviet Union's support of Hitler's occupation of the Rhineland.
    D. the Soviet Union and Germany's cooperation at the Munich Conference.
    E. Germany and the Soviet Union's support for General Franco in 1939.

72. Which of the following has been one reason for opposition toward a common European currency?

   A. Nationalists believe that unity may destroy their countries' unique identities and their ability to control their economies.

   B. Fear of backlash from hostile nations

   C. The United States' negative reaction to European unity

   D. An unstable economy

   E. Unwillingness of formerly communist nations to agree to the terms necessary to achieve European unity

73. The liberties of Englishmen constitute "an *entailed inheritance* derived to us from our forefathers, and to be transmitted to our posterity; as an estate specially belonging to people of this kingdom,…"

Which of the following men would support the ideas in this passage?

   A. Jean-Jacques Rousseau

   B. Thomas Hobbes

   C. Edmund Burke

   D. John Locke

   E. Voltaire

74. "Population, when unchecked, increases in a geometrical rate. Subsistence only increased in an arithmetical ratio."

The ideas in this passage are most associated with

   A. David Ricardo.

   B. Thomas Malthus.

   C. Louis Blanc.

   D. John Locke.

   E. Karl Marx.

75. The Reform Bills of 1832, 1867, 1884, 1918, and 1928 in Britain resulted in

   A. the expansion of voting rights among men and women.

   B. the limiting of the power of the House of Commons.

   C. an increase in the power of the House of Lords.

   D. establishment of guidelines on the role of the monarchy in Great Britain.

   E. establishment of guidelines on the role of government in the economy.

76. Which best describes the philosophers of the Enlightenment?

   A. They were mainly from England and Italy.

   B. They were enthusiastic supporters of the Catholic Church.

   C. They supported absolutism.

   D. They wanted to reform society and used satire to spread their message.

   E. They rejected reason and stressed emotion.

77. Which was a major goal of the Jesuits?

   A. Combating heresy and spreading the Catholic faith

   B. Stopping the sale of indulgences

   C. Stressing the Bible as the source of salvation

   D. Demonstrating that good works were not necessary for salvation

   E. Getting rid of the seven sacraments

78. Which of the following contributed to the outbreak of the nationalist movement in the Hapsburg Empire?

   A. A common language

   B. Active support by Emperor Franz Joseph I

   C. The role of German nationalists in creating a secret national organization

   D. Several national groups, such as the Serbs, Czechs, and Slovenes, occupying the same region

   E. Support of England and France

79. The fifteenth century gave rise to the following powerful leaders EXCEPT

   A. Louis XI of France.

   B. Henry VII of England.

   C. the Medicis in Florence.

   D. Ferdinand and Isabella of Spain.

   E. Charles I of England.

80. The Hungarian nationalist who led the fight for independence against Austria in the nineteenth century was

   A. Lajos Kossuth.

   B. Ferdinand I.

   C. János Kádár.

   D. Eduard Benes.

   E. Imre Nagy.

Section II: Part A—Document-Based Questions

(Suggested writing time—45 minutes)
Percent of Section II score—45%

Directions: The following question is based on the accompanying Documents 1 through 10. (Some of the documents have been edited for the purpose of this exercise.) This question is designed to test your ability to work with historical documents. As you analyze the documents, take into account both the sources of the documents and the authors' points of view. Write an essay on the following topic that integrates your analysis of the documents. Do not simply summarize the documents individually. You may refer to relevant historical facts and developments not mentioned in the documents.

1. Assess the following statement:

   The Industrial Revolution in the 1700s and 1800s caused immense suffering for the workers in English society.

   Historical Background: Arnold Toynbee coined the phrase "Industrial Revolution" to explain the economic development in England during the eighteenth and nineteenth centuries. To many, industrialization became synonymous with progress, but for others, it created many problems. Critics attacked the Industrial Revolution for altering the nature of the workplace, the workforce, and the living conditions of the people.

Document 1

What time did you begin to work at a factory?—When I was six years old. . . .

What kind of mill is it?—Flax-mill. . . .

What were your hours of labour in that mill?—From 5 in the morning till 9 at night, when they were thronged.

For how long a time together have you worked that excessive length of time?—For about half a year.

What were your usual hours of labour when you were not so thronged?—From 6 in the morning till 7 at night.

What time was allowed for your meals?—Forty minutes at noon.

Had you any time to get your breakfast or drinking?—No, we got it as we could.

And when your work was bad, you hardly had anytime to eat at all?—No; we were obliged to leave it or take it home, and when we did not take it, the overlooker took it, and gave it to his pigs.

Were the children beat up to their labour there?—Yes.

With what?—A strap; I have seen the overlooker go to the top end of the room, where the little girls hug the can to the backminders; he has taken a strap, and a whistle in his mouth, and sometimes he has got a chain and chained them, and strapped them all down the room. . . .

What was his reason for that?—He was angry.

Had the children committed any fault?—They were too slow.

Were the children excessively fatigued at that time?—Yes, it was in the afternoon.

Were the girls so struck as to leave marks upon their skin?—Yes . . . they were afraid of losing their work.

If the parents were to complain of this excessive ill-usage, the probable consequence would be the loss of the situation of the child?—Yes. . . .

Source: Testimony before the Sadler Committee (1831–1832).

Document 2

They come forth: the mine delivers its gang . . . Infants of four and five years of age, many of them girls, pretty and still soft and timid; entrusted with the fulfillment of responsible duties. . . . Their labour indeed is not severe, for that would be impossible, but it is passed in darkness and in solitude. . . . Hour after hour elapses, and all that reminds the infant trappers of the world they have quitted, and that which they have joined, is the passage of the coal-wagons for which they open the air-doors of the galleries, and on keeping which doors constantly closed, except at this moment of passage, the safety of the mine and the lives of the persons employed in it entirely depend.

Source: Benjamin Disraeli, *Sybil* (1865).

Document 3

Nothing shows in a clearer point of view the credulity of mankind . . . than the ready faith which was given to the tales of cruelty exercised by proprietors of cotton-mills towards young children. . . .

I have visited many factories . . . and I never saw a single instance of corporal chastisement inflicted on a child, or indeed did I ever see children in ill-humor. They seemed to be always cheerful and alert, taking pleasure in the light play of their muscles . . . the work of these lively elves seemed to resemble a sport, in which habit gave them a pleasing dexterity. Conscious of their skill, they were delighted to show it off to any stranger. As to exhaustion by the day's work, they evinced no trace of it on emerging from the mill in the evening; for they immediately began to skip about any neighboring playground, and to commence their little amusements with the same alacrity as boys issuing from a school. It is moreover my firm convictions that . . . children . . . would thrive better when employed in our modern factories than if left at home in apartments too often ill aired, damp, and cold. . . .

Source: Andrew Ure, *The Philosophy of Manufacturers* (1835).

Document 4

The little town of Hyde was at the beginning of the century a little hamlet of only 800 people, on the summit of a barren hill, the soil of which did not yield sufficient food for the inhabitants. The brothers Ashton have peopled and enriched this desert. . . . Mr. T. Ashton employs 1500 work people (in his factories). The young women are well and decently clothed. . . The houses inhabited by the work people form long and large streets. Mr. Aston has built 300 of them, which he lets (rents) for . . . 75 cents per week. . . . Everywhere is to be observed a cleanliness, which indicates order and comfort.

Source: Leon Faucher, *Manchester in 1844*.

Document 5

The employment of women at once breaks up the family; for when the wife spends twelve or thirteen hours every day in the mill, and the husband works the same length of time there or elsewhere, what becomes of the children? They grow up like wild weeds; they are put out to nurse for a shilling or eighteen pence a week, and how they are treated may be imagined. . . . That the general mortality among young children must be increased by the employment of the mothers is self-evident, and is placed beyond all doubt by notorious facts.

Women often return to the mill three or four days after confinement (for childbirth), leaving the baby, of course; in the dinner hour they must hurry home to feed the child and eat something. . . .

Source: Friedrich Engels, *The Impact of the Factory System on Women and the Family* (1892).

Document 6

The village contains about 1500 inhabitants, of whom all who are capable of work are employed in and about the mills. Of these there are 500 children who are entirely fed, clothed, and educated by Mr. Dale. The others live with their parents in the village and have a weekly allowance for their work. The healthy appearance of these children has frequently attracted the attention of the traveler. Special regulations, adopted by Mr. Dale, have made this factory very different from the others in this kingdom. Out of the nearly 3,000 children employed in the mill from 1785–1797, only fourteen have died.

Source: Society for Bettering the Condition and Increasing the Comforts of the Poor (1797).

Document 7

I am forced to admit that instead of being exaggerated, it is far from black enough to convey a true impression of the filth, ruin, and uninhabitableness, the defiance of all considerations of cleanliness, ventilation, and health which characterizes the construction of this single district, containing at least twenty to thirty thousand inhabitants. And such a district exists in the heart of the second city of England, the first manufacturing city of the world. If any one wishes to see in how little space a human being can move, how little air—and such air!—he can breathe, how little of civilization he may share and yet live, it is only necessary to travel hither. True, this is the Old Town, and the people of Manchester emphasize the fact whenever any one mentions to them the frightful condition of this Hell upon Earth; but what does that prove? Everything which here arouses horror and indignation is of recent origin, belongs to the industrial epoch.

Source: Friedrich Engels, *The Condition of the Working Class in England in 1844* (1844).

Document 8

. . . In most parts of England poor children are a burthen to their parents and to the parish; here the parish, which would else have to support them, is rid of all expense; they get their bread almost as soon as they can run about, and by the time they are seven or eight years old bring in money. . . . I was looking, while he spoke, at the unnatural dexterity with which the fingers of these little creatures were playing in the machinery, half giddy myself with the noise and the endless motion; and when he told me there was no rest in these walls, day or night, I thought that if Dante had peopled one of his hells with children, here was a scene worthy to have supplied him with new images of torment. . . . These children then said, 'have no time to receive instruction.' 'That, sir, he replied 'is the evil . . . you see them till they marry, and then they know nothing about domestic work, not even how to mend a stocking or boil a potato. But we are remedying this now, and send the children to school for an hour after they have done work.' . . . 'manufacturers are favourable to population, the poor are not afraid of having a family here, the parishes therefore have always plenty to apprentice, and we take them as fast as they can supply us.' . . .

Source: Robert Southey, *Letters from England* (1807).

Document 9

Cause of Death	Under 13 years of age	From 13 up to 18 years of age	Over 18 years of age
Fell down the shafts	13	12	31
Fell down the shaft from the rope breaking	1	-	2
Fell out when ascending	-	-	3
Drawn over the pulley	3	-	3
Fall of stone out of a skip down the shaft	1	-	3
Drowned in the mines	3	4	15
Fall of stones, coal, and rubbish in the mines	14	14	69
Injuries in coal pits, the nature of which is not specified	6	3	32
Crushed in coal pits	-	1	1
Explosion of gas	13	18	49
Suffocation of choke-damp	-	2	6
Explosion of gunpowder	-	1	3
By tram-wagons	4	5	12
Total	**58**	**60**	**229**

Source: John Saville, "Child Labor," *Working conditions in the Victorian Age: Common Cause of Death in Coal Mines*.

Document 10

As to the conclusions I have come to from the working of my mill for 11 instead of 12 hours each day, as previously, I am quite satisfied that both as much yarn and cloth may be produced at quite as low a cost in 11 as in 12 hours. It is my intention to make a further reduction to 10½ hours, without the slightest fear of suffering loss. I find the hands work with greater energy and spirit; they are more cheerful, and happy. . . .

Source: *Parliamentary Papers*, 1845, XXV, pp. 456–7. A factory owner's view of industrialization.

Section II: Part B—Thematic Essays

(Suggested planning and writing time—70 minutes)
Percent of Section II score—55%

Directions: You are to answer TWO questions, one from each group of three questions below. Make your selections carefully, choosing the questions that you are best prepared to answer thoroughly in the time permitted. You should spend 5 minutes organizing or outlining each essay. In writing your essays, use specific examples to support your answer. If time permits when you finish writing, check your work. Be certain to number your answers as the questions are numbered below.

Group 1

Choose ONE question from this group. The suggested writing time for this question is 30 minutes. You are advised to spend 5 minutes planning your answer in the area below.

1. Discuss the role of women in the Renaissance.

2. Crane Brinton's book, *The Anatomy of Revolution,* asserts that revolutions follow a certain pattern: moderate, radical, and reactionary, ending with the emergence of a powerful leader. Assess this thesis in regard to the French Revolution.

3. Compare and contrast mercantilism with *laissez-faire.*

Group 2

Choose ONE question from this group. The suggested writing time for this question is 30 minutes. You are advised to spend 5 minutes planning your answer in the area below.

1. Discuss the factors that contributed to the economic recovery of Western Europe after World War II.

2. Discuss the conditions that led to the rise of fascism in Italy and Nazism in Germany.

3. Compare and contrast the unification of Germany with the unification of Italy.

Answer Key for Practice Exam II

Section I: Multiple-Choice Questions

1. D	28. D	55. E
2. C	29. E	56. A
3. E	30. C	57. B
4. A	31. A	58. B
5. B	32. E	59. C
6. C	33. C	60. A
7. A	34. B	61. E
8. D	35. B	62. B
9. C	36. A	63. B
10. C	37. A	64. E
11. A	38. C	65. A
12. C	39. A	66. E
13. A	40. B	67. A
14. E	41. D	68. A
15. B	42. D	69. A
16. E	43. B	70. B
17. A	44. A	71. A
18. B	45. B	72. A
19. E	46. C	73. C
20. D	47. C	74. B
21. C	48. A	75. A
22. C	49. D	76. D
23. D	50. B	77. A
24. D	51. E	78. D
25. B	52. B	79. E
26. D	53. B	80. A
27. B	54. C	

Section II: Free-Response Essays

Student essays and analyses appear beginning on page 321.

Answers and Explanations for Practice Exam II

Section I: Multiple-Choice Questions

1. **D.** *Détente* did not result in the revocation of the Brezhnev Doctrine; rather it refers to a period of relaxation in tension between the United States and the Soviet Union during the 1970s when Leonid Brezhnev was leader. The Brezhnev Doctrine claimed that the Soviet Union had the right to intervene in the affairs of any socialist country that needed it to do so. Brezhnev had intervened in Czechoslovakia in 1968 to end reform efforts by Alexander Dubček to lift censorship as well as trade with Western European countries. Likewise, in 1979, the Soviet Union invaded Afghanistan in order to keep the Communists in power. During the *détente* era, the SALT Accords limited the spread of nuclear weapons. President Nixon's visit to Moscow and Brezhnev's visit to the United States were both tense. The Helsinki Pact signed in 1975 was an agreement among the United States, Canada, the Soviet Union, and 33 European nations formally recognizing the division of Europe in the Cold War era.

2. **C.** The beginning of World War I was sparked by the assassination of Archduke Francis Ferdinand of Austria-Hungary. On June 28, 1914, Archduke Ferdinand and his wife were assassinated by a Serbian nationalist named Gavrilo Princip. When Serbia refused to agree to all of Austria's demands, the chain reaction that developed plunged Europe into World War I. Nicholas II was czar of Russia. Bismarck was chancellor of Prussia and had helped to unify Germany. Emperor Franz Joseph I was the leader of Austria-Hungary and Kaiser Wilhelm II was the leader of the German Empire.

3. **E.** During the Renaissance, the Church was not the dominant institution in society. During the Middle Ages, the Church played a major role in society because it provided religious, economic, and political leadership. By the time of the Renaissance, the influence of the Church began to decline as kings in France and England began to centralize more power and tried to control the influence of the Church. The Renaissance, which glorified the individual and insisted that the secular world was just as important as the religious world, also challenged the position of the Church. Society began to study the civilizations of Greece and Rome, which seemed to provide a better understanding of the fifteenth-century world than the philosophy of the Middle Ages. The Church in the Renaissance was important but was not the single focus of the people.

4. **A.** At the Congress of Vienna in 1814–1815, Prince Klemens von Metternich insisted that Italy was only a "geographic expression." After the congress, Italy was divided into separate states, with Austria annexing the rich, industrialized provinces of Lombardy and Venetia. In the south, the Spanish Bourbon family ruled the Kingdom of the Two Sicilies. Cavour was the prime minister of Piedmont-Sardinia who used war and diplomacy to unite Italy. Bismarck was the chancellor of Prussia whose policy led to the unification of Germany. Louis Napoleon and Napoleon I were both supporters of Italian unification.

5. **B.** The *lettres de cachet* were symbols of the absolutism of the French monarchy during the Old Regime. They were letters signed by the king and countersigned by the Secretary of State in France authorizing someone's imprisonment or exile without a recourse to a court of law. The Constituent Assembly in the French Revolution abolished them. *Lettres de cachet* were a method to ensure absolute control of the French monarch; they were not concerned with toleration, or economic or political attempts to overthrow the monarchy.

6. **C.** The Final Solution refers to Hitler's plan to exterminate Europe's Jewish population. Hitler's National Socialist Program called for the disenfranchising of all Jews, the systematic organizing of the persecution of the Jews, the boycotting of Jews, expelling them from public life, and finally annihilating them. Beginning in November 1935, the Nazis implemented laws that stripped Jews of their civil rights and shipped them to concentration camps. In July 1941, Heinrich Himmler and other Nazi leaders implemented plans (the Final Solution) to exterminate all the Jews in Europe and Hitler's empire. In the next four years, the Nazis rounded up Jews by the thousands and sent them to concentration camps such as Dachau in Germany and Auschwitz in Poland. Operation Barbarossa refers to Hitler's plan to invade Russia, and D-Day refers to the Allied plan to invade Germany through France. There are no specific terms to describe the Allied plan to attack German cities nor for Hitler's invasion of Poland.

7. **A.** The Protestant Reformation was similar to the Renaissance because it emphasized the importance of the individual and faith in the ability of human reason. Humanist writers believed in the ability of individuals to bring about change and stressed the use of reason rather than the acceptance of dogma as the basis of life. Erasmus' *The Praise of Folly* was critical of many Church practices because they were based on superstition and ignorance. Luther and Calvin, leaders of the Protestant Reformation, believed in the power of the individual to read the Bible and determine Church doctrine and practices. As in the Renaissance, Reformation leaders believed in glorifying the individual and his rationality. The influence of the Church declined during the Protestant Reformation, which ended the religious unity of Europe. The role of political rulers, however, expanded during the Reformation as they gained control of Church lands. The Reformation did not focus on classics nor was Florence the intellectual and cultural center. Catholics in Southern Europe and Protestants in Northern Europe developed their own distinct cultural centers.

8. **D.** The Renaissance (fifteenth century) and the Enlightenment (eighteenth century) were similar in that both produced cultural changes, or altered the way people looked at the world. The Renaissance encouraged a secular view of the world, while the Enlightenment promoted the belief that human reason could uncover the plan that governed the universe. Belief in the power of the individual led to the rise of Humanism during the Renaissance and the rise of philosophers during the Enlightenment. The ideals of the Renaissance and the Enlightenment also affected the arts and sciences of the era. Neither of these periods promoted traditional values or democracy, nor did they encourage religion as a force in society. Both attacked traditional abuses that undermined society. Both were optimistic about the importance of life.

9. **C.** Great Britain was not a member of the original European Common Market. Britain ended its traditional policy of aloofness from European affairs and began to seek membership in the late 1960s. President Charles de Gaulle of France vetoed British entrance in 1967. However, in 1973, Britain became a member.

10. **C.** A characteristic of English absolutism in the seventeenth century was that it limited the power of the king. English absolutism developed along constitutional lines, by means of the Bill of Rights (1689), which meant that the power resided in the state (Parliament), and that the elections were to be free from the Crown's control. The English monarchs were not successful in ruling without Parliament (Charles I was beheaded and James II was expelled for trying to rule absolutely), nor did they depend upon the Anglican Church for absolute control. The Tudors were popular rulers, but the Stuarts were unpopular because they tried to rule absolutely and pursued a foreign policy of friendship with Spain. In 1642, the Puritans led the revolt against Charles I because they opposed his efforts to rule absolutely.

11. **A.** Louis Blanc promoted a program that included national government-supported workshops. Blanc was a socialist who looked for solutions to problems created by the Industrial Revolution by reorganizing the economy. Blanc believed that the full power of the state should be directed toward setting up national workshops and factories to guarantee full employment. Blanc did not call for the formation of a workers' union nor did he approve of the government seizure of property through worldwide revolution. He did not promote unemployment insurance, but he did endorse state-supported manufacturing centers in which workers would labor for themselves without the intervention of private capitalists.

12. **C.** Japan never became a subject of imperialism. Japan's government realized that after Commodore Perry's visit to Japan in 1853, Japan had to modernize or, like China, it would fall prey to Western imperialism. In 1868, the Meiji Restoration helped to make Japan strong enough to compete with the Western European powers. The Japanese leaders adopted Western technology, built up a modern army based on the Prussian model, constructed a large navy, and promoted manufacturing. The Japanese demonstrated their power by defeating Russia in the Russo-Japanese War of 1904–1905. Japan's victory shattered the myth of supremacy of the European race. India and Egypt came under British rule in the eighteenth and nineteenth centuries, and Morocco came under French power in the nineteenth century. China began to be divided up by European nations after its defeat in the Opium War of 1839–1842.

13. **A.** France's July Revolution of 1830—in response to King Charles X's suspension of the legislature, limitations on the right to vote, and restrictions of the press—caused Prince Klemens von Metternich to make this statement. He believed that this uprising would have a horrible influence on the rest of Europe and devastating effects not only on France but also on the rest of the continent. Metternich would not have seen the election of Louis-Philippe as king or Napoleon as president of France as a threat to Europe because they did not start a series of other revolutions outside of France. The Peterloo Massacre took place in Manchester, England, in 1819, and involved the deaths and injuries of innocent people who had peacefully gathered to petition Parliament. This massacre did not spark revolts outside of England.

14. **E.** The most important officials in Russia's provisional government in 1917 were the Liberals and Socialists. On March 15, 1917, Czar Nicholas II abdicated and a provisional government headed by Liberal Democrat Prince Georgy Lvov, and later in July by the Moderate Socialist Alexander Kerensky, was established. Dominated by the middle-class Liberals, the provisional government quickly guaranteed civil liberties such as freedom of the press and speech and sought to establish a Western European style of democracy. Both the Liberals and Socialists rejected social revolution, and considered the continuation of the war to be the most important objective. However, the failure of the provisional government to implement social reform resulted in the loss of support among workers and peasants. The Bolsheviks, Mensheviks, and Czarists did not have a major role in the provisional government. Lenin, who was the leader of the Bolsheviks (Communists), was in Switzerland and did not arrive in Russia until April 1917, when the Germans provided him safe passage into Russia.

15. **B.** Yugoslavia's success in not falling under Soviet control was due to the fact that Yugoslavia did not border on the Soviet Union. Although Josip Broz Tito (1892–1980) was as much a nationalist as a communist and insisted on developing his own national policies (which angered Stalin and resulted in Yugoslavia's expulsion from the international Communist movement), Yugoslavia did not border the Soviet Union like Poland, Hungary, and Czechoslovakia; this made it difficult for Stalin to control Yugoslavia. In addition, Tito had the support of the people and was able to resist Soviet pressure while developing his own form of communism that held together Yugoslavia's different ethnic groups and also won aid from the West. Tito did not pursue an aggressive military campaign against the Soviet Union nor was there a treaty between the two countries. Tito also did not receive protection from England or military aid from the United States. He was successful in holding the country together by not allowing each state to develop its own separate government. After Tito's death in 1980, Yugoslavia broke up into different nation states, which led to civil war and chaos in the region.

16. **E.** After the dissolution of the Soviet Union, Russia dramatically cut its military spending. The army was depleted by the long war in Chechnya and Afghanistan. The military-industrial sector had employed one of every five Soviet adults. The drastic cuts left millions unemployed, but these groups were too weak to attempt an overthrow of the government. In October 1993, the military backed Boris Yeltsin, the Russian President, when an impasse between the President and Parliament crippled the government. Pro-Parliament rioters who rampaged through Moscow were crushed by Yeltsin with the support of the military establishment. Russia confronted problems during Yeltsin's presidency: 800-percent inflation; a declining life expectancy; and, in 1994, the necessity to fight Chechnyan rebels. Yeltsin's reputed drinking habits contributed to uncertainty in the government and his erratic behavior.

17. **A.** Giuseppe Garibaldi was the author of this passage. Garibaldi was a military leader who invaded Sicily with his army of 1,000 Red Shirts and, once joined by rebels in Southern Italy, they conquered Sicily. Garibaldi then crossed to the Italian mainland and gave permission to unite the Two Sicilies with the Kingdom of Piedmont-Sardinia. Mazzini was the founder of Young Italy which was dedicated to the liberation of Italy. Cavour was Prime Minister of Piedmont-Sardinia and Victor Emmanuel was the first king of united Italy. Napoleon III was French leader from 1848 to 1871.

18. **B.** The terms, "White Man's Burden" and "Scramble for Africa," refer to the time period known as the Age of Imperialism. The Age of Imperialism covers the time span between 1870 and 1914 when European states established vast empires, mainly in Africa, but also in Asia and the Middle East. The "White Man's Burden" was a term used by the nineteenth-century British poet Rudyard Kipling, expressing the belief that Europeans had an obligation to civilize the uncivilized people in Africa. "Scramble for Africa" described how Europe divided up the continent of Africa during this time period. None of the other answers describe these terms.

19. **E.** A factor in the success of the Tudor monarchy in England was that the Tudors ruled absolutely while also consulting Parliament. When Henry broke with the Roman Catholic Church, he asked Parliament's support to legalize his actions; he also met with Parliament regularly to confirm laws and to seek its approval on levying taxes. Elizabeth I, like her father, also consulted Parliament but controlled with a firm hand. The Tudors' skillful handling of Parliament made them popular and successful leaders. The Tudors were not actively involved in acquiring colonies, nor were they friendly with Catholic Spain considering Henry VIII's divorce from his Spanish wife, Catherine of Aragon.

20. **D.** Charles "Turnip" Townshend is correctly associated with crop rotation. This process improved upon the older methods of crop rotation such as the medieval three-field system. In the 1750s, Townshend won the nickname "Turnip" Townshend for urging farmers to grow turnips, which restored exhausted soil. By using his system of draining extensively, heavy use of manure, and sowing of crops in regular rotation without fallowing, the farmers were able to produce larger crops. Crop rotation helped to conserve soil fertility and made more land available for production. Jethro Tull invented the seed drill. Robert Blackwell developed the scientific breeding of animals. Charles Newbold invented the cast-iron plow, and John Deere invented the self-cleaning plow.

21. **C.** The Edict of Nantes granted religious freedom to the Huguenots, a Calvinist minority living in France. From 1562 to 1589, frequent religious conflicts existed between the Catholic majority and the Huguenots, which culminated in the St. Bartholomew Day Massacre in which more than 20,000 Huguenots were killed. In 1589, Henry IV of Navarre, a Calvinist leader, issued the Edict of Nantes to end the religious wars in France and allow religious and civil freedom to the Protestant minority. There were no Baptists or Anglicans in France; Jews were denied religious freedom and were not affected by the edict.

22. **C.** The invention of movable metal type and the printing press were instrumental in spreading the ideas of the Renaissance from Italy to other parts of the world. In 1450, Johannes Gutenberg, a German printer, invented movable metal type and the printing press. Compared to the medieval hand-copying of books, the printing press increased output and was much cheaper. Presses sprang up in Italy, Germany, England, and the Netherlands. As books became more readily available, more people learned to read and write. The increased circulation of books by Italian writers helped to spread the ideas of the Renaissance to other parts of Europe. By 1500, the printing press had turned out more than 20 million volumes. The Medici family promoted art in Italy but not outside of the Italian Peninsula. Students traveled to Italy to learn about the Renaissance, but humanists did not travel outside of Italy. Patronage of painters in Italy and the opening of new schools to teach Renaissance ideals had a limited influence.

23. **D.** Isaac Newton is considered the greatest figure of the Scientific Revolution because he developed mathematical laws to explain the orderly manner in which the planets revolved around the sun. In 1687, Newton published his work, *Principia Mathematica,* in which he described the universe as a giant clock that worked in ways that could be expressed mathematically. Newton's laws of universal gravitation rejected the medieval view of the universe, which was God-centered, instead showing that man could understand the universe around him by using his reason, and that theology was not needed to understand the forces of nature. Sir Francis Bacon introduced Scientific Method.

24. **D.** Soviet domination of Eastern Europe following World War II was most directly the result of Soviet military occupation of the region. As the Red Army marched toward Berlin and pushed German troops out of Eastern Europe, Soviet troops remained in the region. Wanting to create a buffer zone to protect Russia from future invasions, Stalin insisted at the wartime conferences of Teheran, Yalta, and Potsdam that whoever occupied the territory would control the area. Communists in Poland and elsewhere in Eastern Europe, backed by the Red Army, destroyed the opposition and openly established pro-Stalin Communist governments in Eastern Europe. Fearing future conflict, the Western powers were unwilling to interfere. The United States followed a policy of containment, not isolationism. A democratic movement would not develop in Eastern Europe until the 1980s, nor was the United Nations involved in the problems in Eastern Europe.

25. **B.** World War I had a definite impact on the growth of employment in England. It has been estimated that by January 1916 over 26 million men had volunteered for the British Army. World War I created the need for these military men and also opened up job opportunities on the home front, especially for women. The number of women employed increased from 3,224,600 in July 1914 to 4,814,600 by the end of the war. These women were employed in a variety of activities. Those individuals who were not in the army also found job opportunities, as the war lasted for four years. During World War I there were no economic opportunities in the colonies nor were the British investing in the United States. American businesses were not investing in England during wartime but the American government was providing economic assistance to England. The assembly line had no impact on the growth of employment.

26. **D.** Russia's emergence as a leading world power was not a result of World War I, but instead occurred after World War II. In 1917, the Communists overthrew Czar Nicholas II and established the first Communist government on the European continent, after which Lenin and his Communist followers faced a number of obstacles, including a three-year civil war, famine, and the disbandment of the Russian Empire. The Communists did not establish firm control in Russia until 1921.

27. **B.** Hitler's first violation of the Treaty of Versailles was his remilitarization of Germany. In March 1935, Hitler dramatically repudiated the provisions of the Treaty of Versailles that intended to keep Germany disarmed, and openly built up the German armed forces. France, Great Britain, and later Italy protested the violation of an international treaty but did nothing specifically about it. Soon after, England entered into a naval agreement with Germany. Hitler occupied the Rhineland in 1936 and annexed Austria in 1938—again violations against the Treaty of Versailles that the world chose to ignore. The formation of the Rome-Berlin Axis and the invasion of Russia were not connected to the Treaty of Versailles.

28. **D.** The immediate effect of the Declaration of Pillnitz was that France declared war on Austria. The Declaration of Pillnitz was issued by the king of Prussia and the emperor of Austria in 1791 and stated that Prussia and Austria would intervene in order to protect the French monarchy from the rebels. The revolutionaries in France took this threat of intervention very seriously; the Legislative Assembly of France declared war first on Austria, and then on Prussia, Britain, and other countries. The declaration did not allocate military support and financial support from other European nations, nor did it declare that the people of Prussia and Austria should begin revolutions of their own or declare war on one another.

29. **E.** John Wycliffe and Jan Hus were not successful in trying to reform the Catholic Church. Wycliffe, an English priest, and Hus, a Bohemian religious leader, condemned the wealth of the Church, the pope's religious authority, and the Bible as supreme authority. Both of these men were harshly persecuted and denounced by the pope; Hus was burned at the stake for his beliefs, but his followers, known as the Hussites, fought the Church for many years before they were defeated. These two unsuccessful reformers paved the way for the success of Martin Luther. Selling indulgences (accepting money for Church pardons), simony (selling of Church positions), the Great Schism of 1378 to 1417 (rival popes), and nepotism (appointing relatives to Church positions) all contributed to the Protestant Reformation.

30. **C.** The Peace of Westphalia ended the Thirty Years' War (1618–1648), a religious war in central Europe between Protestant and Catholic rulers. The Peace of Westphalia did not deny religious freedom for Lutherans, nor did it revoke the Peace of Augsburg—rather, it reaffirmed it, giving Lutheran as well as Catholic rulers the right to determine the religion of their people. The German princes remained strong; at the end of the war, there were over 300 states with no central government. Germany, in fact, was divided for the next 200 years. The power of the papacy actually declined because the states gained power as they assumed greater control of both the Protestant and Catholic Churches.

31. **A.** In 1888 an American cartoonist depicted John Bull (England) as the octopus of imperialism, grabbing land on every continent. The left hand is poised to take over Egypt. The cartoon also reinforces the notion that the sun never set on the British Empire because of its extensive possessions throughout the world. Nationalism, ethnocentrism, industrialism, and isolationism are not illustrated in this cartoon about British imperialism.

32. **E.** A major issue dividing the delegates at the Frankfurt Assembly of 1848 was the struggle between the *Grossdeutsche* delegates who wanted to include the German-speaking province of Austria under German rule and the *Kleindeutsche* delegates who wanted to exclude it and include only Prussia with the small German states. When the Austrians opposed any division of their territory, the delegates decided on a united Germany that excluded Austria, a crisis that further weakened the Frankfurt Assembly. The assembly had no conflict about whether or not to address relations with France or how to establish closer ties with Russia because its focus was on Germany alone. Neither the status of religion, nor the Zollverein, was a cause of conflict.

33. **C.** *Perestroika* refers to economic restructuring. Gorbachev's program included less government planning, more power to local factory managers to make production decisions, the ability of some citizens to operate small retail businesses, and permission to farmers to grow some food that could be sold on the free market. *Perestroika* does not refer to the introduction of a police state in certain violent regions; lowered price caps on agricultural goods; rations for necessities; or free elections.

34. **B.** Northern Humanists interpreted the ideas of the Italian Renaissance by paying more attention to Biblical and early Christian themes. Like the Italian Humanists, Northern Humanists stressed the classics but believed that the revival of learning should be used to bring about religious and moral change by combining the ideas of the ancient world with Christian culture. Writers such as Desiderius Erasmus and Sir Thomas More promoted broad reforms based on Christian ideals.

35. **B.** Nicholas Copernicus, the Polish scientist, is represented by this statue. His Heliocentric Theory established the principle that the sun, not the earth, was the center of the universe. Johannes Kepler was a German astronomer. René Descartes was a French mathematician, and Francis Bacon was an English scientist and philosopher. Tycho Brahe was a Danish astronomer.

36. **A.** John Calvin believed in the doctrine of predestination, the essence of which is that man is born a sinner and that God has already determined who is going to be saved and who is damned. Those who were predestined for salvation could be identified by their virtuous life, even by their material success. Calvin, like Luther, thought that people should read and interpret the Bible for themselves with no need for priests and saints. Calvin rejected the idea that doing good deeds would influence one's afterlife, since God had predestined who would be saved; Calvin also rejected the importance of the sacraments.

37. **A.** The Industrial Revolution began in England because the country was rich in natural resources, including water power and coal to fuel steam power; iron ore to make machines, tools, and buildings; rivers for domestic transport of goods; and good harbors to facilitate trade with the rest of the continent and the world. England's available supply of workers came not from the migration from the colonies but from the Agricultural Revolution, which provided workers who were no longer needed on the farms. The English government encouraged businesses to invest but never assumed control of productive resources. Adam Smith's philosophy of *laissez-faire* (limited government interference) influenced the government. Until the mid-nineteenth century, the British government did not adopt a social policy of helping the workers.

38. **C.** One of the effects of the Great Depression was the attraction of supporters to the Nazi Party (the National Socialist German Workers' Party, or NSDAP), one of the many political parties under the Weimar Republic. After listening to Hitler blame the Depression on the Jews and the injustices of the Treaty of Versailles, many Germans began to support the Nazi Party.

In 1932, with six million Germans unemployed, the Nazi Party pooled over 12 million votes, or 37 percent of the vote, and became the largest party in the Reichstag (the German Parliament). On January 30, 1933, German President Hindenburg asked Hitler to become chancellor. The other options are wrong for the following reasons: the Fascist Party had gained control of Italy in 1922 before the Great Depression occurred; the Depression did not affect Russia in the way it did other European countries; many people in England and France were attracted to communism because they lost faith in the ability of democracy to solve the Depression's economic problems; and the Great Depression did not lead to large-scale migration to the United States because of the poor economic conditions there.

39. **A.** The food riots in Manchester, England, caused by a temporary depression after the Napoleonic War, led to the Peterloo Massacre, also called the Manchester Massacre, which took place on August 16, 1819. The Peterloo Massacre led to repressive measures. Parliament passed the Six Acts, which banned demonstrations and imposed censorship. Eventually, beginning in 1832, Parliament began to make changes such as lowering qualifications for voting, repealing the Corn Laws, limiting the power of the House of Lords, and instituting programs to help the poor. These changes would take place throughout the nineteenth and early twentieth centuries.

40. **B.** In the early 1990s, Czechoslovakia peacefully divided into two independent nations. After the downfall of the Soviet Union, ethnic tensions in some of the former satellites emerged; however, Václav Havel, a dissident playwright, and others were able to control ethnic and national tensions that might have destroyed the post-Communist government. Havel was elected president of Czechoslovakia and was famous for his bloodless "Velvet Revolution"—"a peaceful divorce" that split Czechoslovakia into the Czech Republic and Slovakia. The goal of rejoining the West, especially the European Union and NATO, was a powerful force toward this peaceful transition. The Czech Republic joined NATO in 1999 and the European Union in 2004. In the 1990s, Bosnia and Herzegovina were involved in a civil war, but the Czech Republic was not involved. The Warsaw Pact ended in 1991, and Czechoslovakia never had nuclear weapons.

41. **D.** Louis XIV's finance minister, Jean-Baptiste Colbert (1619–1683), helped to advance France's prosperity by his economic policies. Colbert's goal was to make France self-sufficient by achieving a favorable balance of trade and to centralize the economy through government control of trade and industry. He also encouraged French industry by introducing high foreign tariffs and creating a strong merchant marine. France's strong economic position enabled Louis XIV to pursue an aggressive foreign policy and make France the center of culture in the seventeenth century. Colbert supported the monarch and did not promote equality for all classes; in fact, under Colbert, the peasant class was hit hard by the government's heavy taxation. Colbert's main focus was on the economy rather than the government's relationship with the Church; moreover, he did not have an impact on peace in Europe. During Louis XIV's long reign, France was involved in four major wars.

42. **D.** All of the following are associated with Bismarck and the unification of Germany *except* the Berlin Conference of 1884. Bismarck and Jules Ferry, prime minister of France, convened the Conference in 1884–1885 to establish the basic rules for colonizing Africa. The Berlin Conference led to the scramble for Africa. Helmuth von Moltke was a Prussian general chief of staff who strengthened the armed forces that enabled Bismarck to achieve military success. The Danish War, the Austro-Prussian War, and the Franco-Prussian War were all steps in the unification of Germany.

43. **B.** Jeanne-Elizabeth Schmahl founded the French Union for Women's Suffrage. She rejected the militant tactics of the English movement and favored legal protest. She is not associated with any artistic, musical, social reform or the suffrage movement in England.

44. **A.** Frederick the Great of Prussia is considered an Enlightened Despot, an absolute monarch who adopted the ideals of the Enlightenment to bring about social and political changes. Frederick the Great was an absolute ruler who supported literature, music, and science, tolerated religious differences, reduced censorship, improved education, and ordered equal treatment for all persons. He also had swamps drained and introduced new agricultural methods that helped peasants grow new crops such as potatoes. He was motivated by the desire to make his country stronger and his own government more effective. He was not a believer in democracy, however. Louis XIV of France and James I of England and Alexander I were absolute monarchs. Charles V was a Holy Roman Emperor who believed in absolutism.

45. **B.** James Joyce is associated with the term "stream of consciousness" in his landmark novel, *Ulysses* (1922), and its controversial successor, *Finnegan's Wake* (1939). In *Ulysses,* Joyce focuses on a single day in the lives of three Dubliners. Joyce broke with normal sentence structure and vocabulary, trying to mirror the workings of the human mind. Using the stream-of-consciousness technique, Joyce explored his characters' random thoughts and feelings without imposing any logic or order. Ernest Hemingway and F. Scott Fitzgerald are connected with the school of writers known as "The Lost Generation." T. S. Eliot explored his discontent with the modern world in his poem, *The Waste Land.* Erich Maria Remarque's novel, *All Quiet on the Western Front,* explores the horrors of World War I.

46. **C.** In the 1800s, the English Parliament primarily represented the interests of the landed aristocracy. England was not a true democracy in the nineteenth century; only about 5 percent of the population had the right to elect the members of the House of Commons. Voting was limited to men who owned a substantial amount of property. Women could not vote and as a result, the upper landed aristocracy ran the government. In addition, the House of Lords, which was made up of hereditary nobles and high-ranking clergy of the Anglican Church, had the right to veto any laws passed by the House of Commons. The middle class, urban workers, and capitalist owners would gradually gain the right to vote through the passage of the Reform Bills of 1832, 1867, and 1884. The Anglican clergy was part of the House of Lords but the landed aristocracy ran the government, not the clergy.

47. **C.** Critics of the New Imperialism never asserted that imperialism was benefiting the colonies at the expense of the economy of the mother country. Rather, the critics claimed that imperialism only benefited the capitalists, not the entire nation. Lenin, for instance, called imperialism the last stage of capitalism. Other critics insisted that imperialism was undemocratic because it violated the principles of self-government as well as the culture of the people. These critics also rejected the idea of Social Darwinism and insisted that profits were the main motive behind the exploitation of these regions.

48. **A.** Henry VIII (b.1491, ruled 1509–1547) led the Protestant Reformation in England by making the king, not the pope, the head of the Church. Henry VIII broke with the Catholic Church in 1527, when the pope refused to grant him a divorce from his Spanish wife, Catherine of Aragon. In 1534, working through Parliament, King Henry passed the Act of Supremacy, which took control of the English Church. He shut down the monasteries and took over Church lands, thus strengthening the monarchy. He retained most Catholic forms of worship: sacraments were not abolished, and priests were allowed to perform services on Sunday.

49. **D.** Napoleon accomplished many things as emperor, except strengthening the role and status of women in France. The Napoleonic Code, although embodying principles of the Enlightenment—such as equality for all citizens before the law, religious toleration, and advancement based upon merit—lost women many of the rights that they had gained during the French Revolution. The code considered women as minors who could not exercise the rights of citizenship.

50. **B.** The Lateran Treaty between Mussolini and Pius XII was to end the dispute between Italian Catholics and the Fascist government over the seizure of Church land during the unification of Italy. The pact established Catholicism as the state religion and acknowledged the existence of Vatican City, which is about a square mile, as an independent state that is not legally within Italy. The papacy gained independence from national or secular authority. The Lateran Treaty strengthened Mussolini's influence over the Catholics, who composed 99 percent of the population.

51. **E.** The formation of NATO was not an event associated with Nikita Khrushchev. Khrushchev was the leader of the Soviet Union from 1956 to 1964; NATO, on the other hand, was formed in 1949 during the Stalin Era. Khrushchev attacked Stalin's cult of personality and supported a "thaw" in the Cold War by allowing greater intellectual freedom. Although his anti-Stalin campaign led to failed uprisings in Hungary and Poland, his policy of peaceful coexistence also led to a number of Summit meetings at Geneva and Vienna to discuss East/West relations.

52. **B.** Voltaire's statement, *"écrasez l'infâme,"* refers to the Catholic Church. Born François-Marie Arouet (1694–1778), Voltaire challenged the authority of the Catholic Church, attacking its beliefs and practices. He hated all forms of religious intolerance and promoted simply the idea of "love God and your neighbor as yourself." In *Candide*, Voltaire wrote against the evils of organized religion and was subsequently imprisoned for his views. Voltaire was not a believer in social and economic equality in human affairs. Like most writers of the Enlightenment, he was suspicious of the middle class, the military, and the poor. Voltaire believed in the importance of laws to protect the freedom of the weak against the ambitions of the stronger.

53. **B.** A major theme of Machiavelli's 1513 work, *The Prince,* is that the end justifies the means. *The Prince* functions as an instruction guide on how a ruler should rule, stating that a ruler should not be moral but should do what is best for the state, and use any means necessary to maintain power, and assure the success of the government. Machiavelli did not dismiss loyalty as long as it was used to help a ruler rule effectively. He believed, however, that human beings are selfish and out to advance only their own interests. For this reason, Machiavelli dismissed honesty and prayers as a way to promote diplomacy or full virtue. He admired the Roman Republic and dreamed of a united Italy.

54. **C.** One result of the Sadler Committee was that it led to the passage of legislation regulating the employment of children in factories. In 1832, Michael Sadler, a British legislator, conducted a parliamentary investigation of conditions in the textile factories. The Sadler Committee discovered that children worked 12 to 14 hours per day and were regularly abused by factory owners. The immediate effects of the investigation was the passage of the Factory Act of 1833, which prohibited employers from hiring children under the age of nine, prevented children under the age of 13 from working longer than nine hours per day, and allowed children from 13 to 18 to work no more than 12 hours per day in the textile industry. The Sadler Committee only investigated the textile industry and did not address the issue of unions, minimum wage, social legislation, and the nationalization of iron and steel.

55. **E.** Charles I (ruled from 1625 to 1640) did not request money from Parliament for his military expedition against Spain. The Stuarts had established a friendly relationship with Spain. In 1637, Charles I tried to impose Anglicanism on Calvinists living in Scotland. They revolted and Charles was forced to call Parliament to raise money for the war. Parliament refused after three weeks of open debate. During his reign, Charles I disregarded the Petition of Rights for 11 years but was unable to levy taxes. The Long Parliament (1640–1660) did eventually pass laws that limited the power of the king, but when he needed additional money for his military expedition against Spain, he requested a forced loan from his wealthier subjects. Several members of the gentry refused to vote for the loans and Charles threw them into jail. In 1628, Parliament again declined to give Charles additional resources unless he signed the Petition of Rights.

56. **A.** Ludwig van Beethoven who composed nine symphonies was master of Romanticism in music. Extending and breaking open classical forms, Beethoven used contrasting themes and tones to produce dramatic conflict and inspiring resolution. Beethoven's range was tremendous. His works included symphonies, chamber music, sonatas for violin and piano, masses, an opera and many great songs. His expanded use of the orchestra was a revolutionary movement from the controlled and formal compositions of the Enlightenment. Nicolò Paganini was a master of the violin and Franz Liszt was a great pianist. Victor Hugo was a French novelist. Igor Stravinsky was an important Russian composer of the twentieth century.

57. **B.** Britain declared war on Germany when Germany invaded Belgium. Belgium was a neutral country whose neutrality had been recognized by all the major powers of Europe since 1839. England felt committed to protect Belgium, fearing that a powerful Germany would threaten British national interests on the European continent. Britain's decision was not based on Austria's ultimatum to Serbia, Italy's declaration of neutrality, or Russia's support of Serbia.

58. **B.** As a result of the Sepoy Mutiny in 1857, the British assumed direct control of India in 1858, ending the rule of the British East India Company. The British introduced social, educational, and technological reforms that helped India become the "Brightest Jewel of the Crown." However, the British policy was always motivated by how the colony would benefit the mother country. The Sepoy Mutiny did not result in recognizing either Hinduism or Islam as the state religion. Neither democracy nor independence was introduced in India.

59. **C.** The Scientific Revolution did not lead to a widespread growth of knowledge among the general population; it actually had little impact on the economic life and living standards of the masses until the late eighteenth century. The Scientific Revolution of the seventeenth century was primarily an intellectual revolution, which led to the formation of societies such as the Royal Society of London, the purpose of which was to promote the growth of scientific ideas among different countries. The Scientific Revolution led to the scientific method of observation, which opened up a greater knowledge of the physical world in which the sun and not the earth was the center of the universe. The heliocentric theory of the universe replaced the belief in the Aristotelian/medieval view of the earth as the center of the universe.

60. **A.** The painting of *Guernica* by Pablo Picasso was inspired by the Spanish Civil War. Hitler and Mussolini supported General Francisco Franco in his struggle for power against the Spanish Loyalists, who included democrats, republicans, and communists. In 1937, the bombing of a Spanish town, Guernica, by German bombers led to the death of 1,600 people. Picasso's work of art captured the brutality of the event. Picasso never painted a work of art about Mussolini's support of the Spanish Fascists, Hitler's rise to power, Italy's invasion of Ethiopia, or the Nazi-Soviet Non-Aggression Pact.

61. **E.** The *Ausgleich,* or Compromise of 1867, did not provide for a uniform educational and monetary system. It did, however, establish the Dual Monarchy under which Austria and Hungary became separate states. Under the Ausgleich, each country had its own government and independence in local matters such as education, but was joined together on common issues such as foreign affairs, military defense, and finance. The delegates of the two parliaments met together alternatively in Vienna and Budapest, and both Austrians and Hungarians were appointed to this common ministry; also, Francis Joseph I became both emperor of Austria and king of Hungary.

62. **B.** Louis XIV's reign eventually forced the Huguenots to leave France because he destroyed their property and took away their civil rights. Seeing the Protestant minority as a threat to religious unity, in 1685, Louis XIV canceled the Edict of Nantes, which in 1598 had granted religious toleration to the Huguenots. In response, thousands of artisans and business people fled the country. This loss of some of the most prosperous of Louis' subjects had an adverse effect on the economy. The Huguenots were not sent to French colonies but fled to the New World, where many of them settled in New York. They never became trusted advisors of Louis XIV, nor were they forced to live in poverty.

63. **B.** This passage is part of Article 231 of the Treaty of Versailles. In Article 231, Germany accepted responsibility for the war by signing the "War Guilt" clause, and as a result was obligated to pay reparations to the Allies for the cost of the war. The final reparations bill came to $132 billion, which Germany had to pay over 30 years. The Atlantic Charter was a joint statement of principle issued by Franklin D. Roosevelt of the United States and Winston Churchill of Great Britain in 1941. The charter contained many of the ideas of Wilson's Fourteen Points. The charter of the League of Nations (1919) described the function of the League and how it was to be organized. The Treaty of Frankfurt (1871) ended the Franco-Prussian War and the Treaty of Westphalia (1648) concluded the Thirty Years' War.

64. **E.** An important result of the Revolution of 1848 in France was the election of Louis Napoleon, also known as Napoleon III, as president of the Republic. In February of 1848, riots broke out in Paris, which led to the abdication of King Louis-Philippe. A group of liberals, radicals, and socialists proclaimed the Second Republic with a strong president and a one-house legislature elected by universal male suffrage. The division among the different groups and the bitter legacy of the class warfare of June 1848 influenced the presidential election in December. The overwhelming winner was Louis Napoleon, the nephew of Napoleon I. Louis Napoleon attracted the working class by presenting himself as a man who cared about social issues such as poverty. Weary of instability, the French welcomed a strong personality who would bring peace to France. The Revolution of 1848 did not result in the return of the Bourbons or the return of Charles X from England. In June, the National Assembly shut down the National Workshops that had contributed to the class warfare. Austria, which experienced its own series of revolutions, did not intervene.

65. **A.** Arnold Toynbee coined the term "Industrial Revolution" in 1880. Toynbee used this term to describe the rapid growth of the use of machinery that dramatically affected agriculture, industry, and transportation. Historians tend to refer to the economic development in England during the eighteenth and nineteenth centuries as stages of economic growth in which total productivity was increasing, and productivity per man was also increasing. Saint-Simon was a French reformer who promoted the end of private property. Max Weber was a German writer who attributed the rise of the middle class in Europe to the Protestant work ethic promoted by Calvinism. Jacob Burckhardt was a historian who wrote about the Renaissance. Leopold von Ranke was a famous historian who introduced the seminar method of teaching.

66. **E.** The official abolishment of the sacraments was not a result of the Catholic or Counter Reformation. The Council of Trent (1545–1563) was part of the Counter Reformation which reaffirmed the dogma of the Church. The council, which met intermittently for about twenty years, reasserted the validity of the seven sacraments, ended the abuses within the Church, called for more religious art, and created the Index of Prohibited Books, which included the writings of Erasmus and Galileo. It also revived the Inquisition and attacked heretics.

67. **A.** Great Britain was the only country that remained outside of Napoleon's European empire by 1807. Napoleon's conquests redrew the map of Europe; he annexed some areas to France, including the Netherlands and Belgium, and even included parts of Italy and Germany in his empire. Napoleon cut Prussian territory in half and forced alliances on European powers from Madrid to Moscow. In 1805, he tried to invade England, but the French fleet was defeated at the Battle of Trafalgar. Napoleon even tried to reduce Britain's commerce by closing European ports to British goods. However, Napoleon was ultimately unsuccessful in making Great Britain a part of his empire.

68. **A.** Humanist writers focused on glorifying the individual and worldly subjects. Humanist writers believed that man was the measure of all things, and they had faith in man's unlimited potential to achieve success; they also believed in the creative powers of man and were concerned mostly with secular subjects rather than strictly religious themes. Writers such as Petrarch and Castiglione wrote about love and courtly behavior; others like Mirandola and Bruni stressed the importance of man's role in a secular society. Humanist writers focused on how the classical societies of ancient Greece and Rome were models for them rather than the system of feudalism. Humanist writers encouraged the positive effects of education and used the classics as a way to understand their society.

69. **A.** The Balkans were known as the "powder keg" of Europe at the beginning of the twentieth century. Home to many different ethnic groups and having a long history of ethnic uprisings and clashes, the Balkan Peninsula in the southeastern corner of Europe was an explosion waiting to happen. Nationalism was a powerful force in the Balkans as each group wanted to extend its borders. These nationalist sentiments became wrapped up with ambitions of the European powers to divide up the Ottoman Empire, which included the Balkan region. Thus, England and France sometimes supported Russia against the Ottomans. Germany supported Austrian authority over national groups but encouraged the Ottomans because of their strategic location at the eastern end of the Mediterranean. This intrigue—combined with the demand of the subject nationalities of the Serbians, Croatians, and Bulgarians—made the situation more intense.

70. B. During the Cold War (1947–1989), the United States and the Soviet Union were reluctant to become involved in direct conflict because of the potential for global nuclear destruction. Recognizing that mutual interests necessitated avoiding nuclear war, the United States and the Soviet Union even established a hotline that enabled their two leaders to speak directly with each other to avoid any misunderstandings. During the Cold War, the United States and the Soviet Union never directly confronted each other but used their influence to support groups that promoted their own interests. During the Korean War, the United States supported South Korea, and the Soviet Union with China supported North Korea. In the Middle East and in the Third World, the two countries supported governments that were pro-West or pro-Communist, respectively. The Cuban Missile Crisis of 1962 between the United States and the Soviet Union was the closest the two nations came to a direct conflict with each other. The United Nations' effectiveness as a world policeman depended upon the support of both the United States and the Soviet Union.

71. A. The cartoon of a wedding picture representing Hitler as the groom and Stalin as the bride symbolizes the Nazi-Soviet Non-Aggression Pact. In August 1939, the world was shocked to learn that Hitler had signed a ten-year Non-Aggression Pact with Stalin. This pact protected Germany from a two-front war, which had been an issue in World War I. The cartoon also suggests that the honeymoon between these two leaders would be short-lived. The formation of the Pact of Steel, the Soviet Union's support of Hitler's occupation of the Rhineland, the Soviet Union and Germany's cooperation at the Munich Conference, and Germany and the Soviet Union's support for General Franco in 1939 are historically inaccurate and not depicted in this cartoon.

72. A. Nationalists are opposed to European unity because they believe it will destroy their countries' unique identities. In 1991, the European Union signed the Treaty of Maastricht, agreeing to introduce a common currency (euro) by 2002. The treaty, however, allowed member nations to choose whether and when to adopt the single currency. Great Britain, Denmark, and Sweden were the only nations to agree not to adopt the euro, believing that their currency reflects their national identity. Some members of the British Conservative Party also believe that Britain should be in Europe but not run by Europe. They are critical of a common currency because they fear that bankers and financial leaders of Europe will make decisions that can have a negative effect on his country. William Hague and others believe that a single currency should be opposed until there are federal structures in place to manage it more democratically. There have been vigorous debates within the countries of Sweden, Denmark, and Britain about the Euro, but not hostility. The United States understands the economic threat of the European Union but has not been opposed to the concept. The members of the European Union believe that by coordinating their economic polices they can improve their economies, which have been in a slump for the past few years. Former communist nations, such as Poland, Hungary, and other Eastern European countries, entered the European Union in 2004.

73. C. In 1790, Edmund Burke published *Reflections on the Revolution in France* because he was deeply troubled by the events of the French Revolution. His book was one of the greatest intellectual defenses of conservatism. He defended inherited privileges in general and those of the English monarchy and aristocracy. He predicted that reform like that occurring in France would lead to "chaos and tyranny."Rousseau, Locke, and Voltaire were Enlightenment writers who were committed to bringing changes within society. Hobbes was an English writer who supported royal absolutism and believed that the role of the government was to protect man from destroying himself. All of these men had died before the beginning of the French Revolution in 1789.

74. B. Thomas Malthus would agree with the ideas expressed in this passage. In *An Essay on the Principle of Population* (1798), Malthus asserted that the population tended to increase more rapidly than the food supply. Without wars and epidemics to destroy the surplus population, the poor would suffer. Malthus encouraged people to have small families in order to stop the population growth. David Ricardo was associated with the "iron laws of wages" that forced workers to accept lower wages. Louis Blanc was a French reformer who advocated National Workshops during the French Revolution of 1848. John Locke was a seventeenth-century philosopher who wrote *Two Treatises of Government* to demonstrate his support for the Glorious Revolution of 1690. Locke believed in the social contract theory of government. Karl Marx wrote *The Communist Manifesto*.

75. **A.** The Reform Bills of 1832, 1867, 1884, 1918, and 1928 resulted in the expansion of voting rights among men and women. The Reform Bill of 1832 was the first step toward evolutionary democracy in England; reducing property qualifications for voters increased the number of voters from 500,000 to 800,000. The Reform Bill of 1867 further reduced property qualifications for voting to enfranchise the city workers. By 1884, agricultural workers had received the right to vote. In 1918, all men over the age of 21 and women over the age of 30 were able to vote, and in 1928, all women over the age of 21 were granted the franchise. These reform bills did not specifically address the issues of the power of the House of Commons or the House of Lords or the role of the monarchy or the government in Great Britain.

76. **D.** The philosophers of the Enlightenment tried to apply the ideas of science and the Enlightenment to reform society and used satire to spread their message. Writers such as Voltaire and Montesquieu wrote satire because they were fearful that direct attacks would lead to their imprisonment. The philosophers were primarily from France and attacked the organized structure of the Church. They did not support democracy over absolutism but supported the idea that human institutions should conform to logic and reason. The philosophers thought that reason, and not emotion, would provide an understanding of the meaning of the world.

77. **A.** A major goal of the Jesuits was to combat heresy and spread the Catholic faith. Ignatius Loyola, who founded the Jesuits in 1534, believed that he was a soldier of God. The Jesuits received vigorous training in education and philosophy, and were expected to have absolute obedience to the Church. Led by Loyola, the Jesuits became advisers to Catholic kings and spread their message to Asia, Africa, the Americas, and parts of southern Germany. They also used the Inquisition, especially in Spain and Italy, to combat heresy. The Council of Trent had prohibited the sale of indulgences, rejected the belief that the Bible was the source of salvation, and reaffirmed the importance of good works and the seven sacraments.

78. **D.** The outbreak of the nationalist movement in the Hapsburg Empire occurred because several national groups, such as Serbs, Czechs, and Slovenes, occupied the same region. The chief problem for Austria and Hungary was the question of governing many different nationalities and different minorities within the two countries. The Ausgleich, or Compromise of 1867, which made Austria and Hungary separate states, treated Austria as a German nation state and Hungary as a Magyar nation state. However, Germans comprised less than one-half of the people of Austria, as did the Magyars of Hungary. Austria also included the Slovenes and Czechs, as did the Magyars of Hungary, who also included Czechs and Poles.

79. **E.** Charles I of England was the Stuart king who ruled during the seventeenth century. He tried to govern without Parliament, which led to a civil war in England from 1642 to 1649. In 1649, Charles I was beheaded. Louis XI of France, Henry VII of England, the Medici family of Florence, and Ferdinand and Isabella of Spain were all powerful leaders during the Renaissance in Europe. All of these leaders consolidated power, which promoted a sense of authority and leadership. They established dominance by curbing the power of the nobles and centralizing their control.

80. **A.** Lajos Kossuth (1802–1894) was the Hungarian nationalist and fiery orator who led the fight for independence against Austria in the nineteenth century. Kossuth's liberal and nationalist program against Austria led to his arrest in 1837, but popular pressure forced Metternich to release him in 1840. Kossuth was one of the principle figures of the Hungarian Revolt in 1848 against the Austrian government. When the Austrian government prepared to move against Hungary, Kossuth became head of the Hungarian government of national defense. In April 1849, the Hungarian government declared its independence and Kossuth became governor-president. The Hungarians won several victories but when Russian troops intervened in 1849, Kossuth was forced to resign; he fled to Turkey and later to England. Ferdinand I was the emperor of Austria who agreed to the Hungarian demands for independence but abdicated in March 1848. János Kádár was a Hungarian political leader who was placed into power by Khrushchev in 1956 after the Soviets had crushed the revolt led by Imre Nagy. Eduard Benes was the leader of Czechoslovakia before World War II.

Section II: Free-Response Essays

Part A: First Sample Student DBQ Essay

The Industrial Revolution was a turning point in history. Until the mid-1750s, most people in Great Britain had worked the land using simple basic tools and had lived in rural towns. By 1850, many country villages had grown into industrial towns and these cities swelled with workers who labored in factories. Work in the factories affected families as well as the quality of life in these industrial towns. The Industrial Revolution in Great Britain would cause immense problems for the working class people.

In the 1750s, the market town of Manchester, England, had a population of about 45,000 people. Within a few years, it exploded into a center of textile industry and by 1850, had swelled to about 300,000. Visitors to the town were horrified at the living conditions. In 1845, Friedrich Engels noted that Manchester was like "Hell on Earth" (Doc. 7). Others found exactly the opposite. In the town of Hyde, the houses were pleasant and everything seemed clean and orderly (Doc. 4). Although Engels was a Socialist and blamed these poor conditions on industrialization (Doc. 8), he was accurate in pointing out the inhumane conditions in the city. There were no plants and no sanitary and building codes to control the growth of cities. Cholera and other diseases spread rapidly. Alex de Tocqueville, the French aristocrat who visited Manchester in 1835, described the black smoke that blanketed the city and how the homes of the poor were scattered in random order around the factories. He believed that in Manchester, "civilized man turned almost into a savage."

At the heart of the industrial city was the factory. The factory work, unlike the farm work which changed with the seasons, was very structured and the same week after week. Hours were long. Shifts lasted from 12 to 16 hours (Doc. 1). Women made up much of the new industrial work force. Many employers preferred women who were often paid less than men, even for the same work. Factory work created special problems for women. The new jobs forced them out of the homes for 12 hours a day and many of them had to return to work a few days after giving birth. Women also had to run home to feed their children during dinner. Engels asserted that "the employment of women at once breaks up the family" (Doc. 5).

The Industrial Revolution greatly affected children. Factories and mines hired many boys and girls. Benjamin Disraeli, a novelist and prime minister of Great Britain (1868; 1874–80), described the horrible conditions of young girls of four and five who were forced to work in the coal mines (Doc. 2). Disraeli was a reformer who was hoping to gain the working class support for a group of reforming aristocrats in the Conservative Party.

In 1832, Michael Sadler, a British legislator, began a parliamentary investigation into the conditions in the textile industry in order to expose the abuses of child labor. He found many children began work at six years old and usually worked from five in the morning until nine in the evening (Doc. 1). They worked six days a week, with only a half hour for lunch and an hour for dinner. Children were often beaten simply because factory owners thought they did not work hard enough and wanted to keep them awake. Other factory owners were just angry at them. Many children were afraid to report these instances because their parents might lose their jobs.

Factory owners scoffed at reports of poor working conditions and cruelty to children. One British manufacturer indicated that he was going to reduce work hours to $10\frac{1}{2}$ because he wanted his workers to be happy and cheerful and that it was more productive (Doc. 10). The Society for Bettering the Conditions and Increasing the Comfort of the Poor pointed out that there were factories where children were well treated and not abused (Doc. 6). Furthermore, wealthy manufacturers insisted that the children were not beaten and that working in a factory was better than being home in a cold and damp apartment (Doc. 3). The question of child labor was difficult because parents had come to depend upon the children's extra income to survive. Some factory owners thought that children working in the factories took the burden off the parents because children provided money for the family and removed the problem of how they would be fed (Doc. 8). These business men, of course, glossed over the fact that children needed to be educated, insisting that one hour a day was enough (Doc. 8).

Industry also posed a question of safety. Factories were seldom well lit or clean. Machines caused injuries in numerous ways. The most dangerous conditions were found in the mines. Frequent accidents and damp conditions affected the workers. In 1838, over 347 workers died in work-related accidents in coal mines (Doc. 9). The Ashley Mines Commission Report would highlight these problems and lead to laws regulating employment of children in mines and factories.

Tocqueville's comments about Manchester that "from this filthy sewer pure gold flows" shows the best and worst of the city influenced by the Industrial Revolution. The Industrial Revolution caused immense suffering for the working class of the city. However, the gold that flowed from the factories led to the rise of a middle class who changed the social structure of Great Britain which in turn raised the living standards of the workers.

Reader's Comments on Part A: First Sample Student DBQ Essay

- The thesis is clear and well developed.
- The student uses all the documents and analyzes them rather than just describing them.
- The student effectively uses outside information such as the Sadler Report, Ashley Commission, and Tocqueville.
- The conclusion is good.

Possible student score: 8–9

Part A: Second Sample Student DBQ Essay

The Industrial Revolution had a profound effect on Great Britain. In the 1700s and 1800s, economic development would lead to changes in the lives of workers and children as well as life in the cities.

The growth of cities led to the rise of factories around these towns. Workers in these factories usually toiled 12 to 16 hours per day and were given very little time for lunch and dinner (Doc. 1). The factories also employed many children. Children were forced to work long hours and were often beaten if they did not work hard enough (Doc. 1).

Women were also employed in these factories. Employers found women easier to manage and thought that women could more easily adapt to machines than men. Women working in the factories caused disruption within the family. Many women had to leave their children who were taken care of by others. Some women had to run home in between the dinner hour to feed their children (Doc. 5).

Working in factories was difficult and many children and workers were hurt. Factories were poorly ventilated, workers were exposed to constant danger of injuries, and there were no laws to protect them. Children working in mines suffered many accidents (Doc. 9).

Many factory owners believed that children working in factories helped society because it made sure that the children were able to earn money and they did not become a burden to society (Doc. 8). Others claimed that children were not mistreated and working in the factories was better than living in damp apartments (Doc. 3).

The Industrial Revolution also led to the growth of cities. In Manchester, England, the quality of life was uneven. The city grew to over 70,000 people by the beginning of the nineteenth century. Visitors to the city had mixed emotions. Some criticized the poor conditions (Doc. 7), while others praised how good the city appeared (Doc. 4).

The Industrial Revolution would initially cause suffering and pain. However, reformers would bring about changes in the social structure that would help to bring positive benefits to the working people of Great Britain.

Reader's Comments on Part A: Second Sample Student DBQ Essay

- The thesis is superficial.
- The student doesn't analyze any of the documents.
- There is no use of information.
- Organization of the argument is poor.

Possible student score: 4–5

Part B: First Sample Student Thematic Essay, Group 1–1

According to Baldassare Castiglione's book, The Courtier (1528), upper-class women were expected to know the classics and be charming but were not expected to seek fame. Their role was to inspire art but rarely create it. Upper-class Renaissance women were better educated than the women of the Middle Ages. However, they had less influence than medieval women. In terms of the kind of work that they performed, access to property, and their role in shaping their society, women in the Renaissance ruling class generally had less power than comparable women in the feudal age.

During the Middle Ages, few women could read or write outside of the convent. In the cities of the Renaissance, upper-class girls received an education similar to boys. Young ladies studied the writings of ancient Greece and Rome. Some women could even speak one or two modern languages, such as French or Spanish.

Laurea Cereta (1469–1499) illustrated the success and failure of Renaissance women. She was well educated and knew languages, philosophy, and mathematics. However, like all women of the Renaissance, she had to choose between marriage and full social participation or else study and withdraw from the world. She chose marriage. Cereta and other women of the urban upper middle class, in addition to the classical education, received training in painting, music, and dance. However, it was expected that their education would prepare them for the social function of running a household. An educated woman was supposed to know how to attract a husband and run a good household, whereas an educated man was supposed to know how to rule and participate in public affairs. Thus, Renaissance women were supposed to be decorative, affable, and charming.

A few women, such as Isabella d'Este, did exercise some power. Born into the ruling class of Ferrara, she married the ruler of another city state, Mantua. She brought many Renaissance artists to her court and created an art collection that was famous throughout Europe. She was also skilled in politics. When her husband was taken captive, she defended Mantua and won his freedom.

Women's status also declined in regard to love and sex. In the medieval books, manners shaped the man to please the woman. According to Castiglione, the women were supposed to make themselves pleasing to men. Renaissance Humanists laid the foundation for the bourgeoisie double standard, men were supposed to act in the public sector and women belonged in the home.

The Renaissance had very little impact on the lives of ordinary women. Women continued to perform economic functions, such as working on the farms or helping their husbands run businesses. Women continued to work as housekeepers and midwives. Since educational opportunities were limited, very few women as well as men received an education. This educational divide would create a distinct class difference between the "educated elite" who promoted the arts and the mass of people who supported "popular culture."

The Renaissance is the golden age of art and literature but for women it was an era of mixed blessings. Upper-class women were better educated but their role in society became well defined and their influence declined in comparison to the medieval period.

Reader's Comments on Part B: First Sample

Student Thematic Essay, Group 1–1

- The student uses good details to support the thesis statement.
- The response is well organized.
- The essay gives a good comparison between the Middle Ages and the Renaissance.
- The student's analysis of the role of ordinary women is good.
- The essay's discussion of relationships between men and women reinforces the thesis statement.

Possible student score: 8–9

Part B: Second Sample Student Thematic Essay, Group 1–1

The role of women in the Renaissance declined. Upper-class women were well educated and learned the classics of ancient Greece and Rome. Women received the same education as young men. Some young women even learned how to speak modern languages such as Spanish or French.

The purpose of Renaissance education was to prepare women for the function of running a household. Women were not expected to participate in the power structure but were expected to support men in their public function.

Thus Renaissance women received better educational opportunities than women in the Middle Ages, but their role in society was limited. A woman's fulfillment was in getting married and being a good house organizer. The role of Renaissance women was to enhance the position of their husband.

There were some women such as Artemisia Gentileschi, who achieved international renown for her painting, but she was the exception, not the rule. Women were not expected to seek fame. Furthermore, the job of women was to make themselves pleasing to men since the women's role was to manage the home. The life of ordinary women was not greatly affected by the Renaissance. Ordinary women continued to work in agriculture and industry. They received very little education and their role in society was not altered.

Reader's Comments on Part B: Second Sample Student Thematic Essay, Group 1–1

- The thesis is superficial.
- The essay never goes into depth regarding the role of women in comparison to men.
- The essay gives good facts to support the discussion of women who achieved fame.
- The student gives little analysis of the role of ordinary women.
- The essay needs more in-depth analysis, such as how women were expected to support their men, the importance of Castiglione's book, *The Courtier,* and how women were expected to be charming but not seek fame.

Possible student score: 3–4

Part B: First Sample Student Thematic Essay, Group 1–2

The French Revolution follows Crane Brinton's thesis that all revolutions go through three stages: Moderate, Radical, and Reactionary, which ultimately lead to the rise of dictatorships and a period of stability.

In May 1789, Louis XVI called the Estates General (the French Parliament), which had not met since 1614 to help him solve the nation's financial crisis. A six week deadlock over voting ended when the Third Estate (middle class) declared itself the National Assembly and took the "Tennis Court Oath" not to disband until they had written a constitution. The French Revolution had begun and had entered its Moderate Stage. The king consented to the formation of the National Assembly where voting would be per capita, not by unit. During this Moderate Stage, the National Assembly would take steps to end the abuses of the Old Regime. The National Assembly abolished feudalism and passed the Declaration of the Rights of Man and of the Citizen, which guaranteed freedom of speech, religion, and due process to all men. The principles of the declaration were captured by the slogan of "Liberty, Equality, and Fraternity." The National Assembly also passed the Civil Constitution of the

Clergy, which ended papal authority over the French church and dissolved monasteries and convents. This attack on the Church turned many people against the revolution and made the Church a bitter enemy of the revolution. In 1791, the National Assembly wrote a constitution that provided for a limited monarchy and a legislative assembly whose members had to be property owners and elected by taxpaying citizens. By 1791, the middle class and many peasants were satisfied with the revolution. However, there were many groups in France that were dissatisfied and were opposed to a limited constitutional monarchy.

In 1792, the French Revolution entered its Radical Stage when the National Convention, which had replaced the National Assembly, abolished the monarchy and proclaimed a French Republic. There was a split in the convention. The Jacobins, led by Maximilien Robespierre, wanted a centralized government with the power to help the poor and control the economy. The Girondists (a more moderate group) wanted a middle class republic. In 1793, Louis XVI and Marie Antoinette were beheaded. This act sent shock waves through all of Europe and a coalition of European nations was formed to stop the spread of the revolution. Faced with economic difficulties at home (rising prices and unemployment) and the fear of foreign invasion, the Jacobins created the Committee of Public Safety which had dictatorial powers. The goal of this Twelve Man Committee of Public Safety was to save the revolution from foreign invasion and domestic enemies. Military service became mandatory and over 1.1 million men rallied to their country. In the meantime, the Committee of Public Safety instituted a Reign of Terror (July 1793–1794). All persons suspected of treason were put to death. Over 40,000 people were killed. Food rationing was introduced, monetary controls were set up to stop inflation, and all material was censored. Robespierre, known as Mr. Incorruptible, was the architect of the Reign of Terror and proclaimed a republic of virtue. He wanted to de-Christianize France and turn the Cathedral of Notre Dame into the Temple of Reason. By 1794, the Reign of Terror was out of control and the people turned against the government. In March 1794, Robespierre executed Danton, one of the Jacobin Committee leaders, for urging an end to the Reign of Terror. Fearful of what would happen next, the National Convention arrested Robespierre. He was put to death, thus ending the Radical Stage of the Revolution.

In 1795, France entered the Reactionary Stage. The National Convention drew up the Constitution of 1795. This constitution set up a five-man Directory with a two-house legislature that was elected by male citizens who owned property. The Directory held power from 1795–1799. It was a weak, dictatorial, and corrupt government that faced serious problems. The sans-culottes and the aristocracy were critical of the government's policies. When rising bread prices stirred riots in October 1795, the Directory ordered Napoleon, who was a strong leader and happened to be in Paris, to crush the riots. He saved the government but ultimately he would end up destroying the government. In 1799, Napoleon, who considered himself to be a "Son of the Revolution," took control of France as First Consul and later became emperor for life. Many people in France, especially the middle class, supported Napoleon because he restored stability after years of chaos.

The French Revolution, which began with moderate efforts to reform the French government, progressed to the Radical Stage of terror and concluded with a return to stability in the person of Napoleon. The emergence of Napoleon would lend stability at the expense of political freedom.

Reader's Comments on Part B: First Sample Student Thematic Essay, Group 1–2

- The thesis statement is clear and well developed.
- The student effectively assesses each stage of the revolution.
- The student makes excellent use of specific facts (*Declaration of the Rights of Man and of the Citizen,* Reign of Terror, and Directory).
- The essay lacks depth on the appeal of Napoleon.
- The student's showing the loss of freedom makes both the summary and conclusion effective.

Possible student score: 7–8

Part B: Second Sample Student Thematic Essay, Group 1–2

The French Revolution, like all revolutions, followed a moderate, radical, and reactionary stage. After the reactionary stage, a strong ruler emerged.

France in 1789 was in chaos. Louis XVI called the Estates General. There were immediate problems which led to a new government called the National Assembly. The National Assembly ended the Old Regime and passed laws granting civil rights to people. The National Assembly also limited the power of the Catholic Church and created a limited monarchy. The National Convention in 1792 abolished the monarchy and set up a republic which began the Radical Stage. The Radical Stage included the Reign of Terror. Robespierre, a Jacobin, led the Reign of Terror, which resulted in the loss of over 40,000 people. Robespierre also wanted to create a Republic of Virtue. He was beheaded in 1794 and thus ended the Radical Stage.

The Reactionary Stage began with the selection of the Directory to lead France. The Directory was a weak government because voting was restricted to male property owners. The Directory was corrupt and was unable to deal with the economic problems facing the nation. In the midst of this chaos, Napoleon, a victorious general, promised the people a return to order and stability. In 1799, Napoleon seized power and by 1804, became emperor. Napoleon's one-man rule had established order at the expense of freedom.

Reader's Comments on Part B: Second Sample Student Thematic Essay, Group 1–2

- The thesis statement is weak.
- The student's use of facts is extremely limited. The student gives a cursory mention of *Declaration of Rights of Man and Citizen* and the end of feudalism.
- The content of the essay is too general.

Possible student score: 3–4

Part B: First Sample Student Thematic Essay, Group 1–3

Mercantilism was an economic policy that influenced Europe from the sixteenth to the eighteenth century during the era of colonization and the rise of absolutism. Laissez faire was an outgrowth of the philosophy of the Enlightenment and became the economic theory associated with the Industrial Revolution and laid the foundation for the system of capitalism.

During the 1500s and 1600s, European nations adapted the economic policy of mercantilism. The theory of mercantilism was based on the fact that a country's power depended primarily on how much wealth a nation accumulated. The accumulation of wealth would strengthen the national economy. The core of mercantilism included a belief that a nation's wealth was measured in its supply of gold and silver. The supply of gold and silver depended upon a favorable balance of trade, which required that a country had to export more than it imported. Mercantilism went hand in hand with colonization; colonies were central to the mercantile system. In addition to providing gold and silver, colonies also served as a source of raw materials and markets for manufactured goods from the mother country. Colonies existed for the benefit of the mother country. Governments passed strict navigation laws regulating trade and forbidding the colonies to set up industries to manufacture goods or trade with other countries. Thus, political absolutism that had extended over the country was extended into the economic area. The government also adapted a single national currency, standard weights and measures, and sold monopolies to larger producers in certain industries as well as overseas trading empires. As the wealth of a nation increased, the power and prestige of the nation or monarch would be enhanced.

In the eighteenth century, physiocrats (Enlightenment thinkers who searched for a natural law to explain economics) rejected the ideas associated with mercantilism. They insisted that the government end its restriction of trade and ease its regulation of the economy. They also wanted industry and businesses to manufacture and sell goods free from government interference. These physiocrats supported a free market unregulated by the government, hence the term laissez faire (leave business alone). The Enlightenment thinkers criticized the mercantile idea that nations grow wealthy by placing heavy tariffs on foreign goods. They argued that government regulations only interfere with the production of wealth.

Adam Smith (1723–1790), a professor at the University of Glasgow, Scotland, skillfully presented the ideas of laissez faire in the book Wealth of Nations (1776). Smith attacked mercantilism for providing unjust privileges for private monopolies and government favorites. He argued that economic liberty guaranteed economic progress. Smith claimed that the government should not interfere with the economy. He urged that individuals pursuing their own economic interests would benefit the entire nation and lead to expanded resources for the nation. The rising bourgeoisie, or middle class, supported these ideas because it allowed them to increase their economic power at the expense of the aristocracy. Smith's idea that a natural law governed economics would become the foundation of laissez-faire capitalism. The concept of the market place and the importance of the laws of supply and demand would greatly influence Britain and other industrial economies.

Like Smith, economists Thomas Malthus and David Ricardo supported the notion of a natural law for economics. Malthus, in An Essay on the Principle of Population, argued that the population tended to increase more rapidly than the food supply. The only check on population growth was war, disease, and famine. Ricardo, in his Iron Laws of wages, noted that when wages were high, families have more children. But more children increase the supply of labor which leads to lower wages. Like Malthus, Ricardo saw no hope for the poor. Smith, Malthus, and Ricardo opposed any government help for the poor. The supporters of laissez-faire economics believed that only through hard work and effort could individuals improve their position in life.

Mercantilism and laissez faire represent two different types of economic policies. Mercantilism outlines a detailed government policy regulating the economy whose objective is to increase the wealth of the state as well as the power of the ruler. Laissez faire focuses on the importance of individual economic freedom, which benefits the productive resources of the country. Both of these philosophies were never taken to their fullest extent. Mercantile countries, such as England, found it difficult to carry out the navigation laws and followed a policy of benign neglect towards the colonies. Laissez-faire economics was sharply modified by the efforts of social reformers throughout the late nineteenth and twentieth centuries.

Reader's Comments on Part B: First Sample Student Thematic Essay, Group 1–3

- The thesis is well developed in contrasting mercantilism and *laissez-faire*.
- The connection with absolutism and the Enlightenment is very good.
- Inclusion of Malthus and Ricardo demonstrates a good understanding of *laissez-faire*.
- The essay is very analytical.

Possible student score: 8–9

Part B: Second Sample Student Thematic Essay, Group 1–3

Mercantilism and laissez faire were two economic policies reflecting the political and social philosophy of a particular era.

Mercantilism was an economic system that existed in Europe from the sixteenth to the eighteenth century. Mercantilists believed that the wealth of a nation was measured by the supply of gold and silver and that nations must maintain a favorable balance of trade by exporting more goods than they import. Colonies existed for the benefit of the mother country. Colonies provided the raw materials not available in Europe and enriched the mother country by serving as markets for manufactured goods. European nations passed strict navigation laws to ensure that colonies traded only with the mother country.

In 1776, Adam Smith wrote The Wealth of Nations. In this book, Smith presented the idea of laissez faire. Smith argued that laissez faire (leave business alone) would benefit the rising bourgeoisie. The rising middle class wanted the government to discard the policy of mercantilism with its restriction of trade and industry. These capitalists wanted the government to manufacture and sell their goods free from government interference. Smith believed that economic liberty guaranteed economic progress. Unlike mercantilism, which promoted strict government control, laissez faire promoted the idea that each individual would benefit by being able to pursue his own interest. While mercantilism supported the absolute monarchs of Europe from the sixteenth to the eighteenth century, laissez faire provided the foundation for the industrial development of Western society.

Reader's Comments on Part B: Second Sample Student Thematic Essay, Group 1-3

- Thesis statement is superficial—reference to the social and political era is not explained, and issues are addressed weakly.
- Description of mercantilism is good but not analytical.
- Description of *laissez-faire* is weak—lack of connection to the idea of natural law and Enlightenment.
- The essay fails to connect to the ideas of Malthus and Ricardo.
- The student makes little effort to compare and contrast the two systems.

Possible student score: 4–5

Part B: First Sample Student Thematic Essay, Group 2-1

World War II left Europe physically devastated and in a state of economic chaos. Economic conditions in Western Europe were terrible. Simply finding enough food to eat was a constant problem. Runaway inflation and black markets testified to severe shortages and hardships. The economic aid provided by the United States via the Marshall Plan and the close cooperation of the European nations through the Common Market promoted growth and revived the economies of these Western European countries.

Much of Western Europe lay in ruins in 1947. Europe's problems included large-scale unemployment, lack of food, and economic turmoil. The United States was fearful that these conditions could lead to the rise of Communism. In June 1947, Secretary of State John Marshall proposed the European Economic Recovery Program (Marshall Plan). The United States promised to provide food, machines, and other materials to any European country that needed it. The United States also offered aid to the Soviet Union and its satellite nations, but Stalin rejected the offer. He claimed that the Marshall Plan was a way for the United States to extend its economic control over Eastern Europe. In March 1948, Congress approved the Marshall Plan providing $12.5 billion economic assistance to Europe. As the Marshall Plan aid poured into the battered economies of Western Europe, the United States helped the economic recovery get off to a quick start. Furthermore, economic growth became a basic objective of all the Western governments who were determined to avoid the economic chaos of the 1930s. In addition, many workers were willing to work hard for low wages in the hope for a better future.

The spirit of cooperation also helped Europe's recovery from World War II. The close support among European nations required by the Marshall Plan contributed to economic growth. In 1950, French Foreign Minister Robert Schuman proposed an economic union of Western Europe to integrate all European steel production. In 1952, France, West Germany, Belgium, Italy, the Netherlands, and Luxembourg set up the European Coal and Steel

Community. This independent agency set up prices and otherwise regulated the coal and steel industries of member nations. This close cooperation spurred economic growth and also did much to reduce the old rivalries, particularly between France and Germany. In 1957, these same six nations signed the Treaty of Rome to form the Common Market to expand free trade. The goal of the organization was the reduction of all tariffs among the six and also to include the free movement of capital and economic policies and institutions. The Common Market was a great success and added to the economic miracle of Western Europe.

The Marshall Plan and the formation of the Common Market, which abandoned the protectionism of many Western European nations, led to a push towards a united Europe, and contributed to the revival of Europe until the 1960s. By 1963, Western Europe was producing more than $2\frac{1}{2}$ times as much as it had produced before the war. Never before had the European economy grown so fast. Europe had truly undergone an economic miracle.

Reader's Comments on Part B: First Sample Student Thematic Essay, Group 2–1

- The thesis statement is very clear.
- The student makes good use of concrete facts (Marshall Plan, Common Market).
- The overall organization of the essay is good.
- The conclusion is good.

Possible student score: 8–9

Part B: Second Sample Student Thematic Essay, Group 2–1

After World War II, the economic conditions of Western Europe deteriorated. The people of Europe were left with little money and shortages of food. To the rest of the world, it appeared as if Western Europe was in complete chaos with no relief in sight.

New leaders who came to power after the war tried to improve conditions in Western Europe. Christian Democrats played an important role in leadership. They provided effective leadership and authority which helped improve the economy. Socialists and Communists also provided effective leadership and made changes for the better in certain countries. But even with new leaders, Western Europe was still struggling. Outside help finally came from the United States. The United States promised food, economic aid, and military protection for those countries that required it. This support eventually allowed Western Europe to rebuild and rejuvenate itself. Conditions in Europe were not as bad as they had been. The help of the United States made a considerable difference in Europe's economic status.

Even though the aid of the United States had a huge impact on the economy, the governments of Western Europe made a real effort to make economic growth their main priority and to avoid the dangerous times of the 1930s. The economies of Western Europe were further helped by the fact that these countries began to come together to try and improve Europe's economy as a whole rather than focus on individual countries. This sense of unity had a significant impact on their economic recovery.

Reader's Comments on Part B: Second Sample Student Thematic Essay, Group 2–1

- The thesis statement is unclear.
- The essay is too general—there is no specific reference to the Marshall Plan or the European Common Market.
- The student gives very little analysis.

Possible student score: 3–4

Part B: First Sample Student DBQ Essay, Group 2–2

As Europe recovered from World War I, two dictators rose to power in Italy and Germany. Italy's Benito Mussolini attempted to impose a Fascist government on his country, and Germany's Adolf Hitler ruled his country with Nazism.

Before World War I began, Italy appeared ready to move towards a democratic system of government. The existing parliamentary regime had granted universal male suffrage, and the state had a constitution that granted its citizens civil rights. However, several factors weakened Italy's strides towards democracy. The poverty of Italy's many peasants made it hard for them to be truly interested in the growth of Italian nationalism; they were more concerned with the affairs of their smaller villages. There were conflicts between the Catholic Church and Italy—the Church opposed Italy's growing liberalism. As World War I began, so did Italy's socialist movement. Socialists opposed Italy's entry into World War I.

After World War I, Italy was an embittered state. Although they had fought on the side of the Allies with the hopes of expanding Italy's territory, the Treaty of Versailles failed to provide the anticipated territorial gains. Workers and peasants, who had been promised social and land reforms in exchange for their support in the war, did not receive what the government had promised them. The Russian Revolution inspired the growing numbers of Italian Socialists. These Socialists worked with Russian Bolsheviks to seize land and businesses, which in turn scared Italian landowners. At the conclusion of World War I, the pope lifted the ban on Catholics in government.

As more and more conservative Catholics became involved in the government, the political scene in Italy grew more and more confused.

It seemed the perfect time for a charismatic, dominating leader to rise to power in Italy. Benito Mussolini had been a Socialist until he supported Italy's entry into World War I, and fought in World War I. After he returned home, he organized other veterans into a "union of forces"—or Fascists. He began his rise to power by combining nationalism and socialism, and by promising territorial expansion, worker benefits, and land reform for peasants. When his movement—which was similar to the already-established Socialist movement—failed to gain momentum, Mussolini used anti-Socialist propaganda to persuade conservative and middle class Italians to join his cause.

Mussolini began to repress the Socialist movement with increasing violence. He presented himself as the disciplinarian who was necessary to bring stability to Italy. By capitalizing on the fears of the middle class and conservative Italians, Mussolini was able to gain power. In 1922, Mussolini and the Fascists announced a march on Rome to demand that the government make changes. As thousands of Fascists chanted "On to Rome" and swarmed into the city, King Victor Emmanuel II bowed to pressure. Fearing a civil war, he asked Mussolini to form a government as prime minister. Without firing a shot, Mussolini received the legal authority from the king to become the leader of Italy. He received dictatorial powers to rule for one year, but by 1925 had eliminated all opposition through violence and terror.

Adolf Hitler also used the post–World War I climate to rise to power in Germany. Hitler was personally shattered by Germany's defeat in the First World War. A devout nationalist, Hitler was convinced that Germany's defeat was the fault of Jews and Marxists. Like many of the German people, Hitler was particularly bitter that Germany had been forced to accept full blame for the war. At the end of World War I, Hitler joined the German Workers' Party, which also denounced Jews and Marxists and promised an orderly, united German community.

When it appeared that the post–World War I government of the Weimar Republic was on the brink of collapse, Hitler and the German Workers' Party attempted to take control of the government. Although Hitler was put in jail, this revolt planted the first seeds of Nazism. Upon his release from jail, Hitler built his National Socialist German Workers'—or Nazi—Party. By 1928, the Nazi Party grew to include 100,000 members. However, they were still a small movement and in the 1928 election, they received less than 3 percent of the votes in the general election.

Ultimately, the economic crisis in Germany played the greatest role in Hitler's rise to power. In addition to the $132 billion in reparations that Germany was forced to pay the Allied nations, the Great Depression of 1929 hit an already deprived Germany very hard. Unemployment rose to record numbers, and Hitler realized it would greatly help his cause to pay attention to Germany's economic climate. As unemployment rose, the Germans began to panic and turned to the Nazis to solve their problems. Year by year, as the existing German government became less and less effective, the Nazis became more and more prominent. The Weimar Republic was unable to stabilize Germany's plummeting economy, and their attempts at recovery—including slashing prices and wages—were very unpopular.

Hitler also benefited from the inability of Germany's Social Democrats and Communists to compromise. Although both parties together outnumbered the Nazis in the Reichstag, the two groups were unable to see past their differing ideologies. Socialists pleaded for a temporary alliance to block Hitler's rise, but they were unsuccessful—which paved the way for Hitler to reign in Germany.

Although their paths to power were quite different, both Mussolini and Hitler rose to power on the heels of the instability resulting from the First World War. They were able to capitalize on growing anxiety and political infighting—the results of which led to the Second World War.

Reader's Comments on Part B: First Sample Student Thematic Essay, Group 2–2

- The thesis statement is very clear.
- The student gives a good comparison of the two leaders.
- The essay has an excellent analysis of conditions within the two countries.
- The conclusion is good.

Possible student score: 8–9

Part B: Second Sample Student Thematic Essay, Group 2–2

Fascism and Nazism were two systems of government that happened in Italy and Germany after World War I. Fascism was in Italy, and Mussolini led the movement. Mussolini wanted to completely control Italy—he was a dictator. The Italian people listened to him because the country was poor. Italy needed a strong leader, and Mussolini was the right man for the job. He used his charisma to convince the people of Italy that he should rule their country, and after World War I, the king of Italy handed over power to Mussolini. After he got power, Mussolini used violence and intimidation to crush his enemies—the socialists in Italy. Little by little, Mussolini gained complete control of Italy due to his brutal tactics. By the time World War II began, Italy was a dictatorship with Mussolini as the dictator. He had successfully brought fascism to Italy.

In Germany, Adolf Hitler was the reason why Nazism existed. He was also a powerful leader who took total control of his country. The German people were very bitter about what had happened to them after World War I. They had to take all the blame for the war, and they thought this was very unfair. They also had to pay billions of dollars to other countries in Europe, and because of this, their economy was bad and many people lost their jobs. Hitler promised them that all of this would change. He held rallies and riots and made them even angrier about what had happened in World War I. He used this anger to motivate the people of Germany to vote for his Nazi party and to spread Nazi ideas throughout Germany.

Hitler blamed Jews and Communists for what happened in World War I, and he eventually convinced the other German people that Jews and Communists were to blame for World War I. Using these tactics, Hitler was able to spread Nazism throughout Germany and eventually throughout other countries in Europe. Hitler promised the German people that Nazism would solve the economic problems in Germany. He promised the Germans more jobs and better wages. This was a major reason why the German people were so receptive to Hitler's ideas—they were so bitter about what World War I had done to their economy that they were willing to listen to any leader who promised that things would improve. Hitler's dynamic personality was a driving and motivating force for the spread of Nazism.

Fascism rose in Italy because of Mussolini and Nazism rose in Germany because of Hitler. These two men were responsible for the rise of these dictatorial governments, which eventually led to World War II.

Reader's Comments on Part B: Second Sample Student Thematic Essay, Group 2–2

- The thesis statement is superficial.
- The content of the essay is too general.
- The student doesn't analyze the conditions within the two countries.
- The essay is weak overall.

Possible student score: 1–3

Part B: First Sample Student Thematic Essay, Group 2–3

The unification of Germany and the unification of Italy were indicative of the growing spirit of nationalism throughout Europe.

Before 1860, Italy was not a nation. As Metternich, the leader of Austria, expressed, Italy was merely "a geographical expression." Under Metternich, Austria took control of the northern provinces of Lombardy and Venetia. An Italian monarch ruled Sardinia and Piedmont, and Tuscany shared northern and central Italy with several smaller states. The papacy ruled Central Italy and Rome, and a branch of the Bourbons ruled Naples and Sicily, as they had for the past 100 years.

From the beginning to the middle of the nineteenth century, many Italians favored unification, and leaders such as Mazzini and Gioberti attempted to unify Italy through a democratic centralized republic and a federation of states under the power of a pope, respectively. Another consideration was for the independent kingdom of Sardinia-Piedmont to lead Italy. This third alternative appeared to be the most feasible, as a democratic republic seemed too radical an idea and a federation of states ruled by the pope seemed unlikely, especially since the pope had been forced—for a brief span—out of Italy.

From 1850-1861, Camillo di Cavour was Sardinia's dominant figure in government. Cavour came from a noble family and began as a manager of his father's large estates in Piedmont. Before entering politics, Cavour met with much success through various economic ventures including sugar mills, banks, and railroads. When he entered politics after 1848, Cavour only wanted to unify the northern and central Italian states, and did not want to include the Papal States or the Two Sicilies. Cavour realized that because Austria controlled Lombardy and Venetia, he would not be able to unify northern Italy without a powerful ally to force Austria out of these areas. To accomplish this, Cavour forged a secret alliance against Austria with Napoleon III of France.

Armed with this alliance, Cavour enticed Austria into attacking Sardinia and, with France's aid, successfully crushed Austria. However, Napoleon III was disgusted by the nature of war and was criticized by French Catholics for supporting Cavour, the pope's enemy. To appease all sides, Napoleon III signed a compromise peace with Austria that gave Sardinia only Lombardy. An angry Cavour resigned, only to be brought back to Italy by the growing spirit of nationalism throughout the Italian states. Italy ignored Napoleon III's compromise peace and demanded they be joined with Sardinia—eventually, the Italians got their way and Cavour returned to power in 1860.

However, intense patriots such as Giuseppe Garibaldi, believed the Italian unification had further to go. Born into a peasant family, Garibaldi personified romantic nationalism. After a 12-year exile in South America, Garibaldi returned to Italy to fight against Austria. By the end of the war, Garibaldi was a powerful figure in Italian politics. In 1860, Garibaldi's guerrilla band of "Red Shirts" was able to defeat a 20,000-man army and take Palermo. He and his men marched towards Naples and were ready to attack Rome and the pope. As he realized that an attack on Rome would antagonize France, Cavour smartly intercepted Garibaldi before he and his troops got to Rome. Garibaldi did not oppose Cavour and the people of the South voted to join Sardinia. Italy was at last united—at least politically.

As these events occurred in Italy, Germany also struggled with its own process of unification. The unification of Germany spanned several decades. Much like Italy had been, after 1815, the German Confederation was a conglomerate of 39 different sovereign states. Frederick Wilhelm IV of Prussia attempted to unify Germany but Austria—with support from Russia—blocked Wilhelm's attempt. As the nineteenth century progressed, and as economic growth spread throughout the rest of Europe, Prussia was instrumental in helping to form a customs union. The Zollverein, as this union was called, stimulated trade and improved the economies of its member-states. Because it was not economically beneficial or feasible for Austria to join the Zollverein, Austria tried to get the southern German states to leave the Zollverein to no avail. As the members of the Zollverein grew stronger and stronger, Prussia gained more and more of an advantage in its struggle with Austria.

As the German states witnessed the unification of Italy, Prussia changed greatly. The middle-class Prussians wanted to assert parliamentary power over the king. William I—who had replaced Wilhelm—wanted to double the size of Prussia's army. This did not appeal to middle-class Prussians who wanted to not only demilitarize but also wanted to make sure that the army remained under the control of Parliament and did not become its own governing body. By 1862, these middle-class Prussians had successfully won a majority of seats in Parliament and had defeated William I's proposed military budget. Ready to abdicate his throne, William turned to Otto von Bismarck.

The appointment of Bismarck was not met with satisfaction, as Bismarck soon showed that he would rule despite Parliament's disapproval. In order to draw attention away from domestic dissent, Bismarck maneuvered Prussia into a war with Austria. In the span of seven weeks, Prussia defeated Austria. The German Confederation was dissolved and Austria agreed to withdraw from German affairs. An expanded Prussia ruled the new North German Confederation while the mainly Catholic southern states remained independent but formed alliances with Prussia.

After the war, Bismarck restructured the government and chartered a federal constitution for the North German confederation. Each state had local government, but the king of Prussia—William I—became president of the confederation, and the chancellor—Bismarck—reported only to William I. Bismarck also formed a two-house legislature, with each house sharing equally in the making of laws. In a radical move, lower house members were elected by universal male suffrage. This enabled the king and chancellor to bypass the middle class but to also retain power. Realizing that Bismarck had yet to appease the middle class, he made a peace offering by asking Parliament to retroactively approve Prussia's spending from 1862 to 1866. The Parliament readily accepted Bismarck's offer. In 1867, Bismarck brought the four southern German states into a customs parliament and although these states were initially unwilling to go further, Germany was but a few steps away from unity.

The Franco-Prussian war from 1870–1871 was the last piece in the puzzle of German unification. Bismarck was astute enough to realize that war with France was the answer he needed to fully unify Germany. France was becoming alarmed by Prussia's growing power and decided that a war would be a way to assert its power over Prussia. From the very start of the war, the southern German states completely supported Bismarck. Because Bismarck had been so lenient with Austria after Prussia defeated them a few years earlier, Germany was able to easily defeat France's troops. After five months, Bismarck's campaign was successful and Germany was at last united under a two-house legislature, much like the one Bismarck set up in 1867.

Unlike Italy, Germany emerged from its process of unification feeling powerful, cohesive, and very proud. Whereas Cavour had been hesitant and unenthusiastic about bringing the southern Italian states into his new nation, Bismarck forged a war for the very purpose of bringing southern German states into his new empire. Prussia, which had been one of Europe's weaker nations, emerged from the unification of Germany as Europe's powerhouse.

Reader's Comments on Part B: First Sample Student Thematic Essay, Group 2–3

- The thesis is well stated and fully developed.
- The content of the essay is very specific regarding the role of Cavour and Bismarck.
- The student's analysis of the data is excellent, especially regarding Cavour in Italy and Bismarck's relationship with the German states.
- The essay is insightful.

Possible student score: 8–9

Part B: Second Sample Student Thematic Essay, Group 2–3

In the middle of the nineteenth century, two major European nations were unified—Italy and Germany, because of growing nationalism throughout Europe.

Italy was unified because of a man named Cavour. He was the leader of Piedmont and wanted to unite Italy so that he could have more power in Europe. Before Cavour, other leaders had tried to unify Italy but it did not work. One plan was for Italy to be unified and ruled by the pope—but not everyone supported that idea. Another plan was for Italy to be a federation—but many people objected to that idea and thought it was too radical. However, because of the nationalism that was spreading through Europe, many Italians wanted a unified nation.

Cavour helped with this goal of unification. However, he did not want to include all of Italy in this new nation. Cavour thought that only the northern Italian states should be included in a united Italy. However, a patriot from the South—Garibaldi—wanted the South to be a part of Italy. He was ready to fight Cavour and his troops, but Cavour realized it would be better to compromise with Garibaldi. Eventually, Cavour agreed to join the northern and the southern parts of Italy, mostly due to the political influence and public support of Garibaldi. However, even though Italy was unified in name, many people considered the North and the South to be two separate parts—Cavour had only unified Italy to appease Garibaldi's army, and Italy was not truly unified.

German unification was a much longer process than the unification process of Italy. Germany was unified due to the efforts of Bismarck. Bismarck was an aristocratic Prussian who wanted to expand Prussia, and he also wanted to make sure that Austria did not have power over Germany. Before it was unified, Germany was a collection of many independent states, each with their own government. Bismarck set up an economic alliance between Prussia and many of the German states, and Austria was left out of the alliance. Then, Austria and Prussia went to war—and Prussia won in less than two months. Bismarck did not make the Austrians sign a very harsh treaty, but he was able to ensure that Austria did not hold any power over Germany.

Bismarck was a powerful man, and after the war with Austria, he set up a system of government that made him second in command to only the Prussian king. After the war, Bismarck succeeded in bringing together most of Germany. Only the southern German states were not a part of the newly expanded Prussia. Soon after the war between Prussia and Austria was another war—this time between Prussia and France. Bismarck needed this war so that the southern German states would join his newly expanded empire. After a very short war, France was defeated

and the southern German states joined Bismarck's empire. Germany was finally unified.

Nationalism and strong leadership were two things that the Italian and German unification had in common.

However, Germany's process of unification took much longer and Italy's was much less cohesive than Germany's.

Reader's Comments on Part B: Second Sample Student Thematic Essay, Group 2–3

- The thesis statement is not well defined.
- The content of the essay is very superficial.
- The student gives little discussion of important facts, such as the Franco-Prussian War and the role of Garibaldi.
- The essay is weak overall.

Possible student score: 1–3

Sample Practice Exam III

Answer Sheet for Sample Practice Exam III

Remove this sheet and use it to mark your answers for the multiple-choice section of Sample Practice Exam III.

1 Ⓐ Ⓑ Ⓒ Ⓓ Ⓔ   21 Ⓐ Ⓑ Ⓒ Ⓓ Ⓔ   41 Ⓐ Ⓑ Ⓒ Ⓓ Ⓔ   61 Ⓐ Ⓑ Ⓒ Ⓓ Ⓔ
2 Ⓐ Ⓑ Ⓒ Ⓓ Ⓔ   22 Ⓐ Ⓑ Ⓒ Ⓓ Ⓔ   42 Ⓐ Ⓑ Ⓒ Ⓓ Ⓔ   62 Ⓐ Ⓑ Ⓒ Ⓓ Ⓔ
3 Ⓐ Ⓑ Ⓒ Ⓓ Ⓔ   23 Ⓐ Ⓑ Ⓒ Ⓓ Ⓔ   43 Ⓐ Ⓑ Ⓒ Ⓓ Ⓔ   63 Ⓐ Ⓑ Ⓒ Ⓓ Ⓔ
4 Ⓐ Ⓑ Ⓒ Ⓓ Ⓔ   24 Ⓐ Ⓑ Ⓒ Ⓓ Ⓔ   44 Ⓐ Ⓑ Ⓒ Ⓓ Ⓔ   64 Ⓐ Ⓑ Ⓒ Ⓓ Ⓔ
5 Ⓐ Ⓑ Ⓒ Ⓓ Ⓔ   25 Ⓐ Ⓑ Ⓒ Ⓓ Ⓔ   45 Ⓐ Ⓑ Ⓒ Ⓓ Ⓔ   65 Ⓐ Ⓑ Ⓒ Ⓓ Ⓔ
6 Ⓐ Ⓑ Ⓒ Ⓓ Ⓔ   26 Ⓐ Ⓑ Ⓒ Ⓓ Ⓔ   46 Ⓐ Ⓑ Ⓒ Ⓓ Ⓔ   66 Ⓐ Ⓑ Ⓒ Ⓓ Ⓔ
7 Ⓐ Ⓑ Ⓒ Ⓓ Ⓔ   27 Ⓐ Ⓑ Ⓒ Ⓓ Ⓔ   47 Ⓐ Ⓑ Ⓒ Ⓓ Ⓔ   67 Ⓐ Ⓑ Ⓒ Ⓓ Ⓔ
8 Ⓐ Ⓑ Ⓒ Ⓓ Ⓔ   28 Ⓐ Ⓑ Ⓒ Ⓓ Ⓔ   48 Ⓐ Ⓑ Ⓒ Ⓓ Ⓔ   68 Ⓐ Ⓑ Ⓒ Ⓓ Ⓔ
9 Ⓐ Ⓑ Ⓒ Ⓓ Ⓔ   29 Ⓐ Ⓑ Ⓒ Ⓓ Ⓔ   49 Ⓐ Ⓑ Ⓒ Ⓓ Ⓔ   69 Ⓐ Ⓑ Ⓒ Ⓓ Ⓔ
10 Ⓐ Ⓑ Ⓒ Ⓓ Ⓔ   30 Ⓐ Ⓑ Ⓒ Ⓓ Ⓔ   50 Ⓐ Ⓑ Ⓒ Ⓓ Ⓔ   70 Ⓐ Ⓑ Ⓒ Ⓓ Ⓔ
11 Ⓐ Ⓑ Ⓒ Ⓓ Ⓔ   31 Ⓐ Ⓑ Ⓒ Ⓓ Ⓔ   51 Ⓐ Ⓑ Ⓒ Ⓓ Ⓔ   71 Ⓐ Ⓑ Ⓒ Ⓓ Ⓔ
12 Ⓐ Ⓑ Ⓒ Ⓓ Ⓔ   32 Ⓐ Ⓑ Ⓒ Ⓓ Ⓔ   52 Ⓐ Ⓑ Ⓒ Ⓓ Ⓔ   72 Ⓐ Ⓑ Ⓒ Ⓓ Ⓔ
13 Ⓐ Ⓑ Ⓒ Ⓓ Ⓔ   33 Ⓐ Ⓑ Ⓒ Ⓓ Ⓔ   53 Ⓐ Ⓑ Ⓒ Ⓓ Ⓔ   73 Ⓐ Ⓑ Ⓒ Ⓓ Ⓔ
14 Ⓐ Ⓑ Ⓒ Ⓓ Ⓔ   34 Ⓐ Ⓑ Ⓒ Ⓓ Ⓔ   54 Ⓐ Ⓑ Ⓒ Ⓓ Ⓔ   74 Ⓐ Ⓑ Ⓒ Ⓓ Ⓔ
15 Ⓐ Ⓑ Ⓒ Ⓓ Ⓔ   35 Ⓐ Ⓑ Ⓒ Ⓓ Ⓔ   55 Ⓐ Ⓑ Ⓒ Ⓓ Ⓔ   75 Ⓐ Ⓑ Ⓒ Ⓓ Ⓔ
16 Ⓐ Ⓑ Ⓒ Ⓓ Ⓔ   36 Ⓐ Ⓑ Ⓒ Ⓓ Ⓔ   56 Ⓐ Ⓑ Ⓒ Ⓓ Ⓔ   76 Ⓐ Ⓑ Ⓒ Ⓓ Ⓔ
17 Ⓐ Ⓑ Ⓒ Ⓓ Ⓔ   37 Ⓐ Ⓑ Ⓒ Ⓓ Ⓔ   57 Ⓐ Ⓑ Ⓒ Ⓓ Ⓔ   77 Ⓐ Ⓑ Ⓒ Ⓓ Ⓔ
18 Ⓐ Ⓑ Ⓒ Ⓓ Ⓔ   38 Ⓐ Ⓑ Ⓒ Ⓓ Ⓔ   58 Ⓐ Ⓑ Ⓒ Ⓓ Ⓔ   78 Ⓐ Ⓑ Ⓒ Ⓓ Ⓔ
19 Ⓐ Ⓑ Ⓒ Ⓓ Ⓔ   39 Ⓐ Ⓑ Ⓒ Ⓓ Ⓔ   59 Ⓐ Ⓑ Ⓒ Ⓓ Ⓔ   79 Ⓐ Ⓑ Ⓒ Ⓓ Ⓔ
20 Ⓐ Ⓑ Ⓒ Ⓓ Ⓔ   40 Ⓐ Ⓑ Ⓒ Ⓓ Ⓔ   60 Ⓐ Ⓑ Ⓒ Ⓓ Ⓔ   80 Ⓐ Ⓑ Ⓒ Ⓓ Ⓔ

CUT HERE

CUT HERE

Section I: Multiple-Choice Questions

Time: 55 minutes

80 Questions

Percent of total grade = 50%

Directions: Each of the questions or incomplete statements below is followed by five suggested answers or completions. Select the one that is best in each case and then fill in the corresponding oval on the answer sheet.

1. The Soviet invasion in 1979 in which of the following countries led to the end of détente and the United States' boycott of the Olympic games in Russia in 1980?

   A. Poland
   B. Hungary
   C. East Germany
   D. Czechoslovakia
   E. Afghanistan

2. The Medici family helped with the prosperity of Florence by doing all of the following EXCEPT

   A. donating their money to the Church.
   B. sponsoring the arts.
   C. providing political and artistic leadership.
   D. supporting popular causes.
   E. becoming patrons of artists and writers such as Michelangelo, Botticelli, and Giovanni Pico della Mirandola.

3. In 1868, which area in Italy was NOT part of the united Kingdom of Italy?

   A. The Kingdom of the Two Sicilies
   B. Lombardy
   C. Venetia
   D. The Papal States
   E. Tuscany

4. The portrait of this European king who is surrounded by the symbols of his power—the gold flower embroidered on his robe, as well as the sword and the scepter—best represents

A. James I
B. Henry VIII
C. Louis XIV
D. Frederick the Great
E. Philip II

5. Which of the following was NOT a result of the fall of the Berlin Wall in 1989?

   A. The collapse of communism in the Soviet Union
   B. The unification of East and West Germany
   C. The death of Nicolae Ceausescu
   D. The rise of Solidarity in Poland
   E. The election of Václav Havel in Czechoslovakia

6. As a result of the Congress of Vienna, Belgium

   A. was returned to Spain.
   B. was given to France.
   C. was granted independence.
   D. became neutral.
   E. was given to the Netherlands.

7. Johannes Kepler's work on the first three laws of planetary motion that were based on mathematical relations helped to

   A. support Newton's law of gravity.
   B. uphold the Aristotelian view of the universe.
   C. reinforce Galileo's theory of the universe.
   D. prove that Ptolemy's view of the earth as the center of the universe was correct.
   E. support Tycho Brahe's data about the planets moving in an elliptical orbit.

8. The death of Marshall Tito resulted in

   A. a period of peace among the many different ethnic groups of Yugoslavia.
   B. disarmament of Yugoslavia's nuclear weapons.
   C. the unification of Yugoslavia.
   D. a period of chaos in Yugoslavia due to ethnic conflicts.
   E. economic prosperity.

9. Portugal's role in the Age of Discovery included all of the following EXCEPT

   A. exploring overseas lands in the Middle East and Africa.
   B. bringing Christianity to Arab and African lands.
   C. inspiring Spain and other European nations to join the Age of Discovery.
   D. discovering the first water route to India.
   E. developing a unique system of diplomacy to forge relationships with its colonized lands.

10. Mercantilism was an economic policy in which

    A. laws of supply and demand determined the price of goods.
    B. government owned the factors of production.
    C. the workers shared in the profits.
    D. a nation's wealth was measured by its gold and silver.
    E. individuals could follow their own interests for the good of the country.

11. The main reason for the Berlin Conference of 1884–1885 was

    A. to prevent Belgium from taking over all of Africa.
    B. to work with African nations to develop an economic program.
    C. to limit trading practices on the Congo River.
    D. to establish guidelines for dividing up Africa in order to avoid conflicts among European nations.
    E. to allow Italy an opportunity to establish colonies for its surplus population.

12. Which of the following men called for national workshops to guarantee full employment for the workers?

    A. Louis Blanc
    B. Robert Owen
    C. Pierre Proudhon
    D. Charles Fourier
    E. Georg Wilhelm Friedrich Hegel

13. Which is the most accurate statement about the Soviet Union under Lenin?

    A. It was a classless society.
    B. Capitalism was abolished.
    C. The government allowed limited democratic reforms.
    D. The Communist Party had absolute control.
    E. Lenin had selected Stalin as his successor before he died.

14. The 38th Parallel refers to

    A. a condition of the Treaty of Versailles.
    B. the Soviet area of Germany.
    C. officially neutral land.
    D. the point of division between North Korea and South Korea.
    E. safe airspace for Western Bloc aircraft.

15. Milosevic's policy of "ethnic cleansing" was

    A. the forced removal of non-Serbian groups from Serbian-controlled areas.
    B. a way to ensure peace throughout Yugoslavia.
    C. a plan of attack against his neighboring countries.
    D. a treaty with the former Soviet Union.
    E. a way to unite all Serbs and non-Serbs into a greater Yugoslavia.

16. The Seven Weeks' War in 1866 between Austria and Prussia led to

    A. the annexation of Schleswig/Holstein by Prussia.
    B. Austria paying a huge indemnity to Prussia.
    C. Austria recognizing Prussian dominance of the German states.
    D. Napoleon III's decision to support unification of northern and southern Germany.
    E. a quick victory by Austria.

17. The Balfour Declaration of 1917

    A. ended Austria-Hungary's participation in the war.
    B. laid the foundation for the League of Nations.
    C. guaranteed the re-establishment of Belgian neutrality.
    D. declared the right of Jews to a homeland in Palestine.
    E. supported American entrance into World War I.

18. During the Stuart Restoration, what was one accomplishment of Parliament?

    A. They passed the Habeas Corpus Act, prohibiting imprisonment without due cause.
    B. They successfully prevented Charles II's Catholic brother from inheriting the throne.
    C. They revoked Charles II's secret treaty with France.
    D. They limited the power of the monarchy.
    E. They negotiated lucrative treaties with other European nations.

19. Which was considered to be the leading example of the new industrial city of the Industrial Revolution during the late eighteenth and early nineteenth centuries in England?

    A. Manchester
    B. Liverpool
    C. London
    D. Birmingham
    E. Sheffield

20. Machiavelli would most likely support a politician who would

    A. manipulate people and use any means to gain power.
    B. govern his actions by moral considerations.
    C. take actions to weaken the government and let the people govern.
    D. govern with the help of the Church.
    E. take a passive approach when dealing with problems.

21. Enlightened Despots believed in all of the following EXCEPT

    A. reform of the educational system.
    B. use of reason to examine the world.
    C. democracy.
    D. religious toleration.
    E. support of art, literature, and science.

22. Which of the following men was NOT allowed to accept the Nobel Prize in Literature in 1958?

    A. Boris Pasternak
    B. Alexander Solzhenitsyn
    C. Josef Pilsudski
    D. Mikhail Glinka
    E. Sergei Prokofiev

23. In the "Night of the Long Knives" in June 1934, Hitler ordered his SS men and the Gestapo to

    A. arrest all Jews.
    B. destroy the Weimar Republic.
    C. put to death Ernst Roehm, his friend and leader of the Brown Shirts, and 1,000 of his troops.
    D. arrest all members of the Communist Party.
    E. begin occupying the Rhineland.

24. All of the following are included in the Fourteen Points of Woodrow Wilson EXCEPT

    A. the end of secret diplomacy.
    B. freedom of the seas.
    C. reduction of arms.
    D. free trade.
    E. preventing countries from having to pay war reparations.

25. Napoleon's *coup d'état* resulted in

    A. the restoration of the French monarchy.
    B. the restoration of the Directory as the governing body of France.
    C. his defeat and exile.
    D. the formation of the Consulate.
    E. a period of peace in France.

26. A major difference between Calvinists and Lutherans was that John Calvin, unlike Martin Luther, believed

    A. salvation came through faith alone.
    B. the Church was higher than the state and should have a role in the government.
    C. the Bible was not the final authority.
    D. people have free will to do what they think is right.
    E. one's faith has nothing to do with economic status.

27. A major reason for British interest in controlling the Suez Canal was

    A. Egypt's valuable mineral resources.
    B. the strategic location of the Suez Canal.
    C. to spread Christianity to Egypt.
    D. Egypt's value as a marketplace for British goods.
    E. Egypt's control of the spice trade.

28. A major result of the Reform Act of 1832 was

    A. abolishing rotten boroughs.
    B. outlawing the secret ballots.
    C. abolishing the House of Lords' veto power.
    D. government funding for public housing.
    E. extending suffrage to women.

29. The Marshall Plan was

    A. a recovery program that gave over $17 billion in economic aid to European nations.
    B. the United States buildup of nuclear weapons.
    C. a treaty between the nations of NATO and the nations of the Warsaw Pact.
    D. a military invasion of West Germany.
    E. a way for Russia to further increase their control over Eastern European nations.

30. During the Renaissance after the Hundred Years' War, the monarchy in France

    A. was consolidated most effectively by Louis XI.
    B. was overturned by the rise of the bourgeoisie.
    C. was weakened because of the rise of feudal anarchy.
    D. joined with the Church to fix the damages caused by the war.
    E. completely crumbled due to the devastation of the war.

31. All of the following were a result of Napoleon's Russian invasion EXCEPT

    A. Napoleon gained further control over France and other parts of Europe.
    B. Napoleon lost three-fourths of his army.
    C. Napoleon abdicated his throne.
    D. Napoleon was forced into exile.
    E. Louis XVIII was restored to the throne.

32. The Council of Trent supported all of the following statements EXCEPT

    A. salvation was obtained by good works and faith.
    B. the Bible was the source of religious authority and faith.
    C. an individual does not need the guidance of the Church for understanding his or her faith.
    D. seminary education of the clergy is a must in each diocese.
    E. certain books, such as those of Galileo and Erasmus, should not be read.

33. Reformers such as Robert Owen who tried to establish model communities, were known as

    A. Luddites.
    B. communists.
    C. Utopian socialists.
    D. fascists.
    E. anarchists.

34. The Locarno Pact of 1925 referred to

    A. the agreement to end German reparation payments.
    B. the United States joining the League of Nations.
    C. the symbol of a new era of cooperation between France and Germany.
    D. the removal of the War Guilt Clause from the Treaty of Versailles.
    E. the agreement of European nations to denounce war as an instrument of foreign policy.

35. The beautification of Paris during the presidency of Louis Napoleon was under the supervision of

    A. George Haussmann.
    B. Edwin Chadwick.
    C. Louis Pasteur.
    D. Joseph Lister.
    E. Gustav Vasa.

36. In the late 1980s, Mikhail Gorbachev's decision to stop interfering in the internal affairs of Eastern European nations led directly to

    A. the collapse of the free-market economies in the region.
    B. an increase in Cold War tensions.
    C. a renewal of religious violence between Orthodox Christians and Russian Jews.
    D. the collapse of NATO.
    E. the collapse of the Communist governments in the region.

37. All of the following states came into existence after World War I EXCEPT

    A. Albania.
    B. Finland.
    C. Czechoslovakia.
    D. Yugoslavia.
    E. Estonia.

38. *Don Quixote* was

    A. a political manifesto.
    B. a painting that depicted the glory of Spanish colonialism.
    C. a series of maps that depicted Spain's African colonies.
    D. a work of fiction that described Spain in the sixteenth century.
    E. a handbook on protocol in the Spanish court.

39. All of the following statements are true about the united Kingdom of Italy in 1871 EXCEPT

    A. a division existed between the industrial north and agricultural south.
    B. the Catholic Church supported the newly united government.
    C. the government adopted a policy of ambitious nationalism and imperialism.
    D. there was a strong lack of a democratic tradition.
    E. a large population growth led to migration as people were unable to earn a living.

40. One result of Stalin's policy of collectivization was

    A. surplus agricultural crops.
    B. a widespread food shortage.
    C. an increase in exports of agricultural products to Western Europe.
    D. the establishment of a strong agricultural base to support the expansion of the Soviet Union's heavy industry.
    E. a renewed cooperation between Kulaks and the Soviet government.

41. What was a major goal of Peter the Great's foreign policy?

    A. To take complete control of Poland from Prussia
    B. To join an alliance with France against England
    C. To limit the expansion of Austria's influence in the Balkans
    D. To acquire a window on the West along the Baltic Sea
    E. To gain a port on the Black Sea

42. "The Scramble for Africa was due to the growing commercial rivalry which brought home . . . the vital necessity of securing the only remaining fields for industrial enterprises and expansion."

    The author of this passage would support the belief that the motive for imperialism was

    A. religious.
    B. economic.
    C. political.
    D. military.
    E. humanitarian.

43. Which group gained suffrage in England as a result of the Great Reform Bill of 1832?

    A. The middle class
    B. Women
    C. The landed aristocracy
    D. The urban working class
    E. Peasants

44. The Jacobins instituted all of the following EXCEPT

    A. price and wage controls.
    B. the metric system.
    C. food rationing.
    D. de-Christianizing France.
    E. distribution of all land to the peasants.

45. All of the following were results of the Protestant Reformation EXCEPT

    A. a series of religious wars in the sixteenth and seventeenth centuries between Catholics and Protestants.
    B. the religious unity of Europe grew stronger out of the conflict.
    C. the state was seen as superior to the Church.
    D. education and reading increased throughout Europe.
    E. northern Europe became predominately Protestant and southern Europe was mostly Catholic.

46. "Whenever the legislators endeavor to take away and destroy the property of the people or to reduce them to slavery . . . they put themselves into a state of war with the people who are thereupon absolved from any further obedience."

    Which one of the following men would support the ideas in this passage?

    A. Thomas Hobbes
    B. Louis XIV
    C. Charles V
    D. John Locke
    E. Jacques Bousset

47. Which of the following countries did NOT attend the Versailles Conference?

    A. Russia and Germany
    B. Germany and Japan
    C. Russia and Japan
    D. Italy and Germany
    E. Russia and Italy

48. The phrase "peace in our time" refers to

    A. the signing of the Locarno Pact.
    B. the Treaty of Versailles.
    C. the Kellogg-Briand Pact.
    D. the agreement at the Munich Conference of 1938.
    E. the Lateran Pact.

49. Konrad Adenauer was instrumental in

    A. furthering the Communist cause.
    B. negotiating an alliance between the Soviet Union and the Western Bloc.
    C. the disarmament of the Soviet Union.
    D. the economic recovery of Western Germany.
    E. the unification of Germany.

50. The goal of the Royal Society of London, founded in 1660, was to

    A. support the restoration of the British king.
    B. encourage scientific research.
    C. promote overseas exploration.
    D. establish a closer tie between government and scientific research.
    E. use political powers to restrict scientific research.

51. The Renaissance had the following effects on women EXCEPT

    A. the status of upper-class women declined.
    B. the life of the ordinary woman was directly affected.
    C. women's status declined regarding sex and love.
    D. women studied the classics.
    E. women were forbidden from becoming involved in public affairs.

52. "Population, when unchecked, increases in a geometrical rate. Subsistence only increases in an arithmetical ratio."

    The ideas in this passage are most associated with

    A. David Ricardo.
    B. Thomas Malthus.
    C. Louis Blanc.
    D. John Locke.
    E. Karl Marx.

53. Which of the following groups was victimized in the St. Bartholomew's Day Massacre of 1572?

    A. Roundheads
    B. Puritans
    C. French Huguenots
    D. French Jews
    E. Lutherans

54. The purpose of the Maginot Line in France was

    A. to prevent another German invasion by building massive fortifications along the border.
    B. to construct a series of alliances with Eastern European countries to encircle Germany.
    C. to provide work for the unemployed created by the Great Depression.
    D. to prevent the spread of revolutions in the newly formed national governments of Eastern Europe.
    E. to stop the spread of Bolshevism in the newly formed Soviet Union.

55. The Ottoman Empire and the Austrian Empire were most similar in that

    A. both contained multinational ethnic groups.
    B. both were constitutional monarchies.
    C. neither of them was affected by the growth of nationalism in the 1870s.
    D. both tried to promote some economic modernization.
    E. neither of them had a strong, effective military organization.

56. The initial reaction of the Russian government to the fighting that broke out in Chechnya in the 1990s demonstrated that Russia

    A. needs the United States' resources to ensure stability in the region.
    B. has little control over its arsenal of nuclear weapons.
    C. will defend its remaining republics against foreign invasion.
    D. favors reestablishing communism.
    E. is unwilling to grant independence to dissenting ethnic groups.

57. "If anyone wishes to see in how little space a human being can move, how little air and such air . . . he can breathe, how little civilization he may share . . . it is only necessary to travel hither."—Friedrich Engels

    This quotation describes the negative effects of

    A. the Industrial Revolution.
    B. imperialism.
    C. the Glorious Revolution.
    D. the Black Death.
    E. the French Revolution.

58. The political thinkers of the Enlightenment, such as Locke and Rousseau, supported the idea that

   A. government is a social contract designed to protect the rights of the people.
   B. absolute monarchy is the best form of government.
   C. all individuals exist for the benefit of the state.
   D. the power of the king and nobles should be strengthened to ensure stability.
   E. the military is the backbone of society.

59. Which of the following Russian leaders believed in the idea of "permanent revolutions" to ensure the success of Communism?

   A. Joseph Stalin
   B. Vladimir Lenin
   C. Leon Trotsky
   D. Alexander Kerensky
   E. Nikolai Bukharin

60. Which of the following banned freedom of speech and press in the German Confederation in 1819?

   A. *Grossdeutsche*
   B. The Carlsbad Decrees
   C. The Act of the Six Articles
   D. The Holy Alliance
   E. The Six Acts

61. Martin Luther's statement before the Diet of Worms that "my conscience is captive to the Word of God," was referring to his belief in

   A. the need for indulgences.
   B. good works.
   C. the supremacy of the pope.
   D. the supremacy of the Bible over the authority of the pope and the Church.
   E. the seven sacraments.

62. "No man's land is an eerie sight. At early dawn in the pale gray light. Never a house and never a hedge."—James H. Knight-Adkin, *No Man's Land*

   The above quotation describes the situation created by

   A. World War I.
   B. World War II.
   C. the French Revolution.
   D. the Franco-Prussian War.
   E. the Spanish Civil War.

63. Lithuania's declaration of independence in 1990 and the election of Lech Walesa as leader of Poland demonstrated

   A. the continued growth of communism.
   B. increased cooperation between Russia and their allies.
   C. the spirit of self-determination and nationalism.
   D. the influence of the Russian military.
   E. the collapse of NATO.

64. On which of the following movements did Jean-Jacques Rousseau have the greatest influence?

   A. Realism
   B. Romanticism
   C. Mercantilism
   D. Absolutism
   E. Imperialism

65. What was contained in the Atlantic Charter of 1941?

   A. Demands for the unconditional surrender of Germany
   B. A statement about the evils of communism
   C. A plea for the world to open up negotiations to end the war
   D. A statement of British and American principles about their goals in World War II
   E. A statement providing economic aid to the Soviet Union to fight Germany

66. "The Jacobin Revolution is carried on by men of no rank, of no consideration, of wild, savage minds, full of levity, arrogance, and presumption, without morals."

    The ideas in this passage would most likely be associated with

    A. Edmund Burke.
    B. Louis XVI.
    C. Maximilien Robespierre.
    D. Jacques Necker.
    E. Louis XVIII.

67. All of the following were results of the Thirty Years' War EXCEPT

    A. the Edict of Restitution was revoked.
    B. Protestantism was established in Europe.
    C. Calvinism was recognized.
    D. The role of the Church in politics increased.
    E. The concept of the balance of power between nations emerged.

68. Jean Auguste Dominique Ingres' portrait of Napoleon in splendid robes, entitled *Napoleon I on his Imperial Throne,* conveys the image of Napoleon as

    A. the Son of the Revolution.
    B. a democratic ruler.
    C. a god-like figure.
    D. a lover of liberty.
    E. a military leader.

69. Which is a common characteristic of *The Divine Comedy, The Decameron,* and *The Canterbury Tales*?

    A. They were written by Italian Humanists.
    B. They were written in Latin.
    C. They were written in the vernacular.
    D. They were stories about the need to rid Italy of foreign invaders.
    E. They were stories glorifying the heritage of Greece and Rome.

70. The Triple Entente and the Triple Alliance were formed prior to

    A. World War I.
    B. World War II.
    C. the formation of the United Nations.
    D. the formation of the League of Nations.
    E. the signing of the Treaty of Versailles.

71. Willy Brandt, leader of the Social Democratic Party in West Germany, was associated with

    A. containment of communism.
    B. the economic miracle of West Germany.
    C. tough policies towards the Soviet Union.
    D. Ostpolitik.
    E. the destruction of the Berlin Wall.

72. Which event in Italian unification is represented in the following picture?

© Massimo Listri/CORBIS

A. The meeting of Cavour and Garibaldi over the invasion of the Kingdom of the Two Sicilies
B. The meeting of Garibaldi with the representatives of the Papal States
C. Garibaldi's decision to return to Italy
D. Garibaldi's handing over the conquests of southern Italy to Victor Emmanuel to help unite Italy
E. Victor Emmanuel's decision to allow Garibaldi to form a government in the Kingdom of the Two Sicilies

73. The Great Exposition of 1851 held in the Crystal Palace in Britain showed

A. the success of imperialism.
B. the achievements of the government's immigration policy.
C. the success of British socialism.
D. the growth of industry and population of Great Britain.
E. the success of the British military establishment.

74. Which was NOT a result of the Peace of Augsburg?

A. Northern Germany became Lutheran.
B. Southern Germany became Catholic.
C. The prince of each state determined the religion of the subjects.
D. Freedom of religion was not tolerated.
E. Calvinism was recognized as a religion in the German states.

75. The issue of home rule in British politics during the nineteenth century referred to

    A.   using Irish taxes to support the Anglican Church.

    B.   political freedom for the Catholics living in England.

    C.   independence for India.

    D.   self-government for Ireland.

    E.   extension of civil rights for women in England.

76. Which was NOT a belief of Voltaire?

    A.   He admired the British system of government.

    B.   He supported religious tolerance and urged religious freedom.

    C.   He attacked the evils of organized religion.

    D.   He felt that God was a constant influence in the life of each individual.

    E.   He praised Enlightened Despotism.

77. Which of the following allowed the Allies to establish a Second Front in Europe?

    A.   Battle of the Bulge

    B.   Invasion of Normandy

    C.   Allied bombing of Dresden

    D.   Invasion of Italy

    E.   Battle of Stalingrad

78. In which of the following areas was Bismarck considered a pioneer?

    A.   Social and economic reform

    B.   Social reform

    C.   Military reform

    D.   Judicial reform

    E.   Political reform

79. Which of the following men is associated with establishing standards of cleanliness for hospitals in the nineteenth century?

    A.   Louis Pasteur

    B.   Joseph Lister

    C.   Robert Koch

    D.   Edwin Chadwick

    E.   Jeremy Bentham

80. Which of the following leaders is associated with the formation of the Fifth Republic in France?

    A.   Léon Blum

    B.   Charles de Gaulle

    C.   François Mitterrand

    D.   Georges Pompidou

    E.   Édouard Daladier

Section II: Part A—Document-Based Questions

Suggested writing time—45 minutes

Percent of Section II score—45

Directions: The following question is based on the accompanying Documents 1 through 10. (Some of the documents have been edited for the purpose of this exercise.) This question is designed to test your ability to work with historical documents. As you analyze the documents, take into account both the sources of the documents and the authors' points of view. Write an essay on the following topic that integrates your analysis of the documents. Do not simply summarize the documents individually. You may refer to relevant historical facts and developments not mentioned in the documents.

1. Assess the following statement: The Cold War was an inevitable outgrowth of the ideological and political differences between the United States and the Soviet Union.

   Historical Background: The wartime alliance from 1941 to 1945 among the United States, the Soviet Union, and Great Britain against Hitler had been an expedient relationship, whose goal was to destroy Nazism. With the victory over Hitler assured in 1945, Europe became the battleground again for a new war, the Cold War. Between 1945 and 1950, wartime alliances would break down and result in the division of Europe into two hostile camps. The Cold War would determine relations for the next forty years.

Document 1

The USSR still lives in antagonistic 'capitalist encirclement' from which in the long run there can be no permanent peaceful co-existence as stated by Stalin in 1927. . . . at the bottom of the Kremlin's neurotic view of world affairs is traditional and instinctive Russian sense of insecurity. . . . We must see that our public is educated in the realities of Russian situation . . . it must be done by government . . . there would be less hysterical anti-Sovietism in our country if the realities were better understood by the people . . . We must formulate and put forward for other nations a much more positive and constructive picture of the sort of world we would like to see than we have put forward in the past. It is not enough to urge the people to develop political processes similar to our own. Many foreign peoples, in Europe at least, are tired and frightened by experiences of the past, and are less interested in abstract freedom than in security. They are seeking guidance rather than responsibilities. We should be better able than the Russians to give them this. And unless we do, the Russians certainly will.

Source: George Kennan, excerpts from The "Long Telegram" from Moscow, February 22, 1946.

Document 2

It would be wrong to believe that the Second World War broke out accidentally or was a result of the mistakes of some or other statesmen, though mistakes certainly were made. In reality, the war broke out as an inevitable result of the development of world economic and political forces on the basis of modern monopoly capitalism. . . . Marxists have stated more than once that the capitalist system of world economy conceals in itself the elements of general crisis and military clashes . . . Our victory means, in the first place, that our Soviet social system has won, that the Soviet social system successfully withstood the trial in the flames of war and proved its perfect viability. . . . The war has shown that the Soviet social system is a truly popular system, which has grown from the people and enjoys its powerful support, that the Soviet social system is a perfectly viable and stable form of organization of society. . . . The point now is that the Soviet social system has proved more viable and stable than a non-Soviet social system, that the Soviet social system is a better form of organization of society than any non-Soviet social system.

Source: Joseph Stalin, *The Soviet Victory: Capitalism versus Communism*, February 1946.

Document 3

I now come to the . . . danger, which threatens the cottage home and ordinary people, namely tyranny. We cannot be blind to the fact that the liberties enjoyed by individual citizens throughout the United States and British Empire are not valid in a considerable number of countries, some of which are very powerful. . . . A shadow has fallen upon the scenes so lately lighted by the Allied victory. Nobody knows what Soviet Russia and its Communist international organization intends to do in the immediate future, or what are the limits . . . From Stettin in the Baltic to Trieste in the Adriatics, an iron curtain has descended across the continent. Behind that line lie all the capitals of the ancient states of central and eastern Europe. . . . all these famous cities and the populations around them lie in the Soviet sphere and all are subject, in one form or another, not only to Soviet influence but to a very high and increasing measure of control from Moscow. . . .

Source: Winston Churchill, "Iron Curtain Speech," March 5, 1946.

Document 4

In substance, Mr. Churchill now stands in the position of a firebrand of war. And Mr. Churchill is not alone here. He has friends not only in England but also in the United States of America. . . . As a result of the German invasion, the Soviet Union has irrevocably lost . . . 7,000,000 people. . . . the Soviet Union cannot forget them. One can ask therefore, what can be surprising in the fact that the Soviet Union, in a desire to ensure its security for the future, tries to achieve that these countries should have governments whose relations to the Soviet Union are loyal? How can one, without having lost one's reason, qualify these peaceful aspirations of the Soviet Union as 'expansionist tendencies' of our Government? . . .

Source: Joseph Stalin, "Reply to Churchill," *New York Times,* March 14, 1946.

Document 5

. . . The Government of the United States has made frequent protests against coercion and intimidation, in violation of the Yalta agreement, in Poland, Rumania, and Bulgaria. . . . One way of life is based upon the will of the majority, and is distinguished by free institutions, representative governments, . . . The second way of life is based upon the will of a minority forcibly imposed upon the majority. It relies upon terror and oppression, . . . I believe that it must be the policy of the United States to support free peoples who are resisting attempted subjugation by armed minorities or by outside pressures. I believe that we must assist free peoples to work out their own destinies in their own way. . . . The seeds of totalitarian regimes are nurtured by misery and want. They spread and grow in the evil soil of poverty and strife. They reach their full growth when the hope of a people for a better life has died. We must keep that hope alive. . . . I propose giving Greece and Turkey $400 million in aid.

Source: President Harry Truman's Speech to Congress, March, 12, 1947, *Public Papers of the Presidents: Harry S. Truman,* 1947.

Document 6

The truth of the matter is that Europe for the next three or four years . . . must have substantial additional help or face economic social and political deterioration of a very grave character. . . . It is logical that the United States should do whatever it is able to do to assist in the return of normal economic health in the world, without which there can be no political stability and no assured peace. Our policy is directed not against any country or doctrine but against hunger, poverty, desperation, and chaos. Its purpose should be the revival of a working economy in which free institutions can exist. Such assistance, I am convinced, must not be on a piecemeal basis as various crises develop. Any assistance that this Government may render in the future should provide a cure rather than a mere palliative. Any government that is willing to assist in the task of recovery will find full cooperation, I am sure, on the part of the United States Government. Any government which maneuvers to block the recovery of other countries, or groups which seek to perpetuate human misery in order to profit there from politically or otherwise will encounter the opposition of the United States. . . .

Source: *The Marshall Plan: Department of State Bulletin,* June 15, 1947, pp. 1159–1160.

Document 7

. . . the death of Stalin, by shaking the superstructure of discipline, by admitting for a brief moment the clash of several opinions and the consequent opportunity for a slightly larger area of discussion at the summit, has given the communist machinery of politics a momentary opportunity to review some of its errors. But, unless communism ceases to be communism, the process of discipline calls for a new tightening of control, a new struggle to apply the logic of a single man to a world of dark and uncertain phenomena.

Source: Theodore White, *An Assessment of Communism*, 1953.

Document 8

We must assert that in regard to those persons who in their time had opposed the party line, there were often no sufficient reasons for their physical annihilation. . . . Thus, Stalin had sanctioned . . . the most brutal violation of Socialist legality, torture, and oppression.

Source: *Self Renewal: The Attack on Stalin* (June 1956), Congressional Record, 84th Congress, 2nd Session, June 4, 1956, pp. 9390–9402.

Document 9

The 'Communist Logic' . . . is diametrically opposed to our own. Thus, the Communist refers to the iron curtain police states as 'democracies,' and any defensive move on the part of the Western powers is condemned as 'aggression.' The Communist thus builds for himself a topsy-turvy world with a completely distorted set of values. For this reason, it is practically impossible to win an argument with a hard-core Communist. . . . The Communist mind cannot and will not engage in a detached examination of ideas. Talking to a Communist about his own ideas, then, is like listening to a phonograph record. His answers will invariably follow a definite pattern because he can never admit . . . that the basis for his ideas may not be sound.

Source: "How to Spot a Communist," *U.S.A., an American magazine of fact and opinion*, 1955.

Document 10

. . . We believe that in the competition with capitalism socialism will win. . . . We believe that this victory will be won in peaceful competition and not by way of unleashing a war. We have stood, we stand and we will stand by the positions of peaceful competition of states with different social systems. . . . The victory of communism is inevitable! . . . Long live the heroic party of the communists of the Soviet Union, created and tempered in struggle by the great Lenin! Long live the indestructible unity of the international Communist and workers' movement and the fraternal solidarity of the proletarians of all countries! . . . Under the all conquering banner of Marxism-Leninism, under the leadership of the Communist party, forward to the victory of communism!

Source: Nikita Khrushchev's Speech to 22nd Communist Party Congress, *Current Soviet Policies*, IV.

Section II: Part B—Thematic Essays

(Suggested planning and writing time—70 minutes)
Percent of Section II score—55%

Directions: You are to answer TWO questions, one from each group of three questions below. Make your selections carefully, choosing the questions that you are best prepared to answer thoroughly in the time permitted. You should spend 5 minutes organizing or outlining each essay. In writing your essays, use specific examples to support your answer. If time permits when you finish writing, check your work. Be certain to number your answers as the questions are numbered below.

Group 1

Choose ONE question from this group. The suggested writing time for this question is 30 minutes. You are advised to spend 5 minutes planning your answer in the area below.

1. Discuss the reasons for the beginning of the Industrial Revolution in England.

2. Discuss the factors that contributed to the birth of the Renaissance in Italy.

3. Assess and analyze the central concepts of the Enlightenment.

Group 2

Choose ONE question from this group. The suggested writing time for this question is 30 minutes. You are advised to spend 5 minutes planning your answer in the area below.

1. Assess the validity of the following: Democracy in Great Britain was achieved through evolution rather than revolution.

2. Discuss the effectiveness of the Congress of Vienna (1814–1815) and the Versailles Treaty in building a lasting peace.

3. The 1920s has been referred to as the "Era of Disillusionment." Show how the literature of the 1920s reflected this approach.

Answer Key for Practice Exam III

Section I: Multiple-Choice Questions

1. E	28. A	55. A
2. A	29. A	56. E
3. D	30. A	57. A
4. C	31. A	58. A
5. D	32. C	59. C
6. E	33. C	60. B
7. E	34. C	61. D
8. D	35. A	62. A
9. E	36. E	63. C
10. D	37. A	64. B
11. D	38. D	65. D
12. A	39. B	66. A
13. D	40. B	67. D
14. D	41. D	68. C
15. A	42. B	69. C
16. C	43. A	70. A
17. D	44. E	71. D
18. A	45. B	72. D
19. A	46. D	73. D
20. A	47. A	74. E
21. C	48. D	75. D
22. A	49. D	76. D
23. C	50. B	77. B
24. E	51. B	78. B
25. D	52. B	79. B
26. B	53. C	80. B
27. B	54. A	

Section II: Free-Response Essays

Student essays and analysis appear beginning on page 375.

Answers and Explanations for Practice Exam III

Section I: Multiple-Choice Questions

1. **E.** In December 1979, the Soviet Union invaded neighboring Afghanistan to ensure Soviet influence in that country. The invasion abruptly ended the spirit of détente that developed during the 1970s, which had relaxed tension between the United States and Russia. The Afghanistan War drained the Soviet economy and morale at home. The Soviet Union had invaded Poland in 1956 and Hungary in 1916. They invaded Czechoslovakia in 1968 but never invaded East Germany.

2. **A.** While the Medici family often commissioned and paid various artists to decorate or design churches, they did not give their money directly to the Church. The Medicis were a wealthy family who derived much of their fortune from international banking. They came to power in Florence around 1434 at a time when the city's political system was undergoing frequent changes of leadership. Consequently, they maintained power by being politically shrewd and by supporting many popular causes. They also were strong supporters of the arts, which was another way in which they influenced poltical opinions.Nevertheless, without financial support of the Medicis, such great artists as Michelangelo and Botticelli might not have become household names.

3. **D.** In 1868, the Papal States were not part of the united Kingdom of Italy. After the collapse of Rome, Italy had been ruled by a succession of foreign powers: Ostrogoth, Lombard, Frank, Arab, Norman, German, Spanish, Byzantine, and French. By 1815, the country was roughly divided into several regions: the Sardinian Kingdom, which ruled the island of Sardinia and northwestern Italy; the Lombardo-Venetian Kingdom, which was ruled by Austria, in the north; and the Kingdom of the Two Sicilies in the south. During the nineteenth century, Italian nationalism grew in strength, and there was increasing desire for unification. During the years 1859 to 1861, nationalist uprisings deposed local rulers and united most of Italy with Sardinia. On March 17, 1861, the united Kingdom of Italy was proclaimed under the House of Savoy, with the exception of the Papal States and Venice. Venice was added in 1866.

4. **C.** This is a portrait of Louis XIV by Hyacin de Rigaud, conveying the image of a strong monarch in Europe in the 1700s. The high heels made Louis look taller and therefore more powerful.

5. **D.** Solidarity was an independent labor union that was formed in Poland in 1980, nine years before the fall of the Berlin Wall, because of economic hardship faced in the country. In 1980, workers at the Gdansk shipyard went on strike, demanding government recognition of the union. Union leader Lech Walesa became the leader of the strike and also became a national hero when the government gave in to his demands. In April 1989, before the Berlin Wall fell in November 1989, the Communist government legalized Solidarity and agreed to hold Poland's first free election in 50 years. After the fall of the Berlin Wall in 1989, communism fell in Romania and Nicolae Ceausescu and his wife were executed by a military tribunal on December 25, 1989. East and West Germany were united in October 1990. Communism collapsed in the Soviet Union in 1991 and Václav Havel was elected president in 1989.

6. **E.** After the Congress of Vienna in 1815, Belgium was given to the Netherlands. In 1830, a rebellion broke out in Brussels against King William I and Belgium declared her independence. In 1839, Belgium's neutrality was granted by the major powers, including Prussia. Belgium was not returned nor given to either France or Spain after the Congress of Vienna.

7. **E.** Johannes Kepler's work on the first three laws of planetary motion based on mathematical relationships supported Tycho Brahe's data about the planets moving in elliptical orbits. Before Tycho Brahe, astronomers used to observe the planets and the Moon at certain points of their orbits. Brahe, however, carefully measured their full course of movement through the sky. In doing so, he uncovered certain orbital anomalies, which his young assistant at the time, Kepler, was able to incorporate mathematically to demonstrate that the planets moved in elliptical orbits. Brahe still believed the Ptolemaic and Aristotelian view, however, that the earth was the center of the universe, which was shown to be wrong by Copernicus and Galileo.

8. **D.** The death of Marshall Tito in 1980 resulted in a period of chaos in Yugoslavia due to ethnic conflicts. Tito had been viewed as a benevolent father by the multiple ethnic groups and republics that made up the united Yugoslavia. Upon his death, this unity began to disintegrate. An outbreak of ethnic violence among Croats, Muslims, Bosnians, and others soon led to demands for autonomy by the republics. After Tito's death, Yugoslavia suffered economic hardship.

9. **E.** The Portuguese system of exploration did not rely on diplomacy to build relationships with colonized lands, but rather relied on heavily fortified outposts. The Portuguese regarded the non-Christian natives warily, believing that they need not keep any promises to such "infidels," and thus earning a reputation for cruelty. Portuguese explorer Henry the Navigator initiated the search for a sea route to India, which was accomplished by Vasco da Gama. Other Portuguese expeditions also explored parts of Africa and Arabia, bringing Christianity with them. This success inspired neighboring Spain and other European powers to search for their own colonies.

10. **D.** Mercantilism was an economic policy in which a nation's wealth was measured by its reserves of gold and silver. This policy prevailed in the major trading and exploring nations of the sixteenth through eighteenth centuries. These countries believed that by maximizing exports and minimizing imports, they could build vast stores of precious metals from the payments received. This would increase their wealth and power by allowing them to build stronger armies and navies for further overseas conquest. While this implies a high degree of government involvement in trade policy and protection of trade routes, it did not require that governments own the factors of production. As a theory of international trade, mercantilism also says nothing about individual interests or whether workers should share in profits. Mercantilism also artificially distorts supply and demand by limiting imports while encouraging exports.

11. **D.** The main reason for the Berlin Conference of 1884–1885 was to establish guidelines for dividing up Africa in order to avoid conflicts among European nations. After the mid-nineteenth century, the great imperialist powers of Europe began to have a strong interest in further African exploration. This was mainly due to the belief that the African continent might hold vast supplies of raw materials to fuel Europe's greater industrialization. The conference established "spheres of influence" in Africa for England, Austria-Hungary, France, Germany, Russia, America, Portugal, Denmark, the Netherlands, Sweden, Turkey, Spain, Italy, and Belgium. Rather than limit trade, the conference opened trade widely by eliminating most tariffs on African goods and opening the coast to all nations. The Belgians under Leopold II had control of a large portion of the Congo prior to the conference, but there was no fear they would take over all of Africa. African nations did not participate in the conference.

12. **A.** Louis Blanc, the "reformist" socialist, called for national workshops to guarantee full employment for workers in 1848. Robert Owen and Charles Fourier were the pioneering utopian socialists who hoped to build model communities. Hegel was a German philosopher whose ideas of history as a product of conflict between new and old ideas were applied by Karl Marx and Friedrich Engels to social classes to argue for the overthrow of capitalism. Proudhon was a French social theorist who more closely espoused anarchy. Blanc organized a Workers' Party and played a major role in the French Revolution of 1848. The government allowed his national workshops for the unemployed but shut them down in June 1848. The government's decision led to workers' revolts that were eventually suppressed.

13. **D.** The Communist Party had absolute control of the Soviet Union under Lenin, and did not permit even limited democratic reforms. The Soviet Union did not do away with classes under Lenin. Tensions between the rural peasant class and the urban working class were high during his rule. And the leaders of the Communist Party constituted their own elite class. Capitalism was not abolished entirely. Lenin allowed the peasantry to dispose of their surplus goods within the limits of "local trade" and instituted the quasi-capitalist New Economic Policy, which he justified as necessary given the devastation of the recent civil war. Lenin distrusted Stalin toward the end of his life and hoped that Trotsky would succeed him. He hoped to remove Stalin from high Party office but fell ill and died before he could accomplish this. After a power struggle, Stalin consolidated his power. Stalin had Trotsky assassinated in Mexico in 1940.

14. **D.** The 38th Parallel refers to the point of division between North Korea and South Korea. This became the divider of the two Koreas in 1945 with the surrender of Japan in World War II. The United States and Russia, allied against Japan in the Pacific, agreed that north of the 38th Parallel, Japanese forces would surrender to the Soviets. South of it they would surrender to the Americans. In 1950, the Korean War would begin when North Korean troops crossed this line, and the armistice that ended it reestablished the parallel as the border of the two Koreas.

15. **A.** Slobodan Milosevic's policy of "ethnic cleansing" describes the forced removal of non-Serbian groups from Serbian-controlled areas. Milosevic was a former Communist who turned Nationalist and became a national hero to many Serbians within Yugoslavia. He was indicted and tried for war crimes for his policy of forcibly relocating, imprisoning, or killing non-Serbian Muslims and Croats during the Yugoslavian civil wars. He did not attack neighboring countries, but focused on creating a pure Serbian state out of the remains of the old Yugoslavia.

16. **C.** The Seven Weeks' War in 1866 between Austria and Prussia led to Austria's recognition of Prussian dominance over the German states. The war came about shortly after the capture of Schleswig/Holstein from Denmark by a united Prussian and Austrian force. The future of this territory was to have been decided by the Treaty of Gastein in 1865, but both Austria and Prussia accused each other of breaking it, and this led them to fight for dominance of the German states. The Treaty of Prague ended the war. Napoleon III was following the dispute in Germany closely and had his own designs on the territory, but had to shelve these plans in light of the German nationalist movement. He was forced to settle for Luxembourg and a possible French annexation of Belgium.

17. **D.** The Balfour Declaration of 1917 declared the right of Jews to a homeland in Palestine. During the First World War, British policy became gradually committed to the idea of establishing a Jewish home in Palestine. After discussions in the British Cabinet, and consultation with Zionist leaders, the decision was made known in the form of a letter by Lord Arthur James Balfour to Lord Rothschild. The letter represents the first political recognition of Zionist aims by a great power. Woodrow Wilson's Fourteen Points laid the foundation for the League of Nations after World War I.

18. **A.** During the Stuart Restoration, Parliament passed the Habeas Corpus Act in 1679. The act held judges responsible for the well-being of prisoners in their custody, guaranteed speedy trials, and prohibited a person from being tried twice for the same crime. Parliament was not able to prevent Charles II's Catholic brother James II from inheriting the throne in 1685, nor did they revoke Charles II's secret Treaty of Dover, which he struck with the French in 1670. Parliament did not further limit the powers of the monarchy during the Restoration, and did not negotiate lucrative treaties with other European nations.

19. **A.** Manchester was a leading example of the new industrial city. Manchester had ready access to waterpower. It also had available labor from the nearby countryside and an outlet to the sea at Liverpool. Manchester formed the center of Britain's bustling cotton industry. During the 1800s, Manchester's rapid and unplanned population growth (from 25,000 in 1772 to 300000 by 1850) made living conditions intolerable for many poor people who worked there. Liverpool was a seaport city. Birmingham and Sheffield were iron-smelting centers. London was the country's capital and Europe's largest city, with a population of about one million by 1800.

20. **A.** Machiavelli would most likely support a politician who would manipulate people and use any means to gain power. Though Machiavelli wrote his book *The Prince* as advice for Lorenzo de' Medici, its philosophy can be extended to any political leader. Machiavelli suggests that the leader of a state should disregard any moral considerations when acting on behalf of the state, which would include religious considerations on behalf of the Church. Machiavelli would not support taking action to weaken the government, as he saw the sole duty of a leader to be strengthening and preserving the state. He would also not support taking a passive approach to problems. Rather, any approach that solved the problem would be justifiable to Machiavelli, whose theory has often been summarized in the phrase "the ends justify the means."

21. **C.** The Enlightened Despot, a type of ruler first described by the French philosopher Voltaire, had absolute power and thus would not support democracy. Enlightened Despots theoretically governed in the best interests of their subjects and thus would support art, literature, and science, religious toleration, use of reason to examine the world, and education.

22. **A.** Although Nikita Khrushchev had begun a policy of liberalization in 1956, he did not allow the Soviet novelist Boris Pasternak to accept the Nobel Prize in Literature in 1958. His novel *Doctor Zhivago,* which was published in 1956, was a powerful challenge to Communism. Alexander Solzhenitsyn was awarded the Nobel Prize in Literature in 1970 and was exiled from the Soviet Union in 1974. He moved back to Russia in 1994 and died in 2008 at the age of 89. Josef Pilsudski was a Polish revolutionary leader who was the first chief of state of the newly independent country in November 1918. Mikhail Glinka was a nineteenth-century Russian composer. Sergei Prokofiev was a famous Russian composer and pianist of the twentieth century.

23. **C.** To gain the support of the regular army officers, whom he needed to help him retain power, Hitler ordered his SS men and the Gestapo to put to death Ernst Röhm, his friend and leader of the Brown Shirts, and 1,000 of his troops on the "Night of the Long Knives" in June of 1934. The Brown Shirts included many members who wanted to become a revolutionary army to replace the regular German army. The regular army officer corps was very conservative, and the Brown Shirts represented a threat to their tradition and privileges. The Treaty of Versailles had prohibited German troops from entering the Rhineland, but Hitler repudiated this provision and began occupying the region in March 1936. In November 1938, Hitler initiated the harsher phase of Jewish persecution by arresting thousands of Jews in what was known as *Kristallnacht* or "Night of the Broken Glass." The Weimar Republic, the name for Germany's post-Versailles government, was eroded gradually by the rise of Hitler's Nazi Party on the right and the Communist Party on the left. Once installed as chancellor, Hitler finished consolidating his power by blaming Communists for a fire in the Reichstag and arresting many members of the Communist Party in February 1933.

24. **E.** Woodrow Wilson's Fourteen Points did not prevent countries from having to pay war reparations. In fact, the Treaty of Versailles, which ended World War I, called for Germany to pay reparations to the victors. Wilson composed his Fourteen Points as a foundation on which a just peace could be achieved after World War I. The central idea was to establish a degree of self-determination for the successor states that would make up postwar Europe. Thus the points called for freedom of the seas, the end of secret diplomacy, free trade, and a reduction in arms.

25. **D.** Napoleon's *coup d'état* in 1799 overthrew the government of the Directory and resulted in the formation of the Consulate. In imitation of the ancient Roman system, the Consulate was composed of three elected consuls. Napoleon was named First Consul and thus wielded all of the power. He was exiled in 1814 and then returned for 100 days until the Battle of Waterloo forced him into permanent exile.

26. **B.** John Calvin, unlike Martin Luther, believed the Church was higher than the state and should have a role in the government. Calvin believed that societies should be politically structured according to biblical principles. Luther, however, believed that the Church had the power to preach the Gospel and to perform sacraments, but that it should not participate in affairs of the state. Both men believed in free will, salvation by faith alone, that the Bible was the final religious authority, and that economic status did not have a relation to how faithful one was.

27. **B.** A major reason for British interest in controlling the Suez Canal was its strategic location. The Suez was the critical link between the British Empire's territories in India and the British mainland via the Mediterranean Sea. Control by any other nation threatened to divide the British Empire in half and force the British navy and trading ships to have to navigate all the way around Africa to reach India and back. Britain was not interested in Egypt for any other reason, such as minerals, Christianity, spices, or as a marketplace.

28. **A.** A major result of the Reform Act of 1832 was the abolishment of rotten boroughs, which were parliamentary constituencies that had declined significantly in population but still could elect members of Parliament. In addition to this redistricting of Parliament, the Reform Act laid out the property ownership criteria for which men could vote in Parliamentary elections, but did not extend suffrage to women. The act did not address secret ballots, the House of Lords' veto power, or government funding for public housing.

29. **A.** The Marshall Plan was a recovery program that gave over $17 billion in economic aid to European nations. It was so named because it originated in a commencement speech at Harvard in 1947 by Secretary of State George Catlett Marshall. Under what became known as "The Marshall Plan," the United States provided the aid while the countries themselves organized their reconstruction plans. The ultimate goal of the plan was to prevent the spread of communism in Western Europe and to stabilize the continent to make it fertile for the development of democracy and free markets. There was never a treaty between NATO and the Warsaw Pact, the umbrella enemies of the Cold War. West Germany was never militarily invaded.

30. **A.** During the Renaissance after the Hundred Years' War, the monarchy of France was consolidated most effectively by Louis XI. The monarchy had been weakened already by years of war, and the great French nobles held much of the power in the country. Rather than let it crumble or be overturned, Louis XI laid the foundation for absolute monarchy in France, and by promoting industry and commerce, he increased the country's wealth. The rise of the bourgeoisie class actually aided Louis XI in his efforts, as he relied on their support to counterbalance the most powerful of the French nobles.

31. **A.** Napoleon did not gain further control over France and other parts of Europe as a result of his Russian invasion of 1812. Rather, he overextended his armies and lost three-fourths of his troops in both combat and in the harsh Russian winter. With his armies and supplies severely weakened by the Russian campaign, Napoleon lost the Battle of Nations at Leipzig in 1813 to a combined Russian, Austrian, and Prussian army. He was thus forced to abdicate his throne as emperor, the title he had taken in 1804, and flee into exile, whereupon Louis XVIII was restored to the throne.

32. **C.** The Council of Trent, convened in 1545 to definitively state the doctrines of the Roman Catholic Church in response to the "heresies" of the Protestant movements, did not support the idea that individuals could understand faith without Church guidance. In its final decrees issued in 1563, the council did, however, support the belief that salvation was obtained by both good works and faith, that the Bible was the source of religious authority as well as faith, and that seminaries in each diocese must educate the clergy. The council also formulated a list of forbidden books, including works by Galileo and Erasmus.

33. **C.** Reformers such as Robert Owen, who tried to establish model communities, were known as Utopian socialists. These thinkers hoped to establish a world of cooperative communes that would be dedicated to the fair treatment of all individuals. This was in response to the Industrial Revolution and the perceived mistreatment of industrial workers at the hands of wealthy industrialists and factory owners. Luddites were also opponents of the Industrial Revolution who expressed their views by attacking and destroying factories and mills. Communists were a group who believed that all property and means of production should be owned by the state and shared by all. Anarchists believe in the complete overthrow of all systems of government. Fascists believe in consolidating power in a single dictator, with a strong emphasis on nationalism, militarism, and often racism.

34. **C.** The Spirit of Locarno in 1925 referred to a symbol of a new era of cooperation between France and Germany. In 1925, several European nations signed a series of treaties at Locarno, Switzerland. Germany and France, as well as Britain, Italy, and Belgium, agreed to guarantee Germany's western boundaries and they accepted the Versailles settlement's demilitarized zones. The treaties also agreed to settle common border disputes with Poland and Czechoslovakia by peaceful means. The effect of the treaties of Locarno was far reaching and gave Europeans a sense of growing security and stability in international affairs. Efforts were never made to end German reparation payments. The Dawes and Young Plans were designed to reduce but not abolish German reparations. The United States never joined the League of Nations. Article 231 (the War Guilt Clause) was never removed from the Treaty of Versailles. The Kellogg-Briand Pact (1928) outlawed war as an instrument of foreign policy.

35. **A.** George Haussmann supervised the beautification of Paris during the presidency of Louis Napoleon. Under Haussmann, Paris endured a rapid, total, and violent transformation, during which many buildings were demolished and rebuilt and many people forcibly relocated. Edwin Chadwick was an English reformer who campaigned for changes in sanitation, education, and transportation during the nineteenth century. Pasteur was a medical scientist most noted for developing vaccination techniques. Gustav Vasa was the king who united Sweden in the sixteenth century.

36. **E.** In the late 1980s, Mikhail Gorbachev's decision to stop interfering in the internal affairs of Eastern European nations led directly to the collapse of the Communist governments in the region. The satellite states of the Soviet Union depended heavily on financial, military, and diplomatic support from the Soviet Union. When Gorbachev began to hold some of this support back to preserve the Soviet Union's own resources under his policy of glasnost, the smaller states could not maintain communism alone in the face of popular sentiment in favor of free markets and democracy.

37. **A.** Albania did not come into existence after World War I. Albania became an independent state prior to World War I, after a three-year armed struggle by Albanian nationalists against the Ottoman Empire. Its independence was formalized by a conference of the great European powers in London in 1912, which decided its borders. It was not until 1929 that the kingdom of the Serbs, Croats, and Slovenes became known as Yugoslavia. Finland declared and was granted its independence from Russia in December of 1917 following the Russian Revolution, but it would take another year of civil war between Bolshevik-inspired Red forces and so-called White government forces. Estonia's independence from Russia was made official in February of 1920. The creation of Czechoslovakia followed a prolonged struggle by the Czechs against their Austrian rulers. The Treaty of St. Germain in September of 1919 formally recognized the new republic.

38. **D.** *Don Quixote* is a work of fiction, written by Miguel de Cervantes, that describes Spain in the sixteenth century by mocking the type of romantic and chivalrous novels that were so popular at the time. It was not meant to be a political manifesto, nor was it connected to colonialism or Spanish court protocol.

39. **B.** The united Kingdom of Italy in 1871 did not enjoy the support of the Catholic Church. The Church, via the pope, had ruled large parts of Italy for over 1,000 years, until the united Kingdom of Italy seized most of the Papal States between 1869 and 1870. In 1870, the Kingdom, seriously infringing on the Church's sovereignty, annexed Rome itself. Disputes between Italy and what became known as the "prisoner popes" would last until Vatican City was established in 1929.

40. **B.** One result of Stalin's policy of collectivization was a widespread food shortage. Stalin believed collectivization of individual farms would improve productivity and produce more food for the growing industrial labor force; he also hoped that a surplus of crops could be exported to fund industrialization as well. Collectivization was further expected to free many peasants for industrial work in the cities. To this end, Stalin focused particular hostility on the wealthier peasants, or kulaks, resulting in the deportation or disappearance of about one million kulak households. Forced collectivization of the remaining peasants, which was often fiercely resisted, did not have the results Stalin expected; instead, they effected a disastrous disruption of agricultural productivity and a catastrophic famine in 1932–33. The plan backfired and did not achieve its surplus or export goals, nor did it help the Soviet Union's industrial expansion.

41. **D.** One of Peter the Great's major goals in foreign policy was to acquire a window on the West along the Baltic Sea. Thus, in 1700 he started the Northern War with Sweden, in the course of which, St. Petersburg was founded and Russia conquered the vast lands on the Baltic coast. Peter gained access to the Black Sea, though not a port, very early in his reign by defeating the Turks who controlled the mouth of the Don River at the Sea of Azov, which is connected to the Black Sea. Peter was infatuated with the West and traveled extensively in Poland, England, and Austria. He hoped to make Russia more "European" based on these visits and tried to enlist the aid of these countries in fighting the Turks to the south.

42. **B.** The author of this passage would support the belief that the motive for imperialism was economic. The view that nations expand and conquer new territories in order to gain access to raw materials for industrial expansion back home is a purely economic viewpoint. The author of the passage does not attribute the "Scramble for Africa" to religious, political, military, or humanitarian desires but to "industrial enterprise."

43. **A.** As a result of the Great Reform Bill of 1832, the English middle class gained suffrage. The bill set the minimum property requirement for voting. The aristocracy already had the vote, but this requirement enfranchised a large section of the middle class. Women, peasants, and the urban working class who could not meet this requirement did not attain suffrage under the bill.

44. **E.** The Jacobins did not distribute land to the peasants. It was never the intention of the Jacobins to abolish the private ownership of land or to break up the big estates of the rich and divide them among the peasants. The Jacobins recognized that the distribution of land to the peasants would have violated the idea of private property which the revolution had proclaimed. The Jacobins established a planned economy to aid the poor and to help prepare France to fight the European coalition that was trying to stop the spread of the revolution. The Jacobins supported wage controls, food rationing, the metric system, as well as the de-Christianizing of France to ensure the success of the revolution and to promote revolutionary values.

45. **B.** The Protestant Reformation led to more religious division in Europe, which caused a series of religious wars in both the sixteenth and seventeenth centuries between predominately Catholic southern Europe and predominately Protestant northern Europe. Following Luther's belief that the Church did not have a role in state government, the state came to be seen as superior to the Church in many parts of Europe. Education and reading also increased throughout Europe, driven by a renewed focus on religious debate at the same time as the invention of the printing press.

46. **D.** John Locke would support the ideas in this passage. In 1690, he wrote *Two Treatises of Government* to justify the Glorious Revolution, in which he asserted that people entered into a social contract to create a government to protect their basic rights of life, liberty, and property. The power of the government is limited and if the government, which was party to the compact, fails to live up to its purpose, or exceeds its authority, the people have the right to alter or abolish it. Thomas Hobbes, a seventeenth-century English philosopher, wrote *Leviathan* to emphasize his belief that government must be all-powerful and absolute. Louis XIV was the absolute king of France who ruled from 1643 to 1715. Charles V was an absolute Hapsburg monarch of Spain who became the Holy Roman Emperor in 1519. Jacques Bousset was a seventeenth-century French bishop who wrote *Discourse on Universal History* in which he summed up the theory of Divine Right rule.

47. **A.** Neither Russia nor Germany attended the Versailles Conference. In November 1917, the Bolsheviks overthrew the provisional government of Kerensky and set up the first Communist regime in Russia. In March 1918, the Communist government signed the Treaty of Brest-Litovsk that ended Russian participation in World War I. Germany, which had signed an armistice on November 11, 1918, to stop the fighting, was not invited to attend the peace conference. Japan attended the Versailles Conference but was not an integral member of the Big Four meeting among France, England, the United States, and Italy. Italian representatives walked out of the conference because they were upset at the refusal of England and France to give Italy additional territory in Europe and Africa.

48. **D.** The phrase "peace in our time" refers to the agreement at the Munich Conference of 1938. At the conference, Britain and France had agreed to allow Hitler to gain the Sudetenland, a region of Czechoslovakia that he had claimed on the pretext that there was a large German population living there. When British Prime Minister Neville Chamberlain returned to London, he proclaimed he had achieved "peace in our time." Those words would later be used mockingly when it became clear that Britain and France had merely appeased Hitler and failed to stop his expansionist designs. The Treaty of Versailles had ended World War I, and the Locarno Pact was a follow-up to the Treaty of Versailles in 1925 under which England, France, Germany, Italy, Poland, and Belgium made mutual assurances as to borders and demilitarization of the Rhine. This treaty would be known by the phrase "Spirit of Locarno" and symbolized hopes for a new era of peace and goodwill. The Kellogg-Briand Pact was a treaty between the United States and other powers providing for the renunciation of war as an instrument of national policy. The Lateran Pact of 1929, signed by Benito Mussolini, resolved the "prisoner pope" dilemma and granted the Roman Church its own city-state in the Vatican at Rome.

49. **D.** Konrad Adenauer was instrumental in the economic recovery of Western Germany. Adenauer was the chancellor of West Germany from 1949 to 1963. He had been mayor of Cologne and president of the Prussian State Council but was dismissed by the Nazis in 1933. During his term of office as chancellor, the Federal Republic of Germany, as West Germany was known, developed into a stable democracy and into one of the leading industrial and social states. The achievement of national sovereignty, close ties with the free West, reconciliation with France, and the consolidation of the social market economy were all achieved

under Adenauer. He did not preside over the reunification of East and West Germany, which occurred much later in 1990, and did not negotiate any treaties between the Soviet Union and the West.

50. **B.** The goal of the Royal Society of London, founded in 1660, was to encourage scientific research. Its founding fellows included many of the most of the important scientists of the day, including Christopher Wren, who wrote the preamble to its charter. The restoration of Charles II had already happened prior to its founding, and the society was not involved in either overseas expansion or politics.

51. **B.** During the Renaissance, the life of the ordinary woman was not directly affected. Women continued to perform economic functions, such as working on the farms or helping their husbands run businesses. Women also continued to work as housekeepers and midwives. Educational opportunities were limited for ordinary women. Renaissance women studied the classics and received an education similar to boys. However, as Castiglione pointed out in *The Courtier,* upper-class women were expected to know the classics but not to seek fame. It was expected that education would prepare them for the social functions of how to attract a husband and run a good household. An educated man was supposed to know how to rule and participate in public affairs. Renaissance women were supposed to be decorative, affable, and charming. Upper-class roles declined as they had less power than comparable women in the Middle Ages. Women's status declined in regard to sex and love since their main role was to be pleasing as objects to men.

52. **B.** The ideas in this passage are most associated with Thomas Malthus. Malthus believed that humans are capable of reproducing faster than the earth's resources can be expanded to support this growth. Malthus' conclusion was that unless reproduction was regulated, famine would naturally spread globally. His ideas were not popular with social reformers such as the Utopian socialists who believed that under the ideal social system, all of mankind's ills could be solved. David Ricardo was one of the founders of classical economics. John Locke was a philosopher who wrote on both government and economics. Karl Marx was a socialist who formulated the principles of Marxism, and Louis Blanc was a "reformist" socialist who believed that the class problems of capitalism could be solved and a compromise reached with the "bourgeoisie." He advocated National Workshops to help the unemployed.

53. **C.** French Calvinists, also called Huguenots, were the victims of the St. Bartholomew's Day Massacre, in which over 20,000 of them were killed by Catholic factions. The massacres were part of the religious wars in France between different Christian faiths, and did not involve the French Jews. The Puritans were a group of Protestants that arose in the sixteenth century within the Church of England, and the Roundheads were a subset of Puritans who supported Parliament over Charles I in the British civil war, hence neither was involved in the St. Bartholomew's Day Massacre in France. Lutheranism had its following primarily in German territories, whereas Calvinism flourished in France.

54. **A.** The purpose of the Maginot Line was to prevent another German invasion. The Maginot Line was a mighty system of fortifications extending along the eastern frontier of France from the Swiss border to the Belgian border. It was named for André Maginot, the French Minister of War. Construction was begun in 1929 but was not complete at the outbreak of World War II. The Maginot Line offered a sense of security, but it proved of little value to France in the face of German mobile warfare in 1940. The Maginot Line was not a series of alliances nor was it designed to prevent the spread of revolutions. The Maginot Line was not ended to solve an unemployment problem caused by the Great Depression. The sole purpose of this fortification was military.

55. **A.** The Ottoman Empire and the Austrian Empire were most similar in that they both contained multinational ethnic groups. The Ottoman Empire was a blend of many different tribal groups from across Anatolia and modern Turkey, including Turks, Arabs, Slavs, Copts, Persians, Mongols, and Greeks. The Austrian Empire contained Austrian Germans, Hungarians, Slovenes, Poles, Czechs, Slovaks, Ruthenians, Romanians, Serbs, and Croats. In both Austria and the Ottoman Empire, the people practiced the Roman Catholic, Protestant, Eastern Orthodox, and Muslim religions. Both empires were severely weakened by the growth of nationalism in the 1870s. Both empires followed the principle of centralized, absolute authority in the monarch and thus were not constitutional monarchies. Finally, both empires failed to promote economic modernization and fell behind relative to Western Europe, while their militaries were ineffective, as evidenced by Austria's resounding loss to Prussia in the Seven Weeks' War.

56. **E.** The initial reaction of the Russian government to the fighting that broke out in Chechnya in the 1990s demonstrated that Russia is unwilling to grant independence to dissenting ethnic groups. When the largely Muslim population of Chechnya attempted to form their own Muslim republic apart from Russia, it set off a violent guerilla war between federal Russian troops and Chechen fighters. The response to Chechnya was a clear sign to other ethnic groups left in the Russian republic that the Russian government is unwilling to allow further secessions following the initial breakup up the Soviet Union and its republic. Thus far, Russia has maintained control of its nuclear arsenal, though it is a source of concern to the United States. The Russian government does not favor reestablishing communism. The Chechen fighters were not foreign invaders, and thus the Russian reaction did not address how Russia might react to a foreign invasion.

57. **A.** This statement by Friedrich Engels in *The Condition of the Working Class in England in 1844* describes the negative effects of the Industrial Revolution in regard to the horrible living conditions in the new industrial city of Manchester. Manchester, along with the port of Liverpool, formed the center of Britain's bustling cotton industry. In 1750, the town of Manchester numbered 17,000 people, but by 1850, it had swelled to 300,000 people. The rapid, unplanned growth made it a filthy, septic environment for the poor people who worked there. Imperialism describes how a strong country exerts control over a weaker one. The Glorious Revolution of 1688 ended absolute rule in England and led to the creation of a constitutional monarchy. The Black Death, or Bubonic Plague (1347–1350), was a contagious, deadly disease whose death toll is estimated to have exceeded 100 million people in Europe, Asia, and Africa.

58. **A.** The political thinkers of the Enlightenment, such as Locke and Rousseau, supported the idea that government was a social contract designed to protect the rights of the people. Locke's *Two Treatises of Government* and Rousseau's *The Social Contract* claimed that governments were formed to protect the rights of the people and when the government violated the rights of the people, the people had the right to overthrow the government. Rousseau, unlike Locke, was not concerned with individual rights. He emphasized the concept of the general will, the rule of the majority. To enforce the general will, the government has unlimited powers. Absolute monarchy, further strengthening the power of kings and nobles, or putting the state ahead of individuals, are all in contradiction of this principle. While important, they did not see a military as the backbone of society.

59. **C.** Leon Trotsky (Lev Bronstein), one of the principal leaders in the founding of the Soviet Union, developed the theory of permanent revolution. He declared that in Russia, a bourgeoisie and socialist revolution would be combined and that a proletarian revolution in one country would spread throughout the world. He believed that only by encouraging revolution worldwide would Communism be successful in Russia. Stalin coined the phrase "socialism in one country," asserting that the Soviet Union should build up Communism within the country before it could successfully promote revolution worldwide. Vladimir Lenin, the Father of Russian Communism and the first leader of the Soviet Union, was a pragmatic leader whose main concern was to seize power and avoid ideological debates. Lenin's statement, "promises are like the crust of pie, they are made to be broken," summarizes his views. Alexander Kerensky was a Socialist who was the leader of the Provisional Government that the Bolsheviks overthrew in 1917. Nikolai Bukharin was a leading economic theorist who supported Stalin's idea of building socialism in one country.

60. **B.** In 1819 Prince Klemens von Metternich forced the German Confederation to adopt the Carlsbad Decrees, which banned freedom of speech and of the press. *Grossdeutsche* refers to those who supported a larger united Germany that included the German-speaking province of Austria under German rule. The Act of the Six Articles, passed in 1539, it reaffirmed traditional Roman Catholic doctrine on certain issues. Catholic beliefs obligatory in England. The Holy Alliance was created in 1815. It was a coalition of Russia, Austria, and Prussia, the purpose of which was to rule their countries based on Christian principles, while maintaining the absolute monarchy. The Six Acts were passed in England in 1819 to control radical leaders.

61. **D.** Martin Luther's statement before the Diet of Worms reflects his belief in the supremacy of the Bible over the authority of the pope. Luther believed that religious authority rested with the Bible, not the pope. For Luther, the Bible was the final authority because each individual could determine for himself Church doctrines and practices. There was no need for a higher authority. Luther rejected indulgences and good works as a way to achieve salvation. He stressed justification by faith alone. Luther only accepted the sacraments of baptism, communion, and penance.

370

62. **A.** The quotation refers to the situation created by World War I. On the western front, the military stalemate led to trench warfare. The Allies (England, France, and Russia) and the Central Powers (Germany and Austria-Hungary) created a vast system of trenches from the Swiss frontier to the English Channel. The space between the two trenches gained the name "no man's land" and troops occasionally were sent over the top to attack the enemy trenches. When the officers ordered an attack, their men went over the top of the trenches into the bombed-out landscape of "no man's land." Casualties were staggering. At Verdun, both sides lost over 700,000 men. This poem written by Knight-Adkin describes the horrors of World War I in 1917 and does not relate to the French Revolution of 1789, the Franco-Prussian War (1870–71), or the Spanish Civil War (1936–39). Germany's use of *blitzkrieg* (lightning war) in World War II (1939) rendered trench warfare obsolete.

63. **C.** These events demonstrate the spirit of self-determination and nationalism. Lithuania had been an independent state between World War I and World War II until annexed by the Soviet Union in 1940. In March 1990, Lithuania declared its independence. The election of Lech Walesa as leader of Poland also demonstrated the spirit of self-determination. After World War II, Poland was a Soviet satellite and was denied the right of self-government. In 1980, Lech Walesa formed Solidarity in Poland to protest economic hardships. The Polish Communist leadership declared martial law and arrested Walesa and other leaders. In 1989, the Communist government legalized Solidarity and held free democratic elections for the first time in 50 years. On July 4, Solidarity candidates had outpolled Communists. Party members became the first freely elected opposition in a communist country. In 1990, Lech Walesa was elected president of Poland. All of these events showed the decline of communism and a lack of cooperation among Russia and her satellites, as well as Russia's reluctance to use military power to address these issues. Gorbachev was criticized for using military force against Lithuania. NATO is still operational and has not collapsed since the demise of the Soviet Union.

64. **B.** Jean-Jacques Rousseau was a forerunner of the Romantic movement. Like other Enlightenment thinkers, he was committed to individual freedom; however, he attacked the rationalism of the Enlightenment as destroying rather than liberating the individual. Rousseau believed that spontaneous feelings had to complement and correct cold intellect. His ideas greatly influenced the Romantic movement that rebelled against the culture of the Enlightenment in the late eighteenth century. Rousseau and the Romantics, unlike the Enlightenment thinkers, stressed a belief in emotional exuberance over reason as the guide to understanding society. Rousseau did not influence the Realism movement of the late eighteenth century or the economic policies of mercantilism or imperialism of the nineteenth century. His idea of a social contract was opposed to the principles of Absolutism.

65. **D.** The Atlantic Charter of 1941 contained statements of British and American goals and principles which would serve as the basis of the Allied peace plan at the end of World War II. Using the ideals of Wilson's Fourteen Points, British Prime Minister Winston Churchill and United States President Franklin D. Roosevelt called for peace without territorial expansion and pledged to support the rights of all people for free elections and self determination for all liberated nations. They called for the final destruction of Nazi tyranny and called for a permanent system of general security (United Nations). The Casablanca Conference in January 1943 called for the unconditional surrender of Germany. The United States, Great Britain, and Russia had become allies after Germany's invasion of Russia in June 1941. The Atlantic Charter was not a plea to end the war but a commitment to destroy Nazi tyranny. The Lend-Lease Act, not the Atlantic Charter, provided economic aid to Great Britain.

66. **A.** Edmund Burke, a conservative Englishman who wrote *Reflections on the Revolution in France,* would support the ideas in this passage. Burke's book illustrates the French Revolution's destruction of the fabric of French society, and defends inherited privileges in a general and glorified unrepresentative Parliament. Louis XVI was the king of France who was beheaded in January 1793. Maximilien Robespierre was a Jacobin leader who began the Reign of Terror. Jacques Necker was finance minister to Louis XVI who advocated reforming the tax system in 1789 in order for the government to solve its financial crisis. Louis XVIII was the brother of Louis XVI who was selected by the Congress of Vienna to be king of France in 1815.

67. **D.** The role of the Church in politics did not increase as a result of the Thirty Years' War. The Treaty of Westphalia that ended the war marked the end of the idea of the Holy Roman Empire in Europe that was ruled spiritually by a pope and temporally by an emperor. What emerged was a modern Europe composed of a community of many sovereign states. Protestantism became firmly established in many of them, including official recognition of Calvinism alongside Lutheranism. The Edict of Restitution was revoked, and the concept of a balance of power was born between the large states of Spain and France.

68. **C.** Jean Auguste Dominique Ingres' portrait entitled *Napoleon I on his Imperial Throne* conveys the image of Napoleon as a god-like figure. On December 2, 1804, Napoleon, dressed in a splendid robe of purple velvet, walked down the aisle of the Cathedral of Notre Dame. The pope had a crown to place on his head but Napoleon took it from him and placed it on his own head. This defiant gesture showed that Napoleon thought he was more powerful than the pope, who traditionally crowned the rulers of France. This portrait reinforces the majestic and god-like qualities of Napoleon. The portrait does not convey the message that Napoleon was the Son of the Revolution, a democratic ruler, a lover of liberty, or a military leader. This painting projects Napoleon in a regal manner.

69. **C.** Dante's *The Divine Comedy,* Boccaccio's *The Decameron,* and Chaucer's *The Canterbury Tales* were all written in the vernacular: Dante and Boccaccio wrote in Italian and Chaucer wrote in English. Chaucer was an English writer, not an Italian Humanist. None of these stories glorify ancient civilizations or call for getting rid of Italy's foreign invaders. Dante's *The Divine Comedy* describes his imaginary trip through hell, purgatory, and heaven. Boccaccio's *The Decameron* relates the stories of young men and women who had fled Florence to escape the Black Death. Chaucer's *The Canterbury Tales* are stories related by pilgrims journeying to the religious shrines at Canterbury.

70. **A.** The Triple Entente and Triple Alliance were formed prior to World War I in 1914. The Triple Entente was formed in 1907 in response to the growing fear about the rising power of Germany; it did not bind Britain to fight with France and Russia, but it certainly guaranteed that Britain would not fight against them. The Triple Alliance was formed in 1882 when Italy, Austria, and Hungary agreed to a defensive military alliance. By 1907, two rival camps existed in Europe, the Triple Alliance and the Triple Entente. A dispute between the two rival powers could draw the continent into war. The signing of the Treaty of Versailles (1919), the formation of the League of Nations (1920), World War II (1939), and the formation of the United Nations (1945) are not related to the Triple Entente and Triple Alliance.

71. **D.** Willy Brandt, leader of the Social Democratic Party in West Germany, was associated with Ostpolitik. In 1969, Willy Brandt became the chancellor of Germany. Brandt tried to ease tensions with communist neighbors to the east. His policy of Ostpolitik, or Eastern policy, was designed to improve relations with communist Eastern Europe. He opened economic doors to Eastern Europe and led West Germany to reach an agreement to normalize relations with the Soviet Union and Poland in 1972. Brandt's initiative eventually led to the establishment of diplomatic ties between West Germany and East Germany a year later. Brandt's ultimate goal of a unified Germany would not be attainable until 1990. Brandt was not a hardliner towards the Soviet Union nor did he fear the expansion of communism. He never called for the destruction of the Berlin Wall but referred to the structure as a barrier to unification. Konrad Adenauer, German chancellor from 1949 to 1963, is associated with the economic miracle of West Germany.

72. **D.** This picture represents Garibaldi handing over the conquests of southern Italy (Naples and Sicily) to Victor Emmanuel to help unite all of Italy. Giuseppe Garibaldi was an Italian nationalist who, with his band of 1,000 Red Shirts, landed in Sicily in May 1860. Cavour, prime minister of Sardinia, had united northern Italy but had reservations about the area south of Rome. Garibaldi, joined by rebels in southern Italy, soon gained control of the Two Sicilies. Garibaldi's success alarmed Cavour, who feared that Garibaldi might set up a republic in the south. Cavour sent troops to deal with Garibaldi and linked up with him in Naples. For the sake of national interest, Garibaldi put aside his republican sentiments and accepted the plebiscite that united southern and northern Italy. In 1861, Victor Emmanuel was crowned king of Italy. Neither Cavour nor the Papal States are represented in this picture. Garibaldi was already in Italy in 1860 and Cavour and Victor Emmanuel were not in support of a separate government for southern Italy.

73. **D.** The Great Exposition of 1851 held in the Crystal Palace showed the growth of industry and population in Great Britain. The Great Exposition attracted more than six million visitors, many of whom journeyed to London on the newly-built railroad. Companies and countries displayed their products, and prizes were awarded. The variety of British products reinforced the belief that Britain was the workshop of the world. The Great Exposition of 1851 was intended to show the achievements of the Industrial Revolution and was not organized to highlight its imperialistic policies, British socialism, military establishment, or immigration policy.

74. **E.** The Peace of Augsburg did not recognize Calvinism as a major religion in the German states. The Peace of Augsburg (1555) officially recognized Lutheranism, which resulted in northern Germany becoming Lutheran and southern Germany remaining predominantly Catholic. Freedom of religion was not tolerated. Rulers established state churches in which all subjects of the area had to belong. Dissidents, whether Lutherans or Catholics, had to convert or leave. The Treaty of Westphalia would recognize Calvinism as a major religion on the European continent.

75. **D.** The issue of home rule in British politics during the nineteenth century referred to self-government for Ireland. England conquered Ireland during the Middle Ages and, for several hundred years, ruled the country harshly. During the nineteenth century, the Irish continued to press for self-government and independence. The discussion over self-government, or home rule, disrupted English politics. Many were opposed to home rule because of their concern for Ireland's Protestants who made up a small minority of the population. Most Protestants lived in Northern Ireland, known as Ulster. Irish Protestants were fearful about their rights in a country dominated by Catholics. Twice in the late nineteenth century, Parliament defeated William Gladstone's proposals for Irish home rule. In the 1870s, Charles Parnell, an Irish nationalist, rallied Irish members of Parliament to press for home rule. Finally in 1914, Parliament passed a Home Rule Bill but it was delayed when World War I broke out in Europe. In 1922, the British granted independence to the Irish Free State, later called Eire. The largely Protestant Northern country (Ulster) remained under British rule. In 1809, the Disestablishment Act ended taxation of Irish Catholics for the support of the Anglican Church. In 1829, the Catholic Emancipation Act declared Catholics eligible for public office. Women would not be granted civil rights until the beginning of the twentieth century. Home rule or independence for India did not dominate British politics until the twentieth century.

76. **D.** Voltaire believed in a distant God who did not constantly influence the life of each individual. Voltaire thought that God was a clockmaker who built an orderly universe and then let it operate under the laws of science. While in exile in England, Voltaire came to admire the British system of government and that country's policy of religious tolerance. He believed that organized religion only led people to fight wars and commit crimes in the name of their faith. He invented the idea of the Enlightened Despot.

77. **B.** The Invasion of Normandy in France (D-Day) on June 6, 1944, established the Second Front in Europe. The invasion was the largest amphibious assault of the war. The invasion of France meant that Germany was under attack on the Eastern and Western Fronts. The Battle of the Bulge (December 1944) was Germany's last-gasp counterattack in Belgium. The Allied bombing of Dresden (February 1945) in Germany resulted in the deaths of 135,000 people. The Invasion of Italy (September 1943) resulted in the fall of Mussolini but not a Second Front. The Battle of Stalingrad (1942/1943) was a turning point in the war against Germany in Russia but was not the beginning of the Second Front.

78. **B.** German Chancellor Otto von Bismarck played a pioneering role in European social reform. Bismarck actually disliked socialism and in 1875 passed a series of anti-socialist laws to prevent socialist parties from meeting. However, Bismarck was aware that the popular demand for social reform was impossible to oppress fully. Thus Bismarck began a series of welfare programs to improve conditions for German workers, such as medical insurance, sick pay, and old-age pensions. These reforms pleased the working class and took the pressure off Bismarck for more radical reforms. Bismarck made some attempts to reform the German military and political system, but it was his social reforms that were pioneering, in that Europe had seen nothing like them previously.

79. **B.** Joseph Lister was a British surgeon who believed that Louis Pasteur's germ theory of disease might explain why half of all surgical patients died of infection. Prior to Lister's work, hospitals were not sterile places and were institutions where people went to die, not to be cured. In 1865, he ordered that surgical wards be kept spotlessly clean and that wounds be washed in antiseptics. His idea of sterile surgery helped to reduce post-operative infections by about 85 percent. Lister's success established the criteria of cleanliness that other hospitals adopted in the late nineteenth and twentieth centuries. Robert Koch and Louis Pasteur are considered to be the two founders of modern bacteriology. Edwin Chadwick was an English social reformer and Jeremy Bentham was a utilitarian philosopher.

80. **B.** Charles de Gaulle is associated with the rise of the Fifth Republic in France in 1958. The Fourth Republic, which had ruled from 1946, was weak because its multi-party system failed to provide stable and effective government. The government also was unable to solve the Algerian issue. Colonial war in Vietnam and in Algeria had demoralized France. Longtime settlers of Algeria and the French military opposed Algerian nationalists who wanted independence. Fearing civil war, the National Assembly confirmed Charles de Gaulle, who had led the Free French during World War II, as president with unlimited power for six months. He also agreed to submit his constitutional reforms directly to the people. In 1958, de Gaulle's constitution for the Fifth Republic received overwhelming popular approval. The constitution gave de Gaulle strong presidential power whereby the people, instead of the legislature, directly elect the president to a seven-year term by means of a majority vote. In 1962, de Gaulle settled the Algerian crisis by granting Algeria its independence. Throughout the 1960s, de Gaulle worked to restore French prestige and power. In 1969, de Gaulle resigned after his demands for a new constitution to reduce the power of the Senate were rejected. Léon Blum was the leader of the Popular Front in France during the 1930s. François Mitterrand was leader of France from 1981 to 1995. Georges Pompidou became president of France from 1969 to 1974. Édouard Daladier was the French prime minister who attended the Munich Conference in 1938.

Section II: Free-Response Essays

Part A: First Sample Student DBQ Essay

During World War II, the United States and the Soviet Union had joined forces to fight against Germany. The triumphant embrace of American and Russian soldiers on the banks of the Elbe River in defeated Germany, in April 1945, was not representative of the feelings of the leaders of these two countries. The leaders of the United States and the Soviet Union regarded each other in a less than friendly attitude. By 1947, the United States and the Soviet Union would be involved in a contest that became known as the Cold War.

The roots of the Cold War (1947–1990) were an outgrowth of long-standing political and ideological differences between the United States and the Soviet Union. The uneasy relationship between the United States and the Soviet Union was not created at the end of World War II. The roots were primarily philosophical. The United States, founded on democratic principles of the will of the majority and by freedom of individual liberties, was in direct contrast to the totalitarian system created by Communists in Russia under the leadership of Lenin and Stalin.

Although Lenin and Stalin had to make adjustments to Marx's philosophy, they never completely abandoned the belief of a worldwide revolution of workers. The United States, which cherished the principle of individualism and capitalism, felt threatened by Communism and it became a great evil in the American mind. Thus, when the United States and others decided to sleep with the enemy and join Stalin in the crusade against Hitler, Russia became the lesser of two evils.

During World War II, this alliance of expediency began to crack. Stalin was very critical of the Allies for delaying their invasion of German-occupied Europe until 1944 and the Allies (United States and Great Britain) were angry at the Soviet Union for its reluctance to grant free elections in Eastern Europe. Stalin ignored the agreement at Yalta and soon Communist governments gained control in Albania, Bulgaria, Hungary, Czechoslovakia, Romania, Poland, and Yugoslavia. The United States' response to Stalin's actions was to get tough. Harry S. Truman, Roosevelt's successor, decided to cut off all aid to Russia by early 1947. WWII was still going on in the East and the Potsdam Conference had not yet happened. In October 1945, he declared that the United States would never recognize any government established by force against the free will of the people.

In February, George Kennan, chargé d'affaires in Moscow from 1944 to 1946, drafted "The Long Telegram" in which he underscored the centuries-old Russian sense of insecurity and their belief that there was no possibility of peace and coexistence between the United States and Russia (Doc. 1). The "Long Telegram" sounded the alarm over Soviet expansionism and became a warning about the coming Cold War. Kennan, who had been asked by Washington to explain the Soviet's behavior in Eastern Europe, also insisted that the United States assume a leadership role.

Stalin, whose goal was to create a buffer zone in Eastern Europe and spread Communism, became obsessive in the face of a perceived Western encroachment. Stalin believed that World War II was an inevitable result of the development of world economic and political forces on the basis of capitalism (Doc. 2). He insisted that Russia's victory in World War II had proven "that the Soviet system was not doomed to failure" and that it was a better system of government than any other form. These statements reflect Stalin's apprehension and distrust about the United States and Western European countries.

In March 1946, former British Minister Winston Churchill, who had long distrusted Stalin, spoke of the dangers to basic liberties posed by the Soviet system of government. He declared that an "Iron Curtain" (Doc. 3) had descended over Eastern Europe trapping Hungary, Czechoslovakia, Bulgaria, Romania, Poland, and East Germany. Churchill's "Iron Curtain Speech" expressed the growing fear of Communism. The speech also came to represent Europe's division between a democratic Western Europe and a Communist Eastern Europe. Stalin responded by calling Churchill "a firebrand of war" who had friends in the United States. Once again, Stalin also reminded Churchill that the Soviet Union had lost seven million men in World War II, much more than the United States and Britain combined (Doc. 4). Stalin claimed that the Soviet Union was interested in establishing security in the countries of Eastern Europe and posed the question, "How can one, without having lost one's reason, qualify these peaceful aspirations of the Soviet Union as expansionist tendencies?"

Like Churchill, Truman saw Communism as an evil force creeping across Europe and threatening countries around the world. When Stalin began to put pressure on Greece and Turkey, the Greek government requested economic assistance from the United States. In a speech before Congress, President Truman contrasted democracy and Communism and asked for economic aid for Greece and Turkey (Doc. 5). Truman asserted that "it must be the policy of the United States to support free peoples who are resisting attempted subjugation by armed minorities or by outside pressures" (Doc. 5). The policy, known as the Truman Doctrine, was rooted in the idea of containment, limiting Communism to the areas under Soviet control, and resisting its expansion in Europe or elsewhere in the world. George Kennan proposed this approach, believing that Communism would eventually destroy itself. The

Truman Doctrine committed the United States to an active policy of promoting ideological divisions between it and the Soviet Union.

By the spring of 1947, many Americans believed that Stalin was ready to export Communism throughout Europe. In June 1947, George Marshall proposed the Marshall Plan, which provided economic aid to any European country that requested it (Doc. 6). Marshall noted that the policy was directed not against any doctrine but against hunger and poverty (Doc. 6). However, he pointed out that any country that tried to block the recovery of other countries would not get help from the United States. This was an obvious reference to the Soviet Union.

The Marshall Plan, which also advocated the rebuilding of West Germany, was an example of the policy of Soviet containment. Truman offered aid to the Soviet Union and its satellites. Stalin rejected the Marshall Plan and saw containment as encirclement by the capitalist world, which wanted to isolate the Soviet Union. Distrust and tensions between the United States and the Soviet Union continued in 1948 as the Berlin Airlift removed the fear of war. By 1950, people began to assess what the second half of the century might bring. When Joseph Stalin died in 1953, many wondered how this might affect the Cold War. Theodore White, an American journalist, noted, "nothing would really change unless Communism ceases to be Communism" (Doc. 7). The brutal struggle for power in the Soviet Union reinforced this view. The knowledge that the Soviet Union had developed the H-Bomb, several hundred times more lethal than the A-Bomb, added to the fears about the future. The Cold War paranoia was revealed in a United States army publication on "How to Spot a Communist" in 1955 that claimed that "the Communist logic was opposed to our own. There is little hope in talking to them."

There was a "thaw" in the Cold War after 1957, when Nikita Khrushchev became the leader of the Soviet Union and began to dismantle the legacy of Joseph Stalin (Doc. 8). However, the basic antagonism was still beneath the surface. In 1956, Khrushchev claimed that he would bury us. It was during this time that the Berlin Wall was built (1961) and the United States and the Soviet Union almost went to war over Cuba. In 1962, Khrushchev's speech before the 22nd Congress of the Communist Party still contained the arguments outlining the belief that "Communism will destroy capitalism" (Doc. 10). Unlike Stalin, he did not foresee a violent struggle but one in which Communism and capitalism can peacefully coexist with Communism as the winner (Doc. 10).

The Cold War would continue until the 1990s. This 45-year struggle became an ideological struggle between the two systems of government and which one was better. The political problems and conflicts between the United

States and the Soviet Union stemmed from the philosophical differences that divided a democracy, a capitalist system versus a Communist totalitarian system, as practiced by the leaders of the Soviet Union.

Reader's Comments on Part A: First Sample Student DBQ Essay

- The thesis is stated very clearly.
- The student makes excellent use of documents.
- Plenty of factual information is included in the essay.
- The student gives an accurate analysis of information—Kennan's ideas and containment.
- The essay is very good.
- The essay is well detailed.

Possible student score: 8–9

Part A: Second Sample Student DBQ Essay

The Cold War was an ideological struggle between the United States and Russia. In 1947, the wartime alliance between the United States and the Soviet Union broke down over how to reconstruct war-torn Europe. The roots of this conflict were inevitable.

In 1946, Stalin claimed that rivalry was inevitable between capitalism and Communism (Doc. 2). He claimed that the Soviet system was better and destined for victory. George Kennan, in a telegram to Washington, pointed out that the behavior of the Soviet Union was based on insecurities and that the United States needed to exert leadership (Doc. 1).

Winston Churchill reinforced the fear of Communism in March 1946 when he aroused the fear of an "Iron Curtain" that had spread over Eastern Europe (Doc. 3). Churchill's Iron Curtain Speech struck a responsive chord in the United States.

Truman, who feared the spread of Communism, was determined to stop its spread. In 1947, Truman, in an address before Congress, asked for economic aid and military aid to fight Communism in Greece and Turkey (Doc. 5). His policy led to containment, which was designed to stop the spread of Communism. In 1947, the Marshall Plan extended Truman's ideas to all of Europe (Doc. 6).

The Cold War was identified with Joseph Stalin, and his death in 1953 led to speculation about the future of this ideological conflict. Theodore White believed that nothing would change unless Communism changed (Doc. 7). Tensions became relaxed during the late 1950s, when Nikita Khrushchev became leader of the Soviet Union in

1956. He promoted a peaceful coexistence between the United States and the Soviet Union (Doc. 10). However, he like Stalin, believed in the ultimate victory of Communism. The method had changed but not the message.

The Cold War that lasted over 45 years was unavoidable.

Reader's Comments on Part A: Second Sample Student DBQ Essay

- The thesis statement is very weak.
- The student does not analyze the documents/facts.
- The student does not use all the documents.
- Gaps in development of facts and organization of the essay.
- The student gives the topic superficial treatment.

Possible student score: 4–5

Part B: First Sample Student Thematic Essay, Group 1–1

The Industrial Revolution refers to the greatly increased output of machine-made goods that began in England during the eighteenth century. The Industrial Revolution started in England and spread to continental Europe and North America. The roots of industrialization that took place in England grew out of a number of developments.

The Commercial Revolution that spurred the economic expansion of the eighteenth century helped to serve mercantilist England very well. The colonial empire that England built in Asia and the African slave trade provided a growing market for English manufactured goods. England's colonial empire also provided her with a ready access to the raw materials needed for the development of many industries. For example, England's control of India after 1763 provided the cotton necessary for the textile industry.

England had an abundance of its own natural resources. These included waterpower, coal to fuel the new machines, and iron ore to construct machines, tools, and buildings. England was blessed with an abundance of rivers for inland transportation. In an age when it was cheaper to ship goods by water rather than by land, no part of England was more than twenty miles from navigable water. These rivers and the building of the canals provided easy movement of England's enormous deposits of natural resources. Furthermore, there were no tariffs within the country to hamper trade as there were in France before 1789 and in the divided German states.

Agriculture also helped to bring about the Industrial Revolution in England. The Enclosure Movement released a supply of cheap labor for the growing industrial factories. In the 1700s, English farmers were second only to the Dutch in productivity. As English farmers adopted new methods of farming, such as crop rotation and other scientific methods of agriculture, food production increased and food prices declined. This meant that many British families had more income to spend on manufactured goods. Thus, the demand for goods within the country complemented the demand from the colonies.

Britain also had an expanding economy to support industrialization. Industry had grown at less than 1% between 1700 and 1760, but it grew by 3% annually between 1801 and 1831. Business people invested in the manufacture of new inventions. Britain's highly-developed banking system also contributed to the country's industrialization. People were encouraged to invest in new industries and expand their operations.

England's political stability also led to industrial leadership. Unlike eighteenth-century France, the monarchy and aristocracy, which had ruled the country since 1689, provided stable and predictable government. Parliament also passed laws protecting business and helping expansion.

All of these factors contributed to the beginning of the Industrial Revolution in England. Other countries had some advantages. However, Britain had all the factors of production (land, labor, capital/wealth) to produce the goods and services that the Industrial Revolution required.

Reader's Comments on Part B: First Sample Student Thematic Essay, Group 1–1

- The thesis statement is clear and well developed.
- The student analyzes and discusses basic reasons.
- The supporting information of the essay is good (use of river transportation/investment rate/political stability).
- The essay has a good conclusion.

Possible student score: 8–9

Part B: Second Sample Student Thematic Essay, Group 1–1

The Industrial Revolution was an important turning point in our history. The changes that began in Western Europe managed to spread throughout the globe and change the lives of people forever. This Industrial Revolution started in Britain around 1750 and lasted for almost 100 years.

Britain's access to many natural resources contributed to the birth of the Industrial Revolution in this country. Even though it was a small nation, it had large supplies of coal and iron. With the invention and arrival of new machinery came the factor of needing people to actually run the machines. Britain's population had many who were unemployed, ready and willing to mine the coal and iron, build the factories, and run the machines.

Britain had a stable government. This helped to support large economic growth which was imperative for the Industrial Revolution. The well-organized government was able to accommodate the changes that resulted from new technology and not let things get out of control. Britain's government was properly equipped to meet the changes that were occurring.

During the 1700s, Britain's economy prospered immensely. Trade from a growing empire overseas brought in large sums of money. The business class accumulated wealth to invest in things, such as mines, railroads, and factories.

All of these factors helped Britain become the birthplace of the Industrial Revolution. Natural resources, a growing population, good economic conditions, and a stable government allowed Britain to take an early lead in industry. People began to take a real interest in coal, iron, and machinery. Britain paved the way for other countries to follow in their path and bring about immense changes in their own countries.

Reader's Comments on Part B: Second Sample Student Thematic Essay, Group 1–1

- The essay has a superficial thesis statement.
- The student needs to give a more in-depth analysis.
- The essay needs more supporting information.
- The conclusion is weak.

Possible student score: 3–4

Part B: First Sample Student Thematic Essay, Group 1–2

The foundation of the Renaissance was economic growth in Italy from the early eleventh century to the fourteenth century. This growth included population expansion, commerce, and financial development, and increasing political power of self-governing cities. As this economic prosperity continued, artistic endeavors flourished, particularly from the late thirteenth century until the late sixteenth century. Scholars refer to this artistic growth as the Renaissance, and it would not have occurred without the economic growth in Italy.

Northern Italian cities were the leaders in the economic growth in the early eleventh century. By the middle of the twelfth century, Venice—bolstered by its powerful merchant marine—met with much wealth through overseas trade. Venice also benefited greatly from the Fourth Crusade to Constantinople. In 1204, the Venetians and the Crusaders stormed Constantinople and, before sacking the city, were able to bring back thousands of valuable relics that they later sold throughout Europe.

Other northern cities such as Genoa and Milan grew prosperous because of their successful trading with the Middle East and other northern European cities and nations. Because of their geographical position, northern cities were the natural crossroads for trade between the East and the West. Like Venice, Genoa became wealthy due to overseas trade, and in the early fourteenth century, both Genoa and Venice built ships that were able to sail year-round. With these improvements, ships could transport more goods and could travel much quicker. Italian merchants were able to directly buy goods from such lands as England, and then sail to places such as North Africa and sell those goods.

Despite the geographical advantages of such cities as Venice and Genoa, the Renaissance first appeared in the city of Florence. Although it was an inland city without convenient access to naval transportation, by the end of the thirteenth century, Florentine merchants and bankers gained control of papal banking. As papal tax collectors, Florentine mercantile families dominated European banking and had offices in cities from North Africa to London. The profits from these endeavors were funneled back into the city's industries.

The most profitable business venture for Florence was its wool industry. Florentines purchased the finest-quality wool from England and Spain and because they had developed efficient manufacturing techniques for such wool, they were able to produce the highest-quality products. This manufacturing technique brought employment opportunities to thousands of Florentines. The products of these workers' labor brought the highest prices in European, Asian, and African bazaars.

Florence was so strong that it was able to maintain its economic superiority even after King Edward II of England refused to pay his debt to Florence and after the Black Death claimed the lives of almost half of Florence's population. Because their economic foundation was so strong, Florence was able to withstand such setbacks. Their ever-increasing wealth planted the first seeds of the Italian Renaissance, during which painters, philosophers, and all artists were able to flourish.

Reader's Comments on Part B: First Sample Student Thematic Essay, Group 1–2

- The thesis statement is clear and well developed.
- The student gives good supporting data on the role of each Italian city-state, and the importance of Genoa and Venice.
- The student provides good insight about the culture of the period.
- The student's analysis of Florence is good, but lacks mention of the Medici family.
- The essay has an effective summary and conclusion.

Possible student score: 6–7

Part B: Second Sample Student Thematic Essay, Group 1–2

The Renaissance began in Italy in the early fourteenth century. Before the Renaissance began, Italy was the wealthiest nation in Europe. They had many bankers who made money and then they were able to use this money to pay for artists and writers to paint and write.

At the time that the Renaissance began, Italy was organized into small city-states, and each of the city-states had its own form of government. Venice was the richest of Italy's many city-states. Venice is located in Northern Italy and it was able to be rich because it was located near the water. Being by the water meant that Venice could have large fleets of ships. These ships were then able to sail to many different countries and bring goods to many people. People paid high prices for these goods, and Venice made a lot of money. It was only natural that the Renaissance happened in the richest of Italy's city-states. Venice had a plentiful economy and was able to support artists.

Geography was a big factor in the Italian Renaissance. The cities in Northern Italy were the gateway to distant lands in the Middle East and Asia. In order to trade with these nations, other city-states had to pass through the city-states in Northern Italy, and these city-states were able to capitalize and make many profits, which increased their economic prosperity.

Another important northern city was Florence—the birthplace of the Renaissance. Florence was extremely wealthy due to successful overseas trading. The bankers of Florence were Europe's most successful businessmen. They insured that Florence's wealth would be maintained—such wealth would eventually pave the way for the Renaissance to begin.

The Renaissance began in Italy because Italy was the wealthiest nation in Europe. Italians were able to use this wealth to support and encourage the growth of artistic endeavors. Without the wealthy Italian city-states, the Renaissance would not have occurred.

Reader's Comments on Part B: Second Sample Student Thematic Essay, Group 1–2

- The student's thesis statement is weak.
- The student does not explore the role of bankers.
- The role of Venice in the essay is weak.
- The essay gives an adequate analysis of geography.
- The content of the essay is too general.

Possible student score: 3–4

Part B: First Sample Student Thematic Essay, Group 1–3

As the Renaissance blossomed throughout Europe, it gave rise to many important movements, one of which was the Scientific Revolution. Scholars of the Renaissance sought to unearth knowledge in all spheres of life. They discovered the modern scientific method—a theoretical, experimental, and critical way of obtaining knowledge. As these scholars delved deeper into the mysteries of mathematics and science, they began to form communities whose members desired to fully understand life. Although this revolution did not immediately directly affect the everyday lives of Europeans, it did lay the foundation for one of Europe's most important intellectual movements—the Enlightenment. Influenced by the consequences of the Scientific Revolution, the Enlightenment was an innovative worldview that spread through Europe in the eighteenth century and was centered upon several main concepts that all related to methods.

The most fundamental principle of the Enlightenment was that the methods and techniques of modern science could be used to explore and comprehend all aspects of life. Intellectuals of the Enlightenment called this "reason." Reason dictated that nothing was to be accepted on faith alone; people should subject everything in life to rational, critical, and scientific thinking. Reason went hand-in-hand with the scientific method. This rejection of faith-based acceptance often put Enlightenment scholars into direct conflict with churches, whose very beliefs were based on the word of the Bible and Christian theology.

Another important concept of the Enlightenment was that the scientific method could be used to reveal not only the laws of nature but also the laws of human society. The Enlightenment gave birth to the social sciences, which in turn gave birth to the third concept of the Enlightenment: progress. The scholars of the Enlightenment believed that the scientific method, along with their insatiable curiosity and their commitment to reason, held the potential to create better societies and better people. This belief was validated by several economic and social improvements throughout the eighteenth century.

The concepts of the Enlightenment had varying effects on the people of Europe. The secular notions of reason, scientific exploration, and the rejection of blind acceptance based on faith held little merit to the peasants and urban poor. These groups were consumed by their daily struggles to sustain themselves and their families. In fact, many of these people resented the thinkers of the Enlightenment for attacking their traditional beliefs. However, for the urban middle class and the aristocracy, the secular nature of the Enlightenment had profound effects on their lives. In addition to renewing the Renaissance's spirit of worldly explanations, the Enlightenment greatly impacted the culture and way of thinking of the middle class and aristocracy. In years to come, the Enlightenment would continue to shape the concept of the modern mind.

Reader's Comments on Part B: First Sample Student Thematic Essay, Group 1–3

- The thesis statement gives a good background and the connection to the Renaissance is excellent.
- The ideas of Enlightenment in the essay are very clear.
- The student's inclusion of a few Enlightenment thinkers, such as Locke and Rousseau, would have been helpful.
- The essay is very analytical.

Possible student score: 8–9

Part B: Second Sample Student Thematic Essay, Group 1–3

The Enlightenment was a period that came after the Renaissance in Europe. It was very similar to the Renaissance, except that it did not focus as much on art as the Renaissance did. During the Enlightenment, people were encouraged to explore all aspects of life, and were encouraged to gain as much knowledge as possible. This is like the Renaissance, where people wanted to be as learned as possible. The thinkers of the Enlightenment discovered new philosophies and ways of thinking that were very different from what people in Europe thought and believed.

People in the Enlightenment were very scientific and logical in their way of thinking. They were interested in knowledge and facts, and they wanted to get as much knowledge and as many facts as possible. They believed that people were able to become very knowledgeable only through the constant examination of everything. A true Enlightenment thinker would not just accept anything—he would have to discover it for himself. This was a conflict because the church told people to accept things based on faith alone. This was the opposite of what people in the Enlightenment thought. Enlightened people wanted to use facts to discover everything, and they did not believe that faith was a good enough reason to believe in something. They were skeptical of any conclusion that they did not arrive at themselves.

People in the Enlightenment analyzed things using the scientific method, which was a very specific way to analyze. It was very logical and rational, which was another reason why the enlightened thinkers clashed with the church, which did not follow the scientific method.

The Enlightenment greatly affected all of Europe, except for people who continued to follow the church's teachings of faith. Despite conflicts with the church, the people who followed the Enlightenment were inspired by the curiosity of the time. Everyone wanted to gain new knowledge, and the Enlightenment encouraged the intellectual growth of everyone. Europe was never the same after the Enlightenment. It affected people for generations to follow.

Reader's Comments on Part B: Second Sample Student Thematic Essay, Group 1–3

- The thesis statement is not clear—what does 'scientific' mean?
- The student needs to explain in greater detail the conflicts between the people and the church.
- The essay doesn't offer specific effects of the Enlightenment on Europe.
- Overall, the essay is weak.

Possible student score: 3–4

Part B: First Sample Student Thematic Essay, Group 2–1

In the early 1800s, England was a constitutional monarchy, but the British government was not democratic. The British Parliament was made up of the House of Lords and the House of Commons. The House of Lords was hereditary nobles and the House of Commons was elected by less than 5 percent of the people. Voting was limited to men who owned large amounts of property and women could not vote. During the 1800s, democracy gradually expanded so that by the 1900s political democracy would be extended to all groups within Great Britain. In the struggle for democracy, reformers accomplished their purpose by a gradual approach and the art of compromise. In Britain, each opposing side gave in a little to avoid violence. Unlike the French, the British achieved reforms without the bitter bloodshed of revolution. In the 1830s, as revolution flared on the continent, the Whigs, who represented the middle class, and the Tories, who represented nobles and landowners, battled over a reform bill. Parliament leaders in England feared that the revolution of 1830 in France would spread to Britain. The struggle was over extending the suffrage (right to vote) to the emerging middle class. Parliament passed the Great Reform Bill of 1832 and reduced the qualification for voters in order to enfranchise the middle class, thus increasing the number of voters from 500,000 to over 800,000 (still only about 5 percent of the British adult male population). The Bill also abolished the rotten boroughs, or empty districts, which gave thriving new industrial cities more representation.

The Reform Bill did not bring about full democracy but it was a moderate step forward and gave a greater political voice to the middle class. However, the Reform Bill of 1832 did not enfranchise city workers. In the 1830s, workers organized the Chartist Movement to fight for their rights. The Chartists presented their demands called "The People's Charter of 1838." The Chartists demanded universal male suffrage, a secret ballot, annual parliamentary elections, the end of property qualifications for serving in Parliament, and pay for members of Parliament. The Chartists did not call for women's rights. However, women in the Chartist Movement organized the first British Association to work for women's suffrage. The Chartists presented petitions twice to Parliament with over a million signatures. In 1848, as revolutions swept across Europe, the Chartists organized a third march on Parliament. Fearing violence, Parliament suppressed the march. However, the Chartist protests convinced many people that the workers had sound complaints. The Chartist movement died after 1848, but in time Parliament would pass most of the Chartist demands.

Throughout the nineteenth century, workers continued to press for political reform, and Parliament eventually responded. New political parties emerged to support reform efforts. Benjamin Disraeli forged the old Tory Party into the modern Conservative Party and the Whigs, led by William Gladstone, were transformed into the Liberal Party. Both of these men fought for political reform. In 1867, Disraeli supported a bill to extend voting rights to city workers. The Reform Bill of 1867 doubled the size of the electorate. Disraeli had hoped that endorsing this bill would get the working class to support the Conservative Party. Disraeli's hopes never materialized. In the Reform Bill of 1884, Gladstone and the Liberals supported the right to vote for the agricultural workers. By the century's end, almost all of the demands of the now defunct Chartists were achieved except for annual parliamentary elections.

Women in Great Britain, as elsewhere, struggled to gain the right of suffrage against strong opposition. After decades of peaceful efforts, Emmeline Pankhurst in 1903 formed the Women's Social and Political Union. The WSPU became the militant organization for women's rights. Their members led hunger strikes and were imprisoned many times. They cut telegraph wires and committed arson. One WSPU member, Emily Davison, lost her life when she threw herself in front of a horse at the English Derby. Women did not win the right to vote in national elections in Great Britain until after World War I.

The fight for democracy in Great Britain was a long struggle that evolved throughout the nineteenth and early twentieth century. The struggle for democracy was a gradual process in Great Britain but proved more permanent and had a permanent affect on English society. Each of the Reform Bills extended the voting franchise so that all sectors of society became part of the political process.

Reader's Comments on Part B: First Sample Student Thematic Essay, Group 2–1

- The thesis statement is very specific.
- The thesis is well developed—use of facts such as Reform Bills, Chartist Movement.
- The connection with England and revolutions in Europe is good.
- The student gives a detailed analysis of facts.
- The essay is weak on the topic of the women's movement.
- The student needs to develop the conclusion more.

Possible student score: 7–8

Part B: Second Sample Student Thematic Essay, Group 2–1

The development of democracy in Great Britain was an evolutionary one that took 100 years to achieve. Great Britain in the 1800s would evolve from a limited democracy to a full democracy by the 1900s.

In the 1800s, Great Britain was not a true democracy and limited to those who owned property. In 1832, Parliament passed the Reform Bill. This bill extended the franchise to factory owners, bankers, and merchants. The Reform Bill also abolished the rotten boroughs in Great Britain.

In the 1830s, workers formed the Chartist Movement. The Chartist Movement called for suffrage for all men, especially city workers. The Chartists also called for secret ballots and an end to the property qualifications for serving in Parliament. The Chartists did not achieve their goals but throughout the nineteenth century their goals would be implemented.

The Reform Bill of 1867 reduced property qualifications for voting so as to enfranchise city workers. The Conservatives (formerly Tory) Party supported this bill. The Reform Bill of 1884 extended the right to agricultural workers. The Liberal Party led by Prime Minister William Gladstone supported this bill.

By the 1890s, most of England's adult males had the right to vote but women were denied the suffrage. Throughout the 1880s, the fight for women's suffrage became a dominant issue. Led by Emmeline Pankhurst of the Women's Social and Political Union, they became very militant. They committed arson, heckled members of

Parliament, and conducted hunger strikes. By 1918, women over the age of 30 gained the right to vote. It was not until 1928 that all women over 21 could vote.

The growth of democracy in Great Britain was a long struggle that led to an extension of democracy for different groups in British society. The process was evolutionary rather than revolutionary.

Reader's Comments on Part B: Second Sample Student Thematic Essay, Group 2–1

- The thesis statement needs development—What made Great Britain undemocratic?
- The student needs to give more detail on the Reform Bills—Why were they passed?
- The emphasis on women in the essay is weak.
- The conclusion is weak.

Possible student score: 3–4

Part B: First Sample Student Thematic Essay, Group 2–2

The Congress of Vienna of 1814–1815 was a peace conference to reconstruct war-torn Europe following Napoleon's defeat. The Versailles Treaty (1919) was a meeting to reconstruct Europe after Germany's defeat in World War I. The Congress of Vienna would create a framework of peace for Europe that lasted 100 years. The Versailles Treaty did little to build a lasting peace and by 1939, the world was plunged into another major war.

England, Russia, Prussia, Austria, and France attended the Congress of Vienna. Their goal was to turn back the clock to pre-1789 in order to insure order and stability. Although the leaders at the congress had different goals, they agreed to establish a balance of power so that France would be contained and never become strong enough to dominate the continent. The diplomats wanted to restore the power of the monarchs based on the principle of legitimacy. Former rulers deposed by the French Revolution or Napoleon were returned to power. Thus, Louis XVIII, brother of executed Louis XVI, regained the throne. Hereditary rulers were returned to Spain, Holland, the Italian states of Sardinia-Piedmont, and the Two Sicilies. The congress denied many national groups independence and unity. Belgians, Poles, and Finns were handed over to foreign governments. Russia was given part of Poland and Finland, and Holland was forced to give up Ceylon and South Africa to Great Britain but gained Belgium. Austria obtained the Italian provinces of Lombardy and Venetia. All of these steps represented contempt for democracy and a denial of nationalism.

The Congress or Peace of Vienna was a political triumph in many ways. The Peace of Vienna was the most far-reaching diplomatic agreement between the Treaty of Westphalia of 1648 and the Versailles Treaty, which ended

World War I. It had many strong points. It was fair enough so that no one country could hold a grudge. It created a minimum of resentment in France. The Treaty ended two centuries of colonial rivalry and stabilized the international system until the twentieth century. The European Balance of Power would stabilize the international system until the unification of Germany in 1871, and not until World War I (1914) did Europe have another general war. However, the statesmen of Vienna underestimated the growing force of nationalism and failed to see how the Industrial Revolution would change the social and political structure of society. Despite these shortcomings, the Peace of Vienna created a time of peace in Europe for close to 100 years. Only during the Pax Romana did society enjoy such relative harmony.

At the end of World War I in 1918, the Allied countries (England, France, United States, Italy) met at the Palace of Versailles, outside Paris, to draw up a peace treaty to deal with the defeat of the Central Powers (Germany, Austria-Hungary, Turkey, and Bulgaria). The Versailles Treaty dealt with Germany. The Allied countries or Big Four had different objectives at the conference. England and France did not agree with Wilson's vision of peace based on the Fourteen Points. Some of these Fourteen Points included reduced national armies and navies, self-determination, and the formation of a League of Nations. France and England wanted a peace that protected national security. The French were determined to punish Germany. Georges Clemenceau, the French Premier, wanted revenge for all that France had lost. The French had lost more than a million soldiers.

The differences among the United States, Britain, and France led to a heated debate. Finally, on June 28, 1919, the Treaty of Versailles was signed. The treaty was far from the ideals requested by Wilson. A League of Nations was created; Germany accepted sole responsibility for the war and had to pay reparation to the Allied countries. Germany also lost substantial territory and was forced to reduce its armed forces to 100,000 volunteers and was forbidden from having an air force.

The Versailles Treaty that was designed to put an end to the German menace was a failure. Germany was angry and bitter. They resented the War Guilt Clause and felt betrayed by the peace treaty. The treaty transferred German-inhabited territory, such as the Saar to France and Danzig to Poland. Germany lost all of her colonies. While Germany disarmed, the other nations remained armed. The treaty, however, was too severe to conciliate but not severe enough to destroy. From the very beginning, Germany showed no real intention to live up to the treaty and Allied countries believed that parts of the treaty were unenforceable. Other countries were also unhappy with the Versailles Treaty. The United States rejected the treaty and was forced to sign a separate treaty with Germany.

Italy was angry because she would not get all the land she was promised. Japan was upset that the West refused to recognize its claims in China. Russia, under the control of Communism, was also annoyed that they were excluded from the Versailles Conference and that Poland and the Baltic states were carved out of their empire. France was disappointed with England for backing out of a defensive alliance with her. England, by 1919, was beginning to express more fear about the Communists in Russia than the Germans.

The Congress of Vienna created a lasting peace that enabled Europe to grow and prosper throughout the nineteenth century. On the other hand, the Versailles Treaty did not establish a lasting peace but created resentment that sponsored the international climate for two decades and helped spark World War II. Wilson's dream of a lasting peace was never achieved.

Reader's Comments on Part B: First Sample Student Thematic Essay, Group 2–2

- The thesis is very well organized and developed.
- The student's analysis of data is excellent—purpose of the Congress of Vienna and the Versailles Treaty.
- The student's comparison of two treaties is very analytical.
- The overall organization of the essay is good.

Possible student score: 8–9

Part B: Second Sample Student Thematic Essay, Group 2–2

The Congress of Vienna and the Treaty of Versailles were alike in trying to reconstruct Europe, but only the Congress of Vienna achieved its objective.

The Congress of Vienna met to reconstruct Europe after the Napoleonic War. The purpose of the congress was to turn the clock back to the pre-1789 era and to ensure that France never became a powerful force in Europe. To achieve these objectives, the leaders at Vienna restored the former kings to the throne of Spain and the Kingdom of Two Sicilies, and Louis XVIII, brother of Louis XVI to the throne of France. The congress also created nations such as Belgium and the Netherlands to contain French power. The Congress of Vienna ignored the principles of the French Revolution and denied the principle of nationalism and democracy. Nevertheless, the settlement of Vienna created a balance of power that established peace in Europe for almost 100 years.

The Versailles Conference met at the end of World War I to decide how to deal with a defeated Germany. The Allied countries of England, France, the United States, and Italy had different objectives. Italy wanted territory that had been promised to her. England and France wanted to punish Germany and ensure that German power would never threaten Europe again. The United States' main goal was the League of Nations.

The Allies disagreed vigorously during the conference but on June 28, 1919, they signed the Versailles Treaty with Germany. Germany was treated harshly. She had to disarm, give up her colonies, admit war guilt, and also pay reparations for all damages caused by the war. In addition, Germany was forced to transfer German-inhabited territory to France and Poland. The treaty angered the German people who claimed, "they had been stabbed in the back."

The Versailles Treaty, unlike the Congress of Vienna, did not establish a lasting peace. Germany was angry about the harshness of the treaty. The United States rejected the Treaty of Versailles and England and France were unwilling to enforce it. The Versailles Treaty was a temporary truce that created conditions that led to World War II in 1939.

Reader's Comments on Part B: Second Sample Student Thematic Essay, Group 2–2

- The student gives superficial treatment to facts.
- The essay ignores basic facts, such as nationalism and democracy.
- The essay never discusses the role of the Fourteen Points.
- The essay includes little or no analysis.
- Overall, the essay is weak.

Possible student score: 1–3

Part B: First Sample Student Thematic Essay, Group 2–3

The brutality of World War I led to disillusionment in the 1920s about the values of Western civilization, which had been built on the belief in reason and progress. For many people, World War I symbolized a moral breakdown of Western civilization. A general climate of pessimism developed as well as an alienation and fear about the future. Writers expressed their anxieties by creating unsettling visions of the present and the future.

In 1918, Oswald Spengler, a German high school teacher, published The Decline of the West. Spengler believed that every culture experiences a life cycle of growth. For Spengler, Western society was in its old age and was near the end of its life. In 1922, T. S. Eliot, an American living in England, wrote in his famous poem, "The Waste Land," that Western society had lost its spiritual value. The American novelist, Ernest Hemingway, in The Sun Also Rises, describes the emptiness of young people whose lives had been destroyed by war as they struggled to live in a world they did not understand. Austrian-born author Franz Kafka's novels also showed how World War I had affected many writers. His books, <u>The Trial</u> (1925) and <u>The Castle</u> (1926), portray helpless individuals crushed in threatening situations they cannot understand nor escape. Kafka had been writing before World War I but much of his work was published after his death in 1924. His novels struck a responsive chord among many whom Gertrude Stein referred to as "the lost generation."

Some novelists also began to use the stream of consciousness technique to explore the human psyche. Influenced by Sigmund Freud's ideas, writers began to probe a character's thoughts and feelings without imposing logic or order. One famous stream of consciousness novel was Ulysses, which was written by James Joyce and published in 1922. This book focuses on a single day in the life of three men living in Dublin. Joyce broke with conventional grammar and sentence structure and blends words together to mirror the workings of the human mind. The language of Ulysses was intended to reflect the chaos of modern life, which was unintelligible.

World War I created uncertainty about Western society. Before 1914, most people in the West still believed in progress, reason, and the rights of the individual. World War I destroyed this faith and optimism and led to uncertainty and pessimism. The French poet and critic Paul Valery in the early 1920s expressed this feeling best when he wrote, "The storm has died away and still we are restless, uneasy as if the storm was about to break. . . . We fear the future, not without reason."

Reader's Comments on Part B: First Sample Student Thematic Essay, Group 2–3

- The thesis is well developed.
- The essay is well organized.
- The student gives good factual references to Spengler, T. S. Eliot, and other authors.
- The conclusion is excellent.

Possible student score: 8–9

Part B: Second Sample Student Thematic Essay, Group 2–3

The literature of the 1920s expressed the disillusionment of the era. Prior to World War I, people had hope in the future. World War I destroyed this optimism.

In 1922, T. S. Eliot wrote in a poem, "The Wasteland," about this pessimism and lack of hope for the future. In 1924, the Irish poet William Butler Yeats also conveyed a sense of dark times ahead in the poem, "The Second Coming."

Novelists also projected this feeling of uneasiness. Ernest Hemingway wrote about the futility of the young who had lost their innocence and hope because of the horrors of World War I. Throughout the 1920s, there seemed little hope for the future. F. Scott Fitzgerald wrote about the lost generation in his famous book, The Great Gatsby. For him and others of his generation, life was empty as you move from one meaningless experience to another without direction or hope.

Other novelists began to incorporate the ideas of Freud into their writings. Rejecting the emphasis of reason, they used a stream of consciousness to explore the psyche of the individual. Novelists such as Virginia Woolf and James Joyce tried to show that the emotion of the mind, like the modern world, was not intelligent and could not be understood. This uncertainty led to anxiety and fear for the future.

World War I left an indelible mark on society. For the writers of the 1920s, it was reflected in literature that reinforced pessimism, uncertainty, and a loss of hope. Gertrude Stein remarked that the young people who served in World War I were "the lost generation."

Reader's Comments on Part B: Second Sample Student Thematic Essay, Group 2-3

- The thesis is weak and needs development.
- The essay has many redundant phrases.
- The student's analysis of Fitzgerald is brief, but informative.
- The essay gives insufficient elaboration of other authors and their works.
- Overall, the essay is weak.

Possible student score: 3–4

Wiley Publishing, Inc.
End-User License Agreement

READ THIS. You should carefully read these terms and conditions before opening the software packet(s) included with this book "Book". This is a license agreement "Agreement" between you and Wiley Publishing, Inc. "WPI". By opening the accompanying software packet(s), you acknowledge that you have read and accept the following terms and conditions. If you do not agree and do not want to be bound by such terms and conditions, promptly return the Book and the unopened software packet(s) to the place you obtained them for a full refund.

1. **License Grant.** WPI grants to you (either an individual or entity) a nonexclusive license to use one copy of the enclosed software program(s) (collectively, the "Software") solely for your own personal or business purposes on a single computer (whether a standard computer or a workstation component of a multi-user network). The Software is in use on a computer when it is loaded into temporary memory (RAM) or installed into permanent memory (hard disk, CD-ROM, or other storage device). WPI reserves all rights not expressly granted herein.

2. **Ownership.** WPI is the owner of all right, title, and interest, including copyright, in and to the compilation of the Software recorded on the physical packet included with this Book "Software Media". Copyright to the individual programs recorded on the Software Media is owned by the author or other authorized copyright owner of each program. Ownership of the Software and all proprietary rights relating thereto remain with WPI and its licensers.

3. **Restrictions on Use and Transfer.**

   (a) You may only (i) make one copy of the Software for backup or archival purposes, or (ii) transfer the Software to a single hard disk, provided that you keep the original for backup or archival purposes. You may not (i) rent or lease the Software, (ii) copy or reproduce the Software through a LAN or other network system or through any computer subscriber system or bulletin-board system, or (iii) modify, adapt, or create derivative works based on the Software.

   (b) You may not reverse engineer, decompile, or disassemble the Software. You may transfer the Software and user documentation on a permanent basis, provided that the transferee agrees to accept the terms and conditions of this Agreement and you retain no copies. If the Software is an update or has been updated, any transfer must include the most recent update and all prior versions.

4. **Restrictions on Use of Individual Programs.** You must follow the individual requirements and restrictions detailed for each individual program on the Software Media. These limitations are also contained in the individual license agreements recorded on the Software Media. These limitations may include a requirement that after using the program for a specified period of time, the user must pay a registration fee or discontinue use. By opening the Software packet(s), you agree to abide by the licenses and restrictions for these individual programs that are detailed on the Software Media. None of the material on this Software Media or listed in this Book may ever be redistributed, in original or modified form, for commercial purposes.

5. **Limited Warranty.**

   (a) WPI warrants that the Software and Software Media are free from defects in materials and workmanship under normal use for a period of sixty (60) days from the date of purchase of this Book. If WPI receives notification within the warranty period of defects in materials or workmanship, WPI will replace the defective Software Media.

   (b) WPI AND THE AUTHOR(S) OF THE BOOK DISCLAIM ALL OTHER WARRANTIES, EXPRESS OR IMPLIED, INCLUDING WITHOUT LIMITATION IMPLIED WARRANTIES OF MERCHANTABILITY AND FITNESS FOR A PARTICULAR PURPOSE, WITH RESPECT TO THE SOFTWARE, THE PROGRAMS, THE SOURCE CODE CONTAINED THEREIN, AND/OR THE TECHNIQUES DESCRIBED IN THIS BOOK. WPI DOES NOT WARRANT THAT THE FUNCTIONS CONTAINED IN THE SOFTWARE WILL MEET YOUR REQUIREMENTS OR THAT THE OPERATION OF THE SOFTWARE WILL BE ERROR FREE.

   (c) This limited warranty gives you specific legal rights, and you may have other rights that vary from jurisdiction to jurisdiction.

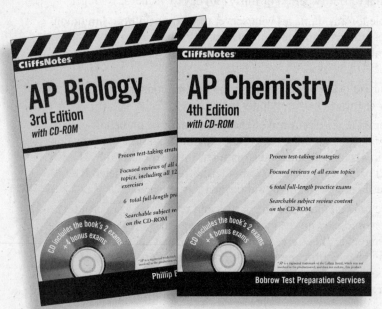